Essentials of Statistics for the Behavioral Sciences

Sixth Edition

Frederick J Gravetter

State University of New York College at Brockport

Larry B. Wallnau

State University of New York College at Brockport

THOMSON

WADSWORTH

Australia · Brazil · Canada · Mexico · Singapore · Spain · United Kingdom · United States

THOMSON

WADSWORTH

Essentials of Statistics for the Behavioral Sciences,
Sixth Edition
Frederick J Gravetter, Larry B. Wallnau

Editor: Erik Evans
Development Editor: Kirk Bomont
Assistant Editor: Gina Kessler
Editorial Assistant: Christina Ganim
Senior Technology Project Manager: Bessie Weiss
Marketing Manager: Karin Sandberg
Marketing Assistant: Melanie Cregger
Marketing Communications Manager: Linda Yip
Project Manager, Editorial Production: Mary Noel
Creative Director: Rob Hugel
Art Director: Vernon T. Boes

Print Buyer: Linda Hsu
Permissions Editor: Bob Kauser
Production Service: Carol O'Connell, Graphic World Inc.
Text Designer: Cheryl Carrington
Cover Designer: Ross Carron
Cover Image: Diebenkorn, Richard (1922–1993) © Copyright. *Ocean Park No. 79,* 1975. Oil on canvas. The Philadelphia Museum of Art/Art Resource, NY. Reprinted with permission.
Compositor: Graphic World Inc.
Printer: Transcontinental Printing/Louiseville

Printed in Canada
1 2 3 4 5 6 7 11 10 09 08 07

For more information about our products, contact us at:
Thomson Learning Academic Resource Center
(+1) 1-800-423-0563

For permission to use material from this text or product, submit a request online at **http://www.thomsonrights.com.**
Any additional questions about permissions can be submitted by e-mail to **thomsonrights@thomson.com.**

Library of Congress Control Number: 2007921807

International Student Edition:
ISBN-13: 978-0-495-38396-3 (Not for sale in the United States)
ISBN-10: 0-495-38396-1

Thomson Higher Education
10 Davis Drive
Belmont, CA 94002-3098
USA

Asia (including India)
Thomson Learning
5 Shenton Way
#01-01 UIC Building
Singapore 068808

Australia/New Zealand
Thomson Learning Australia
102 Dodds Street
Southbank, Victoria 3006
Australia

Canada
Thomson Nelson
1120 Birchmount Road
Toronto, Ontario M1K 5G4
Canada

UK/Europe/Middle East/Africa
Thomson Learning
High Holborn House
50–51 Bedford Row
London WC1R 4LR
United Kingdom

Latin America
Thomson Learning
Seneca, 53
Colonia Polanco
11560 Mexico
D.F. Mexico

Spain (including Portugal)
Thomson Paraninfo
Calle Magallanes, 25
28015 Madrid, Spain

Contents in Brief

Contents

Preface

Many students in the behavioral sciences view the required statistics course as an intimidating obstacle that has been placed in the middle of an otherwise interesting curriculum. They want to learn about human behavior—not about math and science. As a result, the statistics course is seen as irrelevant to their education and career goals. However, as long as the behavioral sciences are founded in science, knowledge of statistics will be necessary. Statistical procedures provide researchers with objective and systematic methods for describing and interpreting their research results. Scientific research is the system that we use to gather information, and statistics are the tools that we use to distill the information into sensible and justified conclusions. The goal of this book is not only to teach the methods of statistics, but also to convey the basic principles of objectivity and logic that are essential for science and valuable for decision making in everyday life.

Those of you who are familiar with previous editions of *Essentials of Statistics for the Behavioral Sciences* will notice that some changes have been made. These changes are summarized in the section entitled "To the Instructor." In revising this text, our students have been foremost in our minds. Over the years, they have provided honest and useful feedback. Their hard work and perseverance has made our writing and teaching most rewarding. We sincerely thank them. Students who are using this edition should please read the section of the preface entitled "To the Student."

ANCILLARIES

Ancillaries for this edition include the following:

- *WebAssign:* New to this edition, WebAssign allows instructors to assign additional homework and study problems to students so they can get even more practice on the most difficult concepts. Guided problems lead students through exercises step-by-step and get students back on track when they make a mistake.

- *Study Guide:* Contains a chapter overview, learning objectives, new terms and concepts, new formulas, step-by-step procedures for problem solving, study hints and cautions, a self-test, and review for each chapter. The Study Guide contains answers for the self-test questions.

- *Book Companion Website:* Additional, free study resources are available online at the book companion website. Practice and reinforce statistical concepts using the Statistics Workshops, chapter quizzes, chapter objectives, interactive flash cards, Web links, and more! Visit http://www.thomsonedu.com/psychology/gravetter.

- *Instructor's Manual with Test Bank:* Contains chapter outlines, annotated learning objectives, lecture suggestions, test items, and solutions to all end-of-chapter problems in the text. Test items are also available as a Word download or for ExamView computerized test bank software.

- *Transparency CD-ROM:* About 90 tables and figures taken directly from the text are available for instructors in PowerPoint.

- *JoinIn Student Response System:* Turn your classroom into an interactive experience with JoinIn polls and quizzes that allow students to respond with "clicker" keypads.

ACKNOWLEDGMENTS

It takes a lot of good, hard-working people to produce a book. Our friends at Wadsworth have made enormous contributions to this textbook. We thank our director, Marcus Boggs; our new editor, Erik Evans; assistant editor, Gina Kessler; editorial assistant, Christina Ganim; development editor, Kirk Bomont; technology project manager, Lauren Keyes; content project manager, Mary Noel; accuracy checker, Sudhir Goel; creative director, Vernon Boes; marketing manager, Karin Sandberg; marketing communications manager, Linda Yip; and marketing assistant, Melanie Cregger.

Reviewers play a very important role in the development of a manuscript. Accordingly, we offer our appreciation to the following colleagues for their assistance with the sixth edition: Noreen Dulin, Vanguard University of South Carolina; David J. Falcone, LaSalle University; Kristin Cotter Mena, University of Houston; Mark Vosvick, University of North Texas; Helga Walz, University of Baltimore; Todd Wiebers, Henderson State University. We would like to thank those who offered their insight on previous editions as well: Delbert Brodie, St. Thomas University; Deborah Carroll, Southern Connecticut State University; Michael Emond, Laurentian University; Jim Evans, Louisiana State University Shreveport; Joel Freund, University of Arkansas; Margarita Garcia-Estevez, Montclair State University; Roberto R. Heredia, Texas A&M University; Scott Hershberger, California State University, Long Beach; Charles Huffman, James Madison University; John Johanson, Winona State University; Mark Johnson, University of Maryland; Katheryn McGuthry, Reinhardt College; Kathryn Oleson, Reed College; Donald Saucier, University of Kentucky; and Richard Wielkiewicz, College of Saint Benedict.

TO THE INSTRUCTOR

Those of you familiar with the previous edition of *Statistics for the Behavioral Sciences* will notice a number of changes in the sixth edition. A new appendix (Appendix D) contains a general introduction to the statistics program SPSS®. In addition, at the end of each chapter for which an SPSS® analysis is feasible, there is a step-by-step set of instructions describing how to enter data, how to run the analysis, and what to look for in the output. Also, all end-of-chapter problem sets have been revised.

The following are examples of the specific and noteworthy revisions:

Chapter 1 More emphasis is placed on data structures and their relationship to statistical techniques and less emphasis on research methodology. Examples have been added to illustrate the different scales of measurement.

Chapter 3 New text acknowledges that most examples of computing the median are based on continuous variables and notes that some of the conventions involving the median can change if a discrete variable is involved.

Chapter 4 Greater emphasis is placed on the definition and concept of variance and standard deviation rather than the computation. Also, the section on degrees of freedom for sample variance has been expanded.

Chapter 5 A new section demonstrates and explains examples of z-score problems other than transforming back and forth between X-scores and z-scores. Also, a new section describes how z-scores can be used with sample data, rather than presenting z-scores exclusively in the context of population distributions.

Chapter 7 Expanded discussion of how the standard deviation and the sample size combine to determine the value of the standard error. Also, a new figure shows how standard error is related to sample size.

Chapter 8 The section on statistical power has been expanded, including a new figure to illustrate the relationship between sample size and power. Also, a new section discusses the different factors that influence the outcome of a hypothesis test (the size of the mean difference, the sample size, and the variability of the scores).

Chapter 9 The section on Cohen's *d* has been revised to clarify that we are now using sample values to obtain an estimate of Cohen's *d* (which is defined in terms of population parameters). Also a discussion has been added on how sample size and sample variance influence the hypothesis test.

Chapter 10 A new section discusses the interpretation of the standard error for a sample mean difference. Also, a new box describes an alternative to using pooled variance to compute the standard error for the independent-measures *t* statistic that eliminates the need for the homogeneity of variance assumption.

Chapter 11 A new section discusses order effects and time-related factors that are potential problems related exclusively to repeated-measures designs.

Chapter 12 The section on the interpretation of a confidence interval has been expanded.

Chapter 13 Increased emphasis is placed on the concepts of analysis of variance rather than the computations.

Chapter 14 New sections demonstrate measures of effect size for both the repeated-measures and the two-factor analysis of variance.

Chapter 15 The phi-coefficient has been added as one more example of a special application of correlation. Also, the presentation of regression has been expanded to include a new section on analysis of regression as an alternative method for evaluating the significance of a relationship.

TO THE STUDENT

A primary goal of this book is to make the task of learning statistics as easy and painless as possible. Among other things, you will notice that the book provides you with a number of opportunities to practice the techniques you will be learning in the form of learning checks, examples, demonstrations, and end-of-chapter problems. We encourage you to take advantage of these opportunities. Read the text rather than just memorize the formulas. We have taken care to present each statistical procedure in a conceptual context that explains why the procedure was developed and when it should be used. If you read this material and gain an understanding of the basic concepts underlying a statistical formula, you will find that learning the formula and how to use it will be much easier. In the following section, "Study Hints," we provide advice that we give our own students. Ask your instructor for advice as well; we are sure that other instructors will have ideas of their own.

Over the years, the students in our classes and other students using our book have given us valuable feedback. If you have any suggestions or comments about this book, you can write to either Professor Frederick Gravetter or Professor Emeritus Larry Wallnau at the Department of Psychology, SUNY College at Brockport, 350 New Campus Drive, Brockport, New York 14420. You can also contact Professor Gravetter directly at fgravett@brockport.edu.

Study Hints You may find some of these tips helpful, as our own students have reported.

- The key to success in a statistics course is to keep up with the material. Each new topic builds on previous topics. If you have learned the previous material, then the new topic is just one small step forward. Without the proper background, however, the new topic can be a complete mystery. If you find that you are falling behind, get help immediately.

- You will learn (and remember) much more if you study for short periods several times per week rather than try to condense all of your studying into one long session. For example, it is far more effective to study half an hour every night than to have a single $3\frac{1}{2}$-hour study session once a week. We cannot even work on *writing* this book without frequent rest breaks.

- Do some work before class. Keep a little ahead of the instructor by reading the appropriate sections before they are presented in class. Although you may not fully understand what you read, you will have a general idea of the topic, which will make the lecture easier to follow. Also, you can identify material that is particularly confusing and then be sure the topic is clarified in class.

- Pay attention and think during class. Although this advice seems obvious, often it is not practiced. Many students spend so much time trying to write down every example presented or every word spoken by the instructor that they do not actually understand and process what is being said. Check with your instructor— there may not be a need to copy every example presented in class, especially if there are many examples like it in the text. Sometimes, we tell our students to put their pens and pencils down for a moment and just listen.

- Test yourself regularly. Do not wait until the end of the chapter or the end of the week to check your knowledge. After each lecture, work some of the end-of-chapter problems, and do the Learning Checks. Review the Demonstration Problems, and be sure you can define the Key Terms. If you are having trouble, get your questions answered *immediately* (reread the section, go to your instructor, or ask questions in class). By doing so, you will be able to move ahead to new material.

- Do not kid yourself! Avoid denial. Many students observe their instructor solve problems in class and think to themselves, "This looks easy, I understand it." Do you really understand it? Can you really do the problem on your own without having to leaf through the pages of a chapter? Although there is nothing wrong with using examples in the text as models for solving problems, you should try working a problem with your book closed to test your level of mastery.

- We realize that many students are embarassed to ask for help. It is our biggest challenge as instructors. You must find a way to overcome this aversion. Perhaps contacting the instructor directly would be a good starting point, if asking questions in class is too anxiety-provoking. You could be pleasantly surprised to find that your instructor does not yell, scold, or bite! Also, your instructor might know of another student who can offer assistance. Peer tutoring can be very helpful.

Frederick J Gravetter
Larry B. Wallnau

About the Authors

Frederick J Gravetter is a Professor of Psychology at the State University of New York College at Brockport. Dr. Gravetter has taught at Brockport since the early 1970s, specializing in statistics, experimental design, and cognitive psychology. He

received his bachelor's degree in mathematics from M.I.T. and his Ph.D. in psychology from Duke University. In addition to publishing this textbook and several research articles, Dr. Gravetter co-authored *Research Methods for the Behavioral Science*s and *Statistics for the Behavioral Sciences*.

Nicki and Fred

Larry B. Wallnau is Professor Emeritus of Psychology at the State University of New York College at Brockport. While teaching at Brockport, he published numerous research articles, primarily on the behavioral effects of psychotropic drugs. With Dr. Gravetter, he co-authored *Statistics for the Behavioral Sciences*. He also has provided editorial consulting for numerous publishers and journals. He routinely gives lectures and demonstrations on service dogs for those with disabilities.

Ben and Larry

C H A P T E R

1

Introduction to Statistics

1.1   STATISTICS, SCIENCE, AND OBSERVATIONS

PREVIEW

Before we begin our discussion of statistics, we ask you to read the following paragraph taken from the philosophy of Wrong Shui (Candappa, 2000).

The Journey to Enlightenment
In Wrong Shui life is seen as a cosmic journey, a struggle to overcome unseen and unexpected obstacles at the end of which the traveler will find illumination and enlightenment. Replicate this quest in your home by moving light switches away from doors and over to the far side of each room.*

Why did we begin a statistics book with a bit of twisted philosophy? Actually, the paragraph is an excellent (and humorous) counterexample for the purpose of this book. Specifically, our goal is to help you avoid stumbling around in the dark by providing lots of easily available light switches and plenty of illumination as you journey through the world of statistics. To accomplish this, we try to present sufficient background and a clear statement of purpose as we introduce each new statistical procedure. Remember that all statistical procedures were developed to serve a purpose. If you understand why a new procedure is needed, you will find it much easier to learn.

The objectives for this first chapter are to provide an introduction to the topic of statistics and to give you some background for the rest of the book. We discuss the role of statistics within the general field of scientific inquiry, and we introduce some of the vocabulary and notation that are necessary for the statistical methods that follow.

As you read through the following chapters, keep in mind that the general topic of statistics follows a well-organized, logically developed progression that leads from basic concepts and definitions to increasingly sophisticated techniques. Thus, the material presented in the early chapters of this book will serve as a foundation for the ma terial that follows. The content of the first nine chapters, for example, provides an essential background and context for the statistical methods presented in Chapter 10. If you turn directly to Chapter 10 without reading the first nine chapters, you will find the material confusing and incomprehensible. However, if you learn and use the background material, you will have a good frame of reference for understanding and incorporating new concepts as they are presented.

DEFINITIONS OF STATISTICS

By one definition, *statistics* consist of facts and figures such as average income, crime rate, birth rate, average snowfall, and so on. These statistics are usually informative and time saving because they condense large quantities of information into a few simple figures. Later in this chapter we return to the notion of calculating statistics (facts and figures) but, for now, we concentrate on a much broader definition of statistics. Specifically, we use the term statistics to refer to a set of mathematical procedures. In this case, we are using the term *statistics* as a shortened version of *statistical procedures*. For example, you are probably using this book for a statistics course in which you will learn about the statistical techniques that are used for research in the behavioral sciences.

Research in psychology (and other fields) involves gathering information. To determine, for example, whether violence on TV has any effect on children's behavior, you

---

*Candappa, R. (2000) *The Little Book of Wrong Shui.* Kansas City: Andrews McMeel Publishing. Reprinted by permission.

would need to gather information about children's behaviors. When researchers finish the task of gathering information, they typically find themselves with pages and pages of measurements such as IQ scores, personality scores, reaction time scores, and so on. The role of statistics is to help researchers make sense of this information. Specifically, statistics serve two general purposes:

1. Statistics are used to organize and summarize the information so that the researcher can see what happened in the research study and can communicate the results to others.

2. Statistics help the researcher to answer the general questions that initiated the research by determining exactly what conclusions are justified based on the results that were obtained.

DEFINITION

The term **statistics** refers to a set of mathematical procedures for organizing, summarizing, and interpreting information.

Statistical procedures help ensure that the information or observations are presented and interpreted in an accurate and informative way. In somewhat grandiose terms, statistics help researchers bring order out of chaos. In addition, statistics provide researchers with a set of standardized techniques that are recognized and understood throughout the scientific community. Thus, the statistical methods used by one researcher will be familiar to other researchers, who can accurately interpret the statistical analyses with a full understanding of how the analysis was done and what the results signify.

1.2 POPULATIONS AND SAMPLES

WHAT ARE THEY?

Scientific research typically begins with a general question about a specific group (or groups) of individuals. For example, a researcher may be interested in the effect of divorce on the self-esteem of preteen children. Or a researcher may want to examine the political attitudes for men compared to women. In the first example, the researcher is interested in the group of *preteen children*. In the second example, the researcher wants to compare the group of *men* with the group of *women*. In statistical terminology, the entire group that a researcher wishes to study is called a *population*.

DEFINITION

A **population** is the set of all the individuals of interest in a particular study.

As you can well imagine, a population can be quite large—for example, the entire set of women on the planet Earth. A researcher might be more specific, limiting the population for study to women who are registered voters in the United States. Perhaps the investigator would like to study the population consisting of women who are heads of state. Populations can obviously vary in size from extremely large to very small, depending on how the investigator defines the population. The population being studied should always be identified by the researcher. In addition, the population need not consist of people—it could be a population of rats, corporations, parts produced in a factory, or anything else an investigator wants to study. In practice, populations are typically very large, such as the population of fourth-grade children in the United States or the population of small businesses.

Although research questions concern an entire population, it usually is impossible for a researcher to examine every individual in the population of interest. Therefore, researchers typically select a smaller, more manageable group from the population and limit their studies to the individuals in the selected group. In statistical terms, a set of individuals selected from a population is called a *sample*. A sample is intended to be representative of its population, and a sample should always be identified in terms of the population from which it was selected.

DEFINITION

A **sample** is a set of individuals selected from a population, usually intended to represent the population in a research study.

Just as we saw with populations, samples can vary in size. For example, one study might examine a sample of only 10 children in a preschool program, and another study might use a sample of more than 1000 registered voters representing the population of a major city.

So far we have talked about a sample being selected from a population. However, this is actually only half of the full relationship between a sample and its population. Specifically, when a researcher finishes examining the sample, the goal is to generalize the results back to the entire population. Remember that the research started with a general question about the population. To answer the question, a researcher studies a sample and then generalizes the results from the sample to the population. The full relationship between a sample and a population is shown in Figure 1.1.

VARIABLES AND DATA

Typically, researchers are interested in specific characteristics of the individuals in the population (or in the sample), or they are interested in outside factors that may influence the individuals. For example, a researcher may be interested in the influence of the weather on people's moods. As the weather changes, do people's moods also change? Something that can change or have different values is called a *variable*.

FIGURE 1.1

The relationship between a population and a sample.

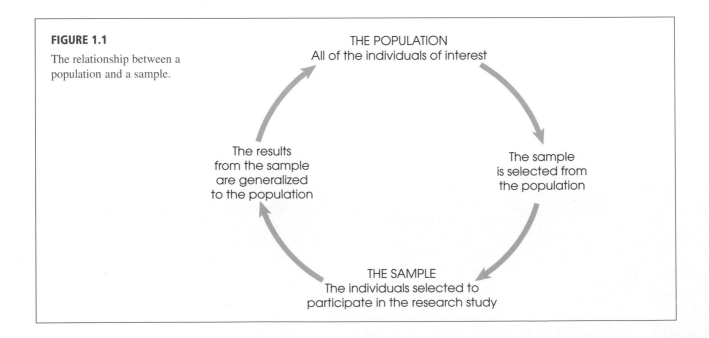

THE POPULATION
All of the individuals of interest

The sample
is selected from
the population

THE SAMPLE
The individuals selected to
participate in the research study

The results
from the sample
are generalized
to the population

D E F I N I T I O N	A **variable** is a characteristic or condition that changes or has different values for different individuals.

Once again, variables can be characteristics that differ from one individual to another, such as height, weight, gender, or personality. Also, variables can be environmental conditions that change such as temperature, time of day, or the size of the room in which the research is being conducted.

In order to demonstrate changes in variables, it is necessary to make measurements of the variables being examined. The measurement obtained for each individual is called a *datum,* or more commonly, a *score* or *raw score*. The complete set of scores is called the *data set* or simply the *data*.

D E F I N I T I O N S	**Data** (plural) are measurements or observations. A **data set** is a collection of measurements or observations. A **datum** (singular) is a single measurement or observation and is commonly called a **score** or **raw score**.

Before we move on, we should make one more point about samples, populations, and data. Earlier, we defined populations and samples in terms of *individuals*. For example, we discussed a population of preteen children and a sample of preschool children. Be forewarned, however, that we will also refer to populations or samples of *scores*. Because research typically involves measuring each individual to obtain a score, every sample (or population) of individuals produces a corresponding sample (or population) of scores.

PARAMETERS AND STATISTICS

When describing data it is necessary to distinguish whether the data come from a population or a sample. A characteristic that describes a population—for example, the population average—is called a *parameter*. On the other hand, a characteristic that describes a sample is called a *statistic*. Thus, the average score for a sample is an example of a statistic. Typically, the research process begins with a question about a population parameter. However, the actual data come from a sample and are used to compute sample statistics.

D E F I N I T I O N S	A **parameter** is a value, usually a numerical value, that describes a population. A parameter may be obtained from a single measurement, or it may be derived from a set of measurements from the population.
	A **statistic** is a value, usually a numerical value, that describes a sample. A statistic may be obtained from a single measurement, or it may be derived from a set of measurements from the sample.

Typically, every population parameter has a corresponding sample statistic, and much of this book is concerned with the relationship between sample statistics and the corresponding population parameters. In Chapter 7, for example, we examine the relationship between the mean obtained for a sample and the mean for the population from which the sample was obtained.

DESCRIPTIVE AND INFERENTIAL STATISTICAL METHODS

Although researchers have developed a variety of different statistical procedures to organize and interpret data, these different procedures can be classified into two general categories. The first category, *descriptive statistics,* consists of statistical procedures that are used to simplify and summarize data.

DEFINITION

Descriptive statistics are statistical procedures used to summarize, organize, and simplify data.

Descriptive statistics are techniques that take raw scores and organize or summarize them in a form that is more manageable. Often the scores are organized in a table or a graph so that it is possible to see the entire set of scores. Another common technique is to summarize a set of scores by computing an average. Note that even if the data set has hundreds of scores, the average provides a single descriptive value for the entire set.

The second general category of statistical techniques is called *inferential statistics*. Inferential statistics are methods that use sample data to make general statements about a population.

DEFINITION

Inferential statistics consist of techniques that allow us to study samples and then make generalizations about the populations from which they were selected.

It usually is not possible to measure everyone in the population. Because populations are typically very large, a sample is selected to represent the population. By analyzing the results from the sample, we hope to make general statements about the population. Typically, researchers use sample statistics as the basis for drawing conclusions about population parameters.

One problem with using samples, however, is that a sample provides only limited information about the population. Although samples are generally *representative* of their populations, a sample is not expected to give a perfectly accurate picture of the whole population. There usually is some discrepancy between a sample statistic and the corresponding population parameter. This discrepancy is called *sampling error*, and it creates another problem to be addressed by inferential statistics (Box 1.1).

DEFINITION

Sampling error is the discrepancy, or amount of error, that exists between a sample statistic and the corresponding population parameter.

The concept of sampling error is illustrated in Figure 1.2. The figure shows a population of 1000 college students and two samples, each with 5 students, that have been selected from the population. Notice that each sample contains different individuals

---

BOX 1.1   THE MARGIN OF ERROR BETWEEN STATISTICS AND PARAMETERS

One common example of sampling error is the error associated with a sample proportion. For example, in newspaper articles reporting results from political polls, you frequently find statements such as this:

Candidate Brown leads the poll with 51% of the vote. Candidate Jones has 42% approval, and the remaining 7% are undecided. This poll was taken from a sample of registered voters and has a margin of error of plus-or-minus 4 percentage points.

The "margin of error" is the sampling error. In this case, the percentages that are reported were obtained from a sample and are being generalized to the whole population. As always, you do not expect the statistics from a sample to be perfect. There always will be some "margin of error" when sample statistics are used to represent population parameters.

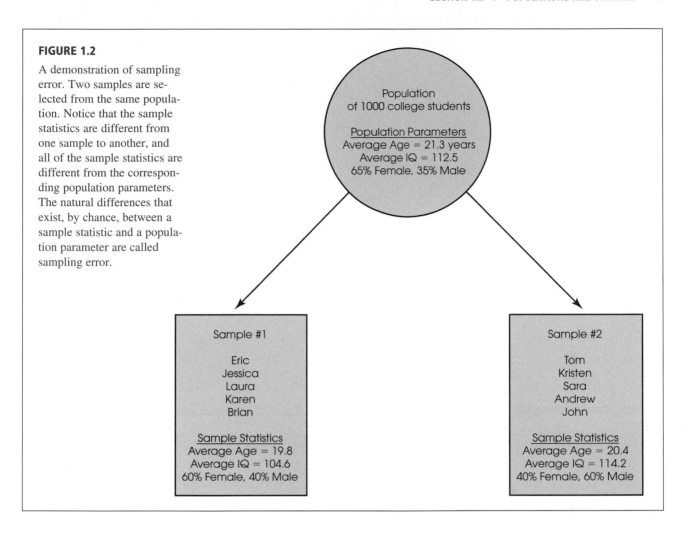

FIGURE 1.2

A demonstration of sampling error. Two samples are selected from the same population. Notice that the sample statistics are different from one sample to another, and all of the sample statistics are different from the corresponding population parameters. The natural differences that exist, by chance, between a sample statistic and a population parameter are called sampling error.

Population of 1000 college students

Population Parameters
Average Age = 21.3 years
Average IQ = 112.5
65% Female, 35% Male

Sample #1

Eric
Jessica
Laura
Karen
Brian

Sample Statistics
Average Age = 19.8
Average IQ = 104.6
60% Female, 40% Male

Sample #2

Tom
Kristen
Sara
Andrew
John

Sample Statistics
Average Age = 20.4
Average IQ = 114.2
40% Female, 60% Male

who have different characteristics. Because the characteristics of each sample depend on the specific people in the sample, the statistics will vary from one sample to another. In addition, neither sample has statistics that are exactly the same as the population parameters. You should also realize that Figure 1.2 shows only two of the hundreds of possible samples. Each sample would contain different individuals and would produce different statistics. This is the basic concept of sampling error: sample statistics vary from one sample to another and typically are different from the corresponding population parameters.

As a further demonstration of sampling error, imagine that your statistics class is separated into two groups by drawing a line from front to back through the middle of the room. Now imagine that you compute the average age (or height, or IQ) for each group. Will the two groups have exactly the same average? Almost certainly they will not. No matter what you chose to measure, you will probably find some difference between the two groups. Should you interpret this difference as meaning that there is a general tendency for older people to sit on the right-hand side of a room? Again, the answer is probably not. It is unlikely that the difference is "caused" by some systematic tendency that leads older people to gravitate to the right (or left) side of a room. Instead, the difference is probably the result of chance. The unpredictable, unsystematic differences that exist from one sample to another are another example of sampling error.

STATISTICS IN THE CONTEXT OF RESEARCH

The following example shows the general stages of a research study and demonstrates how descriptive statistics and inferential statistics are used to organize and interpret the data. At the end of the example, note how sampling error can affect the interpretation of experimental results, and consider why inferential statistical methods are needed to deal with this problem.

EXAMPLE 1.1

Figure 1.3 shows an overview of a general research situation and demonstrates the roles that descriptive and inferential statistics play. The purpose of the research study

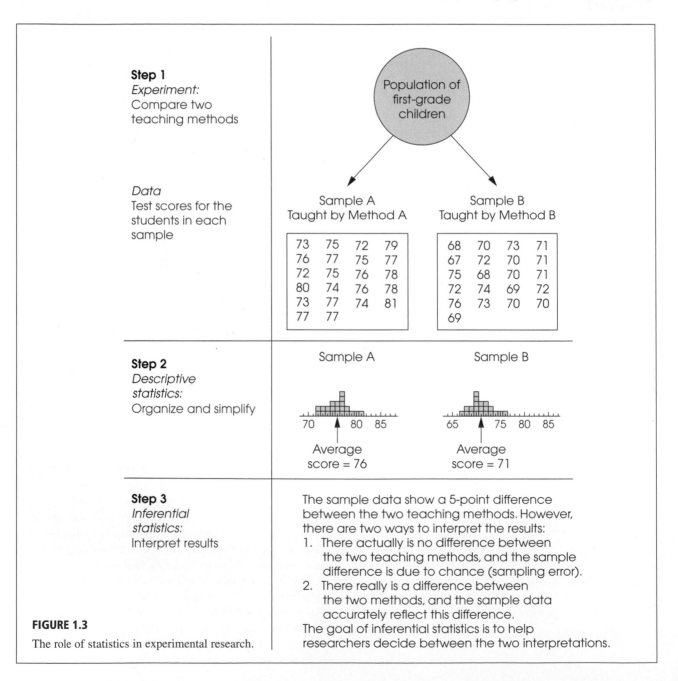

FIGURE 1.3

The role of statistics in experimental research.

is to evaluate the difference between two methods for teaching reading to first-grade children. Two samples are selected from the population of first-grade children. The children in sample A are assigned to teaching method A and the children in sample B are assigned to method B. After 6 months, all of the students are given a standardized reading test. At this point, the researcher has two sets of data: the scores for sample A and the scores for sample B (see Figure 1.3). Now is the time to begin using statistics.

First, descriptive statistics are used to simplify the pages of data. For example, the researcher could draw a graph showing the scores for each sample or compute the average score for each sample. Note that descriptive methods provide a simplified, organized description of the scores. In this example, the students taught by method A averaged 76 on the standardized test, and the students taught by method B averaged only 71.

Once the researcher has described the results, the next step is to interpret the outcome. This is the role of inferential statistics. In this example, the researcher has found a 5-point difference between the two samples. The problem for inferential statistics is to differentiate between the following two interpretations:

1. There is no systematic difference between the two teaching methods, and the 5-point difference between the samples is just an example of sampling error (like the samples in Figure 1.2).

2. There really is a difference between the two teaching methods, and the 5-point difference between the samples was caused by the different methods of teaching.

In simple English, does the 5-point difference between samples provide convincing evidence of a difference between the two teaching methods, or is the 5-point difference just chance? The purpose of inferential statistics is to answer this question.

LEARNING CHECK

1. What is a *population* and what is a *sample?*

2. A characteristic that describes a population, such as the population average, is called a _____.

3. The relationship between a population and a parameter is the same as the relationship between a sample and a _____.

4. Statistical techniques are classified into two general categories. What are the two categories called, and what is the general purpose for the techniques in each category?

5. Briefly define the concept of sampling error.

ANSWERS

1. The population is the entire set of individuals of interest for a particular research study. The sample is the specific set of individuals selected to participate in the study. The sample is expected to be representative of the population.

2. parameter   3. statistic

4. The two categories are descriptive statistics and inferential statistics. Descriptive techniques are intended to organize, simplify, and summarize data. Inferential techniques use sample data to reach general conclusions about populations.

5. Sampling error is the error or discrepancy between the value obtained for a sample statistic and the value for the corresponding population parameter.

1.3   DATA STRUCTURES, RESEARCH METHODS, AND STATISTICS

RELATIONSHIPS BETWEEN VARIABLES

Some research studies are conducted simply to describe individual variables as they exist naturally. For example, a college official may conduct a survey to describe the eating, sleeping, and study habits of a group of college students. Most research, however, is intended to examine the relationship between variables. For example, is there a relationship between sugar consumption and activity level for preschool children? Is there a relationship between the quality of breakfast and academic performance for elementary school children? Is there a relationship between the number of hours of sleep and grade point average for college students? To establish the existence of a relationship, researchers must make observations—that is, measurements of the two variables. The resulting measurements can be classified into two distinct data structures that also help to classify different research methods and different statistical techniques. In the following section we identify and discuss these two data structures.

I. Measuring two variables for each individual: the correlational method   One method for examining the relationship between variables is to observe the two variables as they exist naturally for a set of individuals. That is, simply measure the two variables for each individual. For example, research has demonstrated a relationship between sleep habits, especially wake-up time, and academic performance for college students (Trockel, Barnes, and Egget, 2000). The researchers used a survey to measure wake-up time and school records to measure academic performance for each student. Figure 1.4 shows an example of the kind of data obtained in the study. The researchers then look for consistent patterns in the data to provide evidence for a relationship between variables. For example, as wake-up time changes from one student to another, is there also a tendency for academic performance to change?

Consistent patterns in the data are often easier to see if the scores are presented in a graph. Figure 1.4 also shows the scores for the eight students in a graph called a scatter

(a)

Student	Wake-up Time	Academic Performance
A	11	2.4
B	9	3.6
C	9	3.2
D	12	2.2
E	7	3.8
F	10	2.2
G	10	3.0
H	8	3.0

(b)

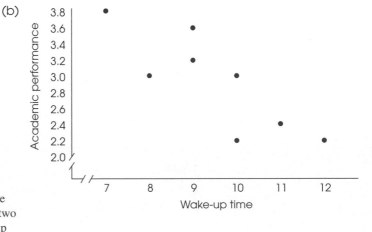

FIGURE 1.4

One of two data structures for studies evaluating the relationship between variables. Note that there are two separate measurements for each individual (wake-up time and academic performance). The same scores are shown in a table (a) and in a graph (b).

plot. In the scatter plot, each individual is represented by a point so that the horizontal position corresponds to the student's wake-up time and the vertical position corresponds to the student's academic performance score. The scatter plot shows a clear relationship between wake-up time and academic performance: as wake-up time increases, academic performance decreases.

A research study that simply measures two variables for each individual and produces the kind of data shown in Figure 1.4 is an example of the *correlational method* or the *correlational research strategy.* The relationship between variables is usually measured and described using a statistic called a correlation. Correlations and the correlational method are discussed in detail in Chapter 15.

DEFINITION

In the **correlational method,** two variables are observed to determine whether there is a relationship between them.

Occasionally, the correlational method produces scores that are not numerical values. For example, a researcher could measure home location (city or suburb) and attitude toward a new budget proposal (for or against) for a group of registered voters. Note that the researcher has two measurements for each individual but neither of the measurements is a numerical score. This type of data is typically summarized in a table showing how many individuals are classified into each of the possible categories. Table 1.1 shows an example of this kind of summary table. The relationship between variables for non-numerical data, such as the data in Table 1.1, is evaluated using a statistical technique known as a *chi-square test.* Chi-square tests are presented in Chapter 16.

II. Comparing two (or more) groups of scores: experimental and non-experimental methods   The second method for examining the relationship between two variables involves the comparison of two or more groups of scores. In this situation, the relationship between variables is examined by using one of the variables to define the groups, then measuring the second variable to obtain scores for each group. For example, one group of elementary school children is given a nutritious breakfast each morning and a second group is given no breakfast. Then, academic performance is measured for each child. An example of the resulting data is shown in Figure 1.5. Note that the researcher will compare the scores for the breakfast group with the scores for the no-breakfast group. A consistent difference between groups provides evidence of a relationship between eating breakfast and academic performance.

When the measurement procedure produces numerical scores, the statistical evaluation typically involves computing the average score for each group and then comparing the averages. The process of computing averages is presented in Chapter 3, and a variety of statistical techniques for comparing averages are presented in Chapters 8–14. If

TABLE 1.1

Correlational data consisting of non-numerical scores. Note that there are two measurements for each individual: home location and attitude. The numbers indicate how many people are in each category. For example, out of the 50 people living in the city, 40 are for the proposal.

		Attitude toward budget proposal		
		For	Against	
Home location	City	40	10	50
	Suburb	20	30	50
		60	40	

FIGURE 1.5

The second data structure for studies evaluating the relationship between variables. Note that one variable is used to define the groups and the second variable is measured to obtain scores within each group.

One variable (breakfast/no breakfast) is used to define groups

A second variable (academic performance) is measured to obtain scores within each group

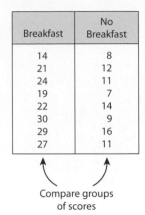

Breakfast	No Breakfast
14	8
21	12
24	11
19	7
22	14
30	9
29	16
27	11

Compare groups of scores

the measurement process simply classifies individuals into nonnumerical categories, the statistical evaluation usually consists of computing proportions for each group and then comparing proportions. Previously, in Table 1.1, we presented an example of nonnumerical data examining the relationship between attitude and home location. The same data can be used to compare the proportions for the two groups. For example, 80% of the people from the city are in favor of the new budget, whereas only 40% of the people from the suburbs are in favor. As before, these data are evaluated using a chi-square test, which is presented in Chapter 16.

THE EXPERIMENTAL METHOD

One specific research method that involves comparing groups of scores is known as the *experimental method* or the *experimental research strategy*. The goal of an experimental study is to demonstrate a cause-and-effect relationship between two variables. Specifically, an experiment attempts to show that changing the value of one variable will cause changes to occur in the second variable. To accomplish this goal, the experimental method has two characteristics that differentiate experiments from other types of research studies:

1. **Manipulation**   The researcher manipulates one variable by changing its value from one level to another. A second variable is observed (measured) to determine whether the manipulation causes changes to occur.

2. **Control**   The researcher must exercise some control over the research situation to ensure that other, extraneous variables do not influence the relationship being examined.

To demonstrate these two characteristics, consider an experiment in which a researcher is examining the effects of room temperature on memory performance. The purpose of the experiment is to determine whether changes in room temperature *cause* changes in memory performance.

The researcher manipulates temperature by creating two or more different treatment conditions. For example, our researcher could set the temperature at 70° for one condition and then change the temperature to 90° for a second condition. The researcher then measures memory performance for a group of individuals (called subjects or participants) in the 70° room and compares their scores with another group that is tested in the 90° room. The structure of this experiment is shown in Figure 1.6.

To be able to say that differences in memory performance are caused by temperature, the researcher must rule out any other possible explanations for the difference.

In more complex experiments, a researcher may systematically manipulate more than one variable and may observe more than one variable. Here we are considering the simplest case, in which only one variable is manipulated and only one variable is observed.

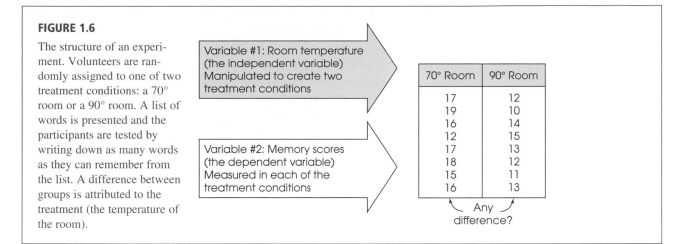

FIGURE 1.6

The structure of an experiment. Volunteers are randomly assigned to one of two treatment conditions: a 70° room or a 90° room. A list of words is presented and the participants are tested by writing down as many words as they can remember from the list. A difference between groups is attributed to the treatment (the temperature of the room).

Variable #1: Room temperature (the independent variable) Manipulated to create two treatment conditions

Variable #2: Memory scores (the dependent variable) Measured in each of the treatment conditions

70° Room	90° Room
17	12
19	10
16	14
12	15
17	13
18	12
15	11
16	13

Any difference?

That is, any other variables that might affect memory performance must be controlled. There are two general categories of variables that researchers must consider:

1. **Participant Variables**   These are characteristics such as age, gender, and intelligence that vary from one individual to another. Whenever an experiment compares different groups of participants (one group in treatment A and a different group in treatment B), researchers must ensure that participant variables do not differ from one group to another. For example, the experiment shown in Figure 1.6 compares memory performance in a 70° room with performance in a 90° room. Suppose, however, that the participants in the 70° room have higher IQs than the participants in the 90° room. In this case, the experiment would be confounded. Specifically, if one group has higher memory scores than the other, the researcher cannot determine whether differences in memory are caused by temperature or are caused by intelligence.

2. **Environmental Variables**   These are characteristics of the environment such as lighting, time of day, and weather conditions. A researcher must ensure that the individuals in treatment A are tested in the same environment as the individuals in treatment B. Using the temperature experiment (see Figure 1.6) as an example, suppose that the individuals in the 70° room were all tested in the morning and the individuals in the 90° room were all tested in the afternoon. Again, this would produce a confounded experiment because the researcher could not determine whether the differences in memory scores were caused by temperature or caused by the time of day.

A research study is *confounded* whenever there is more than one explanation for the results.

Researchers typically use three basic techniques to control other variables. First, the researcher could use *random assignment,* which means that each participant has an equal chance of being assigned to each of the treatment conditions. The goal of random assignment is to distribute the participant characteristics evenly between the two groups so that neither group is noticeably smarter (or older, or faster) than the other. Random assignment can also be used to control environmental variables. For example, participants could be randomly assigned to be tested either in the morning or in the afternoon. Second, the researcher can use *matching* to ensure equivalent groups or equivalent environments. For example, the researcher could measure each particpant's IQ and then assign individuals to groups so that all of the groups have roughly the same average IQ. Finally, the researcher can control variables by *holding them constant.* For example, if an experiment uses only 10-year-old children as particpants (holding age constant), then the researcher can be certain that one group is not noticeably older than another.

DEFINITION

In the **experimental method,** one variable is manipulated, while another variable is observed and measured. To establish a cause-and-effect relationship between the two variables, an experiment attempts to control all other variables to prevent them from influencing the results.

Terminology in the experimental method   Specific names are used for the two variables that are studied by the experimental method. The variable that is manipulated by the experimenter is called the *independent variable.* It can be identified as the treatment conditions to which participants are assigned. For the example in Figure 1.6, temperature is the independent variable. The variable that is observed to assess a possible effect of the manipulation is the *dependent variable.*

DEFINITIONS

The **independent variable** is the variable that is manipulated by the researcher. In behavioral research, the independent variable usually consists of the two (or more) treatment conditions to which subjects are exposed. The independent variable consists of the *antecedent* conditions that were manipulated *prior* to observing the dependent variable.

The **dependent variable** is the one that is observed in order to assess the effect of the treatment.

In psychological research, the dependent variable is typically a measurement or score obtained for each participant. For the temperature experiment (Figure 1.6), the dependent variable is the number of words recalled on the memory test. Differences between groups in performance on the dependent variable suggest that the manipulation had an effect. That is, changes in the dependent variable *depend* on changes in the independent variable.

An experimental study evaluates the relationship between two variables by manipulating one variable (the independent variable) and measuring one variable (the dependent variable). Note that in an experiment only one variable is actually measured. You should realize that this is very different from a correlational study, in which both variables are measured and the data consist of two separate scores for each individual.

Often an experiment will include a condition in which the subjects do not receive any treatment. The scores from these subjects are then compared with scores from subjects who do receive the treatment. The goal of this type of study is to demonstrate that the treatment has an effect by showing that the scores in the treatment condition are substantially different from the scores in the no-treatment condition. In this kind of research, the no-treatment condition is called the *control condition,* and the treatment condition is called the *experimental condition.*

DEFINITIONS

Individuals in a **control condition** do not receive the experimental treatment. Instead, they either receive no treatment or they receive a neutral, placebo treatment. The purpose of a control condition is to provide a baseline for comparison with the experimental condition.

Individuals in the **experimental condition** do receive the experimental treatment.

Note that the independent variable always consists of at least two values. (Something must have at least two different values before you can say that it is "variable.") For the temperature experiment (Figure 1.6), the independent variable is temperature (using values of 90° and 70°). For an experiment with an experimental group and a control group, the independent variable would be treatment versus no treatment.

NONEXPERIMENTAL METHODS: NONEQUIVALENT GROUPS AND PRE–POST STUDIES

There are a number of other research designs that are not true experiments but still examine the relationship between variables by comparing groups of scores. Two examples are shown in Figure 1.7 and are discussed in the following paragraphs. This type of research study is classified as nonexperimental.

The top part of Figure 1.7 shows an example of a *nonequivalent groups* study comparing boys and girls. Notice that this study involves comparing two groups of scores (like an experiment). However, the researcher has no ability to control which participants go into which group—all the males must be in the boy group and all the females must be in the girl group. Because this type of research compares preexisting groups, the researcher cannot control the assignment of participants to groups and cannot ensure equivalent groups. Other examples of nonequivalent group studies include comparing 8-year-old children and 10-year old children; people with an eating disorder and those with no disorder; and children from a single-parent home and those from a two-parent home. Because it is impossible to use techniques like random assignment to ensure equivalent groups, this type of research is not a true experiment.

The bottom part of Figure 1.7 shows an example of a *pre–post* study comparing depression scores before therapy and after therapy. Again, the study is comparing two

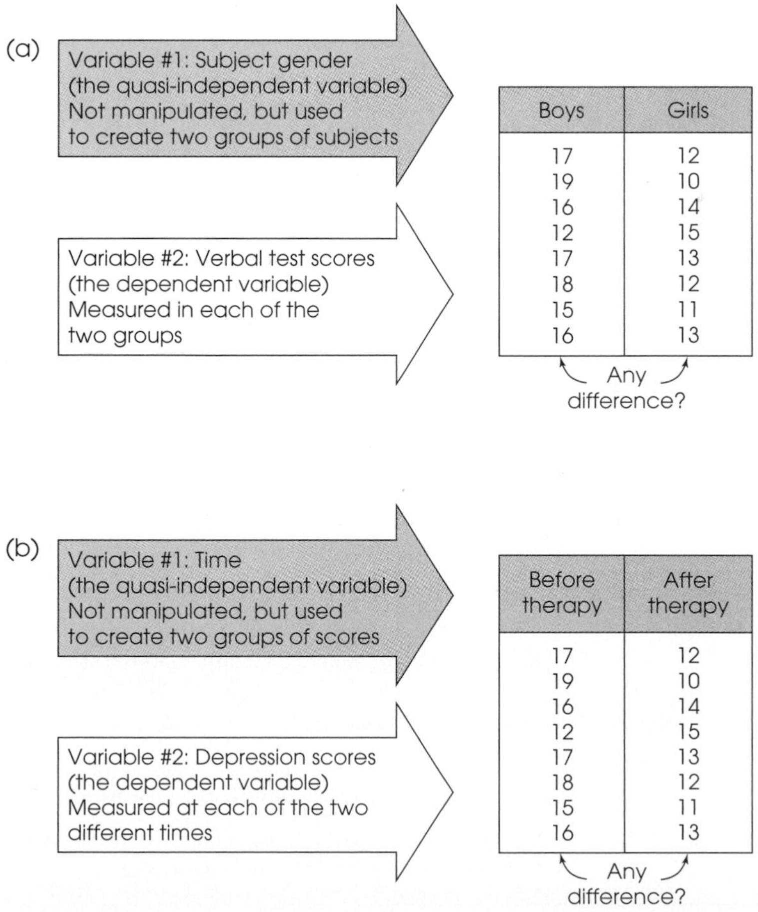

FIGURE 1.7

Two examples of nonexperimental studies that involve comparing two groups of scores. In (a) the study uses two preexisting groups (boys/girls) and measures a dependent variable (verbal scores) in each group. In (b) the study uses time (before/after) to define the two groups and measures a dependent variable (depression) in each group.

(a) Variable #1: Subject gender (the quasi-independent variable) Not manipulated, but used to create two groups of subjects

Variable #2: Verbal test scores (the dependent variable) Measured in each of the two groups

Boys	Girls
17	12
19	10
16	14
12	15
17	13
18	12
15	11
16	13

Any difference?

(b) Variable #1: Time (the quasi-independent variable) Not manipulated, but used to create two groups of scores

Variable #2: Depression scores (the dependent variable) Measured at each of the two different times

Before therapy	After therapy
17	12
19	10
16	14
12	15
17	13
18	12
15	11
16	13

Any difference?

groups of scores (like an experiment). In this study, however, the researcher has no control over the passage of time. The "before" scores are always measured earlier than the "after" scores. Although a difference between the two groups of scores may be caused by the treatment, it is always possible that the scores simply change as time goes by. For example, the depression scores may decrease over time in the same way that the symptoms of a cold disappear over time. In a pre–post study the researcher also has no control over other variables that change with time. For example, the weather could change from dark and gloomy before therapy to bright and sunny after therapy. In this case, the depression scores could improve because of the weather and not because of the therapy. Because the researcher cannot control the passage of time or other variables related to time, this study is not a true experiment.

Although the two research studies shown in Figure 1.7 are not true experiments, you should notice that they produce the same kind of data that are found in an experiment (see Figure 1.6). In each case, one variable is used to create groups, and a second variable is measured to obtain scores within each group. In an experiment, the groups are created by manipulating the independent variable and the scores are the dependent variable. The same terminology is often used to identify the two variables in nonexperimental studies. That is, the variable that is used to create groups is the independent variable and the scores are the dependent variable. For example, the top part of Figure 1.7, gender (boy/girl), is the independent variable and the verbal test scores are the dependent variable. However, you should realize that gender (boy/girl) is not a true independent variable because it is not manipulated. For this reason, the "independent variable" in a nonexperimental study is often called a *quasi-independent variable.*

DEFINITION	In a nonexperimental study, the "independent variable" that is used to create the different groups of scores is often called the **quasi-independent variable.**

Most of the statistical procedures presented in this book are designed for research studies that compare sets of scores like the experimental study in Figure 1.6 and the nonexperimental studies in Figure 1.7. Specifically, we will examine descriptive statistics that summarize and describe the scores in each group, and we will examine inferential statistics that will allow us to use the groups, or samples, to generalize to the entire population.

LEARNING CHECK

1. A researcher observes that elderly people who take regular doses of an anti-inflammatory drug are less likely to be diagnosed with Alzheimer's disease than their peers who do not take the drug. Is this study an example of the correlational method or the experimental method?

2. What two elements are necessary for a research study to be an experiment?

3. The results from an experiment indicate that increasing the amount of indoor lighting during the winter months results in significantly lower levels of depression. Identify the independent variable and the dependent variable for this study.

ANSWERS

1. This is a correlational study. The researcher is simply observing the variables.

2. First, the researcher must manipulate one of the two variables being studied. Second, all other variables that might influence the results must be controlled.

3. The independent variable is the amount of indoor lighting, and the dependent variable is a measure of depression for each individual.

1.4   VARIABLES AND MEASUREMENT

The scores that make up the data from a research study are the result of observing and measuring variables. For example, a researcher may finish a study with a set of IQ scores, personality scores, or reaction time scores. In this section, we will take a closer look at the variables that are being measured and the process of measurement.

CONSTRUCTS AND OPERATIONAL DEFINITIONS

Many of the variables studied by behavioral scientists are actually hypothetical concepts that are used to help describe and interpret behavior. For example, we say that a child does well in school because he or she is *intelligent.* Or we say that someone is anxious in a social situation because he or she has low *self-esteem.* The concepts of "intelligence" and "self-esteem" are called *constructs,* and because they cannot be directly observed, they are hypothetical.

Although constructs such as intelligence are internal characteristics that cannot be directly observed, it is possible to observe and measure behaviors that are representative of the construct. For example, we cannot "see" intelligence but we can see examples of intelligent behavior. The external behaviors can then be used to create an operational definition for the construct. An *operational definition* defines a construct in terms of behaviors that can be measured and observed. For example, your intelligence is defined in terms of your performance on an IQ test.

DEFINITIONS

Constructs are internal attributes or characteristics that cannot be directly observed but are useful for describing and explaining behavior.

An **operational definition** identifies a measurement procedure (a set of operations) for measuring an external behavior and uses the resulting measurements as a definition and a measurement of a hypothetical construct. Note that an operational definition has two components: First, it describes a set of operations for measuring a construct. Second, it defines the construct in terms of the resulting measurements.

DISCRETE AND CONTINUOUS VARIABLES

The variables in a study can be characterized by the type of values that can be assigned to them. A *discrete variable* consists of separate, indivisible categories. For this type of variable, there are no intermediate values between two adjacent categories. Consider the values displayed when dice are rolled. Between neighboring values—for example, seven dots and eight dots—no other values can ever be observed.

DEFINITION

A **discrete variable** consists of separate, indivisible categories. No values can exist between two neighboring categories.

Discrete variables are commonly restricted to whole countable numbers—for example, the number of children in a family or the number of students attending class. If you observe class attendance from day to day, you may count 18 students one day and 19 students the next day. However, it is impossible ever to observe a value between 18 and 19. A discrete variable may also consist of observations that differ qualitatively. For example, a psychologist observing patients may classify some as having panic disorders, others as having dissociative disorders, and some as having psychotic disorders. The type of disorder is a discrete variable because there are distinct and finite categories that can be observed.

On the other hand, many variables are not discrete. Variables such as time, height, and weight are not limited to a fixed set of separate, indivisible categories. You can measure time, for example, in hours, minutes, seconds, or fractions of seconds. These variables are called *continuous* because they can be divided into an infinite number of fractional parts.

DEFINITION

For a **continuous variable**, there are an infinite number of possible values that fall between any two observed values. A continuous variable is divisible into an infinite number of fractional parts.

Suppose, for example, that a researcher is measuring weights for a group of individuals participating in a diet study. Because weight is a continuous variable, it can be pictured as a continuous line (Figure 1.8). Note that there are an infinite number of possible points on the line without any gaps or separations between neighboring points. For any two different points on the line, it is always possible to find a third value that is between the two points.

Two other factors apply to continuous variables:

1. When measuring a continuous variable, it should be very rare to obtain identical measurements for two different individuals. Because a continuous variable has an infinite number of possible values, it should be almost impossible for two people to have exactly the same score. If the data show a substantial number of tied scores, then you should suspect that the measurement procedure is very crude or that the variable is not really continuous.

2. When measuring a continuous variable, each measurement category is actually an *interval* that must be defined by boundaries. For example, two people who both claim to weigh 150 pounds are probably not *exactly* the same weight. However, they are both around 150 pounds. One person may actually weigh 149.6 and the other 150.3. Thus, a score of 150 is not a specific point on the scale but instead is an interval (see Figure 1.8). To differentiate a score of 150 from a score of 149 or 151, we must set up boundaries on the scale of measurement. These boundaries are called *real limits* and are positioned exactly halfway between adjacent scores. Thus, a score of $X = 150$ pounds is actually

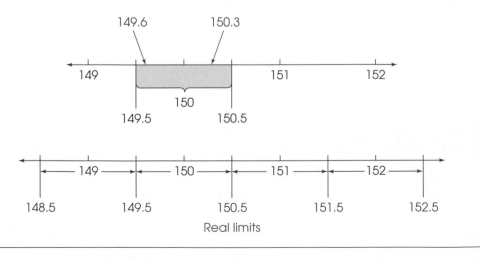

FIGURE 1.8

When measuring weight to the nearest whole pound, 149.6 and 150.3 are assigned the value of 150 (top). Any value in the interval between 149.5 and 150.5 is given the value of 150.

an interval bounded by a *lower real limit* of 149.5 at the bottom and an *upper real limit* of 150.5 at the top. Any individual whose weight falls between these real limits will be assigned a score of $X = 150$.

DEFINITION

Real limits are the boundaries of intervals for scores that are represented on a continuous number line. The real limit separating two adjacent scores is located exactly halfway between the scores. Each score has two real limits. The **upper real limit** is at the top of the interval, and the **lower real limit** is at the bottom.

The concept of real limits applies to any measurement of a continuous variable, even when the score categories are not whole numbers. For example, if you were measuring time to the nearest tenth of a second, the measurement categories would be 31.0, 31.1, 31.2, and so on. Each of these categories represents an interval on the scale that is bounded by real limits. For example, a score of $X = 31.1$ seconds indicates that the actual measurement is in an interval bounded by a lower real limit of 31.05 and an upper real limit of 31.15. Remember that the real limits are always halfway between adjacent categories.

Later in this book, real limits are used for constructing graphs and for various calculations with continuous scales. For now, however, you should realize that real limits are a necessity whenever you make measurements of a continuous variable.

SCALES OF MEASUREMENT

It should be obvious by now that data collection requires that we make measurements of our observations. Measurement involves assigning individuals or events to categories. The categories can simply be names such as male/female or employed/unemployed, or they can be numerical values such as 68 inches or 175 pounds. The complete set of categories makes up a *scale of measurement,* and the relationships between the categories determine different types of scales. The distinctions among the scales are important because they identify the limitations of certain types of measurements and because certain statistical procedures are appropriate for data collected on some scales but not on others. If you were interested in people's heights, for example, you could measure a group of individuals by simply classifying them into three categories: tall, medium, and short. However, this simple classification would not tell you much about the actual heights of the individuals, and these measurements would not give you enough information to calculate an average height for the group. Although the simple classification would be adequate for some purposes, you would need more sophisticated measurements before you could answer more detailed questions. In this section, we examine four different scales of measurement, beginning with the simplest and moving to the most sophisticated.

THE NOMINAL SCALE

The word *nominal* means "having to do with names." Measurement on a nominal scale involves classifying individuals into categories that have different names but that are not related to each other in any systematic way. For example, if you were measuring the academic majors for a group of college students, the categories would be art, biology, business, chemistry, and so on. Each student would be classified in one category according to his or her major. The measurements from a nominal scale allow us to determine whether two individuals are different, but they do not identify either the direction or the size of the difference. If one student is an art major and another is a biology major we can say that they are different, but we cannot say that art is "more than" or "less than" biology and we cannot specify how much difference there is between art and biology. Other examples of nominal scales include classifying people by race, gender, or occupation.

DEFINITION

A **nominal scale** consists of a set of categories that have different names. Measurements on a nominal scale label and categorize observations, but do not make any quantitative distinctions between observations.

Although the categories on a nominal scale are not quantitative values, they are occasionally represented by numbers. For example, the rooms or offices in a building may be identified by numbers. You should realize that the room numbers are simply names and do not reflect any quantitative information. Room 109 is not necessarily bigger than Room 100 and certainly not 9 points bigger. It also is fairly common to use numerical values as a code for nominal categories when data are entered into computer programs. For example, the data from a survey may code males with a 0 and females with a 1. Again, the numerical values are simply names and do not represent any quantitative difference. The scales that follow do reflect an attempt to make quantitative distinctions.

THE ORDINAL SCALE

The categories that make up an *ordinal scale* not only have different names (as in a nominal scale) but also are organized in a fixed order corresponding to differences of magnitude.

DEFINITION

An **ordinal scale** consists of a set of categories that are organized in an ordered sequence. Measurements on an ordinal scale rank observations in terms of size or magnitude.

Often, an ordinal scale consists of a series of ranks (first, second, third, and so on) like the order of finish in a horse race. Occasionally, the categories are identified by verbal labels like small, medium, and large drink sizes at a fast-food restaurant. In either case, the fact that the categories form an ordered sequence means that there is a directional relationship between categories. With measurements from an ordinal scale, you can determine whether two individuals are different and you can determine the direction of difference. However, ordinal measurements do not allow you to determine the magnitude of the difference between two individuals. For example, if Billy is placed in the low-reading group and Tim is placed in the high-reading group, you know that Tim is a better reader, but you do not know how much better. Other examples of ordinal scales include socioeconomic class (upper, middle, lower) and T-shirt sizes (small, medium, large). In addition, ordinal scales are often used to measure variables for which it is difficult to assign numerical scores. For example, people can rank their food preferences but might have trouble explaining "how much" they prefer chocolate ice cream to steak.

THE INTERVAL AND RATIO SCALES

Both an *interval scale* and a *ratio scale* consist of series of ordered categories (like an ordinal scale) with the additional requirement that the categories form a series of intervals that are all exactly the same size. Thus, the scale of measurement consists of a series of equal intervals, such as inches on a ruler. Other examples of interval and ratio scales are the measurement of time in seconds, weight in pounds, and temperature in degrees Fahrenheit. Note that, in each case, one interval (1 inch, 1 second, 1 pound, 1 degree) is the same size, no matter where it is located on the scale. The fact that the intervals are all the same size makes it possible to determine both the size and the direction of the difference between two measurements. For example, you know that a measurement of 80° Fahrenheit is higher than a measure of 60°, and you know that it is exactly 20° higher.

The factor that differentiates an interval scale from a ratio scale is the nature of the zero point. An interval scale has an arbitrary zero point. That is, the value 0 is assigned to a particular location on the scale simply as a matter of convenience or reference. In particular, a value of zero does not indicate a total absence of the variable being measured. For example a temperature of 0 degrees Fahrenheit does not mean that there is no temperature, and it does not prohibit the temperature from going even lower. Interval scales with an arbitrary zero point are relatively rare. The two most common examples are the Fahrenheit and Celsius temperature scales. Other examples include golf scores (above and below par) and relative measures such as above and below average rainfall.

A ratio scale is anchored by a zero point that is not arbitrary but rather is a meaningful value representing none (a complete absence) of the variable being measured. The existence of an absolute, nonabitrary zero point means that we can measure the absolute amount of the variable; that is, we can measure the distance from 0. This makes it possible to compare measurements in terms of ratios. For example, an individual who requires 10 seconds to solve a problem (10 more than 0) has taken twice as much time as an individual who finishes in only 5 seconds (5 more than 0). With a ratio scale, we can measure the direction and the size of the difference between two measurements and we can describe the difference in terms of a ratio. Ratio scales are quite common and include physical measures such as height and weight, as well as variables such as reaction time or the number of errors on a test. The distinction between an interval scale and a ratio scale is demonstrated in Example 1.2.

DEFINITIONS

An **interval scale** consists of ordered categories that are all intervals of exactly the same size. Equal differences between numbers on an interval scale reflect equal differences in magnitude. However, the zero point on an interval scale is arbitrary and does not indicate a zero amount of the variable being measured.

A **ratio scale** is an interval scale with the additional feature of an absolute zero point. With a ratio scale, ratios of numbers do reflect ratios of magnitude.

EXAMPLE 1.2

A researcher obtains measurements of height for a group of 8-year-old boys. Initially, the researcher simply records each child's height in inches, obtaining values such as 44, 51, 49, and so on. These initial measurements constitute a ratio scale. A value of zero represents no height (absolute zero). Also, it is possible to use these measurements to form ratios. For example, a child who is 60 inches tall is one and a half times taller than a child who is 40 inches tall.

Now suppose that the researcher converts the initial measurement into a new scale by calculating the difference between each child's actual height and the average height for this age group. A child who is 1 inch taller than average now gets a score of $+1$; a child 4 inches taller than average gets a score of $+4$. Similarly, a child who is 2 inches shorter than average gets a score of -2. The new scores constitute an interval scale of measurement. A score of zero no longer indicates an absence of height; now it simply means average height.

Notice that both sets of scores involve measurement in inches, and you can compute differences, or intervals, on either scale. For example, there is a 6-inch difference in height between two boys who measure 57 and 51 inches tall on the first scale. Likewise, there is a 6-inch difference between two boys who measure $+9$ and $+3$ on the second scale. However, you should also notice that ratio comparisons are not possible on the second scale. For example, a boy who measures $+9$ is not three times as tall as a boy who measures $+3$.

For our purposes, scales of measurement are important because they influence the kind of statistics that can and cannot be used. For example, if you measure IQ scores for a group of students, it is possible to calculate the average score for the group. On the other hand, if you measure the academic major for each student, you cannot compute the average. (What is the average of three psychology majors, an English major, and two chemistry majors?) The vast majority of the statistical techniques presented in this book are designed for numerical scores from an interval or a ratio scale. For most statistical applications, the distinction between an interval scale and a ratio scale is not important because both scales produce numerical values that permit us to compute differences between scores, to sum scores, and to calculate average scores. On the other hand, measurements from nominal or ordinal scales are typically not numerical values and are not compatible with many basic arithmetic operations. Therefore, alternative statistical techniques are necessary for data from nominal or ordinal scales of measurement (for example, the median and the mode in Chapter 3, the Spearman correlation in Chapter 15, and the chi-square tests in Chapter 16).

LEARNING CHECK

1. The local fast-food restaurant offers small, medium, and large soft drinks. What kind of scale is used to measure the size of the drinks?

2. The Scholastic Achievement Test (SAT) most likely measures aptitude on a(n) _____ scale.

3. In a study on perception of facial expressions, participants must classify the emotions displayed in photographs of people as anger, sadness, joy, disgust, fear, or surprise. Emotional expression is measured on a(n) _____ scale.

4. A researcher studies the factors that determine how many children couples decide to have. The variable, number of children, is a _____ (discrete/continuous) variable.

5. An investigator studies how concept-formation ability changes with age. Age is a _____ (discrete/continuous) variable.

6. **a.** When measuring weight to the nearest pound, what are the real limits for a score of $X = 150$ pounds?
   b. When measuring weight to the nearest $\frac{1}{2}$ pound, what are the real limits for a score of $X = 144.5$ pounds?

ANSWERS   1. ordinal   2. interval   3. nominal   4. discrete   5. continuous

6. **a.** 149.5 and 150.5   **b.** 144.25 and 144.75

1.5 STATISTICAL NOTATION

The measurements obtained in research studies provide the data for statistical analysis. Most of the statistical analyses will use the same general mathematical operations, notation, and basic arithmetic that you have learned during previous years of school. In case you are unsure of your mathematical skills, there is a mathematics review section in Appendix A at the back of this book. The appendix also includes a skills assessment exam (p. 506) to help you determine whether you need the basic mathematics review. In this section, we introduce some of the specialized notation that is used for statistical calculations. In later chapters, additional statistical notation will be introduced as it is needed.

SCORES		
X	X	Y
37	72	165
35	68	151
35	67	160
30	67	160
25	68	146
17	70	160
16	66	133

Measuring a variable in a research study will typically yield a value or a score for each subject. Raw scores are the original, unchanged scores obtained in the study. Scores for a particular variable are represented by the letter X. For example, if performance in your statistics course is measured by tests and you obtain a 35 on the first test, then we could state that $X = 35$. A set of scores can be presented in a column that is headed by X. For example, a list of quiz scores from your class might be presented as shown in the margin (the single column on the left).

When observations are made for two variables, there will be two scores for each subject. The data can be presented as two lists labeled X and Y for the two variables. For example, observations for people's height in inches (variable X) and weight in pounds (variable Y) can be presented as shown in the margin (the double column on the right). Each pair X, Y represents the observations made of a single participant.

It is also useful to specify how many scores are in a set. We will use an uppercase letter N to represent the number of scores in a population and a lowercase letter n to represent the number of scores in a sample. Throughout the remainder of the book you will notice that we often use notational differences to distinguish between samples and populations. For the height and weight data in the preceding table, $n = 7$ for both variables. Note that by using a lowercase letter n, we are implying that these data are a sample.

SUMMATION NOTATION

Many of the computations required in statistics involve adding a set of scores. Because this procedure is used so frequently, a special notation is used to refer to the sum of a set of scores. The Greek letter *sigma*, or Σ, is used to stand for summation. The expression ΣX means to add all the scores for variable X. The summation sign Σ can be read as "the sum of." Thus, ΣX is read "the sum of the scores." For the following set of quiz scores,

$$10, \quad 6, \quad 7, \quad 4$$

$\Sigma X = 27$ and $N = 4$.

To use summation notation correctly, keep in mind the following two points:

1. The summation sign Σ is always followed by a symbol or mathematical expression. The symbol or expression identifies exactly which values are to be summed. To compute ΣX, for example, the symbol following the summation sign is X, and the task is to find the sum of the X values. On the other hand, to compute $\Sigma(X - 1)^2$, the summation sign is followed by a relatively complex mathematical expression, so your first task is to calculate all of the $(X - 1)^2$ values and then sum the results.

2. The summation process is often included with several other mathematical operations, such as multiplication or squaring. To obtain the correct answer, it is essential that the different operations be done in the correct sequence. Following is a list showing the correct *order of operations* for performing mathematical operations. Most of this list should be familiar, but you should note that we have inserted the summation process as the fourth operation in the list.

Order of Mathematical Operations

More information on the order of operations for mathematics is available in the Math Review appendix, page 507.

1. Any calculation contained within parentheses is done first.

2. Squaring (or raising to other exponents) is done second.

3. Multiplying and/or dividing is done third. A series of multiplication and/or division operations should be done in order from left to right.

4. Summation using the Σ notation is done next.

5. Finally, any other addition and/or subtraction is done.

The following examples demonstrate how summation notation will be used in most of the calculations and formulas we will present in this book.

EXAMPLE 1.3   A set of four scores consists of values 3, 1, 7, and 4. We will compute ΣX, ΣX^2, and $(\Sigma X)^2$ for these scores. To help demonstrate the calculations, we will use a computational table showing the original scores (the X values) in the first column. Additional columns can then be added to show additional steps in the series of operations. You should notice that the first three operations in the list (parentheses, squaring, multiplying) all create a new column of values. The last two operations, however, produce a single value corresponding to the sum.

X	X^2
3	9
1	1
7	49
4	16

The table to the left shows the original scores (the X values) and the squared scores (the X^2 values) that are needed to compute ΣX^2.

The first calculation, ΣX, does not include any parentheses, squaring, or multiplication, so we go directly to the summation operation. The X values are listed in the first column of the table, and we simply add the values in this column:

$$\Sigma X = 3 + 1 + 7 + 4 = 15$$

To compute ΣX^2, the correct order of operations is to square each score and then find the sum of the squared values. The computational table shows the original scores and the results obtained from squaring (the first step in the calculation). The second step is to find the sum of the squared values, so we simply add the numbers in the X^2 column.

$$\Sigma X^2 = 9 + 1 + 49 + 16 = 75$$

The final calculation, $(\Sigma X)^2$, includes parentheses, so the first step is to perform the calculation inside the parentheses. Thus, we first find ΣX and then square this sum. Earlier, we computed $\Sigma X = 15$, so

$$(\Sigma X)^2 = (15)^2 = 225$$

EXAMPLE 1.4   We will use the same set of four scores from Example 1.3 and compute $\Sigma(X - 1)$ and $\Sigma(X - 1)^2$. The following computational table will help demonstrate the calculations.

X	$(X - 1)$	$(X - 1)^2$	
3	2	4	The first column lists the
1	0	0	original scores. A second
7	6	36	column lists the $(X - 1)$
4	3	9	values, and a third column
			shows the $(X - 1)^2$ values.

To compute $\Sigma(X - 1)$, the first step is to perform the operation inside the parentheses. Thus, we begin by subtracting one point from each of the X values. The resulting values are listed in the middle column of the table. The next step is to add the $(X - 1)$ values.

$$\Sigma(X - 1) = 2 + 0 + 6 + 3 = 11$$

The calculation of $\Sigma(X - 1)^2$ requires three steps. The first step (inside parentheses) is to subtract 1 point from each X value. The results from this step are shown in the middle column of the computational table. The second step is to square each of the $(X - 1)$ values. The results from this step are shown in the third column of the table. The final step is to add the $(X - 1)^2$ values to obtain

$$\Sigma(X - 1)^2 = 4 + 0 + 36 + 9 = 49$$

Notice that this calculation requires squaring before summing. A common mistake is to add the $(X - 1)$ values and then square the total. Be careful!

E X A M P L E   1 . 5   In both of the preceding examples, and in many other situations, the summation operation is the last step in the calculation. According to the order of operations, parentheses, exponents, and multiplication all come before summation. However, there are situations in which extra addition and subtraction are completed after the summation. For this example we will use the same scores that appeared in the previous two examples, and we will compute $\Sigma X - 1$.

With no parentheses, exponents, or multiplication, the first step is the summation. Thus, we begin by computing ΣX. Earlier we found $\Sigma X = 15$. The next step is to subtract one point from the total. For these data,

$$\Sigma X - 1 = 15 - 1 = 14$$

E X A M P L E   1 . 6   For this example, each individual has two scores. The first score is identified as X, and the second score is Y. With the help of the following computational table, we will compute ΣX, ΣY, and ΣXY.

Person	X	Y	XY
A	3	5	15
B	1	3	3
C	7	4	28
D	4	2	8

To find ΣX, simply add the values in the X column.

$$\Sigma X = 3 + 1 + 7 + 4 = 15$$

Similarly, ΣY is the sum of the Y values.

$$\Sigma Y = 5 + 3 + 4 + 2 = 14$$

To compute ΣXY, the first step is to multiply X times Y for each individual. The resulting products (XY values) are listed in the third column of the table. Finally, we add the products to obtain

$$\Sigma XY = 15 + 3 + 28 + 8 = 54$$

LEARNING CHECK

1. Calculate each value requested for the following scores: 4, 2, 5, 1.
   a. ΣX d. $\Sigma X - 1$
   b. $(\Sigma X)^2$ e. $\Sigma(X - 1)$
   c. ΣX^2 f. $\Sigma(X - 1)^2$

2. Use summation notation to express each of the following calcualtions
   a. Add 2 points to each score, then add the resulting values.
   b. Square each score, then add the squared values.

ANSWERS

1. a. $\Sigma X = 12$ d. $\Sigma X - 1 = 11$
   b. $(\Sigma X)^2 = 144$ e. $\Sigma(X - 1) = 8$
   c. $\Sigma X^2 = 46$ f. $\Sigma(X - 1)^2 = 26$

2. a. $\Sigma(X + 2)$
   b. ΣX^2

SUMMARY

1. The term *statistics* is used to refer to methods for organizing, summarizing, and interpreting data.

2. Scientific questions usually concern a population that is the entire set of individuals one wishes to study. Usually, populations are so large that it is impossible to examine every individual, so most research is conducted with samples. A sample is a group selected from a population, usually for purposes of a research study.

3. A characteristic that describes a sample is called a statistic, and a characteristic that describes a population is called a parameter. Although sample statistics are usually representative of corresponding population parameters, there is typically some discrepancy between a statistic and a parameter. The naturally occurring difference between a statistic and a parameter is called sampling error.

4. Statistical methods can be classified into two broad categories: descriptive statistics, which organize and summarize data, and inferential statistics, which use sample data to draw inferences about populations.

5. The correlational method examines relationships between variables by measuring two different variables for each individual. This method allows researchers to measure and describe relationships, but cannot produce a cause-and-effect explanation for the relationship.

6. The experimental method examines relationships between variables by manipulating one variable to create different treatment conditions and then measuring a second variable to obtain a set of scores in each condition. All other variables are controlled to prevent them from influencing the relationship. The intent of the experimental method is to demonstrate a cause-and-effect relationship between variables.

7. Nonexperimental studies also examine relationships between variables by comparing groups of scores, but they do not have the rigor of true experiments and cannot produce cause-and-effect explanations. Instead of manipulating a variable to create different groups, a nonexperimental study uses a preexisting participant characteristic (such as male/female) or the passage of time (before/after) to create the groups being compared.

8. A measurement scale consists of a set of categories that are used to classify individuals. A nominal scale consists of categories that differ only in name and are not differentiated in terms of magnitude or direction. In an ordinal scale, the categories are differentiated in terms of direction, forming an ordered series. An interval scale consists of an ordered series of categories that are all equal-sized intervals. With an interval scale, it is possible to differentiate direction and magnitude (or distance) between categories. Finally, a ratio scale is an interval scale for which the zero point indicates none of the variable being measured. With a ratio scale, ratios of measurements reflect ratios of magnitude.

9. A discrete variable consists of indivisible categories, often whole numbers that vary in countable steps.

10. A continuous variable consists of categories that are infinitely divisible. Each score corresponds to an interval on the scale. The boundaries that separate intervals are called real limits and are located exactly halfway between adjacent scores.

11. The letter X is used to represent scores for a variable. If a second variable is used, Y represents its scores. The letter N is used as the symbol for the number of scores in a population; n is the symbol for a sample.

12. The Greek letter sigma (Σ) is used to stand for summation. Therefore, the expression ΣX is read "the sum of the scores." Summation is a mathematical operation (like addition or multiplication) and must be performed in its proper place in the order of operations; summation occurs after parentheses, exponents, and multiplying/dividing have been completed.

KEY TERMS

statistics

population

sample

variable

data

data set

datum

raw score

parameter

statistic

descriptive statistics

inferential statistics

sampling error

correlational method

experimental method

independent variable

dependent variable

control condition

experimental condition

quasi-independent variable

construct

operational definition

discrete variable

continuous variable

real limits

upper real limit

lower real limit

nominal scale

ordinal scale

interval scale

ratio scale

RESOURCES

The Wadsworth Publishing Company provides a website containing practice quizzes for every chapter in this book as well as a series of workshops and other resources that correspond to the main topic areas. Go to www.thomsonedu.com/psychology/gravetter, scroll down to the box showing the front cover of your textbook, and click on "Companion Site" under "Students." In the left-hand column you will find a variety of learning exercises for Chapter 1, including a tutorial quiz. Also in the left-hand column, under Book Resources, you will find a link to the Workshops. For Chapter 1, there is a workshop that reviews the scales of measurement. To get there, click on the Workshop link, then click on *Scales of Measurement*. To find materials for other chapters, you begin by selecting the desired chapter at the top of the page.

At the end of each chapter we will remind you about the Web resources. Again, there is a tutorial quiz for every chapter, and we will notify you whenever there is a workshop that is related to the chapter content.

WebTUTOR

For those using WebTutor along with this book, there is a WebTutor section corresponding to this chapter. The WebTutor contains a brief summary of Chapter 1, hints for learning the new material and for avoiding common errors, and sample exam items including solutions.

The Statistical Package for the Social Sciences, known as SPSS, is a computer program that performs most of the statistical calculations that are presented in this book, and is commonly available on college and university computer systems. Appendix D contains a general introduction to SPSS. In the Resource section at the end of each chapter for which SPSS is applicable, there are step-by-step instructions for using SPSS to perform the statistical operations presented in the chapter.

FOCUS ON PROBLEM SOLVING

1. It may help to simplify summation notation if you observe that the summation sign is always followed by a symbol or symbolic expression—for example, ΣX or $\Sigma(X + 3)$. This symbol specifies which values you are to add. If you use the symbol as a column heading and list all the appropriate values in the column, your task is simply to add up the numbers in the column. To find $\Sigma(X + 3)$ for example, start a column headed with $(X + 3)$ next to the column of Xs. List all the $(X + 3)$ values; then find the total for the column.

2. Often, summation notation is part of a relatively complex mathematical expression that requires several steps of calculation. The series of steps must be performed according to the order of mathematical operations (see page 23). The best procedure is to use a computational table that begins with the original X values listed in the first column. Then, each step in the calculation creates a new column of values. For example, computing $\Sigma(X - 1)^2$ requires three steps and produces a computational table with three columns (see Example 1.4).

STEP 1   The first step in the calculation is to subtract 1 from each X. A new column is added to the computational table to list each of the $(X - 1)$ values.

STEP 2   The second step is to square each $(X - 1)$ value. Again, a new column is added to list each of the $(X - 1)^2$ values.

STEP 3   The third step is to add the $(X - 1)^2$ values, so you simply add the numbers in the $(X - 1)^2$ column.

Note that summation (step 3) produces a single number. All of the other steps before summation produce a set of values corresponding to a new column in the computational table.

DEMONSTRATION 1.1

SUMMATION NOTATION

A set of data consists of the following scores:

        7   3   9   5   4

For these data, find the following values:
   a. ΣX **b.** $(\Sigma X)^2$ **c.** ΣX^2 **d.** $\Sigma X + 5$ **e.** $\Sigma(X - 2)$

Compute ΣX   To compute Σ*X*, we simply add all of the scores in the group. For these data, we obtain

$$\Sigma X = 7 + 3 + 9 + 5 + 4 = 28$$

Compute (ΣX)²   The key to determining the value of $(\Sigma X)^2$ is the presence of parentheses. The rule is to perform the operations that are inside the parentheses first.

STEP 1   Find the sum of the scores, Σ*X*.

STEP 2   Square the total.
We have already determined that Σ*X* is 28. Squaring this total, we obtain

$$(\Sigma X)^2 = (28)^2 = 784$$

Compute ΣX²   Calculating the sum of the squared scores, ΣX^2, involves two steps.

STEP 1   Square each score.

STEP 2   Add the squared values.

X	X²
7	49
3	9
9	81
5	25
4	16

These steps are most easily accomplished by constructing a computational table. The first column has the heading *X* and lists the scores. The second column is labeled X^2 and contains the squared value for each score. For this example, the table is presented in the margin. To find the value for ΣX^2, we add the values in the X^2 column.

$$\Sigma X^2 = 49 + 9 + 81 + 25 + 16 = 180$$

Compute ΣX + 5   In this expression, there are no parentheses. Thus, the summation sign is applied only to the *X* values.

STEP 1   Find the sum of *X*.

STEP 2   Add the constant 5 to the total from step 1.
Earlier we found that the sum of the scores is 28. For Σ*X* + 5, we obtain the following:

$$\Sigma X + 5 = 28 + 5 = 33$$

Compute Σ(X − 2)   The summation sign is followed by an expression with parentheses. In this case, *X* − 2 is treated as a single expression, and the summation sign applies to the (*X* − 2) values.

STEP 1   Subtract 2 from every score.

STEP 2   Add these new values.
This problem can be done by using a computational table with two columns, headed *X* and *X* − 2, respectively.

X	X − 2
7	5
3	1
9	7
5	3
4	2

To determine the value for $\Sigma(X - 2)$, we add the numbers in the $X - 2$ column.

$$\Sigma(X - 2) = 5 + 1 + 7 + 3 + 2 = 18$$

PROBLEMS

*1. Statistical methods are classified into two major categories: descriptive and inferential. Describe the general purpose for the statistical methods in each category.

2. Briefly explain how correlational research differs from other research studies that are evaluating the relationship between two variables.

3. A researcher is interested in the effects of humidity on the eating behavior of rats. A group of 25 rats is housed in a controlled environment and the researcher measures the amount of food consumed by each rat with the humidity set at 20% and again with the humidity set at 80%. For this study
   a. identify the population.
   b. identify the sample.

4. Define the terms population, sample, parameter, and statistic. Explain the relationships among the terms.

5. Identify the two elements of an experiment that make this type of research study different from other research methods.

6. Define the concept of *sampling error*. Be sure that your definition includes the concepts of *statistic* and *parameter*.

7. Dr. Jones conducted a study examining the relationship between the quality of breakfast and academic performance for a sample of $n = 20$ first-grade students. The students were divided into two equivalent groups. One group was given a nutritious breakfast each morning for 6 weeks and the other group was given a non-nutritious breakfast each day during the same period. Academic performance was measured by each child's grades at the end of the 6-week period to determine whether there was any difference between the two groups. Is this an example of a correlational or an experimental study? Explain your answer.

8. A research study comparing college alcohol use in the United States and Canada reports that more Canadian students drink but American students drink more (Kuo, Adlaf, Lee, Gliksman, Demers, and Wechsler, 2002). Is this study an example of an experiment? Explain why or why not.

9. To test the effectiveness of a new growth hormone, a researcher selects a sample of $n = 20$ newborn rats. Ten of the rats receive regular injections of the hormone and the other 10 serve as a no-treatment control group. Except for the hormone injections, the two groups receive exactly the same treatment. After 6 months, the researcher weighs each rat and computes the average weight for each group. If the average weight for the hormone group is greater than the average for the control group, can the researcher *automatically* conclude that the hormone has an effect? (Hint: What other factor might explain why the two groups have different averages?)

10. Oxytocin is a naturally occurring brain chemical that is nicknamed the "love hormone" because it seems to play a role in the formation of social relationships such as mating pairs and parent-child bonding. A recent study demonstrated that oxytocin appears to increase people's tendency to trust others (Kosfeld, Heinrichs, Zak, Fischbacher, and Fehr, 2005). Using an investment game, the study demonstrated that people who inhaled oxytocin were more likely to give their money to a trustee compared to people who inhaled an inactive placebo. For this experimental study, identify the independent variable and the dependent variable.

11. A researcher would like to evaluate the claim that large doses of vitamin C can help prevent the common cold. One group of participants is given a large dose of the vitamin (500 mg per day), and a second group is given a placebo (sugar pill). The researcher records the number of colds each individual experiences during the 3-month winter season.

---

*Solutions for odd-numbered problems are provided in Appendix C.

a. Identify the dependent variable for this study.

b. Is the dependent variable discrete or continuous?

c. What scale of measurement (nominal, ordinal, interval, or ratio) is used to measure the dependent variable?

12. Dr. Jones conducted a study examining the relationship between the quality of breakfast and academic performance for a sample of $n = 20$ first-grade students. The quality of breakfast was determined by interviewing each child's parents, and academic performance was measured by each child's most recent grades. Is this an example of a correlational or an experimental study? Explain your answer.

13. Experimental research is intended to demonstrate a cause-and-effect relationship between two variables. What are the names given to the two variables in an experiment? Define each variable.

14. Define and differentiate between a discrete variable and a continuous variable.

15. Research has shown that supplements high in antioxidants (strawberry, spinach, and especially blueberry) can actually reverse some effects of aging (Joseph et al., 1999). In a typical study, one group of elderly rats receives the supplement and a second group is given an inactive placebo. Both groups are then tested on a variety of motor-behavior tasks. One common task is the Morris water maze, which measures how much time it takes for a rat to find a submerged platform in a pool of opaque water. The results generally show that the older rats receiving the supplements are able to locate the platform much faster than their peers who are not receiving supplements.

a. Identify the independent and dependent variables for this study.

b. What scale of measurement is used for the dependent variable?

16. Four scales of measurement were introduced in this chapter: nominal, ordinal, interval, and ratio.

a. What additional information is obtained from measurements on an ordinal scale compared to measurements on a nominal scale?

b. What additional information is obtained from measurements on an interval scale compared to measurements on an ordinal scale?

c. What additional information is obtained from measurements on a ratio scale compared to measurements on an interval scale?

17. Define or give an example of a hypothetical construct. Explain why operational definitions are needed to define and to measure constructs.

18. Each of the following summation expressions requires a specific sequence of step-by-step mathematical operations. For each expression, list the series of steps necessary to complete the calculation. For example, the expression $\Sigma(X + 4)$ requires two steps: (1) add 4 points to each score, and (2) add the resulting values.

a. ΣX^2

b. $(\Sigma X)^2$

c. $\Sigma(X - 1)$

d. $\Sigma(X - 1)^2$

19. Use summation notation to express each of the following calculations:

a. Add the scores, and then add 3 points to the total.

b. Subtract 2 points from each score, and square the result. Then add the squared values.

c. Square each score, and add the squared values. Then subtract 10 points from the sum.

20. Use summation notation to express each of the following calculations:

a. Square each score, then add the squared values.

b. Add the scores, then square the sum.

c. Add two points to each score, then add the resulting values.

d. Add the scores, then subtract 6 points from the total.

21. For the following set of scores, find the value of each expression:

a. ΣX

b. ΣX^2

c. $\Sigma(X + 1)$

d. $\Sigma(X + 1)^2$

X
2
5
0
4

22. For the following scores, find the value of each expression:

a. ΣX

b. ΣX^2

c. $(\Sigma X)^2$

d. $\Sigma(X - 1)$

X
6
1
3
4
2

23. For the following set of scores, find the value of each expression:

a. ΣX^2
b. $(\Sigma X)^2$
c. $\Sigma(X - 3)$
d. $\Sigma(X - 3)^2$

X
9
1
1
1

24. For the following set of scores, find the value of each expression:

a. ΣX
b. ΣX^2
c. $\Sigma(X + 3)$

X
5
−1
0
−3
−1

25. Two scores, X and Y, are recorded for each of $n = 5$ subjects. For these scores, find the value of each expression.

a. ΣX
b. ΣY
c. ΣXY

Subject	X	Y
A	3	7
B	5	4
C	0	3
D	8	1
E	6	5

CHAPTER

2

Frequency Distributions

Tools You Will Need

The following items are considered essential background material for this chapter. If you doubt your knowledge of any of these items, you should review the appropriate chapter or section before proceeding.

- Proportions (math review, Appendix A)
  - Fractions
  - Decimals
  - Percentages
- Scales of measurement (Chapter 1): Nominal, ordinal, interval, and ratio
- Continuous and discrete variables (Chapter 1)
- Real limits (Chapter 1)

2.1   OVERVIEW

When a researcher finishes the data collection phase of an experiment, the results usually consist of pages of numbers. The immediate problem for the researcher is to organize the scores into some comprehensible form so that any trends in the data can be seen easily and communicated to others. This is the job of descriptive statistics: to simplify the organization and presentation of data. One of the most common procedures for organizing a set of data is to place the scores in a *frequency distribution*.

DEFINITION

A **frequency distribution** is an organized tabulation of the number of individuals located in each category on the scale of measurement.

A frequency distribution takes a disorganized set of scores and places them in order from highest to lowest, grouping together all individuals who have the same score. If the highest score is $X = 10$, for example, the frequency distribution groups together all the 10s, then all the 9s, then the 8s, and so on. Thus, a frequency distribution allows the researcher to see "at a glance" the entire set of scores. It shows whether the scores are generally high or low, whether they are concentrated in one area or spread out across the entire scale, and generally provides an organized picture of the data. In addition to providing a picture of the entire set of scores, a frequency distribution allows you to see the location of any individual score relative to all of the other scores in the set.

A frequency distribution can be structured either as a table or as a graph, but in either case the distribution presents the same two elements:

1. The set of categories that make up the original measurement scale.

2. A record of the frequency, or number of individuals in each category.

Thus, a frequency distribution presents a picture of how the individual scores are distributed on the measurement scale—hence the name *frequency distribution*.

2.2   FREQUENCY DISTRIBUTION TABLES

It is customary to list categories from highest to lowest, but this is an arbitrary arrangement. Many computer programs will list categories from lowest to highest.

The simplest frequency distribution table presents the measurement scale by listing the different measurement categories (X values) in a column from highest to lowest. Beside each X value, we indicate the frequency, or the number of times that particular measurement occurred in the data. It is customary to use an X as the column heading for the categories and an f as the column heading for the frequencies. An example of a frequency distribution table follows.

EXAMPLE 2.1

The following set of $N = 20$ scores was obtained from a 10-point statistics quiz. We will organize these scores by constructing a frequency distribution table. Scores:

8, 9, 8, 7, 10, 9, 6, 4, 9, 8,

7, 8, 10, 9, 8, 6, 9, 7, 8, 8

X	f
10	2
9	5
8	7
7	3
6	2
5	0
4	1

1. The highest score is $X = 10$, and the lowest score is $X = 4$. Therefore, the first column of the table will list the categories that make up the scale of measurement (X values) from 10 down to 4. Notice that all of the possible values are listed in the table. For example, no one had a score of $X = 5$, but this value is included. With an ordinal, interval, or ratio scale, the categories are listed in order (usually highest to lowest). For a nominal scale, the categories can be listed in any order.

2. The frequency associated with each score is recorded in the second column. For example, two people had scores of $X = 6$, so there is a 2 in the f column beside $X = 6$.

Because the table organizes the scores, it is possible to see very quickly the general quiz results. For example, there were only two perfect scores, but most of the class had high grades (8s and 9s). With one exception (the score of $X = 4$), it appears that the class has learned the material fairly well.

Notice that the X values in a frequency distribution table represent the scale of measurement, *not* the actual set of scores. For example, the X column lists the value 10 only one time, but the frequency column indicates that there are actually two values of $X = 10$. Also, the X column lists a value of $X = 5$, but the frequency column indicates that no one actually had a score of $X = 5$.

You also should notice that the frequencies can be used to find the total number of scores in the distribution. By adding up the frequencies, you will obtain the total number of individuals:

$$\Sigma f = N$$

OBTAINING ΣX FROM A FREQUENCY DISTRIBUTION TABLE

There may be times when you need to compute the sum of the scores, ΣX, or perform other computations for a set of scores that has been organized into a frequency distribution table. Such calculations can present a problem because many students tend to disregard the frequencies and use only the values listed in the X column of the table. However, it is essential that you use the information in both the X column and the f column to obtain the full set of scores.

When it is necessary to perform calculations for scores that have been organized into a frequency distribution table, the safest procedure is to take the individual scores out of the table before you begin any computations. Consider the frequency distribution table for Example 2.1. The table shows that the distribution has two 10s, five 9s, seven 8s, and so on. If you simply list all of the individual scores, then you can safely proceed with calculations such as finding ΣX or ΣX^2. Note that the complete set contains $N = \Sigma f = 20$ scores and your list should contain 20 values. For example, to compute ΣX you simply add all 20 of the scores:

$$\Sigma X = 10 + 10 + 9 + 9 + 9 + 9 + 9 + 8 + 8 + 8 + 8 + 8 + 8 + 8 + \cdots$$

For the data in Example 2.1, you should obtain $\Sigma X = 158$. Try it yourself. Similarly, to obtain ΣX^2 you simply square each of the 20 scores and then add the squared values.

$$\Sigma X^2 = 10^2 + 10^2 + 9^2 + 9^2 + 9^2 + 9^2 + 9^2 + 8^2 + 8^2 + 8^2 + \\ 8^2 + 8^2 + 8^2 + 8^2 + \cdots$$

This time you should obtain $\Sigma X^2 = 1288$.

An alternative way to get ΣX from a frequency distribution table is to multiply each X value by its frequency and then add these products. This sum may be expressed in symbols as $\Sigma f X$. The computation is summarized as follows for the data in Example 2.1:

Caution: Doing calculations within the table works well for ΣX but can lead to errors for more complex formulas.

X	f	fX	
10	2	20	(The two 10s total 20)
9	5	45	(The five 9s total 45)
8	7	56	(The seven 8s total 56)
7	3	21	(The three 7s total 21)
6	2	12	(The two 6s total 12)
5	0	0	(There are no 5s)
4	1	4	(The one 4 totals 4)

$$\Sigma f X = 158$$

No matter which method you use to find ΣX, the important point is that you must use the information given in the frequency column in addition to the information in the X column.

PROPORTIONS AND PERCENTAGES

In addition to the two basic columns of a frequency distribution, there are other measures that describe the distribution of scores and can be incorporated into the table. The two most common are proportion and percentage.

Proportion measures the fraction of the total group that is associated with each score. In Example 2.1, there were two individuals with $X = 6$. Thus, 2 out of 20 people had $X = 6$, so the proportion would be $\frac{2}{20} = 0.10$. In general, the proportion associated with each score is

$$\text{proportion} = p = \frac{f}{N}$$

Because proportions describe the frequency (f) in relation to the total number (N), they often are called *relative frequencies*. Although proportions can be expressed as fractions (for example, $\frac{2}{20}$), they more commonly appear as decimals. A column of proportions, headed with a p, can be added to the basic frequency distribution table (see Example 2.2).

In addition to using frequencies (f) and proportions (p), researchers often describe a distribution of scores with percentages. For example, an instructor might describe the results of an exam by saying that 15% of the class earned As, 23% Bs, and so on. To compute the percentage associated with each score, you first find the proportion (p) and then multiply by 100:

$$\text{percentage} = p(100) = \frac{f}{N}(100)$$

Percentages can be included in a frequency distribution table by adding a column headed with % (see Example 2.2).

EXAMPLE 2.2   The frequency distribution table from Example 2.1 is repeated here. This time we have added columns showing the proportion (p) and the percentage (%) associated with each score.

X	f	$p = f/N$	$\% = p(100)$
10	2	2/20 = 0.10	10%
9	5	5/20 = 0.25	25%
8	7	7/20 = 0.35	35%
7	3	3/20 = 0.15	15%
6	2	2/20 = 0.10	10%
5	0	0/20 = 0	0%
4	1	1/20 = 0.05	5%

LEARNING CHECK

1. Place the following scores in a frequency distribution table.

    2, 3, 1, 2, 5, 4, 5, 5, 1, 4, 2, 2

2. Find the number of scores (n), the sum of the scores (ΣX), and the sum of the squared scores (ΣX^2) for the sample in the following frequency distribution table.

X	f
5	1
4	1
3	2
2	3
1	1

ANSWERS   1.

X	f
5	3
4	2
3	1
2	4
1	2

2. $n = \Sigma f = 8$, $\Sigma X = 22$, and $\Sigma X^2 = 72$ (Note: To obtain ΣX^2 you must square each of the eight scores then add the eight squared values.)

GROUPED FREQUENCY DISTRIBUTION TABLES

When a set of data covers a wide range of values, it is unreasonable to list all the individual scores in a frequency distribution table. For example, a set of exam scores ranges from a low of $X = 41$ to a high of $X = 96$. These scores cover a *range* of more than 50 points.

When the scores are whole numbers, the total number of rows for a regular table can be obtained by finding the difference between the highest and the lowest scores and adding 1:

rows = highest − lowest + 1

If we were to list all the individual scores from $X = 96$ down to $X = 41$, it would take 56 rows to complete the frequency distribution table. Although this would organize and simplify the data, the table would be long and cumbersome. Remember: The purpose for constructing a table is to obtain a relatively simple, organized picture of the data. This can be accomplished by grouping the scores into intervals and then listing the intervals in the table instead of listing each individual score. For example, we could construct a table showing the number of students who had scores in the 90s, the number with scores in the 80s, and so on. The result is called a *grouped frequency distribution table* because we are presenting groups of scores rather than individual values. The groups, or intervals, are called *class intervals*.

There are several rules that help guide you in the construction of a grouped frequency distribution table. These rules should be considered as guidelines rather than absolute requirements, but they do help produce a simple, well-organized, and easily understood table.

RULE 1   The grouped frequency distribution table should have about 10 class intervals. If a table has many more than 10 intervals, it becomes cumbersome and defeats the purpose of a frequency distribution table. On the other hand, if you have too few intervals, you begin to lose information about the distribution of the scores. At the extreme, with only one interval, the table would not tell you anything about how the scores are distributed. Remember that the purpose of a frequency distribution is to help a researcher see the data. With too few or too many intervals, the table will not provide a clear picture. You should note that 10 intervals is a general guide. If you are constructing a table on a blackboard, for example, you probably will want only 5 or 6 intervals. If the table is to be printed in a scientific report, you may want 12 or 15 intervals. In each case, your goal is to present a table that is relatively easy to see and understand.

RULE 2   The width of each interval should be a relatively simple number. For example, 2, 5, 10, or 20 would be a good choice for the interval width. Notice that it is easy to count by 5s or 10s. These numbers are easy to understand and make it possible for someone to see quickly how you have divided the range.

RULE 3   The bottom score in each class interval should be a multiple of the width. If you are using a width of 10 points, for example, the intervals should start with 10, 20, 30, 40, and so on. Again, this makes it easier for someone to understand how the table has been constructed.

RULE 4   All intervals should be the same width. They should cover the range of scores completely with no gaps and no overlaps, so that any particular score belongs in exactly one interval.

The application of these rules is demonstrated in Example 2.3.

EXAMPLE 2.3   An instructor has obtained the set of $N = 25$ exam scores shown here. To help organize these scores, we will place them in a frequency distribution table. The scores are:

Remember, when the scores are whole numbers, the number of rows is determined by

highest − lowest + 1

82, 75, 88, 93, 53, 84, 87, 58, 72, 94, 69, 84, 61,
91, 64, 87, 84, 70, 76, 89, 75, 80, 73, 78, 60

The first step is to determine the range of scores. For these data, the smallest score is $X = 53$ and the largest score is $X = 94$, so a total of 42 rows would be needed for a table that lists each individual score. Because 42 rows would not provide a simple table, we will have to group the scores into class intervals.

The best method for finding a good interval width is a systematic trial-and-error approach that uses rules 1 and 2 simultaneously. According to rule 1, we want about 10 intervals; according to rule 2, we want the interval width to be a simple number. For this example, the scores cover a range of 42 points, so we will try several different interval widths to see how many intervals are needed to cover this range. For example, if we try a width of 2, how many intervals would it take to cover the range of scores? With each interval only 2 points wide, we would need 21 intervals to cover the range. This is too many. What about an interval width of 5? What about a width of 10? The following table shows how many intervals would be needed for these possible widths:

Because the bottom interval usually extends below the lowest score and the top interval extends beyond the highest score, you often will need slightly more than the computed number of intervals.

Width	Number of Intervals Needed to Cover a Range of 42 Points	
2	21	(too many)
5	9	(OK)
10	5	(too few)

Notice that an interval width of 5 will result in about 10 intervals, which is exactly what we want.

The next step is to actually identify the intervals. The lowest score for these data is $X = 53$, so the lowest interval should contain this value. Because the interval should have a multiple of 5 as its bottom score, the interval would be 50 to 54. Notice that the interval contains five values (50, 51, 52, 53, 54) so it does have a width of 5. The next interval would start at 55 and go to 59. The complete frequency distribution table showing all of the class intervals is presented in Table 2.1.

Once the class intervals are listed, you complete the table by adding a column of frequencies, proportions, or percentages. The values in the frequency column indicate the number of individuals whose scores are located in that class interval. For this example, there were three students with scores in the 60–64 interval, so the frequency for this class interval is $f = 3$ (see Table 2.1).

Finally, you should note that after the scores have been placed in a grouped table, you lose information about the specific value for any individual score. For example, Table 2.1 shows that one person had a score between 65 and 69, but the table does not identify the exact value for the score. In general, the wider the class intervals are, the more information is lost. In Table 2.1 the interval width is 5 points, and the table shows that there are three people with scores in the lower 60s and one person with a

TABLE 2.1

A grouped frequency distribution table showing the data from Example 2.3. The original scores range from a high of $X = 94$ to a low of $X = 53$. This range has been divided into 9 intervals with each interval exactly 5 points wide. The frequency column (f) lists the number of individuals with scores in each of the class intervals.

X	f
90–94	3
85–89	4
80–84	5
75–79	4
70–74	3
65–69	1
60–64	3
55–59	1
50–54	1

score in the upper 60s. This information would be lost if the interval width was increased to 10 points. With an interval width of 10, all of the 60s would be grouped together into one interval labeled 60–69. The table would show a frequency of four people in the 60–69 interval, but it would not tell whether the scores were in the upper 60s or the lower 60s.

REAL LIMITS AND FREQUENCY DISTRIBUTIONS

Recall from Chapter 1 that a continuous variable has an infinite number of possible values and can be represented by a number line that is continuous and contains an infinite number of points. However, when a continuous variable is measured, the resulting measurements correspond to *intervals* on the number line rather than single points. For example, a score of $X = 8$ for a continuous variable actually represents an interval bounded by the real limits 7.5 and 8.5. Thus, a frequency distribution table showing a frequency of $f = 3$ individuals all assigned a score of $X = 8$ does not mean that all three individuals had exactly the same measurement. Instead, you should realize that the three measurements are simply located in the same interval between 7.5 and 8.5.

The concept of real limits also applies to the class intervals of a grouped frequency distribution table. For example, a class interval of 40–49 contains scores from $X = 40$ to $X = 49$. These values are called the *apparent limits* of the interval because it appears that they form the upper and lower boundaries for the class interval. But $X = 40$ is actually an interval from 39.5 to 40.5. Similarly, $X = 49$ is an interval from 48.5 to 49.5. Therefore, the real limits of the interval are 39.5 (the lower real limit) and 49.5 (the upper real limit). Notice that the next higher class interval is 50–59, which has a lower real limit of 49.5. Thus, the two intervals meet at the real limit 49.5, so there are no gaps in the scale. You also should notice that the width of each class interval becomes easier to understand when you consider the real limits of an interval. For example, the interval 50–54 has real limits of 49.5 and 54.5. The distance between these two real limits (5 points) is the width of the interval.

LEARNING CHECK

1. A set of scores ranges from a high of $X = 142$ to a low of $X = 65$.

   a. Explain why it would not be reasonable to display these scores in a *regular* frequency distribution table.

   b. Determine what interval width is most appropriate for a grouped frequency distribution for this set of scores.

   c. What range of values would form the bottom interval for the grouped table?

2. Using only the frequency distribution table presented in Table 2.1, how many individuals had a score of $X = 73$?

ANSWERS

1. **a.** It would require a table with 78 rows to list all the individual score values. This is too many rows.

   b. An interval width of 10 points is probably best. With a width of 10, it would require 8 intervals to cover the range of scores. In some circumstances, an interval width of 5 points (requiring 16 intervals) might be appropriate.

   c. With a width of 10, the bottom interval would be 60–69.

2. After a set of scores has been summarized in a grouped table, you cannot determine the frequency for any specific score. There is no way to determine how many individuals had $X = 73$ from the table alone. (You can say that *at most* three people had $X = 73$.)

2.3   FREQUENCY DISTRIBUTION GRAPHS

A frequency distribution graph is basically a picture showing the information available in a frequency distribution table. We will consider several different types of graphs, but all start with two perpendicular lines called *axes*. The horizontal line is called the *X*-axis, or the abscissa. The vertical line is called the *Y*-axis, or the ordinate. The measurement scale (set of *X* values) is listed along the *X*-axis in increasing value from left to right. The frequencies are listed on the *Y*-axis in increasing value from bottom to top. As a general rule, the point where the two axes intersect should have a value of zero for both the scores and the frequencies. A final general rule is that the graph should be constructed so that its height (*Y*-axis) is approximately two-thirds to three-quarters of its length (*X*-axis). Violating these guidelines can result in graphs that give a misleading picture of the data (see Box 2.1).

GRAPHS FOR INTERVAL OR RATIO DATA

The first graphs that we will consider are designed to be used with numerical scores that have been measured on an interval or a ratio scale of measurement. The two types of graph in this category are called *histograms* and *polygons*.

Histograms   To construct a histogram, you first list the numerical scores (the categories of measurement) along the *X*-axis. Then you draw a bar above each *X* value so that

a. The height of the bar corresponds to the frequency for that category.

b. The width of the bar extends to the real limits of the category.

Because the bars extend to the real limits for each category, adjacent bars touch so that there are no spaces or gaps between bars. An example of a histogram is shown in Figure 2.1.

When data have been grouped into class intervals, you can construct a frequency distribution histogram by drawing a bar above each interval so that the width of the bar extends to the real limits of the interval (the lower real limit of the lowest score and the upper real limit of the highest score in the interval). This process is demonstrated in Figure 2.2.

For the two histograms shown in Figures 2.1 and 2.2, notice that the values on both the vertical and horizontal axes are clearly marked and that both axes are labeled. Also note that, whenever possible, the units of measurement are specified; for example,

FIGURE 2.1

An example of a frequency distribution histogram. The same set of quiz scores is presented in a frequency distribution table and in a histogram.

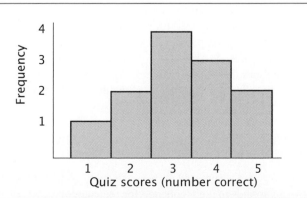

X	f
5	2
4	3
3	4
2	2
1	1

FIGURE 2.2

An example of a frequency distribution histogram for grouped data. The same set of children's heights is presented in a frequency distribution table and in a histogram.

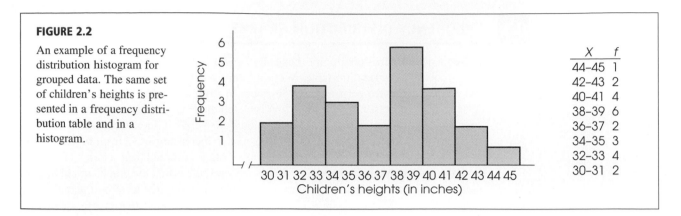

X	f
44–45	1
42–43	2
40–41	4
38–39	6
36–37	2
34–35	3
32–33	4
30–31	2

FIGURE 2.3

A frequency distribution in which each individual is represented by a block placed directly above the individual's score. For example, three people had scores of X = 2.

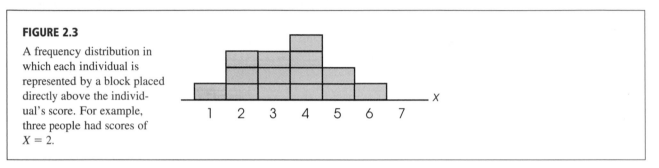

Figure 2.2 shows a distribution of heights measured in inches. Finally, notice that the horizontal axis in Figure 2.2 does not list all of the possible heights starting from zero and going up to 48 inches. Instead, the graph clearly shows a break between zero and 30, indicating that some scores have been omitted.

A modified histogram A slight modification to the traditional histogram produces a very easy to draw and simple to understand sketch of a frequency distribution. Instead of drawing a bar above each score, the modification consists of drawing a stack of blocks. Each block represents one individual, so the number of blocks above each score corresponds to the frequency for that score. An example is shown in Figure 2.3.

Note that the number of blocks in each stack makes it very easy to see the absolute frequency for each category. In addition it is easy to see the exact difference in frequency from one category to another. In Figure 2.3, for example, it is easy to see that there are exactly two more people with scores of X = 2 than with scores of X = 1. Because the frequencies are clearly displayed by the number of blocks, this type of display eliminates the need for a vertical line (the Y-axis) showing frequencies. In general, this kind of graph provides a simple and concrete picture of the distribution for a sample of scores. Note that we will often use this kind of graph to show sample data throughout the rest of the book. You should also note, however, that this kind of display simply provides a sketch of the distribution and is not a substitute for an accurately drawn histogram with two labeled axes.

Polygons To construct a polygon, you begin by listing the numerical scores (the categories of measurement) along the X-axis. Then,

a. A dot is centered above each score so that the vertical position of the dot corresponds to the frequency for the category.

b. A continuous line is drawn from dot to dot to connect the series of dots.

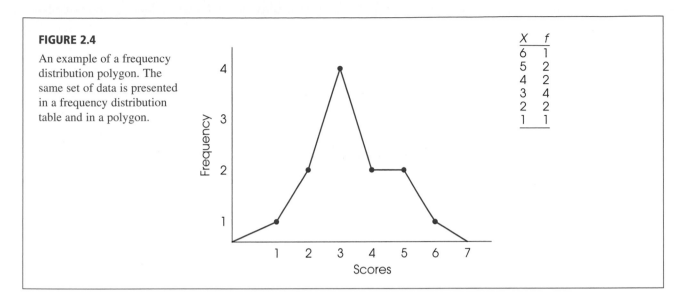

FIGURE 2.4

An example of a frequency distribution polygon. The same set of data is presented in a frequency distribution table and in a polygon.

X	f
6	1
5	2
4	2
3	4
2	2
1	1

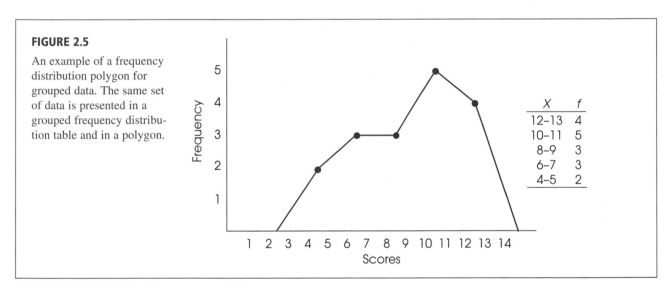

FIGURE 2.5

An example of a frequency distribution polygon for grouped data. The same set of data is presented in a grouped frequency distribution table and in a polygon.

X	f
12–13	4
10–11	5
8–9	3
6–7	3
4–5	2

c. The graph is completed by drawing a line down to the *X*-axis (zero frequency) at each end of the range of scores. The final lines are usually drawn so that they reach the *X*-axis at a point that is one category below the lowest score on the left side and one category above the highest score on the right side. An example of a polygon is shown in Figure 2.4.

A polygon also can be used with data that have been grouped into class intervals. For a grouped distribution, you position each dot directly above the midpoint of the class interval. The midpoint can be found by averaging the highest and the lowest scores in the interval. For example, a class interval that is listed as 20–29 would have a midpoint of 24.5.

$$midpoint = \frac{20 + 29}{2} = \frac{49}{2} = 24.5$$

An example of a frequency distribution polygon with grouped data is shown in Figure 2.5.

GRAPHS FOR NOMINAL OR ORDINAL DATA

When the scores are measured on a nominal or ordinal scale (usually non-numerical values), the frequency distribution can be displayed in a *bar graph.*

Bar graphs   A bar graph is essentially the same as a histogram, except that spaces are left between adjacent bars. For a nominal scale, the space between bars emphasizes that the scale consists of separate, distinct categories. For ordinal scales, separate bars are used because you cannot assume that the categories are all the same size.

To construct a bar graph, list the categories of measurement along the *X*-axis and then draw a bar above each category so that the height of the bar correponds to the frequency for the category. An example of a bar graph is shown in Figure 2.6.

GRAPHS FOR POPULATION DISTRIBUTIONS

When you can obtain an exact frequency for each score in a population, you can construct frequency distribution graphs that are exactly the same as the histograms, polygons, and bar graphs that are typically used for samples. For example, if a population is defined as a specific group of *N* = 50 people, we could easily determine how many have IQs of *X* = 110. However, if we are interested in the entire population of adults in the United States, it would be impossible to obtain an exact count of the number of people with an IQ of 110. Although it is still possible to construct graphs showing frequency distributions for extremely large populations, the graphs usually involve two special features: relative frequencies and smooth curves.

Relative frequencies   Although you usually cannot find the absolute frequency for each score in a population, you very often can obtain *relative frequencies.* For example, you may not know exactly how many fish are in the lake, but after years of fishing you do know that there are twice as many bluegill as there are bass. You can represent these relative frequencies in a bar graph by making the bar above bluegill two times taller than the bar above bass (Figure 2.7). Notice that the graph does not show the absolute number of fish. Instead, it shows the relative number of bluegill and bass.

Smooth curves   When a population consists of numerical scores from an interval or a ratio scale, it is customary to draw the distribution with a smooth curve instead of the jagged, step-wise shapes that occur with histograms and polygons. The smooth curve indicates that you are not connecting a series of dots (real frequencies) but instead are

FIGURE 2.6

A bar graph showing the distribution of personality types in a sample of college students. Because personality type is a discrete variable measured on a nominal scale, the graph is drawn with space between the bars.

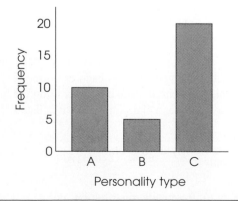

FIGURE 2.7

A frequency distribution showing the relative frequency for two types of fish. Notice that the exact number of fish is not reported; the graph simply says that there are twice as many bluegill as there are bass.

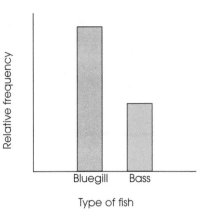

FIGURE 2.8

The population distribution of IQ scores: an example of a normal distribution.

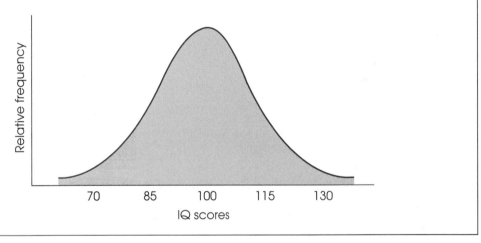

showing the relative changes that occur from one score to the next. One commonly occurring population distribution is the normal curve. The word *normal* refers to a specific shape that can be precisely defined by an equation. Less precisely, we can describe a normal distribution as being symmetrical, with the greatest frequency in the middle and relatively smaller frequencies as you move toward either extreme. A good example of a normal distribution is the population distribution for IQ scores shown in Figure 2.8. Because normal-shaped distributions occur commonly and because this shape is mathematically guaranteed in certain situations, we give it extensive attention throughout this book.

In the future, we will be referring to *distributions of scores.* Whenever the term *distribution* appears, you should conjure up an image of a frequency distribution graph. The graph provides a picture showing exactly where the individual scores are located. To make this concept more concrete, you might find it useful to think of the graph as showing a pile of individuals just like we showed a pile of blocks in Figure 2.3. For the population of IQ scores shown in Figure 2.8, the pile is highest at an IQ score around 100 because most people have average IQs. There are only a few individuals piled up at an IQ of 130; it must be lonely at the top.

| BOX 2.1 | THE USE AND MISUSE OF GRAPHS |

Although graphs are intended to provide an accurate picture of a set of data, they can be used to exaggerate or misrepresent a set of scores. These misrepresentations generally result from failing to follow the basic rules for graph construction. The following example demonstrates how the same set of data can be presented in two entirely different ways by manipulating the structure of a graph.

For the past several years, the city has kept records of the number of major felonies. The data are summarized as follows:

Year	Number of major felonies
2003	218
2004	225
2005	229

These same data are shown in two different graphs in Figure 2.9. In the first graph, we have exaggerated the height, and we started numbering the Y-axis at 210 rather than at zero. As a result, the graph seems to indicate a rapid rise in the crime rate over the 3-year period. In the second graph, we have stretched out the X-axis and used zero as the starting point for the Y-axis. The result is a graph that shows little change in the crime rate over the 3-year period.

Which graph is correct? The answer is that neither one is very good. Remember that the purpose of a graph is to provide an accurate display of the data. The first graph in Figure 2.9 exaggerates the differences between years, and the second graph conceals the differences. Some compromise is needed. Also note that in some cases a graph may not be the best way to display information. For these data, for example, showing the numbers in a table would be better than either graph.

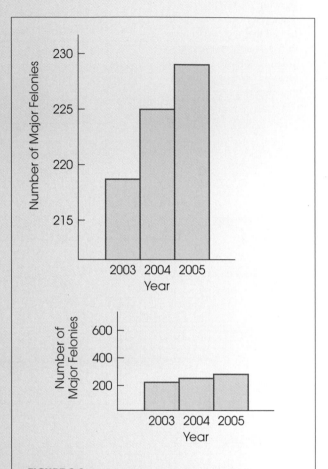

FIGURE 2.9

Two graphs showing the number of major felonies in a city over a 3-year period. Both graphs show exactly the same data. However, the first graph gives the appearance that the crime rate is high and rising rapidly. The second graph gives the impression that the crime rate is low and has not changed over the 3-year period.

2.4 THE SHAPE OF A FREQUENCY DISTRIBUTION

Rather than drawing a complete frequency distribution graph, researchers often simply describe a distribution by listing its characteristics. There are three characteristics that completely describe any distribution: shape, central tendency, and variability. In simple terms, central tendency measures where the center of the distribution is located. Variability tells whether the scores are spread over a wide range or are clustered together. Central tendency and variability will be covered in detail in Chapters 3 and 4. Technically, the shape of a distribution is defined by an equation that prescribes the exact relationship between each X and Y value on the graph. However, we will rely on a few less-precise terms that will serve to describe the shape of most distributions.

Nearly all distributions can be classified as being either symmetrical or skewed.

DEFINITIONS

In a **symmetrical distribution,** it is possible to draw a vertical line through the middle so that one side of the distribution is a mirror image of the other (Figure 2.10).

In a **skewed distribution,** the scores tend to pile up toward one end of the scale and taper off gradually at the other end (see Figure 2.10).

The section where the scores taper off toward one end of a distribution is called the **tail** of the distribution.

A skewed distribution with the tail on the right-hand side is said to be **positively skewed** because the tail points toward the positive (above-zero) end of the X-axis. If the tail points to the left, the distribution is said to be **negatively skewed** (see Figure 2.10).

For a very difficult exam, most scores will tend to be low, with only a few individuals earning high scores. This will produce a positively skewed distribution. Similarly, a very easy exam will tend to produce a negatively skewed distribution, with most of the students earning high scores and only a few with low values.

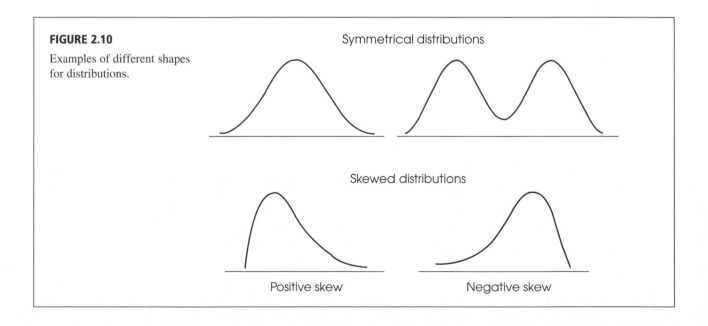

FIGURE 2.10

Examples of different shapes for distributions.

Symmetrical distributions

Skewed distributions

Positive skew   Negative skew

LEARNING CHECK

1. Sketch a frequency distribution histogram and a frequency distribution polygon for the data in the following table:

X	f
5	4
4	6
3	3
2	1
1	1

2. Describe the shape of the distribution in Exercise 1.

3. What type of graph would be appropriate to show the number of gold medals, silver medals, and bronze medals won by the United States during the 2000 Olympics?

4. The results from a recent exam show that most students had high scores in the 80s and 90s, and only a few students had scores in the 50s, 60s, and 70s. What is the shape of this distribution of scores?

ANSWERS

1. The graphs are shown in Figure 2.11.

2. The distribution is negatively skewed.

3. A bar graph is appropriate for ordinal data.

4. It is negatively skewed.

FIGURE 2.11

Answers to Learning Check Exercise 1.

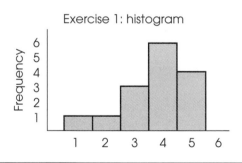
Exercise 1: histogram

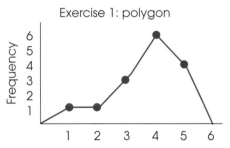
Exercise 1: polygon

SUMMARY

1. The goal of descriptive statistics is to simplify the organization and presentation of data. One descriptive technique is to place the data in a frequency distribution table or graph that shows exactly how many individuals (or scores) are located in each category on the scale of measurement.

2. A frequency distribution table lists the categories that make up the scale of measurement (the X values) in one column. Beside each X value, in a second column, is the frequency or number of individuals in that category. The table may include a proportion column showing the relative frequency for each category:

$$\text{proportion} = p = \frac{f}{N}$$

The table may include a percentage column showing the percentage associated with each X value:

$$\text{percentage} = p(100) = \frac{f}{N}(100)$$

3. It is recommended that a frequency distribution table have a maximum of 10 to 15 rows to keep it simple. If the scores cover a range that is wider than this suggested maximum, it is customary to divide the range into sections called class intervals. These intervals are then listed in the frequency distribution table along with the frequency or number of individuals with scores in each interval. The result is called a grouped frequency distribution. The guidelines for constructing a grouped frequency distribution table are as follows:

   a. There should be about 10 intervals.

   b. The width of each interval should be a simple number (e.g., 2, 5, or 10).

   c. The bottom score in each interval should be a multiple of the width.

   d. All intervals should be the same width, and they should cover the range of scores with no gaps.

4. A frequency distribution graph lists scores on the horizontal axis and frequencies on the vertical axis. The type of graph used to display a distribution depends on the scale of measurement used. For interval or ratio scales, you should use a histogram or a polygon. For a histogram, a bar is drawn above each score so that the height of the bar corresponds to the frequency. Each bar extends to the real limits of the score, so that adjacent bars touch. For a polygon, a dot is placed above the midpoint of each score or class interval so that the height of the dot corresponds to the frequency; then lines are drawn to connect the dots. Bar graphs are used with nominal or ordinal scales. Bar graphs are similar to histograms except that gaps are left between adjacent bars.

5. Shape is one of the basic characteristics used to describe a distribution of scores. Most distributions can be classified as either symmetrical or skewed. A skewed distribution that tails off to the right is said to be positively skewed. If it tails off to the left, it is negatively skewed.

KEY TERMS

frequency distribution

grouped frequency distribution

range

class interval

apparent limits

histogram

polygon

bar graph

relative frequency

symmetrical distribution

positively skewed distribution

negatively skewed distribution

tail(s) of a distribution

RESOURCES

There are a tutorial quiz and other learning exercises for Chapter 2 at the Wadsworth website, www.thomsonedu.com/psychology/gravetter. See page 27 for more information about accessing items on the website.

WebTUTOR

For those using WebTutor along with this book, there is a WebTutor section corresponding to this chapter. The WebTutor contains a brief summary of Chapter 2, hints for learning the new material and for avoiding common errors, and sample exam items including solutions.

General instructions for using SPSS are presented in Appendix D. Following are detailed instructions for using SPSS to produce **Frequency Distribution Tables or Graphs.**

Frequency Distribution Tables

Data Entry

1. Enter all the scores in one column of the data editor, probably VAR00001.

Data Analysis

1. Click **Analyze** on the tool bar, select **Descriptive Statistics,** and click on **Frequencies.**
2. Highlight the column label for the set of scores (VAR00001) in the left box and click the arrow to move it into the **Variable** box.
3. Be sure that the option to **Display Frequency Table** is selected.
4. Click **OK.**

SPSS Output

The frequency distribution table will list the score values in a column from smallest to largest, with the percentage and cumulative percentage also listed for each score. Score values that do not occur (zero frequencies) are not included in the table, and the program does not group scores into class intervals (all values are listed).

Frequency Distribution Histograms or Bar Graphs

Data Entry

1. Enter all the scores in one column of the data editor, probably VAR00001.

Data Analysis

1. Click **Analyze** on the tool bar, select **Descriptive Statistics,** and click on **Frequencies.**
2. Highlight the column label for the set of scores (VAR00001) in the left box and click the arrow to move it into the **Variable** box.
3. Click **Charts.**
4. Select either **Bar Graphs** or **Histogram.**
5. Click **Continue.**
6. Click **OK.**

SPSS Output

After a brief delay, SPSS will display a frequency distribution table and a graph. Note that SPSS will often produce a histogram that groups the scores in unpredictable intervals. A bar graph will usually produce a clearer picture of the actual frequency associated with each score.

FOCUS ON PROBLEM SOLVING

1. The reason for constructing frequency distributions is to put a disorganized set of raw data into a comprehensible, organized format. Because several different types of frequency distribution tables and graphs are available, one problem is deciding which type should be used. Tables have the advantage of being easier to construct, but graphs generally give a better picture of the data and are easier to understand.

    To help you decide exactly which type of frequency distribution is best, consider the following points:

    a. What is the range of scores? With a wide range, you will need to group the scores into class intervals.

    b. What is the scale of measurement? With an interval or a ratio scale, you can use a polygon or a histogram. With a nominal or an ordinal scale, you must use a bar graph.

2. When using a grouped frequency distribution table, a common mistake is to calculate the interval width by using the highest and lowest values that define each interval. For example, some students are tricked into thinking that an interval identified as 20–24 is only 4 points wide. To determine the correct interval width, you can

    a. Count the individual scores in the interval. For this example, the scores are 20, 21, 22, 23, and 24 for a total of 5 values. Thus, the interval width is 5 points.

    b. Use the real limits to determine the real width of the interval. For example, an interval identified as 20–24 has a lower real limit of 19.5 and an upper real limit of 24.5 (halfway to the next score). Using the real limits, the interval width is

    $$24.5 - 19.5 = 5 \text{ points}$$

DEMONSTRATION 2.1

A GROUPED FREQUENCY DISTRIBUTION TABLE

For the following set of $N = 20$ scores, construct a grouped frequency distribution table using an interval width of 5 points. The scores are:

14, 8, 27, 16, 10, 22, 9, 13, 16, 12,
10, 9, 15, 17, 6, 14, 11, 18, 14, 11

STEP 1 Set up the class intervals.

The largest score in this distribution is $X = 27$, and the lowest is $X = 6$. Therefore, a frequency distribution table for these data would have 22 rows and would be too large. A grouped frequency distribution table would be better. We have asked specifically for an interval width of 5 points, and the resulting table will have five rows.

X
25–29
20–24
15–19
10–14
5–9

STEP 2 Determine the frequencies for each interval.
Examine the scores, and count how many fall into the class interval of 25–29. Cross out each score that you have already counted. Record the frequency for this class interval. Now repeat this process for the remaining intervals. The result is the following table:

X	f	
25–29	1	(the score $X = 27$)
20–24	1	($X = 22$)
15–19	5	(the scores $X = 16, 16, 15, 17,$ and 18)
10–14	9	($X = 14, 10, 13, 12, 10, 14, 11, 14,$ and 11)
5–9	4	($X = 8, 9, 9,$ and 6)

PROBLEMS

1. Under what circumstances should you use a grouped frequency distribution instead of a regular frequency distribution?

2. What information is available about the data in a regular frequency distribution table that is not available in a grouped table?

3. Place the following scores in a frequency distribution table. Include columns for proportion (p) and percentage (%) in your table. The scores are:

$$4, \quad 6, \quad 2, \quad 9, \quad 8, \quad 6, \quad 5, \quad 7, \quad 7, \quad 3$$
$$6, \quad 6, \quad 7, \quad 3, \quad 7, \quad 4, \quad 5, \quad 8, \quad 6, \quad 5$$

4. Construct a grouped frequency distribution table for the following scores, which range from a high of 97 to a low of 56.

85, 92, 66, 81, 84, 79, 97, 88, 72, 83, 56, 85, 93, 76, 70

89, 91, 84, 74, 92, 95, 80, 77, 85, 93, 68, 88, 84, 86, 79

5. For the following scores, the lowest value is $X = 13$. Place the scores in a frequency distribution table using
a. An interval width of 5.
b. An interval width of 10.

21,	40,	18,	37,	32,	52,	33,	24,	13
57,	41,	47,	32,	43,	58,	16,	38,	31
47,	29,	49,	54,	22,	39,	34,	45,	20

6. Construct a grouped frequency distribution table to organize the following set of scores, which range from 88 to 470.

319,	241,	104,	165,	97,	452,	280
88,	225,	396,	271,	233,	470,	356
159,	266,	112,	293,	174,	268,	153

7. The following are reading comprehension ratings for a third-grade class of 20 students:

$$5, \quad 4, \quad 4, \quad 2, \quad 6, \quad 4, \quad 5, \quad 3, \quad 3, \quad 6$$
$$4, \quad 1, \quad 7, \quad 4, \quad 3, \quad 5, \quad 4, \quad 7, \quad 4, \quad 2$$

a. Construct a frequency distribution table to organize the scores.
b. Draw a frequency distribution histogram for these data.

8. Find each value requested for the set of scores summarized in the following table:
a. n
b. ΣX
c. ΣX^2

X	f
4	2
3	2
2	4
1	2
0	1

9. For the following set of quiz scores:

$$3, \quad 5, \quad 4, \quad 6, \quad 2, \quad 3, \quad 4, \quad 1, \quad 4, \quad 3,$$
$$7, \quad 7, \quad 3, \quad 4, \quad 5, \quad 8, \quad 2, \quad 4, \quad 7, \quad 10$$

a. Construct a frequency distribution table to organize the scores.
b. Draw a frequency distribution histogram for these data.

10. Sketch a histogram and a polygon showing the distribution of scores presented in the following table:

X	f
5	1
4	5
3	6
2	3
1	2

11. Describe the difference in appearance between a bar graph and a histogram, and describe the circumstances under which each type of graph should be used.

12. An instructor at the state college recorded the academic major for each student in a psychology class and obtained the following results:

Psych	Bio	Soc	Engl	Psych
Health	Phys Ed	Psych	Art	Psych
Soc	Health	Psych	Phys Ed	Soc
Hist	Psych	Art	Health	Psych
Nurs	Soc	Psych	Psych	Pol Sci

    a. Construct a frequency distribution table for these data.
    b. What type of graph would be appropriate to show the frequency distribution for these data?

13. Place the following set of scores in a frequency distribution table:

1, 3, 1, 1, 4, 1, 4, 5, 6, 2, 1, 1, 5,
1, 3, 2, 1, 6, 2, 4, 5, 2, 3, 2, 3

Compute the proportion and the percentage of individuals with each score. From your frequency distribution table, you should be able to identify the shape of this distribution.

14. Find each of the following values for the set of scores shown in the frequency distribution graph.
    a. N
    b. ΣX

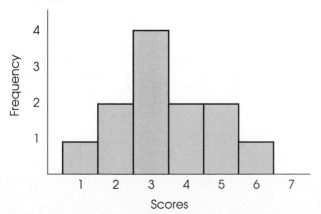

15. A set of scores has been organized into the following frequency distribution table. Find each of the following values for the original set of scores:
    a. n
    b. ΣX
    c. ΣX^2

X	f
5	1
4	0
3	4
2	3
1	2

16. For the following set of scores:

5, 6, 2, 3, 6, 5, 6,
4, 1, 5, 6, 3, 4

    a. Construct a frequency distribution table.
    b. Sketch a polygon showing the distribution.
    c. Describe the distribution using the following characteristics:
        (1) What is the shape of the distribution?
        (2) What score best identifies the center (average) for the distribution?
        (3) Are the scores clustered together, or are they spread out across the scale?

17. The following table shows the frequency distribution of birth-order position for a sample of $n = 24$ students.
    a. What kind of graph would be appropriate for showing this distribution?
    b. Sketch the frequency distribution graph.

Birth-order Position	f
1st born	12
2nd born	5
3rd born	6
4th born	0
5th born	1

18. Mental imagery has been shown to be very effective for improving memory. In one demonstration study, two groups of participants were presented with a list of 20 words. One group was given instructions to use mental images to help them remember the words, and the second group was given no special instructions. After the list was presented, each person was asked to recall as many words as possible. The scores for the two groups are as follows:

Imagery group				
18	19	18	17	19
13	20	17	18	18
20	18	14	19	16

No-instruction group				
11	12	16	12	10
13	14	12	10	8
13	10	11	14	12

   a. Sketch a histogram showing the distribution of scores for each group (two separate graphs).
   b. Describe each graph by identifying the shape of the distribution and the approximate center of the distribution.
   c. Based on the appearance of the two distributions, what is the effect of using mental images on the level of performance for this memory task?

19. The following data are quiz scores from two different sections of an introductory statistics course:

Section I			Section II		
9	6	8	4	7	8
10	8	3	6	3	7
7	8	8	4	6	5
7	5	10	10	3	6
9	6	7	7	4	6

   a. Organize the scores from each section in a frequency distribution histogram.
   b. Describe the general differences between the two distributions.

20. Schmidt (1994) conducted a series of experiments examining the effects of humor on memory. In one study, participants were shown a list of sentences, of which half were humorous and half were nonhumorous. Schmidt then measured the number of each type of sentence recalled by each participant. Following are hypothetical results similar to those obtained by Schmidt.

Number of Sentences Recalled							
Humorous sentences				Nonhumorous sentences			
4	5	2	4	5	2	4	2
6	7	6	6	2	3	1	6
2	5	4	3	3	2	3	3
1	3	5	5	4	1	5	3

   a. Identify the independent variable and the dependent variable for this experiment.
   b. Sketch a polygon showing the data for the humorous sentences.
   c. On the same graph, sketch a polygon for the nonhumorous sentences. (Use a solid line for one polygon and a dashed line for the other.)
   d. Looking at your graph, does it appear that humor has an influence on memory for sentences?

21. A psychologist would like to examine the effects of prior experience on learning a new task. Two groups of rats were compared. One group had participated in a variety of learning experiments over the past 4 months, and the other group had just arrived at the psychology department with no prior research experience. All the rats were tested on a discrimination learning problem and the psychologist recorded the number of errors each animal made before it solved the problem. The data are as follows:

Experienced rats:
 9, 8, 8, 10, 7, 9, 11, 7, 9, 10
10, 8, 9, 9, 8, 10, 9, 8, 9, 8

Inexperienced rats:
13, 11, 12, 10, 14, 12, 13, 10, 9, 13
 9, 12, 12, 10, 13, 12, 11, 12, 10, 14

   a. Sketch a polygon showing the frequency distribution for the experienced rats. On the same graph, sketch a polygon showing the distribution for the inexperienced rats. (Use a solid line for one graph and a dashed line for the other.)
   b. Do the inexperienced rats consistently make more errors than the experienced rats do?

C H A P T E R

3

Central Tendency

Tools You Will Need

The following items are considered essential background material for this chapter. If you doubt your knowledge of any of these items, you should review the appropriate chapter or section before proceeding.

- Summation notation (Chapter 1)
- Frequency distributions (Chapter 2)

3.1   OVERVIEW

The general purpose of descriptive statistical methods is to organize and summarize a set of scores. Perhaps the most common method for summarizing and describing a distribution is to find a single value that defines the average score and can serve as a representative for the entire distribution. In statistics, the concept of an average or representative score is called *central tendency*. The goal in measuring central tendency is to describe a distribution of scores by determining a single value that identifies the center of the distribution. Ideally, this central value will be the score that is the best representative value for all of the individuals in the distribution.

DEFINITION

> **Central tendency** is a statistical measure to determine a single score that defines the center of a distribution. The goal of central tendency is to find the single score that is most typical or most representative of the entire group.

In everyday language, the goal of central tendency is to identify the "average" or "typical" individual. This average value can then be used to provide a simple description of the entire population or sample. For example, the average family income in Greenwich, Connecticut, is more than $225,000. Obviously, not everyone in Greenwich makes this income, but the average should give you a good idea of the neighborhood. Measures of central tendency are also useful for making comparisons between groups of individuals or between sets of figures. For example, weather data indicate that for Seattle, Washington, the average yearly temperature is 53° and the average annual precipitation is 34 inches. By comparison, the average temperature in Phoenix, Arizona, is 71° and the average precipitation is 7.4 inches. The point of these examples is to demonstrate the great advantage of being able to describe a large set of data with a single, representative number. Central tendency characterizes what is typical for a large population and in doing so makes large amounts of data more digestible. Statisticians sometimes use the expression "number crunching" to illustrate this aspect of data description. That is, we take a distribution consisting of many scores and "crunch" them down to a single value that describes them all.

Unfortunately, there is no single, standard procedure for determining central tendency. The problem is that no single measure will always produce a central, representative value in every situation. The three distributions shown in Figure 3.1 should help demonstrate this fact. Before we discuss the three distributions, take a moment to look at the figure and try to identify the "center" or the "most representative score" for each distribution.

1. The first distribution [Figure 3.1(a)] is symmetrical, with the scores forming a distinct pile centered around $X = 5$. For this type of distribution, it is easy to identify the "center," and most people would agree that the value $X = 5$ is an appropriate measure of central tendency.

2. In the second distribution [Figure 3.1(b)], however, problems begin to appear. Now the scores form a negatively skewed distribution, piling up at the high end of the scale around $X = 8$, but tapering off to the left all the way down to $X = 1$. Where is the "center" in this case? Some people might select $X = 8$ as the center because more individuals had this score than any other single value. However, $X = 8$ is clearly not in the middle of the distribution. In fact, the majority of the scores (10 out of 16) have values less than 8, so it seems reasonable that the "center" should be defined by a value that is less than 8.

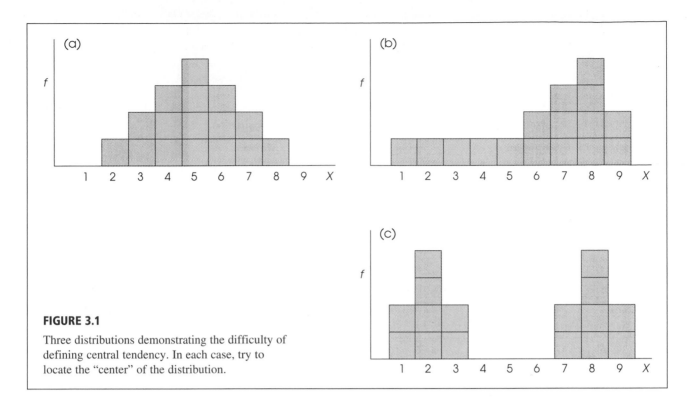

FIGURE 3.1

Three distributions demonstrating the difficulty of defining central tendency. In each case, try to locate the "center" of the distribution.

3. Now consider the third distribution [Figure 3.1(c)]. Again, the distribution is symmetrical, but now there are two distinct piles of scores. Because the distribution is symmetrical with $X = 5$ as the midpoint, you may choose $X = 5$ as the "center." However, none of the scores is located at $X = 5$ (or even close), so this value is not particularly good as a representative score. On the other hand, because there are two separate piles of scores with one group centered at $X = 2$ and the other centered at $X = 8$, it is tempting to say that this distribution has two centers. But can there be two centers?

Clearly, there are problems defining the "center" of a distribution. Occasionally, you will find a nice, neat distribution like the one shown in Figure 3.1(a), for which everyone will agree on the center. But you should realize that other distributions are possible and that there may be different opinions concerning the definition of the center. To deal with these problems, statisticians have developed three different methods for measuring central tendency: the mean, the median, and the mode. They are computed differently and have different characteristics. To decide which of the three measures is best for any particular distribution, you should keep in mind that the general purpose of central tendency is to find the single most representative score. Each of the three measures we will present has been developed to work best in a specific situation. We will examine this issue in more detail after we introduce the three measures.

3.2 THE MEAN

The *mean*, commonly known as the arithmetic average, is computed by adding all the scores in the distribution and dividing by the number of scores. The mean for a population will be identified by the Greek letter mu, μ (pronounced "mew"), and the mean for a sample is identified by M or $\overline{X}$ (read "x-bar").

For years, the convention in statistics textbooks was to use $\overline{X}$ to represent the mean for a sample. However, in manuscripts and in published research reports the letter M is the standard notation for a sample mean. Because you will encounter the letter M when reading research reports and because you should use the letter M when writing research reports, we have decided to use the same notation in this text. Keep in mind that the $\overline{X}$ notation is still appropriate for identifying a sample mean, and you may find it used on occasion, especially in textbooks.

DEFINITION

The **mean** for a distribution is the sum of the scores divided by the number of scores.

The formula for the *population mean* is

$$\mu = \frac{\Sigma X}{N} \tag{3.1}$$

First, sum all the scores in the population, and then divide by N. For a sample, the computation is done the same way, but the formula for the *sample mean* uses symbols that signify sample values:

$$\text{sample mean} = M = \frac{\Sigma X}{n} \tag{3.2}$$

In general, we will use Greek letters to identify characteristics of a population and letters of our own alphabet to stand for sample values. If a mean is identified with the symbol M, you should realize that we are dealing with a sample. Also note that n is used as the symbol for the number of scores in the sample.

EXAMPLE 3.1

For a population of $N = 4$ scores,

3,   7,   4,   6

the mean is

$$\mu = \frac{\Sigma X}{N} = \frac{20}{4} = 5$$

ALTERNATIVE DEFINITIONS FOR THE MEAN

Although the procedure of adding the scores and dividing by the number provides a useful definition of the mean, there are two alternative definitions that may give you a better understanding of this important measure of central tendency.

The first alternative is to think of the mean as the amount each individual would get if the total (ΣX) were divided equally among all the individuals (N) in the distribution. This somewhat socialistic viewpoint is particularly useful in problems where you know the mean and must find the total. Consider the following example.

EXAMPLE 3.2

A group of $n = 6$ boys buys a box of baseball cards at a garage sale and discovers that the box contains a total of 180 cards. If the boys divide the cards equally among themselves, how many cards will each boy get? You should recognize that this problem represents the standard procedure for computing the mean. Specifically, the total (ΣX) is divided by the number (n) to produce the mean, $\frac{180}{6} = 30$ cards for each boy.

You should also recognize that this example demonstrates that it is possible to define the mean as the amount that each individual gets when the total is distributed equally. This new definition can be useful for some problems involving the mean. Consider the following example.

This time we have a group of $n = 4$ boys and we measure the amount of money that each boy has. The data produce a mean of $M = \$5$. Given this information, what is the total amount of money for the whole group? Although you do not know exactly how much money each boy has, the new definition of the mean tells you that if they pool their money together and then distribute the total equally, each boy will get $5. For each of $n = 4$ boys to get $5, the total must be $4(\$5) = \$20$. To check this answer, use the formula for the mean:

$$M = \frac{\Sigma X}{n} = \frac{\$20}{4} = \$5$$

The second alternative definition of the mean describes the mean as a balance point for a distribution. Consider the population consisting of $N = 4$ scores (2, 2, 6, 10). For this population, $\Sigma X = 20$ and $N = 4$, so $\mu = \frac{20}{4} = 5$. Figure 3.2 shows this population drawn as a histogram, with each score represented by a box that is sitting on a seesaw. If the seesaw is positioned so that it pivots at a point equal to the mean, then it will be balanced and will rest level.

The reason the seesaw is balanced over the mean becomes clear when we measure the distance of each box (score) from the mean:

Score	Distance from the Mean
$X = 2$	3 points below the mean
$X = 2$	3 points below the mean
$X = 6$	1 point above the mean
$X = 10$	5 points above the mean

Notice that the mean balances the distances. That is, the total distance below the mean is the same as the total distance above the mean:

3 points below + 3 points below = 6 points below

1 point above + 5 points above = 6 points above

Because the mean serves as a balance point, the value of the mean will always be located somewhere between the highest score and the lowest score; that is, the mean can

FIGURE 3.2

The frequency distribution shown as a seesaw balanced at the mean.

Based on G. H. Weinberg, J. A. Schumaker, & D. Oltman (1981). *Statistics: An Intuitive Approach* (p. 14). Belmont, Calif.: Wadsworth.

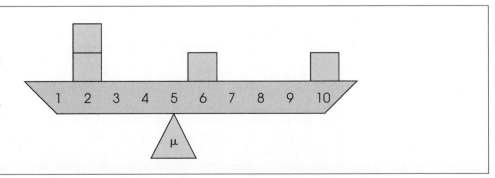

never be outside the range of scores. If the lowest score in a distribution is $X = 8$ and the highest is $X = 15$, then the mean *must* be between 8 and 15. If you calculate a value that is outside this range, then you have made an error.

The image of a seesaw with the mean at the balance point is also useful for determining how a distribution is affected if a new score is added or if an existing score is removed. For the distribution in Figure 3.2, for example, what would happen to the mean (balance point) if a new score were added at $X = 10$?

THE WEIGHTED MEAN

Often it is necessary to combine two sets of scores and then find the overall mean for the combined group. Suppose that we begin with two separate samples. The first sample has $n = 12$ scores and a mean of $M = 6$. The second sample has $n = 8$ and $M = 7$. If the two samples are combined, what is the mean for the total group?

To calculate the overall mean, we will need two values: the overall sum of the scores for the combined group (ΣX) and the total number of scores in the combined group (n). To determine the overall sum, we will simply find the sum of the scores for the first sample (ΣX_1) and the sum for the second sample (ΣX_2) and then add the two sums together. Similarly, the total number of scores in the combined group can be found by adding the number in the first sample (n_1) and the number in the second sample (n_2). With these two values, we can compute the mean using the basic formula

$$\text{overall mean} = M = \frac{\Sigma X \text{ (overall sum for the combined group)}}{n \text{ (total number in the combined group)}}$$

$$= \frac{\Sigma X_1 + \Sigma X_2}{n_1 + n_2}$$

The first sample has $n = 12$ and $M = 6$. Therefore, the total for this sample must be $\Sigma X = 72$. (Remember that when the total is distributed equally, each person gets the mean. For each of 12 people to get $M = 6$, the total must be 72.) In the same way, the second sample has $n = 8$ and $M = 7$, so the total must be $\Sigma X = 56$. Using these values, we obtain an overall mean of

$$\text{overall mean} = M = \frac{\Sigma X_1 + \Sigma X_2}{n_1 + n_2} = \frac{72 + 56}{12 + 8} = \frac{128}{20} = 6.4$$

The following table summarizes the calculations.

First Sample	Second Sample	Combined Sample
$n = 12$	$n = 8$	$n = 20$ (12 + 8)
$\Sigma X = 72$	$\Sigma X = 56$	$\Sigma X = 128$ (72 + 56)
$M = 6$	$M = 7$	$M = 6.4$

Note that the overall mean is not halfway between the original two sample means. Because the samples are not the same size, one will make a larger contribution to the total group and therefore will carry more weight in determining the overall mean. For this reason, the overall mean we have calculated is called the *weighted mean*. In this example, the overall mean of $M = 6.4$ is closer to the value of $M = 6$ (the larger sample) than it is to $M = 7$ (the smaller sample).

In summary, when two samples are combined, the weighted mean is obtained as follows:

STEP 1   Determine the grand total of all the scores in both samples. This sum is obtained by adding the sum of the scores for the first sample (ΣX_1) and the sum of the scores for the second sample (ΣX_2).

STEP 2   Determine the total number of scores in both samples. This value is obtained by adding the number in the first sample (n_1) and the number in the second sample (n_2).

STEP 3   Divide the sum of all the scores (step 1) by the total number of scores (step 2). Expressed as an equation,

$$\text{weighted mean} = \frac{\text{combined sum}}{\text{combined } n} = \frac{\Sigma X_1 + \Sigma X_2}{n_1 + n_2}$$

COMPUTING THE MEAN FROM A FREQUENCY DISTRIBUTION TABLE

When a set of scores has been organized in a frequency distribution table, the calculation of the mean is usually easier if you first remove the individual scores from the table. Table 3.1 shows a distribution of quiz scores organized in a frequency distribution table. To compute the mean for this distribution you must be careful to use both the X values in the first column and the frequencies in the second column. The values in the table show that the distribution consists of one 10, two 9s, four 8s, and one 6, for a total of $n = 8$ scores. Remember that you can determine the number of scores by adding the frequencies, $n = \Sigma f$. To find the sum of the scores, you must be careful to add all eight scores:

$$\Sigma X = 10 + 9 + 9 + 8 + 8 + 8 + 8 + 6 = 66$$

Note that you can also find the sum of the scores by computing ΣfX as we demonstrated in Chapter 2 (p. 36). Once you have found ΣX and n, you compute the mean as usual. For these data,

$$M = \frac{\Sigma X}{n} = \frac{66}{8} = 8.25$$

TABLE 3.1

Statistics quiz scores for a section of $n = 8$ students.

Quiz Score (X)	f	fX
10	1	10
9	2	18
8	4	32
7	0	0
6	1	6

LEARNING CHECK

1. A sample of $n = 6$ scores has a mean of $M = 10$. What is the value of ΣX for this sample?

2. A sample has a mean of $M = 8$ and the sum of the scores is $\Sigma X = 40$. How many scores are in the sample?

3. One sample has $n = 3$ scores with a mean of $M = 4$. A second sample has $n = 7$ scores with a mean of $M = 6$. If the two samples are combined, what is the mean for the combined sample?

4. A sample has a mean of $M = 35$. If one individual with a score of $X = 50$ is removed from the sample, then the sample mean will increase. (True or false?)

5. Find the values for n, ΣX, and M for the sample that is summarized in the following frequency distribution table.

X	f
5	1
4	2
3	2
2	4
1	1

ANSWERS

1. $\Sigma X = 60$

2. $n = 5$

3. The first sample has $n = 3$ and $\Sigma X = 12$. The second sample has $n = 7$ and $\Sigma X = 42$. The combined sample will have $n = 10$ and $\Sigma X = 54$, so the mean will be $54/10 = 5.4$.

4. False. Removing a high score (one above the mean) will cause the mean to decrease.

5. For this sample $n = 10$, $\Sigma X = 28$, and $M = 28/10 = 2.8$.

CHARACTERISTICS OF THE MEAN

The mean has many characteristics that will be important in future discussions. In general, these characteristics result from the fact that every score in the distribution contributes to the value of the mean. Specifically, every score must be added into the total in order to compute the mean. We will now discuss four of the more important characteristics.

Changing a score Changing the value of any score will change the mean. For example, a sample of quiz scores for a psychology lab section consists of 9, 8, 7, 5, and 1. Note that the sample consists of $n = 5$ scores with $\Sigma X = 30$. The mean for this sample is

$$M = \frac{\Sigma X}{n} = \frac{30}{5} = 6.00$$

Now suppose that the score of $X = 1$ is changed to $X = 8$. Note that we have added 7 points to this individual's score, which will also add 7 points to the total (ΣX). After changing the score, the new distribution consists of

9,   8,   7,   5,   8

There are still $n = 5$ scores, but now the total is $\Sigma X = 37$. Thus, the new mean is

$$M = \frac{\Sigma X}{n} = \frac{37}{5} = 7.40$$

Notice that changing a single score in the sample has produced a new mean. You should recognize that changing any score will also change the value of ΣX (the sum of the scores), and thus will always change the value of the mean.

Introducing a new score or removing a score   In general, the mean is determined by two values: ΣX and N (or n). Whenever either of these values is changed, the mean also will be changed. In the preceding example, the value of one score was changed. This produced a change in the total (ΣX) and therefore changed the mean. If you add a new score (or take away a score), you will change both ΣX and n, and you must compute the new mean using the changed values.

Usually, but not always, adding a new score or removing an existing score will change the mean. The exception is when the new score (or the removed score) is exactly equal to the mean. It is easy to visualize the effect of adding or removing a score if you remember that the mean is defined as the balance point for the distribution. Figure 3.3 shows a distribution of scores represented as boxes on a seesaw that is balanced at the mean, $\mu = 7$. Imagine what would happen if we added a new score (a new box) at $X = 10$. Clearly, the seesaw would tip to the right and we would need to slide the pivot point (the mean) higher to restore balance. Thus, adding a new score that is larger than the current mean will cause an increase in the value of the mean.

Again using Figure 3.3, imagine what would happen if we removed the score (the box) that is located at $X = 9$. This time the seesaw would tip to the left and we would have to move the mean lower to restore balance. Thus, removing a score that is greater than the current mean will cause a decrease in the value of the mean.

Finally, consider what would happen to the seesaw if we added a new score (or removed an existing score) located exactly at the mean. It should be clear that the seesaw would not tilt in either direction so the mean would stay in exactly the same place.

The following example demonstrates exactly how the new mean is computed when a new score is added to an existing sample.

EXAMPLE 3.3

Remember that the mean is the amount each person gets when the total is divided equally. If each of four people has 7, then the total must be 28.

We begin with a sample of $n = 4$ scores with a mean of $M = 7$. Notice that this sample must have $\Sigma X = 28$. The problem is to determine what happens to the sample mean if a new score of $X = 12$ is added to the sample.

To find the new sample mean, we must first determine the new values for n and ΣX. In each case, we begin with the original sample and then consider the impact of adding a new score. The original sample had $n = 4$ scores, so adding one new score brings us to $n = 5$. Similarly, the original sample had $\Sigma X = 28$. We added $X = 12$, so the new total is $\Sigma X = 28 + 12 = 40$. Finally, the new mean is computed using the new values for n and ΣX.

FIGURE 3.3

A distribution of $N = 5$ scores that is balanced with a mean of $\mu = 7$.

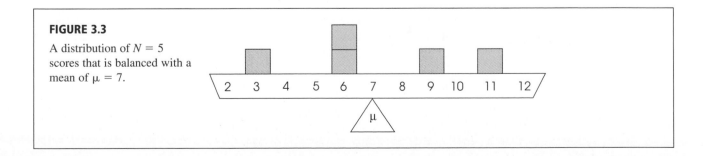

$$M = \frac{\Sigma X}{n} = \frac{40}{5} = 8$$

The entire process can be summarized as follows:

Original Sample	New Sample Adding $X = 12$
$n = 4$	$n = 5$
$\Sigma X = 28$	$\Sigma X = 40$
$M = 28/4 = 7$	$M = 40/5 = 8$

Adding or subtracting a constant from each score   If a constant value is added to every score in a distribution, the same constant will be added to the mean. Similarly, if you subtract a constant from every score, the same constant will be subtracted from the mean.

Consider the feeding scores for a sample of $n = 6$ rats shown in Table 3.2. The scores show the amount of food each rat ate during a 24-hour test period. The first column shows food consumption before the rats were injected with a diet drug. Note that the total amount is $\Sigma X = 26$ grams for $n = 6$ rats, so the mean is $M = 4.33$. The following day, the rats are injected with an experimental drug that reduces appetite. Suppose that the effect of the drug is to subtract a constant (2 points) from each rat's feeding score. The resulting scores are shown in the final column in the table. Note that these scores (after the drug) total $\Sigma X = 14$ grams for $n = 6$ rats, so the new mean is $M = 2.33$. Subtracting 2 points from each score has also subtracted 2 points from the mean, from $M = 4.33$ to $M = 2.33$. (It is important to note that experimental effects are practically never as simple as the adding or subtracting of a constant. Nonetheless, the principle of this characteristic of the mean is important and will be addressed in later chapters when we are using statistics to evaluate the effects of experimental manipulations.)

Multiplying or dividing each score by a constant   If every score in a distribution is multiplied by (or divided by) a constant value, the mean will change in the same way.

Multiplying (or dividing) each score by a constant value is a common method for changing the unit of measurement. To change a set of measurements from minutes to seconds, for example, you multiply by 60; to change from inches to feet, you divide by 12. Table 3.3 shows how a sample of $n = 5$ scores originally measured in yards would be transformed into a set of scores measured in feet. The first column shows the original scores that total $\Sigma X = 50$ with $M = 10$ yards. In the second column, each of the

TABLE 3.2

Amount of food (in grams) consumed before and after diet drug injections.

Rat's Identification	Before Drug Consumption	After Drug Consumption
A	6	4
B	3	1
C	5	3
D	3	1
E	4	2
F	5	3
	$\Sigma X = 26$	$\Sigma X = 14$
	$M = 4.33$	$M = 2.33$

original values has been multiplied by 3 (to change from yards to feet), and the resulting values total $\Sigma X = 150$, with $M = 30$ feet. Multiplying each score by 3 has also caused the mean to be multiplied by 3. You should realize, however, that although the numerical values for the individual scores and the sample mean have been multiplied, the actual measurements are not changed.

TABLE 3.3

Measurement of five pieces of rope.

Original Measurement in Yards	Conversion to Feet (Multiply by 3)
10	30
9	27
12	36
8	24
11	33
$\Sigma X = 50$	$\Sigma X = 150$
$M = 10$ yards	$M = 30$ feet

LEARNING CHECK

1. **a.** Compute the mean for the following sample of scores:

$$6, \quad 1, \quad 8, \quad 0, \quad 5$$

   b. Add 4 points to each score, and then compute the mean.

   c. Multiply each of the original scores by 5, and then compute the mean.

2. A population has a mean of $\mu = 80$.

   a. If 6 points were added to every score, what would be the value for the new mean?

   b. If every score were multiplied by 2, what would be the value for the new mean?

3. A sample of $n = 5$ scores has a mean of $M = 8$. If you added a new score of $X = 2$ to the sample, what value would you obtain for the new sample mean?

ANSWERS

1. **a.** $M = \frac{20}{5} = 4$ **b.** $M = \frac{40}{5} = 8$ **c.** $M = \frac{100}{5} = 20$

2. **a.** The new mean would be 86.   **b.** The new mean would be 160.

3. The original sample has $n = 5$ and $\Sigma X = 40$. With the new score, the sample has $n = 6$ and $\Sigma X = 42$. The new mean is $\frac{42}{6} = 7$.

3.3 THE MEDIAN

The second measure of central tendency we will consider is called the *median*. The median is the score that divides a distribution exactly in half. If the scores are listed in order from smallest to largest, the median is the midpoint of the list.

DEFINITION

The **median** is the score that divides a distribution in half so that 50% of the individuals in the distribution have scores at or below the median.

Earlier, when we introduced the mean, specific symbols and notation were used to identify the mean and to differentiate a sample mean and a population mean. For the median, however, there are no symbols or notation. Instead, the median is simply iden-

By "midpoint" we mean that the scores are being divided into two equal-sized groups. We are not locating the midpoint between the highest and lowest X values.

tified by the word *median*. In addition, the definition and the computations for the median are identical for a sample and for a population.

The goal of the median is to determine the midpoint of the distribution. This commonsense goal is demonstrated in the following two examples which show how the median for most distributions can be found simply by counting scores.

EXAMPLE 3.4   This example demonstrates the calculation of the median when n is an odd number. With an odd number of scores, you list the scores in order (lowest to highest), and the median is the middle score in the list. Consider the following set of $N = 5$ scores, which have been listed in order:

$$3, \quad 5, \quad 8, \quad 10, \quad 11$$

The middle score is $X = 8$, so the median is equal to 8.0. In a graph, the median divides the space or area of the graph in half (Figure 3.4). The amount of area above the median consists of $2\frac{1}{2}$ "boxes," the same as the area below the median (shaded portion).

EXAMPLE 3.5   This example demonstrates the calculation of the median when n is an even number. With an even number of scores in the distribution, you list the scores in order (lowest to highest) and then locate the median by finding the average of the middle two scores. Consider the following population:

$$3, \quad 3, \quad 4, \quad 5, \quad 7, \quad 8$$

Now we select the middle pair of scores (4 and 5), add them together, and divide by 2:

$$\text{median} = \frac{4 + 5}{2} = \frac{9}{2} = 4.5$$

In terms of a graph, we see again that the median divides the area of the distribution exactly in half (Figure 3.5). There are three scores (or boxes) above the median and three below the median.

FIGURE 3.4

The median divides the area in the graph exactly in half.

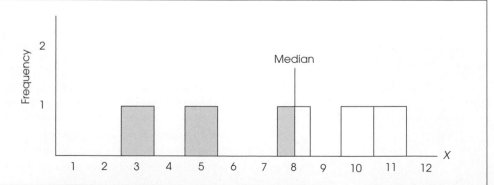

FIGURE 3.5

The median divides the area in the graph exactly in half.

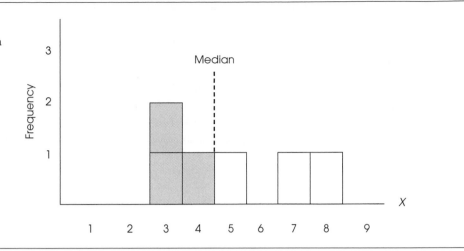

FINDING THE PRECISE MIDPOINT OF A DISTRIBUTION

The simple technique of listing scores to determine the median works well for most distributions. However, in some situations, it is possible to divide a distribution in half by splitting one of the measurement categories into fractional parts so that *exactly* 50% of the distribution is above (and below) a specific point. The following example demonstrates this process.

E X A M P L E 3 . 6

Figure 3.6(a) shows a distribution with $n = 4$ scores. For this distribution, the median is 2 whether you list the scores in order or use the concept of exactly 50%. When the scores are listed in order, the middle two scores are both $X = 2$ so the median is 2. On the other hand, if you draw a vertical line through the graph at $X = 2.00$, it divides the distribution exactly in half, with exactly 2 boxes below the line (one whole box and two half-boxes) and exactly 2 boxes above the line.

FIGURE 3.6

For the distribution in part (a), the median is 2. Note that a line drawn at $X = 2.00$ divides the distribution exactly in half, with two boxes on each side of the line. For the distribution in part (b) there are $n = 5$ boxes. To divide the distribution exactly in half, the median should be located at $X = 2.25$.

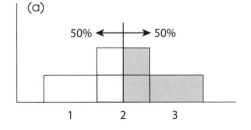

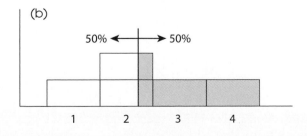

Now consider what happens when we add a new score at $X = 4$. The new distribution with $n = 5$ scores is shown in Figure 3.6(b). If you list the five scores in order, the middle score (the median) is $X = 2$. However, it should be obvious that the 50% point is no longer located at $X = 2.00$. The total distribution now consists of five boxes, and the precise midpoint (the median) is now located at $X = 2.25$. A vertical line drawn at 2.25 has exactly 2.50 boxes above it (two whole boxes and two quarter-boxes) and exactly 2.50 boxes below it.

Finding the precise midpoint of a distribution by dividing scores into fractional parts is sensible for continuous variables, however, it is not inappropriate for discrete variables. You should recall that a continuous variable is infinitely divisible, for example, the amount of time required to solve a problem. A discrete variable, on the other hand, is composed of separate, indivisible categories, for example the number of children in a household. If the scores shown in Figure 3.6(b) were measures of time in seconds, it would be sensible to report the median precisely as $X = 2.25$ seconds. However, if the scores corresponded to the number of children in each household (a discrete variable), it would not be sensible to split the categories. For a discrete variable, list the scores in order and find the middle score. For the distribution in Figure 3.6(b), the median would be reported as $X = 2$ children.

THE MEDIAN, THE MEAN, AND THE MIDDLE

Earlier, we defined the mean as the "balance point" for a distribution because the distances above the mean must have the same total as the distances below the mean. One consequence of this definition is that the mean is always located inside the group of scores; that is, there always will be at least one score above the mean and at least one score below the mean. You should notice, however, that the concept of a balance point focuses on distances rather than scores. In particular, it is possible to have a distribution where the vast majority of the scores are located on one side of the mean. Figure 3.7 shows a distribution of $N = 6$ scores in which 5 out of 6 scores have values less than the mean. In this figure, the total of the distances above the mean is 8 points and the total of the distances below the mean is 8 points. Although it is reasonable to say that the mean is located in the middle of the distribution if you use the concept of distance to define the term "middle," you should realize that the mean is not necessarily located at the exact center of the group of scores.

The median, on the other hand, defines the middle of the distribution in terms of scores. In particular, the median is located so that half of the scores are on one side and half are on the other side. For the distribution in Figure 3.7, for example, the median is located at $X = 2.5$, with exactly 3 scores above this value and exactly 3 scores below.

FIGURE 3.7

A population of $N = 6$ scores with a mean of $\mu = 4$. Notice that the mean does not necessarily divide the scores into two equal groups. In this example, 5 out of the 6 scores have values less than the mean.

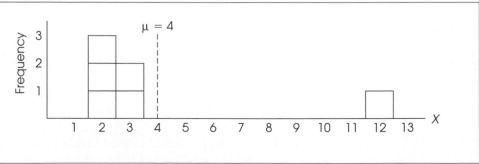

Thus, it is possible to claim that the median is located in the middle of the distribution, provided that the term "middle" is defined by the number of scores.

In summary, the mean and the median are both methods for defining and measuring central tendency. Although they both define the middle of the distribution, they use different definitions of the term "middle."

LEARNING CHECK

1. Find the median for each distribution of scores:

    a. 3, 10, 8, 4, 10, 7, 6

    b. 13, 8, 10, 11, 12, 10

2. If you have a score of 52 on an 80-point exam, then you definitely scored above the median. (True or false?)

3. It is possible for more than 50% of the scores in a distribution to have values greater than the mean. (True or false?)

4. It is possible for more than 50% of the scores in a distribution to have values greater than the median. (True or false?)

ANSWERS

1. **a.** The median is $X = 7$.   **b.** The median is $X = 10.5$.

2. False. The value of the median would depend on where the scores are located.

3. True

4. False

3.4 THE MODE

The final measure of central tendency that we will consider is called the *mode*. In its common usage, the word *mode* means "the customary fashion" or "a popular style." The statistical definition is similar in that the mode is the most commonly occurring value in a group of scores.

DEFINITION

In a frequency distribution, the **mode** is the score or category that has the greatest frequency.

As with the median, there are no symbols or special notation used to identify the mode or to differentiate between a sample mode and a population mode. In addition, the definition of the mode is the same for a population and for a sample distribution.

The mode is a useful measure of central tendency because it can be used to determine the typical or average value for any scale of measurement, including a nominal scale (see Chapter 1). Consider, for example, the data shown in Table 3.4. These data were obtained by asking a sample of 100 students to name their favorite restaurants in town. The result is a sample of $n = 100$ scores with the score for each student corresponding to the restaurant he or she named. For these data, the mode is Luigi's, the restaurant (score) that was named most frequently as a favorite place. Although we can identify a modal response for these data, you should notice that it would be impossible to compute a mean or a median. For example, you cannot add the scores to determine a mean (How much is 5 College Grills plus 42 Luigi's?). Also, it is impossible to list the scores in order because the restaurants do not form any natural order. For example, the College Grill is not "more than" or "less

TABLE 3.4

Favorite restaurants named by a sample of $n = 100$ students. *Caution:* The mode is a score or category, not a frequency. For this example, the mode is Luigi's, not $f = 42$.

Restaurant	f
College Grill	5
George & Harry's	16
Luigi's	42
Oasis Diner	18
Roxbury Inn	7
Sutter's Mill	12

than" the Oasis Diner, they are simply two different restaurants. Thus, it is impossible to obtain the median by finding the midpoint of the list. In general, the mode is the only measure of central tendency that can be used with data from a nominal scale of measurement.

In a frequency distribution graph, the greatest frequency will appear as the tallest part of the figure. To find the mode, you simply identify the score located directly beneath the highest point in the distribution.

Although a distribution will have only one mean and only one median, it is possible to have more than one mode. Specifically, it is possible to have two or more scores that have the same highest frequency. In a frequency distribution graph, the different modes will correspond to distinct, equally high peaks. A distribution with two modes is said to be *bimodal,* and a distribution with more than two modes is called *multimodal.* Occasionally, a distribution with several equally high points is said to have no mode.

Incidentally, a bimodal distribution is often an indication that two separate and distinct groups of individuals exist within the same population (or sample). For example, if you measured height for each person in a set of 100 college students, the resulting distribution would probably have two modes, one corresponding primarily to the males in the group and one corresponding primarily to the females.

Technically, the mode is the score with the absolute highest frequency. However, the term *mode* is often used more casually to refer to scores with relatively high frequencies—that is, scores that correspond to peaks in a distribution even though the peaks are not the absolute highest points. For example, Figure 3.8 shows the number of fish caught at various times during the day. There are two distinct peaks in this distribution, one at 6 A.M. and one at 6 P.M. Each of these values is a mode in the distribution. Note that the two modes do not have identical frequencies. Twelve fish were caught at 6 A.M., and 11 were caught at 6 P.M. Nonetheless, both of these points are called modes. When two modes have unequal frequencies, researchers occasionally will differentiate the two values by calling the taller peak the *major mode,* and the shorter one the *minor mode.*

FIGURE 3.8

The relationship between time of day and number of fish caught.

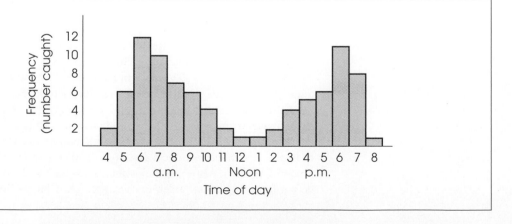

LEARNING CHECK

1. An instructor recorded the number of absences for each student in a class of 20 and obtained the frequency distribution shown in the following table.

Number of Absences (X)	f
7	1
6	0
5	3
4	2
3	3
2	5
1	4
0	2

   a. Using the mean to define central tendency, what is the average number of absences for this class?

   b. Using the mode to define central tendency, what is the average number of absences for this class?

2. In a recent survey comparing picture quality for three brands of color televisions, 63 people preferred brand A, 29 people preferred brand B, and 58 people preferred brand C. What is the mode for this distribution?

3. It is possible for a distribution to have more than one mode. (True or false?)

ANSWERS   1. a. The mean is 2.65.   b. The mode is $X = 2$ absences.

2. The mode is brand A.

3. True

3.5   SELECTING A MEASURE OF CENTRAL TENDENCY

How do you decide which measure of central tendency to use? The answer to this question depends on several factors. Before we discuss these factors, however, note that you usually can compute two or even three measures of central tendency for the same set of data. Although the three measures will often produce similar results, there are situations in which they will be very different (see Section 3.6). Also note that the mean is usually the preferred measure of central tendency. Because the mean uses every score in the distribution, it typically produces a good representative value. Remember that the goal of central tendency is to find the single value that best represents the entire distribution. Besides being a good representative, the mean has the added advantage of being closely related to variance and standard deviation, the most common measures of variability (Chapter 4). This relationship makes the mean a valuable measure for purposes of inferential statistics. For these reasons, and others, the mean generally is considered to be the best of the three measures of central tendency. But there are specific situations in which it is impossible to compute a mean or in which the mean is not particularly representative. It is in these situations that the mode and the median are used.

WHEN TO USE THE MEDIAN   We will consider four situations in which the median serves as a valuable alternative to the mean. In the first three cases, the data consist of numerical values (interval or ratio scales) for which you would normally compute the mean. However, each case also involves a special problem so that it is either impossible to compute the mean, or the calculation of the mean produces a value that is not central or not representative of the distribution. The fourth situation involves measuring central tendency for ordinal data.

Extreme scores or skewed distributions   When a distribution has a few extreme scores, scores that are very different in value from most of the others, then the mean may not be a good representative of the majority of the distribution. The problem comes from the fact that one or two extreme values can have a large influence and cause the mean to be displaced. In this situation, the fact that the mean uses all of the scores equally can be a disadvantage. For example, suppose that a sample of $n = 10$ rats is tested in a T-maze for a food reward. The animals must choose the correct arm of the T (right or left) to find the food in the goal box. The experimenter records the number of errors each rat makes before it solves the maze. Hypothetical data are presented in Figure 3.9.

The mean for this sample is

$$M = \frac{\Sigma X}{n} = \frac{203}{10} = 20.3$$

Notice that the mean is not very representative of any score in this distribution. Most of the scores are clustered between 10 and 13. The extreme score of $X = 100$ (a slow learner) inflates the value of ΣX and distorts the mean.

The median, on the other hand, is not easily affected by extreme scores. For this sample, $n = 10$, so there should be five scores on either side of the median. The median is 11.50. Notice that this is a very representative value. Also note that the median would be unchanged even if the slow learner made 1000 errors instead of only 100. Because it is relatively unaffected by extreme scores, the median commonly is used

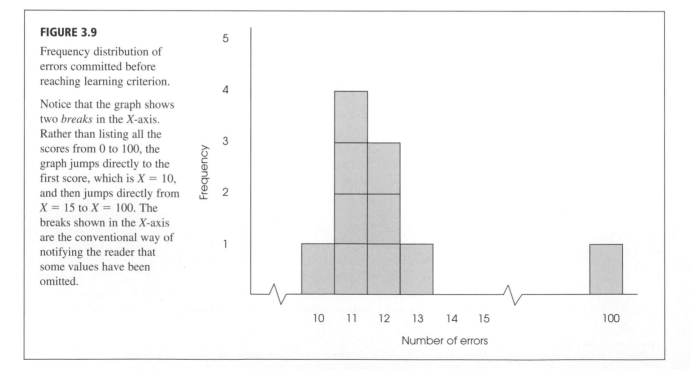

FIGURE 3.9

Frequency distribution of errors committed before reaching learning criterion.

Notice that the graph shows two *breaks* in the X-axis. Rather than listing all the scores from 0 to 100, the graph jumps directly to the first score, which is $X = 10$, and then jumps directly from $X = 15$ to $X = 100$. The breaks shown in the X-axis are the conventional way of notifying the reader that some values have been omitted.

when reporting the average value for a skewed distribution. For example, the distribution of personal incomes is very skewed, with a small segment of the population earning incomes that are astronomical. These extreme values distort the mean, so that it is not very representative of the salaries that most of us earn. As in the previous example, the median is the preferred measure of central tendency when extreme scores exist.

Undetermined values   Occasionally, you will encounter a situation in which an individual has an unknown or undetermined score. In psychology, this often occurs in learning experiments in which you are measuring the number of errors (or amount of time) required for an individual to solve a particular problem. For example, suppose that a sample of $n = 6$ people were asked to assemble a wooden puzzle as quickly as possible. The experimenter records how long (in minutes) it takes each individual to arrange all the pieces to complete the puzzle. Table 3.5 presents the outcome of this experiment.

Notice that person 6 never completed the puzzle. After an hour, this person still showed no sign of solving the puzzle, so the experimenter stopped him or her. This person has an undetermined score. (There are two important points to be noted. First, the experimenter should not throw out this individual's score. The whole purpose for using a sample is to gain a picture of the population, and this individual tells us that part of the population cannot solve the puzzle. Second, this person should not be given a score of $X = 60$ minutes. Even though the experimenter stopped the individual after 1 hour, the person did not finish the puzzle. The score that is recorded is the amount of time needed to finish. For this individual, we do not know how long this is.)

It is impossible to compute the mean for these data because of the undetermined value. We cannot calculate the ΣX part of the formula for the mean. However, it is possible to compute the median. For these data, the median is 12.5. Three scores are below the median, and three scores (including the undetermined value) are above the median.

Open-ended distributions   A distribution is said to be *open-ended* when there is no upper limit (or lower limit) for one of the categories. The table at the left provides an example of an open-ended distribution, showing the number of children in each family for a sample of $n = 20$ households. The top category in this distribution shows that three of the families have "5 or more" children. This is an open-ended category. Notice that it is impossible to compute a mean for these data because you cannot find ΣX (the total number of children for all 20 families). However, you can find the median. Listing the 20 scores in order produces $X = 1$ and $X = 2$ as the middle two scores. For these data, the median is 1.5.

Number of Children (X)	f
5 or more	3
4	2
3	2
2	3
1	6
0	4

Ordinal scale   Many researchers believe that it is not appropriate to use the mean to describe central tendency for ordinal data. When scores are measured on an ordinal scale, the median is always appropriate and is usually the preferred measure of central tendency.

TABLE 3.5

Amount of time to complete puzzle.

Person	Time (Min.)
1	8
2	11
3	12
4	13
5	17
6	Never finished

You should recall that ordinal measurements allow you to determine direction (greater than or less than) but do not allow you to determine distance. The median is compatible with this type of measurement because it is defined by direction: half of the stores are above the median and half are below the median. The mean, on the other hand, defines central tendency in terms of distance. Remember that the mean is the balance point for the distribution, so that the distances above the mean are exactly balanced by the distances below the mean. Because the mean is defined in terms of distances, and because ordinal scales do not measure distance, it is not appropriate to compute a mean for scores from an ordinal scale.

WHEN TO USE THE MODE

We will consider three situations in which the mode is commonly used as an alternative to the mean, or is used in conjunction with the mean to describe central tendency.

Nominal scales   The primary advantage of the mode is that it can be used to measure and describe central tendency for data that are measured on a nominal scale. Recall that the categories that make up a nominal scale are differentiated only by name. Because nominal scales do not measure quantity, it is impossible to compute a mean or a median for data from a nominal scale. Therefore, the mode is the only option for describing central tendency for nominal data.

Discrete variables   Recall that discrete variables are those that exist only in whole, indivisible categories. Often, discrete variables are numerical values, such as the number of children in a family or the number of rooms in a house. When these variables produce numerical scores, it is possible to calculate means. In this situation, the calculated means will usually be fractional values that cannot actually exist. For example, computing means will generate results such as "the average family has 2.4 children and a house with 5.33 rooms." On the other hand, the mode always identifies the most typical case and, therefore, it produces more sensible measures of central tendency. Using the mode, our conclusion would be "the typical, or modal, family has 2 children and a house with 5 rooms." In many situations, especially with discrete variables, people are more comfortable using the realistic, whole-number values produced by the mode.

Describing shape   Because the mode requires little or no calculation, it is often included as a supplementary measure along with the mean or median as a no-cost extra. The value of the mode (or modes) in this situation is that it gives an indication of the shape of the distribution as well as a measure of central tendency. Remember that the mode identifies the location of the peak (or peaks) in the frequency distribution graph. For example, if you are told that a set of exam scores has a mean of 72 and a mode of 80, you should have a better picture of the distribution than would be available from the mean alone (see Section 3.6).

IN THE LITERATURE
REPORTING MEASURES OF CENTRAL TENDENCY

Measures of central tendency are commonly used in the behavioral sciences to summarize and describe the results of a research study. For example, a researcher may report the sample means from two different treatments or the median score for a large sample. These values may be reported in verbal descriptions of the results, in tables, or in graphs.

TABLE 3.6

The mean number of errors made on the task for treatment and control groups according to gender.

	Treatment	Control
Females	1.45	8.36
Males	3.83	14.77

In reporting results, many behavioral science journals use guidelines adopted by the American Psychological Association (APA), as outlined in the *Publication Manual of the American Psychological Association* (2001). We will refer to the APA manual from time to time in describing how data and research results are reported in the scientific literature. The APA style typically uses the letter *M* as the symbol for the sample mean. Thus, a study might state

The treatment group showed fewer errors ($M = 2.56$) on the task than the control group ($M = 11.76$).

When there are many means to report, tables with headings provide an organized and more easily understood presentation. Table 3.6 illustrates this point.

The median can be reported using the abbreviation *Mdn,* as in "Mdn = 8.5 errors," or it can simply be reported in narrative text, as follows:

The median number of errors for the treatment group was 8.5, compared to a median of 13 for the control group.

There is no special symbol or convention for reporting the mode. If mentioned at all, the mode is usually just reported in narrative text.

The modal hair color was blonde, with 23 out of 50 participants in this category.

PRESENTING MEANS AND MEDIANS IN GRAPHS

Graphs also can be used to report and compare measures of central tendency. Usually, graphs are used to display values obtained for sample means, but occasionally you will see sample medians reported in graphs (modes are rarely, if ever, shown in a graph). The value of a graph is that it allows several means (or medians) to be shown simultaneously so it is possible to make quick comparisons between groups or treatment conditions. When preparing a graph, it is customary to list the values for the different groups or treatment conditions on the horizontal axis. Typically, these are the different values that make up the independent variable or the quasi-independent variable. Values for the dependent variable (the scores) are listed on the vertical axis. The means (or medians) are then displayed using a *line graph,* a *histogram,* or a *bar graph,* depending on the scale of measurement used for the independent variable.

Figure 3.10 shows an example of a graph displaying the relationship between drug dose (the independent variable) and food consumption (the dependent variable). In this study, there were five different drug doses (treatment conditions) and they are listed along the horizontal axis. The five means appear as points in the graph. To construct this graph, a point was placed above each treatment condition so that the vertical position of the point corresponds to the mean score for the treatment condition. The points are then connected with straight lines and the resulting graph is called a *line graph.* A line graph is used when the values on the horizontal axis are measured on an interval or a ratio scale. An alternative to the line graph is a *histogram.* For this example, the histogram would show a bar above each drug dose so that the height of each bar corresponds to the mean food consumption for that group, with no space between adjacent bars.

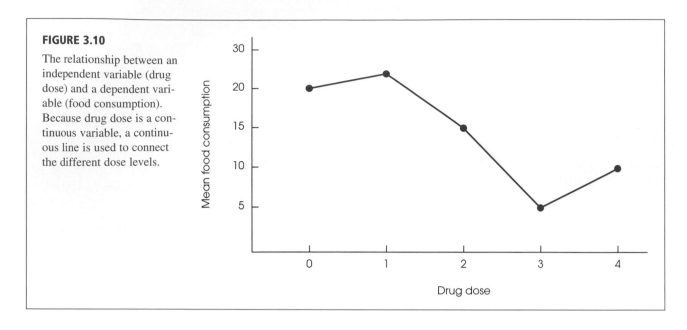

FIGURE 3.10

The relationship between an independent variable (drug dose) and a dependent variable (food consumption). Because drug dose is a continuous variable, a continuous line is used to connect the different dose levels.

Figure 3.11 shows a bar graph displaying the median selling price for single-family homes in different regions of the United States. Bar graphs are used to present means (or medians) when the groups or treatments shown on the horizontal axis are measured on a nominal or an ordinal scale. To construct a bar graph, you simply draw a bar directly above each group or treatment so that the height of the bar corresponds to the mean (or median) for that group or treatment. For a bar graph, a space is left between adjacent bars to indicate that the scale of measurement is nominal or ordinal.

When constructing graphs of any type, you should recall the basic rules we introduced in Chapter 2:

1. The height of a graph should be approximately two-thirds to three-quarters of its length.

2. Normally, you start numbering both the X-axis and the Y-axis with zero at the point where the two axes intersect. However, when a value of zero is part of the data, it is common to move the zero point away from the intersection so that the graph does not overlap the axes (see Figure 3.10).

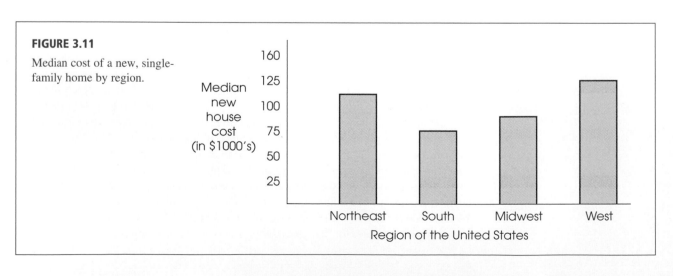

FIGURE 3.11

Median cost of a new, single-family home by region.

Following these rules will help produce a graph that provides an accurate presentation of the information in a set of data. Although it is possible to construct graphs that distort the results of a study (see Box 2.1), researchers have an ethical responsibility to present an honest and accurate report of their research results.   ❏

3.6 CENTRAL TENDENCY AND THE SHAPE OF THE DISTRIBUTION

We have identified three different measures of central tendency, and often a researcher will calculate all three for a single set of data. Because the mean, the median, and the mode are all trying to measure the same thing (central tendency), it is reasonable to expect that these three values should be related. In fact, there are some consistent and predictable relationships among the three measures of central tendency. Specifically, there are situations in which all three measures will have exactly the same value. On the other hand, there are situations in which the three measures are predictably different. In part, the relationships among the mean, median, and mode are determined by the shape of the distribution. We will consider two general types of distributions.

SYMMETRICAL DISTRIBUTIONS

For a *symmetrical distribution,* the right-hand side of the graph will be a mirror image of the left-hand side. By definition, the median will be exactly at the center of a symmetrical distribution because exactly half of the area in the graph will be on either side of the center. The mean also will be exactly at the center of a symmetrical distribution because each score on the left side of the distribution is perfectly balanced by a corresponding score (the mirror image) on the right side. As a result, the mean (the balance point) will be located at the center of the distribution. Thus, for any symmetrical distribution, the mean and the median will be the same [Figure 3.12].

If a symmetrical distribution has only one mode, it will also be exactly in the center of the distribution. In this case, all three measures of central tendency, the mean, the median, and the mode, will have the same value. On the other hand, a bimodal distribution that is symmetrical [see Figure 3.12(b)] will have the mean and the median together in the center with the modes on each side. A rectangular distribution [see Figure 3.12(c)] has no mode because all *X* values occur with the same frequency. Still, the mean and the median will be in the center of the distribution and equivalent in value.

FIGURE 3.12

Measures of central tendency for three symmetrical distributions: normal, bimodal, and rectangular.

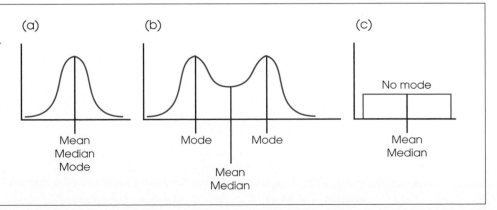

SKEWED DISTRIBUTIONS

The positions of the mean, median, and mode are not as consistently predictable in distributions of discrete variables (see Von Hippel, 2005).

Distributions are not always symmetrical; quite often, they are lopsided or *skewed*. For example, Figure 3.13(a) shows a *positively skewed* distribution. In *skewed distributions,* especially distributions for continuous variables, there is a strong tendency for the mean, median, and mode to be located in predictable positions. In Figure 3.13(a), for example, the peak (highest frequency) is on the left-hand side. This is the position of the mode. However, it should be clear that the vertical line drawn at the mode does not divide the distribution into two equal parts. In order to have exactly 50% of the distribution on each side, the median must be located to the right of the mode. Finally, the mean will be located to the right of the median because it is influenced most by extreme scores and will be displaced farthest to the right by the scores in the tail. Therefore, in a positively skewed distribution, the order of the three measures of central tendency from smallest to largest (left to right) will be the mode, the median, and the mean.

Negatively skewed distributions are lopsided in the opposite direction, with the scores piling up on the right-hand side and the tail tapering off to the left. The grades on an easy exam, for example, will tend to form a negatively skewed distribution [see Figure 3.13(b)]. For a distribution with negative skew, the mode is on the right-hand side (with the peak), while the mean is displaced on the left by the extreme scores in the tail. As before, the median is located between the mean and the mode. In order from smallest value to largest value (left to right), the three measures of central tendency will be the mean, the median, and the mode for a negatively skewed distribution.

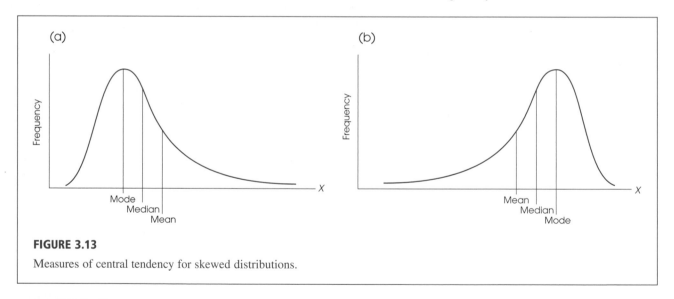

FIGURE 3.13

Measures of central tendency for skewed distributions.

LEARNING CHECK

1. Which measure of central tendency is most likely to be affected by one or two extreme scores in a distribution? (mean, median, or mode)

2. The mode is the correct way to measure central tendency for data from a nominal scale. (True or false?)

3. If a graph is used to show the means obtained from an experiment, the different treatment conditions (the independent variable) should be listed on the vertical axis. (True or false?)

4. A distribution has a mean of 75 and a median of 70. This distribution is probably positively skewed. (True or false?)

ANSWERS   1. Mean   2. True   3 False   4. True

SUMMARY

1. The purpose of central tendency is to determine the single value that identifies the center of the distribution and best represents the entire set of scores. The three standard measures of central tendency are the mode, the median, and the mean.

2. The mean is the arithmetic average. It is computed by adding all the scores and then dividing by the number of scores. Conceptually, the mean is obtained by dividing the total (ΣX) equally among the number of individuals (N or n). The mean can also be defined as the balance point for the distribution. The distances above the mean are exactly balanced by the distances below the mean. Although the calculation is the same for a population or a sample mean, a population mean is identified by the symbol μ, and a sample mean is identified by M. In most situations with numerical scores from an interval or a ratio scale, the mean is the preferred measure of central tendency.

3. Changing any score in the distribution will cause the mean to be changed. When a constant value is added to (or subtracted from) every score in a distribution, the same constant value is added to (or subtracted from) the mean. If every score is multiplied by a constant, the mean will be multiplied by the same constant.

4. The median is the value that divides a distribution exactly in half. If the scores are listed in order, the median is the midpoint of the list. The median is the preferred measure of central tendency when a distribution has a few extreme scores that displace the value of the mean. The median also is used when there are undetermined (infinite) scores that make it impossible to compute a mean. Finally, the median is the preferred measure of central tendency for data from an ordinal scale.

5. The mode is the most frequently occurring score in a distribution. It is easily located by finding the peak in a frequency distribution graph. For data measured on a nominal scale, the mode is the appropriate measure of central tendency. It is possible for a distribution to have more than one mode.

6. For symmetrical distributions, the mean will equal the median. If there is only one mode, then it will have the same value, too.

7. For skewed distributions, the mode will be located toward the side where the scores pile up, and the mean will be displaced toward the extreme scores in the tail. The median usually will be located between these two values.

KEY TERMS

central tendency

population mean (μ)

sample mean (M)

weighted mean

median

mode

bimodal

multimodal

major mode

minor mode

line graph

symmetrical distribution

skewed distribution

positive skew

negative skew

RESOURCES

There are a tutorial quiz and other learning exercises for Chapter 3 at the Wadsworth website, www.thomsonedu.com/psychology/gravetter. The site also includes a work-shop titled *Central Tendency and Variability* that reviews the basic concept of the mean and introduces the concept of variability that will be presented in Chapter 4. See page 27 for more information about accessing items on the website.

WebTUTOR

For those using WebTutor along with this book, there is a WebTutor section corresponding to this chapter. The WebTutor contains a brief summary of Chapter 3, hints for learning the new material, cautions about common errors, and sample exam items including solutions.

General instructions for using SPSS are presented in Appendix D. Following are detailed instructions for using SPSS to compute the **Mean and ΣX** for a set of scores.

Data Entry

1. Enter all of the scores in one column of the data editor, probably VAR00001.

Data Analysis

1. Click **Analyze** on the tool bar, select **Descriptive Statistics,** and click on **Descriptives.**
2. Highlight the column label for the set of scores (VAR00001) in the left box and click the arrow to move it into the **Variable** box.
3. If you want ΣX as well as the mean, click on the **Options** box, select **Sum,** then click **Continue.**
4. Click **OK.**

SPSS Output

SPSS will produce a summary table listing the number of scores (N), the maximum and minimum scores, the sum of the scores (if you selected this option), the mean, and the standard deviation. Note: The standard deviation is a measure of variability that is presented in Chapter 4.

FOCUS ON PROBLEM SOLVING

1. Because there are three different measures of central tendency, your first problem is to decide which one is best for your specific set of data. Usually the mean is the preferred measure, but the median may provide a more representative value if you are working with a skewed distribution. With data measured on a nominal scale, you must use the mode.

2. Although the three measures of central tendency appear to be very simple to calculate, there is always a chance for errors. The most common sources of error are listed next.
   a. Many students find it very difficult to compute the mean for data presented in a frequency distribution table. They tend to ignore the frequencies in the table and simply average the score values listed in the X column. You must use the frequencies *and* the scores! Remember that the number of scores is found by $N = \Sigma f$, and the sum of all N scores is found by $\Sigma f X$. For the distribution shown in the margin, the mean is $\frac{24}{10} = 2.40$.
   b. The median is the midpoint of the distribution of scores, not the midpoint of the scale of measurement. For a 100-point test, for example, many students incorrectly assume that the median must be $X = 50$. To find the median, you must have the *complete set* of individual scores. The median separates the individuals into two equal-sized groups.

X	f
4	1
3	4
2	3
1	2

   c. The most common error with the mode is for students to report the highest frequency in a distribution rather than the score with the highest frequency. Remember that the purpose of central tendency is to find the most representative score. For the distribution in the margin, the mode is $X = 3$, not $f = 4$.

DEMONSTRATION 3.1

COMPUTING MEASURES OF CENTRAL TENDENCY

For the following sample data, find the mean, median, and mode. The scores are:

$$5, \quad 6, \quad 9, \quad 11, \quad 5, \quad 11, \quad 8, \quad 14, \quad 2, \quad 11$$

Compute the mean   Calculating the mean involves two steps:

1. Obtain the sum of the scores, ΣX.
2. Divide the sum by the number of scores, n.

For these data, the sum of the scores is as follows:

$$\Sigma X = 5 + 6 + 9 + 11 + 5 + 11 + 8 + 14 + 2 + 11 = 82$$

We can also observe that $n = 10$. Therefore, the mean of this sample is obtained by

$$M = \frac{\Sigma X}{n} = \frac{82}{10} = 8.2$$

Find the median   The median divides the distribution in half, in that half of the scores are above or equal to the median and half are below or equal to it. In this demonstration, $n = 10$. Thus, the median should be a value that has 5 scores above it and 5 scores below it.

STEP 1   Arrange the scores in order.

$$2, \quad 5, \quad 5, \quad 6, \quad 8, \quad 9, \quad 11, \quad 11, \quad 11, \quad 14$$

STEP 2   With an even number of scores, compute the average of the middle two scores. The middle scores are $X = 8$ and $X = 9$.

$$\text{median} = \frac{8 + 9}{2} = \frac{17}{2} = 8.5$$

Find the mode   The mode is the X value that has the highest frequency. Looking at the data, we can readily determine that $X = 11$ is the score that occurs most frequently.

PROBLEMS

1. Explain the general purpose for measuring central tendency.

2. Identify the circumstances in which the median rather than the mean is the preferred measure of central tendency.

3. Under what circumstances will the mean, the median, and the mode all have the same value?

4. Under what circumstances is the mode the preferred measure of central tendency?

5. Explain why the mean is often not a good measure of central tendency for a skewed distribution.

6. Explain what is meant by each of the following statements:
   a. The mean is the *balance point* of the distribution.
   b. The median is the *midpoint* of the distribution.

7. A sample of $n = 8$ scores has a mean of $M = 6$. What is the value of ΣX for this sample?

8. Find the mean, median, and mode for the set of scores in the following frequency distribution table:

X	f
10	2
9	3
8	5
7	6
6	3
5	1

9. Find the mean, median, and mode for the following sample of scores:

2, 3, 3, 1, 2, 5, 2, 3, 4, 2

10. Find the mean, median, and mode for the following sample of scores:

7, 5, 9, 7, 7, 8, 6, 8, 10, 7, 4, 6

11. Find the mean, median, and mode for the set of scores in the following frequency distribution table:

X	f
5	1
4	5
3	4
2	1
1	1

12. A sample of $n = 6$ scores has a mean of $M = 10$. If one score is changed from $X = 14$ to $X = 2$, what will be the value for the new sample mean?

13. A population of $N = 10$ scores has a mean of $\mu = 24$. If one person with a score of $X = 42$ is removed from the sample, what will be the value for the new mean?

14. A population of $N = 25$ scores has a mean of $\mu = 10$. What is the value of ΣX for this population?

15. A population of $N = 8$ scores has a mean of $\mu = 20$. If one score is changed from $X = 14$ to $X = 30$, what will be the value for the new mean?

16. A sample of $n = 7$ scores has a mean of $M = 5$. After one new score is added to the sample, the new mean is found to be $M = 7$. What is the value of the new score? (Hint: Compare the values for ΣX before and after the score was added.)

17. A population of $N = 10$ scores has a mean of $\mu = 9$. One score is removed from the sample and the new mean is found to be $\mu = 8$. What is the value of the score that was removed?

18. A sample of $n = 20$ scores has a mean of $M = 6$. If one new person with a score of $X = 27$ is added to the sample, what will be the value for the new mean?

19. A sample of $n = 5$ scores has a mean of $M = 8$. If one new person with a score of $X = 2$ is added to the sample, what will be the value for the new mean?

20. One sample of $n = 20$ scores has a mean of $M = 50$. A second sample of $n = 5$ scores has a mean of $M = 10$. If the two samples are combined, what is the mean for the combined sample?

21. For each of the following situations, identify the measure of central tendency (mean, median, or mode) that would provide the best description of the "average" score:
   a. The college recorded the age of each student who graduated last spring. Although the majority of the students were in their early 20s, a few mature students were in their 40s, 50s, and 60s.
   b. A researcher asked each participant to select his or her favorite color from a set of eight color patches.
   c. A professor uses a standardized test to measure verbal skill for a sample of new college freshmen.

22. One question on a student survey asks: In a typical week, how many times do you eat at a fast food restaurant? The following frequency distribution table summarizes the results for a sample of $n = 20$ students.

Number of times per week	f
5 or more	2
4	2
3	3
2	6
1	4
0	3

   a. Find the mode for this distribution.
   b. Find the median for the distribution.
   c. Explain why you cannot compute the mean number of times using the data in the table.

23. To evaluate the effectiveness of a treatment, researchers will often measure individuals before and after treatment, and record the amount of difference between the two scores. If the differences average around zero, it is an indication that the treatment has no effect. However, if the differences are consistently positive (or consistently negative), it suggests that the treatment does have an effect. For example, Kerr, Walsh, and Baxter (2003) evaluated the effectiveness of acupuncture treatment by measuring pain for a group of participants before and after a 6-week treatment program. Hypothetical data, similar to the results

of the study, are as follows. Note that each score measures the difference in pain level after treatment compared to the pain level before treatment.

$$-3, \ -4, \ -3, \ -2, \ -5, \ -4, \ -6, \ +1, \ -4, \ -3$$
$$-4, \ -5, \ -4, \ -2, \ -5, \ -3, \ +2, \ -4, \ -1, \quad 0$$

a. Sketch a histogram showing the frequency distribution for the difference scores.

b. Compute the mean for the sample of $n = 20$ difference scores.

c. Does it appear that the acupuncture treatment had an effect on pain?

24. Does it ever seem to you that the weather is nice during the work week, but lousy on the weekend? Cerveny and Balling (1988) have confirmed that this is not your imagination—pollution accumulating during the work week most likely spoils the weekend weather for people on the Atlantic coast. Consider the following hypothetical data showing the daily amount of rainfall for 10 weeks during the summer.

Week	Average Daily Rainfall on Weekdays (Mon.–Fri.)	Average Daily Rainfall on Weekends (Sat.–Sun.)
1	1.2	1.5
2	0.6	2.0
3	0.0	1.8
4	1.6	1.5
5	0.8	2.2
6	2.1	2.4
7	0.2	0.8
8	0.9	1.6
9	1.1	1.2
10	1.4	1.7

a. Calculate the average daily rainfall (the mean) during the week, and the average daily rainfall for weekends.

b. Based on the two means, does there appear to be a pattern in the data?

25. A sample of $n = 7$ scores has a mean of $M = 8$. A second sample has $n = 3$ scores and a mean of $M = 12$. If the two samples are combined, what is the mean for the combined sample?

26. One sample has a mean of $M = 4$ and a second sample has a mean of $M = 8$. The two samples are combined into a single set of scores.

a. What is the mean for the combined set if both of the original samples have $n = 7$ scores?

b. What is the mean for the combined set if the first sample has $n = 3$ and the second sample has $n = 7$?

c. What is the mean for the combined set if the first sample has $n = 7$ and the second sample has $n = 3$?

CHAPTER

4

Variability

Tools You Will Need

The following items are considered essential background material for this chapter. If you doubt your knowledge of any of these items, you should review the appropriate chapter or section before proceeding.

- Summation notation (Chapter 1)
- Central tendency (Chapter 3)
  - Mean
  - Median

4.1   OVERVIEW

The term *variability* has much the same meaning in statistics as it has in everyday language; to say that things are variable means that they are not all the same. In statistics, our goal is to measure the amount of variability for a particular set of scores, a distribution. In simple terms, if the scores in a distribution are all the same, then there is no variability. If there are small differences between scores, then the variability is small, and if there are large differences between scores, then the variability is large.

DEFINITION   **Variability** provides a quantitative measure of the degree to which scores in a distribution are spread out or clustered together.

Figure 4.1 shows two distributions of familiar values: Part (a) shows the distribution of adult male heights (in inches), and part (b) shows the distribution of adult male weights (in pounds). Notice that the two distributions differ in terms of central tendency. The mean height is 70 inches (5 feet, 10 inches) and the mean weight is 170 pounds. In addition, notice that the distributions differ in terms of variability. For example, most heights are clustered close together, within 5 or 6 inches of the mean. On the other hand, weights are spread over a much wider range. In the weight distribution it is not unusual to find individuals who are located more than 30 pounds away from the mean, and it would not be surprising to find two individuals whose weights differ by more than 30 or 40 pounds. The purpose for measuring variability is to

FIGURE 4.1

Population distributions of adult heights and adult weights.

NOTE: For simplicity, we have omitted the vertical axis for these graphs. As always, the height of any point on the curve indicates the relative frequency for that particular score.

(a)   The distribution of adult heights (in inches)

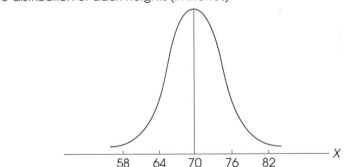

(b)   The distribution of adult weights (in pounds)

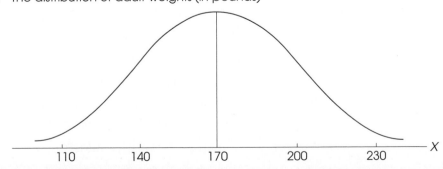

obtain an objective measure of how the scores are spread out in a distribution. In general, a good measure of variability will serve two purposes:

1. Variability describes the distribution. Specifically, it tells whether the scores are clustered close together or are spread out over a large distance. Usually, variability is defined in terms of *distance*. It tells how much distance to expect between one score and another, or how much distance to expect between an individual score and the mean. For example, we know that most adults' heights are clustered close together, within 5 or 6 inches of the average. Although more extreme heights exist, they are relatively rare.

2. Variability measures how well an individual score (or group of scores) represents the entire distribution. This aspect of variability is very important for inferential statistics where relatively small samples are used to answer questions about populations. For example, suppose that you selected a sample of one person to represent the entire population. Because most adult heights are within a few inches of the population average (the distances are small), there is a very good chance that you would select someone whose height is within 6 inches of the population mean. On the other hand, the scores are much more spread out (greater distances) in the distribution of adult weights. In this case, you probably would *not* obtain someone whose weight was within 6 pounds of the population mean. Thus, variability provides information about how much error to expect if you are using a sample to represent a population.

In this chapter, we consider three different measures of variability: the range, the interquartile range, and the standard deviation. Of these three, the standard deviation (and the related measure of variance) is by far the most important.

4.2   THE RANGE AND INTERQUARTILE RANGE

The *range* is the distance between the largest score (X_{max}) and the smallest score in the distribution (X_{min}). In determining this distance, you must also take into account the real limits of the maximum and minimum X values. The range therefore is computed as the difference between the upper real limit (URL) for X_{max} and the lower real limit (LRL) for X_{min}:

$$\text{range} = \text{URL } X_{max} - \text{LRL } X_{min}$$

DEFINITION
> The **range** is the difference between the upper real limit of the largest (maximum) X value and the lower real limit of the smallest (minimum) X value.

For example, consider the following data:

3,   7,   12,   8,   5,   10

When the scores in a distribution are whole numbers, the range also can be obtained as follows:

$$\text{range} = \text{highest } X$$
$$- \text{lowest } X + 1$$

For these data, $X_{max} = 12$, with an upper real limit of 12.5, and $X_{min} = 3$, with a lower real limit of 2.5. Thus, the range equals

$$\text{range} = \text{URL } X_{max} - \text{LRL } X_{min}$$
$$= 12.5 - 2.5 = 10$$

The range is perhaps the most obvious way of describing how spread out the scores are—simply find the distance between the maximum and the minimum scores. The problem with using the range as a measure of variability is that it is completely determined by the two extreme values and ignores the other scores in the distribution. Thus, a distribution with one unusually large (or small) score will have a large range even if the other scores are actually clustered close together.

Because the range does not consider all the scores in the distribution, it often does not give an accurate description of the variability for the entire distribution. For this reason, the range is considered to be a crude and unreliable measure of variability.

One way to avoid the excessive influence of one or two extreme scores is to measure variability with the *interquartile range.* The interquartile range ignores extreme scores; instead, it measures the range covered by the middle 50% of the distribution.

To find the interquartile range, you first locate the boundary that separates the lowest 25% of the distribution from the rest. This boundary is called the first quartile and is identified as $Q1$. Next, you locate the boundary that separates the top 25% of the distribution from the rest. This boundary is called the third quartile, $Q3$, because it separates the bottom three-quarters from the top quarter of the distribution. Finally, the interquartile range is defined as the distance between $Q1$ and $Q3$.

DEFINITION

The **interquartile range** is the range covered by the middle 50% of the distribution.

$$\text{interquartile range} = Q3 - Q1$$

The simplest method for finding the values of $Q1$ and $Q3$ is to construct a frequency distribution histogram in which each score is represented by a box (Figure 4.2). Then determine exactly how many boxes are needed to make up exactly one-quarter of the whole set. With a total of $n = 16$ scores (boxes), for example, one-quarter is exactly

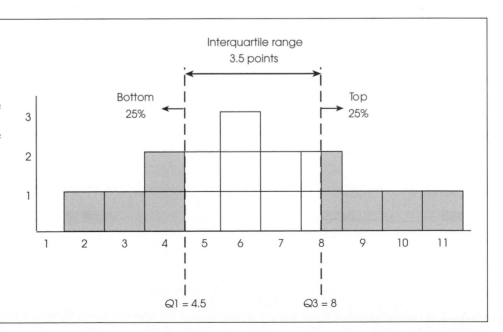

FIGURE 4.2

Frequency distribution for a population of $N = 16$ scores. The first quartile is $Q1 = 4.5$. The third quartile is $Q3 = 8.0$. The interquartile range is 3.5 points. Note that the third quartile ($Q3$) divides the two boxes at $X = 8$ exactly in half, so that a total of 4 boxes are above $Q3$ and 12 boxes are below it.

4 boxes. In this case, the first quartile separates the lowest 4 boxes (25%) from the rest, and the third quartile separates the lowest 12 boxes (75%) from the highest 4 boxes. Usually you can simply count boxes or fractions of boxes to locate $Q1$ and $Q3$.

After the quartiles have been determined, the interquartile range is defined as the distance between the first quartile and the third quartile. For the distribution in Figure 4.2, the interquartile range is

$$Q3 - Q1 = 8 - 4.5 = 3.5 \text{ points}$$

When the interquartile range is used to describe variability, it commonly is transformed into the *semi-interquartile range*. As the name implies, the semi-interquartile range is one-half of the interquartile range. Conceptually, the semi-interquartile range measures the distance from the middle of the distribution to the boundaries that define the middle 50%.

DEFINITION   The **semi-interquartile range** is half of the interquartile range:

$$\text{semi-interquartile range} = \frac{Q3 - Q1}{2}$$

For the distribution in Figure 4.2 the interquartile range is 3.5 points. The semi-interquartile range is half of this distance:

$$\text{semi-interquartile range} = \frac{3.5}{2} = 1.75$$

Because the semi-interquartile range (or interquartile range) is derived from the middle 50% of the distribution, it is not likely to be influenced by extreme scores, and therefore gives a better and more stable measure of variability than the range. However, the semi-interquartile range *only* considers the middle 50% of the scores and completely disregards the other 50%. Therefore, it does not give a complete picture of the variability for the entire set of scores. Like the range, the semi-interquartile range is considered to be a somewhat crude measure of variability.

LEARNING CHECK

1. For the following data, find the range and the semi-interquartile range:

   3,   4,   5,   7,   9,   10,   11,   13

2. Consider the distribution of Exercise 1, except replace the score of 13 with a score of 100. What are the new values for the range and the semi-interquartile range? In comparing the answer to the one in Exercise 1, what can you conclude about these measures of variability?

ANSWERS

1. Range = URL X_{max} − LRL X_{min} = 13.5 − 2.5 = 11; semi-interquartile range = $(Q3 - Q1)/2 = (10.5 - 4.5)/2 = 3$.

2. Range = 98; semi-interquartile range = 3. The range is greatly affected by extreme scores in the distribution.

4.3 STANDARD DEVIATION AND VARIANCE FOR A POPULATION

The standard deviation is the most commonly used and the most important measure of variability. Standard deviation uses the mean of the distribution as a reference point and measures variability by considering the distance between each score and the mean. It determines whether the scores are generally near or far from the mean. That is, are the scores clustered together or scattered? In simple terms, the standard deviation approximates the average distance from the mean.

Although the concept of standard deviation is straightforward, the actual equations will appear complex. Therefore, we will begin by looking at the logic that leads to these equations. If you remember that our goal is to measure the standard, or typical, distance from the mean, then this logic and the equations that follow should be easier to remember.

STEP 1   The first step in finding the standard distance from the mean is to determine the *deviation,* or distance from the mean, for each individual score. By definition, the deviation for each score is the difference between the score and the mean.

D E F I N I T I O N   **Deviation** is distance from the mean:

$$\text{deviation score} = X - \mu$$

For a distribution of scores with $\mu = 50$, if your score is $X = 53$, then your *deviation score* is

$$X - \mu = 53 - 50 = 3$$

If your score is $X = 45$, then your deviation score is

$$X - \mu = 45 - 50 = -5$$

Notice that there are two parts to a deviation score: the sign ($+$ or $-$) and the number. The sign tells the direction from the mean—that is, whether the score is located above ($+$) or below ($-$) the mean. The number gives the actual distance from the mean. For example, a deviation score of -6 corresponds to a score that is below the mean by 6 points.

STEP 2   Because our goal is to compute a measure of the standard distance from the mean, the obvious next step is to calculate the mean of the deviation scores. To compute this mean, you first add up the deviation scores and then divide by N. This process is demonstrated in the following example.

E X A M P L E 4 . 1   We start with the following set of $N = 4$ scores. These scores add up to $\Sigma X = 12$, so the mean is $\mu = \frac{12}{4} = 3$. For each score, we have computed the deviation.

X	$X - \mu$
8	$+5$
1	-2
3	0
0	-3
	$0 = \Sigma(X - \mu)$

Note that the deviation scores add up to zero. This should not be surprising if you remember that the mean serves as a balance point for the distribution. The total of the distances above the mean is exactly equal to the total of the distances below the mean (see page 59). Thus, the total for the positive deviations is exactly equal to the total for the negative deviations, and the complete set of deviations will always add up to zero.

Because the mean of the deviations is always zero, it is of no value as a measure of variability. It is zero whether the scores are grouped together or are all scattered out. (You should note, however, that the constant value of zero can be useful in other ways. Whenever you are working with deviation scores, you can check your calculations by making sure that the deviation scores add up to zero.)

S T E P   3   The average of the deviation scores will not work as a measure of variability because it is always zero. Clearly, this problem results from the positive and negative values canceling each other out. The solution is to get rid of the signs ($+$ and $-$). The standard procedure for accomplishing this is to square each deviation score. Using the squared values, you then compute the *mean squared deviation,* which is called *variance.*

D E F I N I T I O N   **Population variance** equals the mean squared deviation. Variance is the average squared distance from the mean.

Note that the process of squaring deviation scores does more than simply get rid of plus and minus signs. It results in a measure of variability based on *squared* distances. Although variance is valuable for some of the *inferential* statistical methods covered later, the mean squared distance is not the best *descriptive* measure for variability.

S T E P   4   Remember that our goal is to compute a measure of the standard distance from the mean. Variance, which measures the average squared distance from the mean, is not exactly what we want. The final step simply makes a correction for having squared all the distances. The new measure, the *standard deviation,* is the square root of the variance.

D E F I N I T I O N   **Standard deviation** $= \sqrt{\text{variance}}$

Figure 4.3 shows the overall process of computing standard deviation and variance. Remember that our goal is to measure variability by finding the standard distance from the mean. However, we cannot simply calculate the average of the distances because this value will always be zero. Therefore, we begin by squaring each distance, then we find the average of the squared distances, and finally we take the square root to obtain a measure of the standard distance. Technically, the standard deviation is the square root of the average squared deviation. Conceptually, however, the standard deviation provides a measure of the average distance from the mean.

Although we still have not presented any formulas for variance or standard deviation, you should be able to compute these two statistical values from their definitions. The following example demonstrates this process.

E X A M P L E   4 . 2   We will calculate the variance and standard deviation for the following population of $N = 5$ scores:

1,   9,   5,   8,   7

FIGURE 4.3

The calculation of variance and standard deviation.

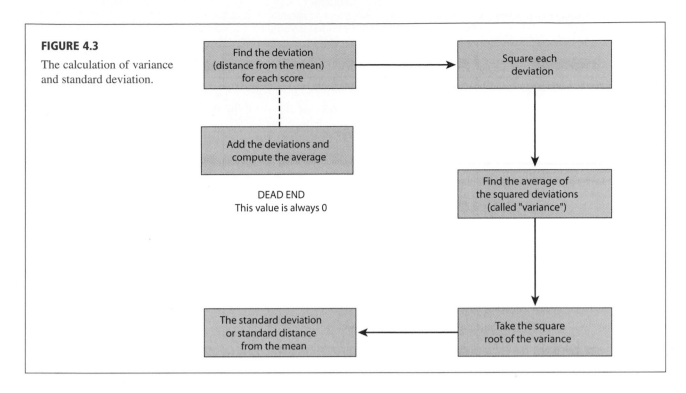

These five scores add up to $\Sigma X = 30$, so the mean is $\frac{30}{5} = 6$. Before doing any other calculations, remember that the purpose of standard deviation is to measure the standard distance from the mean. The scores we have been working with are shown in a histogram in Figure 4.4 so that you can see the distances more clearly. Note that the scores closest to the mean are only 1 point away. Also, the score farthest from the mean is 5 points away. For this distribution, the largest distance from the mean is 5 points and the smallest distance is 1 point. Thus, the standard distance should be somewhere between 1 and 5. By looking at a distribution in this way, you should be able to make a rough estimate of the standard deviation. In this case, the standard deviation should be between 1 and 5, probably around 3 points.

Making a preliminary judgment of the standard deviation can help you avoid errors in calculation. For example, if you calculated the standard deviation for the

FIGURE 4.4

A frequency distribution histogram for a population of $N = 5$ scores. The mean for this population is $\mu = 6$. The smallest distance from the mean is 1 point, and the largest distance is 5 points. The standard distance (or standard deviation) should be between 1 and 5 points.

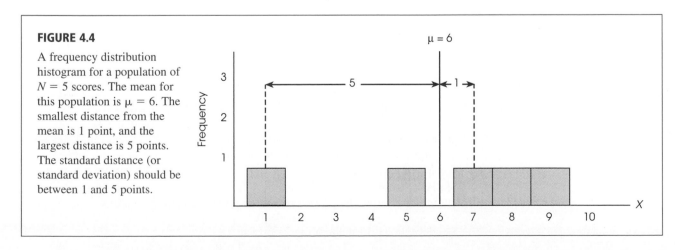

scores in Figure 4.4 and obtained a value of 12, you should realize immediately that you have made an error. (If the biggest deviation is only 5 points, then it is impossible for the standard deviation to be 12.)

Now we start the calculations. The first step is to find the deviation (distance from the mean) for each score and then square the deviations. Using the population mean $\mu = 6$, these calculations are shown in the following table.

Score X	Deviation $X - \mu$	Squared Deviation $(X - \mu)^2$
1	−5	25
9	3	9
5	−1	1
8	2	4
7	1	1

$40 =$ the sum of the squared deviations

For this set of $N = 5$ scores, the squared deviations add up to 40. The mean of the squared deviations, the variance, is $\frac{40}{5} = 8$, and the standard deviation is $\sqrt{8} = 2.83$. Note that the value we obtained for the standard deviation is in excellent agreement with our preliminary estimate of the standard distance from the mean.

FORMULAS FOR POPULATION VARIANCE AND STANDARD DEVIATION

The concepts of standard deviation and variance are the same for both samples and populations. However, the details of the calculations differ slightly, depending on whether you have data from a sample or from a complete population. We first consider the formulas for populations and then look at samples in Section 4.4.

The sum of squared deviations (SS)   Recall that variance is defined as the mean of the squared deviations. This mean is computed exactly the same way you compute any mean: First find the sum, and then divide by the number of scores.

$$\text{Variance} = \text{mean squared deviation} = \frac{\text{sum of squared deviations}}{\text{number of scores}}$$

The value in the numerator of this equation, the sum of the squared deviations, is a basic component of variability, and we will focus on it. To simplify things, it is identified by the notation *SS* (for sum of squared deviations), and it generally is referred to as the *sum of squares*.

DEFINITION   *SS,* or **sum of squares,** is the sum of the squared deviation scores.

You will need to know two formulas to compute *SS.* These formulas are algebraically equivalent (they always produce the same answer), but they look different and are used in different situations.

The first of these formulas is called the definitional formula because the terms in the formula literally define the process of adding up the squared deviations:

definitional formula: $SS = \Sigma(X - \mu)^2$ (4.1)

Note that the formula instructs you to perform a sequence of calculations:

1. Find each deviation score, $(X - \mu)$.
2. Square each deviation score, $(X - \mu)^2$.
3. Sum the squared deviations.

The result is *SS,* the sum of the squared deviations. The following example demonstrates using this formula.

EXAMPLE 4.3 We will compute *SS* for the following set of $N = 4$ scores. These scores have a sum of $\Sigma X = 8$, so the mean is $\mu = \frac{8}{4} = 2$. The following table shows the deviation and the squared deviation for each score. The sum of the squared deviation is $SS = 22$.

Score	Deviation	Squared Deviation	
X	$X - \mu$	$(X - \mu)^2$	
1	−1	1	$\Sigma X = 8$
0	−2	4	$\mu = 2$
6	+4	16	
1	−1	1	
		$22 = \Sigma(X - \mu)^2$	

Although the definitional formula is the most direct method for computing *SS,* it can be awkward to use. In particular, when the mean is not a whole number, the deviations will all contain decimals or fractions, and the calculations become difficult. In addition, calculations with decimal values introduce the opportunity for rounding error, which makes the results less accurate. For these reasons, an alternative formula has been developed for computing *SS.* The alternative, known as the computational formula, performs calculations with the scores (not the deviations) and therefore minimizes the complications of decimals and fractions.

$$\text{computational formula: } SS = \Sigma X^2 - \frac{(\Sigma X)^2}{N} \tag{4.2}$$

The first part of this formula directs you to square each score and then add the squared values, ΣX^2. In the second part of the formula, you find the sum of the scores, ΣX, then square this total and divide the result by N. Finally, subtract the second part from the first. The use of this formula is shown in Example 4.4 with the same scores that we used to demonstrate the definitional formula.

EXAMPLE 4.4 The computational formula is used to calculate *SS* for the same set of $N = 4$ scores we used in Example 4.3. First, compute ΣX. Then square each score, and compute ΣX^2. These calculations are shown in the following table. The two sums are used in the formula to compute *SS.*

X	X²
1	1
0	0
6	36
1	1
ΣX = 8	ΣX² = 38

$$SS = \Sigma X^2 - \frac{(\Sigma X)^2}{N}$$

$$= 38 - \frac{(8)^2}{4}$$

$$= 38 - \frac{64}{4}$$

$$= 38 - 16$$

$$= 22$$

Note that the two formulas produce exactly the same value for *SS*. Although the formulas look different, they are in fact equivalent. The definitional formula provides the most direct representation of the concept of *SS;* however, this formula can be awkward to use, especially if the mean includes a fraction or decimal value. If you have a small group of scores and the mean is a whole number, then the definitional formula is fine; otherwise use the computational formula.

VARIANCE AND STANDARD DEVIATION

In the same way that sum of squares, or *SS,* is used to refer to the sum of squared deviations, the term *mean square,* or *MS,* is often used to refer to variance, which is the mean squared deviation.

With the definition and calculation of *SS* behind you, the equations for variance and standard deviation become relatively simple. Remember that variance is defined as the mean squared deviation. The mean is the sum divided by *N,* so the equation for the *population variance* is

$$\text{variance} = \frac{SS}{N}$$

Standard deviation is the square root of variance, so the equation for the *population standard deviation* is

$$\text{standard deviation} = \sqrt{\frac{SS}{N}}$$

There is one final bit of notation before we work completely through an example computing *SS,* variance, and standard deviation. Like the mean (μ), variance and standard deviation are parameters of a population and will be identified by Greek letters. To identify the standard deviation, we use the Greek letter sigma (the Greek letter *s,* standing for standard deviation). The capital letter sigma (Σ) has been used already, so we now use the lowercase sigma, σ, as the symbol for the population standard deviation. To emphasize the relationship between standard deviation and variance, we use σ^2 as the symbol for population variance (standard deviation is the square root of the variance). Thus,

$$\text{population standard deviation} = \sigma = \sqrt{\sigma^2} = \sqrt{\frac{SS}{N}} \tag{4.3}$$

$$\text{population variance} = \sigma^2 = \frac{SS}{N} \tag{4.4}$$

Using the definitional formula for *SS,* the complete calculation of population variance can be expressed as

$$\text{population variance} = \sigma^2 = \frac{\Sigma(X - \mu)^2}{N} \tag{4.5}$$

GRAPHIC REPRESENTATION OF THE MEAN AND STANDARD DEVIATION

In frequency distribution graphs, we identify the position of the population mean by drawing a vertical line and labeling it with μ (Figure 4.5). Because the standard deviation measures distance from the mean, it will be represented by a line drawn from the mean outward for a distance equal to the standard deviation (see Figure 4.5). For rough sketches, you can identify the mean with a vertical line in the middle of the distribution. The standard deviation line should extend approximately halfway from the mean to the most extreme score. (*Note:* In Figure 4.5 we show the standard deviation as a line pointing to the right. You should realize that we could have drawn the line pointing to the left, or we could have drawn two lines, with one pointing to the right and one pointing to the left. In each case, the goal is to show the standard distance from the mean.)

FIGURE 4.5

The graphic representation of a population with a mean of $\mu = 40$ and a standard deviation of $\mu = 4$.

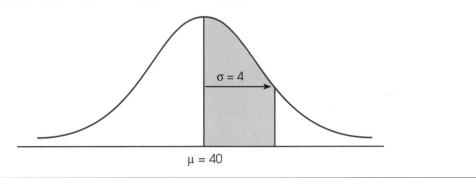

$\sigma = 4$

$\mu = 40$

LEARNING CHECK

1. Write brief definitions of variance and standard deviation.

2. Find *SS*, variance, and standard deviation for the following population of $N = 5$ scores: 10, 10, 10, 10, 10. (*Note:* You should be able to answer this question without doing any calculations.)

3. **a.** Sketch a frequency distribution histogram for the following population of scores: 1, 3, 3, 9. Using this histogram, make an estimate of the standard deviation (i.e., the standard distance from the mean).

   b. Calculate *SS*, variance, and standard deviation for these scores. How well does your estimate from part (a) compare with the real standard deviation?

ANSWERS

1. Variance is the mean squared distance from the mean. Standard deviation is the square root of variance and provides a measure of the standard distance from the mean.

2. Because there is no variability in the population, *SS*, variance, and standard deviation are all equal to zero.

3. **a.** Your sketch should show a mean of $\mu = 4$. The score closest to the mean is $X = 3$, and the farthest score is $X = 9$. The standard deviation should be somewhere between 1 point and 5 points.

   b. For this population, $SS = 36$; the variance is $\frac{36}{4} = 9$; the standard deviation is $\sqrt{9} = 3$.

4.4   STANDARD DEVIATION AND VARIANCE FOR SAMPLES

A sample statistic is said to be *biased* if, on the average, it consistently overestimates or underestimates the corresponding population parameter.

The goal of inferential statistics is to use the limited information from samples to draw general conclusions about populations. The basic assumption of this process is that samples should be representative of the populations from which they come. This assumption poses a special problem for variability because samples consistently tend to be less variable than their populations. An example of this general tendency is shown in Figure 4.6. Notice that a few extreme scores in the population tend to make the population variability relatively large. However, these extreme values are unlikely to be obtained when you are selecting a sample, which means that the sample variability is relatively small. The fact that a sample tends to be less variable than its population means that sample variability gives a *biased* estimate of population variability. This bias is in the direction of underestimating the population value rather than being right on the mark. Fortunately, the bias in sample variability is consistent and predictable, which means it can be corrected. For example, if the speedometer in your car consistently shows speeds that are 5 mph slower than you are actually going, it does not mean that the speedometer is useless. It simply means that you must make an adjustment to the speedometer reading to get an accurate speed. In the same way, we will make an adjustment in the calculation of sample variance. The purpose of the adjustment is to make the resulting value for sample variance an accurate and unbiased representative of the population variance.

The calculations of variance and standard deviation for a sample follow the same steps that were used to find population variance and standard deviation. Except for minor changes in notation, the first three steps in this process are exactly the same for a sample as they were for a population. That is, the calculation of SS is the same for a

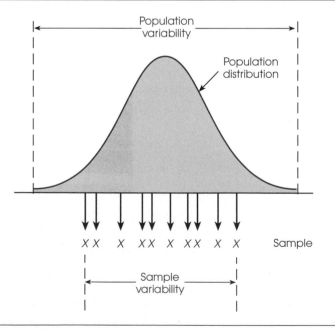

FIGURE 4.6

The population of adult heights forms a normal distribution. If you select a sample from this population, you are most likely to obtain individuals who are near average in height. As a result, the scores in the sample will be less variable (spread out) than the scores in the population.

sample as it is for a population. The changes in notation involve using M for the sample mean instead of μ, and using n (instead of N) for the number of scores. Thus, SS for a sample is found by

1. Find the deviation for each score: deviation $= X - M$
2. Square each deviation: squared deviation $= (X - M)^2$
3. Sum the squared deviations: $SS = \Sigma(X - M)^2$

These three steps can be summarized in a definitional formula for SS:

$$\text{Definitional formula: } SS = \Sigma(X - M)^2 \tag{4.6}$$

The value of SS can also be obtained using the computational formula. Using sample notation, this formula is:

$$\text{Computational formula: } SS = \Sigma X^2 - \frac{(\Sigma X)^2}{n} \tag{4.7}$$

Again, calculating SS for a sample is exactly the same as for a population, except for minor changes in notation. After you compute SS, however, it becomes critical to differentiate between samples and populations. To correct for the bias in sample variability, it is necessary to make an adjustment in the formulas for sample variance and standard deviation. With this in mind, *sample variance* (identified by the symbol s^2) is defined as

$$\text{sample variance} = s^2 = \frac{SS}{n - 1} \tag{4.8}$$

Using the definitional formula for SS, the complete calculation of sample variance can be expressed as

$$\text{sample variance} = s^2 = \frac{\Sigma(X - M)^2}{n - 1} \tag{4.9}$$

Sample standard deviation (identified by the symbol s) is simply the square root of the variance.

$$\text{sample standard deviation} = s = \sqrt{s^2} = \sqrt{\frac{SS}{n - 1}} \tag{4.10}$$

Remember, sample variability tends to underestimate population variability unless some correction is made.

Notice that these sample formulas use $n - 1$ instead of n. This is the adjustment that is necessary to correct for the bias in sample variability. The effect of the adjustment is to increase the value you will obtain. Dividing by a smaller number ($n - 1$ instead of n) produces a larger result and makes sample variance an accurate, or unbiased, estimator of population variance.

A complete example showing the calculation of sample variance and standard deviation will now be worked out.

EXAMPLE 4.5   We have selected a sample of $n = 7$ scores from a population. The scores are 1, 6, 4, 3, 8, 7, 6. The frequency distribution histogram for this sample is shown in Figure 4.7. Before we begin any calculations, you should be able to look at the sample distribution

FIGURE 4.7

The frequency distribution histogram for a sample of $n = 7$ scores. The sample mean is $M = 5$. The smallest distance from the mean is 1 point, and the largest distance from the mean is 4 points. The standard distance (standard deviation) should be between 1 and 4 points, or about 2.5.

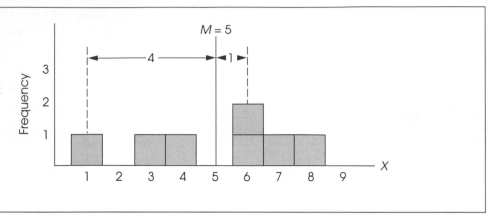

and make a preliminary estimate of the outcome. Remember that standard deviation measures the standard distance from the mean. For this sample the mean is $M = \frac{35}{7} = 5$. The scores closest to the mean are $X = 4$ and $X = 6$, both of which are exactly 1 point away. The score farthest from the mean is $X = 1$, which is 4 points away. With the smallest distance from the mean equal to 1 and the largest distance equal to 4, we should obtain a standard distance somewhere around 2.5 (between 1 and 4).

Now let's begin the calculations. First, we find SS for this sample. Because there are only a few scores and the mean is a whole number, the definitional formula will be easy to use. We begin by finding the deviation (distance from the mean) for each score, then squaring each deviation. The calculations are shown in the following table.

Score X	Deviation $X - M$	Squared Deviation $(X - M)^2$
1	-4	16
6	1	1
4	-1	1
3	-2	4
8	3	9
7	2	4
6	1	1

$36 = SS$ (the sum of the squared deviations)

SS for this sample is 36. Continuing the calculations,

$$\text{sample variance} = s^2 = \frac{SS}{n - 1} = \frac{36}{7 - 1} = 6$$

Finally, the standard deviation is

$$s = \sqrt{s^2} = \sqrt{6} = 2.45$$

Note that the value we obtained is in excellent agreement with our preliminary prediction (see Figure 4.7).

Remember that the formulas for sample variance and standard deviation were constructed so that the sample variability would provide a good estimate of population variability. For this reason, the sample variance is often called *estimated population variance,* and the sample standard deviation is called *estimated population standard deviation.* When you have only a sample to work with, the sample variance and standard deviation provide the best possible estimates of the population variability.

SAMPLE VARIABILITY AND DEGREES OF FREEDOM

Although the concept of a deviation score and the calculation SS are almost exactly the same for samples and populations, the minor differences in notation are really very important. Specifically, with a population, you find the deviation for each score by measuring its distance from the population mean. With a sample, on the other hand, the value of μ is unknown and you must measure distances from the sample mean. This requires that you know the value of M before you can begin to compute deviations. However, knowing the value of M places a restriction on the variability of the scores in the sample. This restriction is demonstrated in the following example.

EXAMPLE 4.6

Consider a sample of $n = 3$ scores with a mean of $M = 5$. The first two scores in the sample can be selected without any restrictions; they are independent of each other and they can have any values. For this demonstration, we will assume that we obtained $X = 2$ for the first score and $X = 9$ for the second. At this point, however, the third score in the sample is restricted.

X	A sample of $n = 3$ scores
2	with a mean of $M = 5$
9	
__	← What is the third score?

In this case, the third score must be $X = 4$. The reason that the third score has to be $X = 4$ is because the entire sample of $n = 3$ scores has a mean of $M = 5$, which means that the total must be $\Sigma X = 15$. The first two scores add up to 11 (9 + 2), so the third score must be $X = 4$.

In Example 4.6, the first two out of three scores were free to have any values, but the final score was dependent on the values chosen for the first two. In general, with a sample of n scores, the first $n - 1$ scores are free to vary, but the final score is restricted. As a result, the sample is said to have $n - 1$ *degrees of freedom.*

DEFINITION

For a sample of n scores, the **degrees of freedom** or **df** for the sample variance are defined as $df = n - 1$. The degrees of freedom determine the number of scores in the sample that are independent and free to vary.

The $n - 1$ degrees of freedom for a sample is the same $n - 1$ that is used in the formulas for sample variance and standard deviation. Remember that variance is defined as the mean squared deviation. As always, this mean is computed by finding the sum and dividing by the number of scores:

$$\text{mean} = \frac{\text{sum}}{\text{number}}$$

To calculate sample variance (mean squared deviation), we find the sum of the squared deviations (SS) and divide by the number of scores that are free to vary. This number is $n - 1 = df$.

$$s^2 = \frac{\text{sum of squared deviations}}{\text{number of scores free to vary}} = \frac{SS}{df} = \frac{SS}{n - 1}$$

Later in this book, we will use the concept of degrees of freedom in other situations. For now, remember that knowing the sample mean places a restriction on sample variability. Only $n - 1$ of the scores are free to vary; $df = n - 1$.

LEARNING CHECK

1. **a.** Sketch a frequency distribution histogram for the following sample of scores: 1, 1, 9, 1. Using your histogram, make an estimate of the standard deviation for this sample.

   b. Calculate *SS*, variance, and standard deviation for this sample. How well does your estimate from part a compare with the real standard deviation?

2. If the scores in the previous exercise were for a population, what value would you obtain for *SS*?

3. Explain why the formulas for sample variance and standard deviation use $n - 1$ instead of *n*.

ANSWERS

1. **a.** Your graph should show a sample mean of $M = 3$. The score farthest from the mean is $X = 9$, and the closest score is $X = 1$. You should estimate the standard deviation to be between 2 points and 6 points.

   b. For this sample, $SS = 48$; the sample variance is $\frac{48}{3} = 16$; the sample standard deviation is $\sqrt{16} = 4$.

2. $SS = 48$ whether the data are from a sample or a population.

3. Without some correction, sample variability is biased because the scores in a sample tend to be less variable than the scores in the population. To correct for this bias, the formulas divide by $n - 1$ instead of *n*.

4.5   MORE ABOUT VARIANCE AND STANDARD DEVIATION

SAMPLE VARIANCE AS AN UNBIASED STATISTIC

Earlier we noted that sample variability tends to underestimate the variability in the corresponding population. To correct for this problem we adjusted the formula for sample variance by dividing by $n - 1$ instead of dividing by *n*. The result of the adjustment is that sample variance provides a much more accurate representation of the population variance. Specifically, the sample variance provides an *unbiased* estimate of the corresponding population variance. This does not mean that each individual sample variance will be exactly equal to its population variance. In fact, some sample variances will overestimate the population value and some will underestimate it. However, the average of all the sample variances will produce an accurate estimate of the population variance. This is the idea behind the concept of an unbiased statistic.

DEFINITIONS

A sample statistic is **unbiased** if the average value of the sample statistic, obtained over many different samples, is equal to the population parameter. On the other hand, if the average value for a sample statistic consistently underestimates or overestimates the corresponding population parameter, then the statistic is **biased**.

The following example demonstrates the concept of biased and unbiased statistics.

EXAMPLE 4.7

Technical note: We have structured this example to mimic "sampling with replacement," which will be covered in Chapter 6.

We begin with a population that consists of exactly $N = 6$ scores: 0, 0, 3, 3, 9, 9. With a few simple calculations you should be able to verify that this population has a mean of $\mu = 4$ and a variance of $\sigma^2 = 14$.

Next, we will select samples of $n = 2$ scores from this population. In fact, we will obtain every single possible sample with $n = 2$. The complete set of samples is listed in Table 4.1. Notice that the samples are listed systematically to ensure that every possible sample is included. We begin by listing all the samples that have $X = 0$ as the first score, then all the samples with $X = 3$ as the first score, and so on. Notice that the table shows a total of 9 samples.

Finally, we have computed the mean and the variance for each sample. Note that we have computed the sample variance two different ways. First, we examine what would happen if there was no correction for bias and the sample variance was computed by simply dividing SS by n. Second, we examine the real sample variances, dividing by $n - 1$ to produce an unbiased measure. You should verify our calculations by computing one or two of the values for yourself. The complete set of sample means and sample variances is presented in Table 4.1.

Now, direct your attention to the column of sample means. For this example, the original population has a mean of $\mu = 4$. Although none of the samples has a mean exactly equal to 4, if you consider the complete set of sample means, you will find that the 9 sample means add up to a total of 36, so the average of the sample means is $\frac{36}{9} = 4$. Note that the average of the sample means is exactly equal to the population mean. This is what is meant by the concept of an unbiased statistic. On average, the sample values provide an accurate representation of the population. In this example, the average of the 9 sample means is exactly equal to the population mean.

Next, consider the column of biased sample variances where we divided by n. For the original population the variance is $\sigma^2 = 14$. The 9 sample variances, however, add up to a total of 63, which produces an average variance of $\frac{63}{9} = 7$. Note that the average of these sample variances is *not* equal to the population variance. If the sample variance is computed by dividing by n, the resulting values will not produce an accurate estimate of the population variance. On average, these sample variances underestimate the population variance and, therefore, are biased statistics.

TABLE 4.1

The set of all the possible samples for $n = 2$ selected from the population described in Example 4.7. The mean is computed for each sample, and the variance is computed two different ways: (1) dividing by n, which is incorrect and produces a biased statistic; and (2) dividing by $n - 1$, which is correct and produces an unbiased statistic.

Sample	First Score	Second Score	Mean M	Biased Variance (Using n)	Unbiased Variance (Using $n - 1$)
1	0	0	0.00	0.00	0.00
2	0	3	1.50	2.25	4.50
3	0	9	4.50	20.25	40.50
4	3	0	1.50	2.25	4.50
5	3	3	3.00	0.00	0.00
6	3	9	6.00	9.00	18.00
7	9	0	4.50	20.25	40.50
8	9	3	6.00	9.00	18.00
9	9	9	9.00	0.00	0.00
		Totals	36.00	63.00	126.00

Finally, consider the column of sample variances that are computed using $n - 1$. Although the population has a variance of $\sigma^2 = 14$, you should notice that none of the samples has a variance exactly equal to 14. However, if you consider the complete set of sample variances, you will find that the 9 values add up to a total of 126, which produces an average variance of $\frac{126}{9} = 14.00$. Thus, the average of the sample variances is exactly equal to the population variance. On average, the sample variance (computed using $n - 1$) produces an accurate, unbiased estimate of the population variance.

In summary, both the sample mean and the sample variance (using $n - 1$) are examples of unbiased statistics. This fact makes the sample mean and sample variance extremely valuable for use as inferential statistics. Although no individual sample is likely to have a mean and variance exactly equal to the population values, both the sample mean and the sample variance, on average, do provide accurate estimates of the corresponding population values.

STANDARD DEVIATION AND DESCRIPTIVE STATISTICS

Because standard deviation requires extensive calculations, there is a tendency to get lost in the arithmetic and forget what standard deviation is and why it is important. Standard deviation is primarily a descriptive measure; it describes how variable, or how spread out, the scores are in a distribution. Behavioral scientists must deal with the variability that comes from studying people and animals. People are not all the same; they have different attitudes, opinions, talents, IQs, and personalities. Although we can calculate the average value for any of these variables, it is equally important to describe the variability. Standard deviation describes variability by measuring *distance from the mean*. In any distribution, some individuals will be close to the mean, and others will be relatively far from the mean. Standard deviation provides a measure of the typical, or standard, distance from the mean.

In addition to describing an entire distribution, standard deviation also allows us to interpret individual scores. We know, for example, that a person with an IQ of 110 is above average but not exceptional; with a standard distance of $\sigma = 15$ points, a score that is 10 points above average is not extreme. If we are comparing heights, on the other hand, a person who is 10 inches taller than average is exceptional; with a small standard deviation of only 4 or 5 inches, a 10-point difference is extreme.

The mean and the standard deviation are the most common values used to describe a set of data. A research report, for example, typically will not list all of the individual scores but rather will summarize the data by reporting the mean and standard deviation. When you are given these two descriptive statistics, you should be able to visualize the entire set of data. For example, consider a sample with a mean of $M = 36$ and a standard deviation of $s = 4$. Although there are several different ways to picture the data, one simple technique is to imagine (or sketch) a histogram in which each score is represented by a box in the graph. For this sample, the data can be pictured as a pile of boxes (scores) with the center of the pile located at a value of $M = 36$. The individual scores or boxes are scattered on both sides of the mean with some of the boxes relatively close to the mean and some farther away. As a rule of thumb, roughly 70% of the scores in a distribution are located within a distance of one standard deviation from the mean, and almost all of the scores (roughly 95%) are within two standard deviations of the mean. In this example, the standard distance from the mean is $s = 4$ points so your image should have most of the boxes within 4 points of the mean, and nearly all of the boxes within 8 points. One possibility for the resulting image is shown in Figure 4.8.

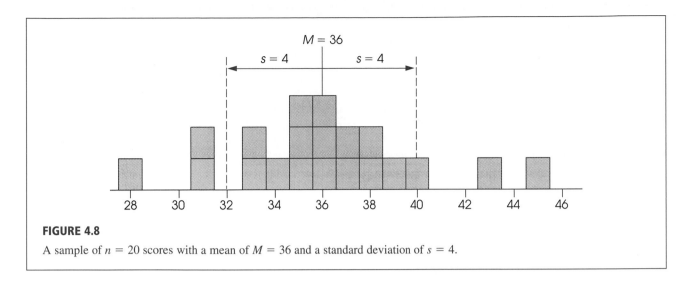

FIGURE 4.8

A sample of $n = 20$ scores with a mean of $M = 36$ and a standard deviation of $s = 4$.

Notice that Figure 4.8 not only shows the mean and the standard deviation, but also uses these two values to reconstruct the underlying scale of measurement (the X values along the horizontal line). The scale of measurement helps complete the picture of the entire distribution and helps to relate each individual score to the rest of the group. In this example, you should realize that a score of $X = 34$ is located near the center of the distribution, only slightly below the mean. On the other hand, a score of $X = 45$ is an extremely high score, located far out in the right-hand tail of the distribution.

The general point of this discussion is that the mean and standard deviation are not simply abstract concepts or mathematical equations. Instead, these two values should be concrete and meaningful, especially in the context of a set of scores. The mean and standard deviation are central concepts for most of the statistics that will be presented in the following chapters. A good understanding of these two statistics will help you with the more complex procedures that follow. (See Box 4.1.)

BOX 4.1   **AN ANALOGY FOR THE MEAN AND THE STANDARD DEVIATION**

Although the basic concepts of the mean and the standard deviation are not overly complex, the following analogy often helps students gain a more complete understanding of these two statistical measures.

In our local community, the site for a new high school was selected because it provides a central location. An alternative site on the western edge of the community was considered, but this site was rejected because it would require extensive busing for students living on the east side. In this example, the location of the high school is analogous to the concept of the mean; just as the high school is located in the center of the community, the mean is located in the center of the distribution of scores.

For each student in the community, it is possible to measure the distance between home and the new high school. Some students live only a few blocks from the new school and others live as much as 3 miles away. The average distance that a student must travel to school was calculated to be 0.80 miles. The average distance from the school is analogous to the concept of the standard deviation; that is, the standard deviation measures the standard distance from an individual score to the mean.

**TRANSFORMATIONS
OF SCALE**

Occasionally, it is convenient to transform a set of scores by adding a constant to each score or by multiplying each score by a constant value. This is done, for example, when you want to "curve" a set of exam scores by adding a fixed amount to each individual's grade or when you want to change the unit of measurement (to convert from minutes to seconds, multiply each X by 60). What happens to the standard deviation when the scores are transformed in this manner?

The easiest way to determine the effect of a transformation is to remember that the standard deviation is a measure of distance. If you select any two scores and see what happens to the distance between them, you also will find out what happens to the standard deviation.

1. Adding a constant to each score will not change the standard deviation   If you begin with a distribution that has $\mu = 40$ and $\sigma = 10$, what happens to σ if you add 5 points to every score? Consider any two scores in this distribution: Suppose, for example, that these are exam scores and that you had $X = 41$ and your friend had $X = 43$. The distance between these two scores is $43 - 41 = 2$ points. After adding the constant, 5 points, to each score, your score would be $X = 46$, and your friend would have $X = 48$. The distance between scores is still 2 points. Adding a constant to every score will not affect any of the distances and, therefore, will not change the standard deviation. This fact can be seen clearly if you imagine a frequency distribution graph. If, for example, you add 10 points to each score, then every score in the graph will be moved 10 points to the right. The result is that the entire distribution is shifted to a new position 10 points up the scale. Note that the mean moves along with the scores and is increased by 10 points. However, the variability does not change because each of the deviation scores $(X - \mu)$ does not change.

2. Multiplying each score by a constant causes the standard deviation to be multiplied by the same constant   Consider the same distribution of exam scores we looked at earlier. If $\mu = 40$ and $\sigma = 10$, what would happen to σ if each score were multiplied by 2? Again, we will look at two scores, $X = 41$ and $X = 43$, with a distance between them equal to 2 points. After all the scores have been multiplied by 2, these scores become $X = 82$ and $X = 86$. Now the distance between scores is 4 points, twice the original distance. Multiplying each score causes each distance to be multiplied, so the standard deviation also is multiplied by the same amount.

IN THE LITERATURE
REPORTING THE STANDARD DEVIATION

In reporting the results of a study, the researcher often provides descriptive information for both central tendency and variability. The dependent variables in psychology research frequently involve measures taken on interval or ratio scales. Thus, the mean (central tendency) and the standard deviation (variability) are commonly reported together. In many journals, especially those following APA style, the symbol SD is used for the sample standard deviation. For example, the results might state:

> Children who viewed the violent cartoon displayed more aggressive responses ($M = 12.45$, $SD = 3.7$) than those who viewed the control cartoon ($M = 4.22$, $SD = 1.04$).

When reporting the descriptive measures for several groups, the findings may be summarized in a table. Table 4.2 illustrates the results of hypothetical data.

TABLE 4.2

The number of aggressive responses in male and female children after viewing cartoons.

	Type of Cartoon	
	Violent	Control
Males	$M = 15.72$	$M = 6.94$
	$SD = 4.43$	$SD = 2.26$
Females	$M = 3.47$	$M = 2.61$
	$SD = 1.12$	$SD = 0.98$

Sometimes the table will also indicate the sample size, *n,* for each group. You should remember that the purpose of the table is to present the data in an organized, concise, and accurate manner. ❏

VARIANCE AND INFERENTIAL STATISTICS

In very general terms, the goal of inferential statistics is to detect meaningful and significant patterns in research results. The basic question is whether the sample data reflect patterns that exist in the population, or do the sample data simply show random fluctuations that occur by chance? Variability plays an important role in the inferential process because the variability in the data influences how easy it is to see patterns. In general, low variability means that existing patterns can be seen clearly, whereas high variability tends to obscure any patterns that might exist. The following two samples provide a simple demonstration of how variance can influence the perception of patterns. Your task is to examine each sample briefly and then estimate the sample mean.

Sample 1 X	Sample 2 X
34	26
35	10
36	64
35	40

After a few seconds of examining sample 1, you should realize that the sample mean is $M = 35$, and you should be very confident that this is an accurate estimate. With sample 2, on the other hand, the task is much more difficult. Although both samples have a mean of $M = 35$, it is much easier to see the mean in sample 1 than it is in sample 2.

The difference between the two samples is variability. In the first sample the scores are all clustered close together and variability is small. In this situation it is easy to see the sample mean. However, the scores in the second sample are spread out over a wide range and variability is large. With high variability, it is not easy to identify the location of the mean. In general, high variability makes it difficult to see any patterns in the data.

The preceding example demonstrates how variability can affect the ability to identify the mean for a single sample. In most research studies, however, the goal is to compare means for two (or more) sets of data. For example:

Is the mean level of depression lower after therapy than it was before therapy?

Is the mean attitude score for men different from the mean score for women?

Is the mean reading achievement score higher for students in a special program than for students in regular classrooms?

In each of these situations, the goal is to find a clear difference between two means that would demonstrate a significant, meaningful pattern in the results. Once again variability plays an important role in determining whether a clear pattern exists. Consider the following data representing hypothetical results from two experiments, each comparing two separate samples. In each case, your task is to determine whether there appears to be any consistent difference between the two samples.

	Experiment A			Experiment B	
	Sample 1	Sample 2		Sample 1	Sample 2
	35	39		31	46
	34	40		15	21
	36	41		57	61
	35	40		37	32

For each experiment, the data have been constructed so that there is a 5-point difference between the two samples: On average, the scores in sample 2 are 5 points higher than the scores in sample 1. The 5-point difference is relatively easy to see in Experiment A, where the variability is low, but the same 5-point difference is relatively difficult to see in Experiment B, where the variability is large. Again, high variability tends to obscure any patterns in the data. This general fact is perhaps even more convincing when the data are presented in a graph. Figure 4.9 shows the two sets of data from Experiments A and B that we just considered. Notice that the data from Experiment A clearly show the 5-point difference between the two samples. One group of scores piles up around 35 and the second group piles up around 40. On the other hand, the two samples from Experiment B [see Figure 4.9(b)] seem to be mixed together randomly with no clear difference between samples. If the two samples represented two different experimental treatments, then the results from Experiment A (low variability) would suggest that there is a real difference between the treatments. However, the results from Experiment B tend to indicate that there is no difference between treatments.

In the context of inferential statistics, the variance that exists in a set of sample data is often classified as *error variance*. This term is used to indicate that the sample variance represents unexplained and uncontrolled differences between scores. As the error variance increases, it becomes more difficult to see any systematic differences or patterns that

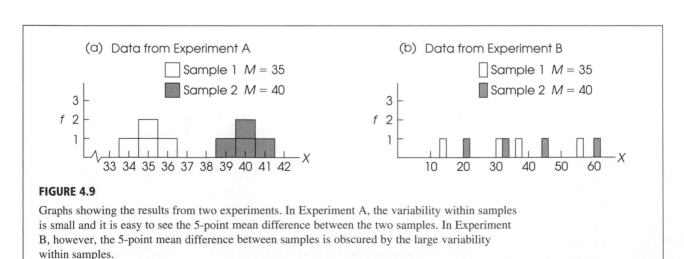

FIGURE 4.9

Graphs showing the results from two experiments. In Experiment A, the variability within samples is small and it is easy to see the 5-point mean difference between the two samples. In Experiment B, however, the 5-point mean difference between samples is obscured by the large variability within samples.

might exist in the data. An analogy is to think of variance as the static that exists on a radio or the "snow" on a television screen. In general, variance makes it difficult to get a clear signal from the data. High variance can make it difficult or impossible to see the mean for a set of scores, to see the mean difference between two sets of data, or to see any meaningful patterns in the results of a research study.

1. What is the difference between a biased and an unbiased statistic?

2. In a population with a mean of $\mu = 50$ and a standard deviation of $\sigma = 10$, would a score of $X = 58$ be considered an extreme value (far out in the tail of the distribution)? What if the standard deviation were $\sigma = 3$?

3. A population has a mean of $\mu = 70$ and a standard deviation of $\sigma = 5$.
   a. If 10 points were added to every score in the population, what would be the new values for the population mean and standard deviation?
   b. If every score in the population were multiplied by 2, what would be the new values for the population mean and standard deviation?

ANSWERS

1. A biased statistic means that, on the average, the value of the statistic does not accurately represent the corresponding population parameter. Instead, the statistic tends to overestimate or underestimate the parameter. An unbiased statistic means that, on the average, the value of the statistic is an accurate representation of the corresponding parameter.

2. With $\sigma = 10$, a score of $X = 58$ would be located in the central section of the distribution (within one standard deviation). With $\sigma = 3$, a score of $X = 58$ would be an extreme value, located more than two standard deviations above the mean.

3. a. The new mean would be $\mu = 80$ but the standard deviation would still be $\sigma = 5$.
   b. The new mean would be $\mu = 140$ and the new standard deviation would be $\sigma = 10$.

SUMMARY

1. The purpose of variability is to determine how spread out the scores are in a distribution. There are four basic measures of variability: the range, the interquartile range, the variance, and the standard deviation.

   The range is the distance from the highest score to the lowest score in a distribution and is defined as the difference between the upper real limit of the largest X and the lower real limit of the smallest X. The interquartile range is the distance covered by the middle 50% of the distribution and is defined as the difference between the third quartile ($Q3$) and the first quartile ($Q1$). Standard deviation and variance are the most commonly used measures of variability. Both of these measures are based on the idea that each score can be described in terms of its deviation or distance from the mean. The variance is the mean of the squared deviations. The standard deviation is the square root of the variance and provides a measure of the standard distance from the mean.

2. To calculate variance or standard deviation, you first need to find the sum of the squared deviations, SS. Except for minor changes in notation, the calculation of SS is identical for samples and populations. There are two methods for calculating SS:

   I. By definition, you can find SS using the following steps:
      a. Find the deviation $(X - \mu)$ for each score.
      b. Square each deviation.
      c. Sum the squared deviations.
      This process can be summarized in a formula as follows:

      definitional formula: $SS = \Sigma(X - \mu)^2$

II. The sum of the squared deviations can also be found using a computational formula, which is especially useful when the mean is not a whole number:

$$\text{computational formula: } SS = \Sigma X^2 - \frac{(\Sigma X)^2}{N}$$

3. Variance is the mean squared deviation and is obtained by finding the sum of the squared deviations and then dividing by the number of scores. For a population, variance is

$$\sigma^2 = \frac{SS}{N}$$

For a sample, only $n - 1$ of the scores are free to vary (degrees of freedom or $df = n - 1$), so sample variance is

$$s^2 = \frac{SS}{n - 1} = \frac{SS}{df}$$

Using $n - 1$ in the sample formula makes the sample variance an accurate and unbiased estimate of the population variance.

4. Standard deviation is the square root of the variance. For a population, this is

$$\sigma = \sqrt{\frac{SS}{N}}$$

Sample standard deviation is

$$s = \sqrt{\frac{SS}{n - 1}} = \sqrt{\frac{SS}{df}}$$

5. Adding a constant value to every score in a distribution will not change the standard deviation. Multiplying every score by a constant, however, will cause the standard deviation to be multiplied by the same constant.

KEY TERMS

variability	deviation score	sum of squares (SS)	degrees of freedom (df)
range	population variance (σ^2)	sample variance (s^2)	biased statistic
interquartile range	population standard deviation (σ)	sample standard deviation (s)	unbiased statistic
semi-interquartile range			

RESOURCES

There are a tutorial quiz and other learning exercises for Chapter 4 at the Wadsworth website, www.thomsonedu.com/psychology/gravetter. The site also includes a workshop titled *Central Tendency and Variability* that examines the basic concepts of variability and the standard deviation, and reviews the concept of central tendency that was covered in Chapter 3. See page 27 for more information about accessing items on the website.

WebTUTOR

For those using WebTutor along with this book, there is a WebTutor section corresponding to this chapter. The WebTutor contains a brief summary of Chapter 4, hints for learning the concepts and formulas for variability, cautions about common errors, and sample exam items including solutions.

General instructions for using SPSS are presented in Appendix D. Following are detailed instructions for using SPSS to compute the **Standard Deviation and Variance** for a sample of scores.

Data Entry

1. Enter all of the scores in one column of the data editor, probably VAR00001.

Data Analysis

1. Click **Analyze** on the tool bar, select **Descriptive Statistics,** and click on **Descriptives.**
2. Highlight the column label for the set of scores (VAR00001) in the left box and click the arrow to move it into the **Variable** box.
3. If you want the variance reported along with the standard deviation, click on the **Options** box, select **Variance,** then click **Continue.**
4. Click **OK.**

SPSS Output

SPSS will produce a summary table listing the number of scores, the maximum and minimum scores, the mean, the standard deviation, and the variance. Caution: SPSS computes the *sample* standard deviation and *sample* variance using $n - 1$. If your scores are intended to be a population, you can multiply the sample standard deviation by the square root of $(n - 1)/n$ to obtain the population standard deviation.

Note: You can also obtain the mean and standard deviation for a sample if you use SPSS to display the scores in a frequency distribution histogram (see the SPSS section at the end of Chapter 2). The mean and standard deviation are displayed beside the graph.

FOCUS ON PROBLEM SOLVING

1. The purpose of variability is to provide a measure of how spread out the scores are in a distribution. Usually this is described by the standard deviation. Because the calculations are relatively complicated, it is wise to make a preliminary estimate of the standard deviation before you begin. Remember that standard deviation provides a measure of the typical, or standard, distance from the mean. Therefore, the standard deviation must have a value somewhere between the largest and the smallest deviation scores. As a rule of thumb, the standard deviation should be about one-fourth of the range.

2. Rather than trying to memorize all the formulas for *SS,* variance, and standard deviation, you should focus on the definitions of these values and the logic that relates them to each other:

   SS is the sum of squared deviations.

   Variance is the mean squared deviation.

   Standard deviation is the square root of variance.

   The only formula you should need to memorize is the computational formula for *SS*.

3. A common error is to use $n - 1$ in the computational formula for *SS* when you have scores from a sample. Remember that the *SS* formula always uses n (or N). After you compute *SS* for a sample, you must correct for the sample bias by using $n - 1$ in the formulas for variance and standard deviation.

DEMONSTRATION 4.1

COMPUTING MEASURES OF VARIABILITY

For the following sample data, compute the variance and standard deviation. The scores are:

$$10, \quad 7, \quad 6, \quad 10, \quad 6, \quad 15$$

STEP 1 **Compute SS, the sum of squared deviations**
We will use the definitional formula: $SS = \Sigma(X - M)^2$. For this sample, the mean is $M = \frac{\Sigma X}{n} = \frac{54}{6} = 9$. The following table shows the deviation and the squared deviation for each score.

X	$X - M$	$(X - M)^2$
10	+1	1
7	−2	4
6	−3	9
10	+1	1
6	−3	9
15	+6	36

SS is the sum of the squared deviations:

$$SS = \Sigma(X - M)^2 = 1 + 4 + 9 + 1 + 9 + 36 = 60$$

STEP 2 **Compute the sample variance**
For sample variance, SS is divided by the degrees of freedom, $df = n - 1$.

$$s^2 = \frac{SS}{n - 1} = \frac{60}{5} = 12$$

STEP 3 **Compute the sample standard deviation**
Standard deviation is simply the square root of the variance.

$$s = \sqrt{12} = 3.46$$

PROBLEMS

1. Can SS ever have a value less than zero? Explain your answer.

2. What does it mean for a sample to have a standard deviation of zero? Describe the scores in such a sample.

3. What does it mean for a sample to have a standard deviation of $s = 5$? Describe the scores in such a sample. (Describe where the scores are located relative to the sample mean.)

4. A population has $\mu = 100$ and $\sigma = 20$. If you select a single score from this population, on the average, how close would it be to the population mean? Explain your answer.

5. In words, explain what is measured by each of the following:
   a. SS
   b. Variance
   c. Standard deviation

6. For the data in the following sample:

    1, 4, 3, 6, 2, 7, 8, 3, 7, 2, 4, 3

    a. Find the median and the semi-interquartile range. (It may help to sketch the frequency distribution histogram.)
    b. Now change the score of $X = 8$ to $X = 18$, and find the new median and semi-interquartile range.
    c. Describe how one extreme score influences the median and semi-interquartile range.

7. On an exam with $\mu = 75$, you obtain a score of $X = 80$.

    a. Would you prefer that the exam distribution had $\sigma = 2$ or $\sigma = 10$? (Sketch each distribution, and locate the position of $X = 80$ in each one.)
    b. If your score is $X = 70$, would you prefer $\sigma = 2$ or $\sigma = 10$? (Again, sketch each distribution to determine how the value of σ affects your position relative to the rest of the class.)

8. Explain what it means to say that the sample variance provides an *unbiased* estimate of the population variance.

9. For the following population of $N = 8$ scores:

    3, 3, 5, 1, 4, 3, 2, 3

    a. Calculate the range, the interquartile range, and the standard deviation.
    b. Add 2 points to every score, then compute the range, the interquartile range, and the standard deviation again. How is variability affected by adding a constant to every score?

10. A normal-shaped population has a mean of $\mu = 80$ and a standard deviation of $\sigma = 20$.

    a. If 10 points were added to every score in the population, what would be the new values for the population mean and standard deviation?
    b. If every score in the original population was multiplied by 2, what would be the new values for the population mean and standard deviation?

11. For the data in the following sample:

    8, 1, 5, 1, 5

    a. Find the mean and the standard deviation.
    b. Now change the score of $X = 8$ to $X = 18$, and find the new mean and standard deviation.
    c. Describe how one extreme score influences the mean and standard deviation.

12. A sample of $n = 20$ scores has a mean of $M = 30$.

    a. If the sample standard deviation is $s = 10$, would a score of $X = 38$ be considered an extreme value (out in the tail of the distribution)?
    b. If the sample standard deviation is $s = 2$, would a score of $X = 38$ be considered an extreme value (out in the tail of the distribution)?

13. There are two different formulas or methods that can be used to calculate SS.

    a. Under what circumstances is the definitional formula easy to use?
    b. Under what circumstances is the computational formula preferred?

14. For the following population of $N = 5$ scores:

    11, 2, 0, 8, 4

    a. Sketch a histogram showing the population distribution.
    b. Locate the value of the population mean in your sketch, and make an estimate of the standard deviation (as done in Example 4.2).
    c. Compute SS, variance, and standard deviation for the population. (How well does your estimate compare with the actual value of σ?)

15. For the following set of scores:

    1, 7, 1, 1

    a. Calculate ΣX and ΣX^2.
    b. Use the two sums from part a and the computational formula to compute SS for the scores.

16. For the following scores:

    1, 0, 4, 1, 1, 5

    a. Calculate the mean. (Note that the value of the mean does not depend on whether the set of scores is considered to be a sample or a population.)
    b. Find the deviation for each score, and check that the deviations sum to zero.
    c. Square each deviation, and compute SS. (Again, note that the value of SS is independent of whether the set of scores is a sample or a population.)

17. Sketch a normal distribution (see Figure 4.5, page 95) with $\mu = 50$ and $\sigma = 20$.

    a. Locate each of the following scores in your sketch, and indicate whether you consider each score to be an extreme value (high or low) or a central value:

    65, 55, 40, 47

    b. Make another sketch showing a distribution with $\mu = 50$, but this time with $\sigma = 2$. Now locate each of the four scores in the new distribution, and indicate whether they are extreme or central. (*Note:* The value of the standard deviation can have a dramatic effect on the location of a score within a distribution.)

18. Suppose that a treatment has the effect of increasing everyone's score by 6 points. Whether this 6-point treatment effect is viewed as a large effect or a small effect depends on the size of the standard deviation. Consider the following two possibilities:
    a. Sketch a normal distribution with a mean of $\mu = 80$ and a standard deviation of $\sigma = 30$. This represents the original population before treatment. On the same figure, sketch a second normal distribution with a mean of $\mu = 86$ and a standard deviation of $\sigma = 30$. This represents the population after the treatment has added 6 points to each person's score. Does the 6-point treatment effect look like a big effect? (Is there a big difference between the two distributions?)
    b. Now sketch a normal distribution with a mean of $\mu = 80$ and a standard deviation of $\sigma = 3$. This represents the original population before treatment. On the same figure, sketch a second normal distribution with a mean of $\mu = 86$ and a standard deviation of $\sigma = 3$. This represents the population after the treatment has added 6 points to each person's score. Does the 6-point treatment effect look like a big effect? (Is there a big difference between the two distributions?)

19. For the following sample of $n = 7$ scores:

    12, 1, 10, 6, 3, 3, 7

    a. Sketch a histogram showing the sample distribution.
    b. Locate the value of the sample mean in your sketch, and make an estimate of the standard deviation (as done in Example 4.5).
    c. Compute SS, variance, and standard deviation for the sample. (How well does your estimate compare with the actual value of s?)

20. Calculate SS, variance, and standard deviation for the following sample of $n = 6$ scores: 11, 0, 8, 2, 4, 5. (*Note:* The definitional formula for SS works well with these scores.)

21. Calculate SS, variance, and standard deviation for the following sample of $n = 9$ scores: 2, 0, 0, 0, 0, 2, 0, 2, 0. (*Note:* The computational formula for SS works best with these scores.)

22. Calculate SS, variance, and standard deviation for the following sample of $n = 4$ scores: 3, 1, 1, 1. (*Note:* The computational formula works best with these scores.)

23. For the following population of $N = 8$ scores:

    10, 1, 2, 5, 9, 7, 2, 4

    a. Sketch a histogram showing the population distribution.

    b. Locate the value of the population mean in your sketch, and make an estimate of the standard deviation (as done in Example 4.2).
    c. Compute SS, variance, and standard deviation for the population. (How well does your estimate compare with the actual value of σ?)

24. Calculate SS, variance, and standard deviation for the following population of $N = 8$ scores: 0, 1, 0, 3, 6, 0, 2, 0. (*Note:* The computational formula for SS works well with these scores.)

25. Calculate SS, variance, and standard deviation for the following sample of $n = 4$ scores: 4, 0, 1, 1. (*Note:* The computational formula for SS works well with these scores.)

26. For the following population of $N = 6$ scores:

    5, 0, 9, 3, 8, 5

    a. Sketch a histogram showing the population distribution.
    b. Locate the value of the population mean in your sketch, and make an estimate of the standard deviation (as done in Example 4.2).
    c. Compute SS, variance, and standard deviation for the population. (How well does your estimate compare with the actual value of σ?)

27. A recent study reports that older adults who got regular physical exercise (as measured by a pedometer) experienced fewer symptoms of depression, even when tested 2 years later (Fukukawa, Nakashima, Tsubio, Kozakai, Doyo, Naoakira, Ando, & Shimokata, 2004). Following are hypothetical data similar to the results obtained in this study.
    a. Calculate the mean and standard deviation for each group of scores.
    b. Based on the statistics from part a, does there appear to be a difference between the two groups?

Regular Exercise	No Regular Exercise
1	5
3	4
4	6
3	3
5	5
2	7
3	6
4	6

CHAPTER

5

z-Scores: Location of Scores and Standardized Distributions

Tools You Will Need

The following items are considered essential background material for this chapter. If you doubt your knowledge of any of these items, you should review the appropriate chapter and section before proceeding.

- The mean (Chapter 3)
- The standard deviation (Chapter 4)
- Basic algebra (math review, Appendix A)

5.1   INTRODUCTION TO *z*-SCORES

In the previous two chapters, we introduced the concepts of the mean and the standard deviation as methods for describing an entire distribution of scores. Now we will shift attention to the individual scores within a distribution. In this chapter, we introduce a statistical technique that uses the mean and the standard deviation to transform each score (*X* value) into a *z-score* or a *standard score*. The purpose of *z*-scores, or standard scores, is to identify and describe the exact location of every score in a distribution.

The following example demonstrates why *z*-scores are useful and introduces the general concept of transforming *X* values into *z*-scores.

E X A M P L E   5 . 1   Suppose you received a score of $X = 76$ on a statistics exam. How did you do? It should be clear that you need more information to predict your grade. Your score of $X = 76$ could be one of the best scores in the class, or it might be the lowest score in the distribution. To find the location of your score, you must have information about the other scores in the distribution. It would be useful, for example, to know the mean for the class. If the mean were $\mu = 70$, you would be in a much better position than if the mean were $\mu = 85$. Obviously, your position relative to the rest of the class depends on the mean. However, the mean by itself is not sufficient to tell you the exact location of your score. Suppose you know that the mean for the statistics exam is $\mu = 70$ and your score is $X = 76$. At this point, you know that your score is six points above the mean, but you still do not know exactly where it is located. Six points may be a relatively big distance and you may have one of the highest scores in the class, or six points may be a relatively small distance and you are only slightly above the average. Figure 5.1 shows two possible distributions of exam scores. Both distributions have a mean of $\mu = 70$, but for one distribution, the standard deviation is $\sigma = 3$, and for the other, $\sigma = 12$. Note that the relative location of $X = 76$ is very

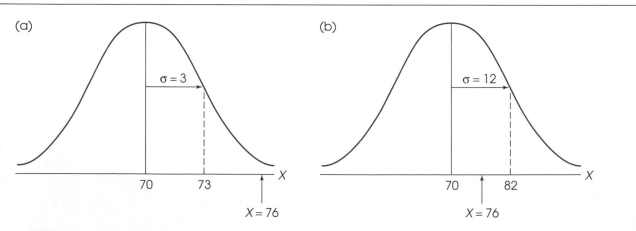

FIGURE 5.1

Two distributions of exam scores. For both distributions, $\mu = 70$, but for one distribution, $\sigma = 3$, and for the other, $\sigma = 12$. The position of $X = 76$ is very different for these two distributions.

different for these two distributions. When the standard deviation is $\sigma = 3$, your score of $X = 76$ is in the extreme right-hand tail, one of the highest scores in the distribution. However, in the other distribution, where $\sigma = 12$, your score is only slightly above average. Thus, the relative location of your score within the distribution depends on the standard deviation as well as the mean.

The purpose of the preceding example is to demonstrate that a score *by itself* does not necessarily provide much information about its position within a distribution. These original, unchanged scores that are the direct result of measurement are often called *raw scores*. To make raw scores more meaningful, they are often transformed into new values that contain more information. This transformation is one purpose for *z*-scores. In particular, we transform X values into *z*-scores so that the resulting *z*-scores tell exactly where the original scores are located.

A second purpose for *z*-scores is to *standardize* an entire distribution. A common example of a standardized distribution is the distribution of IQ scores. Although there are several different tests for measuring IQ, the tests usually are standardized so that they have a mean of 100 and a standard deviation of 15. Because all the different tests are standardized, it is possible to understand and compare IQ scores even though they come from different tests. For example, we all understand that an IQ score of 95 is a little below average, *no matter which IQ test was used*. Similarly, an IQ of 145 is extremely high, *no matter which IQ test was used*. In general terms, the process of standardizing takes different distributions and makes them equivalent. The advantage of this process is that it is possible to compare distributions even though they may have been quite different before standardization.

In summary, the process of transforming X values into *z*-scores serves two useful purposes:

1. Each *z*-score will tell the exact location of the original X value within the distribution.

2. The *z*-scores will form a standardized distribution that can be directly compared to other distributions that also have been transformed into *z*-scores.

Each of these purposes will be discussed in the following sections.

5.2   *z*-SCORES AND LOCATION IN A DISTRIBUTION

One of the primary purposes of a *z*-score is to describe the exact location of a score within a distribution. The *z*-score accomplishes this goal by transforming each X value into a signed number ($+$ or $-$) so that

1. The *sign* tells whether the score is located above ($+$) or below ($-$) the mean, and

2. The *number* tells the distance between the score and the mean in terms of the number of standard deviations.

Thus, in a distribution of IQ scores with $\mu = 100$ and $\sigma = 15$, a score of $X = 130$ would be transformed into $z = +2.00$. The *z* value indicates that the score is located above the mean ($+$) by a distance of 2 standard deviations (30 points).

DEFINITION

A **z-score** specifies the precise location of each *X* value within a distribution. The sign of the *z*-score (+ or −) signifies whether the score is above the mean (positive) or below the mean (negative). The numerical value of the *z*-score specifies the distance from the mean by counting the number of standard deviations between *X* and μ.

Notice that a *z*-score always consists of two parts: a sign (+ or −) and a magnitude. Both parts are necessary to describe completely where a raw score is located within a distribution.

Whenever you are working with *z*-scores, you should imagine or draw a picture similar to Figure 5.2. Although you should realize that not all distributions are normal, we will use the normal shape as an example when showing *z*-scores.

Figure 5.2 shows a population distribution with various positions identified by their *z*-score values. Notice that all *z*-scores above the mean are positive and all *z*-scores below the mean are negative. The sign of a *z*-score tells you immediately whether the score is located above or below the mean. Also, note that a *z*-score of *z* = +1.00 corresponds to a position exactly 1 standard deviation above the mean. A *z*-score of *z* = +2.00 is always located exactly 2 standard deviations above the mean. The numerical value of the *z*-score tells you the number of standard deviations from the mean. Finally, you should notice that Figure 5.2 does not give any specific values for the population mean or the standard deviation. The locations identified by *z*-scores are the same for *all distributions,* no matter what mean or standard deviation the distributions may have.

Now we can return to the two distributions shown in Figure 5.1 and use a *z*-score to describe the position of *X* = 76 within each distribution as follows:

In Figure 5.1(a), the score *X* = 76 corresponds to a *z*-score of *z* = +2.00. That is, the score is located above the mean by exactly 2 standard deviations.

In Figure 5.1(b), the score *X* = 76 corresponds to a *z*-score of *z* = +0.50. In this distribution, the score is located above the mean by exactly $\frac{1}{2}$ standard deviation.

FIGURE 5.2

The relationship between *z*-score values and locations in a population distribution.

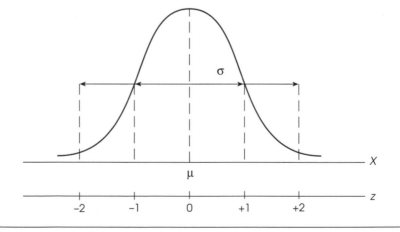

LEARNING CHECK

1. A negative *z*-score always indicates a location below the mean. (True or false?)

2. What *z*-score value identifies each of the following locations in a distribution?

   a. Above the mean by 2 standard deviations

   b. Below the mean by $\frac{1}{2}$ standard deviation

    c. Above the mean by $\frac{1}{4}$ standard deviation

    d. Below the mean by 3 standard deviations

3. For a population with $\mu = 50$ and $\sigma = 10$, find the z-score for each of the following scores:

    a. $X = 55$ **b.** $X = 40$ **c.** $X = 30$

4. For a population with $\mu = 50$ and $\sigma = 10$, find the X value corresponding to each of the following z-scores:

    a. $z = +1.00$ **b.** $z = -0.50$ **c.** $z = +2.00$

ANSWERS
1. True
2. a. $z = +2$ **b.** $z = -\frac{1}{2}$ or -0.50 **c.** $z = +\frac{1}{4}$ or $+0.25$ **d.** $z = -3$
3. a. $z = +0.50$ **b.** $z = -1.00$ **c.** $z = -2.00$
4. a. $X = 60$ **b.** $X = 45$ **c.** $X = 70$

THE z-SCORE FORMULA

The z-score definition is adequate for transforming back and forth from X values to z-scores as long as the arithmetic is easy to do in your head. For more complicated values, it is best to have an equation to help structure the calculations. Fortunately, the relationship between X values and z-scores can be easily expressed in a formula. The formula for transforming scores into z-scores is

$$z = \frac{X - \mu}{\sigma} \tag{5.1}$$

The numerator of the equation, $X - \mu$, is a *deviation score* (Chapter 4, page 89); it measures the distance in points between X and μ and indicates whether X is located above or below the mean. The deviation score is then divided by σ because we want the z-score to measure distance in terms of standard deviation units. The formula performs exactly the same arithmetic that is used with the z-score definition, and it provides a structured equation to organize the calculations when the numbers are more difficult. The following examples demonstrate the use of the z-score formula.

EXAMPLE 5.2

A distribution of scores has a mean of $\mu = 100$ and a standard deviation of $\sigma = 10$. What z-score corresponds to a score of $X = 120$ in this distribution?

According to the definition, the z-score will have a value of $+2$ because the score is located above the mean by exactly 2 standard deviations. Using the z-score formula, we obtain

$$z = \frac{X - \mu}{\sigma} = \frac{120 - 100}{10} = \frac{20}{10} = 2.00$$

The formula produces exactly the same result that is obtained using the z-score definition.

EXAMPLE 5.3

A distribution of scores has a mean of $\mu = 86$ and a standard deviation of $\sigma = 7$. What z-score corresponds to a score of $X = 95$ in this distribution?

Note that this problem is not particularly easy, especially if you try to use the z-score definition and perform the calculations in your head. However, the z-score formula organizes the numbers and allows you to finish the final arithmetic with your calculator. Using the formula, we obtain

$$z = \frac{X - \mu}{\sigma} = \frac{95 - 86}{7} = \frac{9}{7} = 1.29$$

According to the formula, a score of $X = 95$ corresponds to $z = 1.29$. The z-score indicates a location that is above the mean (positive) by slightly more than $1\frac{1}{4}$ standard deviations.

DETERMINING A RAW SCORE (X) FROM A z-SCORE

Although the z-score equation (Formula 5.1) works well for transforming X values into z-scores, it can be awkward when you are trying to work in the opposite direction and change z-scores back into X values. In general it is easier to use the definition of a z-score, rather than a formula, when you are changing z-scores into X values. Remember, the z-score describes exactly where the score is located by identifying the direction and distance from the mean. It is possible, however, to express this definition as a formula, and we will use a sample problem to demonstrate how the formula can be created.

> For a distribution with a mean of $\mu = 60$ and a standard deviation of $\sigma = 5$, what X value corresponds to a z-score of $z = -2.00$?

To solve this problem, we will use the z-score definition and carefully monitor the step-by-step process. The value of the z-score indicates that X is located 2 standard deviations below the mean. Thus, the first step in the calculation is to determine the distance corresponding to 2 standard deviations. This distance is obtained by multiplying the z-score value (-2) by the standard deviation value (5). In symbols,

$$z\sigma = (-2)(5) = -10 \text{ points}$$

(Our score is located below the mean by 10 points.)

The next step is to start at the mean and go down by 10 points to find the value of X. In symbols,

$$X = \mu - 10 = 60 - 10 = 50$$

The two steps can be combined to form a single formula:

$$X = \mu + z\sigma \tag{5.2}$$

Note that the value of $z\sigma$ is the *deviation* of X. In the example, this value was -10, or 10 points below the mean. Formula 5.2 simply combines the mean and the deviation from the mean to determine the exact value of X.

Finally, you should realize that Formula 5.1 and Formula 5.2 are actually two different versions of the same equation. If you begin with either formula and use algebra to shuffle the terms around, you will soon end up with the other formula. We will leave this as an exercise for those who want to try it.

OTHER RELATIONSHIPS BETWEEN z, X, μ, AND σ

In most cases, we simply transform scores (X values) into z-scores, or change z-scores back into X values. However, you should realize that a z-score establishes a relationship between the score, the mean, and the standard deviation. This relationship can be used to answer a variety of different questions about scores and the distributions in which they are located. The following two examples demonstrate some possibilities.

EXAMPLE 5.4   In a population with a mean of $\mu = 65$, a score of $X = 59$ corresponds to $z = -2.00$. What is the standard deviation for the population?

To answer the question, we begin with the *z*-score value. A *z*-score of -2.00 indicates that the corresponding score is located below the mean by a distance of 2 standard deviations. By simple subtraction, you can also determine that the score ($X = 59$) is located below the mean ($\mu = 65$) by a distance of 6 points. Thus, 2 standard deviations correspond to a distance of 6 points, which means that 1 standard deviation must be $\sigma = 3$.

EXAMPLE 5.5   In a population with a standard deviation of $\sigma = 4$, a score of $X = 33$ corresponds to $z = +1.50$. What is the mean for the population?

Again, we begin with the *z*-score value. In this case, a *z*-score of $+1.50$ indicates that the score is located above the mean by a distance corresponding to 1.50 standard deviations. With a standard deviation of $\sigma = 4$, this distance is $(1.50)(4) = 6$ points. Thus, the score is located 6 points above the mean. The score is $X = 33$, so the mean must be $\mu = 27$.

LEARNING CHECK

1. A distribution of scores has a mean of $\mu = 80$ and a standard deviation of $\sigma = 12$. Find the *z*-score value corresponding to each of the following scores. *Note:* You may use the *z*-score definition or Formula 5.1 to determine these values.

    a. $X = 98$ **b.** $X = 86$ **c.** $X = 77$ **d.** $X = 75$

2. A distribution of scores has a mean of $\mu = 80$ and a standard deviation of $\sigma = 12$. Find the X value corresponding to each of the following *z*-scores. *Note:* You may use the *z*-score definition or Formula 5.2 to determine these values.

    a. $z = -1.25$ **b.** $z = 2.50$ **c.** $z = -0.75$ **d.** $z = 1.00$

3. In a population with a mean of $\mu = 55$, a score of $X = 65$ corresponds to $z = 2.00$. What is the standard deviation for the population?

4. In a population with a standard deviation of $\sigma = 10$, a score of $X = 30$ corresponds to $z = -0.50$. What is the mean for the population?

ANSWERS

1. **a.** $z = 1.50$ **b.** $z = 0.50$ **c.** $z = -0.25$ **d.** $z = -0.42$

2. **a.** $X = 65$ **b.** $X = 110$ **c.** $X = 71$ **d.** $X = 92$

3. $\sigma = 5$

4. $\mu = 35$

5.3   USING *z*-SCORES TO STANDARDIZE A DISTRIBUTION

It is possible to transform every X value in a distribution into a corresponding *z*-score. The result of this process is that the entire distribution of X values is transformed into a distribution of *z*-scores (Figure 5.3). The new distribution of *z*-scores has characteristics that make the *z-score transformation* a very useful tool. Specifically, if every X value is transformed into a *z*-score, then the distribution of *z*-scores will have the following properties:

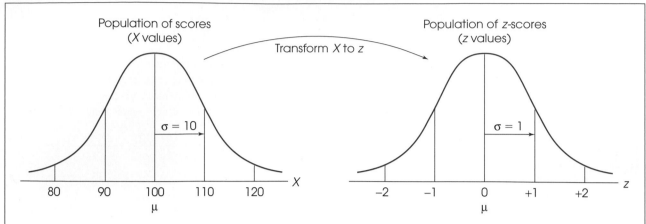

FIGURE 5.3

An entire population of scores is transformed into z-scores. The transformation does not change the shape of the population, but the mean is transformed into a value of 0 and the standard deviation is transformed to a value of 1.

    1. Shape. The shape of the z-score distribution will be the same as the original distribution of raw scores. If the original distribution is negatively skewed, for example, then the z-score distribution will also be negatively skewed. If the original distribution is normal, the distribution of z-scores will also be normal. Transforming raw scores into z-scores does not change anyone's position in the distribution. For example, any raw score that is above the mean by 1 standard deviation will be transformed to a z-score of +1.00, which is still above the mean by 1 standard deviation. Transforming a distribution from X values to z values does not move scores from one position to another; the procedure simply relabels each score (see Figure 5.3). Because each individual score stays in its same position within the distribution, the overall shape of the distribution does not change.

    2. The Mean. The z-score distribution will *always* have a mean of zero. In Figure 5.3, the original distribution of X values has a mean of $\mu = 100$. When this value, $X = 100$, is transformed into a z-score, the result is

$$z = \frac{X - \mu}{\sigma} = \frac{100 - 100}{10} = 0$$

Thus, the original population mean is transformed into a value of zero in the z-score distribution. The fact that the z-score distribution has a mean of zero makes it easy to identify locations. Recall from the definition of z-scores that all positive values are above the mean and all negative values are below the mean. A value of zero makes the mean a convenient reference point.

    3. The Standard Deviation. The distribution of z-scores will *always* have a standard deviation of 1. In Figure 5.3, the original distribution of X values has $\mu = 100$ and $\sigma = 10$. In this distribution, a value of $X = 110$ is above the mean by exactly 10 points or 1 standard deviation. When $X = 110$ is transformed, it becomes $z = +1.00$, which is above the mean by exactly 1 point in the z-score distribution. Thus, the standard deviation corresponds to a 10-point distance in the X distribution and is trans-

FIGURE 5.4

Following a z-score transformation, the X-axis is relabeled in z-score units. The distance that is equivalent to 1 standard deviation on the X-axis (σ = 10 points in this example) corresponds to 1 point on the z-score scale.

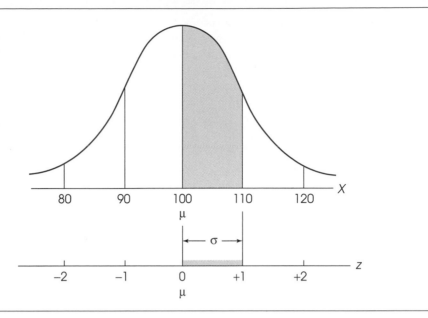

formed into a 1-point distance in the z-score distribution. The advantage of having a standard deviation of 1 is that the numerical value of a z-score is exactly the same as the number of standard deviations from the mean. For example, a z-score value of 2 is exactly 2 standard deviations from the mean.

In Figure 5.3, we showed the z-score transformation as a process that changed a distribution of X values into a new distribution of z-scores. In fact, there is no need to create a whole new distribution. Instead, you can think of the z-score transformation as simply *relabeling* the values along the X-axis. That is, after a z-score transformation, you still have the same distribution, but now each individual is labeled with a z-score instead of an X value. Figure 5.4 demonstrates this concept with a single distribution that has two sets of labels: the X values along one line and the corresponding z-scores along another line. Notice that the mean for the distribution of z-scores is zero and the standard deviation is 1.

When *any* distribution (with any mean or standard deviation) is transformed into z-scores, the resulting distribution will always have a mean of $\mu = 0$ and a standard deviation of $\sigma = 1$. Because all z-score distributions have the same mean and the same standard deviation, the z-score distribution is called a *standardized distribution*.

DEFINITION

A **standardized distribution** is composed of scores that have been transformed to create predetermined values for μ and σ. Standardized distributions are used to make dissimilar distributions comparable.

A z-score distribution is an example of a standardized distribution with $\mu = 0$ and $\sigma = 1$. That is, when any distribution (with any mean or standard deviation) is transformed into z-scores, the transformed distribution will always have $\mu = 0$ and $\sigma = 1$. The advantage of standardizing is that it makes it possible to compare different scores or different individuals even though they may come from completely different distributions.

USING *z*-SCORES FOR MAKING COMPARISONS

When two scores come from different distributions, it is impossible to make any direct comparison between them. Suppose, for example, Bob received a score of $X = 60$ on a psychology exam and a score of $X = 56$ on a biology test. For which course should Bob expect the better grade?

Because the scores come from two different distributions, you cannot make any direct comparison. Without additional information, it is even impossible to determine whether Bob is above or below the mean in either distribution. Before you can begin to make comparisons, you must know the values for the mean and standard deviation for each distribution. Suppose the biology scores had $\mu = 48$ and $\sigma = 4$, and the psychology scores had $\mu = 50$ and $\sigma = 10$. With this new information, you could sketch the two distributions, locate Bob's score in each distribution, and compare the two locations.

Instead of drawing the two distributions to determine where Bob's two scores are located, we simply can compute the two *z*-scores to find the two locations. For psychology, Bob's *z*-score is

Be sure to use the μ and σ values for the distribution to which X belongs.

$$z = \frac{X - \mu}{\sigma} = \frac{60 - 50}{10} = \frac{10}{10} = +1.0$$

For biology, Bob's *z*-score is

$$z = \frac{56 - 48}{4} = \frac{8}{4} = +2.0$$

Note that Bob's *z*-score for biology is $+2.0$, which means that his test score is 2 standard deviations above the class mean. On the other hand, his *z*-score is $+1.0$ for psychology, or 1 standard deviation above the mean. In terms of relative class standing, Bob is doing much better in the biology class.

Notice that we cannot compare Bob's two exam scores ($X = 60$ and $X = 56$) because the scores come from different distributions with different means and standard deviations. However, we can compare the two *z*-scores because all distributions of *z*-scores have the same mean ($\mu = 0$) and the same standard deviation ($\sigma = 1$).

LEARNING CHECK

1. A normal-shaped distribution with $\mu = 50$ and $\sigma = 8$ is transformed into *z*-scores. Describe the shape, mean, and standard deviation for the *z*-score distribution.

2. Why is it possible to compare scores from different distributions after the distributions have been transformed into *z*-scores?

3. A set of mathematics exam scores has $\mu = 70$ and $\sigma = 8$. A set of English exam scores has $\mu = 74$ and $\sigma = 16$. For which exam would a score of $X = 78$ have a higher standing?

4. What is the advantage of having $\mu = 0$ for a distribution of *z*-scores?

ANSWERS

1. The *z*-score distribution would be normal (same shape) with $\mu = 0$ and $\sigma = 1$.

2. Comparison is possible because the two distributions will have the same mean ($\mu = 0$) and the same standard deviation ($\sigma = 1$) after transformation.

3. $z = 1.00$ for the mathematics exam, which is a higher standing than $z = 0.25$ for the English exam.

4. With $\mu = 0$, you know immediately that any positive value is above the mean and any negative value is below the mean.

5.4   OTHER STANDARDIZED DISTRIBUTIONS BASED ON z-SCORES

TRANSFORMING z-SCORES TO A DISTRIBUTION WITH A PREDETERMINED μ AND σ

Although z-score distributions have distinct advantages, many people find them cumbersome because they contain negative values and decimals. For this reason, it is common to standardize a distribution by transforming the scores into a new distribution with a predetermined mean and standard deviation that are whole round numbers. The goal is to create a new (standardized) distribution that has "simple" values for the mean and standard deviation but does not change any individual's location within the distribution. Standardized scores of this type are frequently used in psychological or educational testing. For example, raw scores of the Scholastic Aptitude Test (SAT) are transformed to a standardized distribution that has $\mu = 500$ and $\sigma = 100$. For intelligence tests, raw scores are frequently converted to standard scores that have a mean of 100 and a standard deviation of 15. Because most IQ tests are standardized so that they have the same mean and standard deviation, it is possible to compare IQ scores even though they may come from different tests.

The procedure for standardizing a distribution to create new values for μ and σ involves two-steps:

1. The original raw scores are transformed into z-scores.

2. The z-scores are then transformed into new X values so that the specific μ and σ are attained.

This procedure ensures that each individual has exactly the same z-score location in the new distribution as in the original distribution. The following example demonstrates the standardization procedure.

EXAMPLE 5.6   An instructor gives an exam to a psychology class. For this exam, the distribution of raw scores has a mean of $\mu = 57$ with $\sigma = 14$. The instructor would like to simplify the distribution by transforming all scores into a new, standardized distribution with $\mu = 50$ and $\sigma = 10$. To demonstrate this process, we will consider what happens to two specific students: Maria, who has a raw score of $X = 64$ in the original distribution; and Joe, whose original raw score is $X = 43$.

STEP 1   Transform each of the original raw scores into z-scores. For Maria, $X = 64$, so her z-score is

$$z = \frac{X - \mu}{\sigma} = \frac{64 - 57}{14} = +0.5$$

Remember: The values of μ and σ are for the distribution from which X was taken.

For Joe, $X = 43$, and his z-score is

$$z = \frac{X - \mu}{\sigma} = \frac{43 - 57}{14} = -1.0$$

STEP 2   Change each z-score into an X value in the new standardized distribution which has a mean of $\mu = 50$ and a standard deviation of $\sigma = 10$.

Maria's z-score, $z = +0.50$, indicates that she is located above the mean by $\frac{1}{2}$ standard deviation. In the new, standardized distribution, this location corresponds to $X = 55$ (above the mean by 5 points).

Joe's *z*-score, $z = -1.00$, indicates that he is located below the mean by exactly 1 standard deviation. In the new distribution, this location corresponds to $X = 40$ (below the mean by 10 points).

The results of this two-step transformation process are summarized in Table 5.1. Note that Joe, for example, has exactly the same *z*-score ($z = -1.00$) in both the original distribution and the new standardized distribution. This means that Joe's position relative to the other students in the class has not changed.

TABLE 5.1

A demonstration of how two individual scores are changed when a distribution is standardized. See Example 5.6.

	Original Scores $\mu = 57$ and $\sigma = 14$	*z*-Score Location	Standardized Scores $\mu = 50$ and $\sigma = 10$
Maria	$X = 64$ $\longrightarrow$	$z = +0.50$ $\longrightarrow$	$X = 55$
Joe	$X = 43$ $\longrightarrow$	$z = -1.00$ $\longrightarrow$	$X = 40$

Figure 5.5 provides another demonstration of the concept that standardizing a distribution does not change the individual positions within the distribution. The figure shows the original exam scores from Example 5.6, with a mean of $\mu = 57$ and a standard deviation of $\sigma = 14$. In the original distribution, Joe is located at a score of $X = 43$. In addition to the original scores, we have included a second scale showing the *z*-score value for each location in the distribution. In terms of *z*-scores, Joe is located at a value of $z = -1.00$. Finally, we have added a third scale showing the *standardized scores* where the mean is $\mu = 50$ and the standard deviation is $\sigma = 10$. For the standardized scores, Joe is located at $X = 40$. Note that Joe is always in the same place in

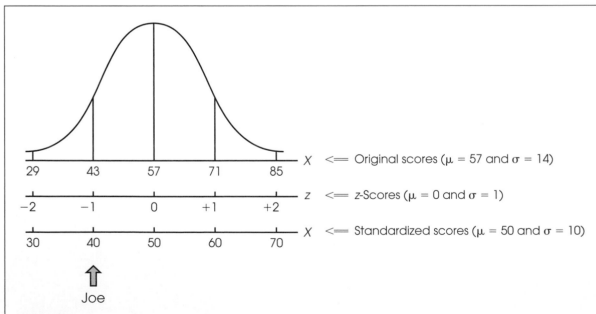

FIGURE 5.5

The distribution of exam scores from Example 5.6. The original distribution was standardized to produce a new distribution with $\mu = 50$ and $\sigma = 10$. Note that each individual is identified by an original score, a *z*-score, and a new, standardized score. For example, Joe has an original score of 43, a *z*-score of -1.00, and a standardized score of 40.

the distribution. The only thing that changes is the number that is assigned to Joe: For the original scores, Joe is at 43; for the z-scores, Joe is at -1.00; and for the standardized scores, Joe is at 40.

LEARNING CHECK

1. A population has $\mu = 37$ and $\sigma = 2$. If this distribution is transformed into a new distribution with $\mu = 100$ and $\sigma = 20$, what new values will be obtained for each of the following scores: 35, 36, 37, 38, 39?

2. For the following population, $\mu = 7$ and $\sigma = 4$. The scores are 2, 4, 6, 10, 13.
   a. Transform this distribution so $\mu = 50$ and $\sigma = 20$.
   b. Compute μ and σ for the new population. (You should obtain $\mu = 50$ and $\sigma = 20$.)

ANSWERS

1. The five scores 35, 36, 37, 38, and 39 are transformed into 80, 90, 100, 110, and 120, respectively.

2. **a.** The original scores, 2, 4, 6, 10, and 13, are transformed into 25, 35, 45, 65, and 80, respectively.
   b. The new scores add up to $\Sigma X = 250$, so the mean is $\frac{250}{5} = 50$. The *SS* for the transformed scores is 2000, the variance is 400, and the new standard deviation is 20.

5.5   COMPUTING z-SCORES FOR SAMPLES

Although z-scores are most commonly used in the context of a population, the same principles can be used to identify individual locations within a sample. The definition of a z-score is the same for a sample as for a population, provided that you use the sample mean and the sample standard deviation to specify each z-score location. Thus, for a sample, each *X* value is transformed into a z-score so that

1. The sign of the z-score indicates whether the *X* value is above (+) or below (−) the sample mean, and

2. The numerical value of the z-score identifies the distance between the score and the sample mean in terms of the sample standard deviation.

Expressed as a formula, each X value in a sample can be transformed into a z-score as follows:

$$z = \frac{X - M}{s}$$

If an entire sample is transformed into z-scores, the distribution of z-scores will have the same characteristics that exist for a population. Specifically, the entire sample of z-scores will have a mean of $M_z = 0$ and a standard deviation of $s_z = 1$. Note that the set of z-scores is considered to be a sample (just like the set of *X* values) and the sample formulas must be used to compute variance and standard deviation. The following example demonstrates the process of transforming scores in a sample into z-scores.

EXAMPLE 5.7   We begin with a sample of $n = 5$ scores: 0, 2, 4, 4, 5. With a few simple calculations, you should be able to verify that the sample mean is $M = 3$, with $SS = 16$, $s^2 = 4$, and $s = 2$. Using the sample mean and the sample standard deviation, we can convert each X value into a z-score as shown in the following table.

X	z
0	−1.50
2	−0.50
4	+0.50
4	+0.50
5	+1.00

Notice that the set of z-scores is considered to be a sample and the variance is computed using the sample formula with $df = n - 1$.

Again, a few simple calculations demonstrate that the sum of the z-score values is $\Sigma z = 0$, so the mean is $M_z = 0$. Also, the z-scores have $SS = 4.00$, so the variance for the sample of z-scores is $SS/(n - 1) = \frac{4}{4} = 1.00$ and the standard deviation is $s_z = \sqrt{1.00} = 1.00$. As always, the distribution of z-scores has a mean of 0 and a standard deviation of 1.

5.6 LOOKING AHEAD TO INFERENTIAL STATISTICS

Recall that inferential statistics are techniques that use the information from samples to answer questions about populations. In later chapters, we will use inferential statistics to help interpret the results from a research study. A typical research study begins with a question about how a treatment will affect the individuals in a population. Because it is usually impossible to study an entire population, the researcher selects a sample and administers the treatment to the individuals in the sample. To evaluate the effect of the treatment, the researcher simply compares the sample with the original population (Figure 5.6). If the individuals in the sample are noticeably different from the individ-

FIGURE 5.6

A diagram of a research study. The goal of the study is to evaluate the effect of a treatment. A sample is selected from the population and the treatment is administered to the sample. If, after treatment, the individuals in the sample are noticeably different from the individuals in the original population, then we have evidence that the treatment does have an effect.

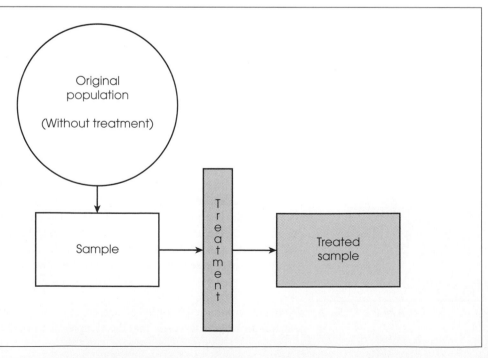

uals in the original population, the researcher has evidence that the treatment has had an effect. On the other hand, if the sample is not noticeably different from the original population, it would appear that the treatment has no effect.

Notice that the interpretation of the research results depends on whether the sample is *noticeably different* from the population. One technique for deciding whether or not a sample is noticeably different is to use *z*-scores. For example, an individual with a *z*-score near 0 is located in the center of the population and would be considered to be a fairly typical or representative individual. However, an individual with an extreme *z*-score, beyond +2.00 or −2.00 for example, would be considered "noticeably different" from most of the individuals in the population (Figure 5.7). Thus, we can use *z*-scores to help decide whether the treatment has caused a change. Specifically, if the individuals who receive the treatment in a research study tend to have extreme *z*-scores, we can conclude that the treatment does appear to have an effect. The following example demonstrates this process.

EXAMPLE 5.8   A researcher is evaluating the effect of a new growth hormone. It is known that regular adult rats weigh an average of $\mu = 400$ grams. The weights vary from rat to rat, and the distribution of weights is normal with a standard deviation of $\sigma = 20$ grams. The population distribution is shown in Figure 5.7. The researcher selects one newborn rat and injects the rat with the growth hormone. When the rat reaches maturity, it is weighed to determine whether there is any evidence that the hormone has an effect.

First, assume that the hormone-injected rat weighs $X = 418$ grams. Although this is more than the average nontreated rat ($\mu = 400$ grams), is it convincing evidence that the hormone has effect? If you look at the distribution in Figure 5.7, you should realize that a rat weighing 418 grams is not noticeably different from the regular rats that did not receive any hormone injection. Specifically, our injected rat would be located near the center of the distribution, with a *z*-score of

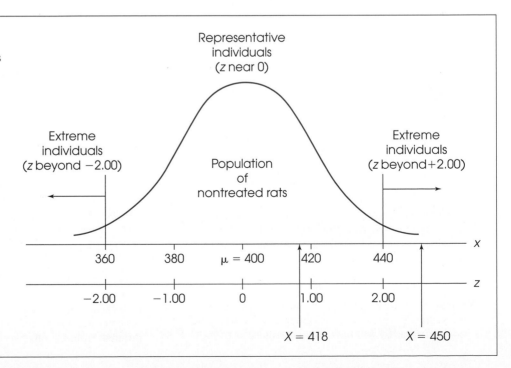

FIGURE 5.7

The distribution of weights for the population of adult rats. Note that individuals with *z*-scores near 0 are typical or representative. However, individuals with *z*-scores beyond +2.00 or −2.00 are extreme and noticeably different from most of the others in the distribution.

Representative individuals (*z* near 0)

Extreme individuals (*z* beyond −2.00)

Extreme individuals (*z* beyond +2.00)

Population of nontreated rats

360   380 $\mu = 400$ 420   440   *x*

−2.00   −1.00   0   1.00   2.00   *z*

$X = 418$ $X = 450$

$$z = \frac{X - \mu}{\sigma} = \frac{418 - 400}{20} = \frac{18}{20} = 0.90$$

Because the injected rat still looks the same as a regular, nontreated rat, the conclusion is that the hormone does not appear to have an effect.

Now, assume that our injected rat weighs $X = 450$ grams as an adult. In the distribution of regular rats (Figure 5.7), this animal would have a *z*-score of

$$z = \frac{X - \mu}{\sigma} = \frac{450 - 400}{20} = \frac{50}{20} = 2.50$$

In this case, the hormone-injected rat is substantially bigger than most ordinary rats, and it would be reasonable to conclude that the hormone does have an effect on weight.

In the preceding example, we used *z*-scores to help interpret the results obtained from a sample. Specifically, if the individuals who receive the treatment in a research study have extreme *z*-scores compared to those who do not receive the treatment, we can conclude that the treatment does appear to have an effect. The example, however, used rather vague definitions to determine which *z*-score values are noticeably different and which are not. Although it is reasonable to describe individuals with *z*-scores near 0 as "highly representative" of the population, and individuals with *z*-scores beyond ± 2.00 as "extreme," you should realize that these *z*-score boundaries are arbitrary numbers. In the following chapter we will introduce *probability*, which will give us a rationale for deciding exactly where to set the boundaries.

SUMMARY

1. Each X value can be transformed into a *z*-score that specifies the exact location of X within the distribution. The sign of the *z*-score indicates whether the location is above (positive) or below (negative) the mean. The numerical value of the *z*-score specifies the number of standard deviations between X and μ.

2. The *z*-score formula is used to transform X values into *z*-scores:

$$z = \frac{X - \mu}{\sigma}$$

3. To transform *z*-scores back into X values, it usually is easier to use the *z*-score definition rather than a formula. However, the *z*-score formula can be transformed into a new equation,

$$X = \mu + z\sigma$$

4. When an entire distribution of X values is transformed into *z*-scores, the result is a distribution of *z*-scores. The *z*-score distribution will have the same shape as the

distribution of raw scores, and it always will have a mean of 0 and a standard deviation of 1.

5. When comparing raw scores from different distributions, it is necessary to standardize the distributions with a *z*-score transformation. The distributions will then be comparable because they will have the same parameters ($\mu = 0$, $\sigma = 1$). In practice, it is necessary to transform only those raw scores that are being compared.

6. In certain situations, such as psychological testing, a distribution may be standardized by converting the original X values into *z*-scores and then converting the *z*-scores into a new distribution of scores with predetermined values for the mean and the standard deviation.

7. In inferential statistics, *z*-scores provide an objective method for determining how well a specific score represents its population. A *z*-score near 0 indicates that the score is close to the population mean and therefore is representative. A *z*-score beyond $+2.00$ (or -2.00) indicates that the score is extreme and is noticeably different from the other scores in the distribution.

KEY TERMS

raw score	deviation score	standardized distribution	standardized score
z-score	z-score transformation		

RESOURCES

There are a tutorial quiz and other learning exercises for Chapter 5 at the Wadsworth website, www.thomsonedu.com/psychology/gravetter. The site also includes a workshop titled z-scores that examines the basic concepts and calculations underlying z-scores. See page 27 for more information about accessing items on the website.

WebTUTOR

For those using WebTutor along with this book, there is a WebTutor section corresponding to this chapter. The WebTutor contains a brief summary of Chapter 5, hints for learning about z-scores, cautions about common errors, and sample exam items including solutions.

SPSS

General instructions for using SPSS are presented in Appendix D. Following are detailed instructions for using SPSS to **Transform X Values into z-Scores for a Sample.**

Data Entry

1. Enter all of the scores in one column of the data editor, probably VAR00001.

Data Analysis

1. Click **Analyze** on the tool bar, select **Descriptive Statistics,** and click on **Descriptives.**
2. Highlight the column label for the set of scores (VAR0001) in the left box and click the arrow to move it into the **Variable** box.
3. Click the box to **Save standardized values as variables** at the bottom of the **Descriptives** screen.
4. Click **OK.**

SPSS Output

The program will produce the usual output display listing the number of scores (N), the maximum and minimum scores, the mean, and the standard deviation. However, if you go back to the Data Editor (use the tool bar at the bottom of the screen), SPSS will have produced a new column showing the z-score corresponding to each of the original X values.

Caution: The SPSS program computes the *z*-scores using the sample standard deviation instead of the population standard deviation. For most applications, these "sample *z*-scores" serve the same purpose as regular *z*-scores; that is, they standardize the distribution so that the sample mean is zero and the sample standard deviation is one, and they identify specific locations within the sample distribution. However, if your set of scores is intended to be a population, SPSS will not produce the correct *z*-score values. You can convert the SPSS values into regular *z*-scores by multiplying each *z*-score value by the square root of $n/(n-1)$.

FOCUS ON PROBLEM SOLVING

1. When you are converting an *X* value to a *z*-score (or vice versa), do not rely entirely on the formula. You can avoid careless mistakes if you use the definition of a *z*-score (sign and numerical value) to make a preliminary estimate of the answer before you begin computations. For example, a *z*-score of $z = -0.85$ identifies a score located *below* the mean by almost 1 standard deviation. When computing the *X* value for this *z*-score, be sure that your answer is smaller than the mean, and check that the distance between *X* and μ is slightly less than the standard deviation.

2. When comparing scores from distributions that have different standard deviations, it is important to be sure that you use the correct value for σ in the *z*-score formula. Use the σ value for the distribution from which the raw score in question was taken.

3. Remember that a *z*-score specifies a relative position within the context of a specific distribution. A *z*-score is a relative value, not an absolute value. For example, a *z*-score of $z = -2.0$ does not necessarily suggest a very low raw score—it simply means that the raw score is among the lowest within that specific group.

DEMONSTRATION 5.1

TRANSFORMING *X* VALUES INTO *z*-SCORES

A distribution of scores has a mean of $\mu = 60$ with $\sigma = 12$. Find the *z*-score for $X = 75$.

STEP 1   Determine the sign of the *z*-score.
First, determine whether *X* is above or below the mean. This will determine the sign of the *z*-score. For this demonstration, *X* is larger than (above) μ, so the *z*-score will be positive.

STEP 2   Convert the distance between *X* and μ into standard deviation units.
For $X = 75$ and $\mu = 60$, the distance between *X* and μ is 15 points. With $\sigma = 12$ points, this distance corresponds to $\frac{15}{12} = 1.25$ standard deviations.

STEP 3   Combine the sign from step 1 with the numerical value from step 2.
The score is above the mean (+) by a distance of 1.25 standard deviations. Thus,

$$z = +1.25$$

STEP 4   Confirm the answer using the *z*-score formula.
For this example, $X = 75$, $\mu = 60$, and $\sigma = 12$.

$$z = \frac{X - \mu}{\sigma} = \frac{75 - 60}{12} = \frac{+15}{12} = +1.25$$

DEMONSTRATION 5.2

CONVERTING z-SCORES TO X VALUES

For a population with $\mu = 60$ and $\sigma = 12$, what is the X value corresponding to $z = -0.50$?

Notice that in this situation we know the z-score and must find X.

STEP 1   Locate X in relation to the mean.

A z-score of -0.50 indicates a location below the mean by half of a standard deviation.

STEP 2   Convert the distance from standard deviation units to points.

With $\sigma = 12$, half of a standard deviation is 6 points.

STEP 3   Identify the X value.

The value we want is located below the mean by 6 points. The mean is $\mu = 60$, so the score must be $X = 54$

PROBLEMS

1. A distribution has a standard deviation of $\sigma = 4$. Describe the location of each of the following z-scores in terms of its position relative to the mean. For example, $z = +1.00$ is a location that is four points above the mean.
   a. $z = +2.00$
   b. $z = +0.50$
   c. $z = -2.00$
   d. $z = -0.50$

2. For a population with $\mu = 50$ and $\sigma = 10$,
   a. Find the z-score for each of the following X values. (Note: You should be able to find these values using the definition of a z-score. You should not need to use a formula or do any serious calculations.)

$X = 55$	$X = 60$	$X = 75$
$X = 45$	$X = 30$	$X = 35$

   b. Find the score (X value) that corresponds to each of the following z-scores. (Again, you should be able to find these values without any formula or serious calculations.)

$z = 1.00$	$z = 0.80$	$z = 1.50$
$z = -0.50$	$z = -0.30$	$z = -1.50$

3. What information is provided by the sign $(+/-)$ of a z-score? What information is provided by the numerical value of the z-score?

4. For a population with a mean of $\mu = 100$ and a standard deviation of $\sigma = 10$,
   a. Find the z-score for each of the following X values.

$X = 105$	$X = 120$	$X = 130$
$X = 90$	$X = 85$	$X = 60$

   b. Find the score (X value) that corresponds to each of the following z-scores.

$z = -1.00$	$z = -0.50$	$z = 2.00$
$z = 0.70$	$z = 1.50$	$z = -1.50$

5. Find the X value corresponding to $z = 1.50$ for each of the following distributions.
   a. $\mu = 40$ and $\sigma = 6$
   b. $\mu = 40$ and $\sigma = 20$
   c. $\mu = 80$ and $\sigma = 4$
   d. $\mu = 80$ and $\sigma = 8$

6. A sample has a mean of $M = 40$ and a standard deviation of $s = 4$. Find the z-score for each of the following X values from this sample.

$X = 44$	$X = 42$	$X = 48$
$X = 28$	$X = 50$	$X = 46$

7. For a population with $\mu = 60$ and $\sigma = 9$, find the *z*-score for each of the following *X* values. (Note: You probably will need to use a formula and a calculator to find these values.)

$$X = 65 \qquad X = 70 \qquad X = 53$$
$$X = 48 \qquad X = 75 \qquad X = 58$$

8. Find the *z*-score corresponding to a score of $X = 60$ for each of the following distributions.
   a. $\mu = 50$ and $\sigma = 10$
   b. $\mu = 50$ and $\sigma = 5$
   c. $\mu = 70$ and $\sigma = 20$
   d. $\mu = 70$ and $\sigma = 5$

9. A population has a mean of $\mu = 40$ and a standard deviation of $\sigma = 12$.
   a. For this population, find the *z*-score for each of the following *X* values.

$$X = 43 \qquad X = 49 \qquad X = 52$$
$$X = 34 \qquad X = 28 \qquad X = 64$$

   b. For the same population, find the score (*X* value) that corresponds to each of the following *z*-scores.

$$z = 0.75 \qquad z = 1.50 \qquad z = -2.00$$
$$z = -0.25 \qquad z = -0.50 \qquad z = 1.25$$

10. A distribution has a standard deviation of $\sigma = 8$. Find the *z*-score for each of the following locations in the distribution.
   a. Above the mean by 4 points.
   b. Above the mean by 16 points.
   c. Below the mean by 8 points.
   d. Below the mean by 12 points.

11. A sample has a mean of $M = 80$ and a standard deviation of $s = 5$. For this sample, find the *X* value corresponding to each of the following *z*-scores.

$$z = 0.80 \qquad z = 1.20 \qquad z = 2.00$$
$$z = -0.40 \qquad z = -0.60 \qquad z = -1.80$$

12. For a population with a standard deviation of $\sigma = 10$, a score of $X = 44$ corresponds to $z = -0.50$. What is the population mean?

13. For a population with a mean of $\mu = 70$, a score of $X = 64$ corresponds to $z = -2.00$. What is the population standard deviation?

14. For a sample with a mean of $M = 85$, a score of $X = 90$ corresponds to $z = 0.50$. What is the sample standard deviation?

15. A score that is 4 points above the mean corresponds to a *z*-score of $z = 0.50$. What is the population standard deviation?

16. A score that is 6 points below the mean corresponds to a *z*-score of $z = -2.00$. What is the population standard deviation?

17. For a sample with a standard deviation of $s = 6$, a score of $X = 65$ corresponds to $z = 1.50$. What is the sample mean?

18. In a population of exam scores, a score of $X = 88$ corresponds to $z = +2.00$ and a score of $X = 79$ corresponds to $z = -1.00$. Find the mean and standard deviation for the population. (*Hint:* Sketch the distribution and locate the two scores on your sketch.)

19. In a distribution of scores, $X = 62$ corresponds to $z = +0.50$, and $X = 52$ corresponds to $z = -2.00$. Find the mean and standard deviation for the distribution.

20. Which of the following exam scores should lead to the better grade?
   a. A score of $X = 55$ on an exam with $\mu = 60$ and $\sigma = 5$.
   b. A score of $X = 40$ on an exam with $\mu = 50$ and $\sigma = 20$.
   Explain your answer.

21. Which of the following exam scores should lead to the better grade?
   a. A score of $X = 43$ on an exam with $\mu = 40$ and $\sigma = 2$.
   b. A score of $X = 60$ on an exam with $\mu = 50$ and $\sigma = 20$.
   Explain your answer.

22. Suppose that you have a score of $X = 75$ on an exam with $\mu = 80$. Which standard deviation would give you a better grade: $\sigma = 2$ or $\sigma = 10$?

23. Suppose that you have a score of $X = 75$ on an exam with $\mu = 70$. Which standard deviation would give you a better grade: $\sigma = 2$ or $\sigma = 10$?

24. For each of the following populations, would a score of $X = 50$ be considered a central score (near the middle of the distribution) or an extreme score (far out in the tail of the distribution)?
   a. $\mu = 45$ and $\sigma = 10$
   b. $\mu = 40$ and $\sigma = 2$
   c. $\mu = 55$ and $\sigma = 2$
   d. $\mu = 60$ and $\sigma = 20$

25. A population consists of the following $N = 6$ scores: 6, 1, 3, 4, 7, and 3.
    a. Compute μ and σ for the population.
    b. Find the z-score for each score in the population.
    c. Transform the original population into a new population of $N = 6$ scores with a mean of $\mu = 50$ and a standard deviation of $\sigma = 10$.

26. A population consists of the following $N = 5$ scores: 0, 6, 4, 3, and 12.
    a. Compute μ and σ for the population.
    b. Find the z-score for each score in the population.
    c. Transform the original population into a new population of $N = 5$ scores with a mean of $\mu = 60$ and a standard deviation of $\sigma = 8$.

27. A distribution with a mean of $\mu = 64$ and a standard deviation of $\sigma = 4$ is being transformed into a standardized distribution with $\mu = 100$ and $\sigma = 20$. Find the new, standardized score for each of the following values from the original population.
    a. $X = 60$ b. $X = 52$
    c. $X = 72$ d. $X = 66$

28. A distribution with a mean of $\mu = 38$ and a standard deviation of $\sigma = 20$ is being transformed into a standardized distribution with $\mu = 50$ and $\sigma = 10$. Find the new, standardized score for each of the following values from the original population.
    a. $X = 48$ b. $X = 40$
    c. $X = 30$ d. $X = 18$

CHAPTER

6

Probability

Tools You Will Need

The following items are considered essential background material for this chapter. If you doubt your knowledge of any of these items, you should review the appropriate chapter or section before proceeding.

- Proportions (math review, Appendix A)
  - Fractions
  - Decimals
  - Percentages
- Basic algebra (math review, Appendix A)
- Upper and lower real limits (Chapters 1 and 2)
- z-Scores (Chapter 5)

6.1 INTRODUCTION TO PROBABILITY

In Chapter 1, we introduced the idea that research studies begin with a general question about an entire population, but the actual research is conducted using a sample. In this situation, the role of inferential statistics is to use the sample data as the basis for answering questions about the population. To accomplish this goal, inferential procedures are typically built around the concept of probability. Specifically, the relationships between samples and populations are usually defined in terms of probability. Suppose, for example, you are selecting a single marble from a jar that contains 50 black and 50 white marbles. (In this example, the jar of marbles is the *population* and the single marble to be selected is the *sample*.) Although you cannot guarantee the exact outcome of your sample, it is possible to talk about the potential outcomes in terms of probabilities. In this case, you have a 50-50 chance of getting either color. Now consider another jar (population) that has 90 black and only 10 white marbles. Again, you cannot specify the exact outcome of a sample, but now you know that the sample probably will be a black marble. By knowing the makeup of a population, we can determine the probability of obtaining specific samples. In this way, probability gives us a connection between populations and samples, and this connection will be the foundation for the inferential statistics to be presented in the chapters that follow.

You may have noticed that the preceding examples begin with a population and then use probability to describe the samples that could be obtained. This is exactly backward from what we want to do with inferential statistics. Remember that the goal of inferential statistics is to begin with a sample and then answer general questions about the population. We will reach this goal in a two-stage process. In the first stage, we develop probability as a bridge from populations to samples. This stage involves identifying the types of samples that probably would be obtained from a specific population. Once this bridge is established, we simply reverse the probability rules to allow us to move from samples to populations (Figure 6.1). The process of reversing the probability relationship can be demonstrated by considering again the two jars of marbles we looked at earlier. (Jar 1 has 50 black and 50 white marbles; jar 2 has 90 black and only 10 white marbles.) This time, suppose you are blindfolded when the sample is selected and your task is to use the sample to help you to decide which jar was used. If you select a sample of $n = 4$ marbles and all are black, where did the

FIGURE 6.1

The role of probability in inferential statistics. Probability is used to predict what kind of samples are likely to be obtained from a population. Thus, probability establishes a connection between samples and populations. Inferential statistics rely on this connection when they use sample data as the basis for making conclusions about populations.

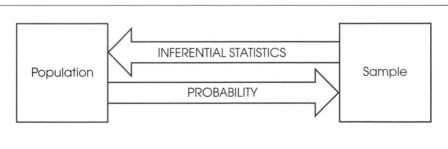

sample come from? It should be clear that it would be relatively unlikely (low probability) to obtain this sample from jar 1; in four draws, you almost certainly would get at least 1 white marble. On the other hand, this sample would have a high probability of coming from jar 2, where nearly all the marbles are black. Your decision therefore is that the sample probably came from jar 2. Note that you now are using the sample to make an inference about the population.

PROBABILITY DEFINITION

Probability is a huge topic that extends far beyond the limits of introductory statistics, and we will not attempt to examine it all here. Instead, we will concentrate on the few concepts and definitions that are needed for an introduction to inferential statistics. We begin with a relatively simple definition of probability.

D E F I N I T I O N

For a situation in which several different outcomes are possible, the **probability** for any specific outcome is defined as a fraction or a proportion of all the possible outcomes. If the possible outcomes are identified as A, B, C, D, and so on, then

$$\text{probability of } A = \frac{\text{number of outcomes classified as } A}{\text{total number of possible outcomes}}$$

For example, if you are selecting a card from a complete deck, there are 52 possible outcomes. The probability of selecting the king of hearts is $p = \frac{1}{52}$. The probability of selecting an ace is $p = \frac{4}{52}$ because there are 4 aces in the deck.

To simplify the discussion of probability, we will use a notation system that eliminates a lot of the words. The probability of a specific outcome will be expressed with a p (for probability) followed by the specific outcome in parentheses. For example, the probability of selecting a king from a deck of cards will be written as p(king). The probability of obtaining heads for a coin toss will be written as p(heads).

Note that probability is defined as a proportion, or a part of the whole. This definition makes it possible to restate any probability problem as a proportion problem. For example, the probability problem "What is the probability of selecting a king from a deck of cards?" can be restated as "What proportion of the whole deck consists of kings?" In each case, the answer is $\frac{4}{52}$, or "4 out of 52." This translation from probability to proportion may seem trivial now, but it will be a great aid when the probability problems become more complex. In most situations, we are concerned with the probability of obtaining a particular sample from a population. The terminology of *sample* and *population* will not change the basic definition of probability. For example, the whole deck of cards can be considered as a population, and the single card we select is the sample.

The definition we are using identifies probability as a fraction or a proportion. If you work directly from this definition, the probability values you obtain will be expressed as fractions. For example, if you are selecting a card at random,

$$p(\text{spade}) = \frac{13}{52} = \frac{1}{4}$$

Of if you are tossing a coin,

$$p(\text{heads}) = \frac{1}{2}$$

You should be aware that these fractions can be expressed equally well as either decimals or percentages:

If you are unsure how to convert
from fractions to decimals or
percentages, you should review
the section on proportions in the
math review, Appendix A.

$$p = \frac{1}{4} = 0.25 = 25\%$$

$$p = \frac{1}{2} = 0.50 = 50\%$$

By convention, probability values most often are expressed as decimal values. But you should realize that any of these three forms is acceptable.

You also should note that all the possible probability values are contained in a limited range. At one extreme, when an event never occurs, the probability is zero or 0%. At the other extreme, when an event always occurs, the probability is 1, or 100%. For example, suppose that you have a jar containing 10 white marbles. The probability of randomly selecting a black marble is

$$p(\text{black}) = \frac{0}{10} = 0$$

The probability of selecting a white marble is

$$p(\text{white}) = \frac{10}{10} = 1$$

RANDOM SAMPLING For the preceding definition of probability to be accurate, it is necessary that the outcomes be obtained by a process called *random sampling*.

D E F I N I T I O N

> A **random sample** requires that each individual in the population has an *equal chance* of being selected. A second requirement, necessary for many statistical formulas, states that the probabilities must *stay constant* from one selection to the next if more than one individual is selected.

Each of the two requirements for random sampling has some interesting consequences. The first ensures that there is no bias in the selection process. For a population with N individuals, each individual must have the same probability, $p = \frac{1}{N}$, of being selected. This means, for example, that you would not get a random sample of people in your city by selecting names from a yacht club membership list. Similarly, you would not get a random sample of college students by selecting individuals from your psychology classes. You also should note that the first requirement of random sampling prohibits you from applying the definition of probability to situations where the possible outcomes are not equally likely. Consider, for example, the question of whether you will win a million dollars in the lottery tomorrow. There are only two possible alternatives.

1. You will win.

2. You will not win.

However, the two alternatives are not equally likely, so you cannot conclude that the probability of winning the lottery is one out of two, or $p = \frac{1}{2}$.

The second requirement also is more interesting than may be apparent at first glance. Consider, for example, the selection of $n = 2$ cards from a complete deck. For the first draw, the probability of obtaining the jack of diamonds is

$$p(\text{jack of diamonds}) = \frac{1}{52}$$

Now, for the second draw, what is the probability of obtaining the jack of diamonds? Assuming that you still are holding the first card, there are two possibilities:

$$p(\text{jack of diamonds}) = \frac{1}{51} \text{ if the first card was not the jack of diamonds}$$

or

$$p(\text{jack of diamonds}) = 0 \text{ if the first card was the jack of diamonds}$$

In either case, the probability is different from its value for the first draw. This contradicts the requirement for random sampling, which says that the probability must stay constant. To keep the probabilities from changing from one selection to the next, it is necessary to replace each sample before you make the next selection. This is called *sampling with replacement*. The second requirement for random samples (constant probability) demands that you sample with replacement.

(*Note:* The definition that we are using identifies one type of random sampling, often called a *simple random sample* or an *independent random sample*. This kind of sampling is important for the mathematical foundation of many of the statistics we will encounter later. However, you should realize that other definitions exist for the concept of random sampling. In particular, it is very common to define random sampling without the requirement of constant probabilities—that is, without replacement. In addition, there are many other sampling techniques that are used when researchers are selecting individuals to participate in research studies.)

PROBABILITY AND FREQUENCY DISTRIBUTIONS

The situations in which we are concerned with probability usually involve a population of scores that can be displayed in a frequency distribution graph. If you think of the graph as representing the entire population, then different portions of the graph will represent different portions of the population. Because probabilities and proportions are equivalent, a particular portion of the graph corresponds to a particular probability in the population. Thus, whenever a population is presented in a frequency distribution graph, it is possible to represent probabilities as proportions of the graph. The relationship between graphs and probabilities is demonstrated in the following example.

EXAMPLE 6.1

We will use a very simple population that contains only $N = 10$ scores with values 1, 1, 2, 3, 3, 4, 4, 4, 5, 6. This population is shown in the frequency distribution graph in Figure 6.2. If you are taking a random sample of $n = 1$ score from this population, what is the probability of obtaining an individual with a score greater than 4? In probability notation,

$$p(X > 4) = ?$$

FIGURE 6.2

A frequency distribution histogram for a population that consists of $N = 10$ scores. The shaded part of the figure indicates the portion of the whole population that corresponds to scores greater than $X = 4$. The shaded portion is two-tenths $\left(p = \frac{2}{10}\right)$ of the whole distribution.

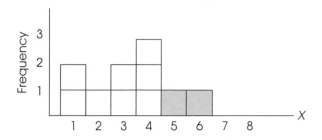

Using the definition of probability, there are 2 scores that meet this criterion out of the total group of $N = 10$ scores, so the answer would be $p = \frac{2}{10}$. This answer can be obtained directly from the frequency distribution graph if you recall that probability and proportion measure the same thing. Looking at the graph (Figure 6.2), what proportion of the population consists of scores greater than 4? The answer is the shaded part of the distribution—that is, 2 squares out of the total of 10 squares in the distribution. Notice that we now are defining probability as a proportion of *area* in the frequency distribution graph. This provides a very concrete and graphic way of representing probability.

Using the same population once again, what is the probability of selecting an individual with a score less than 5? In symbols,

$$p(X < 5) = ?$$

Going directly to the distribution in Figure 6.2, we now want to know what part of the graph is not shaded. The unshaded portion consists of 8 out of the 10 blocks $\left(\frac{8}{10}\right.$ of the area of the graph$\left.\right)$, so the answer is $p = \frac{8}{10}$.

LEARNING CHECK

1. The animal colony in the psychology department contains 20 male rats and 30 female rats. Of the 20 males, 15 are white and 5 are spotted. Of the 30 females, 15 are white, and 15 are spotted. Suppose that you randomly select 1 rat from this colony.
   a. What is the probability of obtaining a female?
   b. What is the probability of obtaining a white male?
   c. Which selection is more likely, a spotted male or a spotted female?

2. A jar contains 10 red marbles and 30 blue marbles.
   a. If you randomly select 1 marble from the jar, what is the probability of obtaining a red marble?
   b. If you take a *random sample* of $n = 3$ marbles from the jar and the first two marbles are both blue, what is the probability that the third marble will be red?

3. Suppose that you are going to select a random sample of $n = 1$ score from the distribution in Figure 6.2. Find the following probabilities:
   a. $p(X > 2)$ b. $p(X > 5)$ c. $p(X < 3)$

ANSWERS   1. a. $p = \frac{30}{50} = 0.60$ b. $p = \frac{15}{50} = 0.30$

   c. A spotted female ($p = 0.30$) is more likely than a spotted male ($p = 0.10$).

2. a. $p = \frac{10}{40} = 0.25$

   b. $p = \frac{10}{40} = 0.25$ Remember that random sampling requires sampling with replacement.

3. a. $p = \frac{7}{10} = 0.70$ b. $p = \frac{1}{10} = 0.10$ c. $p = \frac{3}{10} = 0.30$

6.2   PROBABILITY AND THE NORMAL DISTRIBUTION

The normal distribution was first introduced in Chapter 2 as an example of a commonly occurring shape for population distributions. An example of a normal distribution is shown in Figure 6.3.

Note that the normal distribution is symmetrical, with the highest frequency in the middle and frequencies tapering off as you move toward either extreme. Although the exact shape for the normal distribution is defined by an equation (see Figure 6.3), the normal shape can also be described by the proportions of area contained in each section of the distribution. Statisticians often identify sections of a normal distribution by using z-scores. Figure 6.4 shows a normal distribution with several sections marked in z-score units. You should recall that z-scores measure positions in a distribution in terms of standard deviations from the mean. (Thus, $z = +1$ is 1 standard deviation above the mean, $z = +2$ is 2 standard deviations above the mean, and so on.) The graph shows the percentage of scores that fall in each of these sections. For example, the section between the mean ($z = 0$) and the point that is 1 standard deviation above the mean ($z = 1$) contains 34.13% of the scores. Similarly, 13.59% of the scores fall between

FIGURE 6.3

The normal distribution. The exact shape of the normal distribution is specified by an equation relating each X value (score) with each Y value (frequency). The equation is

$$Y = \frac{1}{\sqrt{2\pi\sigma^2}} e^{-(X-\mu)^2/2\sigma^2}$$

(π and e are mathematical constants.) In simpler terms, the normal distribution is symmetrical with a single mode in the middle. The frequency tapers off as you move farther from the middle in either direction.

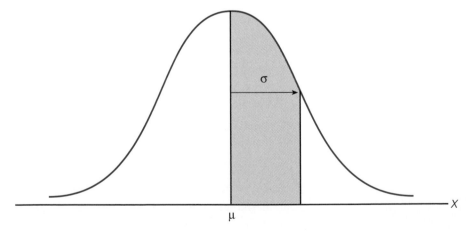

FIGURE 6.4

The normal distribution following a *z*-score transformation.

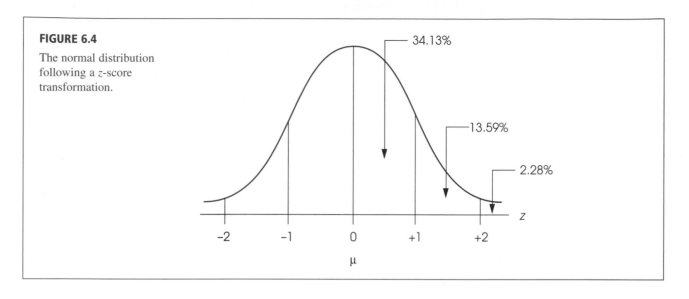

1 and 2 standard deviations from the mean. In this way it is possible to define a normal distribution in terms of its proportions; that is, a distribution is normal if and only if it has all the right proportions.

There are two additional points to be made about the distribution shown in Figure 6.4. First, you should realize that the sections on the left side of the distribution have exactly the same areas as the corresponding sections on the right side because the normal distribution is symmetrical. Second, because the locations in the distribution are identified by *z*-scores, the percentages shown in the figure apply to *any normal distribution* regardless of the values for the mean and the standard deviation. Remember: When any distribution is transformed into *z*-scores, the mean becomes zero and the standard deviation becomes one.

Because the normal distribution is a good model for many naturally occurring distributions and because this shape is guaranteed in some circumstances (as you will see in Chapter 7), we will devote considerable attention to this particular distribution.

The process of answering probability questions about a normal distribution is introduced in the following example.

EXAMPLE 6.2   Assume that the population of adult heights forms a normal-shaped distribution with a mean of $\mu = 68$ inches and a standard deviation of $\sigma = 6$ inches. Given this information about the population and the known proportions for a normal distribution (see Figure 6.4), we can determine the probabilities associated with specific samples. For example, what is the probability of randomly selecting an individual from this population who is taller than 6 feet 8 inches ($X = 80$ inches)?

Restating this question in probability notation, we get

$$p(X > 80) = ?$$

We will follow a step-by-step process to find the answer to this question.

1. First, the probability question is translated into a proportion question: Out of all possible adult heights, what proportion consists of values greater than 80 inches?

2. The set of "all possible adult heights" is simply the population distribution. This population is shown in Figure 6.5(a). The mean is $\mu = 68$, so the score

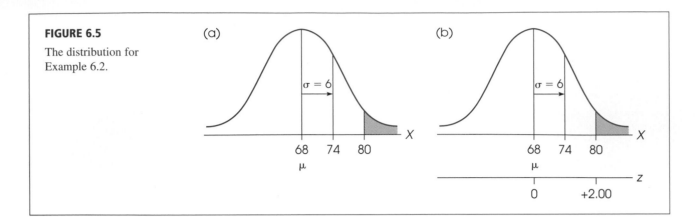

FIGURE 6.5

The distribution for Example 6.2.

$X = 80$ is to the right of the mean. Because we are interested in all heights greater than 80, we shade in the area to the right of 80. This area represents the proportion we are trying to determine.

3. Identify the exact position of $X = 80$ by computing a z-score. For this example,

$$z = \frac{X - \mu}{\sigma} = \frac{80 - 68}{6} = \frac{12}{6} = 2.00$$

That is, a height of $X = 80$ inches is exactly 2 standard deviations above the mean and corresponds to a z-score of $z = +2.00$ [see Figure 6.5(b)].

4. The proportion we are trying to determine may now be expressed in terms of its z-score:

$$p(z > 2.00) = ?$$

According to the proportions shown in Figure 6.4, all normal distributions, regardless of the values for μ and σ, will have 2.28% of the scores in the tail beyond $z = +2.00$. Thus, for the population of adult heights,

$$p(X > 80) = p(z > +2.00) = 2.28\%$$

THE UNIT NORMAL TABLE   Before we attempt any more probability questions, we must introduce a more useful tool than the graph of the normal distribution shown in Figure 6.4. The graph shows proportions for only a few selected z-score values. A more complete listing of z-scores and proportions is provided in the *unit normal table*. This table lists proportions of the normal distribution for a full range of possible z-score values.

The complete unit normal table is provided in Appendix B Table B.1, and part of the table is reproduced in Figure 6.6. Notice that the table is structured in a four-column format. The first column (A) lists z-score values corresponding to different positions in a normal distribution. If you imagine a vertical line drawn through a normal distribution, then the exact location of the line can be described by one of the z-score values listed in column A. You should also realize that a vertical line will separate the distribution into two sections: a larger section called the *body* and a smaller section called the *tail*. Columns B and C in the table identify the proportion of the distribution in each of the two sections. Column B presents the proportion in the body (the larger portion), and column C presents the proportion in the tail. Finally, we have added a fourth column, col-

FIGURE 6.6

A portion of the unit normal table. This table lists proportions of the normal distribution corresponding to each z-score value. Column A of the table lists z-scores. Column B lists the proportion in the body of the normal distribution up to the z-score value. Column C lists the proportion of the normal distribution that is located in the tail of the distribution beyond the z-score value. Column D lists the proportion between the mean and the z-score value.

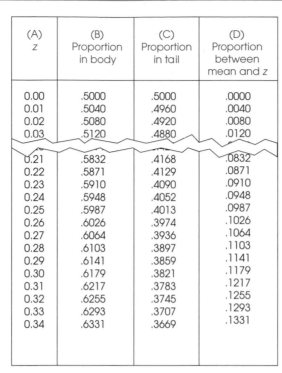

(A) z	(B) Proportion in body	(C) Proportion in tail	(D) Proportion between mean and z
0.00	.5000	.5000	.0000
0.01	.5040	.4960	.0040
0.02	.5080	.4920	.0080
0.03	.5120	.4880	.0120
0.21	.5832	.4168	.0832
0.22	.5871	.4129	.0871
0.23	.5910	.4090	.0910
0.24	.5948	.4052	.0948
0.25	.5987	.4013	.0987
0.26	.6026	.3974	.1026
0.27	.6064	.3936	.1064
0.28	.6103	.3897	.1103
0.29	.6141	.3859	.1141
0.30	.6179	.3821	.1179
0.31	.6217	.3783	.1217
0.32	.6255	.3745	.1255
0.33	.6293	.3707	.1293
0.34	.6331	.3669	.1331

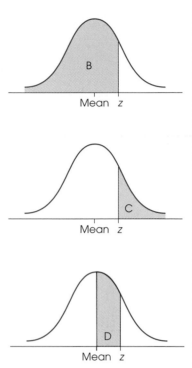

umn D, that identifies the proportion of the distribution *between* the mean and the z-score. Using the portion of the table shown in Figure 6.6, you should verify that a vertical line drawn through a normal distribution at $z = +0.25$ will separate the distribution into two sections with the larger section containing 0.5987 (59.87%) of the distribution and the smaller section containing 0.4013 (40.13%) of the distribution. Also, there is exactly 0.0987 (9.87%) of the distribution between the mean and $z = +0.25$.

To make full use of the unit normal table, there are a few facts to keep in mind:

1. The *body* always corresponds to the larger part of the distribution whether it is on the right-hand side or the left-hand side. Similarly, the *tail* is always the smaller section whether it is on the right or the left.

2. Because the normal distribution is symmetrical, the proportions on the right-hand side are exactly the same as the corresponding proportions on the left-hand side. For example, the proportion in the right-hand tail beyond $z = +1.00$ is exactly the same as the proportion in the left-hand tail beyond $z = -1.00$.

3. Although the z-score values will change signs ($+$ and $-$) from one side to the other, the proportions will always be positive. Thus, column C in the table always lists the proportion in the tail whether it is the right-hand tail or the left-hand tail.

PROBABILITIES, PROPORTIONS, AND z-SCORES

The unit normal table lists relationships between z-score locations and proportions in a normal distribution. For any z-score location, you can use the table to look up the corresponding proportions. Similarly, if you know the proportions, you can use the table to look up the specific z-score location. Because we have defined probability as equivalent to proportion, you can also use the unit normal table to look up probabilities for normal distributions. The following examples demonstrate a variety of different ways that the unit normal table can be used.

Finding proportions/probabilities for specific z-score values   For each of the following examples, we begin with a specific z-score value and then use the unit normal table to find probabilities or proportions associated with the z-score.

EXAMPLE 6.3A   What proportion of the normal distribution corresponds to z-score values greater than $z = 1.00$? First, you should sketch the distribution and shade in the area you are trying to determine. This is shown in Figure 6.7(a). In this case, the shaded portion is the tail of the distribution beyond $z = 1.00$. To find this shaded area, you simply look up $z = 1.00$ in column A of the unit normal table. Then you read column C (tail) for the proportion. Using the table in Appendix B, you should find that the answer is 0.1587.

You also should notice that this same problem could have been phrased as a probability question. Specifically, we could have asked, "For a normal distribution, what is the probability of selecting a z-score value greater than $z = +1.00$?" Again, the answer is $p(z > 1.00) = 0.1587$ (or 15.87%).

EXAMPLE 6.3B   For a normal distribution, what is the probability of selecting a z-score less than $z = 1.50$? In symbols, $p(z < 1.50) = ?$ Our goal is to determine what proportion of the normal distribution corresponds to z-scores less than 1.50. A normal distribution is shown in Figure 6.7(b) and $z = 1.50$ is located in the distribution. Note that we have shaded all the values to the left of (less than) $z = 1.50$. This is the portion we are trying to find. Clearly the shaded portion is more than 50% so it corresponds to the body of the distribution. Therefore, we find $z = 1.50$ in the unit normal table and read the proportion from column B. The answer is $p(z < 1.50) = 0.9332$ (or 93.32%).

EXAMPLE 6.3C   Many problems will require that you find proportions for negative z-scores. For example, what proportion of the normal distribution corresponds to the tail beyond $z = -0.50$? That is, $p(z < -0.50)$. This portion has been shaded in Figure 6.7(c). To answer questions with negative z-scores, simply remember that the normal distribu-

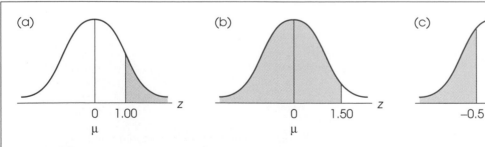
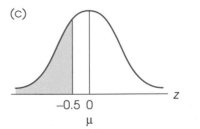

FIGURE 6.7
The distributions for Example 6.3A–6.3C.

Moving to the left on the *X*-axis results in smaller *X* values and smaller *z*-scores. Thus, a *z*-score of −3.00 reflects a smaller value than a *z*-score of −1.

tion is symmetrical with a *z*-score of zero at the mean, positive values to the right, and negative values to the left. The proportion in the left tail beyond $z = -0.50$ is identical to the proportion in the right tail beyond $z = +0.50$. To find this proportion, look up $z = 0.50$ in column A, and find the proportion in column C (tail). You should get an answer of 0.3085 (30.85%).

Finding the *z*-score location that corresponds to specific proportions   The preceding examples all involved using a *z*-score value in column A to look up a proportion in column B or C. You should realize, however, that the table also allows you to begin with a known proportion and then look up the corresponding *z*-score. In general, the unit normal table can be used for two purposes:

1. If you know a specific location (*z*-score) in a normal distribution, you can use the table to look up the corresponding proportions.

2. If you know a specific proportion (or proportions), you can use the table to look up the exact *z*-score location in the distribution.

The following examples demonstrate how the table can be used to find specific *z*-scores if you begin with known proportions.

EXAMPLE 6.4A   For a normal distribution, what *z*-score separates the top 10% from the remainder of the distribution? To answer this question, we have sketched a normal distribution [Figure 6.8(a)] and drawn a vertical line that separates the highest 10% (approximately) from the rest. The problem is to locate the exact position of this line. For this distribution, we know that the tail contains 0.1000 (10%) and the body contains 0.9000 (90%). To find the *z*-score value, you simply locate 0.1000 in column C or 0.9000 in column B of the unit normal table. Note that you probably will not find the exact proportion, but you can use the closest value listed in the table. For example, you will not find 0.1000 listed in column C but you can use 0.1003, which is listed. Once you have found the correct proportion in the table, simply read the corresponding *z*-score. For this example, the *z*-score that separates the extreme 10% in the tail is $z = 1.28$. At this point you must be careful because the table does not differentiate between the right-hand tail and the left-hand tail of the distribution. Specifically, the final answer could be either $z = +1.28$, which separates 10% in the right-hand tail, or $z = -1.28$, which separates 10% in the left-hand tail. For this problem we want the right-hand tail (the highest 10%), so the *z*-score value is $z = +1.28$.

FIGURE 6.8

The distributions for Examples 6.4A and 6.4B.

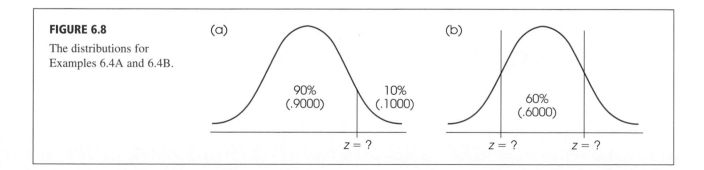

EXAMPLE 6.4B For a normal distribution, what z-score values form the boundaries that separate the middle 60% of the distribution from the rest of the scores?

Again, we have sketched a normal distribution [Figure 6.8(b)] and drawn vertical lines in the approximate locations. For this example, we want slightly more than half of the distribution in the central section, with the remainder split equally between the two tails. The problem is to find the z-score values that define the exact locations for the lines. To find the z-score values, we begin with the known proportions: 0.6000 in the center and 0.4000 divided equally between the two tails. Although these proportions can be used in several different ways, this example provides an opportunity to demonstrate how column D in the table can be used to solve problems. For this problem, the 0.6000 in the center can be divided in half with exactly 0.3000 to the right of the mean and exactly 0.3000 to the left. Each of these sections corresponds to the proportion listed in column D. Looking in column D for a value of 0.3000, you will discover that this exact proportion is not in the table, but the closest value is 0.2995. Reading across the row to column A, you should find a z-score value of $z = 0.84$. Looking again at the sketch [Figure 6.8(b)], you can see that the right-hand line is located at $z = +0.84$ and the left-hand line is located at $z = -0.84$.

You may have noticed that we have sketched distributions for each of the preceding problems. As a general rule, you should always sketch a distribution, locate the mean with a vertical line, and shade in the portion you are trying to determine. Look at your sketch. It will indicate which columns to use in the unit normal table. If you make a habit of drawing sketches, you will avoid careless errors in using the table.

LEARNING CHECK

1. Find the proportion of the normal distribution that is associated with the following sections of a graph:

   a. $z < +1.00$ **b.** $z > +0.80$ **c.** $z < -2.00$ **d.** $z > -0.33$

   e. $z > -0.50$

2. For a normal distribution, find the z-score location that separates the distribution as follows:

   a. Separate the highest 30% from the rest of the distribution.
   b. Separate the lowest 40% from the rest of the distribution.
   c. Separate the highest 75% from the rest of the distribution.

ANSWERS

1. **a.** 0.8413   **b.** 0.2119   **c.** 0.0228   **d.** 0.6293   **e.** 0.6915

2. **a.** $z = 0.52$ **b.** $z = -0.25$ **c.** $z = -0.67$

6.3 PROBABILITIES AND PROPORTIONS FOR SCORES FROM A NORMAL DISTRIBUTION

In the preceding section, we used the unit normal table to find probabilities and proportions corresponding to specific z-score values. In most situations, however, it will be necessary to find probabilities for specific X values. Consider the following example:

It is known that IQ scores form a normal distribution with $\mu = 100$ and $\sigma = 15$. Given this information, what is the probability of randomly selecting an individual with an IQ score less than 130?

This problem is asking for a specific probability or proportion of a normal distribution. However, before we can look up the answer in the unit normal table, we must first transform the IQ scores (*X* values) into *z*-scores. Thus, to solve this new kind of probability problem, we must add one new step to the process. Specifically, to answer probability questions about scores (*X* values) from a normal distribution, you must use the following two-step procedure:

1. Transform the *X* values into *z*-scores.

2. Use the unit normal table to look up the proportions corresponding to the *z*-score values.

Caution: The unit normal table can be used only with normal-shaped distributions. If a distribution is not normal, transforming to *z*-scores will not make it normal.

This process is demonstrated in the following examples. Once again, we suggest that you sketch the distribution and shade the portion you are trying to find to avoid careless mistakes.

EXAMPLE 6.5   We will now answer the probability question about IQ scores that we presented earlier. Specifically, what is the probability of randomly selecting an individual with an IQ score less than 130?

$$p(X < 130) = ?$$

Restated in terms of proportions, we want to find the proportion of the IQ distribution that corresponds to scores less than 130. The distribution is drawn in Figure 6.9, and the portion we want has been shaded.

The first step is to change the *X* values into *z*-scores. In particular, the score of *X* = 130 is changed to

$$z = \frac{X - \mu}{\sigma} = \frac{130 - 100}{15} = \frac{30}{15} = 2.00$$

Next, look up the *z*-score value in the unit normal table. Because we want the proportion of the distribution in the body to the left of *X* = 130 (see Figure 6.9), the answer will be found in column B. Consulting the table, we see that a *z*-score of 2.00 corresponds to a proportion of 0.9772. The probability of randomly selecting an individual with an IQ less than 130 is 0.9772:

$$p(X < 130) = 0.9772 \text{ (or 97.72\%)}$$

Finally, notice that we phrased this question in terms of a *probability*. Specifically, we asked, "What is the probability of selecting an individual with an IQ less than

FIGURE 6.9

The distribution of IQ scores. The problem is to find the probability or proportion of the distribution corresponding to scores less than 130.

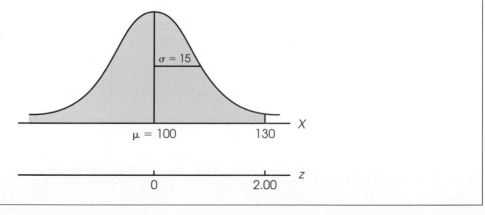

BOX
6.1

PROBABILITIES, PROPORTIONS, AND PERCENTILE RANKS

Thus far we have discussed parts of distributions in terms of proportions and probabilities. However, there is another set of terminology that deals with many of the same concepts. Specifically, the *percentile rank* for a specific score is defined as the percentage of the individuals in the distribution who have scores that are less than or equal to the specific score. For example, if 70% of the individuals have scores of $X = 45$ or lower, then $X = 45$ has a percentile rank of 70%. When a score is referred to by its percentile rank, the score is called a *percentile*. For example, a score with a percentile rank of 70% is called the 70th percentile.

Using this terminology, it is possible to rephrase some of the probability problems that we have been

working. In Example 6.5, the problem is presented as "What is the probability of randomly selecting an individual with an IQ score less than 130?" Exactly the same question could be phrased as "What is the percentile rank for an IQ score of 130?" In each case, we are looking for the proportion of the distribution corresponding to scores equal to or less than 130. Similarly, Example 6.8 asks "What is the minimum score necessary to be in the top 15% of the SAT?" Because this score separates the top 15% from the bottom 85%, the same question could be rephrased as "What is the 85th percentile for the distribution of SAT scores?"

130?" However, the same question can be phrased in terms of a *proportion:* "What proportion of the individuals in the population have IQ scores less than 130?" Both versions ask exactly the same question and produce exactly the same answer. A third alternative for presenting the same question is introduced in Box 6.1.

Finding proportions/probabilities located between two scores The next example demonstrates the process of finding the probability of selecting a score that is located *between* two specific values. Although these problems can be solved using the proportions of columns B and C (body and tail), they are often easier to solve with the proportions listed in column D.

EXAMPLE 6.6 The highway department conducted a study measuring driving speeds on a local section of interstate highway. They found an average speed of $\mu = 58$ miles per hour with a standard deviation of $\sigma = 10$. The distribution was approximately normal. Given this information, what proportion of the cars are traveling between 55 and 65 miles per hour? Using probability notation, we can express the problem as

$$p(55 < X < 65) = ?$$

The distribution of driving speeds is shown in Figure 6.10 with the appropriate area shaded. The first step is to determine the z-score corresponding to the X value at each end of the interval.

$$\text{For } X = 55: \quad z = \frac{X - \mu}{\sigma} = \frac{55 - 58}{10} = \frac{-3}{10} = -0.30$$

$$\text{For } X = 65: \quad z = \frac{X - \mu}{\sigma} = \frac{65 - 58}{10} = \frac{7}{10} = 0.70$$

Looking again at Figure 6.10, we see that the proportion we are seeking can be divided into two sections: (1) the area left of the mean, and (2) the area right of the

FIGURE 6.10

The distribution for Example 6.6.

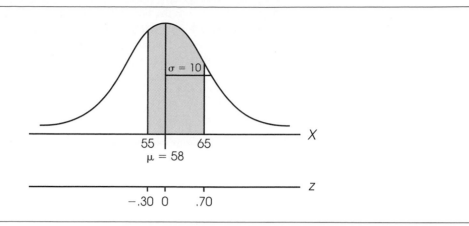

mean. The first area is the proportion between the mean and $z = -0.30$ and the second is the proportion between the mean and $z = +0.70$. Using column D of the unit normal table, these two proportions are 0.1179 and 0.2580. The total proportion is obtained by adding these two sections:

$$p(55 < X < 65) = p(-0.30 < z < +0.70) = 0.1179 + 0.2580 = 0.3759$$

EXAMPLE 6.7 Using the same distribution of driving speeds from the previous example, what proportion of cars are traveling between 65 and 75 miles per hour?

$$p(65 < X < 75) = ?$$

The distribution is shown in Figure 6.11 with the appropriate area shaded. Again, we start by determining the z-score corresponding to each end of the interval.

$$\text{For } X = 65: \quad z = \frac{X - \mu}{\sigma} = \frac{65 - 58}{10} = \frac{7}{10} = 0.70$$

$$\text{For } X = 75: \quad z = \frac{X - \mu}{\sigma} = \frac{75 - 58}{10} = \frac{17}{10} = 1.70$$

FIGURE 6.11

The distribution for Example 6.7.

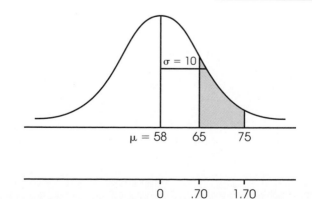

According to column D in the unit normal table, the proportion between the mean and $z = 1.70$ is $p = 0.4554$. Note that this proportion includes the section that we want, but it also includes an extra, unwanted section between the mean and $z = 0.70$. Again, using column D, we see that the unwanted section is $p = 0.2580$. To obtain the correct answer, we subtract the unwanted portion from the total proportion between the mean and $z = 1.70$.

$$p(65 < X < 75) = p(0.70 < z < 1.70) = 0.4554 - 0.2580 = 0.1974$$

Finding scores corresponding to specific proportions or probabilities   In the previous two examples, the problem was to find the proportion or probability corresponding to specific X values. The two-step process for finding these proportions is shown in Figure 6.12. Thus far, we have only considered examples that move in a clockwise direction around the triangle shown in the figure; that is, we start with an X value that is transformed into a z-score, and then we use the unit normal table to look up the appropriate proportion. You should realize, however, that it is possible to reverse this two-step process so that we move backward, or counterclockwise, around the triangle. This reverse process will allow us to find the score (X value) corresponding to a specific proportion in the distribution. Following the lines in Figure 6.12, we will begin with a specific proportion, use the unit normal table to look up the corresponding z-score, and then transform the z-score into an X value. The following example demonstrates this process.

EXAMPLE 6.8   Scores on the SAT form a normal distribution with $\mu = 500$ and $\sigma = 100$. What is the minimum score necessary to be in the top 15% of the SAT distribution? (An alternative form of the same question is presented in Box 6.1.) This problem is shown graphically in Figure 6.13.

In this problem, we begin with a proportion (15% = 0.15), and we are looking for a score. According to the map in Figure 6.12, we can move from p (proportion) to X (score) via z-scores. The first step is to use the unit normal table to find the z-score that corresponds to a proportion of 0.15. Because the proportion is located beyond z in the tail of the distribution, we will look in column C for a proportion of 0.1500. Note that you may not find 0.1500 exactly, but locate the closest value possible. In this case, the closest value in the table is 0.1492, and the z-score that corresponds to this proportion is $z = 1.04$.

FIGURE 6.12

Determining probabilities or proportions for a normal distribution is shown as a two-step process with z-scores as an intermediate stop along the way. Note that you cannot move directly along the dashed line between X values and probabilities or proportions. Instead, you must follow the solid lines around the corner.

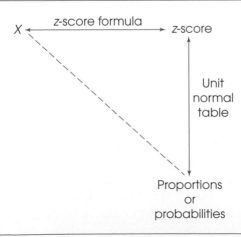

FIGURE 6.13

The distribution of SAT scores. The problem is to locate the score that separates the top 15% from the rest of the distribution. A line is drawn to divide the distribution roughly into 15% and 85% sections.

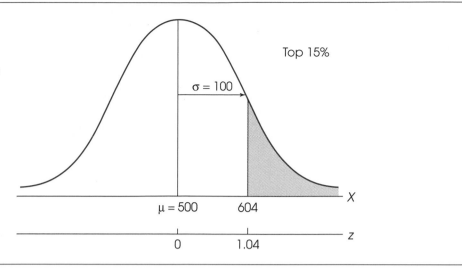

The next step is to determine whether the z-score is positive or negative. Remember that the table does not specify the sign of the z-score. Looking at the graph in Figure 6.13, you should realize that the score we want is above the mean, so the z-score is positive, $z = +1.04$.

Now you are ready for the last stage of the solution—that is, changing the z-score into an X value. By definition, a z-score of $z = +1.04$ corresponds to an X value that is located above the mean (+) by 1.04 standard deviations. One standard deviation is $\sigma = 100$ points, so 1.04 standard deviations is

$$1.04\sigma = 1.04(100) = 104 \text{ points}$$

Thus, our score is located 104 points above the mean. With a mean of $\mu = 500$, the score is $X = 500 + 104 = 604$. The conclusion for this example is that you must have an SAT score of at least 604 to be in the top 15% of the distribution.

EXAMPLE 6.9 This time the problem is to find the range of values that defines the middle 80% of the distribution of SAT scores. The distribution is shown in Figure 6.14 with the appropriate section shaded.

The 80% (0.8000) in the middle of the distribution can be split in half with 0.4000 to the right of the mean and 0.4000 to the left. Looking up 0.4000 in column D of the unit normal table, you will discover that the exact proportion is not listed but the closest value is 0.3997. Reading across to column A, the corresponding z-score is $z = 1.28$. Thus, the z-score at the right-hand boundary is $z = +1.28$ and the z-score at the left boundary is $z = -1.28$. In either case, a z-score of 1.28 indicates a location that is 1.28 standard deviations away from the mean. In this case,

$$1.28\sigma = 1.28(100) = 128 \text{ points}$$

Therefore, the right-hand boundary ($z = +1.28$) is $X = 500 + 128 = 628$. The left-hand boundary ($z = -1.28$) is $X = 500 - 128 = 372$. The middle 80% of the distribution corresponds to X values between 372 and 628.

FIGURE 6.14

The distribution of SAT scores. The problem is to find the scores that determine the middle 80%.

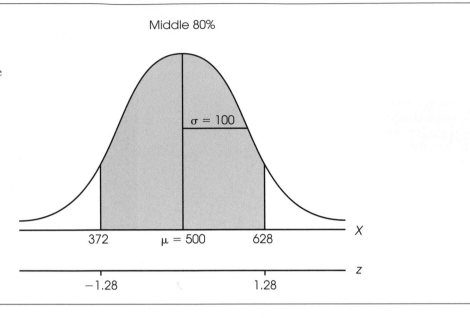

---

1. For a normal distribution with a mean of 80 and a standard deviation of 10, find each probability value requested.

   a. $p(X > 85) = ?$ **b.** $p(X < 95) = ?$
   c. $p(X > 70) = ?$ **d.** $p(75 < X < 100) = ?$

2. For a normal distribution with a mean of 100 and a standard deviation of 20, find each value requested.

   a. What score separates the top 40% from the bottom 60% of the distribution?
   b. What is the minimum score needed to be in the top 5% of the distribution?
   c. What scores form the boundaries for the middle 60% of the distribution?

3. What is the probability of selecting a score greater than 45 from a positively skewed distribution with $\mu = 40$ and $\sigma = 10$? (Be careful.)

ANSWERS   **1. a.** $p = 0.3085$ (30.85%)   **b.** $p = 0.9332$ (93.32%)   **c.** $p = 0.8413$ (84.13%)
   d. $p = 0.6687$ (66.87%)

2. a. $z = +0.25$; $X = 105$ **b.** $z = +1.64$; $X = 132.8$

   c. $z = \pm 0.84$; boundaries are 83.2 and 116.8

3. You cannot obtain the answer. The unit normal table cannot be used to answer this question because the distribution is not normal.

6.4   LOOKING AHEAD TO INFERENTIAL STATISTICS

Probability forms a direct link between samples and the populations from which they come. As we noted at the beginning of this chapter, this link will be the foundation for the inferential statistics in future chapters. The following example provides a brief preview of how probability will be used in the context of inferential statistics.

We ended Chapter 5 with a demonstration of how inferential statistics are used to help interpret the results of a research study. A general research situation was shown in Figure 5.6 and is repeated here in Figure 6.15. The research begins with a population that forms a normal distribution with a mean of $\mu = 400$ and a standard deviation of $\sigma = 20$. A sample is selected from the population and a treatment is administered to the sample. The goal for the study is to evaluate the effect of the treatment.

To determine whether the treatment has an effect, the researcher will simply compare the treated sample with the original population. If the individuals in the sample have scores around 400 (the original population mean), then we must conclude that the treatment appears to have no effect. On the other hand, if the treated individuals have scores that are noticeably different from 400, then the researcher has evidence that the treatment does have an effect. Notice that the study is using a sample to help answer a question about a population; this is the essence of inferential statistics.

The problem for the researcher is determining exactly what is meant by "noticeably different" from 400. If a treated individual has a score of $X = 415$, is that enough to say that the treatment has an effect? What about $X = 420$ or $X = 450$? In Chapter 5, we suggested that z-scores provide one method for solving this problem. Specifically, we suggested that a z-score value beyond $z = 2.00$ (or -2.00) was an extreme value and therefore noticeably different. However, the choice of $z = \pm 2.00$ was purely arbitrary. Now we have another tool, *probability,* to help us decide exactly where to set the boundaries.

Figure 6.16 shows the original population from our hypothetical research study. Note that most of the scores are located close to $\mu = 400$. Also note that we have added boundaries separating the middle 95% of the distribution from the extreme 5% in the tails. The boundaries are located at $z = +1.96$ and $z = -1.96$. (The boundary for the extreme .0250 in the right-hand tail is $z = +1.96$, and for the extreme .0250 in the left-hand tail it is $z = -1.96$. Combined, the two tails account for 0.0500 or 5% of the distribution.)

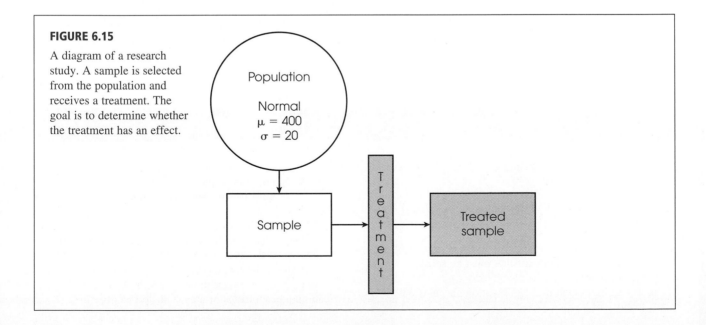

FIGURE 6.15

A diagram of a research study. A sample is selected from the population and receives a treatment. The goal is to determine whether the treatment has an effect.

FIGURE 6.16

Using probability to evaluate a treatment effect. Values that are extremely unlikely to be obtained from the original population are viewed as evidence of a treatment effect.

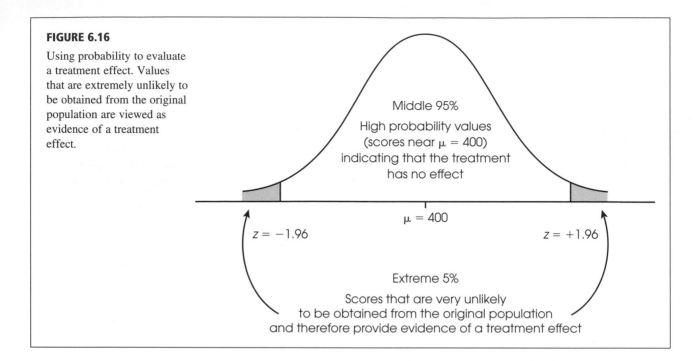

Middle 95%
High probability values
(scores near μ = 400)
indicating that the treatment
has no effect

μ = 400

z = −1.96   z = +1.96

Extreme 5%
Scores that are very unlikely
to be obtained from the original population
and therefore provide evidence of a treatment effect

The boundaries set at $z = \pm1.96$ provide objective criteria for deciding whether our sample provides evidence that the treatment has an effect. Specifically, we will use the sample data to help decide between the following two alternatives:

1. The treatment has no effect and the scores still average $\mu = 400$.

2. The treatment does have an effect that changes the scores so they no longer average $\mu = 400$.

If the first alternative is correct, then the sample should be close to 400. According to Figure 6.16, any sample between the ±1.96 boundaries is considered close to 400 and will support this alternative. On the other hand, a sample beyond the ±1.96 boundaries is significantly different from $\mu = 400$. Specifically, this kind of sample is very unlikely (probability less than 5%) to occur if there is no treatment effect. Therefore, if we obtain a sample that is beyond the ±1.96 boundaries, we can reject the first alternative and conclude that the treatment does have an effect.

SUMMARY

1. The probability of a particular event A is defined as a fraction or proportion:

$$p(A) = \frac{\text{number of outcomes classified as } A}{\text{total number of possible outcomes}}$$

2. This definition is accurate only for a random sample. There are two requirements that must be satisfied for a random sample:
   a. Every individual in the population has an equal chance of being selected.

   b. When more than one individual is being selected, the probabilities must stay constant. This means there must be sampling with replacement.

3. All probability problems can be restated as proportion problems. The "probability of selecting a king from a deck of cards" is equivalent to the "proportion of the deck that consists of kings." For frequency distributions, probability questions can be answered by determining proportions of area. The "probability of

selecting an individual with an IQ greater than 108" is equivalent to the "proportion of the whole population that consists of individuals with IQs above 108."

4. For normal distributions, probabilities (proportions) can be found in the unit normal table. The table provides a listing of the proportions of a normal distribution that correspond to each z-score value. With the table, it is possible to move between X values and probabilities using a two-step procedure:

   a. The z-score formula (Chapter 5) allows you to transform X to z or to change z back to X.

   b. The unit normal table allows you to look up the probability (proportion) corresponding to each z-score or the z-score corresponding to each probability.

5. Percentiles and percentile ranks measure the relative standing of a score within a distribution (see Box 6.1). Percentile rank is the percentage of individuals with scores at or below a particular X value. A percentile is an X value that is identified by its rank. The percentile rank always corresponds to the proportion to the left of the score in question.

KEY TERMS

probability	sampling with replacement	percentile rank
random sample	unit normal table	percentile

RESOURCES

There are a tutorial quiz and other learning exercises for Chapter 6 at the Wadsworth website, www.thomsonedu.com/psychology/gravetter. See page 27 for more information about accessing items on the website.

For those using WebTutor along with this book, there is a WebTutor section corresponding to this chapter. The WebTutor contains a brief summary of Chapter 6, hints for learning about probability, cautions about common errors, and sample exam items including solutions.

SPSS

The statistics computer package SPSS is not structured to compute probabilities. However, the program does report probability values as part of the inferential statistics that we will examine later in this book. In the context of inferential statistics, the probabilities are called *significance levels,* and they warn researchers about the probability of misinterpreting their research results.

FOCUS ON PROBLEM SOLVING

1. We have defined probability as being equivalent to a proportion, which means that you can restate every probability problem as a proportion problem. This definition is particularly useful when you are working with frequency distribution graphs where the popu-

lation is represented by the whole graph and probabilities (proportions) are represented by portions of the graph. When working problems with the normal distribution, you always should start with a sketch of the distribution. You should shade the portion of the graph that reflects the proportion you are looking for.

2. When using the unit normal table, you must remember that the proportions in the table (columns B, C, and D) correspond to specific portions of the distribution. This is important because you will often need to translate the proportions from a problem into specific proportions provided in the table. Also, remember that the table allows you to move back and forth between *z*-scores and proportions. You can look up a given *z* to find a proportion, or you can look up a given proportion to find the corresponding *z*-score.

3. Remember that the unit normal table shows only positive *z*-scores in column A. However, because the normal distribution is symmetrical, the proportions in the table apply to both positive and negative *z*-score values.

4. A common error for students is to use negative values for proportions on the left-hand side of the normal distribution. Proportions (or probabilities) are always positive: 10% is 10% whether it is in the left or right tail of the distribution.

5. The proportions in the unit normal table are accurate only for normal distributions. If a distribution is not normal, you cannot use the table.

DEMONSTRATION 6.1

FINDING PROBABILITY FROM THE UNIT NORMAL TABLE

A population is normally distributed with a mean of $\mu = 45$ and a standard deviation of $\sigma = 4$. What is the probability of randomly selecting a score that is greater than 43? In other words, what proportion of the distribution consists of scores greater than 43?

STEP 1   Sketch the distribution.

You should always start by sketching the distribution, identifying the mean and standard deviation ($\mu = 45$ and $\sigma = 4$ in this example). You should also find the approximate location of the specified score and draw a vertical line through the distribution at that score. The score of $X = 43$ is lower than the mean, and, therefore, it should be placed somewhere to the left of the mean. Figure 6.17(a) shows the preliminary sketch.

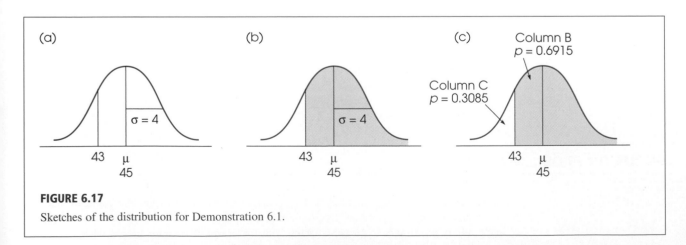

FIGURE 6.17

Sketches of the distribution for Demonstration 6.1.

STEP 2   Shade in the distribution.

Read the problem again to determine whether you want the proportion greater than the score (to the right of your vertical line) or less than the score (to the left of the line). Then shade in the appropriate portion of the distribution. In this demonstration, we are considering scores greater than 43. Thus, we shade in the distribution to the right of this score [Figure 6.17(b)]. Notice that if the shaded area covers more than half of the distribution, then the probability should be greater than 0.5000.

STEP 3   Transform the X value to a z-score.

Remember: To get a probability from the unit normal table, we must first convert the X value to a z-score.

$$z = \frac{X - \mu}{\sigma} = \frac{43 - 45}{4} = \frac{-2}{4} = -0.5$$

STEP 4   Consult the unit normal table.

Look up the z-score (ignoring the sign) in the unit normal table. Find the proportions in the table that are associated with the z-score, and write the proportions in the appropriate regions on the figure. Remember that column B gives the proportion of area in the body of the distribution (more than 50%), and column C gives the area in the tail beyond z. Figure 6.17(c) shows the proportions for different regions of the normal distribution.

STEP 5   Determine the probability.

If one of the proportions in step 4 corresponds exactly to the entire shaded area, then that proportion is your answer. Otherwise, you will need to do some additional arithmetic. In this example, the proportion in the shaded area is given in column B:

$$p(X > 43) = 0.6915$$

PROBLEMS

1. What requirements must be satisfied to have a *random sample*?

2. What is sampling with replacement, and why is it used?

3. A jar contains 20 red marbles, of which 10 are large and 10 are small, and 30 blue marbles, of which 10 are large and 20 are small. If 1 marble is randomly selected from the jar,
   a. What is the probability of obtaining a blue marble?
   b. What is the probability of obtaining a large marble?
   c. What is the probability of obtaining a large blue marble?

4. For each of the following z-scores, sketch a normal distribution and draw a vertical line at the location of the z-score. Then, determine whether the body is to the right or the left of the line and find the proportion in the body.
   a. $z = 1.00$ b. $z = -0.50$
   c. $z = 1.50$ d. $z = -2.00$

5. For a normal distribution, identify the z-score location that would separate the distribution into two sections so that there is
   a. 10% in the tail on the right-hand side.
   b. 20% in the tail on the right-hand side.
   c. 20% in the tail on the left-hand side.
   d. 30% in the tail on the left-hand side.

6. A kindergarten class consists of 14 boys and 11 girls. If the teacher selects children from the class using *random sampling,*
   a. What is the probability that the first child selected will be a girl?
   b. If the teacher selects a random sample of $n = 3$ children and the first two children are both boys, what is the probability that the third child selected will be a girl?

7. For each of the following z-scores, sketch a normal distribution and draw a vertical line at the location of the z-score. Then, determine whether the tail is to the right or the left of the line and find the proportion in the tail.
   a. $z = 1.50$
   b. $z = -1.75$
   c. $z = 0.20$
   d. $z = -0.50$

8. For a normal distribution, identify the z-score location that would separate the distribution into two sections so that there is
   a. 70% in the body on the right-hand side.
   b. 80% in the body on the right-hand side.
   c. 75% in the body on the left-hand side.
   d. 90% in the body on the left-hand side.

9. Find each of the following probabilities for a normal distribution.
   a. $p(z > 1.00)$
   b. $p(z > 0.80)$
   c. $p(z < -0.25)$
   d. $p(z < -1.25)$

10. A normal distribution has $\mu = 80$ and $\sigma = 20$. For each of the following scores, indicate whether the tail of the distribution is located to the right or the left of the score, and find the proportion of the distribution located in the tail.
    a. $X = 85$
    b. $X = 92$
    c. $X = 70$
    d. $X = 64$

11. Answer each of the following for a positively skewed distribution. (*Caution:* This is a trick question.)
    a. Find the proportion of the distribution located in the tail beyond $z = 2.00$.
    b. What z-score value separates the top 40% of the distribution from the rest?

12. Find each of the following probabilities for a normal distribution.
    a. $p(z > -1.00)$
    b. $p(z > -0.80)$
    c. $p(z < 0.25)$
    d. $p(z < 1.25)$

13. What proportion of a normal distribution is located
    a. Between $z = 0.50$ and $z = -0.50$.
    b. Between $z = 1.00$ and $z = -1.00$.
    c. Between $z = 0$ and $z = -1.50$.
    d. Between $z = 1.75$ and $z = -0.25$.

14. For a normal distribution, find the z-score values that separate
    a. The middle 60% of the distribution from the 40% in the tails.
    b. The middle 70% of the distribution from the 30% in the tails.
    c. The middle 80% of the distribution from the 20% in the tails.
    d. The middle 90% of the distribution from the 10% in the tails.

15. The distribution of SAT scores is normal with $\mu = 500$ and $\sigma = 100$.
    a. What SAT score, X value, separates the top 10% from the rest of the distribution?
    b. What SAT score, X value, separates the top 30% from the rest of the distribution?
    c. What SAT score, X value, separates the top 40% from the rest of the distribution?

16. A normal distribution has a mean of $\mu = 60$ and a standard deviation of $\sigma = 20$. For each of the following scores, indicate whether the tail of the distribution is to the left or right of the score, and find the proportion of the distribution in the tail.
    a. $X = 75$
    b. $X = 65$
    c. $X = 50$
    d. $X = 30$

17. A normal distribution has a mean of $\mu = 80$ and a standard deviation of $\sigma = 10$. For each of the following scores, indicate whether the body of the distribution is to the left or right of the score, and find the proportion of the distribution in the body.
    a. $X = 85$
    b. $X = 92$
    c. $X = 78$
    d. $X = 72$

18. The distribution of scores on the SAT is approximately normal with a mean of $\mu = 500$ and a standard deviation of $\sigma = 100$. For the population of students who have taken the SAT,
    a. What proportion have SAT scores greater than 700?
    b. What proportion have SAT scores greater than 550?
    c. What is the minimum SAT score needed to be in the highest 10% of the population?
    d. If the state college only accepts students from the top 60% of the SAT distribution, what is the minimum SAT score needed to be accepted?

19. The distribution of IQ scores is normal with $\mu = 100$ and $\sigma = 15$. What proportion of the population has IQ scores
    a. Greater than 115?
    b. Greater than 130?
    c. Greater than 145?

20. Laboratory rats commit an average of $\mu = 40$ errors before they solve a standardized maze problem. The distribution of error scores is approximately normal with a standard deviation of $\sigma = 8$. A researcher is testing the effect of a new dietary supplement on intelligence. A newborn rat is selected and is given the supplement daily until it reaches maturity. The rat is then tested on the maze and finishes with a total of $X = 24$ errors.
    a. What is the probability that a regular rat (without the supplement) would solve the maze with a score less than or equal to $X = 24$ errors?

b. Is it reasonable to conclude that the rat with the supplement is smarter than the vast majority of regular rats?

c. Does it appear that the supplement has an effect on intelligence? Explain your answer.

21. IQ scores form a normal distribution with a mean of $\mu = 100$ and a standard deviation of $\sigma = 15$. What is the minimum IQ needed

  a. To be in the top 5% of the population?

  b. To be in the top 10% of the population?

  c. To be in the top 25% of the population?

22. Information from the Department of Motor Vehicles indicates that the average age of licensed drivers is $\mu = 39.7$ years with a standard deviation of $\sigma = 12.5$ years. Assuming that the distribution of drivers' ages is approximately normal,

  a. What proportion of licensed drivers are more than 50 years old?

  b. What proportion of licensed drivers are less than 30 years old?

23. Drivers pay an average of $\mu = \$690$ per year for automobile insurance. The distribution of insurance payments is approximately normal with a standard deviation of $\sigma = \$110$.

  a. What proportion of drivers pay more than $800 per year for insurance?

  b. What is the probability of randomly selecting a driver who pays less than $600 per year for insurance?

24. A consumer survey indicates that the average household spends $\mu = \$155$ on groceries each week. The distribution of spending amounts is approximately normal with a standard deviation of $\sigma = \$25$. Based on this distribution,

  a. What proportion of the population spends more than $175 per week on groceries?

  b. What is the probability of randomly selecting a family that spends less than $100 per week on groceries?

  c. How much money do you need to spend on groceries each week to be in the top 20% of the distribution?

CHAPTER

7

Probability and Samples: The Distribution of Sample Means

Tools You Will Need

The following items are considered essential background material for this chapter. If you doubt your knowledge of any of these items, you should review the appropriate chapter and section before proceeding.

- Random sampling (Chapter 6)

- Probability and the normal distribution (Chapter 6)

- *z*-Scores (Chapter 5)

7.1   OVERVIEW

The preceding two chapters presented the topics of z-scores and probability. Whenever a score is selected from a population, you should be able to compute a z-score that describes exactly where the score is located in the distribution. And, if the population is normal, you should be able to determine the probability value for obtaining any individual score. In a normal distribution, for example, any score located in the tail of the distribution beyond $z = +2.00$ is an extreme value, and a score this large has a probability of only $p = 0.0228$.

However, the z-scores and probabilities that we have considered so far are limited to situations in which the sample consists of a single score. Most research studies use much larger samples such as $n = 25$ preschool children or $n = 100$ laboratory rats. In this chapter we will extend the concepts of z-scores and probability to cover situations with larger samples. In particular, we will introduce a procedure for transforming a sample mean into a z-score. Thus, a researcher will be able to compute a z-score that describes an entire sample. As always, a z-score value near zero indicates a central, representative sample; a z-value beyond $+2.00$ or -2.00 indicates an extreme sample. Thus, it will be possible to describe how any specific sample is related to all the other possible samples. In addition, we will be able to use the z-score values to look up probabilities for obtaining certain samples, no matter how many scores the sample contains.

In general, the difficulty of working with samples is that a sample provides an incomplete picture of the population. Suppose, for example, a researcher selects a sample of $n = 25$ students from the state college. Although the sample should be representative of the entire student population, there will almost certainly be some segments of the population that are not included in the sample. In addition, any statistics that are computed for the sample will not be identical to the corresponding parameters for the entire population. For example, the average IQ for the sample of 25 students will not be the same as the overall mean IQ for the entire population. This difference, or *error* between sample statistics and the corresponding population parameters, is called *sampling error* and was illustrated in Figure 1.2 (page 7).

DEFINITION

Sampling error is the natural discrepancy, or amount of error, between a sample statistic and its corresponding population parameter.

Furthermore, samples are variable; they are not all the same. If you take two separate samples from the same population, the samples will be different. They will contain different individuals, they will have different scores, and they will have different sample means. How can you tell which sample gives the best description of the population? Can you even predict how well a sample will describe its population? What is the probability of selecting a sample that has a certain sample mean? These questions can be answered once we establish the set of rules that relate samples to populations.

7.2   THE DISTRIBUTION OF SAMPLE MEANS

As noted, two separate samples probably will be different even though they are taken from the same population. The samples will have different individuals, different scores, different means, and so on. In most cases, it is possible to obtain thousands of different samples from one population. With all these different samples coming from the same population, it may seem hopeless to try to establish some simple rules for the relationships between samples and populations. Fortunately, however, the huge set of possible samples forms a relatively simple and orderly pattern that makes it possible to predict the characteristics of a sample with some accuracy. The ability to predict sample characteristics is based on the *distribution of sample means*.

D E F I N I T I O N

The **distribution of sample means** is the collection of sample means for all the possible random samples of a particular size (*n*) that can be obtained from a population.

Notice that the distribution of sample means contains *all the possible samples*. It is necessary to have all the possible values to compute probabilities. For example, if the entire set contains exactly 100 samples, then the probability of obtaining any specific sample is 1 out of 100: $p = \frac{1}{100}$ (Box 7.1).

Also, you should notice that the distribution of sample means is different from distributions we have considered before. Until now we always have discussed distributions of scores; now the values in the distribution are not scores, but statistics (sample means). Because statistics are obtained from samples, a distribution of statistics is referred to as a *sampling distribution*.

D E F I N I T I O N

A **sampling distribution** is a distribution of statistics obtained by selecting all the possible samples of a specific size from a population.

Thus, the distribution of sample means is an example of a sampling distribution. In fact, it often is called the sampling distribution of *M*.

If you actually wanted to construct the distribution of sample means, you would first select a random sample of a specific size (*n*) from a population, calculate the sample mean, and place the sample mean in a frequency distribution. Then you select another

---

BOX 7.1	**PROBABILITY AND THE DISTRIBUTION OF SAMPLE MEANS**

I have a bad habit of losing playing cards. This habit is compounded by the fact that I always save the old deck in the hope that someday I will find the missing cards. As a result, I have a drawer filled with partial decks of playing cards. Suppose that I take one of these almost-complete decks, shuffle the cards carefully, and then randomly select one card. What is the probability that I will draw a king?

You should realize that it is impossible to answer this probability question. To find the probability of selecting a king, you must know how many cards are in the deck and exactly which cards are missing. (It is crucial that you know whether or not any kings are missing.) The point of this simple example is that any probability question requires that you have complete

information about the population from which the sample is being selected. In this case, you must know all the possible cards in the deck before you can find the probability for selecting any specific card.

In this chapter, we are examining probability and sample means. In order to find the probability for any specific sample mean, you first must know *all the possible sample means*. Therefore, we begin by defining and describing the set of all possible sample means that can be obtained from a particular population. Once we have specified the complete set of all possible sample means (i.e., the distribution of sample means), we will be able to find the probability of selecting any specific sample mean.

random sample with the same number of scores. Again, you calculate the sample mean and add it to your distribution. You continue selecting samples and calculating means, over and over, until you have the complete set of all the possible random samples. At this point, your frequency distribution will show the distribution of sample means.

We demonstrate the process of constructing a distribution of sample means in Example 7.1, but first we use common sense and a little logic to predict the general characteristics of the distribution.

1. The sample means should pile up around the population mean. Samples are not expected to be perfect, but they are representative of the population. As a result, most of the sample means should be relatively close to the population mean.

2. The pile of sample means should tend to form a normal-shaped distribution. Logically, most of the samples should have means close to μ, and it should be relatively rare to find sample means that are substantially different from μ. As a result, the sample means should pile up in the center of the distribution (around μ) and the frequencies should taper off as the distance between M and μ increases. This describes a normal-shaped distribution.

3. In general, the larger the sample size, the closer the sample means should be to the population mean, μ. Logically, a large sample should be a better representative than a small sample. Thus, the sample means obtained with a large sample size should cluster relatively close to the population mean; the means obtained from small samples should be more widely scattered.

As you will see, each of these three commonsense characteristics is an accurate description of the distribution of sample means. The following example demonstrates the process of constructing the distribution of sample means by repeatedly selecting samples from a population.

EXAMPLE 7.1

Remember that random sampling requires sampling with replacement.

Consider a population that consists of only 4 scores: 2, 4, 6, 8. This population is pictured in the frequency distribution histogram in Figure 7.1.

We are going to use this population as the basis for constructing the distribution of sample means for $n = 2$. Remember: This distribution is the collection of sample means from all the possible random samples of $n = 2$ from this population. We begin by looking at all the possible samples. For this example, there are 16 different samples, and they are all listed in Table 7.1. Notice that the samples are listed systematically. First, we list all the possible samples with $X = 2$ as the first score, then all the possible samples with $X = 4$ as the first score, and so on. In this way, we are sure that we have all of the possible random samples.

FIGURE 7.1

Frequency distribution histogram for a population of 4 scores: 2, 4, 6, 8.

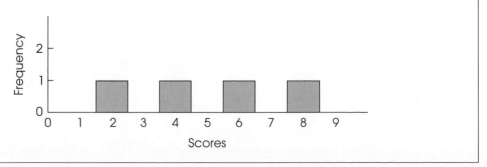

TABLE 7.1

All the possible samples of $n = 2$ scores that can be obtained from the population presented in Figure 7.1. Notice that the table lists *random samples*. This requires sampling with replacement, so it is possible to select the same score twice.

| | Scores | | Sample Mean |
Sample	First	Second	(*M*)
1	2	2	2
2	2	4	3
3	2	6	4
4	2	8	5
5	4	2	3
6	4	4	4
7	4	6	5
8	4	8	6
9	6	2	4
10	6	4	5
11	6	6	6
12	6	8	7
13	8	2	5
14	8	4	6
15	8	6	7
16	8	8	8

Next, we compute the mean, *M*, for each of the 16 samples (see the last column of Table 7.1). The 16 means are then placed in a frequency distribution histogram in Figure 7.2. This is the distribution of sample means. Note that the distribution in Figure 7.2 demonstrates two of the characteristics that we predicted for the distribution of sample means.

1. The sample means pile up around the population mean. For this example, the population mean is $\mu = 5$, and the sample means are clustered around a value of 5. It should not surprise you that the sample means tend to approximate the population mean. After all, samples are supposed to be representative of the population.

2. The distribution of sample means is approximately normal in shape. This is a characteristic that will be discussed in detail later and will be extremely useful because we already know a great deal about probabilities and the normal distribution (Chapter 6).

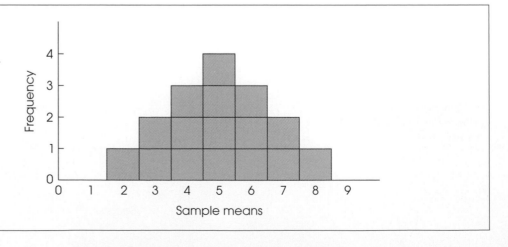

FIGURE 7.2

The distribution of sample means for $n = 2$. The distribution shows the 16 sample means from Table 7.1.

Remember that our goal in this chapter is to answer probability questions about samples with $n > 1$.

Finally, you should notice that we can use the distribution of sample means to answer probability questions about sample means (see Box 7.1). For example, if you take a sample of $n = 2$ scores from the original population, what is the probability of obtaining a sample mean greater than 7? In symbols,

$$p(M > 7) = ?$$

Because probability is equivalent to proportion, the probability question can be restated as follows: What proportion of all the possible sample means have values greater than 7? In this form, the question is easily answered by looking at the distribution of sample means. All the possible sample means are pictured (see Figure 7.2), and only 1 out of the 16 means has a value greater than 7. The answer, therefore, is 1 out of 16, or $p = \frac{1}{16}$.

THE CENTRAL LIMIT THEOREM

Example 7.1 demonstrates the construction of the distribution of sample means for an overly simplified situation with a very small population and samples that each contain only $n = 2$ scores. In more realistic circumstances, with larger populations and larger samples, the number of possible samples will increase dramatically and it will be virtually impossible to actually obtain every possible random sample. Fortunately, it is possible to determine exactly what the distribution of sample means will look like without taking hundreds or thousands of samples. Specifically, a mathematical proposition known as the *central limit theorem* provides a precise description of the distribution that would be obtained if you selected every possible sample, calculated every sample mean, and constructed the distribution of the sample mean. This important and useful theorem serves as a cornerstone for much of inferential statistics. Following is the essence of the theorem.

Central limit theorem: For any population with mean μ and standard deviation σ, the distribution of sample means for sample size n will have a mean of μ and a standard deviation of $\sigma/\sqrt{n}$ and will approach a normal distribution as n approaches infinity.

The value of this theorem comes from two simple facts. First, it describes the distribution of sample means for *any population,* no matter what shape, mean, or standard deviation. Second, the distribution of sample means "approaches" a normal distribution very rapidly. By the time the sample size reaches $n = 30$, the distribution is almost perfectly normal.

Note that the central limit theorem describes the distribution of sample means by identifying the three basic characteristics that describe any distribution: shape, central tendency, and variability. We will examine each of these.

THE SHAPE OF THE DISTRIBUTION OF SAMPLE MEANS

It has been observed that the distribution of sample means tends to be a normal distribution. In fact, this distribution will be almost perfectly normal if either of the following two conditions is satisfied:

1. The population from which the samples are selected is a normal distribution.

2. The number of scores (n) in each sample is relatively large, around 30 or more.

(As n gets larger, the distribution of sample means will closely approximate a normal distribution. When $n > 30$, the distribution is almost normal regardless of the shape of the original population.)

The fact that the distribution of sample means tends to be normal should not be surprising. Whenever you take a sample from a population, you expect the sample mean to be near to the population mean. When you take lots of different samples, you expect the sample means to "pile up" around μ, resulting in a normal-shaped distribution. You can see this tendency emerging (although it is not yet normal) in Figure 7.2.

THE MEAN OF THE DISTRIBUTION OF SAMPLE MEANS: THE EXPECTED VALUE OF *M*

The expected value of *M* is often identified by the symbol μ_M, signifying the "mean of the sample means." However, μ_M is always equal to μ, so we will continue to use the symbol μ to refer to the mean for the population of scores and the mean for the distribution of sample means.

As we noted in Example 7.1, the distribution of sample means is centered around the mean of the population from which the samples were obtained. In fact, the average value of all the sample means is exactly equal to the value of the population mean. This fact should be intuitively reasonable; the sample means are expected to be close to the population mean, and they do tend to pile up around μ. The formal statement of this phenomenon is that the mean of the distribution of sample means always will be identical to the population mean. This mean value is called the *expected value of* M.

In commonsense terms, a sample mean is "expected" to be near its population mean. When all of the possible sample means are obtained, the average value will be identical to μ.

The fact that the average value of *M* is equal to μ was first introduced in Chapter 4 (page 101) in the context of *biased* versus *unbiased* statistics. The sample mean is an example of an unbiased statistic, which means that on average the sample statistic produces a value that is exactly equal to the corresponding population parameter. In this case, the average value of all the sample means is exactly equal to μ.

DEFINITION

The mean of the distribution of sample means is equal to μ (the population mean) and is called the **expected value of** *M*.

THE STANDARD ERROR OF *M*

So far, we have considered the shape and the central tendency of the distribution of sample means. To completely describe this distribution, we need one more characteristic, variability. The value we will be working with is the standard deviation for the distribution of sample means, and it is called the *standard error of* M. Remember that a sample is not expected to provide a perfectly accurate reflection of its population. Although a sample mean should be representative of the population mean, there typically will be some error between the sample and the population. The standard error measures exactly how much difference should be expected on average between a sample mean, *M* and the population mean, μ.

DEFINITION

The standard deviation of the distribution of sample means is called the **standard error of** *M*. The standard error measures the standard amount of difference between a sample mean (*M*) and the population mean (μ).

standard error of $M = \sigma_M$ = standard distance between M and μ

The notation that is used to identify the standard error is σ_M. The σ indicates that we are measuring a standard deviation or a standard distance from the mean. The subscript *M* indicates that we are measuring the standard deviation for a distribution of sample means. The standard error is an extremely valuable measure because it specifies precisely how well a sample mean estimates its population mean—that is, how much error you should expect, on the average, between *M* and μ. Remember that one basic reason for taking samples is to use the sample data to answer questions about the population.

However, you do not expect a sample to provide a perfectly accurate picture of the population. There always will be some discrepancy or error between a sample statistic and the corresponding population parameter. Now we are able to calculate exactly how much error to expect. For any sample size (*n*), we can compute the standard error, which measures the average distance between a sample mean and the population mean.

The magnitude of the standard error is determined by two factors: (1) the size of the sample and (2) the standard deviation of the population from which the sample is selected. We will examine each of these factors.

The sample size   Earlier we predicted, based on common sense, that the distribution of sample means would be tightly clustered around μ for large samples and more widely scattered for smaller samples. It should be intuitively reasonable that the size of a sample should influence how accurately the sample represents its population. Specifically, a large sample should be more accurate than a small sample. In general, as the sample size increases, the error between the sample mean and the population mean should decrease. This rule is also known as the *law of large numbers*.

DEFINITION

> The **law of large numbers** states that the larger the sample size (*n*), the more probable it is that the sample mean will be close to the population mean.

The population standard deviation   As we noted earlier, there is an inverse relationship between the sample size and the standard error: bigger samples have smaller error, and smaller samples have bigger error. At the extreme, the smallest possible sample (and the largest standard error) occurs when the sample consists of *n* = 1 score. At this extreme, the sample is a single score, *X*, and the sample mean is also *X*. In this case, the standard error measures the standard distance between the score, *X*, and the population mean, μ. However, we already know the standard distance between *X* and μ is the standard deviation. By definition, σ is the standard distance between *X* and μ. Thus, when *n* = 1, the standard error and the standard deviation are identical.

When *n* = 1, standard error = σ_M = σ = standard deviation

You can think of the standard deviation as the "starting point" for standard error. When *n* = 1, the standard error and the standard deviation are the same: σ_M = σ. As sample size increases beyond *n* = 1, the sample becomes a more accurate representative of the population, and the standard error decreases. The formula for standard error expresses this relationship between standard deviation and sample size (*n*).

$$\text{standard error} = \sigma_M = \frac{\sigma}{\sqrt{n}} \tag{7.1}$$

Note that the formula satisfies all of the requirements for the standard error. Specifically,

a. As sample size (*n*) increases, the size of the standard error decreases. (Larger samples are more accurate.)

b. When the sample consists of a single score (*n* = 1), the standard error is the same as the standard deviation (σ_M = σ).

In Equation 7.1 and in most of the preceding discussion, we have defined standard error in terms of the population standard deviation. However, the population standard deviation (σ) and the population variance (σ^2) are directly related, and it is easy to

FIGURE 7.3

The relationship between standard error and sample size. As the sample size is increased, there is less error between the sample mean and the population mean.

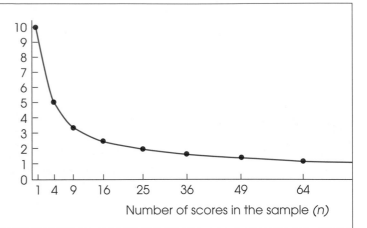

Standard Error (based on $\sigma = 10$)

Standard distance between a sample mean and the population mean

Number of scores in the sample (n)

substitute variance into the equation for standard error. Using the simple equality $\sigma = \sqrt{\sigma^2}$, the equation for standard error can be rewritten as follows:

$$\text{standard error} = \sigma_M = \frac{\sigma}{\sqrt{n}} = \frac{\sqrt{\sigma^2}}{\sqrt{n}} = \sqrt{\frac{\sigma^2}{n}} \qquad (7.2)$$

Throughout the rest of this chapter (and in Chapter 8), we will continue to define standard error in terms of the standard deviation (Equation 7.1). However, in later chapters (starting in Chapter 9) the formula based on variance (Equation 7.2) will become more useful.

Figure 7.3 illustrates the general relationship between standard error and sample size. Again, the basic concept is that the larger a sample is, the more accurately it represents its population. Also note that the standard error decreases in relation to the *square root* of the sample size. As a result, researchers can substantially reduce error by increasing sample size up to around $n = 30$. However, increasing sample size beyond $n = 30$ does not produce much additional improvement in how well the sample represents the population.

THREE DIFFERENT DISTRIBUTIONS

Before we move forward with our discussion of the distribution of sample means, we will pause for a moment to emphasize the idea that we are now dealing with three distinct distributions. First, we have the original population of scores. This population contains the scores for thousands or millions of individual people, and it has its own shape, mean, and standard deviation. For example, the population of IQ scores consists of millions of individual IQ scores that form a normal distribution with a mean of $\mu = 100$ and a standard deviation of $\sigma = 15$. Next, we have the sample that is selected from the population. The sample consists of a small set of scores for a few people who have been selected to represent the entire population. The sample also has its own shape, mean, and standard deviation. For example, we could select a sample of $n = 25$ people, measure each individual's IQ score, and then calculate the sample mean and the sample standard deviation for the set of 25 scores. An example of a population and a sample are shown in Figure 7.4. The third distribution is the distribution of sample means. This is a theoretical distribution consisting of the sample means obtained from all the possible random samples of a specific size, and it has its own shape, mean, and standard deviation. For example, the distribution of sample means for $n = 25$ IQ scores would be normal with a mean (expected value) of $\mu = 100$ and a standard deviation (standard error) of $\sigma_M = 15/\sqrt{25} = 3$. Note that the mean for our sample is one of the values contained in the distribution of sample means. Figure 7.4 also shows the distribution of sample means based on samples of $n = 25$ IQ scores.

FIGURE 7.4

Three distributions. Part (a) shows the population of IQ scores. Part (b) shows a sample of $n = 25$ IQ scores. Part (c) shows the distribution of sample means for samples of $n = 25$ scores. Note that the sample mean from part (b) is one of the thousands of sample means in the part (c) distribution.

(a) Original population of IQ scores.

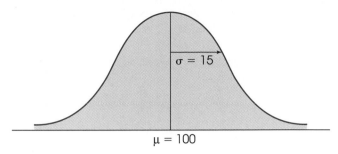

(b) A sample of $n = 25$ IQ scores.

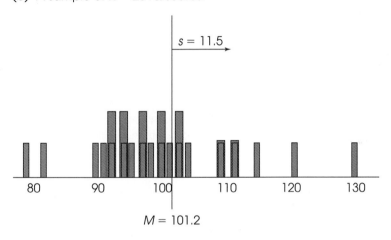

(c) The distribution of sample means. Sample means for all the possible random samples of $n = 25$ IQ scores.

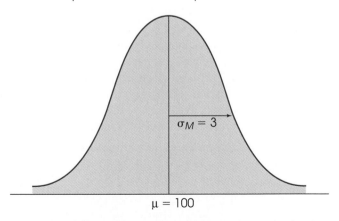

LEARNING CHECK

1. A population of scores is normal with $\mu = 80$ and $\sigma = 20$.

   a. Describe the distribution of sample means for samples of size $n = 16$ selected from this population. (Describe shape, central tendency, and variability for the distribution.)

   b. How would the distribution of sample means be changed if the sample size were $n = 100$ instead of $n = 16$?

2. As sample size increases, the value of the standard error also increases. (True or false?)

3. Under what circumstances will the distribution of sample means be a normal-shaped distribution?

ANSWERS **1. a.** The distribution of sample means is normal with a mean (expected value) of $\mu = 80$ and a standard error of $\sigma_M = 20/\sqrt{16} = 5$.

b. The distribution would still be normal with a mean of 80 but the standard error would be reduced to $\sigma_M = 20/\sqrt{100} = 2$.

2. False. Standard error decreases as n increases.

3. The distribution of sample means will be normal if the sample size is relatively large (around $n = 30$ or more) or if the population of scores is normal.

7.3 PROBABILITY AND THE DISTRIBUTION OF SAMPLE MEANS

The primary use of the distribution of sample means is to find the probability associated with any specific sample. Recall that probability is equivalent to proportion. Because the distribution of sample means presents the entire set of all possible Ms, we can use proportions of this distribution to determine probabilities. The following example demonstrates this process.

E X A M P L E   7 . 2

Caution: Whenever you have a probability question about a sample mean, you must use the distribution of sample means.

The population of scores on the SAT forms a normal distribution with $\mu = 500$ and $\sigma = 100$. If you take a random sample of $n = 25$ students, what is the probability that the sample mean will be greater than $M = 540$?

First, you can restate this probability question as a proportion question: Out of all the possible sample means, what proportion have values greater than 540? You know about "all the possible sample means;" this is simply the distribution of sample means. The problem is to find a specific portion of this distribution.

Although we cannot construct the distribution of sample means by repeatedly taking samples and calculating means (as in Example 7.1), we know exactly what the distribution looks like based on the information from the central limit theorem. Specifically, the distribution of sample means has the following characteristics:

a. The distribution is normal because the population of SAT scores is normal.

b. The distribution has a mean of 500 because the population mean is $\mu = 500$.

c. For $n = 25$, the distribution has a standard error of $\sigma_M = 20$:

$$\sigma_M = \frac{\sigma}{\sqrt{n}} = \frac{100}{\sqrt{25}} = \frac{100}{5} = 20$$

This distribution of sample means is shown in Figure 7.5.

We are interested in sample means greater than 540 (the shaded area in Figure 7.5), so the next step is to use a z-score to locate the exact position of $M = 540$ in the distribution. The value 540 is located above the mean by 40 points, which is exactly 2 standard deviations (in this case, exactly 2 standard errors). Thus, the z-score for $M = 540$ is $z = +2.00$.

FIGURE 7.5

The distribution of sample means for $n = 25$. Samples were selected from a normal population with $\mu = 500$ and $\sigma = 100$.

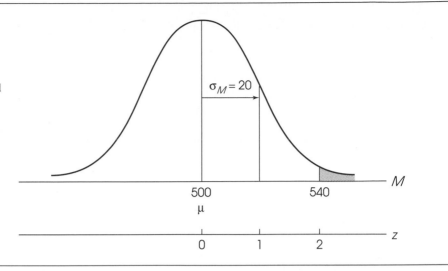

Because this distribution of sample means is normal, you can use the unit normal table to find the probability associated with $z = +2.00$. The table indicates that 0.0228 of the distribution is located in the tail of the distribution beyond $z = +2.00$. Our conclusion is that it is very unlikely, $p = 0.0228$ (2.28%), to obtain a random sample of $n = 25$ students with an average SAT score greater than 540.

A z-SCORE FOR SAMPLE MEANS

As demonstrated in Example 7.2, it is possible to use a z-score to describe the position of any specific sample within the distribution of sample means. The z-score tells exactly where a specific sample is located in relation to all the other possible samples that could have been obtained. A z-score of $z = +2.00$, for example, indicates that the sample mean is much larger than usually would be expected: It is greater than the expected value of M by twice the standard distance. The z-score for each sample mean can be computed by using the standard z-score formula with a few minor changes. First, the value we are locating is a sample mean rather than a score, so the formula uses M in place of X. Second, the standard deviation for this distribution is measured by the standard error, so the formula uses σ_M in place of σ (Box 7.2). The resulting formula, giving the z-score value corresponding to any sample mean, is

Caution: When computing z for a single score, use the standard deviation, σ. When computing z for a sample mean, you must use the standard error, σ_M.

$$z = \frac{M - \mu}{\sigma_M} \tag{7.3}$$

Every sample mean has a z-score that describes its position in the distribution of sample means. Using z-scores and the unit normal table, it is possible to find the probability associated with any specific sample mean (as in Example 7.2). Example 7.3 demonstrates that it also is possible to make quantitative predictions about the kinds of samples that should be obtained from any population.

EXAMPLE 7.3

Once again, the distribution of SAT scores forms a normal distribution with a mean of $\mu = 500$ and a standard deviation of $\sigma = 100$. For this example, we are going to determine what kind of sample mean is likely to be obtained as the average SAT score for a random sample of $n = 25$ students.

BOX 7.2	THE DIFFERENCE BETWEEN STANDARD DEVIATION AND STANDARD ERROR

A constant source of confusion for many students is the difference between standard deviation and standard error. Remember that standard deviation measures the standard distance between a *score* and the population mean, $X - \mu$. Whenever you are working with a distribution of scores, the standard deviation is the appropriate measure of variability. Standard error, on the other hand, measures the standard distance between a *sample mean* and the population mean, $M - \mu$. Whenever you have a question concerning a sample, the standard error is the appropriate measure of variability.

If you still find the distinction confusing, there is a simple solution. Namely, if you always use standard error, you always will be right. Consider the formula for standard error:

$$\text{standard error} = \sigma_M = \frac{\sigma}{\sqrt{n}}$$

If you are working with a single score, then $n = 1$, and the standard error becomes

$$\text{standard error} = \sigma_M = \frac{\sigma}{\sqrt{n}} = \frac{\sigma}{\sqrt{1}}$$

$$= \sigma = \text{standard deviation}$$

Thus, standard error always measures the standard distance from the population mean, whether you have a sample of $n = 1$ or $n = 100$.

First, we expect the sample mean to be *around* $\mu = 500$. For this example, however, we will be more specific, and determine the exact range of values that is expected for our sample mean 80% of the time. We begin with the distribution of sample means. Remember that this distribution is the collection of all the possible sample means, and it will show which samples are likely to be obtained and which are not.

As demonstrated in Example 7.2, the distribution of sample means for $n = 25$ will be normal with an expected value of $\mu = 500$ and a standard error of $\sigma_M = 20$. The distribution of sample means is shown in Figure 7.6. Looking at the distribution, it should be clear that a sample of $n = 25$ students should have a mean SAT score around 500. To be more precise, we can determine the range of values that is expected 80% of the time by locating the middle 80% of the distribution. Because the distribution is normal, we can use the unit normal table. The 80% in the middle is split in half with 40% (0.4000) to the right of the mean and 40% (0.4000) to the left. Looking in column D of the table (proportion between the mean and z) for 0.4000, we find a corresponding z-score value of $z = 1.28$. Thus, the z-score boundaries for the middle 80% are $z = +1.28$ and $z = -1.28$. By definition, a z-score of 1.28 represents a location that is 1.28 standard deviations (or standard errors) from the mean. With a standard error of 20 parts, the distance from the mean is $1.28(20) = 25.6$ points. The mean is $\mu = 500$, so a distance of 25.6 in both directions produces a range of values from 474.4 to 525.6.

Thus, 80% of all the possible sample means are contained in a range between 474.4 and 525.6. If we select a sample of $n = 25$ students, we can be 80% confident that the mean SAT score for the sample will be in this range.

The point of Example 7.3 is that the distribution of sample means makes it possible to predict the value that ought to be obtained for a sample mean. We know, for example, that a sample of $n = 25$ students ought to have a mean SAT score around 500. More specifically, we are 80% confident that the value of the sample mean will be between 474.4 and 525.6. The ability to predict sample means in this way will be a valuable tool for the inferential statistics that follow.

FIGURE 7.6

The middle 80% of the distribution of sample means for $n = 25$. Samples were selected from a normal population with $\mu = 500$ and $\sigma = 100$.

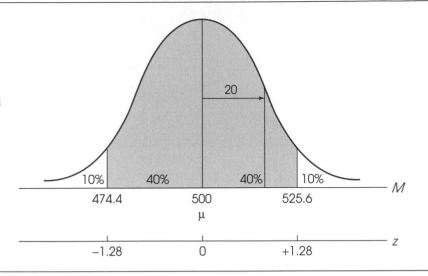

LEARNING CHECK

1. A population has $\mu = 80$ and $\sigma = 12$. Find the z-score corresponding to each of the following sample means:

   a. $M = 84$ for a sample of $n = 9$ scores

   b. $M = 74$ for a sample of $n = 16$ scores

   c. $M = 81$ for a sample of $n = 36$ scores

2. A random sample of $n = 25$ scores is selected from a normal population with $\mu = 90$ and $\sigma = 10$.

   a. What is the probability that the sample mean will have a value greater than 94?

   b. What is the probability that the sample mean will have a value less than 91?

3. A positively skewed distribution has $\mu = 60$ and $\sigma = 8$.

   a. What is the probability of obtaining a sample mean greater than $M = 62$ for a sample of $n = 4$ scores? (Be careful. This is a trick question.)

   b. What is the probability of obtaining a sample mean greater than $M = 62$ for a sample of $n = 64$ scores?

ANSWERS

1. **a.** The standard error is $12/\sqrt{9} = 4$. The z-score is $z = +1.00$.

   b. The standard error is $12/\sqrt{16} = 3$. The z-score is $z = -2.00$.

   c. The standard error is $12/\sqrt{36} = 2$. The z-score is $z = +0.50$.

2. **a.** The standard error is $10/\sqrt{25} = 2$. A mean of $M = 94$ corresponds to $z = +2.00$, and $p = 0.0228$.

   b. A mean of $M = 91$ corresponds to $z = +0.50$, and $p = 0.6915$.

3. **a.** The distribution of sample means does not satisfy either of the criteria for being normal. Therefore, you cannot use the unit normal table, and it is impossible to find the probability.

   b. With $n = 64$, the distribution of sample means is nearly normal. The standard error is $8/\sqrt{64} = 1$, the z-score is $+2.00$, and the probability is 0.0228.

7.4 MORE ABOUT STANDARD ERROR

At the beginning of this chapter, we introduced the idea that it is possible to obtain thousands of different samples from a single population. Each sample will have its own individuals, its own scores, and its own sample mean. The distribution of sample means provides a method for organizing all of the different sample means into a single picture that shows how the sample means are related to each other and how they are related to the overall population mean. Figure 7.7 shows a prototypical distribution of sample means. To emphasize the fact that the distribution contains many different samples, we have constructed this figure so that the distribution is made up of hundreds of small boxes, each box representing a single sample mean. Also notice that the sample means tend to pile up around the population mean (μ), forming a normal-shaped distribution as predicted by the central limit theorem.

The distribution shown in Figure 7.7 provides a concrete example for reviewing the general concepts of sampling error and standard error. Although the following points may seem obvious, they are intended to provide you with a better understanding of these two statistical concepts.

1. Sampling Error.   The general concept of sampling error is that a sample typically will not provide a perfectly accurate representation of its population. More specifically, there typically will be some discrepancy (or error) between a statistic computed for a sample and the corresponding parameter for the population. As you look at Figure 7.7, notice that the individual sample means are not exactly equal to the population mean. In fact, 50% of the samples have means that are smaller than μ (the entire left-hand side of the distribution). Similarly, 50% of the samples produce means that overestimate the true population mean. In general, there will be some discrepancy, or *sampling error,* between the mean for a sample and the mean for the population from which the sample was obtained.

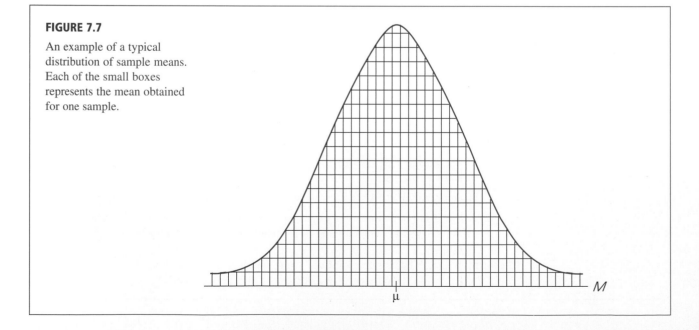

FIGURE 7.7

An example of a typical distribution of sample means. Each of the small boxes represents the mean obtained for one sample.

2. Standard Error. Again, looking at Figure 7.7, notice that most of the sample means are relatively close to the population mean (those in the center of the distribution). These samples provide a fairly accurate representation of the population. On the other hand, some samples will produce means that are out in the tails of the distribution, relatively far way from the population mean. These extreme sample means do not accurately represent the population. For each individual sample, you can measure the error (or distance) between the sample mean and the population mean. For some samples, the error will be relatively small, but for other samples, the error will be relatively large. The *standard error* provides a way to measure the "average" or standard distance between a sample mean and the population mean.

Thus, the standard error provides a method for defining and measuring sampling error. Knowing the standard error gives researchers a good indication of how accurately their sample data represent the populations they are studying. In most research situations, for example, the population mean is unknown, and the researcher selects a sample to help obtain information about the unknown population. Specifically, the sample mean provides information about the value of the unknown population mean. The sample mean is not expected to give a perfectly accurate representation of the population mean; there will be some error, and the standard error tells *exactly how much error,* on average, should exist between the sample mean and the unknown population mean. The following example demonstrates the use of the standard error and provides additional information about the relationship between standard error and standard deviation.

EXAMPLE 7.4   We will begin with a population that is normally distributed with a mean of $\mu = 80$ and a standard deviation of $\sigma = 20$. Next, we will take a sample from this population and examine how accurately the sample mean represents the population mean. More specifically, we will examine how sample size affects accuracy by considering three different samples: one with $n = 1$ score, one with $n = 4$ scores, and one with $n = 100$ scores.

Figure 7.8 shows the distributions of sample means based on samples of $n = 1$, $n = 4$, and $n = 100$. Each distribution shows the collection of all possible sample

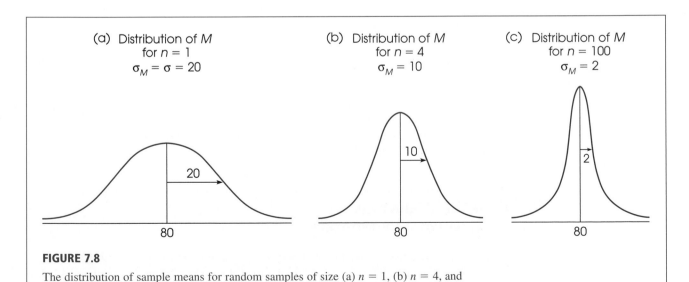

FIGURE 7.8

The distribution of sample means for random samples of size (a) $n = 1$, (b) $n = 4$, and (c) $n = 100$ obtained from a normal population with $\mu = 80$ and $\sigma = 20$. Notice that the size of the standard error decreases as the sample size increases.

means that could be obtained for that particular sample size. Notice that all three sampling distributions are normal (because the original population is normal), and all three have the same mean, $\mu = 80$, which is the expected value of M. However, the three distributions differ greatly with respect to variability. We will consider each one separately.

The smallest sample size is $n = 1$. When a sample consists of a single score, the mean for the sample will equal the value of that score, $M = X$. Thus, when $n = 1$, the distribution of sample means is identical to the original population of scores. In this case, the standard error for the distribution of sample means is equal to the standard deviation for the original population. Equation 7.1 confirms this observation.

$$\sigma_M = \frac{\sigma}{\sqrt{n}} = \frac{20}{\sqrt{1}} = 20$$

As we noted earlier, the population standard deviation is the "starting point" for the standard error. With the smallest possible sample, $n = 1$, the standard error is equal to the standard deviation [see Figure 7.8(a)].

As the sample size increases, however, the standard error gets smaller. For $n = 4$, the standard error is

$$\sigma_M = \frac{\sigma}{\sqrt{n}} = \frac{20}{\sqrt{4}} = \frac{20}{2} = 10$$

That is, the typical (or standard) distance between M and μ is 10 points. Figure 7.8(b) illustrates this distribution. Notice that the sample means in this distribution approximate the population mean more closely than in the previous distribution where $n = 1$.

With a sample of $n = 100$, the standard error is still smaller.

$$\sigma_M = \frac{\sigma}{\sqrt{n}} = \frac{20}{\sqrt{100}} = \frac{20}{10} = 2$$

A sample of $n = 100$ scores should provide a sample mean that is a much better estimate of μ than you would obtain with a sample of $n = 4$ or $n = 1$. As shown in Figure 7.8(c), there is very little error between M and μ (you would expect only a 2-point error, on average). The sample means pile up very close to μ.

In summary, this example illustrates that with the smallest possible sample ($n = 1$), the standard error and the population standard deviation are the same. When sample size is increased, the standard error gets smaller, and the sample means tend to approximate μ more closely. Thus, standard error defines the relationship between sample size and the accuracy with which M represents μ.

IN THE LITERATURE
REPORTING STANDARD ERROR

As we will see later, standard error plays a very important role in inferential statistics. Because of its crucial role, the standard error for a sample mean, rather than the sample standard deviation, is often reported in scientific papers. Scientific journals vary in how they refer to the standard error, but frequently the symbols *SE* and *SEM* (for standard error of the mean) are used. The standard error is reported in two ways.

TABLE 7.2

The mean self-consciousness scores for participants who were working in front of a video camera and those who were not (controls)

	n	Mean	SE
Control	17	32.23	2.31
Camera	15	45.17	2.78

Much like the standard deviation, it may be reported in a table along with the sample means (Table 7.2). Alternatively, the standard error may be reported in graphs.

Figure 7.9 illustrates the use of a bar graph to display information about the sample mean and the standard error. In this experiment, two samples (groups A and B) are given different treatments, and then the subjects' scores on a dependent variable are recorded. The mean for group A is $M = 15$, and for group B, it is $M = 30$. For both samples, the standard error of M is $\sigma_M = 4$. Note that the mean is represented by the height of the bar, and the standard error is depicted on the graph by brackets at the top of each bar. Each bracket extends 1 standard error above and 1 standard error below the sample mean. Thus, the graph illustrates the mean for each group plus or minus 1 standard error ($M \pm SE$). When you glance at Figure 7.9, not only do you get a "picture" of the sample means, but also you get an idea of how much error you should expect for those means.

Figure 7.10 shows how sample means and standard error are displayed on a line graph. In this study, two samples (groups A and B) receive different treatments and

FIGURE 7.9

The mean ($\pm SE$) score for treatment groups A and B.

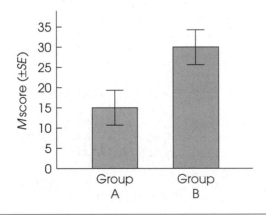

FIGURE 7.10

The mean ($\pm SE$) number of mistakes made for groups A and B on each trial.

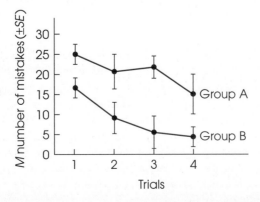

then are tested on a task for four trials. The number of mistakes committed on each trial is recorded for all subjects. The graph shows the mean (M) number of mistakes committed for each group on each trial. The brackets show the size of the standard error for each sample mean. Again, the brackets extend 1 standard error above and below the value of the mean.   ❏

LEARNING CHECK

1. A population has a standard deviation of $\sigma = 20$.

    a. If a single score is selected from this population, how close, on average, would you expect the score to be to the population mean?

    b. If a sample of $n = 4$ scores is selected from the population, how close, on average, would you expect the sample mean to be to the population mean?

    c. If a sample of $n = 25$ scores is selected from the population, how close, on average, would you expect the sample mean to be to the population mean?

2. Can the magnitude of the standard error ever be larger than the population standard deviation? Explain your answer.

3. A researcher plans to select a random sample of $n = 36$ individuals from a population with a standard deviation of $\sigma = 18$. On average, how much error should the researcher expect between the sample mean and the population mean?

4. A researcher plans to select a random sample from a population with a standard deviation of $\sigma = 20$.

    a. How large a sample is needed to have a standard error of 10 points or less?

    b. How large a sample is needed if the researcher wants the standard error to be 2 points or less?

ANSWERS

1. **a.** The standard deviation, $\sigma = 20$, measures the standard distance between a score and the mean.

    b. The standard error is $20/\sqrt{4} = 10$ points.

    c. The standard error is $20/\sqrt{25} = 4$ points.

2. No. The standard error is always less than or equal to the standard deviation. The two values are equal only when $n = 1$.

3. The standard error is $18/\sqrt{36} = 3$ points.

4. **a.** A sample of $n = 4$ or larger.

    b. A sample of $n = 100$ or larger.

7.5   LOOKING AHEAD TO INFERENTIAL STATISTICS

Inferential statistics are methods that use sample data as the basis for drawing general conclusions about populations. However, we have noted that a sample is not expected to give a perfectly accurate reflection of its population. In particular, there will be some error or discrepancy between a sample statistic and the corresponding population parameter. In this chapter, we have observed that a sample mean will not be exactly equal to the population mean. The standard error of M specifies how much difference is expected on average between the mean for a sample and the mean for the population.

The natural differences that exist between samples and populations introduce a certain amount of uncertainty and error into all inferential processes. For example, there is always a margin of error that must be considered whenever a researcher uses a sample mean as the basis for drawing a conclusion about a population mean. Remember that the sample mean is not perfect. In the next seven chapters we will introduce a variety of statistical methods that all use sample means to draw inferences about population means.

In each case, the distribution of sample means and the standard error will be critical elements in the inferential process. Before we begin this series of chapters, we pause briefly to demonstrate how the distribution of sample means, along with z-scores and probability, can help us use sample means to draw inferences about population means.

EXAMPLE 7.5   Suppose that a psychologist is planning a research study to evaluate the effect of a new growth hormone. It is known that regular, adult rats (with no hormone) weigh an average of $\mu = 400$ grams. Of course, not all rats are the same size, and the distribution of their weights is normal with $\sigma = 20$. The psychologist plans to select a sample of $n = 25$ newborn rats, inject them with the hormone, and then measure their weights when they become adults. The structure of this research study is shown in Figure 7.11.

The psychologist will make a decision about the effect of the hormone by comparing the sample of treated rats with the regular untreated rats in the original population. If the treated rats in the sample are noticeably different from untreated rats, then the researcher has evidence that the hormone has an effect. The problem is to determine exactly how much difference is necessary before we can say that the sample is *noticeably different*.

The distribution of sample means and the standard error can help researchers make this decision. In particular, the distribution of sample means can be used to show exactly what would be expected for a sample of rats who do not receive any hormone injections. This allows researchers to make a simple comparison between

   a. The sample of treated rats (from the research study)

   b. Samples of untreated rats (from the distribution of sample means)

FIGURE 7.11

The structure of the research study described in Example 7.5. The purpose of the study is to determine whether the treatment (a growth hormone) has an effect on weight for rats.

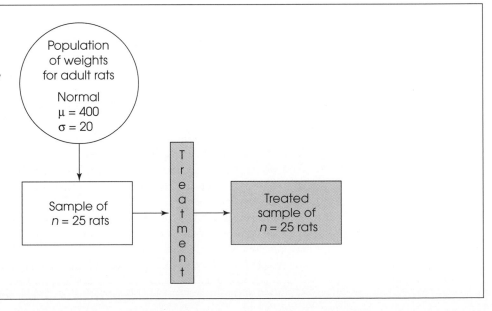

FIGURE 7.12

The distribution of sample means for samples of $n = 25$ untreated rats (from Example 7.5).

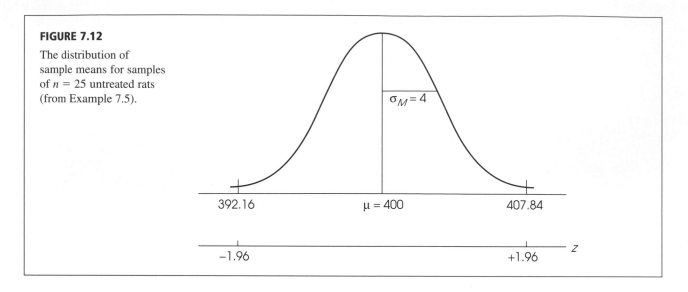

If our treated sample is noticeably different from the untreated samples, then we will have evidence that the treatment has an effect. On the other hand, if our treated sample still looks like one of the untreated samples, then we must conclude that the treatment does not appear to have any effect.

For this example, the distribution of sample means for $n = 25$ untreated rats will have the following characteristics:

1. It will be a normal distribution, because the population of rat weights is normal.

2. It will have an expected value of 400, because the population mean for untreated rats is $\mu = 400$.

3. It will have a standard error of $\sigma_M = 20/\sqrt{25} = 20/5 = 4$, because the population standard deviation is $\sigma = 20$ and the sample size is $n = 25$.

The distribution of sample means is shown in Figure 7.12. Notice that a sample of $n = 25$ untreated rats (without the hormone) should have a mean weight around 400 grams. To be more precise, we can use z-scores to determine the middle 95% of all the possible sample means. As demonstrated in Chapter 6 (page 153), the middle 95% of a normal distribution is located between z-score boundaries of $z = +1.96$ and $z = -1.96$ (check the unit normal table). These z-score boundaries are shown in Figure 7.12. With a standard error of $\sigma = 4$ points, a z-score of $z = 1.96$ corresponds to a distance of $1.96(4) = 7.84$ points from the mean. Thus, the z-score boundaries of ± 1.96 correspond to sample means of 392.16 and 407.84.

Thus, a sample of untreated rats is almost guaranteed (95% probability) to have a sample mean between 392.16 and 407.84. If our sample has a mean within this range, then we must conclude that our sample of treated rats does not look any different from a sample of untreated rats. In this case, we conclude that the hormone does not appear to have any effect.

On the other hand, if the mean for the treated sample is outside the 95% range, then we can conclude that our sample of treated rats is noticeably different from the samples that would be obtained for $n = 25$ rats without any treatment. In this case, the research results provide evidence that the treatment has an effect.

In Example 7.5 we used the distribution of sample means, together with z-scores and probability, to provide a description of what is reasonable to expect for an untreated sample. Then, we evaluated the effect of a treatment by determining whether or not the treated sample was noticeably different from an untreated sample. This procedure forms the foundation for the inferential technique known as *hypothesis testing* that is introduced in Chapter 8.

STANDARD ERROR AS A MEASURE OF RELIABILITY

The research situation shown in Figure 7.11 introduces one final issue concerning sample means and standard error. In Figure 7.11, as in most research studies, the researcher must rely on a *single* sample to provide an accurate representation of the population being investigated. As we have noted, however, if you take two different samples from the same population, you will get different individuals with different scores and different sample means. Thus, every researcher must face the nagging question, "If I had taken a different sample, would I have obtained different results?"

The importance of this question is directly related to the degree of similarity among all the different samples. For example, if there is a high level of consistency from one sample to another, then a researcher can be reasonably confident that the specific sample being studied will provide a good measurement of the population. That is, when all the samples are similar, then it does not matter which one you have selected. On the other hand, if there are big differences from one sample to another, then the researcher is left with some doubts about the accuracy of his/her specific sample. In this case, a different sample could have produced vastly different results.

In this context, the standard error can be viewed as a measure of the *reliability* of a sample mean. The term *reliability* refers to the consistency of different measurements of the same thing. More specifically, a measurement procedure is said to be reliable if you make two different measurements of the same thing and obtain identical (or nearly identical) values. If you view a sample as a "measurement" of a population, then a sample mean is a "measurement" of a population mean. If the means from different samples are all nearly identical, then the sample mean provides a reliable measure of the population. On the other hand, if there are big differences from one sample to another, then the sample mean is an unreliable measure of the population mean.

Earlier, in Figure 7.8, we showed how the size of the standard error is related to sample size. The same figure can now be used to demonstrate how standard error provides a measure of reliability for a sample mean.

Look back at Figure 7.8(b), and see that it shows a distribution of sample means based on $n = 4$ scores. In this distribution, the standard error is $\sigma_M = 10$, and it is relatively easy to find two samples with means that differ by 10 or 20 points. In this situation, a researcher cannot be confident that the mean for any individual sample is reliable; that is, a different sample could provide a very different mean.

Now consider what happens when the sample size is increased. Figure 7.8(c) shows the distribution of sample means based on $n = 100$. For this distribution, the standard error is $\sigma_M = 2$. With a larger sample and a smaller standard error, all of the sample means are clustered close together. With $n = 100$, a researcher can be much more confident that the mean for any individual sample is reliable; that is, if a second sample were taken, it would probably produce a sample mean that is essentially equivalent to the mean for the first sample.

LEARNING CHECK

1. A population forms a normal distribution with a mean of $\mu = 50$ and a standard deviation of $\sigma = 10$.

   a. A sample of $n = 4$ scores from this population has a mean of $M = 55$. Would you describe this as a relatively typical sample or is the mean an extreme value? Explain your answer.

   b. If the sample from part a had $n = 25$ scores, would it be considered typical or extreme?

2. The scores from a depression questionnaire form a normal distribution with a mean of $\mu = 80$ and a standard deviation of $\sigma = 10$.

   a. If the questionnaire is given to a sample of $n = 25$ people, what range of values for the sample mean would be expected 95% of the time?

   b. What range of values would have a 95% probability if the sample size were $n = 100$?

3. An automobile manufacturer claims that a newly introduced model will average $\mu = 45$ miles per gallon with $\sigma = 2$. A sample of $n = 4$ cars is tested and averages only $M = 42$ miles per gallon. Is this sample mean likely to occur if the manufacturer's claim is true? Specifically, is the sample mean within the range of values that would be expected 95% of the time? (Assume that the distribution of mileage scores is normal.)

ANSWERS

1. a. With $n = 4$ the standard error is 5, and the sample mean corresponds to $z = 1.00$. This is a relatively typical value.

   b. With $n = 25$ the standard error is 2, and the sample mean corresponds to $z = 2.50$. This is an extreme value.

2. a. With $n = 25$ the standard error is $\sigma_M = 2$ points. Using $z = 1.96$, the 95% range extends from 76.08 to 83.92.

   b. With $n = 100$ the standard error is only 1 point and the range extends from 78.04 to 81.96.

3. With $n = 4$, the standard error is $\sigma_M = 1$. If the real mean is $\mu = 45$, then 95% of all sample means should be within $1.96(1) = 1.96$ points of $\mu = 45$. This is a range of values from 43.04 to 46.96. Our sample mean is outside this range, so it is not the kind of sample that ought to be obtained if the manufacturer's claim is true.

SUMMARY

1. The distribution of sample means is defined as the set of Ms for all the possible random samples for a specific sample size (n) that can be obtained from a given population. According to the *central limit theorem*, the parameters of the distribution of sample means are as follows:

   a. *Shape*. The distribution of sample means will be normal if either one of the following two conditions is satisfied:

   (1) The population from which the samples are selected is normal.

   (2) The size of the samples is relatively large (around $n = 30$ or more).

   b. *Central Tendency*. The mean of the distribution of sample means will be identical to the mean of the population from which the samples are selected. The mean of the distribution of sample means is called the expected value of M.

   c. *Variability*. The standard deviation of the distribution of sample means is called the standard error of M and is defined by the formula

   $$\sigma_M = \frac{\sigma}{\sqrt{n}} \quad \text{or} \quad \sigma_M = \sqrt{\frac{\sigma^2}{n}}$$

   Standard error measures the standard distance between a sample mean (M) and the population mean (μ).

2. One of the most important concepts in this chapter is standard error. The standard error is the standard deviation of the distribution of sample means. It measures the standard distance between a sample mean (M) and the population mean (μ). The standard error tells how much error to expect if you are using a sample mean to estimate a population mean.

3. The location of each M in the distribution of sample means can be specified by a z-score:

$$z = \frac{M - \mu}{\sigma_M}$$

Because the distribution of sample means tends to be normal, we can use these z-scores and the unit normal table to find probabilities for specific sample means. In particular, we can identify which sample means are likely and which are very unlikely to be obtained from any given population. This ability to find probabilities for samples is the basis for the inferential statistics in the chapters ahead.

4. In general terms, the standard error measures how much discrepancy you should expect between a sample statistic and a population parameter. Statistical inference involves using sample statistics to make a general conclusion about a population parameter. Thus, standard error plays a crucial role in inferential statistics.

KEY TERMS

sampling error

distribution of sample means

sampling distribution

central limit theorem

expected value of M

standard error of M

law of large numbers

RESOURCES

There are a tutorial quiz and other learning exercises for Chapter 7 at the Wadsworth website, www.thomsonedu.com/psychology/gravetter. The site also provides access to two workshops entitled *Standard Error* and *Central Limit Theorem* that review the material covered in Chapter 7. See page 27 for more information about accessing items on the website.

WebTUTOR

For those using WebTutor along with this book, there is a WebTutor section corresponding to this chapter. The WebTutor contains a brief summary of Chapter 7, hints for learning about the distribution of sample means, cautions about common errors, and sample exam items including solutions.

SPSS

The statistical computer package SPSS is not structured to compute the standard error or a z-score for a sample mean. In later chapters, however, we introduce new inferential statistics that are included in SPSS. When these new statistics are computed, SPSS typically includes a report of standard error that describes how accurately, on average, the sample represents its population.

FOCUS ON PROBLEM SOLVING

1. Whenever you are working probability questions about sample means, you must use the distribution of sample means. Remember that every probability question can be restated as a proportion question. Probabilities for sample means are equivalent to proportions of the distribution of sample means.

2. When computing probabilities for sample means, the most common error is to use standard deviation (σ) instead of standard error (σ_M) in the z-score formula. Standard deviation measures the typical deviation (or "error") for a single score. Standard error measures the typical deviation (or error) for a sample. Remember: The larger the sample is, the more accurately the sample represents the population. Thus, sample size (n) is a critical part of the standard error.

$$\text{Standard error} = \sigma_M = \frac{\sigma}{\sqrt{n}}$$

3. Although the distribution of sample means is often normal, it is not always a normal distribution. Check the criteria to be certain the distribution is normal before you use the unit normal table to find probabilities (see item 1a of the Summary). Remember that all probability problems with a normal distribution are easier if you sketch the distribution and shade in the area of interest.

DEMONSTRATION 7.1

PROBABILITY AND THE DISTRIBUTION OF SAMPLE MEANS

For a normally distributed population with $\mu = 60$ and $\sigma = 12$, what is the probability of selecting a random sample of $n = 36$ scores with a sample mean greater than 64?
   In symbols, for $n = 36$

$$p(M > 64) = ?$$

Notice that we may rephrase the probability question as a proportion question. Out of all the possible sample means for $n = 36$, what proportion has values greater than 64?

STEP 1   Sketch the distribution.
   We are looking for a specific proportion of *all possible sample means*. Therefore, we begin with a sketch of the distribution of sample means, including the expected value, $\mu = 60$, and the standard error

$$\sigma_M = \frac{\sigma}{\sqrt{n}} = \frac{12}{\sqrt{36}} = \frac{12}{6} = 2$$

The sample mean, $M = 64$, is located in the tail on the right-hand side of the distribution. Figure 7.13(a) shows the preliminary sketch.

STEP 2   Shade the appropriate area of the distribution.
   In this example we are looking for the proportion greater than $M = 64$, so we shade the area on the right-hand side of $M = 64$. See Figure 7.13(b).

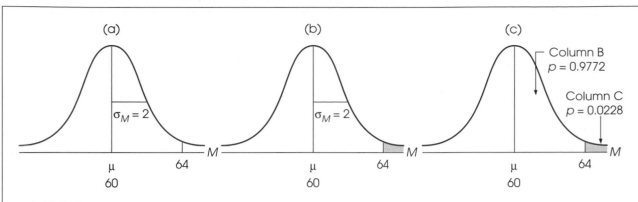

FIGURE 7.13

Sketches of the distributions for Demonstration 7.1.

STEP 3 Compute the z-score for the sample mean.

Using the z-score formula for sample means, including the standard error in the denominator, we obtain

$$z = \frac{M - \mu}{\sigma_M} = \frac{64 - 60}{2} = \frac{4}{2} = 2.00$$

STEP 4 Consult the unit normal table.

Look up the z-score in the unit normal table, and note the two proportions in columns B and C. Jot them down in the appropriate areas of the distribution [Figure 7.13(c)]. For this demonstration, the value in column C (the tail beyond z) corresponds exactly to the proportion we want (the shaded area). Thus, for $n = 36$,

$$p(M > 64) = p(z > +2.00) = 0.0228$$

PROBLEMS

1. Describe the shape, expected value, and standard error for the distribution of sample means for samples of $n = 36$ scores selected from a population with a mean of $\mu = 80$ and a standard deviation of $\sigma = 24$.

2. The distribution of sample means is not always a normal distribution. Under what circumstances will the distribution of sample means *not* be normal?

3. Briefly define each of the following:
   a. Distribution of sample means
   b. Expected value of M
   c. Standard error of M

4. For a sample selected from a population with a mean of $\mu = 50$ and a standard deviation of $\sigma = 10$:
   a. What is the expected value of M and the standard error of M for a sample of $n = 4$ scores?
   b. What is the expected value of M and the standard error of M for a sample of $n = 25$ scores?

5. The distribution of SAT scores is normal with $\mu = 500$ and $\sigma = 100$. If you select a random sample from this population, on average, how much error would you expect between the sample mean and the population mean for each of the following samples?
   a. A sample of $n = 4$ scores
   b. A sample of $n = 25$ scores
   c. A sample of $n = 100$ scores

6. For a population with a standard deviation of $\sigma = 20$:
   a. How large a sample would be needed to have a standard error less than 10 points?
   b. How large a sample would be needed to have a standard error less than 4 points?
   c. How large a sample would be needed to have a standard error less than 2 points?

7. A sample of $n = 25$ scores is selected from a population. What is the value for the population standard deviation if the standard error for the sample mean is
   a. $\sigma_M = 1$?
   b. $\sigma_M = 2$?
   c. $\sigma_M = 10$?

8. A population has a mean of $\mu = 100$ and a standard deviation of $\sigma = 20$. Find the z-score corresponding to each of the following sample means obtained from this population.
   a. $M = 102$ for a sample of $n = 4$ scores
   b. $M = 102$ for a sample of $n = 100$ scores
   c. $M = 95$ for a sample of $n = 16$ scores
   d. $M = 95$ for a sample of $n = 25$ scores

9. The following samples were obtained from a population with a mean of $\mu = 40$ and a standard deviation of $\sigma = 8$. Find the z-score corresponding to each sample mean.
   a. A sample of $n = 4$ scores with $M = 38$
   b. A sample of $n = 16$ scores with $M = 38$
   c. A sample of $n = 64$ scores with $M = 38$

10. A random sample is obtained from a population with a mean of $\mu = 50$ and a standard deviation of $\sigma = 12$.
   a. For a sample of $n = 4$ scores, would a sample mean of $M = 55$ be considered an extreme value or is it a fairly typical sample mean?
   b. For a sample of $n = 36$ scores, would a sample mean of $M = 55$ be considered an extreme value or is it a fairly typical sample mean?

11. A random sample is obtained from a population with a mean of $\mu = 100$ and a standard deviation of $\sigma = 20$.
   a. How much error would you expect between the sample mean and the population mean for a sample of $n = 4$ scores?
   b. How much error would you expect for a sample of $n = 16$ scores?
   c. How much error would be expected for a sample of $n = 100$ scores?

12. A random sample is obtained from a normal population with a mean of $\mu = 80$ and a standard deviation of $\sigma = 8$. Which of the following outcomes is more likely? Explain your answer.
   a. A sample mean greater than $M = 86$ for a sample of $n = 4$ scores.
   b. A sample mean greater than $M = 84$ for a sample of $n = 16$ scores.

13. A population forms a normal distribution with a mean of $\mu = 60$ and a standard deviation of $\sigma = 12$.
   a. What is the probability of randomly selecting a score from this population with a value greater than $X = 63$?
   b. What is the probability of randomly selecting a sample of $n = 4$ scores with a sample mean greater than $M = 63$?
   c. What is the probability of randomly selecting a sample of $n = 36$ scores with a sample mean greater than $M = 63$?

14. IQ scores form a normal distribution with $\mu = 100$ and $\sigma = 15$. If a random sample is selected from this population, on average, how much distance would you expect between the sample mean and the population mean for each of the following samples?
   a. A sample of $n = 9$ scores
   b. A sample of $n = 25$ scores
   c. A sample of $n = 100$ scores

15. For a normal-shaped distribution with $\mu = 50$ and $\sigma = 8$:
   a. Find $p(M > 46)$ for a sample of $n = 16$ scores.
   b. Find $p(M > 52)$ for a sample of $n = 4$ scores.
   c. Find $p(M > 52)$ for a sample of $n = 64$ scores.

16. For a normal-shaped distribution with $\mu = 50$ and $\sigma = 8$:
   a. What proportion of the scores have values between 46 and 54?
   b. For samples of $n = 4$, what proportion of the samples means have values between 46 and 54?
   c. For sample of $n = 16$, what proportion of the sample mean have values between 46 and 54?

17. A random sample of $n = 16$ scores is selected from a normal distribution with a mean of $\mu = 50$ and a standard deviation of $\sigma = 10$.
   a. What is the probability that the sample mean will have a value between 45 and 55?
   b. What is the probability that the sample mean will have a value between 48 and 52?
   c. What range of values contains the middle 95% of all the possible sample means for $n = 16$?

18. The average age for licensed drivers in the county is $\mu = 42.6$ years with a standard deviation of $\sigma = 12$. The distribution is approximately normal.
   a. A researcher obtained a sample of $n = 36$ drivers who received parking tickets. The average age for these drivers was $M = 40.7$. Is this a reasonable outcome for a sample of $n = 36$ or is this sample mean an extreme value?
   b. The same researcher also obtained a sample of $n = 16$ drivers who received speeding tickets. The average age for this sample was $M = 34.4$. Is this a reasonable outcome for a sample of $n = 16$, or is

the sample mean very different from what would usually be expected? (Again, compute the z-score for the sample mean.)

19. A normally distributed population has a mean of $\mu = 80$ and a standard deviation of $\sigma = 20$. Calculate the z-score for each of the following samples. Based on the z-score value, determine whether the sample mean is a typical, representative value or an extreme value for samples of this size.
   a. A sample of $n = 4$ scores with a mean of $M = 90$
   b. A sample of $n = 25$ scores with a mean of $M = 84$
   c. A sample of $n = 100$ scores with a mean of $M = 84$

20. A population forms a normal distribution with a mean of $\mu = 75$ and a standard deviation of $\sigma = 20$.
   a. Sketch the distribution of sample means for samples of $n = 25$ from this population.
   b. What proportion of the sample means for $n = 25$ have values less than 80? In other words, find $p(M < 80)$ for $n = 25$.
   c. Sketch the distribution of sample means for samples of $n = 100$.
   d. What proportion of the sample means for $n = 100$ have values greater than 79? In other words, find $p(M > 79)$ for $n = 100$.

21. People are selected to serve on juries by randomly picking names from the list of registered voters. The average age for registered voters in the county is $\mu = 39.7$ years with a standard deviation of $\sigma = 12.4$. A statistician randomly selects a sample of $n = 16$ people who are currently serving on juries. The average age for the individuals in the sample is $M = 48.9$ years.
   a. How likely is it to obtain a random sample of $n = 16$ jurors with an average age greater than or equal to 48.9?
   b. Is it reasonable to conclude that this set of $n = 16$ people is not a representative random sample of registered voters?

22. Welsh, Davis, Burke, and Williams (2002) conducted a study to evaluate the effectiveness of a carbohydrate-electrolyte drink on sports performance and endurance. Experienced athletes were given either a carbohydrate-electrolyte drink or a placebo while they were tested on a series of high-intensity exercises. One measure was how much time it took for the athletes to run to fatigue. Data similar to the results obtained in the study are shown in the following table.

Time to Run to Fatigue (in minutes)		
	Mean	SE
Placebo	21.7	2.2
Carbohydrate-electrolyte	28.6	2.7

   a. Construct a bar graph that incorporates all of the information in the table.
   b. Looking at your graph, do you think that the carbohydrate-electrolyte drink helps performance?

23. A normal-shaped distribution has $\mu = 80$ and $\sigma = 15$.
   a. Sketch the distribution of sample means for samples of $n = 25$ scores from this population.
   b. What are the z-score values that form the boundaries for the middle 95% of the distribution of sample means?
   c. Compute the z-score for $M = 89$ for a sample of $n = 25$ scores. Is this sample mean in the middle 95% of the distribution?
   d. Compute the z-score for $M = 84$ for a sample of $n = 25$ scores. Is this sample mean in the middle 95% of the distribution?

24. The distribution of SAT scores is normal with a mean of $\mu = 500$ and a standard deviation of $\sigma = 100$. If the mean SAT score is computed for a sample of $n = 100$ students,
   a. What range of values should contain the sample mean 90% of the time? (That is, find the middle 90% of the distribution of sample means.)
   b. What range of values should contain the sample mean 95% of the time?
   c. What range of values should contain the sample mean 99% of the time?

25. Research examining sleep behavior demonstrates a relationship between age and average amount of sleep. The following data show the mean amount of sleep and the standard error for five samples representing five different ages. Sketch a line graph showing these data, including the standard error for each sample mean.
   1 year: $M = 13$ hours with $SE = 2$
   5 years: $M = 11$ hours with $SE = 1\frac{1}{2}$
   10 years: $M = 10$ hours with $SE = 1\frac{1}{2}$
   15 years: $M = 8\frac{1}{2}$ hours with $SE = 1$
   20 years: $M = 8$ hours with $SE = 1$

CHAPTER

8

Introduction to Hypothesis Testing

Tools You Will Need

The following items are considered essential background material for this chapter. If you doubt your knowledge of any of these items, you should review the appropriate chapter or section before proceeding.

- z-Scores (Chapter 5)
- Distribution of sample means (Chapter 7)
  - Expected value
  - Standard error
  - Probability of sample means

8.1   THE LOGIC OF HYPOTHESIS TESTING

It usually is impossible or impractical for a researcher to observe every individual in a population. Therefore, researchers usually collect data from a sample and then use the sample data to help answer questions about the population. Hypothesis testing is a statistical procedure that allows researchers to use sample data to draw inferences about the population of interest.

Hypothesis testing is one of the most commonly used inferential procedures. In fact, most of the remainder of this book examines hypothesis testing in a variety of different situations and applications. Although the details of a hypothesis test change from one situation to another, the general process remains constant. In this chapter, we introduce the general procedure for a hypothesis test. You should notice that we use the statistical techniques that have been developed in the preceding three chapters—that is, we will combine the concepts of *z*-scores, probability, and the distribution of sample means to create a new statistical procedure known as a *hypothesis test*.

DEFINITION

A **hypothesis test** is a statistical method that uses sample data to evaluate a hypothesis about a population.

In very simple terms, the logic underlying the hypothesis-testing procedure is as follows:

1. First, we state a hypothesis about a population. Usually the hypothesis concerns the value of a population parameter. For example, we might hypothesize that the mean IQ for registered voters in the United States is $\mu = 110$.

2. Before we actually select a sample, we use the hypothesis to predict the characteristics that the sample should have. For example, if we hypothesize that the population mean IQ is $\mu = 110$, then we would predict that our sample should have a mean *around* 110. Remember: The sample should be similar to the population, but you should always expect a certain amount of error.

3. Next, we obtain a random sample from the population. For example, we might select a random sample of $n = 200$ registered voters and compute the mean IQ for the sample.

4. Finally, we compare the obtained sample data with the prediction that was made from the hypothesis. If the sample mean is consistent with the prediction, we will conclude that the hypothesis is reasonable. But if there is a big discrepancy between the data and the prediction, we will decide that the hypothesis is wrong.

A hypothesis test is typically used in the context of a research study. That is, a researcher completes a research study and then uses a hypothesis test to evaluate the results. Depending on the type of research and the type of data, the details of the hypothesis test will change from one research situation to another. In later chapters, we will examine different versions of hypothesis testing that are used for different kinds of research. For now, however, we will focus on the basic elements that are common to all hypothesis tests. To accomplish this general goal, we will examine a hypothesis test as it applies to the simplest possible research study. In particular, we will look at the situation in which a researcher is using one sample to examine one unknown population.

The unknown population   Figure 8.1 shows the general research situation that we will use to introduce the process of hypothesis testing. Notice that the researcher begins

FIGURE 8.1

The basic experimental situation for hypothesis testing. It is assumed that the parameter μ is known for the population before treatment. The purpose of the experiment is to determine whether the treatment has an effect on the population mean.

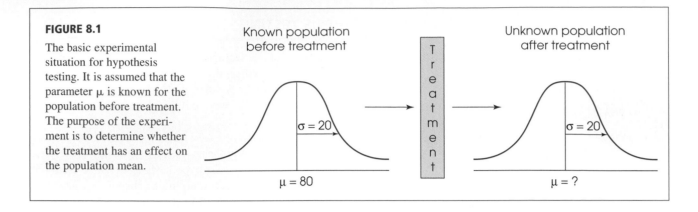

with a known population. This is the set of individuals as they exist *before treatment*. For this example, we are assuming that the original set of scores forms a normal distribution with $\mu = 80$ and $\sigma = 20$. The purpose of the research is to determine the effect of the treatment on the individuals in the population. That is, the goal is to determine what happens to the population *after the treatment is administered*.

To simplify the hypothesis-testing situation, one basic assumption is made about the effect of the treatment: If the treatment has any effect, it is simply to add a constant amount to (or subtract a constant amount from) each individual's score. You should recall from Chapters 3 and 4 that adding (or subtracting) a constant will change the mean but will not change the shape of the population, nor will it change the standard deviation. Thus, we will assume that the population after treatment has the same shape as the original population and the same standard deviation as the original population. This assumption is incorporated into the situation shown in Figure 8.1.

Note that the unknown population, after treatment, is the focus of the research question. Specifically, the purpose of the research is to determine what would happen if the treatment were administered to every individual in the population.

The sample in the research study   The goal of the hypothesis test is to determine whether the treatment has any effect on the individuals in the population (see Figure 8.1). Usually, however, we cannot administer the treatment to the entire population so the actual research study is conducted using a sample. Figure 8.2 shows the structure of the research study from the point of view of the hypothesis test. The original population, before treatment, is shown on the left-hand side. The unknown population, after treatment, is shown on the right-hand side. Note that the unknown population is actually *hypothetical* (the treatment is never administered to the entire population). Instead, we are asking *what if* the treatment were administered to the entire population. However, we do have a *real* sample that has received the treatment, and we will use this sample to evaluate a hypothesis about the unknown population mean.

A hypothesis test is a formalized procedure that follows a standard series of operations. In this way, researchers have a standardized method for evaluating the results of their research studies. Other researchers will recognize and understand exactly how the data were evaluated and how conclusions were reached. To emphasize the formal structure of a hypothesis test, we will present hypothesis testing as a four-step process that is used throughout the rest of the book. The following example provides a concrete foundation for introducing the hypothesis-testing procedure.

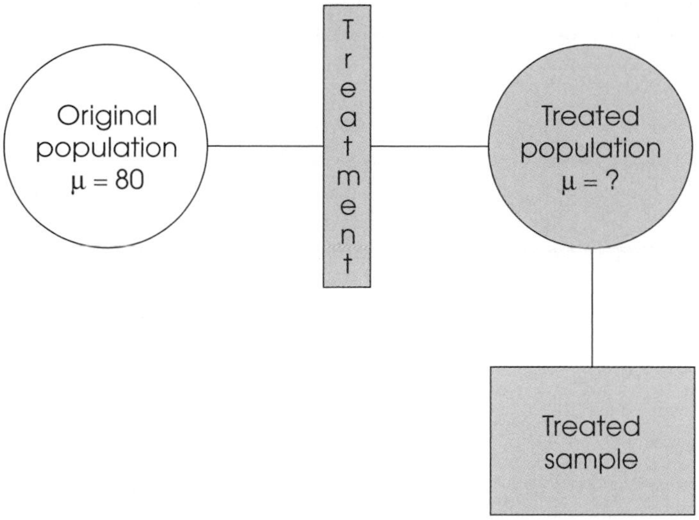

FIGURE 8.2

The research situation from the point of view of the hypothesis test. A treatment is administered to a sample and the treated sample is compared with the original untreated population. The hypothesis test is concerned with the unknown population that would exist if the treatment were administered to the entire population.

E X A M P L E   8 . 1   Researchers have noted that certain food supplements (such as blueberries) that contain antioxidants can reduce and even reverse age-related declines in neuronal and cognitive function in laboratory rats (Joseph, Shukitt-Hale, Denisova, et al., 1999). Based on these results, one might theorize that the same supplements might also benefit elderly humans. Suppose a researcher is interested in testing this theory.

Standardized neuropsychological tests such as the Wisconsin Card Sorting Test can be used to measure conceptual thinking ability and mental flexibility (Heaton, Chelune, Talley, Kay, & Curtis, 1993). Performance on this type of test declines gradually with age. Suppose our researcher selects a test for which adults older than 65 have an average score of $\mu = 80$ with a standard deviation of $\sigma = 20$. The distribution of test scores is approximately normal. The researcher's plan is to obtain a sample of $n = 25$ adults who are older than 65, and give each participant a daily dose of a blueberry supplement that is very high in antioxidants. After taking the supplement for 6 months, the participants will be given the neuropsychological test to measure their level of cognitive function. If the mean score for the sample is noticeably different from the mean for the general population of elderly adults, the researcher can conclude that the supplement does appear to have an effect on cognitive function. On the other hand, if the sample mean is around 80 (the same as the general population mean), the researcher must conclude that the supplement does not appear to have any effect.

Figure 8.2 depicts the research situation that was described in the preceding example. Notice that the population after treatment is unknown. Specifically, we do not know what will happen to the mean score if the entire population of elderly adults is given the blueberry supplement. However, we do have a sample of $n = 25$ participants who have received the supplement and we can use this sample to help draw inferences about the unknown population. The following four steps outline the hypothesis-testing procedure that allows us to use sample data to answer questions about an unknown population.

STEP 1: STATE THE HYPOTHESES

The goal of inferential statistics is to make general statements about the population by using sample data. Therefore, when testing hypotheses, we make our predictions about the population parameters.

As the name implies, the process of hypothesis testing begins by stating a hypothesis about the unknown population. Actually, we state two opposing hypotheses. Notice that both hypotheses are stated in terms of population parameters.

The first and most important of the two hypotheses is called the *null hypothesis*. The null hypothesis states that the treatment has no effect. In general, the null hypothesis states that there is no change, no effect, no difference—nothing happened, hence the name *null*. The null hypothesis is identified by the symbol H_0. (The H stands for *hypothesis*, and the zero subscript indicates that this is the *zero-effect*, null hypothesis.) For the study in Example 8.1, the null hypothesis states that the blueberry supplement has no effect on cognitive functioning for the population of adults who are more than 65 years old. In symbols, this hypothesis is

$$H_0: \quad \mu_{\text{with supplement}} = 80 \qquad \text{(Even with the supplement, the mean test score still will be 80.)}$$

DEFINITION

The **null hypothesis** (H_0) states that in the general population there is no change, no difference, or no relationship. In the context of an experiment, H_0 predicts that the independent variable (treatment) will have *no effect* on the dependent variable for the population.

The second hypothesis is simply the opposite of the null hypothesis, and it is called the *scientific* or *alternative hypothesis* (H_1). This hypothesis states that the treatment has an effect on the dependent variable.

DEFINITION

The **alternative hypothesis** (H_1) states that there is a change, a difference, or a relationship for the general population. In the context of an experiment, H_1 predicts that the independent variable (treatment) *will have an effect* on the dependent variable.

The null hypothesis and the alternative hypothesis are mutually exclusive and exhaustive. They cannot both be true. The data will determine which one should be rejected.

For this example, the alternative hypothesis states that the supplement does have an effect on cognitive functioning for the population and will cause a change in the mean score. In symbols, the alternative hypothesis is represented as

$$H_1: \quad \mu_{\text{with supplement}} \neq 80 \qquad \text{(With the supplement, the mean test score will be different from 80.)}$$

Notice that the alternative hypothesis simply states that there will be some type of change. It does not specify whether the effect will be increased or decreased test scores. In some circumstances, it is appropriate for the alternative hypothesis to specify the direction of the effect. For example, the researcher might hypothesize that the supplement will increase neuropsychological test scores ($\mu > 80$). This type of hypothesis results in a directional hypothesis test, which will be examined in detail later in this chapter. For now we concentrate on nondirectional tests, for which the hypotheses simply state that the treatment has some effect (H_1) or has no effect (H_0).

STEP 2: SET THE CRITERIA FOR A DECISION

The researcher will eventually use the data from the sample to evaluate the credibility of the null hypothesis. The data will either provide support for the null hypothesis or tend to refute the null hypothesis. In particular, if there is a big discrepancy between the data and the hypothesis, we will conclude that the hypothesis is wrong.

To formalize the decision process, we use the null hypothesis to predict the kind of sample mean that ought to be obtained. Specifically, we determine exactly what sample means are consistent with the null hypothesis and what sample means are at odds with the null hypothesis.

For our example, the null hypothesis states that the supplement has no effect and the population mean is still $\mu = 80$. If this is true, then the sample mean should have a value around 80. Therefore, a sample mean near 80 is consistent with the null hypothesis. On the other hand, a sample mean that is very different from 80 is not consistent with the null hypothesis. To determine exactly what values are "near" 80 and what values are "very different from" 80, we will examine all of the possible sample means that could be obtained if the null hypothesis is true. For our example, this is the distribution of sample means for $n = 25$. According to the null hypothesis, this distribution is centered at $\mu = 80$. The distribution of sample means is then divided into two sections:

1. Sample means that are likely to be obtained if H_0 is true; that is, sample means that are close to the null hypothesis

2. Sample means that are very unlikely to be obtained if H_0 is true; that is, sample means that are very different from the null hypothesis

The distribution of sample means divided into these two sections is shown in Figure 8.3. Notice that the high-probability samples are located in the center of the distribution and have sample means close to the value specified in the null hypothesis. On the other hand, the low-probability samples are located in the extreme tails of the distribution. After the distribution has been divided in this way, we can compare our sample data with the values in the distribution. Specifically, we can determine whether our sample mean is consistent with the null hypothesis (like the values in the center of the distribution) or whether our sample mean is very different from the null hypothesis (like the values in the extreme tails).

FIGURE 8.3

The set of potential samples is divided into those that are likely to be obtained and those that are very unlikely to be obtained if the null hypothesis is true.

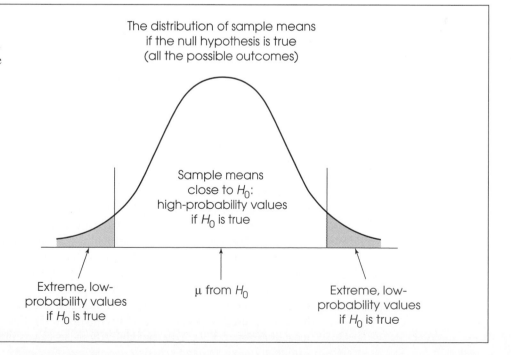

The distribution of sample means if the null hypothesis is true (all the possible outcomes)

Sample means close to H_0: high-probability values if H_0 is true

Extreme, low-probability values if H_0 is true

μ from H_0

Extreme, low-probability values if H_0 is true

The alpha level   To find the boundaries that separate the high-probability samples from the low-probability samples, we must define exactly what is meant by "low" probability and "high" probability. This is accomplished by selecting a specific probability value, which is known as the *level of significance* or the *alpha level* for the hypothesis test. The alpha (α) value is a small probability that is used to identify the low-probability samples. By convention, commonly used alpha levels are $\alpha = .05$ (5%), $\alpha = .01$ (1%), and $\alpha = .001$ (0.1%). For example, with $\alpha = .05$, we separate the most unlikely 5% of the sample means (the extreme values) from the most likely 95% of the sample means (the central values).

With rare exceptions, an alpha level is never larger than .05.

The extremely unlikely values, as defined by the alpha level, make up what is called the *critical region*. These extreme values in the tails of the distribution define outcomes that are inconsistent with the null hypothesis; that is, they are very unlikely to occur if the null hypothesis is true. Whenever the data from a research study produce a sample mean that is located in the critical region, we will conclude that the data are inconsistent with the null hypothesis, and we will reject the null hypothesis.

DEFINITIONS

The **alpha level** or the **level of significance** is a probability value that is used to define the very unlikely sample outcomes if the null hypothesis is true.

The **critical region** is composed of extreme sample values that are very unlikely to be obtained if the null hypothesis is true. The boundaries for the critical region are determined by the alpha level. If sample data fall in the critical region, the null hypothesis is rejected.

Technically, the critical region is defined by sample outcomes that are *very unlikely* to occur if the treatment has no effect (that is, if the null hypothesis is true). Reversing the point of view, we can also define the critical region as sample values that provide *convincing evidence* that the treatment really does have an effect. For our example, the regular population of elderly adults has a mean test score of $\mu = 80$. We selected a sample from this population and administered a treatment (the blueberry supplement) to the individuals in the sample. What kind of sample mean would convince you that the treatment has an effect? It should be obvious that the most convincing evidence would be a sample mean that is really different from $\mu = 80$. In a hypothesis test, the critical region is determined by sample values that are "really different" from the original population.

The boundaries for the critical region   To determine the exact location for the boundaries that define the critical region, we will use the alpha-level probability and the unit normal table. In most cases, the distribution of sample means is normal, and the unit normal table will provide the precise z-score location for the critical region boundaries. With $\alpha = .05$, for example, the boundaries separate the extreme 5% from the middle 95%. Because the extreme 5% is split between two tails of the distribution, there is exactly 2.5% (or 0.0250) in each tail. In the unit normal table, you can look up a proportion of 0.0250 in column C (the tail) and find that the z-score boundary is $z = 1.96$. Thus, for any normal distribution, the extreme 5% is in the tails of the distribution beyond $z = 1.96$ and $z = -1.96$. These values define the boundaries of the critical region for a hypothesis test using $\alpha = .05$ (Figure 8.4).

Similarly, an alpha level of $\alpha = .01$ means that 1% or .0100 is split between the two tails. In this case, the proportion in each tail is .0050, and the corresponding z-score boundaries are $z = \pm2.58$ (±2.57 is equally good). For $\alpha = .001$, the boundaries are located at $z = \pm3.30$. You should verify these values in the unit normal table and be sure that you understand exactly how they are obtained.

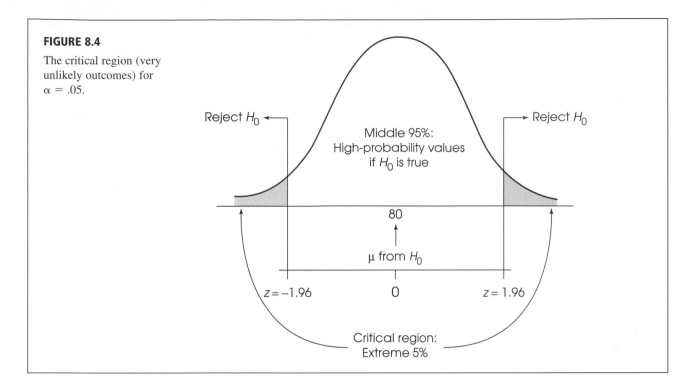

FIGURE 8.4

The critical region (very unlikely outcomes) for $\alpha = .05$.

Reject H_0 ←

Reject H_0 →

Middle 95%:
High-probability values
if H_0 is true

80

↑

μ from H_0

$z = -1.96$ 0 $z = 1.96$

Critical region:
Extreme 5%

STEP 3: COLLECT DATA AND COMPUTE SAMPLE STATISTICS

At this time, we select a sample of adults who are more than 65 years old, and give each one a daily dose of the blueberry supplement. After 6 months, the neuropsychological test is used to measure cognitive function for the sample of participants. Notice that the data are collected *after* the researcher has stated the hypotheses and established the criteria for a decision. This sequence of events helps ensure that a researcher makes an honest, objective evaluation of the data and does not tamper with the decision criteria after the experimental outcome is known.

Next, the raw data from the sample are summarized with the appropriate statistics: For this example, the researcher would compute the sample mean. Now it is possible for the researcher to compare the sample mean (the data) with the null hypothesis. This is the heart of the hypothesis test: comparing the data with the hypothesis.

The comparison is accomplished by computing a z-score that describes exactly where the sample mean is located relative to the hypothesized population mean from H_0. In step 2, we constructed the distribution of sample means that would be expected if the null hypothesis were true—that is, the entire set of sample means that could be obtained if the treatment has no effect (see Figure 8.4). Now we will calculate a z-score that identifies where our sample mean is located in this hypothesized distribution. The z-score formula for a sample mean is

$$z = \frac{M - \mu}{\sigma_M}$$

In the formula, the value of the sample mean (M) is obtained from the sample data, and the value of μ is obtained from the null hypothesis. Thus, the z-score formula can be expressed in words as follows:

$$z = \frac{\text{sample mean} - \text{hypothesized population mean}}{\text{standard error between } M \text{ and } \mu}$$

Notice that the top of the z-score formula measures how much difference there is between the data and the hypothesis. The bottom of the formula measures the standard distance that ought to exist between the sample mean and the population mean.

STEP 4: MAKE A DECISION   In the final step, the researcher uses the z-score value obtained in step 3 to make a decision about the null hypothesis according to the criteria established in step 2. There are two possible decisions, and both are stated in terms of the null hypothesis (Box 8.1).

One possible decision is to *reject the null hypothesis*. This decision is made whenever the sample data fall in the critical region. By definition, a sample value in the critical region indicates that there is a big discrepancy between the sample and the null hypothesis (the sample is in the extreme tail of the distribution). This kind of outcome is very unlikely to occur if the null hypothesis is true, so our conclusion is to reject H_0. In this case, the data provide convincing evidence that the null hypothesis is wrong, and we conclude that the treatment really did have an effect on the individuals in the sample. For the example we have been considering, suppose the sample produced a mean of $M = 92$ after taking the supplement for 6 months. With $n = 25$ and $\sigma = 20$, the standard error for the sample mean is

$$\sigma_M = \frac{\sigma}{\sqrt{n}} = \frac{20}{\sqrt{25}} = \frac{20}{5} = 4$$

The z-score for the sample is

$$z = \frac{M - \mu}{\sigma_M} = \frac{92 - 80}{4} = \frac{12}{4} = 3.00$$

With an alpha level of $\alpha = .05$, this z-score is far beyond the boundary of 1.96. Because the sample z-score is in the critical region, we reject the null hypothesis and conclude that the blueberry supplement did have an effect on cognitive functioning.

BOX 8.1   **REJECTING THE NULL HYPOTHESIS VERSUS PROVING THE ALTERNATIVE HYPOTHESIS**

It may seem awkward to pay so much attention to the null hypothesis. After all, the purpose of most experiments is to show that a treatment does have an effect, and the null hypothesis states that there is no effect. The reason for focusing on the null hypothesis, rather than the alternative hypothesis, comes from the limitations of inferential logic. Remember that we want to use the sample data to draw conclusions, or inferences, about a population. Logically, it is much easier to demonstrate that a universal (population) hypothesis is false than to demonstrate that it is true. This principle is shown more clearly in a simple example. Suppose you make the universal statement "all dogs have four legs" and you intend to test this hypothesis by using a sample of ten dogs. If all the dogs in your sample have four legs, have

you proved the statement? It should be clear that ten four-legged dogs do not prove the general statement to be true. On the other hand, suppose one dog in your sample has only three legs. In this case, you have proved the statement to be false. Again, it is much easier to show that something is false than to prove that it is true.

Hypothesis testing uses this logical principle to achieve its goals. We state the null hypothesis, "the treatment has no effect," and try to show that it is false. The end result still is to demonstrate that the treatment does have an effect. That is, we find support for the alternative hypothesis by disproving (rejecting) the null hypothesis.

The second possibility occurs when the sample data are not in the critical region. In this case, the data are reasonably close to the null hypothesis (in the center of the distribution). Because the data do not provide strong evidence that the null hypothesis is wrong, our conclusion is to *fail to reject the null hypothesis*. This conclusion means that the treatment does not appear to have an effect. For the research study examining the blueberry supplement, suppose our sample produced a mean test score of $M = 84$. As before, the standard error for a sample of $n = 25$ is $\sigma_M = 4$, and the null hypothesis states that $\mu = 80$. These values produce a z-score of

$$z = \frac{M - \mu}{\sigma_M} = \frac{84 - 80}{4} = \frac{4}{4} = 1.00$$

The z-score of 1.00 is not in the critical region. Therefore, we fail to reject the null hypothesis and conclude that the blueberry supplement does not appear to have an effect on cognitive functioning.

The two possible decisions may be easier to understand if you think of a research study as an attempt to gather evidence to prove that a treatment works. From this perspective, the research study has two possible outcomes:

1. You gather enough evidence to demonstrate convincingly that the treatment really works. That is, you reject the null hypothesis and conclude that the treatment does have an effect.

2. The evidence you gather from the research study is not convincing. In this case, all you can do is conclude that there is not enough evidence. The research study has failed to demonstrate that the treatment has an effect, and the statistical decision is to fail to reject the null hypothesis.

A CLOSER LOOK AT THE z-SCORE STATISTIC

The z-score statistic that is used in the hypothesis test is the first specific example of what is called a *test statistic*. The term *test statistic* simply indicates that the sample data are converted into a single, specific statistic that is used to test the hypotheses. In the chapters that follow, we will introduce several other test statistics that are used in a variety of different research situations. However, most of the new test statistics will have the same basic structure and will serve the same purpose as the z-score. We have already described the z-score equation as a formal method for comparing the sample data and the population hypothesis. In this section, we discuss the z-score from two other perspectives that may give you a better understanding of hypothesis testing and the role that z-scores play in this inferential technique. In each case, keep in mind that the z-score will serve as a general model for other test statistics that will come in future chapters.

The z-score formula as a recipe   The z-score formula, like any formula, can be viewed as a recipe. If you follow instructions and use all the right ingredients, the formula will produce a z-score. In the hypothesis-testing situation, however, you do not have all the necessary ingredients. Specifically, you do not know the value for the population mean (μ), which is one component or ingredient in the formula.

This situation is similar to trying to follow a cake recipe where one of the ingredients is not clearly listed. For example, there may be a grease stain that obscures one part of your recipe. In this situation, what do you do? One possibility is to make a hypothesis about the missing ingredient. You might, for example, hypothesize that the missing ingredient is 2 cups of flour. To test the hypothesis, you simply add the rest of the ingredients along with the hypothesized flour and see what happens. If the cake turns out to be good, then you can be reasonably confident that your hypothesis was correct. But if the cake is terrible, then you conclude that your hypothesis was wrong.

In a hypothesis test with z-scores, you do essentially the same thing. You do not know the value for the population mean, μ. Therefore, you make a hypothesis (the null hypothesis) about the unknown value μ and plug it into the formula along with the rest of the ingredients. To evaluate your hypothesis, you simply look at the result. If the formula produces a z-score near zero (which is where z-scores are supposed to be), then you conclude that your hypothesis was correct. On the other hand, if the formula produces an unlikely result (an extremely large or small value), then you conclude that your hypothesis was wrong.

The z-score formula as a ratio   In the context of a hypothesis test, the z-score formula has the following structure:

$$z = \frac{M - \mu}{\sigma_M} = \frac{\text{sample mean } - \text{ hypothesized population mean}}{\text{standard error between } M \text{ and } \mu}$$

Notice that the numerator of the formula involves a direct comparison between the sample data and the null hypothesis. In particular, the numerator measures the obtained difference between the sample mean and the hypothesized population mean. The standard error in the denominator of the formula measures the standard amount of distance that ought to exist between a sample mean and the population mean when there is no treatment effect. Thus, the z-score formula (and most other test statistics) forms a ratio

$$z = \frac{\text{actual difference between the sample } (M) \text{ and the hypothesis } (\mu)}{\text{standard difference between } M \text{ and } \mu \text{ with no treatment effect}}$$

Thus, for example, a z-score of $z = 3.00$ means that the obtained difference between the sample and the hypothesis is 3 times bigger than would be expected if the treatment had no effect.

In general, a large value for a test statistic like the z-score indicates a large discrepancy between the sample data and the null hypothesis. Specifically, a large value indicates that the sample data are very unlikely to have occurred by chance alone. Therefore, when we obtain a large value (in the critical region), we conclude that it must have been caused by a treatment effect.

LEARNING CHECK

1. What does the null hypothesis predict about a population or a treatment effect?

2. Define the *critical region* for a hypothesis test.

3. As the alpha level gets smaller, the size of the critical region also gets smaller. (True or false?)

4. A small value (near zero) for the z-score statistic is evidence that the null hypothesis should be rejected. (True or false?)

5. A decision to reject the null hypothesis means you have demonstrated that the treatment has no effect. (True or false?)

ANSWERS

1. The null hypothesis predicts that the treatment has no effect and the population is unchanged.

2. The critical region consists of sample outcomes that are very unlikely to be obtained if the null hypothesis is true.

3. True. As alpha gets smaller, the critical region is moved farther out into the tails of the distribution.

4. False. A z-score near zero indicates that the data support the null hypothesis.

5. False. Rejecting the null hypothesis means you have concluded that the treatment does have an effect.

8.2   UNCERTAINTY AND ERRORS IN HYPOTHESIS TESTING

Hypothesis testing is an *inferential process,* which means that it uses limited information as the basis for reaching a general conclusion. Specifically, a sample provides only limited or incomplete information about the whole population, and yet a hypothesis test uses a sample to draw a conclusion about the population. In this situation, there is always the possibility that an incorrect conclusion will be made. Although sample data are usually representative of the population, there is always a chance that the sample is misleading and will cause a researcher to make the wrong decision about the research results. In a hypothesis test, there are two different kinds of errors that can be made.

TYPE I ERRORS   It is possible that the data will lead you to reject the null hypothesis when in fact the treatment has no effect. Remember: Samples are not expected to be identical to their populations, and some extreme samples can be very different from the populations they are supposed to represent. If a researcher selects one of these extreme samples by chance, then the data from the sample may give the appearance of a strong treatment effect, even though there is no real effect. In the previous section, for example, we discussed a research study examining how a food supplement that is high in antioxidants affects the cognitive functioning of elderly adults. Suppose the researcher selected a sample of $n = 25$ people who already had cognitive functioning that was well above average. When these people are tested after 6 months of taking the supplement, they will score higher than average on the neuropsychological test even though the blueberry supplement (the treatment) may have had no effect. In this case, the researcher is likely to conclude that the treatment has had an effect, when in fact it really did not. This is an example of what is called a *Type I error.*

DEFINITION   A **Type I error** occurs when a researcher rejects a null hypothesis that is actually true. In a typical research situation, a Type I error means the researcher concludes that a treatment does have an effect when in fact it has no effect.

You should realize that a Type I error is not a stupid mistake in the sense that a researcher is overlooking something that should be perfectly obvious. On the contrary, the researcher is looking at sample data that appear to show a clear treatment effect. The researcher then makes a careful decision based on the available information. The problem is that the information from the sample is misleading.

In most research situations, the consequences of a Type I error can be very serious. Because the researcher has rejected the null hypothesis and believes that the treatment has a real effect, it is likely that the researcher will report or even publish the research results. A Type I error, however, means that this is a false report. Thus, Type I errors lead to false reports in the scientific literature. Other researchers may try to build theories or develop other experiments based on the false results. A lot of precious time and resources may be wasted.

A Type I error occurs when a researcher unknowingly obtains an extreme, nonrepresentative sample. Fortunately, the hypothesis test is structured to minimize the risk that this will occur. Figure 8.4 shows the distribution of sample means and the critical region for the research study we have been discussing. This distribution contains all of the possible sample means for samples of $n = 25$ if the null hypothesis is true. Notice that most of the sample means are near the hypothesized population mean, $\mu = 80$. However, some of the possible sample means are located far out in the tails of the distribution beyond the z-score boundaries of ±1.96. Although it is possible to obtain one of these extreme samples when H_0 is true, it is *very unlikely*. Specifically, the alpha level determines the exact proportion of the sample means that are in the critical region. Thus, the alpha level determines the probability that you will obtain a sample mean in the critical region when H_0 is true. This fact leads to an alternative definition of the alpha level.

DEFINITION   The **alpha level** for a hypothesis test is the probability that the test will lead to a Type I error. That is, the alpha level determines the probability of obtaining sample data in the critical region even though the null hypothesis is true.

In summary, whenever the sample data are in the critical region, the appropriate decision for a hypothesis test is to reject the null hypothesis. Normally this is the correct decision because the treatment has caused the sample to be different from the original population; that is, the treatment effect has pushed the sample mean into the critical region. In this case, the hypothesis test has correctly identified a real treatment effect. Occasionally, however, sample data will be in the critical region just by chance, without any treatment effect. When this occurs, the researcher will make a Type I error; that is, the researcher will conclude that a treatment effect exists, when in fact it does not. Fortunately, the risk of a Type I error is small and is under the control of the researcher. Specifically, the probability of a Type I error is equal to the alpha level.

TYPE II ERRORS

Whenever a researcher rejects the null hypothesis, there is a risk of a Type I error. Similarly, whenever a researcher fails to reject the null hypothesis, there is a risk of a *Type II error*. By definition, a Type II error is the failure to reject a false null hypothesis. In more straightforward English, a Type II error means that a treatment effect really exists, but the hypothesis test fails to detect it.

DEFINITION   A **Type II error** occurs when a researcher fails to reject a null hypothesis that is really false. In a typical research situation, a Type II error means that the hypothesis test has failed to detect a real treatment effect.

A Type II error occurs when the sample mean is not in the critical region even though the treatment has had an effect on the sample. Often this happens when the effect of the treatment is relatively small. In this case, the treatment does influence the sample, but the magnitude of the effect is not big enough to move the sample mean into the critical region. Because the sample is not substantially different from the original population (it is not in the critical region), the statistical decision is to fail to reject the null hypothesis and to conclude that there is not enough evidence to say there is a treatment effect.

TABLE 8.1

Possible outcomes of a statistical decision.

		Actual Situation	
		No Effect, H_0 True	Effect Exists, H_0 False
EXPERIMENTER'S DECISION	Reject H_0	Type I error	Decision correct
	Retain H_0	Decision correct	Type II error

The consequences of a Type II error are usually not as serious as those of a Type I error. In general terms, a Type II error means that the research data do not show the results that the researcher had hoped to obtain. The researcher can accept this outcome and conclude that the treatment either has no effect or has only a small effect that is not worth pursuing, or the researcher can repeat the experiment (usually with some improvements) and try to demonstrate that the treatment really does work.

Unlike a Type I error, it is impossible to determine a single, exact probability value for a Type II error. Instead, the probability of a Type II error depends on a variety of factors and therefore is a function, rather than a specific number. Nonetheless, the probability of a Type II error is represented by the symbol β, the Greek letter *beta*.

In summary, a hypothesis test always leads to one of two decisions:

1. The sample data provide sufficient evidence to reject the null hypothesis and conclude that the treatment has an effect.

2. The sample data do not provide enough evidence to reject the null hypothesis. In this case, you fail to reject H_0 and conclude that the treatment does not appear to have an effect.

In either case, there is a chance that the data are misleading and the decision is wrong. The complete set of decisions and outcomes is shown in Table 8.1. The risk of an error is especially important in the case of a Type I error, which can lead to a false report. Fortunately, the probability of a Type I error is determined by the alpha level, which is completely under the control of the researcher. At the beginning of a hypothesis test, the researcher states the hypotheses and selects the alpha level, which immediately determines the risk that a Type I error will be made.

SELECTING AN ALPHA LEVEL

As you have seen, the alpha level for a hypothesis test serves two very important functions. First, alpha helps determine the boundaries for the critical region by defining the concept of "very unlikely" outcomes. More importantly, alpha determines the probability of a Type I error. When you select a value for alpha at the beginning of a hypothesis test, your decision influences both of these functions.

The primary concern when selecting an alpha level is to minimize the risk of a Type I error. Thus, alpha levels tend to be very small probability values. By convention, the largest permissible value is $\alpha = .05$. When there is no treatment effect, an alpha level of .05 means that there is still a 5% risk, or a 1-in-20 probability, of rejecting the null hypothesis and committing a Type I error. Because the consequences of a Type I error

FIGURE 8.5

The locations of the critical region boundaries for three different levels of significance: $\alpha = .05$, $\alpha = .01$, and $\alpha = .001$.

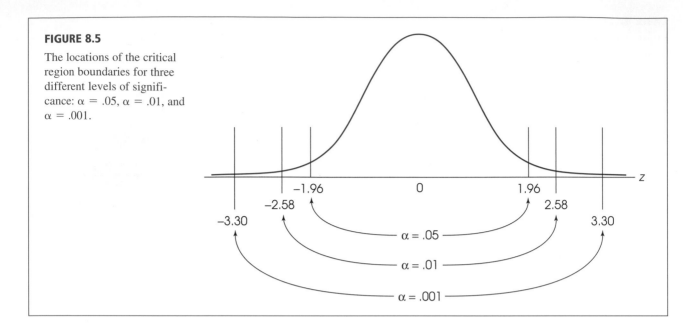

can be relatively serious, many individual researchers and many scientific publications prefer to use a more conservative alpha level such as .01 or .001 to reduce the risk that a false report is published and becomes part of the scientific literature. (For more information on the origins of the .05 level of significance, see the excellent short article by Cowles and Davis, 1982.)

At this point, it may appear that the best strategy for selecting an alpha level is to choose the smallest possible value in order to minimize the risk of a Type I error. However, there is a different kind of risk that develops as the alpha level is lowered. Specifically, a lower alpha level means less risk of a Type I error, but it also means that the hypothesis test demands more evidence from the research results.

The trade-off between the risk of a Type I error and the demands of the test is controlled by the boundaries of the critical region. For the hypothesis test to conclude that the treatment does have an effect, the sample data must be in the critical region. If the treatment really has an effect, it should cause the sample to be different from the original population; essentially, the treatment should push the sample into the critical region. However, as the alpha level is lowered, the boundaries for the critical region move farther out and become more difficult to reach. Figure 8.5 shows how the boundaries for the critical region move farther away as the alpha level decreases. Notice that lower alpha levels produce more extreme boundaries for the critical region. Thus, an extremely small alpha level, such as .000001 (one in a million), would mean almost no risk of a Type I error but would push the critical region so far out that it would become essentially impossible to ever reject the null hypothesis; that is, it would require an enormous treatment effect before the sample data would reach the critical boundaries.

In general, researchers try to maintain a balance between the risk of a Type I error and the demands of the hypothesis test. Alpha levels of .05, .01, and .001 are considered reasonably good values because they provide a low risk of error without placing excessive demands on the research results.

LEARNING CHECK

1. What is a Type I error?

2. Why is the consequence of a Type I error considered serious?

3. If the alpha level is changed from $\alpha = .05$ to $\alpha = .01$, the probability of a Type I error increases. (True or false?)

4. Define a Type II error.

5. What research situation is likely to lead to a Type II error?

ANSWERS

1. A Type I error is rejecting a true null hypothesis—that is, saying that the treatment has an effect when in fact it does not.

2. A Type I error often results in a false report. A researcher reports or publishes a treatment effect that does not exist.

3. False. The probability of a Type I error is α.

4. A Type II error is the failure to reject a false null hypothesis. In terms of a research study, a Type II error occurs when a study fails to detect a treatment effect that really exists.

5. A Type II error is likely to occur when the treatment effect is very small. In this case, a research study is more likely to fail to detect the effect.

8.3 AN EXAMPLE OF A HYPOTHESIS TEST

At this time, we have introduced all the elements of a hypothesis test. In this section, we present a complete example of the hypothesis-testing process and discuss how the results from a hypothesis test are presented in a research report. For purposes of demonstration, the following scenario will be used to provide a concrete background for the hypothesis-testing process.

EXAMPLE 8.2

Alcohol appears to be involved in a variety of birth defects, including low birth weight and retarded growth. A researcher would like to investigate the effect of prenatal alcohol on birth weight. A random sample of $n = 16$ pregnant rats is obtained. The mother rats are given daily doses of alcohol. At birth, one pup is selected from each litter to produce a sample of $n = 16$ newborn rats. The average weight for the sample is $M = 15$ grams. The researcher would like to compare the sample with the general population of rats. It is known that regular newborn rats (not exposed to alcohol) have an average weight of $\mu = 18$ grams. The distribution of weights is normal with $\sigma = 4$. Figure 8.6 shows the overall research situation. Notice that the researcher's question concerns the unknown population that is exposed to alcohol. Also notice that we have a sample representing the unknown population, and we have a hypothesis about the unknown population mean. Specifically, the null hypothesis says that the alcohol has no effect and the unknown mean is still $\mu = 18$. The goal of the hypothesis test is to determine whether the sample data are compatible with the hypothesis.

The following steps outline the hypothesis test that evaluates the effect of alcohol exposure on birth weight.

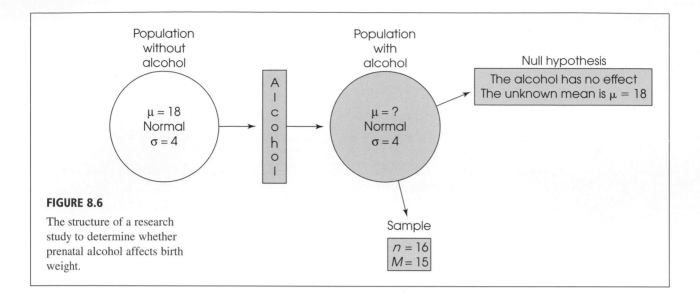

FIGURE 8.6

The structure of a research study to determine whether prenatal alcohol affects birth weight.

STEP 1   *State the hypotheses, and select the alpha level.* Both hypotheses concern the population that is exposed to alcohol, for which the population mean is unknown (the population on the right-hand side of Figure 8.6). The null hypothesis states that exposure to alcohol has no effect on birth weight. Thus, the population of rats with alcohol exposure should have the same mean birth weight as the regular, unexposed rats. In symbols,

$$H_0: \quad \mu_{\text{alcohol exposure}} = 18 \qquad \text{(Even with alcohol exposure, the rats still average 18 grams at birth.)}$$

The alternative hypothesis states that alcohol exposure does affect birth weight, so the exposed population should be different from the regular rats. In symbols,

$$H_1: \quad \mu_{\text{alcohol exposure}} \neq 18 \qquad \text{(Alcohol exposure changes birth weight.)}$$

Notice that both hypotheses concern the unknown population. For this test, we will use an alpha level of $\alpha = .05$. That is, we are taking a 5% risk of committing a Type I error.

STEP 2   *Set the decision criteria by locating the critical region.* By definition, the critical region consists of outcomes that are very unlikely if the null hypothesis is true. To locate the critical region we will go through a three-stage process that is portrayed in Figure 8.7. We begin with the null hypothesis, which states that the alcohol has no effect on newborn rats. If H_0 is true, the population treated with alcohol is the same as the original population: that is, a normal distribution with $\mu = 18$ and $\sigma = 4$. Next, we consider all the possible outcomes for a sample of $n = 16$ newborn rats. This is the distribution of sample means for $n = 16$. For this example, the distribution of sample mean is normal, is centered at $\mu = 18$ (according to H_0), and has a standard error of $\sigma_M = 4/\sqrt{16} = 1$. Finally, we use the distribution of sample means to identify the critical region, which consists of those outcomes that are very unlikely if the null hypothesis is true. With $\alpha = .05$, the critical region consists of the extreme 5% of the distribution. As we saw earlier, for any normal

FIGURE 8.7

Locating the critical region as a three-step process. You begin with the population of scores that is predicted by the null hypothesis. Then, you construct the distribution of sample means for the sample size that is being used. The distribution of sample means corresponds to all the possible outcomes that could be obtained if H_0 is true. Finally, you use z-scores to separate the extreme outcomes (as defined by the alpha level) from the high-probability outcomes. The extreme values determine the critical region.

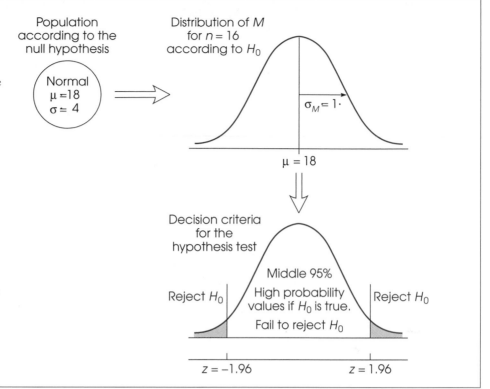

distribution, z-scores of $z = \pm 1.96$ separate the middle 95% from the extreme 5% (a proportion of 0.0250 in each tail). Thus, we have identified the sample means that, according to the null hypothesis, have a high probability of occurrence, and the sample means that are very unlikely to occur. It is the unlikely sample means, those with z-score values beyond ± 1.96, that form the critical region for the test.

STEP 3   *Collect the data, and compute the test statistic.* At this point, we would select our sample of $n = 16$ pups whose mothers had received alcohol during pregnancy. The birth weight would be recorded for each pup and the sample mean computed. As noted, we obtained a sample mean of $M = 15$ grams. The sample mean is then converted to a z-score, which is our test statistic.

$$z = \frac{M - \mu}{\sigma_M} = \frac{15 - 18}{1} = \frac{-3}{1} = -3.00$$

STEP 4   *Make a decision.* The z-score computed in step 3 has a value of -3.00, which is beyond the boundary of -1.96. Therefore, the sample mean is located in the critical region. This is a very unlikely outcome if the null hypothesis is true, so our decision is to reject the null hypothesis. In addition to this statistical decision concerning the null hypothesis, it is customary to state a conclusion about the results of the research study. For this example, we conclude that prenatal exposure to alcohol does have a significant effect on birth weight.

IN THE LITERATURE
REPORTING THE RESULTS OF THE STATISTICAL TEST

A special jargon and notational system are used in published reports of hypothesis tests. When you are reading a scientific journal, for example, you typically will not be told explicitly that the researcher evaluated the data using a z-score as a test statistic with an alpha level of .05. Nor will you be told that "the null hypothesis is rejected." Instead, you will see a statement such as

> The treatment with alcohol had a significant effect on the birth weight of newborn rats, $z = 3.00, p < .05$.

Let us examine this statement piece by piece. First, what is meant by the word *significant*? In statistical tests, a *significant* result means that the null hypothesis has been rejected, which means that the result is very unlikely to have occurred merely by chance. For this example, the null hypothesis would have stated that the alcohol has no effect, however the data clearly indicated that the alcohol did have an effect. Specifically, it is very unlikely that the data would have been obtained if the alcohol did not have an effect.

DEFINITION

A result is said to be **significant** or **statistically significant** if it is very unlikely to occur when the null hypothesis is true. That is, the result is sufficient to reject the null hypothesis. Thus, a treatment has a significant effect if the decision from the hypothesis test is to reject H_0.

Next, what is the meaning of $z = 3.00$? The z indicates that a z-score was used as the test statistic to evaluate the sample data and that its value is 3.00. Finally, what is meant by $p < .05$? This part of the statement is a conventional way of specifying the alpha level that was used for the hypothesis test. More specifically, we are being told that although this result is possible if H_0 is true, it has a very small probability (p) of occurring (less than .05) if there is no treatment effect.

In circumstances where the statistical decision is to *fail to reject* H_0, the report might state that

The APA style does not use a leading zero in a probability value that refers to a level of significance.

> There was no evidence that the alcohol had an effect on birth weight, $z = 1.30, p > .05$.

In this case, we are saying that the obtained result, $z = 1.30$, is not unusual (not in the critical region) and has a relatively high probability of occurring (greater than .05) even if the null hypthesis is true and there is no treatment effect.

Sometimes students become confused trying to differentiate between $p < .05$ and $p > .05$. Remember that you reject the null hypothesis with extreme, low-probability values, located in the critical region in the tails of the distribution. Thus, a significant result that rejects the null hypothesis corresponds to $p < 0.5$ (Figure 8.8).

When a hypothesis test is conducted using a computer program, the printout will often include not only a z-score value but also an exact value for p, the probability that the result occurred without any treatment effect. In this case, researchers are encouraged to report the exact p value instead of using the less-than or greater-than notation. For example, a research report might state that the treatment effect was significant, with $z = 2.45, p = .0142$. When using exact values for p, however, you must still satisfy the traditional criterion for significance; specifically, the p value

FIGURE 8.8

Sample means that fall in the critical region (shaded areas) have a probability *less than* alpha ($p < \alpha$). In this case, H_0 should be rejected. Sample means that do not fall in the critical region have a probability *greater than* alpha ($p > \alpha$).

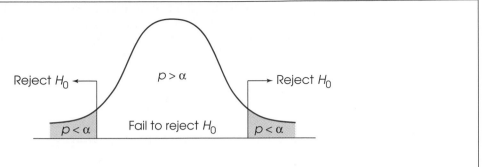

must be smaller than .05 to be considered statistically significant. Remember: The *p* value is the probability that the result would occur if H_0 were true (without any treatment effect), which is also the probability of a Type I error. It is essential that this probability be very small.

Finally, you should notice that in scientific reports, the researcher does not actually state that "the null hypothesis was rejected." Instead, the researcher reports that the effect of the treatment was statistically significant. Likewise, when H_0 is not rejected, one simply states that the treatment effect was not statistically significant or that there was no evidence for a treatment effect. In fact, when you read scientific reports, you will note that the terms *null hypothesis* and *alternative hypothesis* are rarely mentioned. Nevertheless, H_0 and H_1 are part of the logic of hypothesis testing even if they are not formally stated in a scientific report. Because of their central role in the process of hypothesis testing, you should be able to identify and state these hypotheses.   ❏

FACTORS THAT INFLUENCE A HYPOTHESIS TEST

In a hypothesis test, a large value for the *z*-score statistic is an indication that the sample mean, *M*, is very unlikely to have occurred if there is no treatment effect. Thus, a large value for *z* is grounds for concluding that the treatment has a significant effect. However, there are several factors that help determine whether the *z*-score will be large enough to reject H_0. In this section we examine three factors that can influence the outcome of a hypothesis test.

1. The size of the difference between the sample mean and the original population mean. This is the value that appears in the numerator of the *z*-score.

2. The variability of the scores, which is measured by either the standard deviation or the variance. The variability influences the size of the standard error in the denominator of the *z*-score.

3. The number of scores in the sample. This value also influences the size of the standard error in the denominator.

We will use the research study from Example 8.2, shown in Figure 8.6, to examine each of the three factors. The study used a sample of $n = 16$ newborn rats and concluded that alcohol has a significant effect on birth weight, $z = -3.00$, $p < .05$.

The size of the mean difference   The most obvious factor influencing the outcome of a hypothesis test is the size of the mean difference. The amount of difference between the treated sample mean and the original population mean is the clearest indicator of a significant treatment effect. In Figure 8.6, there is a 3-point difference between the sample mean, $M = 15$, and the hypothesized population mean, $\mu = 18$. This difference produced $z = -3.00$, a significant result. Now consider what happens if the sample mean is changed to $M = 17$, reducing the mean difference to only 1 point. The z-score becomes

$$z = \frac{M - \mu}{\sigma_M} = \frac{17 - 18}{1} = \frac{-1}{1} = -1.00$$

Now the z-score is not in the critical region and we fail to reject the null hypothesis. In general, a larger mean difference indicates a larger treatment effect which produces a larger z-score and increases the likelihood of finding a significant effect.

The variability of the scores   In Chapter 4 (page 106) we noted that high variability can make it very difficult to see any clear patterns in the results from a research study. In a hypothesis test, higher variability can reduce the chances of finding a significant treatment effect. For the study in Figure 8.6, the standard deviation is $\sigma = 4$. With a sample of $n = 16$, this produced a standard error of $\sigma_M = 1$ point and a significant z-score of $z = -3.00$. Now consider what happens if the standard deviation is increased to $\sigma = 12$. With the increased variability, the standard error becomes $\sigma_M = 12/\sqrt{16} = 3$ points. Using the same 3-point mean difference from the original example, the new z-score becomes

$$z = \frac{M - \mu}{\sigma_M} = \frac{15 - 18}{3} = \frac{-3}{3} = -1.00$$

The z-score is no longer beyond the critical boundary of 1.96, so the statistical decision is to fail to reject the null hypothesis. The increased variability means that the sample data are no longer sufficient to conclude that the treatment has a significant effect. In general, increasing the variability of the scores will produce a larger standard error and a smaller value (closer to zero) for the z-score. If other factors are held constant, the larger the variability, the lower the likelihood of finding a significant treatment effect.

The number of scores in the sample   The final factor that influences the outcome of a hypothesis test is the number of scores in the sample. The study in Figure 8.6 used a sample of $n = 16$ rats and obtained a standard error of $\sigma_M = 4/\sqrt{16} = 1$ point and a significant z-score of $z = -3.00$. Now consider what happens if we reduce the sample size to only $n = 4$ rats. With $n = 4$, the standard error becomes $\sigma_M = 4/\sqrt{4} = 2$ points, and the z-score becomes

$$z = \frac{M - \mu}{\sigma_M} = \frac{15 - 18}{2} = \frac{-3}{2} = -1.50$$

This z-score is not in the critical region, and now we must conclude that the alcohol does not have a significant effect. In general, increasing the number of scores in the sample will produce a smaller standard error and a larger value for the z-score. If all other factors are held constant, the larger the sample size, the greater the likelihood of finding a significant treatment effect. In simple terms, finding a 3-point treatment effect with a large sample is more convincing than finding a 3-point effect with a small sample.

**ASSUMPTIONS FOR
HYPOTHESIS TESTS
WITH z-SCORES**

The mathematics that are used for a hypothesis test are based on a set of assumptions. When these assumptions are satisfied, you can be confident that the test produces a justified conclusion. However, if the assumptions are not satisfied, the hypothesis test may be compromised. In practice, researchers are not overly concerned with the assumptions underlying a hypothesis test because the tests usually work well even when the assumptions are violated. However, you should be aware of the fundamental conditions that are associated with each type of statistical test to ensure that the test is being used appropriately. The assumptions for hypothesis tests with z-scores are summarized as follows.

Random sampling   It is assumed that the subjects used to obtain the sample data were selected randomly. Remember, we wish to generalize our findings from the sample to the population. We accomplish this task when we use sample data to test a hypothesis about the population. Therefore, the sample must be representative of the population from which it has been drawn. Random sampling helps to ensure that it is representative.

Independent observations   The values in the sample must consist of *independent* observations. In everyday terms, two observations are independent if there is no consistent, predictable relationship between the first observation and the second. More precisely, two events (or observations) are independent if the occurrence of the first event has no effect on the probability of the second event. Specific examples of independence and nonindependence are examined in Box 8.2. Usually, this assumption is satisfied by using a *random* sample, which also helps ensure that the sample is representative of the population and that the results can be generalized to the population.

The value of σ is unchanged by the treatment   A critical part of the z-score formula in a hypothesis is the standard error, σ_M. To compute the value for the standard error, we must know the sample size (n) and the population standard deviation (σ). In a hypothesis test, however, the sample comes from an *unknown* population (see Figures 8.2 and 8.6). If the population is really unknown, it would suggest that we do not know the standard deviation and, therefore, we cannot calculate the standard error. To solve this dilemma, we must make an assumption. Specifically, we assume that the standard deviation for the unknown population (after treatment) is the same as it was for the population before treatment.

Actually, this assumption is the consequence of a more general assumption that is part of many statistical procedures. This general assumption states that the effect of the treatment is to add a constant amount to (or subtract a constant amount from) every score in the population. You should recall that adding (or subtracting) a constant will change the mean but will have no effect on the standard deviation. You also should note that this assumption is a theoretical ideal. In actual experiments, a treatment generally will not show a perfect and consistent additive effect.

Normal sampling distribution   To evaluate hypotheses with z-scores, we have used the unit normal table to identify the critical region. This table can be used only if the distribution of sample means is normal.

BOX 8.2   INDEPENDENT OBSERVATIONS

Independent observations are a basic requirement for nearly all hypothesis tests. The critical concern is that each observation or measurement is not influenced by any other observation or measurement. An example of independent observations is the set of outcomes obtained in a series of coin tosses. Assuming that the coin is balanced, each toss has a 50–50 chance of coming up either heads or tails. More important, each toss is *independent* of the tosses that came before. On the fifth toss, for example, there is a 50% chance of heads, no matter what happened on the previous four tosses; the coin does not remember what happened earlier and is not influenced by the past. (*Note:* Many people fail to believe in the independence of events. For example, after a series of four tails in a row, it is tempting to think that the probability of heads must increase because the coin is overdue to come up heads. This is a mistake, called the "gambler's fallacy." Remember that the coin does not know what happened on the preceding tosses and cannot be influenced by previous outcomes.)

In most research situations, the requirement for independent observations is typically satisfied by using a random sample of separate, unrelated individuals. Thus, the measurement obtained for each individual is not influenced by other subjects in the sample. The following two situations demonstrate circumstances in which the observations are *not* independent.

1. A researcher is interested in examining television preferences for children. To obtain a sample of $n = 20$ children, the researcher selects 4 children from family A, 3 children from family B, 5 children from family C, 2 children from family D, and 6 children from family E.

   It should be obvious that the researcher does *not* have 20 independent observations. Within each family, the children probably share television preference (at least they watch the same shows). Thus, the response for each child is likely to be related to the responses of his or her siblings.

2. A researcher is interested in people's ability to judge distances. A sample of 20 people is obtained. All 20 participants are gathered together in the same room. The researcher asks the first person to estimate the distance between New York and Miami. The second person is asked the same question, then the third person, the fourth person, and so on.

   Again, the observations that the researcher obtains are not independent: The response of each participant is probably influenced by the responses of the previous participants. For example, consistently low estimates by the first few participants could create pressure to conform and thereby increase the probability that the following participants would also produce low estimates.

LEARNING CHECK

1. A researcher would like to know whether room temperature will affect eating behavior in rats. The lab temperature is usually kept at 72°, and under these conditions, the rats eat an average of $\mu = 10$ grams of food each day. The amount of food varies from one rat to another, forming a normal distribution with $\sigma = 2$. The researcher selects a sample of $n = 4$ rats and places them in a room where the temperature is kept at 65°. The daily food consumption for these rats averaged $M = 13$ grams. Do these data indicate that temperature has a significant effect on eating? Test at the .05 level of significance.

2. In a research report, the term *significant* is used when the null hypothesis is rejected. (True or false?)

3. In a research report, the results of a hypothesis test include the phrase "$p < .01$." This means that the test failed to reject the null hypothesis. (True or false?)

ANSWERS

1. The null hypothesis states that temperature has no effect, or $\mu = 10$ grams even at the lower temperature. With $\alpha = .05$, the critical region consists of z-scores beyond $z = \pm1.96$. The sample data produce $z = 3.00$. The decision is to reject H_0 and conclude that temperature has a significant effect on eating behavior.

2. True.

3. False. The probability is *less than* .01, which means it is very unlikely that the result occurred without any treatment effect. In this case, the data are in the critical region, and H_0 is rejected.

8.4 DIRECTIONAL (ONE-TAILED) HYPOTHESIS TESTS

The hypothesis-testing procedure presented in Section 8.3 was the standard, or *two-tailed*, test format. The term *two-tailed* comes from the fact that the critical region is located in both tails of the distribution. This format is by far the most widely accepted procedure for hypothesis testing. Nonetheless, there is an alternative that is discussed in this section.

Usually a researcher begins an experiment with a specific prediction about the direction of the treatment effect. For example, a special training program is expected to *increase* student performance, or alcohol consumption is expected to *slow* reaction times. In these situations, it is possible to state the statistical hypotheses in a manner that incorporates the directional prediction into the statement of H_0 and H_1. The result is a directional test, or what commonly is called a *one-tailed test*.

D E F I N I T I O N

In a **directional hypothesis test**, or a **one-tailed test**, the statistical hypotheses (H_0 and H_1) specify either an increase or a decrease in the population mean score. That is, they make a statement about the direction of the effect.

Suppose, for example, a researcher is using a sample of $n = 16$ laboratory rats to examine the effect of a new diet drug. It is known that under regular circumstances these rats eat an average of 10 grams of food each day. The distribution of food consumption is normal with $\sigma = 4$. The expected effect of the drug is to reduce food consumption. The purpose of the experiment is to determine whether the drug really works.

THE HYPOTHESES FOR A DIRECTIONAL TEST

Because a specific direction is expected for the treatment effect, it is possible for the researcher to perform a directional test. The first step (and the most critical step) is to state the statistical hypotheses. Remember that the null hypothesis states that there is no treatment effect and that the alternative hypothesis says that there is an effect. For this example, the predicted effect is that the drug will reduce food consumption. Thus, the two hypotheses would state:

H_0:   Food consumption is not reduced.

H_1:   Food consumption is reduced.

To express these directional hypotheses in symbols, it usually is easier to begin with the alternative hypothesis. Again, we know that regular rats eat an average of $\mu = 10$ grams of food, and H_1 says that food consumption will be reduced by the diet drug. Therefore, expressed in symbols, H_1 states

H_1: $\mu < 10$ (With the drug, food consumption is less than 10 grams per day.)

The null hypothesis states that the drug does not reduce food consumption:

$$H_0: \quad \mu \geq 10 \quad \text{(With the drug, food consumption is still at least 10 grams per day.)}$$

THE CRITICAL REGION FOR DIRECTIONAL TESTS

The critical region is defined by sample outcomes that are very unlikely to occur if the null hypothesis is true (that is, if the treatment has no effect). Earlier (page 194), we noted that the critical region can also be defined in terms of sample values that provide *convincing evidence* that the treatment really does have an effect. For a directional test, the concept of "convincing evidence" is the simplest way to determine the location of the critical region. In this example, the treatment is intended to reduce food consumption. If untreated rats eat $\mu = 10$ grams per day, then a sample mean that is substantially less than 10 would provide convincing evidence that the treatment worked. Thus, the critical region is located entirely in one tail of the distribution (Figure 8.9), which is why a directional test is commonly called a *one-tailed* test.

Notice that a directional (one-tailed) test requires two changes in the step-by-step hypothesis-testing procedure.

1. In the first step of the hypothesis test, the directional prediction is incorporated into the statement of the hypotheses.

2. In the second step of the process, the critical region is located entirely in one tail of the distribution.

After these two changes, the remainder of a one-tailed test proceeds exactly the same as a regular two-tailed test. Specifically, you calculate the z-score statistic and then make a decision about H_0 depending on whether the z-score is in the critical region.

Next we present a complete example of a one-tailed test. Once again, we use the study evaluating the effect of an antioxidant food supplement (blueberries) on the cognitive functioning of adults older than 65.

EXAMPLE 8.3

Food supplements that are high in antioxidants (like blueberries) have been shown to reduce, and even reverse, age-related declines in cognitive performance for rats. To determine whether the same result applies to humans, a researcher selects a sample of $n = 25$ adults who are more than 65 years old. Each participant is given a daily dose of a blueberry supplement for 6 months. At the end of the 6-month study, the

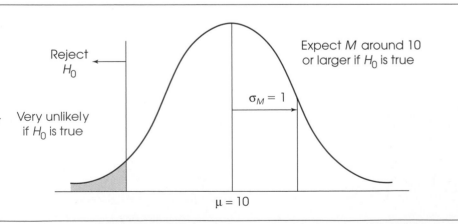

FIGURE 8.9

The distribution of sample means for $n = 16$ if H_0 is true. The null hypothesis states that the drug does not reduce food consumption. A sample mean much smaller than $\mu = 10$ would provide evidence that the drug works and that H_0 should be rejected.

researcher measures cognitive performance for each participant using a standardized neuropsychological test for which adults older than age 65 have an average score of $\mu = 80$ with a standard deviation of $\sigma = 20$. The distribution of test scores is approximately normal. The researcher expects that the blueberry supplement will improve cognitive performance and, therefore, increase scores on the test. For this sample, the average score on the test is $M = 87$.

STEP 1   *State the hypotheses and select* α. Because the researcher is predicting that the supplement will increase scores, it is possible to do a directional test. The null hypothesis states that the treatment will not work as predicted. In symbols,

$$H_0: \quad \mu \leq 80 \qquad \text{(There is no increase in test scores.)}$$

The alternative hypothesis states that the supplement will increase scores. In symbols,

$$H_1: \quad \mu > 80 \qquad \text{(There is an increase in test scores.)}$$

We will use $\alpha = .05$.

STEP 2   *Locate the critical region.* To locate the critical region, we begin with all the possible sample means for $n = 25$ that could be obtained if H_0 is true. This is the distribution of sample means, and it will be normal (because the population of scores is normal), have an expected value of $\mu = 80$ (from H_0), and have a standard error of $\sigma_M = 20/\sqrt{25} = 4$. The distribution is shown in Figure 8.10.

For a one-tailed test with $\alpha = .05$, the entire 5% is in one tail of the distribution. Check the unit normal table with .05 in the tail, and you should find that $z = 1.65$.

The critical region consists of extreme values that are inconsistent with the null hypothesis. Equivalently, the critical region consists of extreme values that provide evidence of a real treatment effect. By either definition, the critical region consists of large values for the sample mean, values much bigger than $\mu = 80$. Thus, the critical region is located entirely in the right-hand tail of the distribution. Using $\alpha = .05$, the most extreme 5% is separated from the rest of the distribution by a z-score of $z = 1.65$ (see Figure 8.10).

STEP 3   *Obtain the sample data and compute the test statistic.* The sample mean of $M = 87$ corresponds to a z-score of

$$z = \frac{M - \mu}{\sigma_M} = \frac{87 - 80}{4} = \frac{7}{4} = 1.75$$

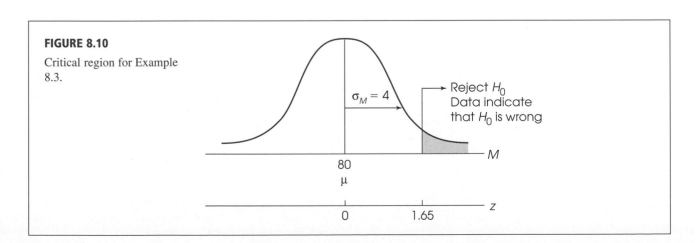

FIGURE 8.10

Critical region for Example 8.3.

STEP 4   *Make a decision.* A z-score of 1.75 is in the critical region (for the one-tailed test). This is a very unlikely outcome if H_0 is true. Our decision is to reject H_0 and conclude that the supplement does produce a significant increase in test scores.

COMPARISON OF
ONE-TAILED VERSUS
TWO-TAILED TESTS

The general goal of hypothesis testing is to determine whether a particular treatment has any effect on a population. The test is performed by selecting a sample, administering the treatment to the sample, and then comparing the result with the original population. If the treated sample is noticeably different from the original population, then we conclude that the treatment has an effect, and we reject H_0. On the other hand, if the treated sample is still similar to the original population, then we conclude that there is no evidence for a treatment effect, and we fail to reject H_0. The critical factor in this decision is the *size of the difference* between the treated sample and the original population. A large difference is evidence that the treatment worked; a small difference is not sufficient to say that the treatment has any effect.

The major distinction between one-tailed and two-tailed tests is in the criteria they use for rejecting H_0. A one-tailed test allows you to reject the null hypothesis when the difference between the sample and the population is relatively small, provided the difference is in the specified direction. A two-tailed test, on the other hand, requires a relatively large difference independent of direction. This point is illustrated in the following example.

EXAMPLE 8.4   Consider again the study in Example 8.3 evaluating the effect of an antioxidant supplement. If we had used a standard two-tailed test, the hypotheses would be

H_0: $\mu = 80$ (The supplement has no effect on test scores.)

H_1: $\mu \neq 80$ (The supplement does have an effect on test scores.)

For a two-tailed test with $\alpha = .05$, the critical region consists of z-scores beyond ± 1.96. The data from Example 8.3 produced a sample mean of $M = 87$ and $z = 1.75$. For the two-tailed test, this z-score is not in the critical region, and we conclude that the supplement does not have a significant effect.

With the two-tailed test in Example 8.4, the 7-point difference between the sample mean and the hypothesized population mean ($M = 87$ and $\mu = 80$) was not big enough to reject the null hypothesis. However, with the one-tailed test in Example 8.3, the same 7-point difference was large enough to reject H_0 and conclude that the treatment had a significant effect.

All researchers agree that one-tailed tests are different from two-tailed tests. However, there are several ways to interpret the difference. One group of researchers contends that a two-tailed test is more rigorous and, therefore, more convincing than a one-tailed test. Remember that the two-tailed test demands more evidence to reject H_0 and thus provides a stronger demonstration that a treatment effect has occurred.

Other researchers feel that one-tailed tests are preferred because they are more sensitive. That is, a relatively small treatment effect may be significant with a one-tailed test but fail to reach significance with a two-tailed test. Also, there is the argument that one-tailed tests are more precise because they test hypotheses about a specific directional effect instead of an indefinite hypothesis about a general effect.

In general, two-tailed tests should be used in research situations when there is no strong directional expectation or when there are two competing predictions. For example, a two-tailed test would be appropriate for a study in which one theory predicts an increase in scores but another theory predicts a decrease. One-tailed tests should be used only in situations where the directional prediction is made before the research is conducted and there is a strong justification for making the directional prediction. In particular, you should never use a one-tailed test as a second attempt to salvage a significant result from a research study for which the first analysis with a two-tailed test failed to reach significance.

LEARNING CHECK

1. A researcher predicts that a treatment will lower scores. If this researcher uses a one-tailed test, will the critical region be in the right- or left-hand tail of the distribution?

2. A psychologist is examining the effects of early sensory deprivation on the development of perceptual discrimination. A sample of $n = 9$ newborn kittens is obtained. These kittens are raised in a completely dark environment for 4 weeks, after which they receive normal visual stimulation. At age 6 months, the kittens are tested on a visual discrimination task. The average score for this sample is $M = 32$. It is known that under normal circumstances kittens score an average of $\mu = 40$ on this task. The distribution of scores is normal with $\sigma = 12$. The researcher is predicting that the early sensory deprivation will reduce the kittens' performance on the discrimination task. Use a one-tailed test with $\alpha = .01$ to test this hypothesis.

ANSWERS

1. The left-hand tail

2. The hypotheses are H_0: $\mu \geq 40$ and H_1: $\mu < 40$. The critical region is determined by z-scores less than -2.33. The z-score for these sample data is $z = -2.00$. Fail to reject H_0.

8.5 CONCERNS ABOUT HYPOTHESIS TESTING: MEASURING EFFECT SIZE

Although hypothesis testing is the most commonly used technique for evaluating and interpreting research data, a number of scientists have expressed a variety of concerns about the hypothesis testing procedure (for example see Loftus, 1996; Hunter, 1997; and Killeen, 2005).

Perhaps the most serious criticism of a hypothesis test concerns the interpretation of a significant result. Actually, there are two serious limitations with using a hypothesis test to establish the significance of a treatment effect. The first concern is that the focus of a hypothesis test is on the data rather than the hypothesis. Specifically, when the null hypothesis is rejected, we are actually making a strong probability statement about the sample data, not about the null hypothesis. A significant result permits the following conclusion: "This specific sample mean is very unlikely ($p < .05$) if the null hypothesis is true." Note that the conclusion does not make any definite statement about the probability of the null hypothesis being true or false. The fact that the data are very unlikely *suggests* that the null hypothesis is also very unlikely, but we do not have any solid grounds for making a probability statement about the null hypothesis. Rejecting the null hypothesis with $\alpha = .05$ does not justify a conclusion that the probability of the null hypothesis being true is less than 5%.

A second concern is that demonstrating a *significant* treatment effect does not necessarily indicate a *substantial* treatment effect. In particular, statistical significance does not provide any real information about the absolute size of a treatment effect. Instead, the hypothesis test has simply established that the results obtained in the research study are very unlikely to have occurred if there is no treatment effect. The hypothesis test reaches this conclusion by (1) calculating the standard error, which measures how much difference is reasonable to expect between M and μ, and (2) demonstrating that the obtained mean difference is substantially bigger than the standard error.

Notice that the test is making a *relative* comparison: the size of the treatment effect is being evaluated relative to the standard error. If the standard error is very small, then the treatment effect can also be very small and still be large enough to be significant. Thus, a significant effect does not necessarily mean a big effect.

The idea that a hypothesis test evaluates the relative size of a treatment effect, rather than the absolute size, is illustrated in the following example.

EXAMPLE 8.5

We begin with a population of scores that forms a normal distribution with $\mu = 50$ and $\sigma = 10$. A sample is selected from the population and a treatment is administered to the sample. After treatment, the sample mean is found to be $M = 51$. Does this sample provide evidence of a statistically significant treatment effect?

Although there is only a 1-point difference between the sample mean and the original population mean, the difference may be enough to be significant. In particular, the outcome of the hypothesis test depends on the sample size.

For example, with a sample of $n = 25$ the standard error is

$$\sigma_M = \frac{\sigma}{\sqrt{n}} = \frac{10}{\sqrt{25}} = \frac{10}{5} = 2.00$$

and the z-score for $M = 51$ is

$$z = \frac{M - \mu}{\sigma_M} = \frac{51 - 50}{2} = \frac{1}{2} = 0.50$$

For an alpha level of .05, the critical region would begin at $z = 1.96$. Our z-score fails to reach the critical region, so we fail to reject the null hypothesis. In this case, the 1-point difference between M and μ is not significant because it is being evaluated relative to a standard error of 2 points.

Now consider the outcome with a sample of $n = 400$. The standard error is

$$\sigma_M = \frac{\sigma}{\sqrt{n}} = \frac{10}{\sqrt{400}} = \frac{10}{20} = 0.50$$

and the z-score for $M = 51$ is

$$z = \frac{M - \mu}{\sigma_M} = \frac{51 - 50}{0.5} = \frac{1}{0.5} = 2.00$$

Now the z-score is beyond the 1.96 boundary, so we reject the null hypothesis and conclude that there is a signficant effect. In this case, the 1-point difference between M and μ is considered statistically significant because it is being evaluated relative to a standard error of only 0.5 points.

The point of Example 8.5 is that a small treatment effect can still be statistically significant. If the sample size is large enough, any treatment effect, no matter how small, can be enough for us to reject the null hypothesis.

MEASURING EFFECT SIZE   As noted in the previous section (point 2), one concern with hypothesis testing is that a hypothesis test does not really evaluate the absolute size of a treatment effect. To correct this problem, it is recommended that whenever researchers report a statistically significant effect, they also provide a report of the effect size (see the guidelines presented by L. Wilkinson and the APA Task Force on Statistical Inference, 1999). Therefore, as we present different hypothesis tests we will also present different options for measuring and reporting *effect size*.

One of the simplest and most direct methods for measuring effect size is *Cohen's* d. Cohen (1988) recommended that effect size can be standardized by measuring the mean difference in terms of the standard deviation. The resulting measure of effect size is computed as

$$\text{Cohen's } d = \frac{\text{mean difference}}{\text{standard deviation}} \tag{8.1}$$

For the *z*-score hypothesis test, the mean difference is simply the difference between the sample mean (after treatment) and the original population mean (before treatment). This is the same mean difference, $M - \mu$, that appears in the numerator of the *z*-score in the test. The standard deviation is included in the calculation to standardize the size of the mean difference in much the same way that *z*-scores standardize locations in a distribution. For example, a 15-point mean difference can be a relatively large treatment effect or a relatively small effect depending on the size of the standard deviation. This phenomenon is demonstrated in Figure 8.11. The top portion of the figure (part a) shows the results of a treatment that produces a 15-point mean difference in SAT scores; before treatment, the average SAT score is 500, and after treatment the average is 515. Notice that the standard deviation for SAT scores is $\sigma = 100$, so the 15-point difference appears to be small. For this example, Cohen's *d* is

$$\text{Cohen's } d = \frac{\text{mean difference}}{\text{standard deviation}} = \frac{15}{100} = 0.15$$

Now consider the treatment effect shown in Figure 8.11(b). This time, the treatment produces a 15-point mean difference in IQ scores; before treatment the average IQ is 100, and after treatment the average is 115. Because IQ scores have a standard deviation of $\sigma = 15$, the 15-point mean difference now appears to be large. For this example, Cohen's *d* is

$$\text{Cohen's } d = \frac{\text{mean difference}}{\text{standard deviation}} = \frac{15}{15} = 1.00$$

Notice that Cohen's *d* measures the size of the treatment effect in terms of the standard deviation. For example, a value of $d = 0.50$ indicates that the treatment changed the mean by half of a standard deviation; similarly, a value of $d = 1.00$ indicates that the size of the treatment effect is equal to one whole standard deviation.

Cohen (1988) also suggested criteria for evaluating the size of a treatment effect as shown in Table 8.2.

As one final demonstration of Cohen's *d*, consider the two hypothesis tests in Example 8.5. For each test, the original population had a mean of $\mu = 50$ with a

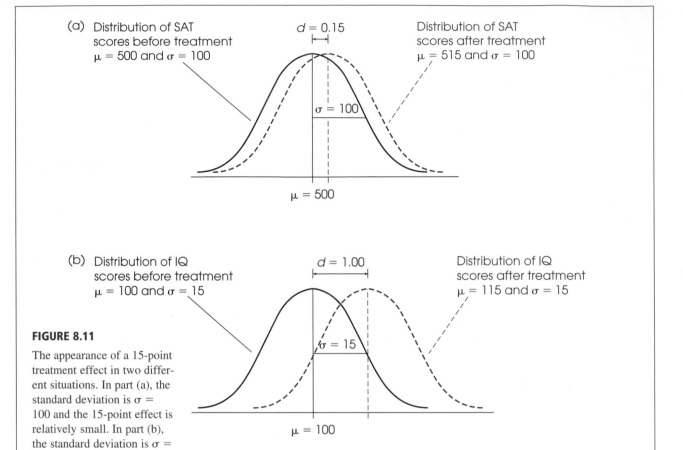

(a) Distribution of SAT scores before treatment $\mu = 500$ and $\sigma = 100$

$d = 0.15$

Distribution of SAT scores after treatment $\mu = 515$ and $\sigma = 100$

$\sigma = 100$

$\mu = 500$

(b) Distribution of IQ scores before treatment $\mu = 100$ and $\sigma = 15$

$d = 1.00$

Distribution of IQ scores after treatment $\mu = 115$ and $\sigma = 15$

$\sigma = 15$

$\mu = 100$

FIGURE 8.11

The appearance of a 15-point treatment effect in two different situations. In part (a), the standard deviation is $\sigma = 100$ and the 15-point effect is relatively small. In part (b), the standard deviation is $\sigma = 15$ and the 15-point effect is relatively large. Cohen's d uses the standard deviation to help measure effect size.

TABLE 8.2

Evaluating effect size with Cohen's d

Magnitude of d	Evaluation of Effect Size
$d = 0.2$	Small effect (mean difference around 0.2 standard deviation)
$d = 0.5$	Medium effect (mean difference around 0.5 standard deviation)
$d = 0.8$	Large effect (mean difference around 0.8 standard deviation)

standard deviation of $\sigma = 10$. For each test, the mean for the treated sample was $M = 51$. Although one test used a sample of $n = 25$ and the other test used a sample of $n = 400$, the sample size is not considered when computing Cohen's d. Therefore, both of the hypothesis tests would produce the same value:

$$\text{Cohen's } d = \frac{\text{mean difference}}{\text{standard deviation}} = \frac{1}{10} = 0.10$$

Notice that Cohen's d simply describes the size of the treatment effect and is not influenced by the number of scores in the sample. For both hypothesis tests, the original mean was 50 and, after treatment, the mean was 51. Thus, treatment appears to have increased the scores by 1 point, which is equal to one-tenth of a standard deviation (Cohen's $d = 0.1$).

LEARNING CHECK

1. Briefly explain why a "statistically significant" effect is not necessarily a "substantial" effect.

2. Compute Cohen's d for the hypothesis test presented in Example 8.2 (page 203).

ANSWERS

1. "Statistically significant" means that the result is greater than would be expected by chance. However, chance is measured by the standard error and, when the sample size is large, the standard error can be very small. In this case, a small treatment effect can still be significant.

2. For Example 8.2, the mean difference is 3 points and the standard deviation is $\sigma = 4$. Cohen's d is 0.75.

8.6 STATISTICAL POWER

Instead of measuring effect size directly, an alternative approach to determining the size or strength of a treatment effect is to measure the power of the statistical test. The *power* of a test is defined as the probability that the test will reject the null hypothesis if the treatment really has an effect.

DEFINITION

> The **power** of a statistical test is the probability that the test will correctly reject a false null hypothesis. That is, power is the probability that the test will identify a treatment effect if one really exists.

Researchers typically calculate power as a means of determining whether a research study is likely to be successful. Thus, researchers usually calculate the power of a hypothesis test *before* they actually conduct the research study. In this way, they can determine the probability that the results will be significant (reject H_0) before investing time and effort in the actual research. To calculate power, however, it is first necessary to make assumptions about a variety of factors that influence the outcome of a hypothesis test. Factors such as the sample size, the size of the treatment effect, and the value chosen for the alpha level can all influence a hypothesis test. The following example demonstrates the calculation of power for a specific research situation.

EXAMPLE 8.6

We start with a normal shaped population with a mean of $\mu = 80$ and a standard deviation of $\sigma = 10$. A researcher plans to select a sample of $n = 25$ individuals from this population and administer a treatment to each individual. It is expected that the treatment will have an 8-point effect; that is, the treatment will add 8 points to each individual's score.

Figure 8.12 shows the null hypothesis and the critical region for this study along with the results that would be obtained with an 8-point effect. The left-hand side of the figure shows what should happen according to the null hypothesis. In this case, the treatment has no effect and the population mean is still $\mu = 80$. On the right-hand

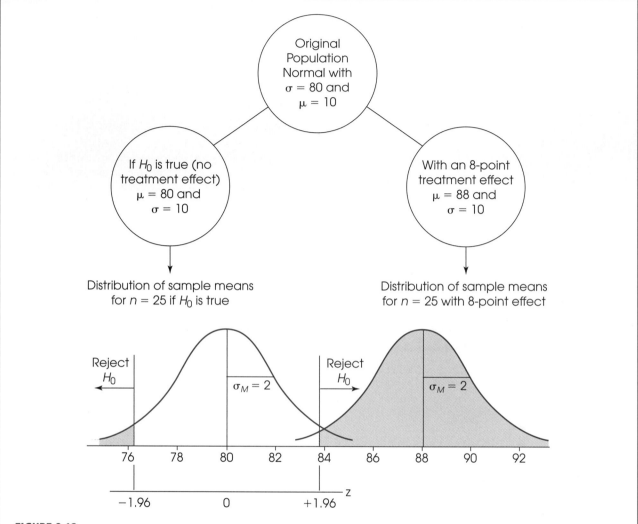

FIGURE 8.12

A demonstration of measuring power for a hypothesis test. The left-hand side shows the distribution of sample means that would occur if the null hypothesis were true. The critical region is defined for this distribution. The right-hand side shows the distribution of sample means that would be obtained if there were an 8-point treatment effect. Notice that if there were an 8-point effect, essentially all of the sample means would be in the critical region. Thus, the probability of rejecting H_0 (the power of the test) would be nearly 100% for an 8-point treatment effect.

side of the figure we show what would really happen if the treatment has an 8-point effect. If the treatment adds 8 points to each person's score, the population mean after treatment will increase to $\mu = 88$.

Next, we look at the distribution of sample means for $n = 25$ for each of the two possible outcomes. According to the null hypothesis, the sample means should be centered around $\mu = 80$. With an 8-point treatment effect, the sample means should be centered around $\mu = 88$. Both distributions have a standard error of

$$\sigma_M = \frac{\sigma}{\sqrt{n}} = \frac{10}{\sqrt{25}} = \frac{10}{5} = 2$$

Notice that the distribution on the left shows all of the possible sample means if the null hypothesis is true. This is the distribution we use to locate the critical region for the hypothesis test. Using $\alpha = .05$, the critical region consists of extreme values in this distribution, specifically sample means beyond $z = 1.96$ or $z = -1.96$. These values are shown in Figure 8.12, and we have shaded all of the sample means located in the critical region.

Now turn your attention to the distribution on the right, which shows all of the possible sample means if there is an 8-point treatment effect. Notice that most of these sample means are located beyond the $z = 1.96$ boundary. This means, that if there is an 8-point treatment effect, you are almost guaranteed to obtain a sample mean in the critical region and reject the null hypothesis. Thus, the power of the test (the probability of rejecting H_0) is close to 100% if there is an 8-point treatment effect.

To calculate the exact value for the power of the test we must determine what portion of the distribution on the right-hand side is shaded. Thus, we must locate the exact boundary for the critical region, then find the probability value in the unit normal table. First, note that the critical boundary of $z = 1.96$ corresponds to a sample mean of $M = 83.92$ [80 + 1.96(2)]. Next, we determine exactly where $M = 83.92$ is located in the right-hand distribution. In this case, the z-score is

$$z = \frac{M - \mu}{\sigma_M} = \frac{83.92 - 88}{2} = \frac{-4.08}{2} = -2.04$$

Finally, look up $z = -2.04$ in the unit normal table and determine that the shaded area ($z > -2.04$) corresponds to $p = 0.9793$ (or 97.93%). Thus, if the treatment has an 8-point effect, 97.93% of all the possible sample means will be in the critical region and we will reject the null hypothesis. In other words, the power of the test is 97.93%. In practical terms, this means that the research study is almost guaranteed to be successful. If the researcher selects a sample of $n = 25$ individuals, and if the treatment really does have an 8-point effect, then 97.93% of the time the hypothesis test will conclude that there is a significant effect.

POWER AND EFFECT SIZE

Logically, it should be clear that power and effect size are related. Figure 8.12 shows the calculation of power for an 8-point treatment effect. Now consider what would happen if the treatment effect were only 4 points. With a 4-point treatment effect, the distribution on the right-hand side would be shifted to the left to be centered at $\mu = 84$. With this new position, many of the treated sample means would no longer be beyond the $z = 1.96$ boundary. In fact, only about 50% of the sample means in the right-hand distribution would be beyond the 1.96 boundary. Thus, with a 4-point treatment effect, there is only a 50% probability that you would select a sample that led to rejecting the null hypothesis. In other words, the power of the test is only about 50% for a 4-point treatment effect. (Again, you can find the z-score corresponding to the exact location of the critical region boundary and look up the probability value for power in the unit normal table. In this case, you should obtain $z = -0.04$ and the power of the test is $p = 0.5160$ or 51.60%.)

In general, as the effect size increases the distribution of sample means on the right-hand side will move even farther to the right so that more and more of the samples are beyond the $z = 1.96$ boundary. Thus, as the effect size increases, the probability of rejecting H_0 also increases, which means that the power of the test increases. Thus, measures of effect size such as Cohen's d and measures of power both provide an indication of the strength or magnitude of a treatment effect.

OTHER FACTORS THAT AFFECT POWER

Although the power of a hypothesis test is directly influenced by the size of the treatment effect, power is not meant to be a pure measure of effect size. Instead, power is influenced by several factors, other than effect size, that are related to the hypothesis test. Some of these factors are considered in the following section.

Sample size   One factor that has a huge influence on power is the size of the sample. In Example 8.6 we demonstrated power for an 8-point treatment effect using a sample of $n = 25$. If the researcher decided to conduct the study using a sample of only $n = 4$, then the power would be dramatically different. With $n = 4$, the standard error for the sample means would be

$$\sigma_M = \frac{\sigma}{\sqrt{n}} = \frac{10}{\sqrt{4}} = \frac{10}{2} = 5$$

Figure 8.13 shows the two distributions of sample means with $n = 4$ and a standard error of $\sigma_M = 5$ points. The distribution on the left is centered at $\mu = 80$ and shows all

FIGURE 8.13

A demonstraion of how sample size affects the power of a hypothesis test. As in Figure 8.12, the left-hand side shows the distribution of sample means if the null hypothesis were true. The critical region is defined for this distribution. The right-hand side shows the distribuution of sample means that would be obtained if there were an 8-point treatment effect. Notice that reducing the sample size to $n = 4$ has reduced the power of the test to less than 50% compared to power of nearly 100% with a sample of $n = 25$ in Figure 8.12.

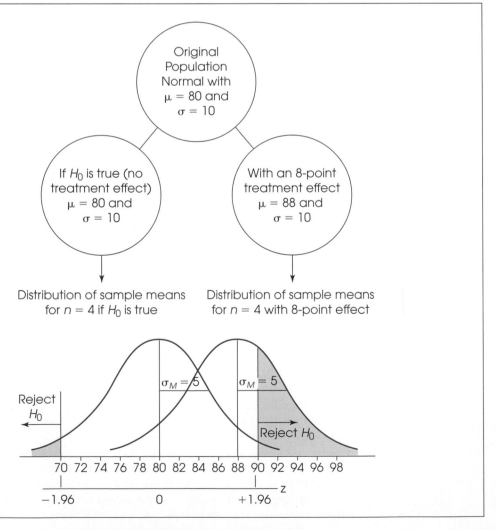

the possible sample means if H_0 is true. As always, this distribution is used to locate the critical boundaries for the hypothesis test. The distribution on the right is centered at $\mu = 88$ and shows all the possible sample means if there is an 8-point treatment effect. Note that less than half of the treated sample means are now located beyond the $z = 1.96$ boundary. Thus, using a sample of $n = 4$, there is less than a 50% probability that the sample mean would be in the critical region and the hypothesis test would detect the 8-point treatment effect. By changing the sample size from $n = 25$ (see Figure 8.12) to $n = 4$ (see Figure 8.13) the power of the test is reduced from nearly 98% to less than 50%.

Alpha level Reducing the alpha level for a hypothesis test will also reduce the power of the test. For example, lowering α from .05 to .01 will lower the power of the hypothesis test. The effect of reducing the alpha level can be seen by referring again to Figure 8.13. In this figure, the boundaries for the critical region are drawn using $\alpha = .05$. Specifically, the critical region on the right-hand side begins at $z = 1.96$. If α were changed to .01, the boundary would be moved farther to the right, out to $z = 2.58$. It should be clear that moving the critical boundary to the right means that a smaller portion of the treatment distribution (the distribution on the right-hand side) will be in the critical region. Thus, there would be a lower probability of rejecting the null hypothesis and a lower value for the power of the test.

One-tailed versus two-tailed tests Changing from a regular two-tailed test to a one-tailed test will increase the power of the hypothesis test. Again, this effect can be seen by referring to Figure 8.13. The figure shows the boundaries for the critical region using a two-tailed test with $\alpha = .05$ so that the critical region on the right-hand side begins at $z = 1.96$. Changing to a one-tailed test would move the critical boundary to the left to a value of $z = 1.65$. Moving the boundary to the left would cause a larger proportion of the treatment distribution to be in the critical region and, therefore, would increase the power of the test.

LEARNING CHECK

1. For a particular hypothesis test, the power is .50 for a 5-point treatment effect. Will the power be greater or less for a 10-point treatment effect?

2. As the power of a test increases, what happens to the probability of a Type II error?

3. If a researcher uses $\alpha = .01$ rather than $\alpha = .05$, then power will increase. (True or false?)

4. What is the effect of increasing sample size on power?

ANSWERS

1. The hypothesis test is more likely to detect a 10-point effect, so power will be greater.

2. As power increases, the probability of a Type II error decreases.

3. False.   4. Power increases as sample size gets larger.

SUMMARY

1. Hypothesis testing is an inferential procedure that uses the data from a sample to draw a general conclusion about a population. The procedure begins with a hypothesis about an unknown population. Then a sample is selected, and the sample data provide evidence that either supports or refutes the hypothesis.

2. In this chapter, we introduced hypothesis testing using the simple situation in which a sample mean is used to test a hypothesis about an unknown population mean. We begin with an unknown population, generally a population that has received a treatment. The question is to determine whether the treatment has an effect on the population mean (see Figure 8.1).

3. Hypothesis testing is structured as a four-step process that is used throughout the remainder of the book.

    a. State the null hypothesis (H_0), and select an alpha level. The null hypothesis states that there is no effect or no change. In this case, H_0 states that the mean for the treated population is the same as the mean before treatment. The alpha level, usually $\alpha = .05$ or $\alpha = .01$, provides a definition of the term *very unlikely* and determines the risk of a Type I error. Also state an alternative hypothesis (H_1), which is the exact opposite of the null hypothesis.

    b. Locate the critical region. The critical region is defined as sample outcomes that would be very unlikely to occur if the null hypothesis is true. The alpha level defines "very unlikely." For example, with $\alpha = .05$, the critical region is defined as sample means in the extreme 5% of the distribution of sample means. When the distribution is normal, the extreme 5% corresponds to z-scores beyond $z = \pm 1.96$.

    c. Collect the data, and compute the test statistic. The sample mean is transformed into a z-score by the formula

    $$z = \frac{M - \mu}{\sigma_M}$$

    The value of μ is obtained from the null hypothesis. The z-score test statistic identifies the location of the sample mean in the distribution of sample means. Expressed in words, the z-score formula is

    $$z = \frac{\text{sample mean} - \text{hypothesized population mean}}{\text{standard error}}$$

    d. Make a decision. If the obtained z-score is in the critical region, reject H_0 because it is very unlikely that these data would be obtained if H_0 were true.

In this case, conclude that the treatment has changed the population mean. If the z-score is not in the critical region, fail to reject H_0 because the data are not significantly different from the null hypothesis. In this case, the data do not provide sufficient evidence to indicate that the treatment has had an effect.

4. Whatever decision is reached in a hypothesis test, there is always a risk of making the incorrect decision. There are two types of errors that can be committed.

    A Type I error is defined as rejecting a true H_0. This is a serious error because it results in falsely reporting a treatment effect. The risk of a Type I error is determined by the alpha level and therefore is under the experimenter's control.

    A Type II error is defined as the failure to reject a false H_0. In this case, the experiment fails to detect an effect that actually occurred. The probability of a Type II error cannot be specified as a single value and depends in part on the size of the treatment effect. It is identified by the symbol β (beta).

5. When a researcher expects that a treatment will change scores in a particular direction (increase or decrease), it is possible to do a directional or one-tailed test. The first step in this procedure is to incorporate the directional prediction into the hypotheses. For example, if the prediction is that a treatment will increase scores, the null hypothesis says that there is no increase and the alternative hypothesis states that there is an increase. To locate the critical region, you must determine what kind of data would refute the null hypothesis by demonstrating that the treatment worked as predicted. These outcomes will be located entirely in one tail of the distribution, so the entire critical region (5% or 1% depending on α) will be in one tail.

6. A one-tailed test is used when there is prior justification for making a directional prediction. These a priori reasons may be previous reports and findings or theoretical considerations. In the absence of the a priori basis, a two-tailed test is appropriate. In this situation, you might be unsure of what to expect in the study, or you might be testing competing theories.

7. In addition to using a hypothesis test to evaluate the *significance* of a treatment effect, it is recommended that you also measure and report the *effect size*. One measure of effect size is Cohen's d, which is a standardized measure of the mean difference. Cohen's d is computed as

$$\text{Cohen's } d = \frac{\text{mean difference}}{\text{standard deviation}}$$

8. The power of a hypothesis test is defined as the probability that the test will correctly reject the null hypothesis.

9. To illustrate the power for a hypothesis test, you must first identify the treatment and null distributions. Also, you must specify the magnitude of the treatment effect. Next, you locate the critical region in the null distribution. The power of the hypothesis test is the portion of the treatment distribution that is located beyond the boundary (critical value) of the critical region.

10. As the size of the treatment effect increases, statistical power increases. Also, power is influenced by several factors that can be controlled by the experimenter:
   a. Increasing the alpha level will increase power.
   b. A one-tailed test will have greater power than a two-tailed test.
   c. A large sample will result in more power than a small sample.

KEY TERMS

hypothesis test	alpha level	Type II error	one-tailed test
null hypothesis	critical region	beta	effect size
alternative hypothesis	test statistic	significant	Cohen's d
level of significance	Type I error	directional test	power

RESOURCES

There are a tutorial quiz and other learning exercises for Chapter 8 at the Wadsworth website, www.thomsonedu.com/psychology/gravetter. The site also provides access to a workshop entitled *Hypothesis Testing* that reviews the concept and logic of hypothesis testing. See page 27 for more information about accessing items on the website.

For those using WebTutor along with this book, there is a WebTutor section corresponding to this chapter. The WebTutor contains a brief summary of Chapter 8, some hints for learning the new material and for avoiding common errors, and a review of the new vocabulary that accompanies hypothesis testing. As usual, WebTutor also presents some sample exam items including solutions.

SPSS

The statistical computer package SPSS is not structured to conduct hypothesis tests using z-scores. In truth, the z-score test presented in this chapter is rarely used in actual research situations. The problem with the z-score test is that it requires that you know the value of the population standard deviation, and this information is usually not available. Researchers rarely have detailed information about the populations that they wish to study. Instead, they must obtain information entirely from samples. In the following chapters we introduce new hypothesis-testing techniques that are based entirely on sample data. These new techniques are included in SPSS.

FOCUS ON PROBLEM SOLVING

1. Hypothesis testing involves a set of logical procedures and rules that enable us to make general statements about a population when all we have are sample data. This logic is reflected in the four steps that have been used throughout this chapter. Hypothesis-testing problems will become easier to tackle when you learn to follow the steps.

S T E P 1   State the hypotheses, and set the alpha level.

S T E P 2   Locate the critical region.

S T E P 3   Compute the z-score for the sample statistic.

S T E P 4   Make a decision about H_0 based on the result of step 3.

A nice benefit of mastering these steps is that all hypothesis tests that will follow use the same basic logic outlined in this chapter.

2. Students often ask, "What alpha level should I use?" Or a student may ask, "Why is an alpha of .05 used?" as opposed to something else. There is no single correct answer to either of these questions. Keep in mind the aim of setting an alpha level in the first place: *to reduce the risk of committing a Type I error.* Therefore, you would not want to set α to something like .20. In that case, you would be taking a 20% risk of committing a Type I error—reporting an effect when one actually does not exist. Most researchers would find this level of risk unacceptable. Instead, researchers generally agree to the convention that $\alpha = .05$ is the greatest risk one should take in making a Type I error. Thus, the .05 level of significance is frequently used and has become the "standard" alpha level. However, some researchers prefer to take even less risk and use alpha levels of .01 and smaller.

3. Take time to consider the implications of your decision about the null hypothesis. The null hypothesis states that there is no effect. Therefore, if your decision is to reject H_0, you should conclude that the sample data provide evidence for a treatment effect. However, it is an entirely different matter if your decision is to fail to reject H_0. Remember that when you fail to reject the null hypothesis, the results are inconclusive. It is impossible to *prove* that H_0 is correct; therefore, you cannot state with certainty that "there is no effect" when H_0 is not rejected. At best, all you can state is that "there is insufficient evidence for an effect" (see Box 8.1).

4. It is very important that you understand the structure of the z-score formula (page 198). It will help you understand many of the other hypothesis tests that will be covered later.

5. When you are doing a directional hypothesis test, read the problem carefully, and watch for key words (such as increase or decrease, raise or lower, and more or less) that tell you which direction the researcher is predicting. The predicted direction will determine the alternative hypothesis (H_1) and the critical region. For example, if a treatment is expected to *increase* scores, H_1 would contain a *greater than* symbol, and the critical region would be in the tail associated with high scores.

DEMONSTRATION 8.1

HYPOTHESIS TEST WITH z

A researcher begins with a known population—in this case, scores on a standardized test that are normally distributed with $\mu = 65$ and $\sigma = 15$. The researcher suspects that special training in reading skills will produce a change in the scores for the individuals in the population. Because it is not feasible to administer the treatment (the special training) to everyone in the population, a sample of $n = 25$ individuals is selected, and the treatment is given to this sample. Following treatment, the average score for this sample is $M = 70$. Is there evidence that the training has an effect on test scores?

STEP 1 State the hypothesis and select an alpha level.

The researcher would like to know what would happen if the special training were given to the entire population. Although this population is unknown, it is possible to make hypotheses about the treated population. The null hypothesis says that the treatment has no effect, so the treated population is identical to the original untreated population. In symbols,

$$H_0: \mu = 65 \qquad \text{(After special training, the mean is still 65.)}$$

The alternative hypothesis states that the treatment does have an effect that causes a change in the population mean. In symbols,

$$H_1: \mu \neq 65 \qquad \text{(After special training, the mean is different from 65.)}$$

At this time, you also select the alpha level. Traditionally, α is set at .05 or .01. If there is particular concern about a Type I error, or if a researcher desires to present overwhelming evidence for a treatment effect, a smaller alpha level can be used (such as $\alpha = .001$). For this demonstration, we will set alpha to .05. Thus, we are taking a 5% risk of committing a Type I error.

STEP 2 Locate the critical region.

We begin by looking at all the possible outcomes that could be obtained if the null hypothesis is true. This is the distribution of sample means for $n = 25$. The distribution will be normal with an expected value of $\mu = 65$ (from H_0) and a standard error of

$$\sigma_M = \frac{\sigma}{\sqrt{n}} = \frac{15}{\sqrt{25}} = \frac{15}{5} = 3$$

With $\alpha = .05$, we want to identify the most unlikely 5% of this distribution. Therefore, we divide the alpha level between the two tails, with 2.5% or $p = 0.0250$ in each tail. According to the unit normal table, the boundaries for the critical region are z-scores of $+1.96$ and -1.96. The distribution and the critical region are shown in Figure 8.14.

STEP 3 Obtain the sample data, and compute the test statistic.

For this demonstration, the researcher obtained a sample mean of $M = 70$. This sample mean corresponds to a z-score of

$$z = \frac{M - \mu}{\sigma_M} = \frac{70 - 65}{3} = \frac{5}{3} = +1.67$$

FIGURE 8.14

The critical region for Demonstration 8.1 consists of the extreme tails with boundaries of $z = -1.96$ and $z = +1.96$.

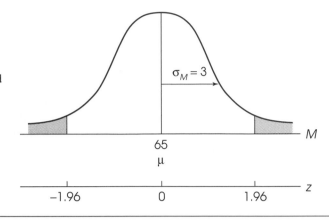

S T E P   4   Make a decision about H_0, and state the conclusion.

The z-score we obtained is not in the critical region. This indicates that our sample mean of $M = 70$ is not an extreme or unusual value to be obtained from a population with $\mu = 65$. Therefore, our statistical decision is to *fail to reject* H_0. Our conclusion for the study is that the data do not provide sufficient evidence that the special training changes test scores.

DEMONSTRATION 8.2

EFFECT SIZE USING COHEN'S *d*

We will compute Cohen's d using the research situation and the data from Demonstration 8.1. Again, the original population mean was $\mu = 65$ and, after treatment (special training), the sample mean was $M = 70$. Thus, there is a 5-point mean difference. Using the population standard deviation, $\sigma = 15$, we obtain an effect size of

$$\text{Cohen's } d = \frac{\text{mean difference}}{\text{standard deviation}} = \frac{5}{15} = 0.33$$

According to Cohen's evaluation standards (see Table 8.2), this is a medium treatment effect.

PROBLEMS

1. Discuss the errors that can be made in hypothesis testing.
   a. What is a Type I error? Why might it occur?
   b. What is a Type II error? How does it happen?

2. Briefly explain the advantage of using an alpha level of .01 versus a level of .05. In general, what is the disadvantage of using a smaller alpha level?

3. In the z-score formula as it is used in a hypothesis test,
   a. Explain what is measured by $M - \mu$ in the numerator.
   b. Explain what is measured by the standard error in the denominator.

4. The term *error* is used two different ways in the context of a hypothesis test. First, there is the concept of standard error, and, second, there is the concept of a Type I error.
   a. What factor can a researcher control that will reduce the risk of a Type I error?
   b. What factor can a researcher control that will reduce the standard error?

5. What happens to the boundaries for the critical region when the alpha level is lowered—for example, from

.05 to .01? Also, what happens to the probability of a Type I error when the alpha level is lowered?

6. The value of the z-score that is obtained for a hypothesis test is influenced by several factors. Some factors influence the size of the numerator of the z-score and other factors influence the size of the standard error in the denominator. For each of the following, indicate whether the factor influences the numerator or denominator of the z-score and determine whether the effect would be to increase the value of z (farther from zero) or decrease the value of z (closer to zero). In each case, assume that all other components of the z-score remain constant.
   a. Increase the sample size.
   b. Increase the population standard deviation.
   c. Increase the difference between the sample mean and the value of μ specified in the null hypothesis.

7. A researcher is testing the effectiveness of a new drug that is intended to improve learning and memory performance. A sample of $n = 16$ rats is obtained, and the rats are administered the drug and then are tested on a standardized learning task. For the general population of rats (with no drug) the average score on the standardized task is $\mu = 50$ with a standard deviation of $\sigma = 10$. The distribution of test scores is normal.
   a. If the drug has a 4-point effect and produces a mean score of $M = 54$ for the sample, is this sufficient to conclude that there is a significant effect using a two-tailed test with $\alpha = .05$?
   b. If there is a 6-point effect with a sample mean of $M = 56$, is this sufficient to conclude that there is a significant effect using a two-tailed test with $\alpha = .05$?

8. Childhood participation in sports, cultural groups, and youth groups appears to be related to improved self-esteem for adolescents (McGee, Williams, Howden-Chapman, Martin, & Kawachi, 2006). In a representative study, a sample of $n = 100$ adolescents with a history of group participation is given a standardized self-esteem questionnaire. For the general population of adolescents, scores on this questionnaire form a normal distribution with a mean of $\mu = 40$ and a standard deviation of $\sigma = 12$. The sample of group-participation adolescents had an average of $M = 43.84$. Does this sample provide enough evidence to conclude that self-esteem scores for group-participation adolescents are significantly different from those of the general population? Use a two-tailed test with $\alpha = .01$.

9. A researcher is evaluating the effectiveness of a new physical education program for elementary school children. The program is designed to reduce competition and increase individual self-esteem. A sample of $n = 16$ children is selected and the children are placed in the new program. After 3 months, each child is given a standardized self-esteem test. For the general population of elementary school children, the scores on the self-esteem test form a normal distribution with $\mu = 40$ and $\sigma = 8$.
   a. If the researcher obtains a sample mean of $M = 42$, is this enough evidence to conclude that the program has a significant effect? Assume a two-tailed test with $\alpha = .05$.
   b. If the sample mean is $M = 44$, is this enough to demonstrate a significant effect? Again, assume a two-tailed test with $\alpha = .05$.
   c. Briefly explain why you reached different conclusions for part a and part b.

10. State College is evaluating a new English composition course for freshmen. A random sample of $n = 25$ freshmen is obtained and the students are placed in the course during their first semester. One year later, a writing sample is obtained for each student and the writing samples are graded using a standardized evaluation technique. The average score for the sample is $M = 76$. For the general population of college students, writing scores form a normal distribution with a mean of $\mu = 70$.
   a. If the writing scores for the population have a standard deviation of $\sigma = 20$, does the sample provide enough evidence to conclude that the new composition course has a significant effect? Assume a two-tailed test with $\alpha = .05$.
   b. If the population standard deviation is $\sigma = 10$, is the sample sufficient to demonstrate a significant effect? Again, assume a two-tailed test with $\alpha = .05$.
   c. Briefly explain why you reached different conclusions for part (a) and part (b).

11. Although there is a popular belief that herbal remedies such as Ginkgo biloba and Ginseng may improve learning and memory in healthy adults, these effects are usually not supported by well-controlled research (Peresson, Bringlov, Nilsson, & Nyberg, 2004). In a typical study, a researcher obtains a sample of $n = 36$ participants and has each person take the herbal supplements every day for 90 days. At the end of the 90 days, each person takes a standardized memory test. For the general population, scores from the test are normally distributed with a mean of $\mu = 80$ and a standard deviation of $\sigma = 18$. The sample of research participants had an average of $M = 84$.
   a. In a sentence, state the null hypothesis being tested.
   b. Using symbols, state the null hypothesis and the alternative hypothesis.
   c. Conduct the hypothesis test using a two-tailed test with $\alpha = .05$.

12. A researcher would like to test the effectiveness of a newly developed growth hormone. The researcher knows that under normal circumstances laboratory rats reach an average weight of $\mu = 950$ grams at 10 weeks of age. The distribution of weights is normal with $\sigma = 30$. A random sample of $n = 25$ newborn rats is obtained, and the hormone is given to each rat. When the rats in the sample reach 10 weeks old, each rat is weighed. The mean weight for this sample is $M = 974$.
    a. Identify the independent and the dependent variables for this study.
    b. Assuming a two-tailed test, state the null hypothesis in a sentence that includes the independent variable and the dependent variable.
    c. Using symbols, state the hypotheses (H_0 and H_1) for the two-tailed test.
    d. Sketch the appropriate distribution, and locate the critical region for $\alpha = .05$.
    e. Calculate the test statistic (z-score) for the sample.
    f. What decision should be made about the null hypothesis, and what decision should be made about the effect of the hormone?

13. There is some evidence that REM sleep, associated with dreaming, may also play a role in learning and memory processing. For example, Smith and Lapp (1991) found increased REM activity for college students during exam periods. Suppose that REM activity for a sample of $n = 16$ students during the final exam period produced an average score of $M = 143$. Regular REM activity for the college population averages $\mu = 110$ with a standard deviation of $\sigma = 50$. The population distribution is approximately normal.
    a. Do the data from this sample provide evidence for a significant increase in REM activity during exams? Use a one-tailed test with $\alpha = .01$.
    b. Compute Cohen's d to estimate the size of the effect.

14. Under some circumstances a 6-point treatment effect can be very large, and in some circumstances it can be very small. Assume that a sample of $n = 16$ individuals is selected from a population with a mean of $\mu = 70$. A treatment is administered to the sample and, after treatment, the sample mean is found to be $M = 76$. Notice that the treatment appears to have increased scores by an average of 6 points.
    a. If the population standard deviation is $\sigma = 20$, is the 6-point effect large enough to be statistically significant? Use a two-tailed test with $\alpha = .05$.
    b. If the population standard deviation is $\sigma = 8$, is the 6-point effect large enough to be statistically significant? Use a two-tailed test with $\alpha = .05$.

15. A psychologist has developed a standardized test for measuring vocabulary skill for 4-year-old children. The scores on the test form a normal distribution with $\mu = 70$ and $\sigma = 20$. A researcher would like to use the test to investigate the hypothesis that children who grow up as an only child develop vocabulary skills at a faster rate than children in larger families. A sample of $n = 25$ only children is obtained and the mean test score for the sample is $M = 77$.
    a. Is this sample sufficient to conclude that vocabulary skills for only children are significantly higher than those for the general population? Use a one-tailed test with $\alpha = .05$.
    b. Is this sample sufficient to conclude that vocabulary skills for only children are significantly different from those for the general population? Use a two-tailed test with $\alpha = .05$.
    c. Explain why the two tests lead to different conclusions.

16. Researchers have often noted increases in violent crimes when it is very hot. In fact, Reifman, Larrick, and Fein (1991) noted that this relationship even extends to baseball. That is, there is a much greater chance of a batter being hit by a pitch when the temperature increases. Consider the following hypothetical data. Suppose that over the past 30 years, during any given week of the major-league season, an average of $\mu = 12$ players are hit by wild pitches. Assume that the distribution is nearly normal with $\sigma = 3$. For a sample of $n = 4$ weeks in which the daily temperature was extremely hot, the weekly average of hit-by-pitch players was $M = 15.5$. Are players more likely to get hit by pitches during hot weeks? Set alpha to .05 for a one-tailed test.

17. A sample of $n = 16$ individuals is selected from a normal population with a mean of $\mu = 48$ and a standard deviation of $\sigma = 12$. After receiving a treatment, the sample mean is found to be $M = 52$.
    a. Compute Cohen's d to evaluate the size of the treatment effect.
    b. If the sample size were $n = 36$, what value would be obtained for Cohen's d? How does sample size influence the measure of effect size?
    c. If the population standard deviation were $\sigma = 24$, what value would be obtained for Cohen's d? How does standard deviation influence the measure of effect size?
    d. If the sample mean were $M = 56$, what value would be obtained for Cohen's d? How does the size of the mean difference influence the measure of effect size?

18. To test the effectiveness of a treatment, a sample of $n = 25$ people is selected from a normal population with a mean of $\mu = 60$. After the treatment is administered to the individuals in the sample, the sample mean is found to be $M = 55$.

a. If the population standard deviation is $\sigma = 10$, can you conclude that the treatment has a significant effect? Use a two-tailed test with $\alpha = .05$.

b. If the population standard deviation is $\sigma = 20$, can you conclude that the treatment has a significant effect? Use a two-tailed test with $\alpha = .05$.

c. Compute Cohen's d to measure effect size for both tests ($\sigma = 20$ and $\sigma = 10$).

d. Briefly describe how the standard deviation influences the outcome of the hypothesis test. How does σ influence measures of effect size?

19. A sample of $n = 9$ individuals was selected from a normally distributed population with a mean of $\mu = 25$ and a standard deviation of $\sigma = 6$. A treatment was administered to the sample and, after treatment, the nine individuals produced the following scores: 36, 27, 30, 33, 22, 30, 30, 24, 38.

a. Calculate the sample mean.

b. Sketch a histogram showing the sample distribution.

c. Does the sample appear to be centered around $\mu = 25$ or does the treatment appear to have moved the scores away from $\mu = 25$?

d. Use a hypothesis test with $\alpha = .05$ to determine whether the treatment had a significant effect.

e. Looking at the sample distribution from part b, determine how big the treatment effect is. Specifically, what is the distance between the sample mean and the original population mean?

f. Compute Cohen's d to measure the size of the treatment effect.

20. A sample of $n = 9$ scores is obtained from a normal population distribution with $\sigma = 12$. The sample mean is $M = 60$.

a. With a two-tailed test and $\alpha = .05$, use the sample data to test the hypothesis that the population mean is $\mu = 65$.

b. With a two-tailed test and $\alpha = .05$, use the sample data to test the hypothesis that the population mean is $\mu = 55$.

c. In parts (a) and (b) of this problem, you should find that $\mu = 65$ and $\mu = 55$ are both acceptable hypotheses. Explain how two different values can both be acceptable.

21. To test the effectiveness of a treatment, a sample is selected from a normal population with a mean of $\mu = 40$ and a standard deviation of $\sigma = 12$. After the treatment is administered to the individuals in the sample, the sample mean is found to be $M = 46$.

a. If the sample consists of $n = 4$ individuals, is this result sufficient to conclude that there is a significant treatment effect? Use a two-tailed test with $\alpha = .05$.

b. If the sample consists of $n = 36$ individuals, is this result sufficient to conclude that there is a significant treatment effect? Use a two-tailed test with $\alpha = .05$.

c. Compute Cohen's d to measure effect size for both tests ($n = 4$ and $n = 36$).

d. Briefly describe how sample size influences the outcome of the hypothesis test. How does sample size influence measures of effect size?

22. Suppose that a researcher normally uses an alpha level of .01 for hypothesis tests, but this time uses an alpha level of .05. What does this change in alpha level do to the amount of power? What does it do to the risk of a Type I error?

23. Explain why power for a hypothesis test can never be less than the alpha level for the test. (*Hint:* Sketch a null distribution, and then add several different treatment distributions to your sketch. What happens to power as the treatment distribution gets very close to the null distribution?)

CHAPTER

9

Introduction to the *t* Statistic

Tools You Will Need

The following items are considered essential background material for this chapter. If you doubt your knowledge of any of these items, you should review the appropriate chapter or section before proceeding.

- Sample standard deviation (Chapter 4)
- Degrees of freedom (Chapter 4)
- Standard error (Chapter 7)
- Hypothesis testing (Chapter 8)

9.1 THE *t* STATISTIC: AN ALTERNATIVE TO *z*

In the previous chapter, we presented the statistical procedures that permit researchers to use a sample mean to test hypotheses about an unknown population. These statistical procedures were based on a few basic concepts, which we summarize as follows:

> Remember that the expected value of the distribution of sample means is μ, the population mean.

1. A sample mean (*M*) is expected more or less to approximate its population mean (μ). This permits us to use the sample mean to test a hypothesis about the population mean.

2. The standard error provides a measure of how well a sample mean approximates the population mean. Specifically, the standard error determines how much difference is reasonable to expect between a sample mean (*M*) and the population mean (μ).

$$\sigma_M = \frac{\sigma}{\sqrt{n}} \qquad \text{or} \qquad \sigma_M = \sqrt{\frac{\sigma^2}{n}}$$

3. To quantify our inferences about the population, we compare the obtained sample mean (*M*) with the hypothesized population mean (μ) by computing a *z*-score test statistic.

$$z = \frac{M - \mu}{\sigma_M} = \frac{\text{obtained difference between data and hypothesis}}{\text{standard distance between } M \text{ and } \mu}$$

The goal of the hypothesis test is to determine whether the obtained result is significantly greater than would be expected by chance. When the *z*-scores form a normal distribution, we are able to use the unit normal table (Appendix B) to find the critical region for the hypothesis test.

THE PROBLEM WITH *z*-SCORES

The shortcoming of using a *z*-score as an inferential statistic is that the *z*-score formula requires more information than is usually available. Specifically, a *z*-score requires that we know the value of the population standard deviation (or variance), which is needed to compute the standard error. In most situations, however, the standard deviation for the population is not known. In fact, the whole reason for conducting a hypothesis test is to gain knowledge about an *unknown* population. This situation appears to create a paradox: You want to use a *z*-score to find out about an unknown population, but you must know about the population before you can compute a *z*-score. Fortunately, there is a relatively simple solution to this problem. When the variability for the population is not known, we use the sample variability in its place.

INTRODUCING THE *t* STATISTIC

In Chapter 4, the sample variance was developed specifically to provide an unbiased estimate of the corresponding population variance. Recall the formulas for sample variance and sample standard deviation as follows:

> The concept of degrees of freedom, *df* = *n* − 1, was introduced in Chapter 4 (page 99) and is discussed later in this chapter (page 235).

$$\text{sample variance} = s^2 = \frac{SS}{n - 1} = \frac{SS}{df}$$

$$\text{sample standard deviation} = s = \sqrt{\frac{SS}{n - 1}} = \sqrt{\frac{SS}{df}}$$

Using the sample values, we can now *estimate* the standard error. Recall from Chapters 7 and 8 that the value of the standard error can be computed using either standard deviation or variance:

$$\text{standard error} = \sigma_M = \frac{\sigma}{\sqrt{n}} \quad \text{or} \quad \sigma_M = \sqrt{\frac{\sigma^2}{n}}$$

Now we will estimate the standard error by simply substituting the sample variance or standard deviation in place of the unknown population value:

$$\text{estimated standard error} = s_M = \frac{s}{\sqrt{n}} \quad \text{or} \quad s_M = \sqrt{\frac{s^2}{n}} \quad (9.1)$$

Notice that the symbol for the *estimated standard error of* M is s_M instead of σ_M, indicating that the estimated value is computed from sample data rather than from the actual population parameter.

DEFINITION

The **estimated standard error** (s_M) is used as an estimate of the real standard error σ_M when the value of σ is unknown. It is computed from the sample variance or sample standard deviation and provides an estimate of the standard distance between a sample mean *M* and the population mean μ.

Finally, you should recognize that we have shown formulas for standard error (actual or estimated) using both the standard deviation and the variance. In the past (Chapters 7 and 8), we concentrated on the formula using the standard deviation. At this point, however, we will shift our focus to the formula based on variance. Thus, throughout the remainder of this chapter, and in following chapters, the estimated standard error of *M* typically is presented and computed using

$$s_M = \sqrt{\frac{s^2}{n}}$$

There are two reasons for making this shift from standard deviation to variance:

1. In Chapter 4 (page 100) we saw that the sample variance is an *unbiased* statistic; on average, the sample variance (s^2) will provide an accurate and unbiased estimate of the population variance (σ^2). Therefore, the most accurate way to estimate the standard error is to use the sample variance to estimate the population variance.

2. In future chapters we will encounter other versions of the *t* statistic that require variance (instead of standard deviation) in the formulas for estimated standard error. To maximize the similarity from one version to another, we will use variance in the formula for *all* of the different *t* statistics. Thus, whenever we present a *t* statistic, the estimated standard error will be computed as

$$\text{estimated standard error} = \sqrt{\frac{\text{sample variance}}{\text{sample size}}}$$

Now we can substitute the estimated standard error in the denominator of the *z*-score formula. The result is a new test statistic called a *t statistic*:

$$t = \frac{M - \mu}{s_M} \quad (9.2)$$

D E F I N I T I O N

The *t* **statistic** is used to test hypotheses about an unknown population mean μ when the value of σ is unknown. The formula for the *t* statistic has the same structure as the *z*-score formula, except that the *t* statistic uses the estimated standard error in the denominator.

The only difference between the *t* formula and the *z*-score formula is that the *z*-score uses the actual population variance, σ^2 (or the standard deviation), and the *t* formula uses the corresponding sample variance (or standard deviation) when the population value is not known.

$$z = \frac{M - \mu}{\sigma_M} = \frac{M - \mu}{\sqrt{\sigma^2/n}} \qquad t = \frac{M - \mu}{s_M} = \frac{M - \mu}{\sqrt{s^2/n}}$$

DEGREES OF FREEDOM AND THE *t* STATISTIC

In this chapter, we have introduced the *t* statistic as a substitute for a *z*-score. The basic difference between these two is that the *t* statistic uses sample variance (s^2) and the *z*-score uses the population variance (σ^2). To determine how well a *t* statistic approximates a *z*-score, we must determine how well the sample variance approximates the population variance.

In Chapter 4, we introduced the concept of degrees of freedom (page 99). Reviewing briefly, you must know the sample mean before you can compute sample variance. This places a restriction on sample variability such that only $n - 1$ scores in a sample are independent and free to vary. The value $n - 1$ is called the *degrees of freedom* (or *df*) for the sample variance.

$$\text{degrees of freedom} = df = n - 1 \tag{9.3}$$

D E F I N I T I O N

Degrees of freedom describe the number of scores in a sample that are independent and free to vary. Because the sample mean places a restriction on the value of one score in the sample, there are $n - 1$ degrees of freedom for the sample (see Chapter 4).

The greater the value of *df* for a sample, the better s^2 represents σ^2, and the better the *t* statistic approximates the *z*-score. This should make sense because the larger the sample (*n*) is, the better the sample represents its population. Thus, the degrees of freedom associated with s^2 also describe how well *t* represents *z*.

THE *t* DISTRIBUTION

Every sample from a population can be used to compute a *z*-score or a *t* statistic. If you select all the possible samples of a particular size (*n*), and compute the *z*-score for each sample mean, then the entire set of *z*-scores will form a *z*-score distribution. As we saw in Chapter 7, the distribution of *z*-scores for sample means tends to be a normal distribution. In the same way, you can compute the *t* statistic for every sample, the entire set of *t* values will form a *t* *distribution*. The *t* distribution will approximate a normal distribution in the same way that a *t* statistic approximates a *z*-score. How well a *t* distribution approximates a normal distribution is determined by degrees of freedom. In general, the greater the sample size (*n*) is, the larger the degrees of freedom ($n - 1$) are, and the better the *t* distribution approximates the normal distribution (Figure 9.1).

FIGURE 9.1

Distributions of the *t* statistic for different values of degrees of freedom are compared to a normal *z*-score distribution. Like the normal distribution, *t* distributions are bell-shaped and symmetrical and have a mean of zero. However, *t* distributions have more variability, indicated by the flatter and more spread-out shape. The larger the value of *df* is, the more closely the *t* distribution approximates a normal distribution.

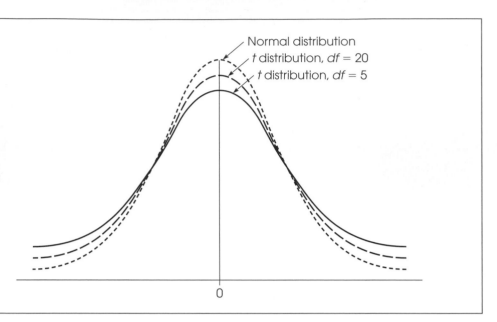

Normal distribution
t distribution, *df* = 20
t distribution, *df* = 5

0

THE SHAPE OF THE
_t_ DISTRIBUTION

The exact shape of a *t* distribution changes with degrees of freedom. In fact, statisticians speak of a "family" of *t* distributions. That is, there is a different sampling distribution of *t* (a distribution of all possible sample *t* values) for each possible number of degrees of freedom. As *df* gets very large, the *t* distribution gets closer in shape to a normal *z*-score distribution. A quick glance at Figure 9.1 reveals that distributions of *t* are bell-shaped and symmetrical and have a mean of zero. However, the *t* distribution has more variability than a normal *z* distribution, especially when *df* values are small (see Figure 9.1). The *t* distribution tends to be flatter and more spread out, whereas the normal *z* distribution has more of a central peak.

The reason that the *t* distribution is flatter and more variable than the normal *z*-score distribution becomes clear if you look at the structure of the formulas for *z* and *t*. For both formulas, *z* and *t*, the top of the formula, $M - \mu$, can take on different values because the sample mean (M) will vary from one sample to another. For *z*-scores, however, the bottom of the formula will not vary, provided that all of the samples are the same size and are selected from the same population. Specifically, all the *z*-scores will have the same standard error in the denominator, $\sigma_M = \sqrt{\sigma^2/n}$, because the population variance and the sample size are the same for every sample. For *t* statistics, on the other hand, the bottom of the formula will vary from one sample to another. Specifically, the sample variance (s^2) will change from one sample to the next, so the estimated standard error will also vary, $s_M = \sqrt{s^2/n}$. Thus, only the numerator of the *z*-score formula varies, but both the numerator and the denomination of the *t* statistic vary. As a result, *t* statistics are more variable than are *z*-scores, and the *t* distribution will be flatter and more spread out. As sample size and *df* increase however, the variability in the *t* distribution decreases, and it more closely resembles a normal distribution.

DETERMINING
PROPORTIONS AND
PROBABILITIES FOR
_t_ DISTRIBUTIONS

Just as we used the unit normal table to locate proportions associated with *z*-scores, we will use a *t* distribution table to find proportions for *t* statistics. The complete *t* distribution table is presented in Appendix B, page 531, and a portion of this table is reproduced in Table 9.1. The two rows at the top of the table show proportions of the

TABLE 9.1

A portion of the *t*-distribution table. The numbers in the table are the values of *t* that separate the tail from the main body of the distribution. Proportions for one or two tails are listed at the top of the table, and *df* values for *t* are listed in the first column.

	Proportion in One Tail					
	0.25	0.10	0.05	0.025	0.01	0.005
	Proportion in Two Tails Combined					
df	0.50	0.20	0.10	0.05	0.02	0.01
1	1.000	3.078	6.314	12.706	31.821	63.657
2	0.816	1.886	2.920	4.303	6.965	9.925
3	0.765	1.638	2.353	3.182	4.541	5.841
4	0.741	1.533	2.132	2.776	3.747	4.604
5	0.727	1.476	2.015	2.571	3.365	4.032
6	0.718	1.440	1.943	2.447	3.143	3.707

t distribution contained in either one or two tails, depending on which row is used. The first column of the table lists degrees of freedom for the *t* statistic. Finally, the numbers in the body of the table are the *t* values that mark the boundary between the tails and the rest of the *t* distribution.

For example, with *df* = 3, exactly 5% of the *t* distribution is located in the tail beyond *t* = 2.353 (Figure 9.2). To find this value, you locate *df* = 3 in the first column and locate 0.05 (5%) in the one-tail proportion row. When you line up these two values in the table, you should find *t* = 2.353. Similarly, 5% of the *t* distribution is located in the tail beyond *t* = −2.353 (see Figure 9.2). Finally, notice that a total of 10% is contained in the two tails beyond *t* = ±2.353 (check the proportion value in the "two-tails combined" row at the top of the table).

A close inspection of the *t* distribution table in Appendix B will demonstrate a point we made earlier: As the value for *df* increases, the *t* distribution becomes more similar to a normal distribution. For example, examine the column containing *t* values for a 0.05 proportion in two tails. You will find that when *df* = 1, the *t* values that separate the extreme 5% (0.05) from the rest of the distribution are *t* = ±12.706.

As you read down the column, however, you should find that the critical *t* values become smaller and smaller, ultimately reaching ±1.96. You should recognize ±1.96 as the *z*-score values that separate the extreme 5% in a normal distribution. Thus, as *df* increases, the proportions in a *t* distribution become more like the proportions in a normal distribution. When the sample size (and degrees of freedom) is sufficiently large, the difference between a *t* distribution and the normal distribution becomes negligible.

FIGURE 9.2

The *t* distribution with *df* = 3. Note that 5% of the distribution is located in the tail beyond *t* = 2.353. Also, 5% is in the tail beyond *t* = −2.353. Thus, a total proportion of 10% (0.10) is in the two tails beyond *t* = ±2.353.

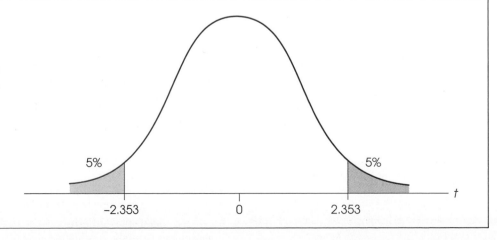

Caution: The *t* distribution table printed in this book has been abridged and does not include entries for every possible *df* value. For example, the table lists *t* values for *df* = 40 and for *df* = 60, but does not list any entries for *df* values between 40 and 60. Occasionally, you will encounter a situation in which your *t* statistic has a *df* value that is not listed in the table. In these situations, you should look up the critical *t* for both of the surrounding *df* values listed and then use the *larger* value for *t*. If, for example, you have *df* = 53 (not listed), look up the critical *t* value for both *df* = 40 and *df* = 60 and *then use the larger t value.* If your sample *t* statistic is greater than the larger value listed, you can be certain that the data are in the critical region, and you can confidently reject the null hypothesis.

LEARNING CHECK

1. Under what circumstances is a *t* statistic used instead of a *z*-score for a hypothesis test?

2. To conduct a hypothesis test with a *z*-score statistic, you must know the variance or the standard deviation for the population of scores. (True or false?)

3. In general, a distribution of *t* statistics is flatter and more spread out than the standard normal distribution. (True or false?)

4. A sample of *n* = 15 scores would produce a *t* statistic with *df* = 16. (True or false?)

5. For *df* = 15, find the value(s) of *t* associated with each of the following:
   a. The top 5% of the distribution.
   b. The middle 95% versus the extreme 5% of the distribution.
   c. The middle 99% versus the extreme 1% of the distribution.

ANSWERS

1. A *t* statistic is used instead of a *z*-score when the population standard deviation and variance are not known.

2. True.

3. True.

4. False. With *n* = 15, the *df* value would be 14.

5. **a.** *t* = +1.753   **b.** *t* = ±2.131   **c.** *t* = ±2.947

9.2 HYPOTHESIS TESTS WITH THE *t* STATISTIC

In the hypothesis-testing situation, we begin with a population with an unknown mean and an unknown variance, often a population that has received some treatment (Figure 9.3). The goal is to use a sample from the treated population (a treated sample) as the basis for determining whether the treatment has any effect.

As always, the null hypothesis states that the treatment has no effect; specifically, H_0 states that the population mean is unchanged. Thus, the null hypothesis provides a specific value for the unknown population mean. The sample data provide a value for the sample mean. Finally, the variance and estimated standard error are computed from the sample data. When these values are used in the *t* formula, the result becomes

$$t = \frac{\text{sample mean} - \text{population mean}}{\text{(from the data)} \quad \text{(hypothesized from } H_0\text{)}}{\text{estimated standard error}}$$
(computed from the sample data)

FIGURE 9.3

The basic experimental situation for using the *t* statistic or the *z*-score is presented. It is assumed that the parameter μ is known for the population before treatment. The purpose of the experiment is to determine whether the treatment has an effect. We ask: Is the population mean after treatment the same as or different from the mean before treatment? A sample is selected from the treated population to help answer this question.

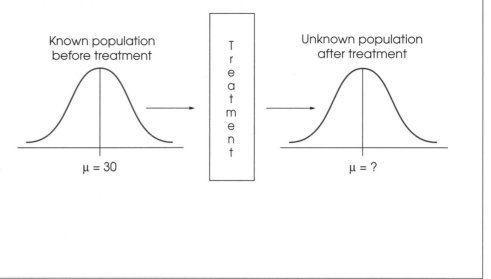

Known population before treatment

μ = 30

Treatment

Unknown population after treatment

μ = ?

As with the *z*-score formula, the *t* statistic forms a ratio. The numerator measures the actual difference between the sample data (*M*) and the population hypothesis (μ). The estimated standard error in the denominator measures how much difference is reasonable to expect between a sample mean and the population mean. When the obtained difference between the data and the hypothesis (numerator) is much greater than expected (denominator), we will obtain a large value for *t* (either large positive or large negative). In this case, we conclude that the data are not consistent with the hypothesis, and our decision is to "reject H_0." On the other hand, when the difference between the data and the hypothesis is small relative to the standard error, we will obtain a *t* statistic near zero, and our decision will be "fail to reject H_0."

HYPOTHESIS-TESTING EXAMPLE

The following research situation will be used to demonstrate the procedures of hypothesis testing with the *t* statistic.

EXAMPLE 9.1

Many studies have shown that direct eye contact and even patterns that look like eyes are avoided by many animals. Some insects, such as moths, have even evolved large eye-spot patterns on their wings to help ward off predators. This research example, modeled after Scaife's (1976) study, examines how eye-spot patterns affect the behavior of moth-eating birds.

A sample of *n* = 9 insectivorous birds is selected. The animals are tested in a box that has two separate chambers (Figure 9.4). The birds are free to roam from one chamber to another through a doorway in a partition. On the wall of one chamber, two large eye-spot patterns have been painted. The other chamber has plain walls.

FIGURE 9.4

Apparatus used in Example 9.1.

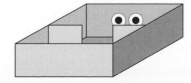

The birds are tested one at a time by placing them in the doorway in the center of the apparatus. Each animal is left in the box for 60 minutes, and the amount of time spent in the plain chamber is recorded. Suppose that the sample of $n = 9$ birds spent an average of $M = 36$ minutes in the plain side with $SS = 228$. Can we conclude that eye-spot patterns have an effect on behavior? Note that while it is possible to predict a value for μ, we have no information about the population standard deviation.

STEP 1   State the hypotheses, and select an alpha level. The null hypothesis states that the eye-spot patterns have no effect on behavior. In this case, the animals should show no preference for either side of the box. That is, they should spend half of the 60-minute test period in the plain chamber. In symbols, the null hypothesis would state that

$$H_0: \quad \mu_{\text{plain side}} = 30 \text{ minutes}$$

The alternative hypothesis states that the eye patterns have an effect on behavior, and the birds will either avoid the painted walls or be attracted to the painted eye spots. (Note that a directional, one-tailed test would specify one of the two alternatives.) The nondirectional alternative hypothesis would be expressed as follows:

$$H_1: \quad \mu_{\text{plain side}} \neq 30 \text{ minutes}$$

We will set the level of significance at $\alpha = .05$ for two tails.

STEP 2   Locate the critical region. The test statistic is a *t* statistic because the population variance is not known. The exact shape of the *t* distribution and, therefore, the proportions under the *t* distribution depend on the number of degrees of freedom associated with the sample. To find the critical region, *df* must be computed:

$$df = n - 1 = 9 - 1 = 8$$

For a two-tailed test at the .05 level of significance and with 8 degrees of freedom, the critical region consists of *t* values greater than $+2.306$ or less than -2.306. Figure 9.5 depicts the critical region in this *t* distribution.

STEP 3   Calculate the test statistic. The *t* statistic typically requires much more computation than is necessary for a *z*-score. Therefore, we recommend that you divide the calculations into a three-stage process as follows:

a.   First, calculate the sample variance. Remember that the population variance is unknown, and you must use the sample value in its place. (This is why we are using a *t* statistic instead of a *z*-score.)

$$s^2 = \frac{SS}{n - 1} = \frac{SS}{df}$$

$$= \frac{288}{8} = 36$$

b.   Next, use the sample variance (s^2) to compute the estimated standard error. This value will be the denominator of the *t* statistic and measures how much error is reasonable to expect between a sample mean and the corresponding population mean.

$$s_M = \sqrt{\frac{s^2}{n}}$$

$$= \sqrt{\frac{36}{9}} = \sqrt{4} = 2$$

FIGURE 9.5

The critical region in the
t distribution for $\alpha = .05$
and *df* = 8.

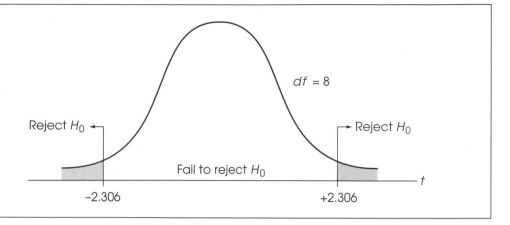

df = 8

Reject H_0 ←   → Reject H_0

Fail to reject H_0

t

−2.306   +2.306

c. Finally, compute the *t* statistic for the sample data.

$$t = \frac{M - \mu}{s_M}$$

$$= \frac{36 - 30}{2} = 3.00$$

STEP 4   Make a decision regarding H_0. The obtained *t* statistic of 3.00 falls into the critical
region on the right-hand side of the *t* distribution (see Figure 9.5). Our statistical
decision is to reject H_0 and conclude that the presence of eye-spot patterns does
influence behavior. Specifically, the average amount of time that the birds spent on
the plain side is *significantly* different from the 30 minutes that would be expected if
the eye spots had no effect. As can be seen from the sample mean, there is a tendency for the birds to avoid the eye spots and spend more time on the plain side of
the box.

ASSUMPTIONS OF THE *t* TEST   Two basic assumptions are necessary for hypothesis tests with the *t* statistic.

1. The values in the sample must consist of *independent* observations.

   In everyday terms, two observations are independent if there is no consistent, predictable relationship between the first observation and the second.
   More precisely, two events (or observations) are independent if the occurrence
   of the first event has no effect on the probability of the second event. We examined specific examples of independence and nonindependence in Box 8.2
   (page 210).

2. The population sampled must be normal.

   This assumption is a necessary part of the mathematics underlying the development of the *t* statistic and the *t* distribution table. However, violating this
   assumption has little practical effect on the results obtained for a *t* statistic,
   especially when the sample size is relatively large. With very small samples, a
   normal population distribution is important. With larger samples, this assumption can be violated without affecting the validity of the hypothesis test. If you
   have reason to suspect that the population distribution is not normal, use a large
   sample to be safe.

9.3   MEASURING EFFECT SIZE FOR THE *t* STATISTIC

In Chapter 8 we noted that one criticism of a hypothesis test is that it does not really evaluate the size of the treatment effect. Instead, a hypothesis test simply determines whether the treatment effect is greater than chance, where "chance" is measured by the standard error. In particular, it is possible for a very small treatment effect to be "statistically significant," especially when the sample size is very large. To correct for this problem, it is recommended that the results from a hypothesis test be accompanied by a report of effect size such as Cohen's *d*.

ESTIMATING COHEN'S *d*

When Cohen's *d* was originally introduced (page 217), the formula was presented as

$$\text{Cohen's } d = \frac{\text{mean difference}}{\text{standard deviation}}$$

Cohen defined this measure of effect size in terms of the population mean difference and the population standard deviation. However, in most situations the population values are not known and you must substitute the corresponding sample values in their place. When this is done, many researchers prefer to identify the calculated value as an "*estimated* d" or name the value after one of the statisticians who first substituted sample statistics into Cohen's formula (e.g., Glass's *g* or Hedges's *g*). For hypothesis tests using the *t* statistic, the standard deviation is not known and we will use the sample standard deviation in its place. With this substitution, the formula for estimating Cohen's *d* becomes

$$\text{estimated } d = \frac{\text{mean difference}}{\text{sample standard deviation}} = \frac{M - \mu}{s} \tag{9.4}$$

The numerator measures that magnitude of the treatment effect by finding the difference between the mean for the treated sample and the mean for the untreated population (μ from H_0). The sample standard deviation in the denominator standardizes the mean difference into standard deviation units. Thus, an estimated *d* of 1.00 indicates that the size of the treatment effect is equivalent to one standard deviation. The following example demonstrates how the estimated *d* is used to measure effect size for a hypothesis test using a *t* statistic.

EXAMPLE 9.2

For the eye-spot study in Example 9.1, the birds averaged $M = 36$ minutes on the plain side of the box. If the eye spots had no effect (as stated by the null hypothesis), the population mean would be $\mu = 30$ minutes. Thus, the results demonstrate that the eye spots had a 6-minute effect on the birds ($36 - 30$). For this study, the sample standard deviation is

$$\text{sample standard deviation} = s = \sqrt{\frac{SS}{df}} = \sqrt{\frac{288}{8}} = \sqrt{36} = 6$$

Thus, Cohen's *d* for this example is estimated to be

$$\text{Cohen's } d = \frac{\text{mean difference}}{\text{sample standard deviation}} = \frac{6}{6} = 1.00$$

According to the standards suggested by Cohen (Table 8.2, page 218), this is a large treatment effect.

To help you visualize what is measured by Cohen's *d*, we have constructed a set of $n = 9$ scores with a mean of $M = 36$ and a standard deviation of $s = 6$ (the same values as in Examples 9.1 and 9.2). The set of scores is shown in Figure 9.6. Notice that the figure also includes a vertical line drawn at $\mu = 30$. Recall that $\mu = 30$ is the value specified by the null hypothesis and identifies what the mean ought to be if the treatment has no effect. Clearly, our sample is not centered around $\mu = 30$. Instead, the scores have been shifted to the right so that the sample mean is $M = 36$. This shift, from 30 to 36, is the 6-point mean difference that was caused by the treatment effect. Also notice that the 6-point mean difference is exactly equal to the standard deviation. Thus, the size of the treatment effect is equal to 1 standard deviation. In other words, Cohen's $d = 1.00$.

MEASURING THE PERCENTAGE OF VARIANCE EXPLAINED, r^2

An alternative method for measuring effect size is to determine how much of the variability in the scores is explained by the treatment effect. The concept behind this measure is that the treatment causes the scores to increase (or decrease), which means that the treatment is causing the scores to vary. If we can measure how much of the variability is explained by the treatment, we will obtain a measure of the size of the treatment effect.

To demonstrate this concept we will use the data from the hypothesis test in Example 9.1. Recall that the null hypothesis stated that the treatment (eye-spot pattern) has no effect on the birds' behavior. According to the null hypothesis, the birds should show no preference between the two sides of the box, and therefore should spend an average of $\mu = 30$ minutes on the plain side. However, if you look at the data in Figure 9.6, the scores are not centered around $\mu = 30$. Instead, the scores are shifted to the right so that they are centered around the sample mean, $M = 36$. This shift is the treatment effect. To measure the size of the treatment effect we will calculate deviations from the mean and the sum of squared deviations, *SS*, two different ways.

Figure 9.7(a) shows the original set of scores. For each score, the deviation from $\mu = 30$ is shown as a colored line. Recall that $\mu = 30$ comes from the null hypothesis and represents the mean that should be obtained if the treatment has no effect. Note that almost all of the scores are located on the right-hand side of $\mu = 30$. This shift to the right is the treatment effect. Specifically, the treatment has caused the birds to spend

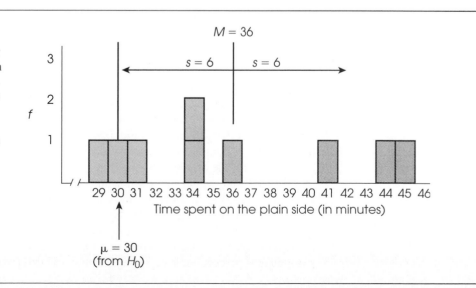

FIGURE 9.6

The sample distribution for the scores that were used in Examples 9.1 and 9.2. The population mean $\mu = 30$ is the value that would be expected if the treatment had no effect. Note that the sample mean is displaced away from $\mu = 30$ by a distance equal to one standard deviation.

FIGURE 9.7

Deviations from μ = 30 (no treatment effect) for the scores in Example 9.1. The colored lines in part (a) show the deviations for the original scores, including the treatment effect. In part (b), the colored lines show the deviations for the adjusted scores after the treatment effect has been removed.

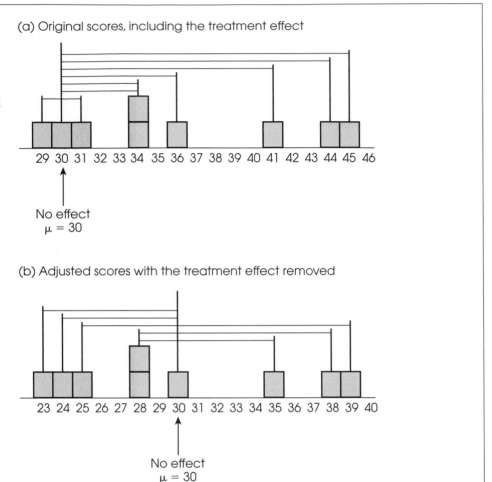

(a) Original scores, including the treatment effect

No effect
μ = 30

(b) Adjusted scores with the treatment effect removed

No effect
μ = 30

more time on the plain side of the box, which means that their scores are generally greater than 30. Thus, the treatment has pushed the scores away from μ = 30 and has increased the size of the deviations.

Next, we will see what happens if the treatment effect is removed. In this example, the treatment has a 6-point effect (the average increases from μ = 30 to $M = 36$). To remove the treatment effect, we will simply subtract 6 points from each score. The adjusted scores are shown in Figure 9.7(b) and, once again, the deviations from μ = 30 are shown as colored lines. First, notice that the adjusted scores are centered at μ = 30, indicating that there is no treatment effect. Also notice that the deviations, the colored lines, are noticeably smaller when the treatment effect is removed.

To measure how much the variability is reduced when the treatment effect is removed, we will compute the sum of squared deviations, *SS,* for each set of scores. The calculations for the original scores [Figure 9.7(a)] are shown in the left-hand columns of Table 9.2, and the calculations for the adjusted scores [Figure 9.7(b)] are shown in the right-hand columns. Note that the total variability, including the treatment effect, is $SS = 612$. However, when the treatment effect is removed, the variability is reduced to $SS = 288$. The difference between these two values, $612 - 288 = 324$ points, is the amount of variability that is accounted for by the treatment effect. This value is usually reported as a proportion or percentage of the total variability:

TABLE 9.2

Calculation of *SS*, the sum of squared deviations, for the data in Figure 9.7. The first three columns show the calculations for the original scores, including the treatment effect. The last three columns show the calculations for the adjusted scores after the treatment effect has been removed.

	Calculation of *SS* Including the Treatment Effect			Calculation of *SS* after the Treatment Effect Is Removed		
Score	Deviation from $\mu = 30$	Squared Deviation	Adjusted Score	Deviation from $\mu = 30$	Squared Deviation
29	−1	1	29 − 6 = 23	−7	49
30	0	0	30 − 6 = 24	−6	36
31	1	1	31 − 6 = 25	−5	25
34	4	16	34 − 6 = 28	−2	4
34	4	16	34 − 6 = 28	−2	4
36	6	36	36 − 6 = 30	0	0
41	11	121	41 − 6 = 35	5	25
44	14	196	44 − 6 = 38	8	64
45	15	225	45 − 6 = 39	9	81
		612 = *SS*			288 = *SS*

$$\frac{\text{variability accounted for}}{\text{total variability}} = \frac{324}{612} = 0.5294 \quad (52.94\%)$$

Thus, removing the treatment effect reduces the variability by 52.94%. This value is called the *percentage of variance accounted for by the treatment* and is identified as r^2.

Rather than computing r^2 directly by comparing two different calculations for *SS*, the value can be found from a single equation based on the outcome of the *t* test.

The letter *r* is the traditional symbol used for a correlation, and the concept of r^2 will be discussed again when we consider correlations in Chapter 15. Also, in the context of *t* statistics, the percentage of variance that we are calling r^2 is often identified by the Greek letter omega squared (ω^2).

$$r^2 = \frac{t^2}{t^2 + df} \tag{9.5}$$

For the hypothesis test in Example 9.1, we obtained $t = 3.00$ with $df = 8$. These values produce

$$r^2 = \frac{3^2}{3^2 + 8} = \frac{9}{17} = 0.5294 \quad (52.94\%)$$

Note that this is exactly the same value we obtained with the direct calculation of the percentage of variability accounted for by the treatment.

Interpreting r^2 In addition to developing the Cohen's *d* measure of effect size, Cohen (1988) also proposed criteria for evaluating the size of a treatment effect that is measured by r^2. The criteria were actually suggested for evaluating the size of a correlation, *r*, but are easily extended to apply to r^2. Cohen's standards for interpreting r^2 are shown in Table 9.3.

According to these standards, the data we constructed for Examples 9.1 and 9.2 show a very large effect size with $r^2 = .5294$.

TABLE 9.3

Criteria for interpreting the value of r^2 as proposed by Cohen (1988).

Percentage of Variance Explained, r^2	
$r^2 = 0.01$	Small effect
$r^2 = 0.09$	Medium effect
$r^2 = 0.25$	Large effect

THE INFLUENCE OF SAMPLE SIZE AND SAMPLE VARIANCE

As we noted in Chapter 8 (page 208), a variety of factors can influence the outcome of a hypothesis test. In particular, the number of scores in the sample and the magnitude of the sample variance both have a large effect on the t statistic and thereby influence the statistical decision. The structure of the t formula makes these factors easier to understand.

$$t = \frac{M - \mu}{s_M} \qquad \text{where } s_M = \sqrt{s^2/n}$$

Because the estimated standard error, s_M, appears in the denominator of the formula, a larger value for s_M will produce a smaller value (closer to zero) for t. Thus, any factor that increases the standard error will also reduce the likelihood of rejecting the null hypothesis and finding a significant treatment effect. The two factors that determine the size of the standard error are the sample variance, s^2, and the sample size, n.

The estimated standard error is directly related to the sample variance so that the larger the variance, the larger the error. Thus, large variance means that you are less likely to obtain a significant treatment effect. In general, large variance is bad for inferential statistics. Large variance means that the scores are widely scattered, which makes it difficult to see any consistent patterns or trends in the data. In general, high variance reduces the likelihood of rejecting the null hypothesis and it reduces measures of effect size.

On the other hand, the estimated standard error is inversely related to the number of scores in the sample. The larger the sample is, the smaller the error is. If all other factors are held constant, large samples tend to produce bigger t statistics and therefore are more likely to produce significant results. For example, a 2-point mean difference with a sample of $n = 4$ may not be convincing evidence of a treatment effect. However, the same 2-point difference with a sample of $n = 100$ is much more compelling.

As a final note, we should remind you that although sample size affects the hypothesis test, this factor has little or no impact on measures of effect size. In particular, estimates of Cohen's d are not influenced at all by sample size, and measures of r^2 are only slightly affected by changes in the size of the sample.

IN THE LITERATURE
REPORTING THE RESULTS OF A t TEST

In Chapter 8, we noted the conventional style for reporting the results of a hypothesis test, according to APA format. First, recall that a scientific report typically uses the term *significant* to indicate that the null hypothesis has been rejected and the term *not significant* to indicate failure to reject H_0. Additionally, there is a prescribed format for reporting the calculated value of the test statistic, degrees of freedom, and alpha level for a t test. This format parallels the style introduced in Chapter 8 (page 206).

In Example 9.1 we calculated a t statistic of 3.00 with $df = 8$, and we decided to reject H_0 with alpha set at .05. Using the same data in Example 9.2, we obtained $r^2 = 52.94\%$ for the percentage of variance explained by the treatment effect. In a scientific report, this information is conveyed in a concise statement, as follows:

> The subjects averaged $M = 36$ minutes on the plain side of the apparatus with $SD = 6.00$. Statistical analysis indicates that the time spent on the side without eye spots was significantly more than would be expected by chance, $t(8) = 3.00$, $p < .05$, $r^2 = 52.94\%$.

In the first statement, the mean ($M = 36$) and the standard deviation ($SD = 6$) are reported as previously noted (Chapter 4, page 104). The next statement provides the results of the statistical analysis. Note that the degrees of freedom are reported in parentheses immediately after the symbol *t*. The value for the obtained *t* statistic follows (3.00), and next is the probability of committing a Type I error (less than 5%). Finally, the effect size is reported, $r^2 = 52.94\%$.

The statement $p < .05$ was explained in Chapter 8, page 206.

Often, researchers will use a computer to perform a hypothesis test like the one in Example 9.1. In addition to calculating the mean, standard deviation, and the *t* statistic for the data, the computer usually calculates and reports the *exact probability* associated with the *t* value. In Example 9.1 we determined that any *t* value beyond ± 2.306 has a probability of less than .05 (see Figure 9.5). Thus, the obtained *t* value, $t = 3.00$, is reported as being very unlikely, $p < .05$. A computer printout, however, would have included an exact probability for our specific *t* value.

Whenever a specific probability value is available, you are encouraged to use it in a research report. For example, a computer analysis of these data reports an exact *p* value of $p = .017$, and the research report would state "$t(8) = 3.00, p = .017$" instead of using the less specific "$p < .05$." As one final caution, we note that occasionally a *t* value is so extreme that the computer reports $p = 0.000$. The zero value does not mean that the probability is literally zero; instead, it means that the computer has rounded off the probability value to three decimal places and obtained a result of 0.000. In this situation, you do not know the exact probability value, but you can report $p < .001$.   ❏

LEARNING CHECK

1. A sample of $n = 16$ individuals is selected from a population with a mean of $\mu = 80$. A treatment is administered to the sample and, after treatment, the sample mean is found to be $M = 86$ with a standard deviation of $s = 8$.

   a. Does the sample provide sufficient evidence to conclude that the treatment has a significant effect? Test with $\alpha = .05$. Also, compute Cohen's *d* and r^2 to measure the effect size.

   b. Now assume the sample has only $n = 4$ individuals, but the mean is still $M = 86$ and the standard deviation is still $s = 8$. Repeat the hypothesis test with $\alpha = .05$ and compute the new measures of effect size (*d* and r^2) for the sample of $n = 4$.

   c. How does sample size influence the outcome of the hypothesis test? How does sample size influence the measures of effect size?

ANSWERS

1. **a.** The estimated standard error is 2 points and the data produce $t = 6/2 = 3.00$. With $df = 15$, the critical values are $t = \pm 2.131$, so the decision is to reject H_0 and conclude that there is a significant treatment effect. For these data, $d = 6/8 = 0.75$ and $r^2 = 9/24 = 0.375$ or 37.5%.

   b. With $n = 4$, the estimated standard error is 4 points and $t = 6/4 = 1.50$. With $df = 3$, the critical boundaries are ± 3.182, so the decision is to fail to reject H_0 and conclude that the treatment does not have a significant effect. The data produce $d = 6/8 = 0.75$ and $r^2 = 2.25/5.25 = 0.429$ (42.9%).

   c. Changing the sample size has a big effect on the outcome of the hypothesis test; the larger sample is more likely to produce a significant effect. However, sample size has no effect on Cohen's *d* and has only a small effect on the value of r^2.

9.4   DIRECTIONAL HYPOTHESES AND ONE-TAILED TESTS

As noted in Chapter 8, the nondirectional (two-tailed) test is more commonly used than the directional (one-tailed) alternative. On the other hand, a directional test may be used in some research situations, such as exploratory investigations or pilot studies or when there is a priori justification (for example, a theory or previous findings). The following example demonstrates a directional hypothesis test with a *t* statistic, using the same experimental situation presented in Example 9.1.

EXAMPLE 9.3   The research question is whether eye-spot patterns will affect the behavior of birds placed in a special testing box. The researcher is expecting the birds to avoid the eye-spot patterns. Therefore, the researcher predicts that the birds will spend most of the hour on the plain side of the box. For this example we will use the same sample data that were used in the original hypothesis test in Example 9.1. Specifically, the researcher tested a sample of $n = 9$ birds and obtained a mean of $M = 36$ minutes spent on the plain side of the box with $SS = 288$.

STEP 1   State the hypotheses, and select an alpha level. With most directional tests, it is usually easier to state the hypothesis in words, including the directional prediction, and then convert the words into symbols. For this example, the researcher is predicting that the eye-spot patterns will cause the birds to *increase* the amount of time they spend in the plain side of the box; that is, more than half of the hour should be spent on the plain side. In general, the null hypothesis states that the predicted effect will not happen. For this study, the null hypothesis states that the birds will *not* spend more than half of the hour on the plain side. In symbols,

$$H_0: \quad \mu_{\text{plain side}} \leq 30 \text{ minutes} \qquad \text{(Not more than half of the hour on the plain side)}$$

Similarly, the alternative states that the treatment will work. In this case, H_1 states that the birds will spend more than half of the hour on the plain side. In symbols,

$$H_1: \quad \mu_{\text{plain side}} > 30 \text{ minutes} \qquad \text{(More than half of the hour on the plain side)}$$

We will set the level of significance at $\alpha = .05$.

STEP 2   Locate the critical region. In this example, the researcher is predicting that the sample mean (*M*) will be greater than 30. Thus, if the birds average more than 30 minutes on the plain side, the data will provide support for the researcher's prediction and will tend to refute the null hypothesis. However, we must still determine exactly how large a value is necessary to reject the null hypothesis. To find the critical value, you must look in the *t* distribution table using the one-tail proportions. With a sample of $n = 9$, the *t* statistic will have $df = 8$; using $\alpha = .05$, you should find a critical value of $t = 1.860$. Therefore, if we obtain a sample mean greater than 30 minutes and the sample mean produces a *t* statistic greater than 1.860, we will reject the null hypothesis and conclude that birds spend significantly more than 30 minutes on the plain side of the box. Figure 9.8 shows the one-tailed critical region for this test.

STEP 3   Calculate the test statistic. The computation of the *t* statistic is the same for either a one-tailed or a two-tailed test. Earlier (in Example 9.1), we found that the data for this experiment produce a test statistic of $t = 3.00$.

FIGURE 9.8

The critical region in the *t* distribution for α = .05, *df* = 8, one-tailed test.

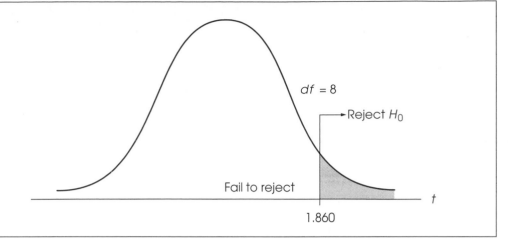

df = 8

Reject H_0

Fail to reject

1.860

t

STEP 4   Make a decision. The test statistic is in the critical region, so we reject H_0. In terms of the experimental variables, we have decided that the birds spent significantly more time on the plain side of the box than on the side with eye-spot patterns.

LEARNING CHECK

1. A researcher would like to evaluate the effect of a new cold medication on reaction time. It is known that under regular circumstances the distribution of reaction times is normal with μ = 200. A sample of *n* = 4 participants is obtained. Each person is given the new cold medication, and 1 hour later reaction time is measured for each individual. The average reaction time for this sample is *M* = 215 with *SS* = 300. On the basis of these data, can the researcher conclude that the cold medication has an effect on reaction time? Test at the .05 level of significance.

  a. State the hypotheses.
  b. Locate the critical region.
  c. Compute the *t* statistic.
  d. Make a decision.

ANSWERS

2. Suppose the researcher in the previous problem predicted that the medication would increase reaction time and decided to use a one-tailed test to evaluate this prediction.

  a. State the hypotheses for the one-tailed test.
  b. Locate the one-tailed critical region for α = .05.
  c. Can the researcher conclude that the cold medication significantly increases reaction time?

1. a. H_0: μ = 200   (The medication has no effect on reaction time.)
       H_1: μ ≠ 200   (Reaction time is changed.)
    b. With *df* = 3 and α = .05, the critical region consists of *t* values beyond ±3.182.

   c. The sample variance is $s^2 = 100$, the standard error is 5, and $t = 3.00$.

   d. The *t* statistic is not in the critical region. Fail to reject the null hypothesis, and conclude that the data do not provide enough evidence to say that the medication affects reaction time.

   2. a. H_0: $\mu \leq 200$ (Reaction time is not increased.)
   H_1: $\mu > 200$ (Reaction time is increased.)

   b. With $df = 3$ and $\alpha = .05$, the one-tailed critical region consists of values beyond $t = +2.353$.

   c. The obtained *t* statistic, $t = 3.00$, is in the critical region. Reject the null hypothesis and conclude that the medication significantly increases reaction time.

SUMMARY

1. The *t* statistic is used instead of a *z*-score for hypothesis testing when the population standard deviation (or variance) is unknown.

2. To compute the *t* statistic, you must first calculate the sample variance (or standard deviation) as a substitute for the unknown population value.

$$\text{sample variance} = s^2 = \frac{SS}{df}$$

Next, the standard error is *estimated* by substituting s^2 in the formula for standard error. The estimated standard error is calculated in the following manner:

$$\text{estimated standard error} = s_M = \sqrt{\frac{s^2}{n}}$$

Finally, a *t* statistic is computed using the estimated standard error. The *t* statistic is used as a substitute for a *z*-score that cannot be computed when the population variance or standard deviation is unknown.

$$t = \frac{M - \mu}{s_M}$$

3. The structure of the *t* formula is similar to that of the *z*-score in that

$$z \text{ or } t = \frac{\text{sample mean} - \text{population mean}}{\text{(estimated) standard error}}$$

For a hypothesis test, you hypothesize a value for the unknown population mean and plug the hypothesized value into the equation along with the sample mean and the estimated standard error, which are computed from the sample data. If the hypothesized mean produces an extreme value for *t,* you conclude that the hypothesis was wrong.

4. The *t* distribution is an approximation of the normal *z* distribution. To evaluate a *t* statistic that is obtained for a sample mean, the critical region must be located in a *t* distribution. There is a family of *t* distributions, with the exact shape of a particular distribution of *t* values depending on degrees of freedom $(n - 1)$. Therefore, the critical *t* values will depend on the value for *df* associated with the *t* test. As *df* increases, the shape of the *t* distribution approaches a normal distribution.

5. When a *t* statistic is used for a hypothesis test, Cohen's *d* can be computed to measure effect size. In this situation, the sample standard deviation is used in the formula to obtain an estimated value for *d*:

$$\text{estimated } d = \frac{\text{mean difference}}{\text{standard deviation}} = \frac{M - \mu}{s}$$

6. A second measure of effect size is r^2, which measures the percentage of the variability that is accounted for by the treatment effect. This value is computed as follows:

$$r^2 = \frac{t^2}{t^2 + df}$$

KEY TERMS

estimated standard error	*t* statistic	degrees of freedom
t distribution	estimated *d*	percentage of variance accounted for by the treatment (r^2)

RESOURCES

There are a tutorial quiz and other learning exercises for Chapter 9 at the Wadsworth website, www.thomsonedu.com/psychology/gravetter. The site also provides access to a workshop entitled *Single-Sample t Test* that reviews the concepts and logic of hypothesis testing with the *t* statistic. See page 27 for more information about accessing items on the website.

For those using WebTutor along with this book, there is a WebTutor section corresponding to this chapter. The WebTutor contains a brief summary of Chapter 9, hints for learning the concepts and the formulas for the *t* score hypothesis test, cautions about common errors, and sample exam items including solutions.

SPSS

General instructions for using SPSS are presented in Appendix D. Following are detailed instructions for using SPSS to perform **the *t* Test** presented in this chapter**.**

Data Entry

1. Enter all of the scores from the sample in one column of the data editor, probably VAR00001.

Data Analysis

1. Click **Analyze** on the tool bar, select **Compare Means,** and click on **One-Sample T Test.**
2. Highlight the column label for the set of scores (VAR0001) in the left box and click the arrow to move it into the **Test Variable(s)** box.
3. In the **Test Value** box at the bottom of the One-Sample *t* Test window, enter the hypothesized value for the population mean from the null hypothesis. *Note:* The value is automatically set at zero until you type in a new value.
4. Click **OK.**

SPSS Output

The program will produce a table of One-Sample Statistics showing the number of scores, the sample mean and standard deviation, and the estimated standard error of the mean. A second table presents the results of the One-Sample Test, including the value of *t*, the degrees of freedom, the level of significance (the *p* value or alpha level for the test), and the size of the mean difference between the sample mean and the hypothesized population mean.

Note: The output also includes the upper and lower boundaries for a 95% confidence interval for the mean difference. Confidence intervals are discussed in Chapter 12 and generally estimate the size of the mean difference.

FOCUS ON PROBLEM SOLVING

1. The first problem we confront in analyzing data is determining the appropriate statistical test. Remember that you can use a *z*-score for the test statistic only when the value for σ is known. If the value for σ is not provided, then you must use the *t* statistic.

2. For a *t* test, students sometimes use the unit normal table to locate the critical region. This, of course, is a mistake. The critical region for a *t* test is obtained by consulting the *t* distribution table. Notice that to use this table you first must compute the value for degrees of freedom (*df*).

3. For the *t* test, the sample variance is used to find the value for estimated standard error. Remember that when computing the sample variance, use $n - 1$ in the denominator (see Chapter 4). When computing estimated standard error, use *n* in the denominator.

DEMONSTRATION 9.1

A HYPOTHESIS TEST WITH THE *t* STATISTIC

A psychologist has prepared an "Optimism Test" that is administered yearly to graduating college seniors. The test measures how each graduating class feels about its future—the higher the score, the more optimistic the class. Last year's class had a mean score of $\mu = 15$. A sample of $n = 9$ seniors from this year's class was selected and tested. The scores for these seniors are 7, 12, 11, 15, 7, 8, 15, 9, and 6, which produce a sample mean of $M = 10$ with $SS = 94$.

On the basis of this sample, can the psychologist conclude that this year's class has a different level of optimism than last year's class?

Note that this hypothesis test will use a *t* statistic because the population variance (σ^2) is not known.

STEP 1   State the hypotheses, and select an alpha level.

The statements for the null hypothesis and the alternative hypothesis follow the same form for the *t* statistic and the *z*-score test.

$$H_0: \quad \mu = 15 \qquad \text{(There is no change.)}$$

$$H_1: \quad \mu \neq 15 \qquad \text{(This year's mean is different.)}$$

For this demonstration, we will use $\alpha = .05$, two tails.

STEP 2   Locate the critical region.

Remember that for hypothesis tests with the *t* statistic, we must consult the *t* distribution table to find the critical *t* values. With a sample of $n = 9$ students, the *t* statistic will have degrees of freedom equal to

$$df = n - 1 = 9 - 1 = 8$$

For a two-tailed test with $\alpha = .05$ and $df = 8$, the critical *t* values are $t = \pm 2.306$. These critical *t* values define the boundaries of the critical region. The obtained *t* value must be more extreme than either of these critical values to reject H_0.

STEP 3   Compute the test statistic. As we have noted, it is easier to separate the calculation of the t statistic into three stages.

Sample variance.

$$s^2 = \frac{SS}{n-1} = \frac{94}{8} = 11.75$$

Estimated standard error. The estimated standard error for these data is

$$s_M = \sqrt{\frac{s^2}{n}} = \sqrt{\frac{11.75}{9}} = 1.14$$

The t statistic. Now that we have the estimated standard error and the sample mean, we can compute the t statistic. For this demonstration,

$$t = \frac{M - \mu}{s_M} = \frac{10 - 15}{1.14} = \frac{-5}{1.14} = -4.39$$

STEP 4   Make a decision about H_0, and state a conclusion.

The t statistic we obtained ($t = -4.39$) is in the critical region. Thus, our sample data are unusual enough to reject the null hypothesis at the .05 level of significance. We can conclude that there is a significant difference in level of optimism between this year's and last year's graduating classes, $t(8) = -4.39$, $p < .05$, two-tailed.

DEMONSTRATION 9.2

EFFECT SIZE: ESTIMATING COHEN'S *d* AND COMPUTING r^2

We will estimate Cohen's d for the same data used for the hypothesis test in Demonstration 9.1. The mean optimism score for the sample from this year's class was 5 points lower than the mean from last year ($M = 10$ versus $\mu = 15$). In Demonstration 9.1 we computed a sample variance of $s^2 = 11.75$, so the standard deviation is $\sqrt{11.75} = 3.43$. With these values,

$$\text{estimated } d = \frac{\text{mean difference}}{\text{standard deviation}} = \frac{5}{3.43} = 1.46$$

To calculate the percentage of variance explained by the treatment effect, r^2, we need the value of t and the df value from the hypothesis test. In Demonstration 9.1 we obtained $t = -4.39$ with $df = 8$. Using these values in Equation 9.5, we obtain

$$r^2 = \frac{t^2}{t^2 + df} = \frac{(-4.39)^2}{(-4.39)^2 + 8} = \frac{19.27}{27.27} = 0.71$$

PROBLEMS

1. A sample of $n = 16$ scores has a mean of $M = 45$ and $SS = 960$.

    a. Calculate the sample standard deviation (s) and the estimated standard error for the sample mean (s_M).

    b. Describe what is measured by the standard deviation and what is measured by the estimated standard error.

2. What is the relationship between the value for degrees of freedom and the shape of the *t* distribution? What happens to the critical value of *t* for a particular alpha level when *df* increases in value?

3. What factor determines whether you should use a *z*-score or a *t* statistic for a hypothesis test?

4. Several factors influence the value obtained for a *t* statistic. Some factors affect the numerator of the *t* statistic and others influence the size of the estimated standard error in the denominator. For each of the following, indicate whether the factor influences the numerator or denominator of the *t* statistic and determine whether the effect would be to increase the value of *t* (farther from zero) or decrease the value of *t* (closer to zero). In each case, assume that all other factors remain constant.
   a. Increase the variability of the scores.
   b. Increase the number of scores in the sample.
   c. Increase the difference between the sample mean and the population mean.

5. Why is a *t* distribution generally more variable than a normal distribution?

6. A sample of $n = 16$ individuals is selected from a population with a mean of $\mu = 78$. A treatment is administered to the individuals in the sample and, after treatment, the sample variance is found to be $s^2 = 144$.
   a. If the treatment has a 4-point effect and produces a sample mean of $M = 82$, is this sufficient to conclude that there is a significant treatment effect using a two-tailed test with $\alpha = .05$?
   b. If the treatment has an 8-point effect and produces a sample mean of $M = 86$, is this sufficient to conclude that there is a significant treatment effect using a two-tailed test with $\alpha = .05$?

7. A random sample of $n = 4$ individuals is obtained from a population with a mean of $\mu = 80$. A treatment is administered to each individual in the sample and, after treatment, each individual is measured. The average score for the treated sample is $M = 86$ with $SS = 192$.
   a. How much difference is there between the mean for the treated sample and the mean for the original population? (*Note:* In a hypothesis test, this value forms the numerator of the *t* statistic.)
   b. How much difference is expected just by chance between the sample mean and its population mean? That is, find the standard error for *M*. (*Note:* In a hypothesis test, this value is the denominator of the *t* statistic.)
   c. Based on the sample data, does the treatment have a significant effect? Use a two-tailed test with $\alpha = .05$.

8. The following sample was obtained from a population with unknown parameters.

   Scores: 1,   5,   1,   1

   a. Compute the sample mean and standard deviation. (Note that these are descriptive values that summarize the sample data.)
   b. Compute the estimated standard error for *M*. (Note that this is an inferential value that describes how accurately the sample mean represents the unknown population mean.)

9. The following sample was obtained from a population with unknown parameters.

   Scores: 6,   12,   0,   3,   4

   a. Compute the sample mean and standard deviation. (Note that these are descriptive values that summarize the sample data.)
   b. Compute the estimated standard error for *M*. (Note that this is an inferential value that describes how accurately the sample mean represents the unknown population mean.)

10. Last fall, a sample of $n = 36$ freshmen was selected to participate in a new 4-hour training program designed to improve study skills. To evaluate the effectiveness of the new program, the sample was compared with the rest of the freshman class. All freshmen must take the same English Language Skills course, and the mean score on the final exam for the entire freshman class was $\mu = 74$. The students in the new program had a mean score of $M = 79.4$ with a standard deviation of $s = 18$.
   a. On the basis of these data, can the college conclude that the students in the new program performed significantly better than the rest of the freshman class? Use a one-tailed test with $\alpha = .05$.
   b. Can the college conclude that the students in the new program are significantly different from the rest of the freshman class? Use a two-tailed test with $\alpha = .05$.

11. A sample is randomly selected from a population with a mean of $\mu = 50$, and a treatment is administered to the individuals in the sample. After treatment, the sample is found to have a mean of $M = 56$ with a standard deviation of $s = 8$.
   a. If there are $n = 4$ individuals in the sample, are the data sufficient to reject H_0 and conclude that the treatment has a significant effect using a two-tailed test with $\alpha = .05$?
   b. If there are $n = 16$ individuals in the sample, are the data sufficient to conclude that the treatment has a significant effect? Again, assume a two-tailed test with $\alpha = .05$.

12. A sample of $n = 25$ individuals is randomly selected from a population with a mean of $\mu = 65$, and a treatment is administered to the individuals in the sample.

After treatment, the sample mean is found to be $M = 70$.

a. If the sample standard deviation is $s = 10$, are the data sufficient to conclude that the treatment has a significant effect using a two-tailed test with $\alpha = .05$?

b. If the sample standard deviation is $s = 20$, are the data sufficient to conclude that the treatment has a significant effect using a two-tailed test with $\alpha = .05$?

13. In a classic study of infant attachment, Harlow (1959) placed infant monkeys in cages with two artificial surrogate mothers. One "mother" was made from bare wire mesh and contained a baby bottle from which the infants could feed. The other mother was made from soft terry cloth and did not provide any access to food. Harlow observed the infant monkeys and recorded how much time per day was spent with each mother. In a typical day, the infants spent a total of 18 hours clinging to one of the two mothers. If there were no preference between the two, you would expect the time to be divided evenly, with an average of $\mu = 9$ hours for each of the mothers. However, the typical monkey spent around 15 hours per day with the terry cloth mother indicating a strong preference for the soft, cuddly mother. Suppose a sample of $n = 9$ infant monkeys averaged $M = 15.3$ hours per day with $SS = 216$ with the terry cloth mother. Is this result sufficient to conclude that the monkeys spent significantly more time with the softer mother than would be expected if there were no preference? Use a two-tailed test with $\alpha = .05$.

14. Belsky, Weinraub, Owen, and Kelly (2001) reported on the effects of preschool childcare on the development of young children. One result suggests that children who spend more time away from their mothers are more likely to show behavioral problems in kindergarten. Using a standardized scale, the average rating of behavioral problems for kindergarten children is $\mu = 35$. A sample of $n = 16$ kindergarten children who had spent at least 20 hours per week in child care during the previous year produced a mean score of $M = 42.7$ with a standard deviation of $s = 6$. Are the data sufficient to conclude that children with a history of child care show significantly more behavioral problems than the average kindergarten child? Use a one-tailed test with $\alpha = .01$.

15. Other research examining the effects of preschool childcare has found that children who spent time in day care, especially high-quality day care, perform better on math and language tests than children who stay home with their mothers (Broberg, Wessels, Lamb, & Hwang, 1997). Typical results, for example, show that a sample of $n = 25$ children who attended day care before starting school had an average score of $M = 87$ with $SS = 1536$ on a standardized math test for which the population mean is $\mu = 81$. Is this sample sufficient to conclude that the children with a history of preschool day care are significantly different from the general population? Use a two-tailed test with $\alpha = .01$.

16. The herbal supplement ginkgo biloba is advertised as producing an increase in physical strength and stamina. To test this claim, a sample of $n = 36$ adults is obtained and each person is instructed to take the regular daily dose of the herb for a period of 30 days. At the end of the 30-day period, each person is tested on a standard treadmill task for which the average, age-adjusted score is $\mu = 15$. The individuals in the sample produce a mean score of $M = 16.9$ with $SS = 1260$.

a. Are these data sufficient to conclude that the herb has a statistically significant effect using a two-tailed test with $\alpha = .05$?

b. What decision would be made if the researcher used a one-tailed test with $\alpha = .05$? (Assume that the herb is expected to increase scores.)

17. A random sample of $n = 16$ scores is obtained from a population with a mean of $\mu = 80$, and a treatment is administered to the sample. After treatment, the sample mean is found to be $M = 82$.

a. Assuming the sample variance is $s^2 = 64$, compute the estimated d and r^2 to measure the size of the treatment effect.

b. Assuming the sample variance is $s^2 = 1600$, compute the estimated d and r^2 to measure the size of the treatment effect.

c. Comparing your answers from parts a and b, how does sample variance influence measures of effect size?

18. An example of the vertical-horizontal illusion is shown in the figure. Although the two lines are exactly the same length, the vertical line appears to be much longer. To examine the strength of this illusion, a researcher prepared an example in which both lines were exactly 10 inches long. The example was shown to individual participants who were told that the horizontal line was 10 inches long and then were asked to estimate the length of the vertical line. For a sample of $n = 25$ participants, the average estimate was $M = 12.2$ inches with a standard deviation of $s = 1.00$.

a. Use a one-tailed hypothesis test with $\alpha = .01$ to demonstrate that the individuals in the sample significantly overestimate the true length of the line. (Note: Accurate estimation would produce a mean of $\mu = 10$ inches.)

b. Calculate the estimated d and r^2, the percentage of variance accounted for, to measure the size of this effect.

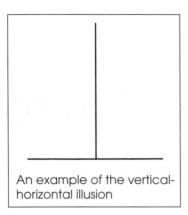

An example of the vertical-horizontal illusion

19. Numerous studies have shown that IQ scores have been increasing, generation by generation, for years (Flynn, 1984, 1999). The increase is called the Flynn Effect, and the data indicate that the increase appears to be about 7 points per decade. To demonstrate this phenomenon, a researcher obtains an IQ test that was written in 1980. At the time the test was prepared, it was standardized to produce a population mean of $\mu = 100$. The researcher administers the test to a random sample of $n = 16$ of today's high school students and obtains a sample mean IQ of $M = 121$ with $SS = 6000$. Is this result sufficient to conclude that today's sample scored significantly higher than would be expected from a population with $\mu = 100$? Use a one-tailed test with $\alpha = .01$.

20. A psychologist would like to determine whether there is a relation between depression and aging. It is known that the general population averages $\mu = 40$ on a standardized depression test. The psychologist obtains a sample of $n = 36$ individuals who are all older than the age of 70. The average depression score for this sample is $M = 44.5$ with $SS = 5040$. On the basis of this sample, can the psychologist conclude that depression for elderly people is significantly different from depression in the general population? Use a two-tailed test at the .05 level of significance.

21. On a standardized spatial skills task, normative data reveal that people typically get $\mu = 15$ correct solutions. A psychologist tests $n = 7$ individuals who have brain injuries in the right cerebral hemisphere. For the following data, determine whether or not right-hemisphere damage results in significantly reduced performance on the spatial skills task. Test with alpha set at .05 with one tail. The data are as follows: 12, 16, 9, 8, 10, 17, 10.

22. People tend to evaluate the quality of their lives relative to others around them. In a demonstration of this phenomenon, Frieswijk, Buunk, Steverink, and Slaets (2004) conducted interviews with frail elderly people. In the interview, each person was compared with fictitious others who were worse off. After the interviews, the elderly people reported more satisfaction with their own lives. Following are hypothetical data similar to those obtained in the research study. The scores are measures on a life-satisfaction scale for a sample of $n = 9$ elderly people who completed the interview. Assume that the average score on this scale is $\mu = 20$. Are the data sufficient to conclude that the people in this sample are significantly more satisfied than others in the general population? Use a one-tailed test with $\alpha = .05$. The life-satisfaction scores for the sample are 18, 23, 24, 22, 19, 27, 23, 26, 25.

23. A researcher would like to examine the effects of humidity on eating behavior. It is known that laboratory rats normally eat an average of $\mu = 21$ grams of food each day. The researcher selects a random sample of $n = 100$ rats and places them in a controlled atmosphere room where the relative humidity is maintained at 90%. The daily food consumption for the sample averages $M = 18.7$ with $SS = 2475$.
   a. Can the researcher conclude that humidity has a significant effect on eating behavior? Use a two-tailed test with $\alpha = .05$.
   b. Compute the estimated d and r^2 to measure the size of the treatment effect.

24. A random sample is obtained from a population with a mean of $\mu = 100$, and a treatment is administered to the sample. After treatment, the sample mean is found to be $M = 104$ and the sample variance is $s^2 = 400$.
   a. Assuming the sample contained $n = 16$ individuals, measure the size of the treatment effect by computing the estimated d and r^2.
   b. Assuming the sample contained $n = 25$ individuals, measure the size of the treatment effect by computing the estimated d and r^2.
   c. Comparing your answers from parts a and b, how does sample size influence measures of effect size?

CHAPTER

10

The *t* Test for Two Independent Samples

Tools You Will Need

The following items are considered essential background material for this chapter. If you doubt your knowledge of any of these items, you should review the appropriate chapter or section before proceeding.

- Sample variance (Chapter 4)

- Standard error formulas (Chapter 7)

- The *t* statistic (Chapter 9)
  - Distribution of *t* values
  - *df* for the *t* statistic
  - Estimated standard error

10.1 OVERVIEW

Until this point, all the inferential statistics we have considered involve using one sample as the basis for drawing conclusions about one population. Although these *single-sample* techniques are used occasionally in real research, most research studies require the comparison of two (or more) sets of data. For example, a social psychologist may want to compare men and women in terms of their political attitudes, an educational psychologist may want to compare two methods for teaching mathematics, or a clinical psychologist may want to evaluate a therapy technique by comparing depression scores for patients before therapy with their scores after therapy. In each case, the research question concerns a mean difference between two sets of data.

There are two general research strategies that can be used to obtain the two sets of data to be compared:

1. The two sets of data could come from two completely separate samples. For example, the study could involve a sample of men compared with a sample of women. Or the study could compare one sample of students taught by method A and a second sample taught by method B.

2. The two sets of data could both come from the same sample. For example, the researcher could obtain one set of scores by measuring depression for a sample of patients before they begin therapy and then obtain a second set of data by measuring the same individuals after 6 weeks of therapy.

The first research strategy, using completely separate samples, is called an *independent-measures* research design or a *between-subjects* design. These terms emphasize the fact that the design involves separate and independent samples and makes a comparison between two groups of individuals. In this chapter, we examine the statistical techniques used to evaluate the data from an independent-measures design. More precisely, we in-

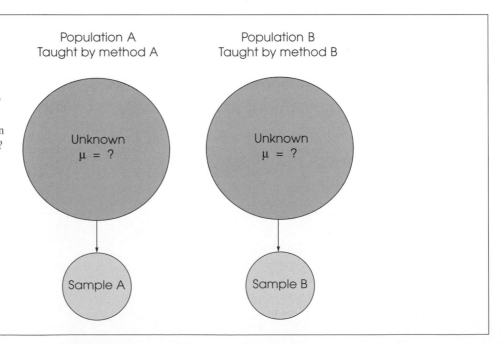

FIGURE 10.1

Do the achievement scores for children taught by method A differ from the scores for children taught by method B? In statistical terms, are the two population means the same or different? Because neither of the two population means is known, it will be necessary to take two samples, one from each population. The first sample will provide information about the mean for the first population, and the second sample will provide information about the second population.

Population A
Taught by method A

Population B
Taught by method B

Unknown
μ = ?

Unknown
μ = ?

Sample A

Sample B

troduce the hypothesis test that allows researchers to use the data from two separate samples to evaluate the mean difference between two populations or between two treatment conditions.

The second research strategy, in which the two sets of data are obtained from the same sample, is called a *repeated-measures* research design or a *within-subjects* design. The statistical analysis for repeated measures are introduced in Chapter 11. Also, at the end of Chapter 11, we discuss some of the advantages and disadvantages of independent-measures versus repeated-measures research designs.

The typical structure of an independent-measures research study is shown in Figure 10.1. Notice that the research study is using two separate samples to answer a question about two populations.

DEFINITION | A research design that uses a separate sample for each treatment condition (or for each population) is called an **independent-measures** research design or a **between-subjects** design.

10.2 THE *t* STATISTIC FOR AN INDEPENDENT-MEASURES RESEARCH DESIGN

Because an independent-measures study involves two separate samples, we will need some special notation to help specify which data go with which sample. This notation involves the use of subscripts, which are small numbers written beside a sample statistic. For example, the number of scores in the first sample is identified by n_1; for the second sample, the number of scores is n_2. The sample means are identified by M_1 and M_2. The sums of squares are SS_1 and SS_2.

THE HYPOTHESES FOR AN INDEPENDENT-MEASURES TEST

The goal of an independent-measures research study is to evaluate the mean difference between two populations (or between two treatment conditions). Using subscripts to differentiate the two populations, the mean for the first population is μ_1, and the second population mean is μ_2. The difference between means is simply $\mu_1 - \mu_2$. As always, the null hypothesis states that there is no change, no effect, or, in this case, no difference. Thus, in symbols, the null hypothesis for the independent-measures test is

$$H_0: \quad \mu_1 - \mu_2 = 0 \qquad \text{(No difference between the population means)}$$

You should notice that the null hypothesis could also be stated as $\mu_1 = \mu_2$. However, the first version of H_0 produces a specific numerical value (zero) that will be used in the calculation of the *t* statistic. Therefore, we prefer to phrase the null hypothesis in terms of the difference between the two population means.

The alternative hypothesis states that there is a mean difference between the two populations,

$$H_1: \quad \mu_1 - \mu_2 \neq 0 \qquad \text{(There is a mean difference.)}$$

Equivalently, the alternative hypothesis can simply state that the two population means are not equal: $\mu_1 \neq \mu_2$.

THE FORMULAS FOR AN
INDEPENDENT-MEASURES
HYPOTHESIS TEST

The independent-measures hypothesis test will be based on another *t* statistic. The formula for this new *t* statistic will have the same general structure as the *t* statistic formula that was introduced in Chapter 9. To help distinguish between the two *t* formulas, we will refer to the original formula (Chapter 9) as the *single-sample* t *statistic* and we will refer to the new formula as the *independent-measures* t *statistic*. Because the new independent-measures *t* will include data from two separate samples and hypotheses about two populations, the formulas may appear to be a bit overpowering. However, the new formulas will be easier to understand if you view them in relation to the single-sample *t* formulas from Chapter 9. In particular, there are two points to remember:

1. The basic structure of the *t* statistic is the same for both the independent-measures and the single-sample hypothesis tests. In both cases,

$$t = \frac{\text{sample statistic} - \text{hypothesized population parameter}}{\text{estimated standard error}}$$

2. The independent-measures *t* is basically a *two-sample* t *that doubles all the elements of the single-sample* t *formulas.*

To demonstrate the second point, we examine the two *t* formulas piece by piece.

The overall *t* formula   The single-sample *t* uses one sample mean to test a hypothesis about one population mean. The sample mean and the population mean appear in the numerator of the *t* formula, which measures how much difference there is between the sample data and the population hypothesis.

$$t = \frac{\begin{array}{cc}\text{sample} & \text{population}\\ \text{mean} & - & \text{mean}\end{array}}{\text{estimated standard error}} = \frac{M - \mu}{s_M}$$

The independent-measures *t* uses the difference between *two* sample means to evaluate the difference between *two* population means. Thus, the independent-measures *t* formula is

$$t = \frac{\begin{array}{cc}\text{sample} & \text{population}\\ \text{mean difference} & - & \text{mean difference}\end{array}}{\text{estimated standard error}} = \frac{(M_1 - M_2) - (\mu_1 - \mu_2)}{s_{(M_1 - M_2)}}$$

In this formula, the value of $M_1 - M_2$ is obtained from the sample data and the value for $\mu_1 - \mu_2$ comes from the null hypothesis. Finally, note that the null hypothesis sets the population mean difference equal to zero, so the independent measures *t* formula can be simplified further,

$$t = \frac{\text{sample mean difference}}{\text{estimated standard error}}$$

In this form, the *t* statistic is a simple ratio comparing the actual mean difference (numerator) with the difference that is expected by chance (denominator).

The estimated standard error   In each of the *t*-score formulas, the standard error in the denominator measures how accurately the sample statistic represents the population parameter. In the single-sample *t* formula, the standard error measures the amount of error expected for a sample mean and is represented by the symbol s_M. For the independent-measures t formula, the standard error measures the amount of error that is expected when you use a sample mean difference $(M_1 - M_2)$ to represent a population mean difference $(\mu_1 - \mu_2)$. The standard error for the sample mean difference is represented by the symbol $s_{(M_1-M_2)}$.

Caution: Do not let the notation for standard error confuse you. In general, standard error measures how accurately a statistic represents a parameter. The symbol for standard error takes the form $s_{\text{statistic}}$. When the statistic is a sample mean, M, the symbol for standard error is s_M. For the independent-measures test, the statistic is a sample mean difference $(M_1 - M_2)$, and the symbol for standard error is $s_{(M_1-M_2)}$. In each case, the standard error tells how much discrepancy is reasonable to expect between the sample statistic and the corresponding population parameter.

Interpreting the estimated standard error   The *estimated standard error of $M_1 - M_2$* that appears in the bottom of the independent-measures t statistic is typically defined as a measure of the standard discrepancy between a sample statistic $(M_1 - M_2)$ and the corresponding population parameter $(\mu_1 - \mu_2)$. In simple terms, samples are not expected to be perfectly accurate, and the standard error measures how much difference is reasonable to expect between a sample statistic and the population parameter.

Sample mean difference $(M_1 - M_2)$ ←—— Estimated standard error (How much difference) ——→   Population mean difference $(\mu_1 - \mu_2)$

When the population mean difference is equal to zero (H_0 is true), we expect the difference between the two sample means to be close to zero. In this case, the estimated standard error measures *how close* the sample mean difference is to zero.

Sample mean difference $(M_1 - M_2)$ ←—— Estimated standard error (How much difference) ——→   0 (If H_0 is true)

Measuring how close the sample mean difference is to zero is equivalent to measuring how much difference there is between the two sample means. That is, we are estimating how much difference is reasonable to expect between M_1 and M_2 if the null hypothesis is true.

M_1 ←—— Estimated standard error (How much difference) ——→ M_2

Thus, when the null hypothesis is true, the independent-measures t statistic can be greatly simplified as follows:

$$t = \frac{\text{sample mean difference}}{\text{estimated standard error}}$$

$$= \frac{\text{actual difference between } M_1 \text{ and } M_2}{\text{standard difference (If } H_0 \text{ is true) between } M_1 \text{ and } M_2}$$

As always, a large value for the t statistic indicates that the difference between the two sample means is larger than would be expected if H_0 is true and there is no difference between the two population means.

CALCULATING THE ESTIMATED STANDARD ERROR

To develop the formula for $s_{(M_1-M_2)}$ we will consider the following three points:

1. Each of the two sample means represents it own population mean, but in each case there is some error.

M_1 approximates μ_1 with some error

M_2 approximates μ_2 with some error

Thus, there are two sources of error.

2. The amount of error associated with each sample mean can be measured by computing the standard error of M. In Chapter 9 (Equation 9.1), we calculated the standard error for a single sample mean as

$$s_M = \sqrt{\frac{s^2}{n}}$$

3. For the independent-measures t statistic, we want to know the total amount of error involved in using *two* sample means to approximate *two* population means. To do this, we will find the error from each sample separately and then add the two errors together. The resulting formula for standard error is

$$s_{(M_1-M_2)} = \sqrt{\frac{s_1^2}{n_1} + \frac{s_2^2}{n_2}} \tag{10.1}$$

Because the independent-measures t statistic uses two sample means, the formula for the estimated standard error simply combines the error for the first sample mean and the error for the second sample mean (Box 10.1).

POOLED VARIANCE

Although Equation 10.1 accurately presents the concept of standard error for the independent-measures t statistic, this formula is limited to situations in which the two samples are exactly the same size (that is, $n_1 = n_2$). In situations in which the two sample sizes are different, the formula is *biased* and, therefore, inappropriate. The bias comes from the fact that Equation 10.1 treats the two sample variances equally. However, when the sample sizes are different, the two sample variances are not equally good and should not be treated equally. In Chapter 7, we introduced the law of large numbers, which states that statistics obtained from large samples tend to be better (more accurate) estimates of population parameters than statistics obtained from small samples. This same fact holds for sample variances: The variance obtained from a large sample will be a more accurate estimate of σ^2 than the variance obtained from a small sample.

An alternative to computing pooled variance is presented in Box 10.3, p 276.

One method for correcting the bias in the sample variances is to combine the two sample variances into a single value called the *pooled variance*. The pooled variance is obtained by averaging or "pooling" the two sample variances using a procedure that allows the bigger sample to carry more weight in determining the final value.

You should recall that when there is only one sample, the sample variance is computed as

$$s^2 = \frac{SS}{df}$$

| BOX 10.1 | THE VARIABILITY OF DIFFERENCE SCORES |

It may seem odd that the independent-measures *t* statistic *adds* together the two sample errors when it *subtracts* to find the difference between the two sample means. The logic behind this apparently unusual procedure is demonstrated here.

We begin with two populations, I and II (Figure 10.2). The scores in population I range from a high of 70 to a low of 50. The scores in population II range from 30 to 20. We will use the range as a measure of how spread out (variable) each population is:

For population I, the scores cover a range of 20 points.

For population II, the scores cover a range of 10 points.

If we randomly select a score from population I and a score from population II and compute the difference between these two scores $(X_1 - X_2)$, what range of values is possible for these differences? To answer this question, we need to find the biggest possible difference and the smallest possible difference. Look at Figure 10.2; the biggest difference occurs when $X_1 = 70$ and $X_2 = 20$. This is a difference of $X_1 - X_2 = 50$ points. The smallest difference occurs when $X_1 = 50$ and $X_2 = 30$. This is a difference of $X_1 - X_2 = 20$ points. Notice that the differences go from a high of 50 to a low of 20. This is a range of 30 points:

range for population I (X_1 scores) = 20 points

range for population II (X_2 scores) = 10 points

range for the differences ($X_1 - X_2$) = 30 points

The variability for the difference scores is found by *adding* together the variabilities for the two populations.

In the independent-measures *t* statistics, we are computing the variability (standard error) for a sample mean difference. To compute this value, we add together the variability for each of the two sample means.

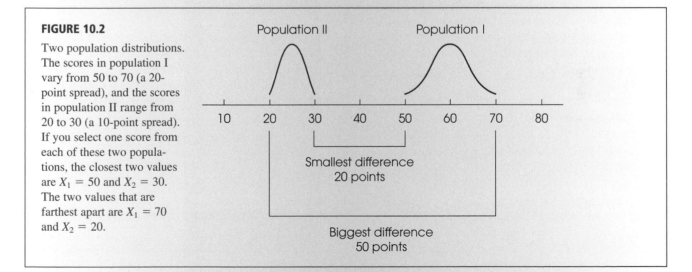

FIGURE 10.2

Two population distributions. The scores in population I vary from 50 to 70 (a 20-point spread), and the scores in population II range from 20 to 30 (a 10-point spread). If you select one score from each of these two populations, the closest two values are $X_1 = 50$ and $X_2 = 30$. The two values that are farthest apart are $X_1 = 70$ and $X_2 = 20$.

For the independent-measures *t* statistic, there are two *SS* values and two *df* values (one from each sample). The values from the two samples are combined to compute what is called the *pooled variance*. The pooled variance is identified by the symbol s_p^2 and is computed as

$$s_p^2 = \frac{SS_1 + SS_2}{df_1 + df_2}$$

(10.2)

With one sample, variance is computed as *SS* divided by *df*. With two samples, the two *SS*s are divided by the two *df*s to compute pooled variance. The pooled variance is an average of the two sample variances, and the value of the pooled variance will always be located between the two sample variances. A more detailed discussion of the pooled variance is presented in Box 10.2.

ESTIMATED STANDARD ERROR

Using the pooled variance in place of the individual sample variances, we can now obtain an unbiased measure of the standard error for a sample mean difference. The resulting formula for the independent-measures estimated standard error is

$$\text{estimated standard error of } M_1 - M_2 = s_{(M_1 - M_2)} = \sqrt{\frac{s_p^2}{n_1} + \frac{s_p^2}{n_2}} \qquad (10.3)$$

Conceptually, this standard error measures how accurately the difference between two sample means represents the difference between the two population means. The formula combines the error for the first sample mean with the error for the second sample mean. Notice that the pooled variance from the two samples is used to compute the standard error for the two samples.

BOX 10.2

A CLOSER LOOK AT THE POOLED VARIANCE

The pooled variance is actually an average of the two sample variances, but the formula is structured so that each sample is weighted by the magnitude of its *df* value. Thus, the larger sample carries more weight in determining the final value. The following examples demonstrate this point.

Equal Sample Size   We begin with two samples that are exactly the same size. The first sample has $n = 6$ scores with $SS = 50$, and the second sample has $n = 6$ scores with $SS = 30$. Individually, the two sample variances are

$$\text{Variance for sample 1:} \quad s^2 = \frac{SS}{df} = \frac{50}{5} = 10$$

$$\text{Variance for sample 2:} \quad s^2 = \frac{SS}{df} = \frac{30}{5} = 6$$

The pooled variance for these two samples is

$$s_p^2 = \frac{SS_1 + SS_2}{df_1 + df_2} = \frac{50 + 30}{5 + 5} = \frac{80}{10} = 8.00$$

Note that the pooled variance is exactly halfway between the two sample variances. Because the two samples are exactly the same size, the pooled variance is simply the average of the two individual sample variances.

Unequal Samples Sizes   Now consider what happens when the samples are not the same size. This time the first sample has $n = 3$ scores with $SS = 20$, and the second sample has $n = 9$ scores with $SS = 48$. Individually, the two sample variances are

$$\text{Variance for sample 1:} \quad s^2 = \frac{SS}{df} = \frac{20}{2} = 10$$

$$\text{Variance for sample 2:} \quad s^2 = \frac{SS}{df} = \frac{48}{8} = 6$$

The pooled variance for these two samples is

$$s_p^2 = \frac{SS_1 + SS_2}{df_1 + df_2} = \frac{20 + 48}{2 + 8} = \frac{68}{10} = 6.80$$

This time the pooled variance is not located halfway between the two sample variances. Instead, the pooled value is closer to the variance for the large sample ($s^2 = 6$) than to the variance for the small sample ($s^2 = 10$). The larger sample carries more weight when the pooled variance is computed.

THE FINAL FORMULA AND DEGREES OF FREEDOM

The complete formula for the independent-measures *t* statistic is as follows:

$$t = \frac{(M_1 - M_2) - (\mu_1 - \mu_2)}{s_{(M_1-M_2)}}$$

$$= \frac{\text{sample mean difference} - \text{population mean difference}}{\text{estimated standard error}} \tag{10.4}$$

In the formula, the estimated standard error in the denominator is calculated using Equation 10.3, and requires calculation of the pooled variance using Equation 10.2.

The degrees of freedom for the independent-measures *t* statistic are determined by the *df* values for the two separate samples:

$$df \text{ for the } t \text{ statistic} = df \text{ for the first sample} + df \text{ for the second sample}$$

$$= df_1 + df_2$$

$$= (n_1 - 1) + (n_2 - 1) \tag{10.5}$$

The independent-measures *t* statistic will be used for hypothesis testing. Specifically, we will use the difference between two sample means $(M_1 - M_2)$ as the basis for testing hypotheses about the difference between two population means $(\mu_1 - \mu_2)$. In this context, the overall structure of the *t* statistic can be reduced to the following:

$$t = \frac{\text{data} - \text{hypothesis}}{\text{error}}$$

This same structure is used for both the single-sample *t* from Chapter 9 and the new independent-measures *t* that was introduced in the preceding pages. Table 10.1 identifies each component of these two *t* statistics and should help reinforce the point that we made earlier in the chapter; that is, the independent-measures *t* statistic simply doubles each aspect of the single-sample *t* statistic.

TABLE 10.1

The basic elements of a *t* statistic for the single-sample *t* and the independent-measures *t*.

	Sample Data	Hypothesized Population Parameter	Estimated Standard Error	Sample Variance
Single-sample *t* statistic	M	μ	$\sqrt{\dfrac{s^2}{n}}$	$s^2 = \dfrac{SS}{df}$
Independent-measures *t* statistic	$(M_1 - M_2)$	$(\mu_1 - \mu_2)$	$\sqrt{\dfrac{s_p^2}{n_1} + \dfrac{s_p^2}{n_2}}$	$s_p^2 = \dfrac{SS_1 + SS_2}{df_1 + df_2}$

LEARNING CHECK

1. Describe the general characteristics of an independent-measures research study.

2. Identify the two sources of error that are reflected in the standard error for the independent-measures *t* statistic.

3. An independent-measures *t* statistic is used to evaluate the mean difference between two treatments using a sample of $n = 10$ in one treatment and a separate sample of $n = 15$ in the other treatment. What is the *df* value for the *t* test?

4. The first sample from an independent-measures research study has $n = 5$ scores with $SS = 40$. The second sample has $n = 5$ scores with $SS = 32$.

   a. Compute the variance for each of the two samples.

   b. Compute the pooled variance for the two samples. (Because the two samples are exactly the same size, you should find that the pooled variance is equal to the average of the two sample variances.)

5. The first sample from an independent-measures research study has $n = 5$ scores with $SS = 40$. The second sample has $n = 7$ scores with $SS = 48$.

   a. Compute the variance for each of the two samples.

   b. Compute the pooled variance for the two samples. (Because the two samples are not the same size, you should find that the pooled variance is not halfway between the two sample variances. Because the larger sample carries more weight, the pooled variance is closer to the variance from the larger sample.)

ANSWERS   1. An independent-measures study uses a separate sample to represent each of the treament conditions or populations being compared.

2. The two sources of error come from the fact that two sample means are being used to represent two population means. Thus, M_1 represents its population mean with some error and M_2 represents its population mean with some error. The two errors combine in the standard error for the independent-measures *t* statistic.

3. The *t* statistic has $df = df_1 + df_2 = 9 + 14 = 23$.

4. a. The first sample has a variance of 10 and the second sample has a variance of 8.

   b. The pooled variance is 9 (exactly halfway between 10 and 8).

5. a. The first sample has a variance of 10 and the second sample has a variance of 8.

   b. The pooled variance is 8.8, which is weighted toward the variance for the larger sample.

10.3   HYPOTHESIS TESTS AND EFFECT SIZE WITH THE INDEPENDENT-MEASURES *t* STATISTIC

The independent-measures *t* statistic uses the data from two separate samples to help decide whether there is a significant mean difference between two populations or between two treatment conditions. A complete example of a hypothesis test with two independent samples follows.

EXAMPLE 10.1

Remember that an independent-measures design means there are separate samples for each treatment condition.

In recent years, psychologists have demonstrated repeatedly that using mental images can greatly improve memory. Here we present a hypothetical experiment designed to examine this phenomenon.

   The psychologist first prepares a list of 40 pairs of nouns (for example, dog/bicycle, grass/door, lamp/piano). Next, two groups of participants are obtained (two separate samples). Participants in one group are given the list for 5 minutes and instructed to memorize the 40 noun pairs. Participants in another group receive the same list of words, but in addition to the regular instructions, they are told to form a mental image for each pair of nouns (imagine a dog riding a bicycle, for example). Note that the two samples are identical except that one group is using mental images to help learn the list.

Later each group is given a memory test in which they are given the first word from each pair and asked to recall the second word. The psychologist records the number of words correctly recalled for each individual. The data from this experiment are as follows. On the basis of these data, can the psychologist conclude that mental images affected memory?

Data (Number of Words Recalled)			
Group 1 (Images)		Group 2 (No Images)	
19	32	23	12
20	30	22	16
24	27	15	19
30	22	16	14
31	25	18	25
$n = 10$		$n = 10$	
$M = 26$		$M = 18$	
$SS = 200$		$SS = 160$	

STEP 1 State the hypotheses, and select the alpha level.

Directional hypotheses could be used and would specify whether imagery should increase or decrease recall scores.

H_0: $\mu_1 - \mu_2 = 0$ (No difference; imagery has no effect.)

H_1: $\mu_1 - \mu_2 \neq 0$ (Imagery produces a difference.)

We will set $\alpha = .05$.

STEP 2 This is an independent-measures design. The *t* statistic for these data will have degrees of freedom determined by

$$df = df_1 + df_2$$
$$= (n_1 - 1) + (n_2 - 1)$$
$$= 9 + 9$$
$$= 18$$

The *t* distribution for $df = 18$ is presented in Figure 10.3. For $\alpha = .05$, the critical region consists of the extreme 5% of the distribution and has boundaries of $t = +2.101$ and $t = -2.101$.

FIGURE 10.3

The *t* distribution with $df = 18$. The critical region for $\alpha = .05$ is shown.

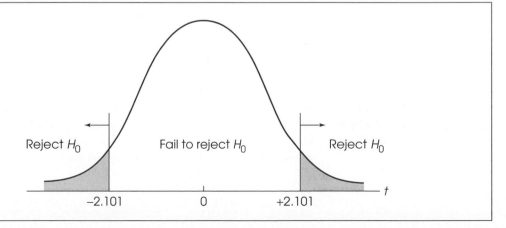

Reject H_0 Fail to reject H_0 Reject H_0

−2.101   0   +2.101   *t*

STEP 3 Obtain the data, and compute the test statistic. The data are as given, so all that remains is to compute the *t* statistic.

As with the single-sample *t* test in Chapter 9, we recommend that the calculations be divided into three parts.

First, find the pooled variance for the two samples:

Caution: The pooled variance combines the two samples to obtain a single estimate of variance. In the formula, the two samples are combined in a single fraction.

$$s_p^2 = \frac{SS_1 + SS_2}{df_1 + df_2}$$

$$= \frac{200 + 160}{9 + 9}$$

$$= \frac{360}{18}$$

$$= 20$$

Caution: The standard error adds the errors from two separate samples. In the formula, these two errors are added as two separate fractions. In this case, the two errors are equal because the sample sizes are the same.

Second, use the pooled variance to compute the estimated standard error:

$$s_{(M_1 - M_2)} = \sqrt{\frac{s_p^2}{n_1} + \frac{s_p^2}{n_2}} = \sqrt{\frac{20}{10} + \frac{20}{10}}$$

$$= \sqrt{2 + 2}$$

$$= \sqrt{4}$$

$$= 2$$

Third, compute the *t* statistic:

$$t = \frac{(M_1 - M_2) - (\mu_1 - \mu_2)}{s_{(M_1 - M_2)}} = \frac{(26 - 18) - 0}{2}$$

$$= \frac{8}{2}$$

$$= 4.00$$

STEP 4 Make a decision. The obtained value ($t = 4.00$) is in the critical region. In this example, the obtained sample mean difference is four times greater than would be expected if there were no treatment effect. In other words, this result is very unlikely if H_0 is true. Therefore, we reject H_0 and conclude that using mental images produced a significant difference in memory performance. More specifically, the group using images recalled significantly more words than the group with no images.

MEASURING EFFECT SIZE FOR THE INDEPENDENT-MEASURES

As noted in Chapters 8 and 9, a hypothesis test is usually accompanied by a report of effect size to provide an indication of the absolute magnitude of the treatment effect. One technique for measuring effect size is Cohen's *d*, which produces a standardized measure of mean difference. In its general form, Cohen's *d* is defined as

$$d = \frac{\text{mean difference}}{\text{standard deviation}}$$

In the context of an independent-measures research study, the difference between the two sample means $(M_1 - M_2)$ is used as the best estimate of the mean difference, and the pooled standard deviation (the square root of the pooled variance) is used to estimate the population standard deviation. Thus, the formula for estimating Cohen's *d* becomes

$$\text{estimated } d = \frac{\text{estimated mean difference}}{\text{estimated standard deviation}} = \frac{M_1 - M_2}{\sqrt{s_p^2}} \tag{10.6}$$

For the data from Example 10.1, the two sample means are 26 and 18, and the pooled variance is 20. The estimated *d* for these data is

$$d = \frac{M_1 - M_2}{\sqrt{s_p^2}} = \frac{26 - 18}{\sqrt{20}} = \frac{8}{4.47} = 1.79$$

Using the criteria established to evaluate Cohen's *d* (see Table 8.2 on page 218), this value indicates a very large treatment effect.

The independent-measures *t* hypothesis test also allows for measuring effect size by computing the percentage of variance accounted for, r^2. As we saw in Chapter 9, r^2 measures how much of the variability in the scores can be explained by the treatment effects. For example, the participants in the imagery study (Example 10.1) have different memory scores. In statistical terms, their scores are variable. However, some of the variability can be explained by knowing which group the scores are in; people in the imagery condition tended to have higher scores than people in the no-imagery condition. By measuring exactly how much of the variability can be explained, we can obtain a measure of how big the treatment effect actually is. The calculation of r^2 for the independent-measures *t* is exactly the same as it was for the single-sample *t* in Chapter 9:

$$r^2 = \frac{t^2}{t^2 + df} \tag{10.7}$$

For the data in Example 10.1 (the imagery study), we obtained $t = 4.00$ with $df = 18$. These values produce an r^2 of

$$r^2 = \frac{4^2}{4^2 + 18} = \frac{16}{16 + 18} = \frac{16}{34} = 0.47$$

According to the standards used to evaluate r^2 (see Table 9.3 on page 245), this value also indicates a very large treatment effect.

Although the value of r^2 is usually obtained by using Equation 10.7, it is possible to determine the percentage of variability directly by computing *SS* values for the set of scores. The following example demonstrates this process using the data from the imagery study in Example 10.1.

EXAMPLE 10.2 The memory study described in Example 10.1 compared memory scores for two groups of participants; one group was instructed to use images and the other group received no imagery instructions. If we assume that the null hypothesis is true and there is no difference between the two treatments (imagery and no-imagery), then there should be no treatment effect to cause a mean difference between the two samples. In this case, the two samples can be combined to form a single set of $n = 20$ scores with an overall mean of $M = 22$. The two samples are shown as a single distribution in Figure 10.4(a).

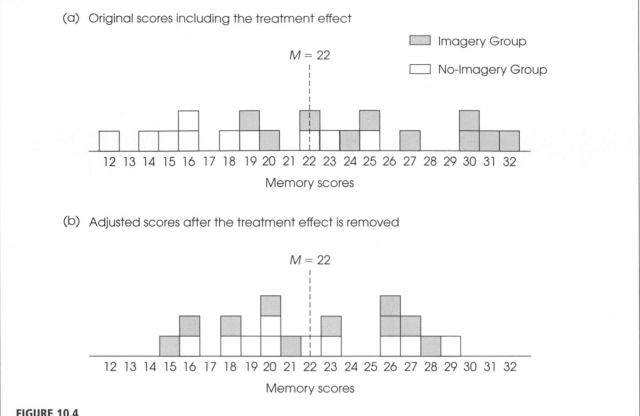

FIGURE 10.4

The two groups of scores from Example 10.1 combined into a single distribution. The original scores, including the treatment effect, are shown in part (a). Part (b) shows the adjusted scores, after the treatment effect has been removed.

For this example, however, there is a treatment effect that causes the imagery group to have higher memory scores than the no-imagery group. Specifically, the imagery group has a mean score of $M = 26$, which is four points higher than the overall mean of $M = 22$. Similarly, the no-imagery group has a mean score of $M = 18$, which is four points lower than the overall mean. Thus, the treatment effect causes the imagery scores to move away from $M = 22$ toward the right, and the no-imagery scores to move away from $M = 22$ toward the left. Notice that the imagery scores are clustered on the right side of the distribution in Figure 10.4(a), and the no-imagery scores are clustered on the left. Thus, the treatment effect has shifted the scores away from the mean and therefore has increased the variability.

To determine how much the treatment effect contributes to the variability, we remove the treatment effect and examine the resulting scores. To remove the treatment effect, we adjust the scores by adding 4 points to each score in the no-imagery group and subtracting 4 points from each score in the imagery group. This adjustment will cause both groups to have a mean of $M = 22$ so there is no mean difference between the two treatments. The adjusted scores are shown in Figure 10.4(b).

It should be clear that the adjusted scores in Figure 10.4(b) are less variable (more closely clustered) than the original scores in Figure 10.4(a). That is, removing the treatment effect has reduced the variability. To determine exactly how much the treatment influences variability, we will compute *SS*, the sum of squared deviations, for each set of scores. For the original set of scores, including the treatment effect, the total variability is $SS = 680$. When the treatment effect is removed, the variability is reduced to $SS = 360$. The difference between these two values, 320 points, is the amount of variability that is explained by the treatment effect. When expressed as a proportion of the total variability, we obtain

$$\frac{\text{variability explained by the treatment}}{\text{total variability}} = \frac{320}{680} = 0.47 = 47\%$$

You should recognize that this is exactly the same value we obtained for r^2 using Equation 10.7.

IN THE LITERATURE
REPORTING THE RESULTS OF AN INDEPENDENT-MEASURES *t* TEST

In Chapter 4 (page 104), we demonstrated how the mean and the standard deviation are reported in APA format. In Chapter 9 (page 246), we illustrated the APA style for reporting the results of a *t* test. Now we will use the APA format to report the results of Example 10.1, an independent-measures *t* test. A concise statement might read as follows:

> The group using mental images recalled more words ($M = 26$, $SD = 4.71$) than the group that did not use mental images ($M = 18$, $SD = 4.22$). This difference was significant, $t(18) = 4.00$, $p < .05$, $d = 1.79$.

You should note that standard deviation is not a step in the computations for the independent-measures *t* test, yet it is useful when providing descriptive statistics for each treatment group. It is easily computed when doing the *t* test because you need *SS* and *df* for both groups to determine the pooled variance. Note that the format for reporting *t* is exactly the same as that described in Chapter 9 (page 246) and that the measure of effect size is reported immediately after the results of the hypothesis test.

Also, as we noted in Chapter 9, if an exact probability is available from a computer analysis, it should be reported. For the data in Example 10.1, the computer analysis reports a probability value of $p = .001$ for $t = 4.00$ with $df = 18$. In the research report, this value would be included as follows:

> The difference was significant, $t(18) = 4.00$, $p = .001$, $d = 1.79$.   ❑

DIRECTIONAL HYPOTHESES AND ONE-TAILED TESTS

When planning an independent-measures experiment, a researcher usually has some expectation or specific prediction for the outcome. For the memory experiment described in Example 10.1, the psychologist clearly expects the group using images to have higher memory scores than the group without images. This kind of directional prediction can be incorporated into the statement of the hypotheses, resulting in a directional, or one-tailed, test. Recall from Chapter 8 that one-tailed tests can be less conservative than two-tailed tests, and should be used when clearly justified by theory or previous findings. The following example demonstrates the procedure for stating hypotheses and locating the critical region for a one-tailed test using the independent-measures *t* statistic.

EXAMPLE 10.3   We will use the same experimental situation that was described in Example 10.1. The researcher is using an independent-measures design to examine the effect of mental images on memory. The prediction is that the imagery group will have higher memory scores.

STEP 1   State the hypotheses and select the alpha level. As always, the null hypothesis says that there is no effect, and the alternative hypothesis says that there is an effect. For this example, the *predicted* effect is that images will produce higher scores. Thus, the two hypotheses are:

$$H_0: \quad \mu_{\text{images}} \leq \mu_{\text{no images}} \qquad \text{(Imagery scores are not higher.)}$$

$$H_1: \quad \mu_{\text{images}} > \mu_{\text{no images}} \qquad \text{(Imagery scores are higher, as predicted.)}$$

Note that it is usually easier to state the hypotheses in words before you try to write them in symbols. Also, it usually is easier to begin with the alternative hypothesis (H_1), which states that the treatment works as predicted. Then the null hypothesis is just the opposite of H_1. Also note that the equal sign goes in the null hypothesis, indicating *no difference* between the two treatment conditions. The idea of zero difference is the essence of the null hypothesis, and the numerical value of zero will be used for ($\mu_1 - \mu_2$) during the calculation of the *t* statistic.

STEP 2   Locate the critical region. For a directional test, the critical region will be located entirely in one tail of the distribution. Rather than trying to determine which tail, positive or negative, is the correct location, we suggest you identify the criteria for the critical region in a two-step process as follows. First, look at the data and determine whether the sample mean difference is in the direction that was predicted. If the answer is no, then the data obviously do not support the predicted treatment effect, and you can stop the analysis. On the other hand, if the difference is in the predicted direction, then the second step is to determine whether the difference is large enough to be significant. To test for significance, simply find the one-tailed critical value in the *t* distribution table. If the calculated *t* statistic is more extreme (either positive or negative) than the critical value, then the difference is significant.

For this example, the imagery group scored 6 points higher, as predicted. With $df = 18$, the one-tailed critical value for $\alpha = .05$ is $t = 1.734$.

STEP 3   Collect the data and calculate the test statistic. The details of the calculations were shown in Example 10.1. The data produce a *t* statistic of $t = 4.00$.

STEP 4   Make a decision. The *t* statistic of $t = 4.00$ is well beyond the critical boundary of $t = 1.734$. Therefore, we reject the null hypothesis and conclude that scores in the imagery condition are significantly higher than scores in the no-imagery condition, as predicted.

LEARNING CHECK

1. A researcher report states that there is a significant difference between treatments for an independent-measures design with $t(28) = 2.27$.

   a. How many individuals participated in the research study? (*Hint:* Start with the *df* value.)

   b. Should the report state that $p > .05$ or $p < .05$?

2. A developmental psychologist would like to examine the difference in verbal skills for 6-year-old girls compared with 6-year-old boys. A sample of $n = 5$ girls and $n = 5$ boys is obtained, and each child is given a standardized verbal abilities test.

The data are as follows:

GIRLS	BOYS
$M = 83$	$M = 71$
$SS = 200$	$SS = 120$

Are these data sufficient to indicate a significant difference in verbal skills for 6-year-old girls and 6-year-old boys? Test at the .05 level of significance.

3. Suppose that the psychologist in the previous question predicted that girls have higher verbal scores at age 5. What value of *t* would be necessary to conclude that girls score significantly higher using a one-tailed test with $\alpha = .01$?

4. Calculate the effect size for the data in Question 2. Compute Cohen's *d* and r^2.

ANSWERS   1. **a.** The $df = 28$, so the total number of participants is 30.

   b. A significant result is indicated by $p < .05$.

2. Pooled variance = 40, the standard error = 4, and $t = 3.00$. With $df = 8$, the decision is to reject the null hypothesis.

3. With $df = 8$ and $\alpha = .01$ the critical value is $t = 2.896$.

4. For these data, $d = 1.90$ (a very large effect size), and $r^2 = 0.53$ (or 53%).

THE ROLE OF SAMPLE VARIANCE IN THE INDEPENDENT-MEASURES *t* TEST

In Chapter 8 and in Chapter 9 (pages 207 and 246) we identified several factors that can influence the outcome of a hypothesis test. One factor that plays an important role is the variability of the scores. In general, high variability reduces the likelihood of obtaining a significant result. The independent-measures *t* test offers an opportunity to present a visual demonstration of this phenomenon.

EXAMPLE 10.4

We will use the data in Figure 10.5 to demonstrate the influence of sample variance. The figure shows the results from a research study comparing two treatments. Notice that the study uses the two separate samples, each with $n = 9$, and there is a 5-point mean difference between the two samples: $M = 8$ for treatment 1 and $M = 13$ for treatment 2. Also notice that there is no overlap between the two distributions; all of the scores for treatment 2 are higher than all of the scores for treatment 1. In this situation, there is a very clear and obvious difference between the two treatments.

For the hypothesis test, the data produce a pooled variance of 1.50 and an estimated standard error of 0.58. The *t* statistic is

$$t = \frac{\text{mean difference}}{\text{estimated standard error}} = \frac{5}{0.58} = 8.62$$

With $df = 16$, this value is far into the critical region (for $\alpha = .05$ or $\alpha = .01$), so we reject the null hypothesis and conclude that there is a significant difference between the two treatments.

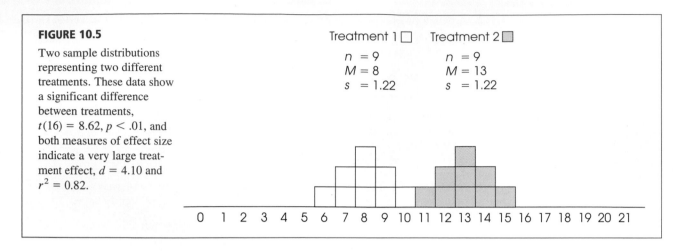

FIGURE 10.5

Two sample distributions representing two different treatments. These data show a significant difference between treatments, $t(16) = 8.62$, $p < .01$, and both measures of effect size indicate a very large treatment effect, $d = 4.10$ and $r^2 = 0.82$.

Now consider the effect of increasing sample variance. Figure 10.6 shows the results from a second research study comparing two treatments. To create these scores we simply increased the variance for the two samples shown in Figure 10.5. Notice that there are still $n = 9$ scores in each sample, and the two sample means are still $M = 8$ and $M = 13$. However, the sample variances have been greatly increased: Each sample now has $s^2 = 44.25$ as compared with $s^2 = 1.5$ for the data in Figure 10.5. Notice that the increased variance means that the scores are now spread out over a wider range, with the result that the two samples are mixed together without any clear distinction between them.

The absence of a clear difference between the two samples is supported by the hypothesis test. The pooled variance is 44.25, the estimated standard error is 3.14, and the independent-measures t statistic is

$$t = \frac{\text{mean difference}}{\text{estimated standard error}} = \frac{5}{3.14} = 1.59$$

With $df = 16$ and $\alpha = .05$, this value is not in the critical region. Therefore, we fail to reject the null hypothesis and conclude that there is no significant difference be-

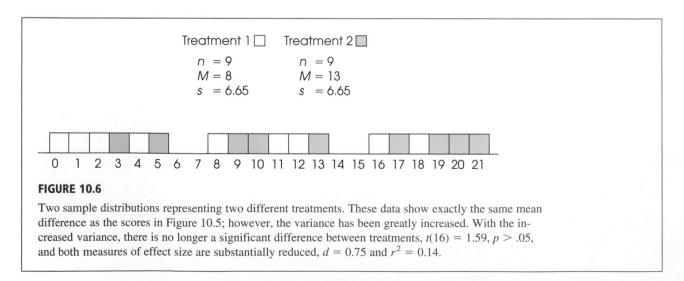

FIGURE 10.6

Two sample distributions representing two different treatments. These data show exactly the same mean difference as the scores in Figure 10.5; however, the variance has been greatly increased. With the increased variance, there is no longer a significant difference between treatments, $t(16) = 1.59$, $p > .05$, and both measures of effect size are substantially reduced, $d = 0.75$ and $r^2 = 0.14$.

tween the two treatments. Although there is still a 5-point difference between sample means (as in Figure 10.5), the 5-point difference is not significant with the increased variance. In general, large sample variance can obscure any mean difference that exists in the data and reduces the likelihood of obtaining a significant difference in a hypothesis test.

10.4 ASSUMPTIONS UNDERLYING THE INDEPENDENT-MEASURES t FORMULA

There are three assumptions that should be satisfied before you use the independent-measures t formula for hypothesis testing:

1. The observations within each sample must be independent (see page 210).

2. The two populations from which the samples are selected must be normal.

3. The two populations from which the samples are selected must have equal variances.

The first two assumptions should be familiar from the single-sample t hypothesis test presented in Chapter 9. As before, the normality assumption is the less important of the two, especially with large samples. When there is reason to suspect that the populations are far from normal, you should compensate by ensuring that the samples are relatively large.

The third assumption is referred to as *homogeneity of variance* and states that the two populations being compared must have the same variance. You may recall a similar assumption for both the z-score and the single-sample t. For those tests, we assumed that the effect of the treatment was to add a constant amount to (or subtract a constant amount from) each individual score. As a result, the population standard deviation after treatment was the same as it had been before treatment. We now are making essentially the same assumption but phrasing it in terms of variances.

Remember: Adding a constant to (or subtracting a constant from) each score does not change the standard deviation.

Recall that the pooled variance in the t-statistic formula is obtained by averaging together the two sample variances. It makes sense to average these two values only if they both are estimating the same population variance—that is, if the homogeneity of variance assumption is satisfied. If the two sample variances represent different population variances, then the average is meaningless. (*Note:* There is no meaning to the value obtained by averaging two unrelated numbers. For example, if I estimate your age and then estimate your weight, there is no point in averaging the two estimates.)

The importance of the homogeneity assumption increases when there is a large discrepancy between the sample sizes. With equal (or nearly equal) sample sizes, this assumption is less critical, but still important.

The homogeneity of variance assumption is quite important because violating this assumption can negate any meaningful interpretation of the data from an independent-measures experiment. Specifically, when you compute the t statistic in a hypothesis test, all the numbers in the formula come from the data except for the population mean difference, which you get from H_0. Thus, you are sure of all the numbers in the formula except one. If you obtain an extreme result for the t statistic (a value in the critical region), you conclude that the hypothesized value was wrong. But consider what happens when you violate the homogeneity of variance assumption. In this case, you have two questionable values in the formula (the hypothesized population value and the meaningless average of the two variances). Now if you obtain an extreme t statistic, you do not know which of these two values is responsible. Specifically, you cannot reject the hypothesis because it may have been the pooled variance that produced the extreme *t* statistic. Without satisfying the homogeneity of variance requirement, you cannot accurately interpret a *t* statistic, and the hypothesis test becomes meaningless.

If you suspect that the homogeneity of variance assumption is not justified, you should not compute an independent-measures *t* statistic using pooled variance. However, there is an alternative formula for the *t* statistic that does not pool the two sample variances and does not require the homogeneity assumption. The alternative formula is presented in Box 10.3.

HARTLEY'S *F*-MAX TEST
How do you know whether the homogeneity of variance assumption is satisfied? One simple test involves just looking at the two sample variances. Logically, if the two population variances are equal, then the two sample variances should be very similar. When the two sample variances are reasonably close, you can be reasonably confident that the homogeneity assumption has been satisfied and proceed with the test. However, if one sample variance is more than three or four times larger than the other, then there is reason for concern. A more objective procedure involves a statistical test to evaluate the homogeneity assumption. Although there are many different statistical methods for determining whether the homogeneity of variance assumption has been satisfied, Hartley's *F*-max test is one of the simplest to compute and to understand. An additional advantage is that this test can also be used to check homogeneity of variance with more than two independent samples. Later, in Chapter 13, we will examine statistical methods for comparing several different samples, and Hartley's test will be useful again.

The following example demonstrates the *F*-max test for two independent samples.

BOX 10.3   **AN ALTERNATIVE TO POOLED VARIANCE**

For years it has been traditional to compute the pooled variance to use in the formula for the independent-measures *t*. However, pooling the sample variances requires that the data satisfy the homogeneity of variance assumption. Specifically, the two distributions from which the samples are obtained must have equal variances. To avoid this assumption, many statisticians recommend an alternative formula for computing the independent-measures *t* statistic that does not require pooled variance or the homogeneity assumption. The alternative procedure consists of two steps:

1. The standard error is computed using the two separate sample variances as in Equation 10.1.

2. The value of degrees of freedom for the *t* statistic is adjusted using the following equation:

$$df = \frac{(V_1 + V_2)^2}{\dfrac{V_1^2}{n_1 - 1} + \dfrac{V_2^2}{n_2 - 1}} \quad \text{where} \quad V_1 = \frac{s_1^2}{n_1} \quad \text{and} \quad V_2 = \frac{s_2^2}{n_2}$$

Decimal values for *df* should be rounded down to the next integer.

Note: The adjustment to degrees of freedom will lower the value of *df*, which pushes the boundaries for the critical region farther out. Thus, the adjustment makes the test more demanding and therefore corrects for the same bias problem that the pooled variance attempts to avoid.

EXAMPLE 10.5   The *F*-max test is based on the principle that a sample variance provides an unbiased estimate of the population variance. Therefore, if the population variances are the same, the sample variances should be very similar. The procedure for using the *F*-max test is as follows:

1. Compute the sample variance, $s^2 = SS/df$, for each of the separate samples.

2. Select the largest and the smallest of these sample variances and compute

$$F\text{-max} = \frac{s^2(\text{largest})}{s^2(\text{smallest})}$$

A relatively large value for *F*-max indicates a large difference between the sample variances. In this case, the data suggest that the population variances are different and that the homogeneity assumption has been violated. On the other hand, a small value of *F*-max (near 1.00) indicates that the sample variances are similar and that the homogeneity assumption is reasonable.

3. The *F*-max value computed for the sample data is compared with the critical value found in Table B.3 (Appendix B). If the sample value is larger than the table value, you conclude that the variances are different and that the homogeneity assumption is not valid.

To locate the critical value in the table, you need to know

   a. k = number of separate samples. (For the independent-measures *t* test, $k = 2$.)

   b. $df = n - 1$ for each sample variance. The Hartley test assumes that all samples are the same size.

   c. The alpha level. The table provides critical values for $\alpha = .05$ and $\alpha = .01$. Generally a test for homogeneity would use the larger alpha level.

Example: Two independent samples each have $n = 10$. The sample variances are 12.34 and 9.15. For these data,

$$F\text{-max} = \frac{s^2(\text{largest})}{s^2(\text{smallest})} = \frac{12.34}{9.15} = 1.35$$

With $\alpha = .05$, $k = 2$, and $df = n - 1 = 9$, the critical value from the table is 4.03. Because the obtained *F*-max is smaller than this critical value, you conclude that the data do not provide evidence that the homogeneity of variance assumption has been violated.

Note: The goal for most hypothesis tests is to reject the null hypothesis to demonstrate a significant difference or a significant treatment effect. However, when testing for homogeneity of variance, the preferred outcome is to fail to reject H_0. Rejecting H_0 with the *F*-max test means that you have found a significant difference between the two population variances which means the homogeneity assumption is violated and you cannot compute the regular *t* statistic using pooled variance.

LEARNING CHECK

1. A researcher is using an independent-measures design to compare two treatment conditions with $n = 8$ participants in each treatment. If the results are evaluated using a one-tailed test with $\alpha = .05$, what is the critical value for *t*?

2. The homogeneity of variance assumption requires that the two sample variances be equal. (True or false?)

3. When you are using an *F*-max test to evaluate the homogeneity of variance assumption, you usually do not want to find a significant difference between the variances. (True or false?)

ANSWERS   1. With $df = 14$, the critical $t = 1.761$.

2. False. The assumption is that the two population variances are equal.

3. True. If there is a significant difference between the two variances, you cannot do the *t* test.

SUMMARY

1. The independent-measures *t* statistic uses the data from two separate samples to draw inferences about the mean difference between two populations or between two different treatment conditions.

2. The formula for the independent-measures *t* statistic has the same structure as the original *z*-score or the single-sample *t*:

$$t = \frac{\text{sample statistic} - \text{population parameter}}{\text{estimated standard error}}$$

For the independent-measures *t*, the sample statistic is the sample mean difference ($M_1 - M_2$). The population parameter is the population mean difference, ($\mu_1 - \mu_2$). The estimated standard error for the sample mean difference is computed by combining the errors for the two sample means. The resulting formula is

$$t = \frac{(M_1 - M_2) - (\mu_1 - \mu_2)}{s_{(M_1 - M_2)}}$$

where the estimated standard error is

$$s_{(M_1 - M_2)} = \sqrt{\frac{s_p^2}{n_1} + \frac{s_p^2}{n_2}}$$

The pooled variance in the formula, s_p^2, is the weighted mean of the two sample variances:

$$s_p^2 = \frac{SS_1 + SS_2}{df_1 + df_2}$$

This *t* statistic has degrees of freedom determined by the sum of the *df* values for the two samples:

$$df = df_1 + df_2$$
$$= (n_1 - 1) + (n_2 - 1)$$

3. For hypothesis testing, the null hypothesis states that there is no difference between the two population means:

$$H_0: \mu_1 = \mu_2 \quad \text{or} \quad \mu_1 - \mu_2 = 0$$

4. When a hypothesis test with an independent-measures *t* statistic indicates a significant difference, it is recommended that you also compute a measure of the effect size. One measure of effect size is Cohen's *d*, which is a standardized measured of the mean difference. For the independent-measures *t* statistic, Cohen's *d* is estimated as follows:

$$\text{estimated } d = \frac{M_1 - M_2}{\sqrt{s_p^2}}$$

A second common measure of effect size is the percentage of variance accounted for by the treatment effect. This measure is identified by r^2 and is computed as

$$r^2 = \frac{t^2}{t^2 + df}$$

5. Appropriate use and interpretation of the *t* statistic using pooled variance require that the data satisfy the homogeneity of variance assumption. This assumption stipulates that the two populations have equal variances. An informal test of the assumption can be made by verifying that the two sample variances are approximately equal. Hartley's *F*-max test provides a statistical technique for determining whether or not the data satisfy the homogeneity assumption. An alternative technique that avoids pooling variances and eliminates the need for the homogeneity assumption is presented in Box 10.3.

KEY TERMS

independent-measures
   research design

repeated-measures
   research design

between-subjects research
   design

within-subjects
   research design

independent-measures
   t statistic

estimated standard error
   of $M_1 - M_2$

pooled variance

homogeneity of variance

RESOURCES

There are a tutorial quiz and other learning exercises for Chapter 10 at the Wadsworth website, www.thomsonedu.com/psychology/gravetter. The site also provides access to a workshop entitled *Independent vs. Repeated t-tests* that compares the t test presented in this chapter with the repeated-measures test presented in Chapter 11. See page 27 for more information about accessing items on the website.

For those using WebTutor along with this book, there is a WebTutor section corresponding to this chapter. The WebTutor contains a brief summary of Chapter 10, hints for learning the concepts and the formulas for the independent-measures t test, cautions about common errors, and sample exam items including solutions.

SPSS

General instructions for using SPSS are presented in Appendix D. Following are detailed instructions for using SPSS to perform **The Independent-Measures t Test** presented in this chapter.

Data Entry

1. The scores are entered in what is called *stacked format,* which means that all the scores from *both samples* are entered in one column of the data editor (probably VAR00001). Enter the scores for sample #2 directly beneath the scores from sample #1 with no gaps or extra spaces.
2. Values are then entered into a second column (VAR00002) to identify the sample or treatment condition corresponding to each of the scores. For example, enter a 1 beside each score from sample #1 and enter a 2 beside each score from sample #2.

Data Analysis

1. Click **Analyze** on the tool bar, select **Compare Means,** and click on **Independent-Samples T Test.**
2. Highlight the column label for the set of scores (VAR0001) in the left box and click the arrow to move it into the **Test Variable(s)** box.
3. Highlight the label from the column containing the sample numbers (VAR0002) in the left box and click the arrow to move it into the **Group Variable** box.
4. Click on **Define Groups.**
5. Assuming that you used the numbers 1 and 2 to identify the two sets of scores, enter the values 1 and 2 into the appropriate group boxes.

6. Click **Continue.**

7. Click **OK.**

SPSS Output

SPSS produces a summary table showing the number of scores, the mean, the standard deviation, and the standard error for each of the two samples. A separate table presents the results of the hypothesis test. SPSS first conducts a test for homogeneity of variance, using Levene's test. This test should *not* be significant (you do not want the two variances to be different), so you want the reported Sig. value to be greater than .05. Next, the results of the independent-measures *t* test are presented using two different assumptions. The top row shows the outcome assuming equal variances, using the pooled variance to compute *t*. The second row does not assume equal variances and computes the *t* statistic using the alternative method presented in Box 10.3. Each row reports the calculated *t* value, the degrees of freedom, the level of significance (the *p* value or alpha level for the test), and the size of the mean difference. Finally, the output includes a report of the standard error for the mean difference (the denominator of the *t* statistic) and a 95% confidence interval for the mean difference. Confidence intervals are presented in Chapter 12 and provide an estimate of the size of the mean difference.

FOCUS ON PROBLEM SOLVING

1. As you learn more about different statistical methods, one basic problem will be deciding which method is appropriate for a particular set of data. Fortunately, it is easy to identify situations in which the independent-measures *t* statistic is used. First, the data will always consist of two separate samples (two *n*s, two *M*s, two *SS*s, and so on). Second, this *t* statistic is always used to answer questions about a mean difference: On the average, is one group different (better, faster, smarter) than the other group? If you examine the data and identify the type of question that a researcher is asking, you should be able to decide whether an independent-measures *t* is appropriate.

2. When computing an independent-measures *t* statistic from sample data, we suggest that you routinely divide the formula into separate stages rather than trying to do all the calculations at once. First, find the pooled variance. Second, compute the standard error. Third, compute the *t* statistic.

3. One of the most common errors for students involves confusing the formulas for pooled variance and standard error. When computing pooled variance, you are "pooling" the two samples together into a single variance. This variance is computed as a *single fraction,* with two *SS* values in the numerator and two *df* values in the denominator. When computing the standard error, you are adding the error from the first sample and the error from the second sample. These two separate errors add as *two separate fractions* under the square root symbol.

DEMONSTRATION 10.1

THE INDEPENDENT-MEASURES *t* TEST

In a study of jury behavior, two samples of participants were provided details about a trial in which the defendant was obviously guilty. Although group 2 received the same details as group 1, the second group was also told that some evidence had been withheld from the jury by the judge. Later the participants were asked to recommend a jail sentence. The length of term suggested by each participant is presented here. Is there a significant difference between the two groups in their responses?

Group 1	Group 2
4	3
4	7
3	8
2	5
5	4
1	7
1	6
4	8

for Group 1: $M = 3$ and $SS = 16$

for Group 2: $M = 6$ and $SS = 24$

There are two separate samples in this study. Therefore, the analysis will use the independent-measures t test.

STEP 1 State the hypothesis, and select an alpha level.

H_0: $\mu_1 - \mu_2 = 0$ (For the population, knowing evidence has been withheld has no effect on the suggested sentence.)

H_1: $\mu_1 - \mu_2 \neq 0$ (For the population, knowledge of withheld evidence has an effect on the jury's response.)

We will set the level of significance to $\alpha = .05$, two tails.

STEP 2 Identify the critical region.

For the independent-measures t statistic, degrees of freedom are determined by

$$df = n_1 + n_2 - 2$$
$$= 8 + 8 - 2$$
$$= 14$$

The t distribution table is consulted, for a two-tailed test with $\alpha = .05$ and $df = 14$. The critical t values are $+2.145$ and -2.145.

STEP 3 Compute the test statistic. As usual, we recommend that the calculation of the t statistic be separated into three stages.

Pooled variance For these data, the pooled variance equals

$$s_p^2 = \frac{SS_1 + SS_2}{df_1 + df_2} = \frac{16 + 24}{7 + 7} = \frac{40}{14} = 2.86$$

Estimated standard error Now we can calculate the estimated standard error for mean differences.

$$s_{(M_1 - M_2)} = \sqrt{\frac{s_p^2}{n_1} + \frac{s_p^2}{n_2}} = \sqrt{\frac{2.86}{8} + \frac{2.86}{8}} = \sqrt{0.358 + 0.358}$$
$$= \sqrt{0.716} = 0.85$$

The* t *statistic   Finally, the *t* statistic can be computed.

$$t = \frac{(M_1 - M_2) - (\mu_1 - \mu_2)}{s_{(M_1-M_2)}} = \frac{(3-6) - 0}{0.85} = \frac{-3}{0.85}$$

$$= -3.53$$

STEP 4   Make a decision about H_0, and state a conclusion.
The obtained *t* value of -3.53 falls in the critical region of the left tail (critical $t = \pm 2.145$). Therefore, the null hypothesis is rejected. The participants that were informed about the withheld evidence gave significantly longer sentences, $t(14) = -3.53$, $p < .05$, two tails.

DEMONSTRATION 10.2

EFFECT SIZE FOR THE INDEPENDENT-MEASURES *t*

We will estimate Cohen's *d* and compute r^2 for the jury decision data in Demonstration 10.1. For these data, the two sample means are $M_1 = 3$ and $M_2 = 6$, and the pooled variance is 2.86. Therefore, our estimate of Cohen's *d* is

$$\text{estimated } d = \frac{M_1 - M_2}{\sqrt{s_p^2}} = \frac{3-6}{\sqrt{2.86}} = \frac{3}{1.69} = 1.78$$

With a *t* value of $t = 3.53$ and $df = 14$, the percentage of variance accounted for is

$$r^2 = \frac{t^2}{t^2 + df} = \frac{(3.53)^2}{(3.53)^2 + 14} = \frac{12.46}{26.46} = 0.47 \quad (\text{or } 47\%)$$

PROBLEMS

1. Describe the general characteristics of a research study for which an independent-measures *t* would be the appropriate test statistic.

2. Several factors influence the value obtained for the independent-measures *t* statistic. Some factors affect the numerator of the *t* statistic and others influence the size of the estimated standard error in the denominator. For each of the following, indicate whether the factor influences the numerator or denominator of the *t* statistic and determine whether the effect would be to increase the value of *t* (farther from zero) or decrease the value of *t* (closer to zero). In each case, assume that all other factors remain constant.
   a. Increase the difference between the two sample means.
   b. Increase the size of the two samples.
   c. Increase the size of the sample variances.

3. One sample has $SS = 48$ and a second sample has $SS = 42$.
   a. Assuming that $n = 4$ for both samples, find each of the sample variances, and calculate the pooled variance. You should find that the pooled variance is exactly halfway between the two sample variances.
   b. Now assume that $n = 4$ for the first sample and $n = 8$ for the second. Find each of the sample variances, and calculate the pooled variance. You should find that the pooled variance is closer to the variance for the larger sample ($n = 8$).

4. One sample has $SS = 35$ and a second sample has $SS = 45$.
   a. Assuming that $n = 6$ for both samples, calculate each of the sample variances, then calculate the pooled variance. Because the samples are the same size, you should find that the pooled variance is exactly halfway between the two sample variances.

b. Now assume that $n = 6$ for the first sample and $n = 16$ for the second. Again, calculate the two sample variances and the pooled variance. You should find that the pooled variance is closer to the variance for the larger sample.

5. Describe the homogeneity of variance assumption, and explain why it is important for the independent-measures hypothesis test.

6. One sample has $n = 4$ scores with $SS = 100$ and a second sample has $n = 8$ scores with $SS = 140$.
   a. Calculate the pooled variance for the two samples.
   b. Calculate the estimated standard error for the sample mean difference.
   c. If the sample mean difference is 6 points, is this enough to reject the null hypothesis for a two-tailed test with $\alpha = .05$?
   d. If the sample mean difference is 9 points, is this enough to reject the null hypothesis for a two-tailed test with $\alpha = .05$?

7. One sample has $n = 15$ with $SS = 1660$, and a second sample has $n = 15$ with $SS = 1700$.
   a. Find the pooled variance for the two samples.
   b. Compute the estimated standard error for the sample mean difference.
   c. If the sample mean difference is 8 points, is this enough to reject the null hypothesis and conclude that there is a significant difference for a two-tailed test at the .05 level?
   d. If the sample mean difference is 12 points, is this enough to indicate a significant difference for a two-tailed test at the .05 level?
   e. Calculate the percentage of variance accounted for (r^2) to measure the effect size for an 8-point mean difference and for a 12-point mean difference.

8. What is measured by the estimated standard error that is used for the independent-measures t statistic?

9. For the independent-measures t test, the sample mean difference ($M_1 - M_2$) is not expected to provide a perfectly accurate estimate of the population mean difference ($\mu_1 - \mu_2$). On average, the discrepancy between the sample value and the population value is measured by the estimated standard error. For each of the following situations, compute the estimated standard error for the sample mean difference.
   a. One sample has $n = 10$ scores with $SS = 400$ and the second sample has $n = 10$ scores with $SS = 410$.
   b. One sample has $n = 7$ scores with $SS = 1064$ and the second sample has $n = 11$ scores with $SS = 1400$.

10. As noted on page 261, when the two population means are equal, the estimated standard error for the independent-measures t test provides a measure of how much difference to expect between two sample means. For each of the following situations, assume that $\mu_1 = \mu_2$ and calculate how much difference should be expected between the two sample means.
    a. One sample has $n = 8$ scores with $SS = 30$ and the second sample has $n = 8$ scores with $SS = 26$.
    b. One sample has $n = 8$ scores with $SS = 150$ and the second sample has $n = 4$ scores with $SS = 90$.

11. The local school district is comparing two methods for teaching mathematics to third-grade children. One class of $n = 20$ students is being taught by method A and another class of $n = 20$ is being taught by method B. At the end of the school year, all of the students take a standardized math achievement test. The scores for the students taught by method A produced a mean of $M = 75$ with $SS = 1800$, and the students taught by method B had a mean of $M = 87$ with $SS = 2000$.
    a. Compute the pooled variance for the two samples.
    b. Take the square root of the pooled variance to obtain a measure of the pooled standard deviation. Using the pooled standard deviation for both groups, you should be able to describe (or sketch) the two sample distributions. Based on your description (or sketch) does there appear to be a difference between the two teaching methods? (That is, are there two separate distributions or do all the scores seem to blend together into a single distribution?)
    c. Perform the hypothesis test, using a two-tailed test with $\alpha = .05$, to determine whether there is a significant difference between the two methods. Do the results of the test agree with your decision from part b?

12. Do you view a chocolate bar as delicious or as fattening? Your attitude may depend on your gender. In a study of American college students, Rozin, Bauer, and Catanese (2003) examined the importance of food as a source of pleasure versus concerns about food associated with weight gain and health. The following results are similar to those obtained in the study. The scores are a measure of concern about the negative aspects of eating.

Males	Females
$n = 6$	$n = 9$
$M = 31$	$M = 45$
$SS = 490$	$SS = 680$

a. Based on these results, is there a significant difference between the attitudes for males and for females? Use a two-tailed test with $\alpha = .05$.

b. Compute r^2, the percentage of variance accounted for by the gender difference, to measure effect size for this study.

13. A researcher is evaluating the pain-relief effectiveness of a new medication by comparing pain tolerance for a sample of $n = 10$ people who receive the medication with pain tolerance for a sample of $n = 10$ people who receive an inactive placebo. The scores for the placebo group produce a mean of $M = 38$ with $SS = 150$.

a. If the scores for the medication group have a mean of $M = 42$ with $SS = 210$, are the data sufficient to conclude that the medication has a significant effect? Use a two-tailed test with $\alpha = .05$.

b. In part a, the medication group averaged 4 points higher than the control group, indicating that the medication had a 4-point effect. If the effect was 8 points, so the medication group had a mean of $M = 46$ with $SS = 210$, would the data be sufficient to conclude that there is a significant effect? Again, use a two-tailed test with $\alpha = .05$.

14. An independent-measures research study was used to compare two treatment conditions with $n = 4$ participants in each treatment. The first treatment had a mean of $M = 58$ with a variance of $s^2 = 28$, and the second treatment had $M = 52$ and $s^2 = 36$. Do these data indicate a significant difference between the two treatments? Use a two-tailed test with $\alpha = .05$. (Note: Because the two samples are the same size, the pooled variance is simply the average of the two sample variances.)

15. The independent-measures study from the previous problem was repeated using larger samples with $n = 16$ participants in each treatment. Assuming that the larger samples produced exactly the same sample means and variances as were obtained in problem 16, are the data sufficient to conclude that there is a significant difference between treatments? Use a two-tailed test with $\alpha = .05$. (Again, the two samples are the same size, so the pooled variance is simply the average of the two sample variances.)

16. When people learn a new task, their performance usually improves when they are tested the next day, but only if they get at least 6 hours of sleep (Stickgold, Whidbee, Schirmer, Patel, & Hobson, 2000). The following data demonstrate this phenomenon. The participants learned a visual discrimination task on one day, and then were tested on the task the following day. Half of the participants were allowed to have at least 6 hours of sleep and the other half were kept awake all night. Is there a significant difference between the two conditions? Use a two-tailed test with $\alpha = .05$.

Performance Scores	
6-hours Sleep	No Sleep
$n = 8$	$n = 8$
$M = 72$	$M = 61$
$SS = 440$	$SS = 456$

17. Harris, Schoen, and Hensley (1992) conducted a research study showing how cultural experience can influence memory. They presented participants with two different versions of stories. One version contained facts or elements that were consistent with a U.S. culture and the second version contained material consistent with a Mexican culture. The results showed that the participants tended to make memory errors for the information that was not consistent with their own culture. Specifically, participants from Mexico either forgot or distorted information that was unique to U.S. culture, and participants from the United States forgot or distorted information that was unique to Mexican culture. The following data represent results similar to those obtained by Harris and Schoen. Is there a significant difference between the two groups? Use a two-tailed test with $\alpha = .05$.

Number of Errors Recalling the Mexican Story	
Participants from Mexico	Participants from the United States
$n = 20$	$n = 20$
$M = 4.1$	$M = 6.9$
$SS = 180$	$SS = 200$

18. In a study examining the permanence of academic learning, Bahrick and Hall (1991) tested knowledge of high school algebra for two groups of participants 50 years after they graduated from high school. One group had received additional college math courses and the other group had received no advanced math courses in college. The following table shows data similar to Bahrick and Hall's results. Do the data indicate a significant difference between the two groups? Use a two-tailed test with $\alpha = .05$.

No College Math	Additional Math
$n = 4$	$n = 8$
$M = 42$	$M = 50$
$SS = 100$	$SS = 140$

19. In a study comparing individual performance with group performance, Laughlin, Zander, Knievel, and Tan (2003) found that groups consistently outperformed the best of the individuals. The task was a letters-to-numbers problem in which an arithmetic problem was presented substituting a letter in place of each digit. Participants had to determine which letters corresponded to each number. Three-person groups competed with individuals and scores were compared for the groups and the best of the individuals. The dependent variable was the number of trials needed to solve each problem. The following data are similar to those obtained in the study.

Groups	Individuals
$n = 15$	$n = 15$
$M = 3.8$	$M = 4.7$
$SS = 15.4$	$SS = 18.2$

a. Based on these results, is there a significant difference between the performance for individuals versus the performance for groups? Use a two-tailed test with $\alpha = .05$.

b. Compute the estimated value of Cohen's d to measure effect size for this study.

20. Friedman and Rosenman (1974) have classified people into two categories: Type A personalities and Type B personalities. Type As are hard-driving, competitive, and ambitious. Type Bs are more relaxed, easy-going people. One factor that differentiates these two groups is the chronically high level of frustration experienced by Type As. To demonstrate this phenomenon, separate samples of Type As and Type Bs are obtained, with $n = 8$ in each sample. The individual participants are all given a frustration inventory measuring level of frustration. The average score for the Type As is $M = 84$ with $SS = 740$, and the Type Bs average $M = 71$ with $SS = 660$. Do these data indicate a significant difference between the two groups? Test at the .01 level of significance.

21. A researcher is comparing the effectiveness of two sets of instructions for assembling a child's bike. A sample of eight fathers is obtained. Half of the fathers are given one set of instructions and the other half receives the second set. The researcher measures how much time is needed for each father to assemble the bike. The scores are the number of minutes needed by each participant.

Instruction Set I	Instruction Set II
8	14
4	10
8	6
4	10

a. Is there a significant difference in time for the two sets of instructions? Use a two-tailed test at the .05 level of significance.

b. Calculate the estimated Cohen's d and r^2 to measure effect size for this study.

22. A researcher conducts an independent-measures research study and obtains $t = 2.070$ with $df = 28$.

a. How many individuals participated in the entire research study?

b. Using a two-tailed test with $\alpha = .05$, is there a significant difference between the two treatment conditions?

c. Compute r^2 to measure the percentage of variance accounted for by the treatment effect.

23. Stephen Schmidt (1994) conducted a series of experiments examining the effects of humor on memory. He collected a set of humorous sentences and then modified each one to produce a nonhumorous version of the same sentence. The humorous sentences were then presented to one group of participants and the nonhumorous sentences were presented to another group. Each group was then given a test to determine how many sentences they could recall. Data similar to those obtained by Schmidt are shown in the following table.

Number of Sentences Recalled							
Humorous Sentences				Nonhumorous Sentences			
4	5	2	4	5	2	4	2
6	7	6	6	2	3	1	5
2	5	4	3	3	2	3	3
3	3	5	3	4	1	5	3

a. Do the data provide enough evidence to conclude that humor has a significant effect on memory? Use a two-tailed test at the .05 level of significance.

b. Calculate Cohen's d to evaluate the size of the effect.

c. Calculate the percentage of variance explained by the treatment, r^2, to measure effect size.

24. In a classic study of problem solving, Duncker (1945) asked participants to mount a candle on a wall in an upright position so that it would burn normally. One group was given a candle, a book of matches, and a box of tacks. A second group was given the same items, except that the tacks and the box were presented separately as two distinct items. The solution to this problem involves using the tacks to mount the box on the wall, creating a shelf for the candle. Duncker reasoned that the first group of participants would have trouble seeing a "new" function for the box (a shelf) because it was already serving a function (holding tacks). For each participant, the amount of time to solve the problem was recorded. Data similar to Duncker's are as follows:

Time to Solve Problem (in sec.)	
Box of Tacks	Tacks and Box Separate
128	42
160	24
113	68
101	35
94	47

Do the data indicate a significant difference between the two conditions? Test at the .01 level of significance.

25. Siegel (1990) found that elderly people who owned dogs were less likely to pay visits to their doctors after upsetting events than were those who did not own pets. Similarly, consider the following hypothetical data. A sample of elderly dog owners is compared to a similar group (in terms of age and health) who do not own dogs. The researcher records the number of visits to the doctor during the past year for each person. The data are as follows:

Control Group	Dog Owners
12	8
10	5
6	9
9	4
15	6
12	
14	

a. Is there a significant difference in the number of doctor visits between dog owners and control subjects? Use a two-tailed test with $\alpha = .05$.

b. Calculate the value of r^2 (percentage of variance accounted for) for these data.

The *t* Test for Two Related Samples

Tools You Will Need

The following items are considered essential background material for this chapter. If you doubt your knowledge of any of these items, you should review the appropriate chapter or section before proceeding.

- Introduction to the *t* statistic (Chapter 9)
  - Estimated standard error
  - Degrees of freedom
  - *t* Distribution
  - Hypothesis tests with the *t* statistic

- Independent-measures design (Chapter 10)

11.1 OVERVIEW

In the previous chapter, we introduced the independent-measures research design as one strategy for comparing two treatment conditions or two populations. The independent-measures design is characterized by the fact that two separate samples are used to obtain the two sets of data that are to be compared. In this chapter, we examine an alternative strategy known as a *repeated-measures design* or a *within-subjects design*. With a repeated-measures design, two sets of data are obtained from the same sample of individuals. For example, a group of patients could be measured before therapy and then measured again after therapy. Or a group of individuals could be tested in a quiet, comfortable environment and then tested again in a noisy, stressful environment to examine the effects of stress on performance. In each case, notice that the same variable is being measured twice for the same set of individuals; that is, we are literally repeating measurements on the same sample.

DEFINITION

A **repeated-measures design** or a **within-subject design** is one in which a single sample of individuals is measured more than once on the same dependent variable. The same subjects are used in all of the treatment conditions.

The main advantage of a repeated-measures study is that it uses exactly the same individuals in all treatment conditions. Thus, there is no risk that the participants in one treatment are substantially different from the participants in another. With an independent-measures design, on the other hand, there is always a risk that the results are biased because the individuals in one sample are systematically different (smarter, faster, more extroverted, and so on) than the individuals in the other sample. At the end of this chapter, we present a more detailed comparison of repeated-measures studies and independent-measures studies, considering the advantages and disadvantages of both types of research.

Occasionally, researchers will try to approximate the advantages of a repeated-measures design by using a technique known as *matched subjects*. A matched-subjects design involves two separate samples, but each individual in one sample is matched one-to-one with an individual in the other sample. Typically, the individuals are matched on one or more variables that are considered to be especially important for the study. For example, a researcher studying verbal learning might want to be certain that the two samples are matched in terms of IQ and gender. In this case, a male participant with an IQ of 120 in one sample would be matched with another male with an IQ of 120 in the other sample. Although the participants in one sample are not *identical* to the participants in the other sample, the matched-subjects design at least ensures that the two samples are equivalent (or matched) with respect to some specific variables.

DEFINITION

In a **matched-subjects** study, each individual in one sample is matched with an individual in the other sample. The matching is done so that the two individuals are equivalent (or nearly equivalent) with respect to a specific variable that the researcher would like to control.

Of course, it is possible to match participants on more than one variable. For example, a researcher could match pairs of subjects on age, gender, race, and IQ. In this case, for example, a 22-year-old white female with an IQ of 115 who was in one sample would

A matched-subjects study occasionally is called a *matched-samples design*. But the subjects in the samples must be matched one-to-one before you can use the statistical techniques in this chapter.

be matched with another 22-year-old white female with an IQ of 115 in the second sample. The more variables that are used, however, the more difficult it is to find matching pairs. The goal of the matching process is to simulate a repeated-measures design as closely as possible. In a repeated-measures design, the matching is perfect because the same individual is used in both conditions. In a matched-subjects design, however, the best you can get is a degree of match that is limited to the variable(s) that are used for the matching process.

In a repeated-measures design, or a matched-subjects design, the data consist of two sets of scores with the scores in one set directly related, one-to-one, with the scores in the second set. For this reason, the two research designs are statistically equivalent and are grouped together under the common name *related-samples* designs (or correlated-samples designs). In this chapter, we focus our discussion on repeated-measures designs because they are overwhelmingly the more common example of related-groups designs. However, you should realize that the statistical techniques used for repeated-measures studies can be applied directly to data from a matched-subjects study.

Now we will examine the statistical techniques that allow a researcher to use the sample data from a repeated-measures study to draw inferences about the general population.

11.2   THE *t* STATISTIC FOR RELATED SAMPLES

The *t* statistic for related samples is structurally similar to the other *t* statistics we have examined. As we shall see, it is essentially the same as the single-sample *t* statistic covered in Chapter 9. One major distinction of the related-samples *t* is that it is based on difference scores rather than raw scores (*X* values). In this section, we examine difference scores and develop the *t* statistic for related samples.

DIFFERENCE SCORES: THE DATA FOR A RELATED-SAMPLES STUDY

Table 11.1 presents hypothetical data from a research study examining how reaction time is affected by a common, over-the-counter cold medication. The first score for each person (X_1) is a measurement of reaction time before the medication was administered. The second score (X_2) is a measure of reaction time one hour after taking the medication. Because we are interested in how the medication affects reaction time, we have computed the difference between the first score and the second score for each individual. The *difference scores*, or *D* values, are shown in the last column of the table.

TABLE 11.1

Reaction time measurements taken before and after taking an over-the-counter cold medication.

Person	Before Medication (X_1)	After Medication (X_2)	Difference *D*
A	215	210	−5
B	221	242	21
C	196	219	23
D	203	228	25

$$\Sigma D = 64$$

Note that M_D is the mean for the sample of *D* scores.

$$M_D = \frac{\Sigma D}{n} = \frac{64}{4} = 16$$

Notice that the difference scores measure the amount of change in reaction time for each person. Typically, the difference scores are obtained by subtracting the first score (before treatment) from the second score (after treatment) for each person:

$$\text{difference score} = D = X_2 - X_1 \tag{11.1}$$

Note that the sign of each D score tells you the direction of the change. Person A, for example, shows a decrease in reaction time after taking the medication (a negative change), but person B shows an increase (a positive change).

The sample of difference scores (D values) will serve as the sample data for the hypothesis test. To compute the t statistic, we will use the number of D scores (n) as well as the sample mean (M_D) and the value of SS for the sample of D scores.

THE HYPOTHESES FOR A RELATED-SAMPLES TEST

The researcher's goal is to use the sample of difference scores to answer questions about the general population. In particular, the researcher would like to know whether there is any difference between the two treatment conditions for the general population. Note that we are interested in a population of *difference scores*. That is, we would like to know what would happen if every individual in the population were measured in two treatment conditions (X_1 and X_2) and a difference score (D) were computed for everyone. Specifically, we are interested in the mean for the population of difference scores. We identify this population mean difference with the symbol μ_D (using the subscript letter D to indicate that we are dealing with D values rather than X scores).

As always, the null hypothesis states that for the general population there is no effect, no change, or no difference. For a repeated-measures study, the null hypothesis states that the mean difference for the general population is zero. In symbols,

$$H_0: \quad \mu_D = 0$$

Again, this hypothesis refers to the mean for the entire population of difference scores. According to this hypothesis, it is possible that some individuals will show positive difference scores and some will show negative scores, but the differences are random and unsystematic and will balance out to zero. In addition, the null hypothesis does not imply that the sample mean difference will be equal to zero. Remember, a sample mean is not expected to be *exactly* the same as the population mean, so even if $\mu_D = 0$ you would not expect M_D to be exactly equal to zero.

The alternative hypothesis states that there is a treatment effect that causes the scores in one treatment condition to be systematically higher (or lower) than the scores in the other condition. In symbols,

$$H_1: \quad \mu_D \neq 0$$

According to H_1, the difference scores for the individuals in the population tend to be systematically positive (or negative), indicating a consistent, predictable difference between the two treatments. See Box 11.1 for further discussion of H_0 and H_1.

THE *t* STATISTIC FOR RELATED SAMPLES

Figure 11.1 shows the general situation that exists for a repeated-measures hypothesis test. You may recognize that we are facing essentially the same situation that we encountered in Chapter 9. In particular, we have a population for which the mean and the standard deviation are unknown, and we have a sample that will be used to test a hypothesis about the unknown population. In Chapter 9, we introduced a t statistic that allowed us to use the sample mean as a basis for testing hypotheses about the population

BOX 11.1	ANALOGIES FOR H_0 AND H_1 IN THE REPEATED-MEASURES TEST

An Analogy for H_0: Intelligence is a fairly stable charac-teristic; that is, you do not get noticeably smarter or dumber from one day to the next. However, if we gave you an IQ test every day for a week, we probably would get seven different numbers. The day-to-day changes in your IQ score are caused by random factors such as your health, your mood, and your luck at guessing an-swers you do not know. Some days your IQ score is slightly higher, and some days it is slightly lower. On average, the day-to-day changes in IQ should balance out to zero. This is the situation that is predicted by the null hypothesis for a repeated-measures test. According to H_0, any changes that occur either for an individual or for a sample are just due to chance, and in the long run, they will average out to zero.

An Analogy for H_1: On the other hand, suppose we evaluate the effects of a fitness training program by measuring the strength of the muscles in your right arm. We will measure your grip strength every day over a 4-week period. We probably will find small differences in your scores from one day to the next, just as we did with the IQ scores. However, the day-to-day changes in grip strength will not be random. Although your grip strength may decrease occasionally, there should be a general trend toward increased strength as you go through the training program. Thus, most of the day-to-day changes should show an increase. This is the situa-tion that is predicted by the alternative hypothesis for the repeated-measures test. According to H_1, the changes that occur are systematic and predictable and will not average out to zero.

FIGURE 11.1

A sample of $n = 4$ people is se-lected from the population. Each individual is measured twice, once in treatment I and once in treatment II, and a difference score, *D*, is computed for each individual. This sample of difference scores is in-tended to represent the population. Note that we are using a sample of difference scores to represent a population of difference scores. Specifically, we are interested in the mean difference for the general population. The null hypothesis states that for the general popula-tion there is no consistent or sys-tematic difference between the two treatments, so the population mean difference is $\mu_D = 0$.

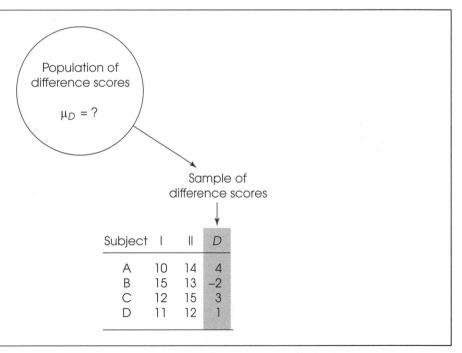

mean. This *t*-statistic formula will be used again here to develop the repeated-measures *t* test. To refresh your memory, the single-sample *t* statistic (Chapter 9) is defined by the formula

$$t = \frac{M - \mu}{s_M}$$

In this formula, the sample mean, *M,* is calculated from the data, and the value for the population mean, μ, is obtained from the null hypothesis. The estimated standard error, s_M, is also calculated from the data and provides a measure of how much difference is reasonable to expect between the sample mean and the population mean.

For the repeated-measures design, the sample data are difference scores and are identified by the letter *D,* rather than *X*. Therefore, we will use *D*s in the formula to emphasize that we are dealing with difference scores instead of *X* values. Also, the population mean that is of interest to us is the population mean difference (the mean amount of change for the entire population), and we identify this parameter with the symbol μ_D. With these simple changes, the *t* formula for the repeated-measures design becomes

$$t = \frac{M_D - \mu_D}{s_{M_D}} \tag{11.2}$$

In this formula, the *estimated standard error, s_{M_D},* is computed in exactly the same way as it is computed for the single-sample *t* statistic. To calculate the estimated standard error, the first step is to compute the variance (or the standard deviation) for the sample of *D* scores.

$$s^2 = \frac{SS}{n-1} = \frac{SS}{df} \qquad \text{or} \qquad s = \sqrt{\frac{SS}{df}}$$

The estimated standard error is then computed using the sample variance (or sample standard deviation) and the sample size, *n*.

$$s_{M_D} = \sqrt{\frac{s^2}{n}} \qquad \text{or} \qquad s_{M_D} = \frac{s}{\sqrt{n}}$$

Notice that all of the calculations are done using the difference scores (the *D* scores) and that there is only one *D* score for each subject. With a sample of *n* subjects, there will be exactly *n D* scores, and the *t* statistic will have $df = n - 1$. Remember that *n* refers to the number of *D* scores, not the number of *X* scores in the original data.

You should also note that the *repeated-measures* t *statistic* is conceptually similar to the *t* statistics we have previously examined:

$$t = \frac{\text{sample statistic} - \text{population parameter}}{\text{estimated standard error}}$$

In this case, the sample data are represented by the sample mean of the difference scores (M_D), the population parameter is the value predicted by H_0 ($\mu_D = 0$), and the amount of sampling error is measured by the standard error of the sample mean (s_{M_D}).

LEARNING CHECK

1. What characteristics differentiate a repeated-measures study from an independent-measures research study?

2. How are the difference scores (*D* values) obtained for a repeated-measures hypothesis test?

3. Stated in words and stated in symbols, what is the null hypothesis for a repeated-measures hypothesis test?

ANSWERS   1. A repeated-measures study obtains two sets of data from one sample by measuring each individual twice. An independent-measures study uses two separate samples to obtain two sets of data.

2. The difference score for each subject is obtained by subtracting the subject's first score from the second score. In symbols, $D = X_2 - X_1$.

3. The null hypothesis states that the mean difference for the entire population is zero. That is, if every individual is measured in both treatments and a difference score is computed for each individual, then the average difference score for the entire population will be equal to zero. In symbols, $\mu_D = 0$.

11.3 HYPOTHESIS TESTS AND EFFECT SIZE FOR THE REPEATED-MEASURES DESIGN

In a repeated-measures study, we are interested in whether there is a systematic difference between the scores in the first treatment condition and the scores in the second treatment condition. The hypothesis test will use the difference scores obtained from a sample to evaluate the overall mean difference, μ_D, for the entire population. According to the null hypothesis, there is no consistent or systematic difference between treatments and $\mu_D = 0$. The alternative hypothesis, on the other hand, says that there is a systematic difference and $\mu_D \neq 0$. The purpose of the hypothesis test is to decide between these two options.

The hypothesis test is based on the repeated-measures t formula,

$$t = \frac{M_D - \mu_D}{s_{M_D}}$$

The numerator measures the actual difference between the data (M_D) and the hypothesis (μ_D), and the denominator measures the standard difference that is expected if H_0 is true. A sample mean that is close to the hypothesized population mean will produce a t statistic near zero, and we will conclude that the data support the null hypothesis. On the other hand, a large value for the t statistic (either positive or negative) indicates that the data do not fit the hypothesis and will result in rejecting H_0.

The hypothesis test with the repeated-measures t statistic follows the same four-step process that we have used for other tests. The complete hypothesis-testing procedure is demonstrated in Example 11.1.

EXAMPLE 11.1   One technique to help people deal with phobias is to have them counteract the feared objects by using imagination to move themselves to a place of safety. In an experimental test of this technique, patients sit in front of a screen and are instructed to relax. Then, they are shown a slide of the feared object (for example, a picture of a spider). The patient signals the researcher as soon as feelings of anxiety begin to arise, and the researcher records the amount of time that the patient was able to endure looking at the slide. The patient then spends two minutes imagining a "safe scene" such as a tropical beach or a familiar room before the slide is presented again. Again the patient signals at the first feelings of anxiety. If patients can tolerate the feared object longer after the imagination exercise, it is viewed as a reduction in the phobia. The data in Table 11.2 summarize the times recorded for a sample of $n = 7$ patients. Do the data indicate that the imagination technique effectively alters phobias?

TABLE 11.2

The amount of time (in seconds) that patients are able to view a feared object before experiencing feelings of anxiety before and after imagination therapy.

Patient	Time Before Imagination	Time After Imagination	D	D^2
A	15	24	+9	81
B	10	23	+13	169
C	7	11	+4	16
D	18	25	+7	49
E	5	14	+9	81
F	9	14	+5	25
G	12	21	+9	81

$\Sigma D = 56$ $\Sigma D^2 = 502$

Because the data consist of difference scores (_D_ values) instead of _X_ scores, the formulas for the mean and _SS_ also use _D_ in place of _X_. However, you should recognize the computational formula for _SS_ that was introduced in Chapter 4.

$$M_D = \frac{\Sigma D}{n} = \frac{56}{7} = 8.00$$

$$SS = \Sigma D^2 - \frac{(\Sigma D)^2}{n} = 502 - \frac{(56)^2}{7}$$

$$= 502 - 448 = 54$$

STEP 1 State the hypotheses, and select the alpha level.

H_0: $\mu_D = 0$ (There is no change in the phobia.)

H_1: $\mu_D \neq 0$ (There is a change.)

For this test, we will use $\alpha = .01$ for the level of significance.

STEP 2 Locate the critical region. For this example, $n = 7$, so the _t_ statistic has $df = n - 1 = 6$. From the _t_ distribution table, you should find that the critical value for $\alpha = .01$ is ± 3.707. The critical region is shown in Figure 11.2.

STEP 3 Calculate the _t_ statistic. Table 11.2 shows the sample data and the calculations for $M_D = 8.00$ and $SS = 54$. As we have done with the other _t_ statistics, we will present the calculation of the _t_ statistic as a three-stage process.

First, compute the sample variance.

$$s^2 = \frac{SS}{n-1} = \frac{54}{6} = 9.00$$

FIGURE 11.2

The critical region for the _t_ distribution with $df = 6$ and $\alpha = .01$.

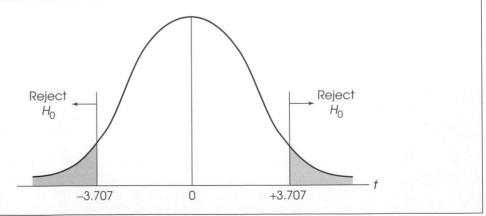

Reject H_0 Reject H_0

−3.707   0   +3.707   _t_

Next, use the sample variance to compute the estimated standard error.

$$s_{M_D} = \sqrt{\frac{s^2}{n}} = \sqrt{\frac{9.00}{7}} = \sqrt{1.29} = 1.14$$

Finally, use the sample mean (M_D) and the hypothesized population mean (μ_D) along with the estimated standard error to compute the value for the t statistic.

$$t = \frac{M_D - \mu_D}{s_{M_D}} = \frac{8.0 - 0}{1.14} = 7.02$$

STEP 4   Make a decision. The t value we obtained falls in the critical region (see Figure 11.2). The researcher rejects the null hypothesis and concludes that the imagination technique does affect the onset of anxiety when patients are exposed to feared objects.

MEASURING EFFECT SIZE FOR THE REPEATED-MEASURES *t*

As we noted with other hypothesis tests, whenever a treatment effect is found to be statistically significant, it is recommended that you also report a measure of the absolute magnitude of the effect. The two commonly used measures of effect size are Cohen's d and r^2, the percentage of variance accounted for. Using the data from Example 11.1, we will demonstrate how these two measures are used to calculate effect size.

In Chapters 8 and 9 we introduced Cohen's d as a standardized measure of the mean difference between treatments. The standardization process simply divides the actual mean difference by the standard deviation. For the repeated-measures t, the sample mean, M_D, is the best estimate of the actual mean difference, and the sample standard deviation (square root of sample variance) provides the best estimate of the actual standard deviation. Thus, we are able to estimate the value of d as follows:

Because we are measuring the size of the effect and not the direction, we have ignored the minus sign for the sample mean difference.

$$\text{estimated } d = \frac{\text{sample mean difference}}{\text{sample standard deviation}} = \frac{M_D}{s} \qquad (11.3)$$

For the repeated-measures study in Example 11.1, $M_D = 8$ and the sample variance was $s^2 = 9$, so the data produce

$$\text{estimated } d = \frac{M_D}{s} = \frac{8.00}{\sqrt{9}} = \frac{8.00}{3} = 2.67$$

Any value greater than 0.80 is considered to be a large effect, and these data are clearly in that category (see Table 8.2 on page 218).

Percentage of variance is computed using the obtained t value and the df value from the hypothesis test, exactly as was done for the independent-measures t (see page 269). For the data in Example 11.1, we obtain

$$r^2 = \frac{t^2}{t^2 + df} = \frac{(7.02)^2}{(7.02)^2 + 6} = \frac{49.28}{55.28} = 0.89 \quad \text{or} \quad 89\%$$

For these data, 89% of the variance in the difference scores is explained by the effect of the imagination technique. More specifically, the imagination produced an increase in tolerance for the feared stimulus so that the difference scores are consistently positive. Thus, the deviations from zero are largely explained by the treatment.

IN THE LITERATURE
REPORTING THE RESULTS OF A REPEATED-MEASURES *t* TEST

As we have seen in Chapters 9 and 10, the APA format for reporting the results of *t* tests consists of a concise statement that incorporates the *t* value, degrees of freedom, and alpha level. One typically includes values for means and standard deviations, either in a statement or a table (Chapter 4). For Example 11.1, we observed a mean difference of $M = 8.00$ with $s = 3$. Also, we obtained a *t* statistic of $t = 7.02$ with $df = 6$, and our decision was to reject the null hypothesis at the .01 level of significance. Finally, we measured effect size by computing the percentage of variance explained and obtained $r^2 = 0.89$. A published report of this study might summarize the results as follows:

> Imagining a safe scene increased the amount of time that patients could tolerate a feared stimulus before feeling anxiety by an average of $M = 8.00$ seconds with $SD = 3$. The treatment effect was statistically significant, $t(6) = 7.02, p < .01, r^2 = 0.89$.

When the hypothesis test is conducted with a computer program, the printout typically includes an exact probability for the level of significance. The *p*-value from the printout is then stated as the level of significance in the research report. However, the data from Example 11.1 produced a significance level of $p = .000$ in the computer printout. In this case, the probability was so small that the computer rounded it off to three decimal points and obtained a value of zero. In this situation you do not know the exact probability value and should report $p < .001$. ❏

DESCRIPTIVE STATISTICS AND THE HYPOTHESIS TEST

Often, a close look at the sample data from a research study will make it easier to see the size of the treatment effect and to understand the outcome of the hypothesis test. In Example 11.1 we obtained a sample of $n = 7$ individuals who produced a mean difference of $M_D = 8.00$ with a standard deviation of $s = 3$ points. The sample mean and standard deviation describe a set of scores centered at $M_D = 8.00$ with most of the scores located within 3 points of the mean. Figure 11.3 shows the actual set of difference scores that were obtained in Example 11.1. In addition to showing the scores in the sample, we have highlighted the position of $\mu_D = 0$; that is, the value specified in the null hypothesis. Notice that the scores in the sample are displaced away from zero. Specifically, the data are not consistent with a population mean of $\mu_D = 0$, which is why we rejected the null hypothesis. In addition, note that the sample mean is located more than 2 standard

---

FIGURE 11.3

The sample of difference scores from Example 11.1. The mean is $M_D = 8$ and the standard deviation is $s = 3$. The data show a consistent increase in scores (positive change) and suggest that $\mu_D = 0$ (no effect) is not a reasonable hypothesis.

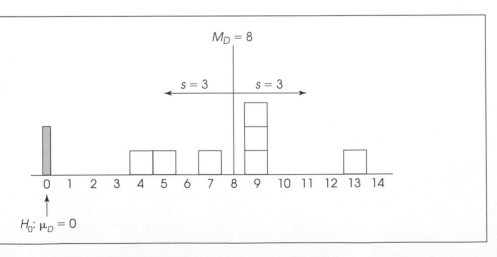

deviations below zero. This distance corresponds to the effect size measured by Cohen's $d = 2.67$. For these data, the picture of the sample distribution (see Figure 11.3) should help you to understand the measure of effect size and the outcome of the hypothesis test.

VARIABILITY AS A MEASURE OF CONSISTENCY FOR THE TREATMENT EFFECT

In a repeated-measures study, the variability of the difference scores becomes a relatively concrete and easy-to-understand concept. In particular, the sample variability describes the *consistency* of the treatment effect. For example, if a treatment consistently adds 7 or 8 points to each individual's score, then the set of difference scores will be clustered around a mean of $M = 8$ with relatively small variability. This is the situation we observed in Example 11.1 (see Figure 11.3), where all the patients increased their tolerance of images of their phobias after imagining a safe place. In this situation, with small variability, it is easy to see the treatment effect and the effect is likely to be significant.

Now consider what happens when variability is large. Figure 11.4 shows a set of difference scores that also have a mean of $M = 8$, but now the variability has been substantially increased. Again, we have highlighted the position of $\mu_D = 0$, which is the value specified in the null hypothesis. Notice that the high variability means that there is no consistent treatment effect. For some participants the treatment produces an increase in scores and for some it produces a decrease. Although these data have exactly the same mean difference ($M_D = 8$) that is shown in Figure 11.3, the mean difference is no longer significant. In the hypothesis test, the high variability increases the size of the estimated standard error and produces $t = 1.76$, which is not near the critical region. As we have noted several times, high variability can obscure patterns in the data. In general, the more variability there is in the sample data, the less likely you are to obtain a significant treatment effect.

DIRECTIONAL HYPOTHESES AND ONE-TAILED TESTS

In many repeated-measures and matched-subjects studies, the researcher has a specific prediction concerning the direction of the treatment effect. For example, in the study described in Example 11.1, the researcher expects the imagination exercise to increase the amount of time that phobia patients can tolerate viewing the feared object. This kind of directional prediction can be incorporated into the statement of the hypotheses, resulting in a directional, or one-tailed, hypothesis test. The following example demonstrates how the hypotheses and critical region are determined for a directional test.

EXAMPLE 11.2

We will reexamine the experiment presented in Example 11.1. The researcher is using a repeated-measures design to investigate the effect of imagining a safe scene on the

---

FIGURE 11.4

A sample of difference scores with a mean difference of $M_D = 8$ and a standard deviation of $s = 12$. The data do not show a consistent increase or decrease in scores, which means that $\mu_D = 0$ (no effect) is a reasonable hypothesis.

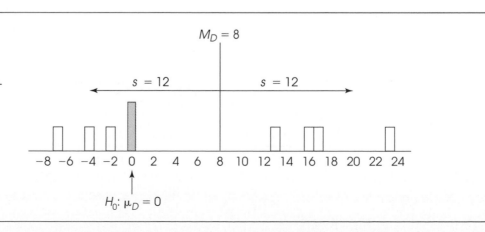

anxiety felt by patients suffering from phobias. The researcher predicts that the imagination technique will increase the amount of time that patients can tolerate viewing the feared stimulus.

STEP 1 State the hypothesis and select the alpha-level. For this example, the researcher predicts that imagining a safe scene will increase the amount of time that patients can tolerate the stimulus. The null hypothesis, on the other hand, says that the amount of time will not be increased but rather will be unchanged or even reduced after imagining a safe scene. In symbols,

$$H_0: \quad \mu \leq 0 \qquad \text{(The amount of time is not increased.)}$$

The alternative hypothesis says that the treatment does work. For this example, H_1 states that imagining a safe scene will increase the amount of time that patients can tolerate the feared stimulus.

$$H_1: \quad \mu > 0 \qquad \text{(The amount of time is increased.)}$$

STEP 2 Locate the critical region. As we demonstrated with the independent-measures *t* statistic (page 272), the critical region for a one-tailed test can be located using a two-stage process. Rather than trying to determine which tail of the distribution contains the critical region, you first look at the sample mean difference to verify that it is in the predicted direction. If not, then the treatment clearly did not work as expected and you can stop the test. If the change is in the correct direction, then the question is whether it is large enough to be significant. For this example, change is in the predicted direction (the researcher predicted an increase in time and the sample mean shows an increase). With $n = 7$, we obtain $df = 6$ and a critical value of $t = 3.143$ for a one-tailed test with $\alpha = .01$. Thus, any *t* statistic beyond 3.143 (positive or negative) will be sufficient to reject H_0.

STEP 3 Compute the *t* statistic. We calculated the *t* statistic in Example 11.1 and obtained $t = 7.02$.

STEP 4 Make a decision. The obtained *t* statistic is well beyond the critical boundary. Therefore, we reject H_0 and conclude that the imagination technique did significantly increase the amount of time that patients could tolerate viewing the feared stimulus.

LEARNING CHECK

1. A researcher would like to examine the effect of hypnosis on cigarette smoking. The researcher selects a sample of smokers ($n = 4$) for the study, and records the number of cigarettes smoked on the day prior to treatment. The participants are then hypnotized and given the posthypnotic suggestion that each time they light a cigarette, they will experience a horrible taste and feel nauseous. The data are as follows:

The Number of Cigarettes Smoked Before and After Hypnosis		
Participant	Before Treatment	After Treatment
1	19	12
2	35	36
3	20	13
4	31	24

    a. Find the difference scores (*D* values) for this sample.

    b. The difference scores have $M_D = -5$ and $SS = 48$. Do the data indicate that hypnosis has a significant effect on cigarette smoking? Test with $\alpha = .05$.

    c. Are the data sufficient to conclude that hypnosis significantly *reduces* cigarette smoking? Use a one-tailed test with $\alpha = .05$.

2. Compute the effect size using both Cohen's *d* and r^2 for the hypnosis treatment in Question 1.

3. A computer printout for a repeated-measures *t* test reports a *p* value of $p = .021$.

    a. Can the researcher claim a significant effect with $\alpha = .01$?

    b. Is the effect significant with $\alpha = .05$?

ANSWERS   **1. a.** The difference scores are $-7, 1, -7, -7$.

    b. For the data, $s^2 = 16$, $s_{M_D} = 2$, and $t = -2.50$. With $\alpha = .05$, we fail to reject H_0; the data do not provide sufficient evidence to conclude that hypnosis has a significant effect on cigarette smoking.

    c. For the directional test, the critical value is $t = -2.353$. The sample data produce a *t* statistic of $t = -2.50$, which is in the critical region. Reject H_0 and conclude that the hypnosis significantly reduced smoking.

2. For the data, $d = -5/4 = -1.25$ and $r^2 = 0.68$.

3. a. The exact *p* value, $p = .021$, is not less than $\alpha = .01$. Therefore, the effect is not significant for $\alpha = .01$ ($p > .01$).

    b. The *p* value is less than .05, so the effect is significant with $\alpha = .05$.

11.4   USES AND ASSUMPTIONS FOR REPEATED-MEASURES *t* TESTS

REPEATED-MEASURES VERSUS INDEPENDENT-MEASURES DESIGNS

In many research situations, it is possible to use either a repeated-measures study or an independent-measures study to compare two treatment conditions. The independent-measures design would use two separate samples (one in each treatment condition) and the repeated-measures design would use only one sample with the same individuals in both treatments. The decision about which design to use is often made by considering the advantages and disadvantages of the two designs. In general, the repeated-measures design has most of the advantages.

Number of subjects   A repeated-measures design typically requires fewer subjects than an independent-measures design. The repeated-measures design uses the subjects more efficiently because each individual is measured in both of the treatment conditions. This can be especially important when there are relatively few subjects available (for example, when you are studying a rare species or individuals in a rare profession).

Study changes over time   The repeated-measures design is especially well suited for studying learning, development, or other changes that take place over time. Remember that this design involves measuring individuals at one time and then returning to measure the same individuals at a later time. In this way, a researcher can observe behaviors that change or develop over time.

Individual differences   The primary advantage of a repeated-measures design is that it reduces or eliminates problems caused by individual differences. *Individual differ-*

ences are characteristics such as age, IQ, gender, and personality that vary from one individual to another. These individual differences can influence the scores obtained in a research study, and they can affect the outcome of a hypothesis test. Consider the data in Table 11.3 . The first set of data represents the results from a typical independent-measures study and the second set represents a repeated-measures study. Note that we have identified each participant by name to help demonstrate the effects of individual differences.

For the independent-measures data, note that every score represents a different person. For the repeated-measures study, on the other hand, the same participants are measured in both of the treatment conditions. This difference between the two designs has some important consequences.

1. We have constructed the data so that both research studies have exactly the same scores and they both show the same 5-point mean difference between treatments. In each case, the researcher would like to conclude that the 5-point difference was caused by the treatments. However, with the independent-measures design, there is always the possibility that the participants in treatment 1 have different characteristics than those in treatment 2. For example, the three participants in treatment 1 may be more intelligent than those in treatment 2 and their higher intelligence caused them to have higher scores. Note that this problem disappears with the repeated-measures design. Specifically, with repeated measures there is no possibility that the participants in one treatment are different from those in another treatment because the same participants are used in all the treatments.

2. Although the two sets of data contain exactly the same scores and have exactly the same 5-point mean difference, you should realize that they are very different in terms of the variance used to compute standard error. For the independent-measures study, you calculate the *SS* or variance for the scores in each of the two separate samples. Note that in each sample there are big differences between subjects. In treatment 1, for example, Bill has a score of 33 and John's score is only 18. These individual differences produce a relatively large sample variance and a large standard error. For the independent-measures study, the standard error is 5.77, which produces a *t* statistic of $t = 0.87$. For these data, the hypothesis test concludes that there is no significant difference between treatments.

In the repeated-measures study, the *SS* and variance are computed for the difference scores. If you examine the repeated-measures data in Table 11.3, you will see that the big differences between John and Bill that exist in treatment 1 and in treatment 2 are eliminated when you get to the difference scores. Because the individual differences are eliminated, the variance and standard error are dramatically reduced. For the repeated-measures study, the standard

TABLE 11.3

Hypothetical data showing the results from an independent-measures study and a repeated-measures study. The two sets of data use exactly the same numerical scores and they both show the same 5-point mean difference between treatments.

Independent-Measures Study (2 Separate Samples)		Repeated-Measures Study (Same Sample in both Treatments)		
Treatment 1	Treatment 2	Treatment 1	Treatment 2	D
(John) $X = 18$	(Sue) $X = 15$	(John) $X = 18$	(John) $X = 15$	−3
(Mary) $X = 27$	(Tom) $X = 20$	(Mary) $X = 27$	(Mary) $X = 20$	−7
(Bill) $X = 33$	(Dave) $X = 28$	(Bill) $X = 33$	(Bill) $X = 28$	−5
$M = 26$	$M = 21$			$M_D = -5$
$SS = 114$	$SS = 86$			$SS = 8$

error is 1.15 and the *t* statistic is $t = -4.35$. With the repeated-measures *t*, the data show a significant difference between treatments. Thus, one big advantage of a repeated-measures study is that it reduces variance by removing individual differences, which increases the chances of finding a significant result.

TIME-RELATED FACTORS AND ORDER EFFECTS

The primary disadvantage of a repeated-measures design is that the structure of the design allows for factors other than the treatment effect to cause a participant's score to change from one treatment to the next. Specifically, in a repeated-measures design, each individual is measured in two different treatment conditions *at two different times*. In this situation, outside factors that change over time may be responsible for changes in the participants' scores. For example, a participant's health or mood may change over time and cause a difference in the participant's scores. Outside factors such as the weather can also change and may have an influence on participants' scores. In general, a repeated-measures study must take place over time, and it is always possible that time-related factors (other than the two treatments) are responsible for causing changes in the participants' scores.

Also, it is possible that participation in the first treatment influences the individual's score in the second treatment. For example, participants may become tired or bored during the first treatment and, therefore, do not perform well in the second treatment. In this situation, the researcher would find a mean difference between the two treatments, however the difference is not caused by the treatments, instead it is caused by fatigue. Changes in scores that are caused by participation in an earlier treatment are called *order effects* and can distort the mean differences found in repeated-measures research studies.

Counterbalancing   One way to deal with time-related factors and order effects is to counterbalance the order of presentation of treatments. That is, the participants are randomly divided into two groups, with one group receiving treatment 1 followed by treatment 2, and the other group receiving treatment 2 followed by treatment 1. The goal of counterbalancing is to distribute any outside effects evenly over the two treatments. For example, if fatigue is a problem, then half of the participants (one of the two groups) will experience fatigue in treatment 1 and the other half will experience fatigue in treatment 2. Thus, fatigue influences the two treatments equally.

Finally, if there is reason to expect strong time-related effects or strong order effects, your best strategy is not to use a repeated-measures design. Instead, use independent-measures (or a matched-subjects design) so that each individual participates in only one treatment and is measured only one time.

ASSUMPTIONS OF THE RELATED-SAMPLES *t* TEST

The related-samples *t* statistic requires two basic assumptions:

1. The observations within each treatment condition must be independent (see page 210). Notice that the assumption of independence refers to the scores *within* each treatment. Inside each treatment, the scores are obtained from different individuals and should be independent of one another.

2. The population distribution of difference scores (*D* values) must be normal.

As before, the normality assumption is not a cause for concern unless the sample size is relatively small. In the case of severe departures from normality, the validity of the *t* test may be compromised with small samples. However, with relatively large samples ($n > 30$), this assumption can be ignored.

LEARNING CHECK

1. What assumptions must be satisfied for repeated-measures *t* tests to be valid?

2. Describe some situations for which a repeated-measures design is well suited.

3. How is a matched-subjects design similar to a repeated-measures design? How do they differ?

4. The data from a research study consist of 10 scores in each of two different treatment conditions. How many individual subjects would be needed to produce these data

   a. For an independent-measures design?

   b. For a repeated-measures design?

   c. For a matched-subjects design?

ANSWERS

1. The observations within a treatment are independent. The population distribution of *D* scores is assumed to be normal.

2. The repeated-measures design is suited to situations in which a particular type of subject is not readily available for study. This design is helpful because it uses fewer subjects (only one sample is needed). Certain questions are addressed more adequately by a repeated-measures design—for example, anytime one would like to study changes across time in the same individuals. Also, when individual differences are large, a repeated-measures design is helpful because it reduces the amount of this type of error in the statistical analysis.

3. They are similar in that the role of individual differences in the experiment is reduced. They differ in that there are two samples in a matched-subjects design and only one in a repeated-measures study.

4. a. The independent-measures design would require 20 subjects (two separate samples with *n* = 10 in each).

   b. The repeated-measures design would require 10 subjects (the same 10 individuals are measured in both treatments).

   c. The matched-subjects design would require 20 subjects (10 matched pairs).

SUMMARY

1. In a related-samples research study, the individuals in one treatment condition are directly related, one-to-one, with the individuals in the other treatment condition(s). The most common related-samples study is a repeated-measures design, in which the same sample of individuals is tested in all of the treatment conditions. This design literally repeats measurements on the same subjects. An alternative is a matched-subjects design, in which the individuals in one sample are matched one-to-one with individuals in another sample. The matching is based on a variable relevant to the study.

2. The repeated-measures *t* test begins by computing a difference between the first and second measurements for each subject (or the difference for each matched pair). The difference scores, or *D* scores, are obtained by

   $$D = X_2 - X_1$$

The sample mean, M_D, and sample variance, s^2, are used to summarize and describe the set of difference scores.

3. The formula for the repeated-measures *t* statistic is

   $$t = \frac{M_D - \mu_D}{s_{M_D}}$$

   In the formula, the null hypothesis specifies $\mu_D = 0$, and the estimated standard error is computed by

   $$s_{M_D} = \sqrt{\frac{s^2}{n}}$$

4. A repeated-measures design may be preferred to an independent-measures study when one wants to observe changes in behavior in the same subjects, as in learning or developmental studies. An important advantage of the repeated-measures design is that it removes or re-

duces individual differences, which in turn lowers sample variability and tends to increase the chances for obtaining a significant result.

5. For a repeated-measures design, effect size can be measured using either r^2 (the percentage of variance accounted for) or Cohen's d (the standardized mean difference). The value of r^2 is computed the same for both independent- and repeated-measures designs,

$$r^2 = \frac{t^2}{t^2 + df}$$

Cohen's d is defined as the sample mean difference divided by standard deviation for both repeated- and independent-measures designs. For repeated-measures studies, Cohen's d is estimated as

$$\text{estimated } d = \frac{M_D}{s}$$

KEY TERMS

repeated-measures design

within-subjects design

matched-subjects design

related-samples design

difference scores

repeated-measures
t statistic

estimated standard error for M_D

individual differences

order effects

RESOURCES

There are a tutorial quiz and other learning exercises for Chapter 11 at the Wadsworth website, www.thomsonedu.com/psychology/gravetter. The site also provides access to a workshop entitled *Independent vs. Repeated t-tests* that compares the *t* test presented in this chapter with the independent-measures test that was presented in Chapter 10. See page 27 for more information about accessing items on the website.

For those using WebTutor along with this book, there is a WebTutor section corresponding to this chapter. The WebTutor contains a brief summary of Chapter 11, hints for learning the concepts and the formulas for the repeated-measures *t* test, cautions about common errors, and sample exam items including solutions.

SPSS

General instructions for using SPSS are presented in Appendix D. Following are detailed instructions for using SPSS to perform **The Repeated-Measures *t* Test** presented in this chapter.

Data Entry

1. Enter the data into two columns (VAR0001 and VAR0002) in the data editor with the first score for each participant in the first column and the second score in the second column. The two scores for each participant must be in the same row.

Data Analysis

1. Click **Analyze** on the tool bar, select **Compare Means,** and click on **Paired-Samples T Test.**
2. Highlight both of the column labels for the two data columns (click on one, then click on the second) and click the arrow to move them into the **Paired Variables** box.
3. Click **OK.**

SPSS Output

SPSS produces a summary table showing descriptive statistics for each of the two sets of scores (the mean, the number of scores, the standard deviation, and the standard error for the mean). The second table shows the correlation between the two sets of scores. Correlations are presented in Chapter 15. The final table presents the results of the repeated-measures *t* test. The output shows the mean and the standard deviation for the difference scores, and the standard error for the mean difference. The table includes a 95% confidence interval that estimates the size of the mean difference (confidence intervals are presented in Chapter 12). Finally, the table reports the value for *t,* the value for *df,* and the level of significance (the *p* value or alpha level for the test).

FOCUS ON PROBLEM SOLVING

1. Once data have been collected, we must then select the appropriate statistical analysis. How can you tell whether the data call for a repeated-measures *t* test? Look at the experiment carefully. Is there only one sample of subjects? Are the same subjects tested a second time? If your answers are yes to both of these questions, then a repeated-measures *t* test should be done. There is only one situation in which the repeated-measures *t* can be used for data from two samples, and that is for *matched-subjects* studies (page 288).

2. The repeated-measures *t* test is based on difference scores. In finding difference scores, be sure you are consistent with your method. That is, you may use either $X_2 - X_1$ or $X_1 - X_2$ to find *D* scores, but you must use the same method for all subjects.

DEMONSTRATION 11.1

A REPEATED-MEASURES *t* TEST

A major oil company would like to improve its tarnished image following a large oil spill. Its marketing department develops a short television commercial and tests it on a sample of $n = 7$ participants. People's attitudes about the company are measured with a short questionnaire, both before and after viewing the commercial. The data are as follows:

Person	X_1 (Before)	X_2 (After)	D (Difference)	
A	15	15	0	
B	11	13	+2	$\Sigma D = 21$
C	10	18	+8	
D	11	12	+1	$M_D = 21/7 = 3.00$
E	14	16	+2	
F	10	10	0	$SS = 74$
G	11	19	+8	

Was there a significant change? Note that participants are being tested twice—once before and once after viewing the commercial. Therefore, we have a repeated-measures experiment.

STEP 1   State the hypotheses, and select an alpha level.

The null hypothesis states that the commercial has no effect on people's attitude, or in symbols,

$$H_0: \quad \mu_D = 0 \quad \text{(The mean difference is zero.)}$$

The alternative hypothesis states that the commercial does alter attitudes about the company, or

$$H_1: \quad \mu_D \neq 0 \quad \text{(There is a mean change in attitudes.)}$$

For this demonstration, we will use an alpha level of .05 for a two-tailed test.

STEP 2   Locate the critical region.

Degrees of freedom for the repeated-measures t test are obtained by the formula

$$df = n - 1$$

For these data, degrees of freedom equal

$$df = 7 - 1 = 6$$

The t distribution table is consulted for a two-tailed test with $\alpha = .05$ for $df = 6$. The critical t values for the critical region are $t = \pm 2.447$.

STEP 3   Compute the test statistic.

Once again, we suggest that the calculation of the t statistic be divided into a three-part process.

*Variance for the **D** scores*   The variance for the sample of D scores is

$$s^2 = \frac{SS}{n - 1} = \frac{74}{6} = 12.33$$

Estimated standard error for $\mathbf{M_D}$ The estimated standard error for the sample mean difference is computed as follows:

$$s_{M_D} = \sqrt{\frac{s^2}{n}} = \sqrt{\frac{12.33}{7}} = \sqrt{1.76} = 1.33$$

*The repeated-measures **t** statistic*   Now we have the information required to calculate the t statistic.

$$t = \frac{M_D - \mu_D}{s_{M_D}} = \frac{3 - 0}{1.33} = 2.26$$

STEP 4   Make a decision about H_0, and state the conclusion.

The obtained t value is not extreme enough to fall in the critical region. Therefore, we fail to reject the null hypothesis. We conclude that there is no evidence that the commercial will change people's attitudes, $t(6) = 2.26$, $p > .05$, two-tailed. (Note that we state that p is *greater than* .05 because we failed to reject H_0.)

DEMONSTRATION 11.2

EFFECT SIZE FOR THE REPEATED-MEASURES *t*

We will estimate Cohen's *d* and calculate r^2 for the data in Demonstration 11.1. The data produced a sample mean difference of $M_D = 3.00$ with a sample variance of $s^2 = 12.33$. Based on these values, Cohen's *d* is

$$\text{estimated } d = \frac{\text{mean difference}}{\text{standard deviation}} = \frac{M_D}{s} = \frac{3.00}{\sqrt{12.33}} = \frac{3.00}{3.51} = 0.86$$

The hypothesis test produced $t = 2.26$ with $df = 6$. Based on these values,

$$r^2 = \frac{t^2}{t^2 + df} = \frac{(2.26)^2}{(2.26)^2 + 6} = \frac{5.11}{11.11} = 0.46 \quad (\text{or } 46\%)$$

PROBLEMS

1. Explain the difference between a matched-subjects design and a repeated-measures design.

2. A researcher conducts an experiment comparing two treatment conditions and obtains data with 10 scores for each treatment condition.
   a. If the researcher used an independent-measures design, how many subjects participated in the experiment?
   b. If the researcher used a repeated-measures design, how many subjects participated in the experiment?
   c. If the researcher used a matched-subjects design, how many subjects participated in the experiment?

3. For the following studies, indicate whether a repeated-measures *t* test is the appropriate analysis. Explain your answers.
   a. A researcher is comparing academic performance for college students who participate in organized sports and those who do not.
   b. A researcher is testing the effectiveness of a new blood-pressure medication by comparing blood-pressure readings before and after each participant takes the medication.
   c. A researcher is examining how light intensity influences color perception. A sample of 50 college students is obtained and each student is asked to judge the differences between color patches under conditions of bright light and dim light.

4. What is the primary advantage of a repeated-measures design over an independent-measures design?

5. A sample of $n = 15$ difference scores from a repeated-measures study has $SS = 840$.
   a. Would a sample mean difference of $M_D = 3$ be large enough to reject the null hypothesis for a two-tailed test with $\alpha = .05$?

   b. Would a sample mean difference of $M_D = 6$ be large enough to reject the null hypothesis for a two-tailed test with $\alpha = .05$?

6. In Chapter 8 (page 191) we presented an example of a research study examining how an antioxidant supplement (such as blueberries) affects the cognitive functioning of elderly adults. In the example, we compared one sample of adults who received the blueberry supplement with the general population. An alternative approach to the research question is to use a repeated-measures design. Suppose a researcher obtains a sample of $n = 16$ adults who are between the ages of 65 and 75. The researcher uses a standardized test to measure cognitive performance for each individual. The participants then begin a 2-month program in which they receive daily doses of the blueberry supplement. At the end of the 2-month period, the researcher again measures cognitive performance for each participant. The results show an average increase in performance of $M_D = 7.4$ with $SS = 1215$. Does this result support the conclusion that the antioxidant supplement has a significant effect on cognitive performance? Use a two-tailed test with $\alpha = .05$.

7. The results of two repeated-measures studies are summarized as follows: The first study produces a sample with $M_D = 4$ and $s = 10$, and the second study produces $M_D = 4$ and $s = 2$. Assume $n = 10$ for both samples. In each case, the sample mean and sample standard deviation should provide enough information for you to visualize (or sketch) the sample distribution (see Figure 11.3).
   a. For each sample, identify where a value of zero is located. (Is zero in the middle of the sample or is it an extreme, unrepresentative value for the sample?)

b. Assuming that the samples are representative of their populations, which of the two samples is more likely to have come from a population with a mean difference of $\mu_D = 0$? (Which sample is more likely to accept a null hypothesis that $\mu_D = 0$?)

8. The results of two repeated-measures studies are summarized as follows: The first study produces a sample with $M_D = 4$ and $s = 9$, and the second study produces $M_D = 12$ and $s = 9$. Assume $n = 10$ for both samples. In each case, the sample mean and sample standard deviation should provide enough information for you to visualize (or sketch) the sample distribution (see Figure 11.3).
   a. For each sample, identify where a value of zero is located. (Is zero in the middle of the sample or is it an extreme, unrepresentative value for the sample?)
   b. Assuming that the samples are representative of their populations, which of the two samples is more likely to have come from a population with a mean difference of $\mu_D = 0$? (Which sample is more likely to accept a null hypothesis that $\mu_D = 0$?)

9. A recent report indicates that physically attractive people are also perceived as being more intelligent (Eagly, Ashmore, Makhijani, & Longo, 1991). As a demonstration of this phenomenon, a researcher obtained a set of 10 photographs, 5 showing men who were judged to be attractive and 5 showing men who were judged as unattractive. The photographs were shown to a sample of $n = 25$ college students and the students were asked to rate the intelligence of the person in the photo on a scale from 1 to 10. For each student, the researcher determined the average rating for the 5 attractive photos and the average for the 5 unattractive photos, and then computed the difference between the two scores. For the entire sample, the average difference was $M_D = 2.7$ (attractive photos rated higher) with $s = 2.00$. Are the data sufficient to conclude that there was a significant difference in perceived intelligence for the two sets of photos? Use a two-tailed test at the .05 level of significance.

10. A sample of difference scores from a repeated-measures experiment has a mean of $M_D = 5$ and a variance of $s^2 = 64$.
   a. If $n = 4$, is this sample sufficient to reject the null hypothesis using a two-tailed test with $\alpha = .05$?
   b. Would you reject H_0 if $n = 16$? Again, assume a two-tailed test with $\alpha = .05$.

11. A researcher uses a repeated-measures study to evaluate the effectiveness of magnetic therapy for treating chronic pain. A sample of $n = 9$ patients is obtained, each of whom has been treated for severe elbow pain for at least 1 year. Each patient is given a questionnaire to evaluate the current level of pain. The patients are then instructed to wear a magnetic band around their elbows for 2 weeks. After the 2-week period, the patients again complete the questionnaire evaluating pain. For this sample, the reported level of pain decreased by an average of $M_D = 12.5$ points with $SS = 1152$. Do these data indicate a significant change in the level of pain? Use a two-tailed test with $\alpha = .01$.

12. Research has shown that losing even one night's sleep can have a significant effect on performance of complex tasks such as problem solving (Linde & Bergstroem, 1992). To demonstrate this phenomenon, a sample of $n = 20$ college students was given a problem-solving task at noon on one day and again at noon on the following day. The students were not permitted any sleep between the two tests. For each student, the difference between the first and second score was recorded. For this sample, the students averaged $M_D = 6.3$ points better on the first test, with SS for the difference scores equal to 2375.
   a. Do the data demonstrate a significant change in problem-solving ability? Use a two-tailed test with $\alpha = .05$.
   b. Compute an estimated d to measure the size of the effect.

13. Strack, Martin, and Stepper (1988) reported that people rate cartoons as funnier when holding a pen in their teeth (which forced them to smile) than when holding a pen in their lips (which forced them to frown). A researcher attempted to replicate this result using a sample of $n = 16$ adults between the ages of 40 and 45. For each person, the researcher recorded the difference between the rating obtained while smiling and the rating obtained while frowning. On average the cartoons were rated as funnier when the participants were smiling, with an average difference of $M_D = 3.6$ with $SS = 960$.
   a. Do the data indicate that the cartoons are rated significantly funnier when the participants are smiling? Use a one-tailed test with $\alpha = .05$.
   b. Compute r^2 to measure the size of the treatment effect.

14. The following data are from a research study comparing two treatment conditions. Do the data indicate a significant difference between treatments? Use a two-tailed test with $\alpha = .05$.
   a. For the first test, assume the data are from an independent-measures study using two separate samples.
   b. For the second test, assume the data are from a repeated-measures study using the same sample of $n = 5$ participants in both treatments.

c. Explain why the 2-point mean difference is significant for one test but not for the other.

Treatment 1	Treatment 2
10	11
2	5
1	2
15	18
7	9
$M = 7$	$M = 9$
$SS = 134$	$SS = 150$

15. A researcher investigates whether single people who own pets are generally happier than singles without pets. A group of non-pet owners is compared to pet owners using a mood inventory. The pet owners are matched one to one with the non-pet owners for income, number of close friendships, and general health. The data are as follows:

Matched Pair	Non-pet Owner	Pet Owner
A	10	15
B	9	9
C	11	10
D	11	19
E	5	17
F	9	15

Is there a significant difference in the mood scores for non-pet owners versus pet owners? Test with $\alpha = .05$ for two tails.

16. The stimulant Ritalin has been shown to increase attention span and improve academic performance in children with ADHD (Evans, Pelham, Smith, et al., 2001). To demonstrate the effectiveness of the drug, a researcher selects a sample of $n = 25$ children diagnosed with the disorder and measures each child's attention span before and after taking the drug. The data show an average increase of attention span of $M_D = 6.8$ minutes with a standard deviation of $s = 5.5$.
   a. Is this result sufficient to conclude that Ritalin has a significant effect on attention span? Use a two-tailed test with $\alpha = .01$.
   b. Compute r^2 and estimate Cohen's d to measure the effect size of the drug.

17. A researcher studies the effect of cognitive psychotherapy on positive self-regard. The number of positive statements made about oneself is recorded for each participant during the first meeting. After

8 weekly therapy sessions, the measures are repeated for each person. For the following data,
   a. Calculate the difference scores and M_D.
   b. Compute SS, sample variance, and estimated standard error.
   c. Is there a significant treatment effect? Use $\alpha = .05$, two tails.

Participant	Before Treatment	After Treatment
A	7	10
B	6	13
C	9	12
D	5	8

18. Another researcher did the exact same study as that described in problem 17, and the data are presented here.
   a. Calculate the difference scores and M_D. Compare the results to part a of the previous problem.
   b. Compute SS, sample variance, and estimated standard error. Compare these results to those of the previous problem.
   c. Is there a significant treatment effect? Use $\alpha = .05$, two tails.
   d. Compare the outcome of part c to that of the previous problem. Explain why the outcomes differ.

Participant	Before Treatment	After Treatment
A	7	3
B	6	14
C	9	11
D	5	15

19. The previous two problems both have the same sample mean difference of $M = 4$ points. However, the two samples have different variances and produce different outcomes for the hypothesis test.
   a. Compute the estimated Cohen's d and r^2 to measure effect size for both sets of data.
   b. Explain how effect size is related to sample variance.

20. A researcher for a cereal company wanted to demonstrate the health benefits of eating oatmeal. A sample of 9 volunteers was obtained and each participant ate a fixed diet without any oatmeal for 30 days. At the end of the 30-day period, cholesterol was measured for each individual. Then the participants began a second 30-day period in which they repeated exactly the same diet except that they added 2 cups of oatmeal each day. After the second 30-day period, cholesterol levels were measured again. The scores for the 9 participants are as

follows: 0, −2, −11, −15, −12, +3, −9, −9, −8 (a negative scores indicates a decrease in cholesterol level).

Are the data sufficient to demonstrate a significant change in cholesterol level after 30 days with an oatmeal diet? Use a two-tailed test with $\alpha = .05$.

21. The level of lymphocytes (white blood cells) in the blood is associated with susceptibility to disease—lower levels indicate greater susceptibility. In a study of the effects of stress on physical well-being, Schleifer and colleagues (1983) recorded the lymphocyte counts for men who were going through a period of extreme emotional stress (the death of a spouse). For a sample of $n = 20$ men, the lymphocyte counts dropped an average of $M_D = 0.09$ with $s = 0.08$. Do these data indicate a significant change? Test at the .05 level of significance.

22. At the Olympic level of competition, even the smallest factors can make the difference between winning and losing. For example, Pelton (1983) has shown that Olympic marksmen shoot much better if they fire between heartbeats, rather than squeezing the trigger during a heartbeat. The small vibration caused by a heartbeat seems to be sufficient to affect the marksman's aim. The following hypothetical data demonstrate this phenomenon. A sample of $n = 6$ Olympic marksmen fires a series of rounds while a researcher records heartbeats. For each marksman, a score is recorded for shots fired during heartbeats and for shots fired between heartbeats. Do the data indicate a significant difference? Test with $\alpha = .05$.

Participant	During Heartbeats	Between Heartbeats
A	93	98
B	90	94
C	95	96
D	92	91
E	95	97
F	91	97

23. Sensory isolation chambers are used to examine the effects of mild sensory deprivation. The chamber is a dark, silent tank where participants float on heavily salted water and are thereby deprived of nearly all external stimulation. Sensory deprivation produces deep relaxation and has been shown to produce temporary increases in sensitivity for vision, hearing, touch, and even taste. The following data represent hearing threshold scores for a group of participants who were tested before and immediately after 1 hour of deprivation. A lower score indicates more sensitive hearing. Do these data indicate that deprivation has a significant effect on hearing threshold? Test at the .05 level of significance.

Participant	Before	After
A	31	30
B	34	31
C	29	29
D	33	29
E	35	32
F	32	34
G	35	28

24. There is some evidence that men have an enzyme that begins to metabolize alcohol in the stomach. Women have lower levels of the enzyme, which means that alcohol passes directly through the stomach and into the bloodstream. As a result, women have a stronger reaction to alcohol and are affected more quickly (Lieber, 1990). To evaluate this phenomenon, a researcher obtains a sample of $n = 10$ men and a corresponding sample of $n = 10$ women. Each individual is tested on a driving simulator task to measure mental alertness. Then, equivalent doses of alcohol are given to each participant (adjusting for body weight), and the driving simulator test is repeated 30 minutes later.
a. For the sample of men, performance on the simulator task declined by an average of $M_D = 2.9$ points with $s = 4.1$. Is this a statistically significant change? Use a two-tailed test with $\alpha = .05$.
b. For the women, performance declined by an average of $M_D = 6.4$ points with $s = 5.2$. Is this a statistically significant change? Use a two-tailed test with $\alpha = .05$.

25. A variety of research results suggest that visual images interfere with visual perception. In one study, Segal and Fusella (1970) had participants watch a screen, looking for brief presentations of a small blue arrow. On some trials, the participants were also asked to form a mental image (for example, imagine a volcano). The results show that participants made more errors while forming images than while not forming images. Data similar to the Segal and Fusella results are as follows. Do the data indicate a significant difference between the two conditions? Use a two-tailed test with $\alpha = 05$.

Participant	Errors with Image	Errors without Image
A	14	4
B	9	2
C	12	10
D	7	8
E	10	6
F	8	6

CHAPTER

12

Estimation

Tools You Will Need

The following items are considered essential background material for this chapter. If you doubt your knowledge of any of these items, you should review the appropriate chapter or section before proceeding.

- Single-sample t statistic (Chapter 9)

- Independent-measures t statistic (Chapter 10)

- Related-samples t statistic (Chapter 11)

12.1 AN OVERVIEW OF ESTIMATION

In Chapter 8, we introduced hypothesis testing as a statistical procedure that allows researchers to use sample data to draw inferences about populations. Hypothesis testing is probably the most frequently used inferential technique, but it is not the only one. In this chapter, we examine the process of estimation, which provides researchers with an additional method for using samples as the basis for drawing general conclusions about populations.

The basic principle underlying all of inferential statistics is that samples are representative of the populations from which they come. The most direct application of this principle is the use of sample values as estimators of the corresponding population values—that is, using statistics to estimate parameters. This process is called *estimation*.

DEFINITION
> The inferential process of using sample statistics to estimate population parameters is called **estimation.**

The use of samples to estimate populations is quite common. For example, you often hear news reports such as "Sixty percent of the general public approves of the president's new budget plan." Clearly, the percentage that is reported was obtained from a sample (they don't ask everyone's opinion), and this sample statistic is being used as an estimate of the population parameter.

We already have encountered estimation in earlier sections of this book. For example, the formula for sample variance (Chapter 4) was developed so that the sample value would give an accurate and unbiased estimate of the population variance. Now we examine the process of using sample means as the basis for estimating population means.

PRECISION AND CONFIDENCE IN ESTIMATION

Before we begin the actual process of estimation, a few general points should be kept in mind. First, a sample will not give a perfect picture of the whole population. A sample is expected to be representative of the population, but there always will be some differences between the sample and the entire population. These differences are referred to as *sampling error*. Second, there are two distinct ways of making estimates. Suppose, for example, you are asked to estimate the age of the authors of this book. If you look in the frontmatter of the book, just before the Contents, you will find pictures of Gravetter and Wallnau. We are roughly the same age, so pick either one of us and estimate how old we are. Note that you could make your estimate using a single value (for example, Gravetter appears to be 55 years old) or you could use a range of values (for example, Wallnau seems to be between 50 and 60 years old). The first estimate, using a single number, is called a *point estimate*.

DEFINITION
> For a **point estimate,** you use a single number as your estimate of an unknown quantity.

Point estimates have the advantage of being very precise; they specify a particular value. On the other hand, you generally do not have much confidence that a point estimate is correct. For example, most of you would not be willing to bet that Gravetter is exactly 55 years old.

The second type of estimate, using a range of values, is called an *interval estimate*. Interval estimates do not have the precision of point estimates, but they do give you more confidence. For example, it would be reasonably safe for you to bet that Wallnau is between 40 and 60 years old. At the extreme, you would be very confident betting that Wallnau is between 30 and 70 years old. Note that there is a trade-off between precision and confidence. As the interval gets wider and wider, your confidence grows. At the same time, however, the precision of the estimate gets worse. We will be using samples to make both point and interval estimates of a population mean. Because the interval estimates are associated with confidence, they usually are called *confidence intervals*.

DEFINITIONS

For an **interval estimate,** you use a range of values as your estimate of an unknown quantity.

When an interval estimate is accompanied by a specific level of confidence (or probability), it is called a **confidence interval.**

Estimation is used in the same general situations in which we have already used hypothesis testing. In fact, there is an estimation procedure that accompanies each of the hypothesis tests we presented in the preceding chapters. Figure 12.1 shows an example of a research situation in which either hypothesis testing or estimation could be used. The figure shows a population with an unknown mean (the population after treatment). A sample is selected from the unknown population. The goal of estimation is to use the sample data to obtain an estimate of the unknown population mean.

COMPARISON OF HYPOTHESIS TESTS AND ESTIMATION

You should recognize that the situation shown in Figure 12.1 is the same situation in which we have used hypothesis tests in the past. In many ways, hypothesis testing and estimation are similar. They both make use of sample data and either z-scores or t statistics to find out about unknown populations. But these two inferential procedures are designed to answer different questions. Using the situation shown in Figure 12.1 as an example, we could use a hypothesis test to evaluate the effect of the treatment. The test would determine whether the treatment has any effect. Notice that this is a yes-no question. The null hypothesis says, "No, there is no treatment effect." The alternative hypothesis says, "Yes, there is a treatment effect."

FIGURE 12.1

The basic research situation for either hypothesis testing or estimation. The goal is to use the sample data to answer questions about the unknown population mean after treatment.

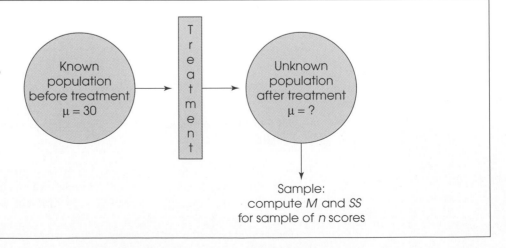

The goal of estimation, on the other hand, is to determine the value of the population mean after treatment. Essentially, estimation will determine *how much* effect the treatment has. If, for example, we obtained a point estimate of $\mu = 38$ for the population after treatment, we could conclude that the effect of the treatment is to increase scores by an average of 8 points (from the original mean of $\mu = 30$ to the post-treatment mean of $\mu = 38$).

WHEN TO USE ESTIMATION   There are three situations in which estimation commonly is used:

1. Estimation is used after a hypothesis test when H_0 is rejected. Remember that when H_0 is rejected, the conclusion is that the treatment does have an effect. The next logical question would be, How much effect? This is exactly the question that estimation is designed to answer.

2. Estimation is used when you already know that there is an effect and simply want to find out how much. For example, the city school board probably knows that a special reading program will help students. However, they want to be sure that the effect is big enough to justify the cost. Estimation is used to determine the size of the treatment effect.

3. Estimation is used when you simply want some basic information about an unknown population. Suppose, for example, you want to know about the political attitudes of students at your college. You could use a sample of students as the basis for estimating the population mean.

THE LOGIC OF ESTIMATION   As we have noted, estimation and hypothesis testing are both *inferential* statistical techniques that involve using sample data as the basis for drawing conclusions about an unknown population. More specifically, a researcher begins with a question about an unknown population parameter. To answer the question, a sample is obtained, and a sample statistic is computed. In general, *statistical inference* involves using sample statistics to help answer questions about population parameters. The general logic underlying the processes of estimation and hypothesis testing is based on the fact that each population parameter has a corresponding sample statistic. In addition, you usually can compute a standard error that measures how much discrepancy is expected, on average, between the statistic and the parameter. For example, a sample mean, M, corresponds to the population mean, μ, with a standard error measured by σ_M or s_M.

In the preceding four chapters we presented four different situations for hypothesis testing: the z-score test, the single-sample t, the independent-measures t, and the repeated-measures t. Although it is possible to do estimation in each of these four situations, we will only consider estimation for the three t statistics. Recall that the general structure of a t statistic is as follows:

$$t = \frac{\substack{\text{sample mean} \\ \text{(or mean difference)}} - \substack{\text{population mean} \\ \text{(or mean difference)}}}{\text{estimated standard error}}$$

This general formula is used both for hypothesis testing and for estimation. In each case, the population mean (or mean difference) is unknown. The purpose for a hypothesis test is to evaluate a hypothesis about the unknown population parameter. The purpose for estimation is to determine the value for the unknown population parameter. Because hypothesis testing and estimation have different goals, they will follow different logical paths. These different paths are outlined as follows:

Hypothesis Test	Estimation
Goal: To test a hypothesis about a population parameter—usually the null hypothesis, which states that the treatment has no effect.	*Goal:* To estimate the value of an unknown population parameter—usually the value for an unknown population mean.
A. For a hypothesis test, you begin by hypothesizing a value for the unknown population parameter. This value is specified in the null hypothesis.	A. For estimation, you do not attempt to calculate *t*. Instead, you begin by estimating what the *t* value ought to be. The strategy for making this estimate is to select a "reasonable" value for *t*. (*Note:* You are not just picking a value for *t*; rather, you are estimating where the sample is located in the distribution.)
B. The hypothesized value is substituted into the formula, and *the value* for *t is computed*.	
C. If the hypothesized value produces a "reasonable" outcome for *t*, we conclude that the hypothesis was "reasonable," and we fail to reject H_0. If the result is an extreme value for *t*, H_0 is rejected.	B. As with hypothesis testing, a "reasonable" value for *t* is defined as a high-probability outcome located near the center of the distribution (see Figure 12.2).
D. A "reasonable" value for *t* is defined by its location in a distribution. In general, "reasonable" values are high-probability outcomes in the center of the distribution. Extreme values with low probability are considered "unreasonable" (Figure 12.2).	C. The "reasonable" value for *t* is substituted into the formula, and *the value for the unknown population parameter is computed*.
	D. Because you used a "reasonable" value for *t* in the formula, it is assumed that the computation will produce a "reasonable" estimate of the population parameter.

Because the goal of the estimation process is to compute a value for the unknown population mean or mean difference, it usually is easier to regroup the terms in the *t* formula so that the population value is isolated on one side of the equation. In algebraic terms, we are solving the equation for the unknown population parameter. The result takes the following form:

$$\begin{array}{l}\text{population mean} \\ \text{(or mean difference)}\end{array} = \begin{array}{l}\text{sample mean} \\ \text{(or mean difference)}\end{array} \pm t(\text{estimated standard error})$$

(12.1)

FIGURE 12.2

For estimation or hypothesis testing, the distribution of *t* statistics is divided into two sections: the middle of the distribution, consisting of high-probability outcomes that are considered "reasonable," and the extreme tails of the distribution, consisting of low-probability, "unreasonable" outcomes.

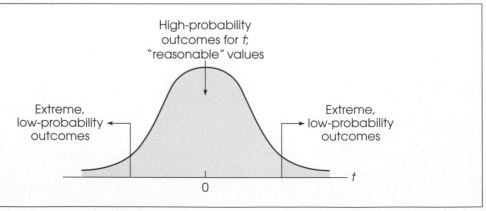

High-probability outcomes for *t;* "reasonable" values

Extreme, low-probability outcomes

Extreme, low-probability outcomes

0   *t*

This is the general equation that we will use for estimation. Consider the following two points about Equation 12.1:

1. On the right-hand side of the equation, the values for the sample mean and the estimated standard error are computed directly from the sample data. Thus, only the value of *t* is unknown. If we can determine this missing value, then we can use the equation to calculate the unknown population mean.

2. Although the specific value for the *t* statistic cannot be determined, we do know what the entire distribution of *t* statistics looks like. We can use the distribution to *estimate* what the *t* statistic ought to be.

   a. For a point estimate, the best bet is to use $t = 0$, the exact center of the distribution. There is no reason to suspect that the sample data are biased (either above average or below average), so $t = 0$ is a sensible value. Also, $t = 0$ is the most likely value, with probabilities decreasing steadily as you move away from zero toward the tails of the distribution.

   b. For an interval estimate, we will use a range of *t* values around zero. For example, to be 90% confident that our estimation is correct, we will simply use the range of *t* values that forms the middle 90% of the distribution. Note that we are estimating that the sample data correspond to a *t* statistic somewhere in the middle 90% of the *t* distribution.

Once we have estimated a value for *t,* then we have all the numbers on the right-hand side of the equation and we can calculate a value for the unknown population mean. Because one of the numbers on the right-hand side is an estimated value, the population mean that we calculate is also an estimated value.

LEARNING CHECK

1. Estimation is used to determine whether a treatment effect exists. (True or false?)

2. Estimation is primarily used to estimate the value of sample statistics. (True or false?)

3. In general, as confidence increases, the precision of an interval estimate decreases. (True or false?)

4. Explain why it would *not* be sensible to use estimation after a hypothesis test in which the decision was "fail to reject the null hypothesis."

ANSWERS

1. False. Estimation is used to determine *how much* effect the treatment has.

2. False. Estimation procedures are used to estimate the value for unknown population parameters.

3. True. There is a trade-off between precision and confidence.

4. If the decision is fail to reject H_0, then you have concluded that there is not a significant treatment effect. In this case, it would not make sense to estimate how much effect there is.

12.2   ESTIMATION WITH THE *t* STATISTIC

In the preceding three chapters, we introduced three different versions of the *t* statistic: the single-sample *t* in Chapter 9, the independent-measures *t* in Chapter 10, and the repeated-measures *t* in Chapter 11. Although the three *t* statistics were introduced in the context of hypothesis testing, they all can be adapted for use in estimation. As we saw in the previous section, the general form of the *t* equation for estimation is as follows:

$$\text{population mean (or mean difference)} = \text{sample mean (or mean difference)} \pm t(\text{estimated standard error})$$

With the single-sample *t*, we will estimate an unknown population mean, μ, using a sample mean, *M*. The estimation formula for the single-sample *t* is

$$\mu = M \pm ts_M \tag{12.2}$$

With the independent-measures *t*, we will estimate the size of the difference between two population means, $\mu_1 - \mu_2$, using the difference between two sample means, $M_1 - M_2$. The estimation formula for the independent-measures *t* is

$$\mu_1 - \mu_2 = M_1 - M_2 \pm ts_{(M_1 - M_2)} \tag{12.3}$$

Finally, the repeated-measures *t* statistic will be used to estimate the mean difference for the general population, μ_D, using the mean difference for a sample, M_D. The estimation formula for the repeated-measures *t* is

$$\mu_D = M_D \pm ts_{M_D} \tag{12.4}$$

To use the *t* statistic formulas for estimation, we must determine all of the values on the right-hand side of the equation (including an estimated value for *t*) and then use these numbers to compute an estimated value for the population mean or mean difference. Specifically, you first compute the sample mean (or mean difference) and the estimated standard error from the sample data. Next, you estimate a value, or a range of values, for *t*. More precisely, you are estimating where the sample data are located in the *t* distribution. These values complete the right-hand side of the equation and allow you to compute an estimated value for the mean (or the mean difference). The following examples demonstrate the estimation procedure with each of the three *t* statistics.

ESTIMATION OF μ FOR SINGLE-SAMPLE STUDIES

In Chapter 9, we introduced single-sample studies and hypothesis testing with the *t* statistic. Now we will use a single-sample study to estimate the value for μ, using point and interval estimates.

EXAMPLE 12.1

For several years researchers have noticed that there appears to be a regular, year-by-year increase in the average IQ for the general population. This phenomenon is called the Flynn effect after the researcher who first reported it (Flynn, 1984, 1999), and it means that psychologists must continuously update IQ tests to keep the population mean at $\mu = 100$. To evaluate the size of the effect, a researcher obtained a 10-year-old IQ test that was standardized to produce a mean IQ of $\mu = 100$ for the population 10 years ago. The test was then given to a sample of $n = 64$ of today's 20-year-old adults. The average score for the sample was $M = 107$ with a standard deviation of $s = 12$. The researcher would like to use the data to estimate how much IQ scores have changed during the past 10 years. Specifically, the researcher would like to make a point estimate and an 80% confidence interval estimate of the population mean for people taking a 10-year-old IQ test. The structure for this research study is shown in Figure 12.3.

FIGURE 12.3

The structure of the research study described in Example 12.1. The goal is to use the sample to estimate the population mean IQ for people taking a 10-year-old IQ test. We can then estimate how much IQ scores have changed during the past 10 years.

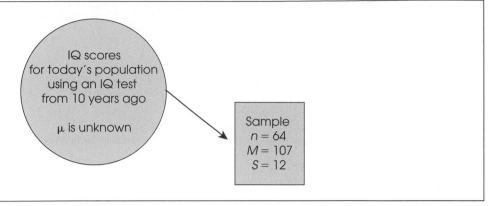

In this example, we are using a single sample to estimate the mean for a single population. In this case, the estimation formula for the single-sample *t* is

$$\mu = M \pm ts_M$$

To use the equation, we must first compute the estimated standard error and then determine the estimated value(s) to be used for the *t* statistic.

Compute the estimated standard error, s_M To compute the estimated standard error, it is first necessary to calculate the sample variance. For this example, we are given a sample standard deviation of $s = 12$, so the sample variance is $s^2 = (12)^2 = 144$. The estimated standard error is

$$s_M = \sqrt{\frac{s^2}{n}} = \sqrt{\frac{144}{64}} = \frac{12}{8} = 1.50$$

The point estimate As noted earlier, a point estimate involves selecting a single value for *t*. Because the *t* distribution is always symmetrically distributed with a mean of zero, we will always use $t = 0$ as the best choice for a point estimate. Using the sample data and the estimate of $t = 0$, we obtain

$$\mu = M \pm ts_M$$
$$= 107 \pm 0(1.50)$$
$$= 107$$

This is our point estimate of the population mean. Note that we simply have used the sample mean, *M,* to estimate the population mean, μ. The sample is the only information that we have about the population, and it provides an unbiased estimate of the population mean (Chapter 7, page 166). That is, on average, the sample mean provides an accurate representation of the population mean. Based on this point estimate, our conclusion is that today's population would have a mean IQ of $\mu = 107$ on an IQ test from 10 years ago. Thus, we are estimating that there has been a 7-point increase in IQ scores (from $\mu = 100$ to $\mu = 107$) during the past decade.

To have 80% in the middle there must be 20% (or .20) in the tails. To find the *t* values, look under two tails, .20 in the *t* table.

The interval estimate For an interval estimate, select a range of *t* values that is determined by the level of confidence. In this example, we want 80% confidence in our estimate of μ. Therefore, we will estimate that the *t* statistic is located somewhere in

FIGURE 12.4

The 80% confidence interval with $df = 60$ is constructed using t values of $t = -1.296$ and $t = +1.296$. The t values are obtained from the table using 20% (0.20) as the proportion remaining in the two tails of the distribution.

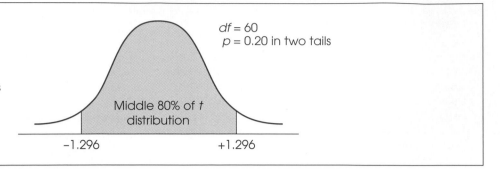

the middle 80% of the t distribution. With $df = n - 1 = 63$, the middle 80% of the distribution is bounded by t values of $+1.296$ and -1.296 (using $df = 60$ from the table). These values are shown in Figure 12.4. Using the sample data and this estimated range of t values, we obtain

$$\mu = M \pm t(s_M) = 107 \pm 1.296(1.50) = 107 \pm 1.944$$

At one end of the interval we obtain 108.944 (107 + 1.944), and at the other end of the interval we obtain 105.056 (107 − 1.944). Our conclusion is that today's population would have a mean IQ between 105.056 and 108.944 if they used an IQ test from 10 years ago. In other words, we are concluding that the mean IQ has increased over the past 10 years, and we are estimating with 80% confidence that the size of the increase is between 5 and 9 points. The confidence comes from the fact that the calculation was based on only one assumption. Specifically, we assumed that the t statistic was located between $+1.296$ and -1.296, and we are 80% confident that this assumption is correct because 80% of all the possible t values are located in this interval. Finally, note that the confidence interval is constructed around the sample mean. As a result, the sample mean, $M = 107$, is located exactly in the center of the interval.

Figure 12.5 provides a visual presentation of the results from Example 12.1. The original population mean from 10 years ago is shown along with the two estimates (point and interval) of today's mean. The estimates clearly indicate that there has been an increase in IQ scores over the past 10 years, and they provide a clear indication of how large the increase is.

FIGURE 12.5

A representation of the estimates made in Example 12.1. Ten years ago the mean IQ was $\mu = 100$. Based on a sample of today's adults, the mean has increased to $\mu = 107$ (point estimate) or somewhere between 105.056 and 108.944 (interval estimate).

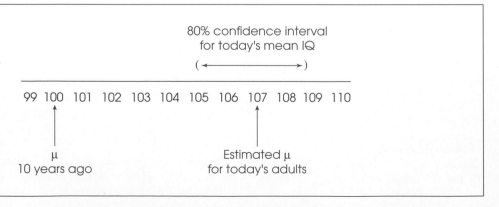

Interpretation of the confidence interval   In the preceding example, we computed an 80% confidence interval to estimate an unknown population mean. We obtained an interval ranging from 105.056 to 108.944, and we are 80% confident that the unknown population mean is located within this interval. You should note, however, that the 80% confidence applies to the *process* of computing the interval rather than the specific end points for the interval. For example, if we repeated the process over and over, we could eventually obtain hundreds of different samples (each with $n = 64$ scores) and we could calculate hundreds of different confidence intervals. However, each interval is computed using the same procedure. Specifically, each interval is centered around its own sample mean, and each interval extends from a value corresponding to $t = -1.296$ at one end to $t = +1.296$ at the other end.

Figure 12.6 shows the distribution of *t* values with the middle 80% highlighted. Note that the value of zero in the middle of the distribution corresponds to the population mean, μ, because $t = 0$ only when the sample mean is exactly equal to the population mean. Also note that all of the *t* values in the middle 80% are within 1.296 points of $t = 0$ (the population mean). Finally, the figure shows two possible samples and their corresponding *t* values.

1. Sample 1 is an example of a sample with a *t* value located inside the 80% boundaries. The 80% confidence interval for sample 1 is centered at the sample mean and extends for a distance corresponding to $t = 1.296$ in both directions. Thus, the confidence interval for sample 1 overlaps $t = 0$ which means that the unknown population mean μ is contained within the interval.

2. Sample 2, on the other hand, corresponds to a *t* value located outside the 80% boundaries. The 80% confidence for sample 2 extends for a distance corresponding to $t = 1.296$ in both directions from the sample mean. This time, however, the interval does not extend far enough to include $t = 0$, which means that the value of μ is not included in the interval.

Out of all the possible samples, 80% will be similar to sample 1. That is, they will correspond to *t* values between ± 1.296 and will produce confidence intervals that contain the population mean. The other 20% of the possible samples will be similar to sample 2. They will correspond to *t* values outside the ± 1.296 boundaries, and they will

FIGURE 12.6

Interpretation of the 80% confidence for an 80% confidence interval. Of all the possible samples, 80% will have *t* scores located in the middle 80% of the distribution and will produce confidence intervals that overlap and contain the population mean. Thus, 80% of all the possible confidence intervals will contain the true value for μ.

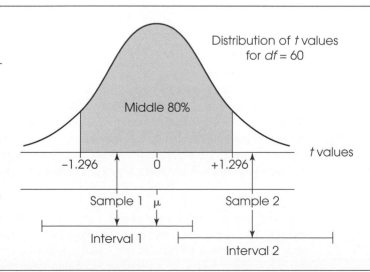

produce confidence intervals that do not contain μ. Thus, out of all the different confidence intervals that we could calculate, 80% will actually contain the population mean and 20% will not.

Note that the population mean, μ, is a constant value. Because the mean does not change, it is incorrect to think that sometimes μ is in a specific interval and sometimes it is not. Instead, the intervals change from one sample to another, so that μ is in some of the intervals and is not in others. The probability that any individual confidence interval actually contains the mean is determined by the level of confidence (the percentage) used to construct the interval.

ESTIMATION OF $\mu_1 - \mu_2$ FOR INDEPENDENT-MEASURES STUDIES

The independent-measures t statistic uses the data from two separate samples to evaluate the mean difference between two populations. In Chapter 10, we used this statistic to answer a yes-no question: Is there any difference between the two population means? With estimation, we ask, *How much* difference? In this case, the independent-measures t statistic is used to estimate the value of $\mu_1 - \mu_2$. The following example demonstrates the process of estimation with the independent-measures t statistic.

EXAMPLE 12.2

Recent studies have allowed psychologists to establish definite links between specific foods and specific brain functions. For example, lecithin (found in soybeans, eggs, and liver) has been shown to increase the concentration of certain brain chemicals that help regulate memory and motor coordination. This experiment is designed to demonstrate the importance of this particular food substance.

The experiment involves two separate samples of newborn rats (an independent-measures experiment). The 10 rats in the first sample are given a normal diet containing standard amounts of lecithin. The 5 rats in the other sample are fed a special diet, which contains almost no lecithin. After 6 months, each of the rats is tested on a specially designed learning problem that requires both memory and motor coordination. The purpose of the experiment is to demonstrate the deficit in performance that results from lecithin deprivation. The score for each animal is the number of errors it makes before it solves the learning problem. The data from this experiment are as follows:

Regular Diet	No-Lecithin Diet
$n = 10$	$n = 5$
$M = 25$	$M = 33$
$SS = 250$	$SS = 140$

Because we fully expect that there will be a significant difference between these two treatments, we will not do the hypothesis test (although you should be able to do it). We want to use these data to obtain an estimate of the size of the difference between the two population means; that is, how much does lecithin affect learning performance? We will use a point estimate and a 95% confidence interval.

The basic equation for estimation with an independent-measures experiment is

$$\mu_1 - \mu_2 = (M_1 - M_2) \pm ts_{(M_1 - M_2)}$$

The first step is to obtain the known values from the sample data. The sample mean difference is easy; one group averaged $M = 25$, and the other averaged $M = 33$, so there is an 8-point difference. Note that it is not important whether we call this a $+8$ or a -8 difference. In either case, the size of the difference is

8 points, and the regular diet group scored lower. Because it is easier to do arithmetic with positive numbers, we will use

$$M_1 - M_2 = 8$$

Compute the standard error   To find the standard error, we first must pool the two variances:

$$s_p^2 = \frac{SS_1 + SS_2}{df_1 + df_2} = \frac{250 + 140}{9 + 4} = \frac{390}{13} = 30$$

Next, the pooled variance is used to compute the standard error:

$$s_{(M_1 - M_2)} = \sqrt{\frac{s_p^2}{n_1} + \frac{s_p^2}{n_2}} = \sqrt{\frac{30}{10} + \frac{30}{5}} = \sqrt{3 + 6} = \sqrt{9} = 3$$

Recall that this standard error combines the error from the first sample and the error from the second sample. Because the first sample is much larger, $n = 10$, it should have less error. This difference shows up in the formula. The larger sample contributes an error of 3 points, and the smaller sample contributes 6 points, which combine for a total error of 9 points under the square root.

Sample 1 has $df = 9$, and sample 2 has $df = 4$. The *t* statistic has $df = 9 + 4 = 13$.

Estimate the value(s) for *t*   The final value needed on the right-hand side of the equation is *t*. The data from this experiment would produce a *t* statistic with $df = 13$. With 13 degrees of freedom, we can sketch the distribution of all the possible *t* values. This distribution is shown in Figure 12.7. The *t* statistic for our data is somewhere in this distribution. The problem is to estimate where. For a point estimate, the best bet is to use $t = 0$. This is the most likely value, located exactly in the middle of the distribution. To gain more confidence in the estimate, you can select a range of *t* values. For 95% confidence, for example, you would estimate that the *t* statistic is somewhere in the middle 95% of the distribution. Checking the table, you find that the middle 95% is bounded by values of $t = +2.160$ and $t = -2.160$.

Using these *t* values and the sample values computed earlier, we now can estimate the magnitude of the performance deficit caused by lecithin deprivation.

Compute the point estimate   For a point estimate, use the single-value (point) estimate of $t = 0$:

$$\mu_1 - \mu_2 = (M_1 - M_2) \pm t s_{(M_1 - M_2)}$$
$$= 8 \pm 0(3)$$
$$= 8$$

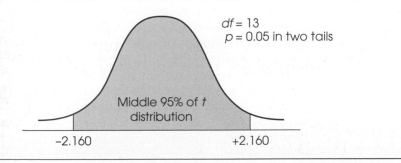

FIGURE 12.7

The distribution of *t* values with $df = 13$. Note that *t* values pile up around zero and that 95% of the values are located between -2.160 and $+2.160$.

$df = 13$
$p = 0.05$ in two tails

Middle 95% of *t* distribution

-2.160 $+2.160$

Note that the result simply uses the sample mean difference to estimate the population mean difference. The conclusion is that lecithin deprivation produces an average of 8 more errors on the learning task. (Based on the fact that the non-deprived animals averaged around 25 errors, an 8-point increase would mean a performance deficit of approximately 30%.)

Construct the interval estimate   For an interval estimate, or confidence interval, use the range of t values. With 95% confidence, at one extreme,

$$\mu_1 - \mu_2 = (M_1 - M_2) + ts_{(M_1-M_2)}$$

$$= 8 + 2.160(3)$$

$$= 8 + 6.48$$

$$= 14.48$$

and at the other extreme,

$$\mu_1 - \mu_2 = (M_1 - M_2) - ts_{(M_1-M_2)}$$

$$= 8 - 2.160(3)$$

$$= 8 - 6.48$$

$$= 1.52$$

This time we conclude that the effect of lecithin deprivation is to increase errors, with an average increase somewhere between 1.52 and 14.48 errors. We are 95% confident of this estimate because our only estimation was the location of the t statistic, and we used the middle 95% of all the possible t values.

Note that the result of the point estimate is to say that lecithin deprivation will increase errors by *exactly* 8 points. To gain confidence, you must lose precision and say that errors will increase by *around* 8 points (for 95% confidence, we say that the average increase will be 8 ± 6.48).

ESTIMATION OF μ_D FOR REPEATED-MEASURES STUDIES

Finally, we turn our attention to the repeated-measures study. Remember that this type of study has a single group of participants, with the same individuals measured in two different treatment conditions. By finding the difference between the score for treatment 1 and the score for treatment 2, we calculate a difference score for each participant.

$$D = X_2 - X_1$$

The mean for the sample of D scores, M_D, is used to estimate the population mean μ_D, which is the mean for the entire population of difference scores.

EXAMPLE 12.3

A research study has demonstrated that self-hypnosis can be an effective treatment for allergies (Langewitz, Izakovic, & Wyler, 2005). The researchers recruited a sample of patients with moderate to severe allergic reactions. The patients were then trained to focus their minds on a specific place, such as a ski slope in the middle of winter, where allergies did not bother them. The participants who practiced this self-hypnosis therapy for the full 2 years of the study were then tested for allergic reactions to pollen under two different conditions: once without self-hypnosis and once after using the self-hypnosis therapy. Hypothetical data, similar to the actual research results, show that allergic reactions averaged $M = 71$ without self-hypnosis and $M = 50$ after using the self-hypnosis therapy. For this sample of $n = 16$ patients, the difference scores averaged $M_D = 21$ points lower when the patients were using self-hypnosis, with $SS = 1215$. We will use these results to estimate how much effect self-hypnosis therapy would have on allergy symptoms for the general population. Specifically, we will make a point estimate and a 90% confidence interval estimate for the population mean difference, μ_D.

You should recognize that this study requires a repeated-measures *t* statistic. For estimation, the repeated-measures *t* equation is as follows:

$$\mu_D = M_D \pm t s_{M_D}$$

The sample mean is $M_D = 21$, so all that remains is to compute the estimated standard error and estimate the appropriate value(s) for *t*.

Compute the standard error   To find the standard error, we first must compute the sample variance:

$$s^2 = \frac{SS}{n-1} = \frac{1215}{15} = 81$$

Now the estimated standard error is

$$s_{M_D} = \sqrt{\frac{s^2}{n}} = \sqrt{\frac{81}{16}} = \frac{9}{4} = 2.25$$

To complete the estimate of μ_D, we must identify the value of *t*. We will consider the point estimate and the interval estimate separately.

Compute the point estimate   To obtain a point estimate, a single value of *t* is selected to approximate the location of M_D. Remember that the *t* distribution is symmetrical and bell-shaped with a mean of zero (see Figure 12.7). Because $t = 0$ is the most frequently occurring value in the distribution, this is the *t* value used for the point estimate. Using this value in the estimation formula gives

$$\mu_D = M_D \pm t s_{M_D} = 21 \pm 0(2.25) = 21$$

For this example, our best estimate is that the self-hypnosis will lower allergy symptoms in the general population by an average of $\mu_D = 21$ points. As noted several times before, the sample mean, $M_D = 21$, provides the best point estimate of the population mean.

Construct the interval estimate   We also want to make an interval estimate in order to be 90% confident that we have accurately estimated the value of μ_D. To get the interval, it is necessary to determine what *t* values form the boundaries of the middle 90% of the *t* distribution. With 90% in the middle, the remaining area in the two tails must total 10% or $p = .10$. Using $df = n - 1 = 15$ and $p = .10$ for two tails, you should find the values $+1.753$ and -1.753 in the *t* table. These values form the boundaries for the middle 90% of the *t* distribution (Figure 12.8). We are confident that the *t* value for our sample is in this range because 90% of all the possible *t* values are there. Using these values in the estimation formula, we obtain the following: On one end of the interval,

$$\mu_D = M_D - t s_{M_D}$$
$$= 21 - 1.753(2.25)$$
$$= 21 - 3.94$$
$$= 17.06$$

FIGURE 12.8

The *t* values for the 90% confidence interval are obtained by consulting the *t* tables for *df* = 15, *p* = 0.10 for two tails.

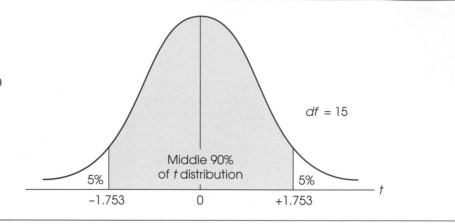

and on the other end of the interval,

$$\mu_D = 21 + 1.753(2.25)$$
$$= 21 + 3.94$$
$$= 24.94$$

Therefore, the researchers can conclude that self-hypnosis therapy would reduce allergy symptoms in the general population by an average of around 21 points. They can be 90% confident that the average reduction is between 17.06 and 24.94 points. Given that the allergy symptoms for untreated patients averaged *M* = 71, this is a reduction of around 30%.

LEARNING CHECK

1. A researcher would like to determine the average reading ability for third-grade students in the local school district. A sample of *n* = 25 students is selected and each student takes a standardized reading achievement test. The average score for the sample is *M* = 72 with *SS* = 2400. Use the sample results to construct a 99% confidence interval for the population mean.

2. A psychologist studies the change in mood from the follicular phase (prior to ovulation) to the luteal phase (after ovulation) during the menstrual cycle. In a repeated-measures study, a sample of *n* = 9 women take a mood questionnaire during each phase. On average, the participants show an increase in dysphoria (negative moods) of M_D = 18 points with *SS* = 152. Determine the 95% confidence interval for population mean change in mood.

3. In families with several children, the first-born tend to be more reserved and serious, whereas the last-born tend to be more outgoing and happy-go-lucky. A psychologist is using a standardized personality inventory to measure the magnitude of this difference. Two samples are used: 8 first-born children and 8 last-born children. Each child is given the personality test. The results are as follows:

First-born	Last-born
M = 11.4	*M* = 13.9
SS = 26	*SS* = 30

a. Use these sample statistics to make a point estimate of the population mean difference in personality for first-born versus last-born children.

b. Make an interval estimate of the population mean difference so that you are 80% confident that the true mean difference is in your interval.

ANSWERS
1. The sample variance is $s^2 = 100$ and the estimated standard error is $s_M = 2$ points. With $df = 24$ and 99% confidence, the t statistic should be between $+2.797$ and -2.797. With 99% confidence, we estimate that the population mean is between 66.406 and 77.594.

2. $s^2 = 19$, $s_{M_D} = 1.45$, $df = 8$, $t = \pm 2.306$; estimate that μ_D is between 14.66 and 21.34.

3. **a.** For a point estimate, use the sample mean difference: $M_1 - M_2 = 2.5$ points.

   b. Pooled variance $= 4$, estimated standard error $= 1$, $df = 14$, $t = \pm 1.345$. The 80% confidence interval is 1.16 to 3.85.

12.3   A FINAL LOOK AT ESTIMATION

FACTORS AFFECTING THE WIDTH OF A CONFIDENCE INTERVAL

Two characteristics of the confidence interval should be noted. First, notice what happens to the width of the interval when you change the level of confidence (the percent confidence). To gain more confidence in your estimate, you must increase the width of the interval. Conversely, to have a smaller interval, you must give up confidence. This is the basic trade-off between precision and confidence that was discussed earlier. In the estimation formula, the percentage of confidence influences the width of the interval by way of the t value. The larger the level of confidence (the percentage), the larger the t value and the larger the interval. This relationship can be seen in Figure 12.8. In the figure, we identified the middle 90% of the t distribution in order to find a 90% confidence interval. It should be obvious that if we were to increase the confidence level to 95%, it would be necessary to increase the range of t values and thereby increase the width of the interval.

Second, note what would happen to the interval width if you had a different sample size. This time the basic rule is as follows: The bigger the sample (n), the smaller the interval. This relationship is straightforward if you consider the sample size as a measure of the amount of information. A bigger sample gives you more information about the population and allows you to make a more precise estimate (a narrower interval). The sample size controls the magnitude of the standard error in the estimation formula. As the sample size increases, the standard error decreases, and the interval gets smaller.

With t statistics, the sample size has an additional effect on the width of a confidence interval. Remember that the exact shape of the t distribution depends on degrees of freedom. As the sample size gets larger, df also gets larger, and the t values associated with any specific percentage of confidence get smaller. This fact simply enhances the general relationship that the larger the sample, the smaller the confidence interval.

ESTIMATION, EFFECT SIZE, AND HYPOTHESIS TESTS

The process of estimation, especially the estimation of mean differences, provides a relatively simple and direct method for evaluating effect size. For example, the outcome of the study in Example 12.3 indicates that self-hypnosis can reduce allergy symptoms by an estimated 21 points, or about 30%. In this case, the estimation process produces a very clear and understandable indication of how large the treatment effect actually is.

In addition to describing the size of a treatment effect, estimation can be used to get an indication of the "significance" of the effect. Example 12.2 presented an independent-

FIGURE 12.9

The 95% confidence interval for the population mean difference ($\mu_1 - \mu_2$) from Example 12.2. Note that $\mu_1 - \mu_2 = 0$ is excluded from the confidence interval, indicating that a zero difference is not an acceptable value (H_0 would be rejected in a hypothesis test).

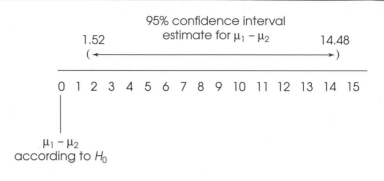

measures research study examining the effect of lecithin on problem-solving performance for rats. Based on the results of this study, it was estimated that the mean difference in performance produced by lecithin was $\mu_1 - \mu_2 = 8$ points. The 95% confidence interval estimated the mean difference to be between 1.52 points and 14.48 points. The confidence interval estimate is shown in Figure 12.9. In addition to the confidence interval for $\mu_1 - \mu_2$, we have marked the spot where the mean difference is equal to zero. You should recognize that a mean difference of zero is exactly what would be predicted by the null hypothesis if we were doing a hypothesis test. You also should realize that a zero difference ($\mu_1 - \mu_2 = 0$) is *outside* the 95% confidence interval. In other words, $\mu_1 - \mu_2 = 0$ is not an acceptable value if we want 95% confidence in our estimate. To conclude that a value of zero is *not acceptable* with 95% confidence is equivalent to concluding that a value of zero is *rejected* with 95% confidence. This conclusion is equivalent to rejecting H_0 with $\alpha = .05$. On the other hand, if a mean difference of zero was included within the 95% confidence interval, then we would have to conclude that $\mu_1 - \mu_2 = 0$ is an acceptable value, which is the same as failing to reject H_0.

LEARNING CHECK

1. If all other factors are held constant, an 80% confidence interval will be wider than a 90% confidence interval. (True or false?)

2. If all other factors are held constant, a confidence interval computed from a sample of $n = 25$ will be wider than a confidence interval from a sample of $n = 100$. (True or false?)

3. A 99% confidence interval for a population mean difference (μ_D) extends from -1.50 to $+3.50$. If a repeated-measures hypothesis test with two tails and $\alpha = .01$ were conducted using the same data, the decision would be to fail to reject the null hypothesis. (True or false?)

ANSWERS

1. False. Greater confidence requires a wider interval.

2. True. The smaller sample will produce a wider interval.

3. True. The value $\mu_D = 0$ is included within the 99% confidence interval, which means that it is an acceptable value with $\alpha = .01$ and would not be rejected.

SUMMARY

1. Estimation is a procedure that uses sample data to obtain an estimate of a population mean or mean difference. The estimate can be either a point estimate (single value) or an interval estimate (range of values). Point estimates have the advantage of precision, but they do not give much confidence. Interval estimates provide confidence, but you lose precision as the interval grows wider.

2. Estimation and hypothesis testing are similar processes: Both use sample data to answer questions about populations. However, these two procedures are designed to answer different questions. Hypothesis testing will tell you whether a treatment effect exists (yes or no). Estimation will tell you how much treatment effect there is.

3. The estimation process begins by solving the t-statistic equation for the unknown population mean (or mean difference).

$$\begin{matrix} \text{population mean} \\ \text{(or mean difference)} \end{matrix} = \begin{matrix} \text{sample mean} \\ \text{(or mean difference)} \end{matrix}$$
$$\pm\ t(\text{estimated standard error})$$

Except for the value of t, the numbers on the right-hand side of the equation are all obtained from the sample data. By using an estimated value for t, you can then compute an estimated value for the population mean (or mean difference). For a point estimate, use $t = 0$. For an interval estimate, first select a level of confidence and then look up the corresponding range of t values from the t-distribution table. For example, for 90% confidence, use the range of t values that determine the middle 90% of the distribution.

4. For a single-sample study, the mean from one sample is used to estimate the mean for the corresponding population.

$$\mu = M \pm ts_M$$

For an independent-measures study, the means from two separate samples are used to estimate the mean difference between two populations.

$$(\mu_1 - \mu_2) = (M_1 - M_2) \pm ts_{(M_1 - M_2)}$$

For a repeated-measures study, the mean from a sample of difference scores (D values) is used to estimate the mean difference for the general population.

$$\mu_D = M_D \pm ts_{M_D}$$

5. The width of a confidence interval is an indication of its precision: A narrow interval is more precise than a wide interval. The interval width is influenced by the sample size and the level of confidence.
   a. As sample size (n) gets larger, the interval width gets smaller (greater precision).
   b. As the percentage confidence increases, the interval width gets larger (less precision).

KEY TERMS

estimation   point estimate   interval estimate   confidence interval

RESOURCES

There are a tutorial quiz and other learning exercises for Chapter 12 at the Wadsworth website, www.thomsonedu.com/psychology/gravetter. See page 27 for more information about accessing items on the website.

WebTUTOR

For those using WebTutor along with this book, there is a WebTutor section corresponding to this chapter. The WebTutor contains a brief summary of Chapter 12, hints for learning the concepts and the formulas for estimation, cautions about common errors, and sample exam items including solutions.

General instructions for using SPSS are presented in Appendix D. The SPSS program can be used to compute **The Confidence Intervals** presented in this chapter. When SPSS is used to perform any of the three t tests presented in this book (single-sample, independent-measures, and repeated-measures), the output automatically includes a 95% confidence interval. If you want a different level of confidence (for example 80%), you can click on the **Options** box and enter your own percentage before clicking the final **OK** for the t test. Detailed instructions for each of the three t tests are presented in the SPSS section at the end of the appropriate chapter (Chapter 9 for the single-sample test, Chapter 10 for the independent-measures test, and Chapter 11 for the repeated-measures test).

FOCUS ON PROBLEM SOLVING

1. Although hypothesis tests and estimation are similar in some respects, remember that they are separate statistical techniques. A hypothesis test is used to determine whether there is evidence for a treatment effect. Estimation is used to determine how much effect a treatment has.

2. When students perform a hypothesis test and estimation with the same set of data, a common error is to take the t statistic from the hypothesis test and use it in the estimation formula. For estimation, the t value is determined by the level of confidence and must be looked up in the appropriate table.

3. Now that you are familiar with several different formulas for hypothesis tests and estimation, one problem will be determining which formula is appropriate for each set of data. When the data consist of a single sample selected from a single population, the appropriate statistic is the single-sample t. For an independent-measures design, you will always have two separate samples. In a repeated-measures design, there is only one sample, but each individual is measured twice so that difference scores can be computed.

DEMONSTRATION 12.1

ESTIMATION WITH A SINGLE-SAMPLE t STATISTIC

A sample of $n = 16$ is randomly selected from a population with unknown parameters.

The sample has a mean of $M = 11$ with $SS = 112$. We will use the sample data to estimate the value of the population mean using a point estimate and a 90% confidence interval. Because we are using a single sample to estimate the mean for a single population, the formula is

$$\mu = M \pm ts_M$$

STEP 1   Compute the sample variance and the estimated standard error, s_M.

Variance. The sample variance is computed for these data.

$$s^2 = \frac{SS}{n - 1} = \frac{112}{16 - 1} = \frac{112}{15} = 7.47$$

Estimated standard error. We can now determine the estimated standard error.

$$s_M = \sqrt{\frac{s^2}{n}} = \sqrt{\frac{7.47}{16}} = \sqrt{0.467} = 0.68$$

STEP 2   Compute the point estimate for μ.

For a point estimate, we use $t = 0$. Using the estimation formula, we obtain

$$\mu = M \pm ts_M$$

$$= 11 \pm 0(0.68)$$

$$= 11 \pm 0 = 11$$

The point estimate for the population mean is $\mu = 11$.

STEP 3   Determine the confidence interval for μ.

For these data, we want the 90% confidence interval. Therefore, we will use a range of t values that form the middle 90% of the distribution. For this demonstration, degrees of freedom are

$$df = n - 1 = 16 - 1 = 15$$

If we are looking for the middle 90% of the distribution, then 10% ($p = 0.10$) would lie in both tails outside of the interval. To find the t values, we look up $p = 0.10$, two tails, for $df = 15$ in the t-distribution table. The t values for the 90% confidence interval are $t = \pm 1.753$.

Using the estimation formula, one end of the confidence interval is

$$\mu = M - ts_M$$

$$= 11 - 1.753(0.68)$$

$$= 11 - 1.19 = 9.81$$

For the other end of the confidence interval, we obtain

$$\mu = M + ts_M$$

$$= 11 + 1.753(0.68)$$

$$= 11 + 1.19 = 12.19$$

Thus, the 90% confidence interval for μ is from 9.81 to 12.19.

DEMONSTRATION 12.2

ESTIMATION WITH THE INDEPENDENT-MEASURES t STATISTIC

Samples are taken from two school districts, and knowledge of American history is tested with a short questionnaire. For the following sample data, estimate the amount of mean difference between the students of these two districts. Specifically, provide a point estimate and a 95% confidence interval for $\mu_1 - \mu_2$.

District A	District B
$n = 4$	$n = 4$
$M = 18$	$M = 10$
$SS = 54$	$SS = 30$

STEP 1   Compute the pooled variance and the estimated standard error, $s_{(M_1 - M_2)}$.

Pooled variance. For pooled variance, we use the SS and df values from both samples. For district A, $df_1 = n_1 - 1 = 3$. For district B, $df_2 = n_2 - 1 = 3$. Pooled variance is

$$s_p^2 = \frac{SS_1 + SS_2}{df_1 + df_2} = \frac{54 + 30}{3 + 3} = \frac{84}{6} = 14$$

Estimated standard error. The estimated standard error for mean difference can now be calculated.

$$s_{(M_1-M_2)} = \sqrt{\frac{s_p^2}{n_1} + \frac{s_p^2}{n_2}} = \sqrt{\frac{14}{4} + \frac{14}{4}} = \sqrt{3.5 + 3.5}$$

$$= \sqrt{7} = 2.65$$

STEP 2   Compute the point estimate for $\mu_1 - \mu_2$.

For the point estimate, we use a t value of zero. Using the sample means and estimated standard error from previous steps, we obtain

$$\mu_1 - \mu_2 = (M_1 - M_2) \pm ts_{(M_1-M_2)}$$

$$= (18 - 10) \pm 0(2.65)$$

$$= 8 \pm 0 = 8$$

STEP 3   Determine the confidence interval for $\mu_1 - \mu_2$.

For the independent-measures t statistic, degrees of freedom are determined by

$$df = n_1 + n_2 - 2$$

For these data, df is

$$df = 4 + 4 - 2 = 6$$

With a 95% level of confidence, 5% of the distribution falls in the tails outside the interval. Therefore, we consult the t-distribution table for $p = 0.05$, two tails, with $df = 6$. The t values from the table are $t = \pm2.447$. On one end of the confidence interval, the population mean difference is

$$\mu_1 - \mu_2 = (M_1 - M_2) - ts_{(M_1-M_2)}$$

$$= (18 - 10) - 2.447(2.65)$$

$$= 8 - 6.48$$

$$= 1.52$$

On the other end of the confidence interval, the population mean difference is

$$\mu_1 - \mu_2 = (M_1 - M_2) + ts_{(M_1-M_2)}$$

$$= (18 - 10) + 2.447(2.65)$$

$$= 8 + 6.48$$

$$= 14.48$$

Thus, the 95% confidence interval for population mean difference is from 1.52 to 14.48.

PROBLEMS

1. Explain how each of the following factors affects the width of a confidence interval:
   a. Increasing the sample size
   b. Increasing the sample variability
   c. Increasing the level of confidence (the percentage of confidence)

2. For the following studies, state whether estimation or hypothesis testing is required. Also, is an independent- or a repeated-measures t statistic appropriate?
   a. A researcher would like to determine whether there is any difference in the amount of homework between senior year of high school and freshman year of college. A sample of high school seniors is surveyed and, 1 year later, the students are surveyed again during their first year of college.
   b. A doctor would like to determine how much a new medication affects sleeping for insomniacs. A sample of people suffering from insomnia is obtained and half are given the new medication and half are given a placebo. Each person records the number of hours of sleep each night for a week.
   c. A teacher would like to know whether a new computer-based education program improves performance for high school math students. Two high school math classes are selected. One class gets the computer program and the other receives regular classroom instruction. At the end of the year, both classes take the same exam.
   d. A researcher would like to determine how much people's moods are affected by seasonal changes. A sample of 100 adults is obtained and each individual is given a mood-analysis questionnaire in the summer and again in the winter.

3. Explain how the purpose of estimation differs from the purpose of a hypothesis test.

4. Explain why it would *not* be reasonable to use estimation after a hypothesis test for which the decision was "fail to reject H_0."

5. A researcher has constructed a 90% confidence interval of 87 ± 10, based on a sample of $n = 25$ scores. Note that this interval is 20 points wide (from 77 to 97).
   a. What would happen to the width of the interval (increase or decrease) if the sample size were increased?
   b. What would happen to the width of the interval (increase or decrease) if the level of confidence (% confidence) were increased?

6. Standardized measures seem to indicate that the average level of anxiety has increased gradually over the past 50 years (Twenge, 2000). In the 1950s, the average score on the Child Manifest Anxiety Scale was $\mu = 15.1$. A sample of $n = 16$ of today's children produces a mean score of $M = 23.3$ with $SS = 240$.
   a. Based on the sample, make a point estimate of the population mean anxiety score for today's children.
   b. Make a 90% confidence interval estimate of today's population mean.

7. An elementary school principal would like to know how many hours the students spend watching TV each day. A sample of $n = 25$ children is selected, and a survey is sent to each child's parents. The results indicate an average of $M = 3.1$ hours per day with a standard deviation of $s = 3.0$.
   a. Make a point estimate of the mean number of hours of TV per day for the population of elementary school children
   b. Make an interval estimate of the mean so that you are 90% confident that the true mean is in your interval.

8. A sample of $n = 9$ scores is obtained from an unknown population. The sample mean is $M = 46$ with a standard deviation of $s = 6$.
   a. Use the sample data to make an 80% confidence interval estimate of the unknown population mean.
   b. Make a 90% confidence interval estimate of μ.
   c. Make a 95% confidence interval estimate of μ.
   d. In general, how is the width of a confidence interval related to the percentage of confidence?

9. Problem 15 in Chapter 9 described a study by Harlow (1959) in which infant monkeys were placed in cages with two artificial "mothers." One mother was made of wire mesh and had a bottle from which the infant could feed, and the second mother was made of soft terry cloth but did not provide any food. Data for a sample of $n = 9$ monkeys showed that the infants spent an average of $M = 15.3$ hours per day with $SS = 216$ with the terry cloth mother. Use the data to estimate how many hours per day would be spent with the terry cloth mother for the entire population of infant monkeys. Make a point estimate and an 80% confidence interval estimate of the population mean.

10. Problem 17 in Chapter 9 described a study showing that children who attended a high-quality daycare program before they enter school perform better on math tests than children who do not have daycare experience. The data showed that a sample of $n = 25$ children who attended day care before starting school had an average score of $M = 87$ with $SS = 1536$ on a standardized math test for which the population mean is $\mu = 81$.
   a. Use the sample data to make a point estimate of the average math test score for the population of children with a history of high-quality daycare. Based on your estimate, how much higher than average do these children score?
   b. Make an interval estimate the population mean score for the daycare children so that you are 95% confident that the true mean is in your interval.

11. A developmental psychologist would like to determine how much fine motor skill improves for children from age 3 to age 4. A random sample of $n = 15$ three-year-old children and a second sample of $n = 15$ four-year-olds are obtained. Each child is given a manual dexterity test that measures fine motor skills. The average score for the older children was $M = 40.6$ with $SS = 430$ and the average for the younger children was $M = 35.4$ with $SS = 410$. Using these data,
   a. Make a point estimate of the population mean difference in fine motor skills.
   b. Make an interval estimate so you are 95% confident that the real mean difference is in your interval.
   c. Make an interval estimate so you are 99% confident that the real mean difference is in your interval.
   d. Based on your answers from b and c, do these data indicate a significant change using a two-tailed test with $\alpha = .05$? Is the difference significant with $\alpha = .01$?

12. There is some evidence suggesting that you are likely to improve your test score if you rethink and change answers on a multiple-choice exam (Johnston, 1975). To examine this phenomenon, a teacher gave the same final exam to two sections of a psychology course. The students in one section were told to turn in their exams immediately after finishing, without changing any of their answers. In the other section, students were encouraged to reconsider each question and to change answers whenever they felt it was appropriate. The average score for the $n = 16$ students in the "no change" section was $M = 75.4$ with $SS = 500$. The average for the $n = 16$ students in the "change" section was $M = 80.6$ with $SS = 460$.
   a. Make a point estimate of the population mean difference between the two test conditions.
   b. Make a 95% confidence interval estimate of the mean difference between the two conditions.

c. Based on your answer to part b, would a two-tailed hypothesis test with $\alpha = .05$ conclude that there is a significant difference between the two conditions? (Is $\mu_1 - \mu_2 = 0$ an acceptable hypothesis?)

13. A common test of short-term memory requires participants to repeat a random string of digits that was presented a few seconds earlier. The number of digits is increased on each trial until the person begins to make mistakes. The longest string that can be reported accurately determines the participant's score. The following data were obtained from a sample of $n = 9$ participants. The scores are 4, 3, 12, 5, 7, 8, 10, 5, 9.
   a. Compute the mean and variance for the sample.
   b. Use the data to make a point estimate of the population mean.
   c. Make an 80% confidence interval estimate of μ.

14. Most adolescents experience a growth spurt when they are between 12 and 15 years old. This period of dramatic growth generally occurs around age 12 for girls and around age 14 for boys. A researcher studying physical development selected a random sample of $n = 9$ girls and a second sample of $n = 16$ boys and recorded the gain in height (in millimeters) between the 14th birthday and 15th birthday for each participant. The girls showed an average gain of $M = 40$ millimeters with $SS = 1152$, and the boys gained an average of $M = 95$ millimeters with $SS = 2160$.
   a. Estimate the population mean growth in 1 year for 14-year-old boys. Make a point estimate and an 80% confidence interval estimate.
   b. Estimate the population mean growth in 1 year for 14-year-old girls. Make a point estimate and an 80% confidence interval estimate.
   c. Estimate the mean difference in growth for boys versus girls during this 1-year-period. Again, make a point estimate and an 80% confidence interval estimate.

15. Problem 14 in Chapter 10 described a study by Rozin, Bauer, and Catanese (2003) comparing attitudes toward eating for male and female college students. The results showed that females are much more concerned about weight gain and other negative aspects of eating than are men. The following data represent the results from one measure of concern about weight gain.

Males	Females
$n = 6$	$n = 9$
$M = 31$	$M = 45$
$SS = 490$	$SS = 680$

a. Use the data to make a point estimate of the population mean difference between males' and females' level of concern about weight gain.

b. Make a 90% confidence interval estimate of the population mean difference.

16. Problem 15 in Chapter 10 described a study by Laughlin, Zander, Knievel, and Tan (2003) showing that groups of three people consistently outperformed the best of the individuals working alone on a letters-to-numbers substitution problem. The following data describe the number of trials needed to solve each problem for a sample of $n = 15$ groups and a sample of $n = 15$ individuals.

Groups	Individuals
$n = 15$	$n = 15$
$M = 3.8$	$M = 4.7$
$SS = 15.4$	$SS = 18.2$

a. Make a point estimate of how much better groups perform than individuals for the general population. (Estimate the mean difference in the number of trials needed for a solution.)

b. Make an interval estimate of the mean difference so that you are 95% confident that the true mean difference is in your interval.

c. Based on your answer to part b, what would be the decision from a hypothesis test evaluating the significance of the mean difference using a two-tailed test with $\alpha = .05$. Explain your answer.

17. Research results suggest that children who show high levels of stimulation seeking as preschoolers, will also show higher IQs as young adolescents (Raine, Reynolds, Verables, and Mednick, 2002). In an attempt to evaluate the size of this effect, a researcher obtained measures of stimulation seeking for a sample of 20 3-year-old children. The children were separated into two groups consisting of the $n = 10$ highest and $n = 10$ lowest stimulation seekers. At age 11, each child was given an IQ test. The IQ scores for the high–stimulation-seeking group had a mean of $M = 113.6$ with $SS = 1210$ and the mean for the low group was $M = 102.4$ with $SS = 1040$. Use the sample data to estimate the population mean difference in IQ at age 11 between children who exhibited high stimulation seeking and children who showed low stimulation seeking at age 3. Make a point estimate and a 90% confidence interval estimate.

18. People's handshakes seem to be related to other aspects of their personalities (Chaplin, Phillips, Brown, Clanton, & Stein, 2000). For example, a firm handshake is negatively related to shyness. To measure the magnitude of this effect, a researcher obtained a sam-

ple of $n = 12$ people who were rated as having firm handshakes and $n = 8$ who were rated as having weak handshakes. Both groups had 50% males and 50% females. Each individual was given a personality test measuring shyness. The average score for the firm handshake group was $M = 43$ with $SS = 1170$ and the average for the weak handshake group was $M = 61$ with $SS = 990$. Use the sample data to estimate how much difference there is in shyness between people with firm handshakes and people with weak handshakes. Make a point estimate and a 95% confidence interval estimate.

19. Although people with schizophrenia often show evidence of brain abnormalities, there is evidence to suggest that the disease is not associated with progressive brain damage (Heaton, Gladsjo, Palmer, Kuck, Marcotte, & Jeste, 2001). To examine this phenomenon, a researcher administered a test designed to measure brain damage to a sample of individuals recently diagnosed with schizophrenia. A year later, the same individuals were given the test again. A higher score indicates more damage. The data are as follows:

Participant	1st Test	2nd Test
A	83	79
B	68	72
C	71	73
D	73	78
E	65	64
F	68	69
G	81	84
H	77	80

a. Make a point estimate of the population mean difference in brain damage during the year.

b. Make a 95% confidence interval estimate of the population mean difference.

20. Problem 12 in Chapter 11 presented data from a study testing the effectiveness of Ritalin for increasing attention span for children with ADHD. Results from a sample of $n = 25$ children showed an average increase of attention span of $M_D = 6.8$ minutes with a standard deviation of $s = 5.5$ after the children were administered the drug.

a. Make a point estimate of the population mean difference in attention span after children with ADHD take Ritalin.

b. Make an interval estimate of the population mean difference so that you are 99% confident that the true mean difference is in your interval.

21. Problem 20 in Chapter 11 described a research study examining the hypothesis that women have a stronger reaction to alcohol and are affected more quickly than men are (Lieber, 1990). The difference appears to be due to an enzyme that begins to metabolize alcohol in the stomach. Because men have more of the enzyme, they metabolize more alcohol than women do before it reaches the bloodstream. A sample of $n = 10$ men and a corresponding sample of $n = 10$ women were tested on a driving simulator task to measure mental alertness. Then, equivalent doses of alcohol are given to each participant (adjusting for body weight), and the driving simulator test was repeated 30 minutes later. For the sample of men, performance on the simulator task declined by an average of $M_D = 2.9$ points with $s = 4.1$. For the women, performance declined by an average of $M_D = 6.4$ points with $s = 5.2$.

   a. Make a 95% confidence interval estimate of the mean difference in performance caused by alcohol for the population of men.

   b. Based on your answer from part a, would a mean difference of $\mu_D = 0$ (no difference) be an acceptable hypothesis for the men assuming a two-tailed test with $\alpha = .05$? Explain your answer.

   c. Make a 95% confidence interval estimate of the mean difference in performance caused by alcohol for the population of women.

   d. Based on your answer from part c, would a mean difference of $\mu_D = 0$ (no difference) be an acceptable hypothesis for the women assuming a two-tailed test with $\alpha = .05$? Explain your answer.

22. A researcher would like to determine how physical endurance is affected by a common herbal supplement. The researcher measures endurance for a sample of $n = 9$ participants. Each individual is then given a 30-day supply of the herbs and, 1 month later, endurance is measured again. For this sample, endurance increased by an average of $M_D = 6$ points with $SS = 216$.

   a. Make a point estimate of the population mean difference in endurance after taking the herbs.

   b. Make a 95% confidence interval estimate of the population mean difference.

23. A researcher would like to estimate how much reaction time is affected by a common over-the-counter cold medication. The researcher measures reaction time for a sample of $n = 36$ particiants. Each is then given a dose of the cold medication and reaction time is measured again. For this sample, reaction time increased after the medication by an average of $M_D = 24$ milliseconds with $s = 8$.

   a. Make a point estimate of the mean difference in reaction time caused by the medicine.

   b. Make a 95% confidence interval estimate of the population mean difference.

CHAPTER

13

Introduction to Analysis of Variance

Tools You Will Need

The following items are considered essential background material for this chapter. If you doubt your knowledge of any of these items, you should review the appropriate chapter or section before proceeding.

- Variability (Chapter 4)
  - Sum of squares
  - Sample variance
  - Degrees of freedom

- Introduction to hypothesis testing (Chapter 8)
  - The logic of hypothesis testing

- Independent-measures t statistic (Chapter 10)

13.1 INTRODUCTION

Analysis of variance (ANOVA) is a hypothesis-testing procedure that is used to evaluate mean differences between two or more treatments (or populations). As with all inferential procedures, ANOVA uses sample data as the basis for drawing general conclusions about populations. It may appear that analysis of variance and *t* tests are simply two different ways of doing exactly the same job: testing for mean differences. In some respects, this is true—both tests use sample data to test hypotheses about population means. However, ANOVA has a tremendous advantage over *t* tests. Specifically, *t* tests are limited to situations in which there are only two treatments to compare. The major advantage of ANOVA is that it can be used to compare *two or more treatments*. Thus, ANOVA provides researchers with much greater flexibility in designing experiments and interpreting results.

Figure 13.1 shows a typical research situation for which analysis of variance would be used. Note that the study involves three samples representing three populations. The goal of the analysis is to determine whether the mean differences observed among the samples provide enough evidence to conclude that there are mean differences among the three populations. Specifically, we must decide between two interpretations:

1. There really are no differences between the populations (or treatments). The observed differences between samples are simply due to chance (sampling error).

2. The populations (or treatments) really do have different means, and these population mean differences are part of the reason that the samples have different means.

You should recognize that these two interpretations correspond to the two hypotheses (null and alternative) that are part of the general hypothesis-testing procedure.

Before we continue, it is necessary to introduce some terminology that is used to describe the research situation shown in Figure 13.1. Recall (from Chapter 1) that when a researcher manipulates a variable to create treatment conditions, the variable is called an *independent variable*. For example, Figure 13.1 could represent a study examining behavior in three different temperature conditions that have been created by the researcher. On the other hand, when a researcher uses a nonmanipulated variable to designate groups, the variable is called a *quasi-independent variable*. For example, the three groups in Figure 13.1 could represent 6-year-old, 8-year-old, and 10-year-old

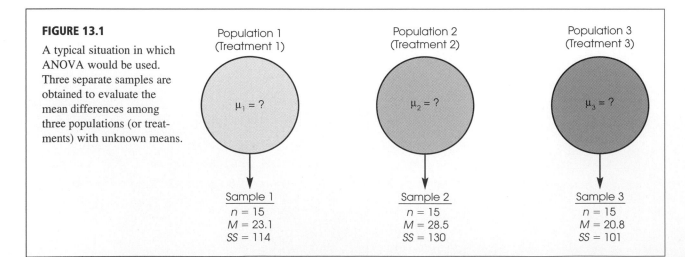

FIGURE 13.1

A typical situation in which ANOVA would be used. Three separate samples are obtained to evaluate the mean differences among three populations (or treatments) with unknown means.

Population 1 (Treatment 1) $\mu_1 = ?$

Population 2 (Treatment 2) $\mu_2 = ?$

Population 3 (Treatment 3) $\mu_3 = ?$

Sample 1
$n = 15$
$M = 23.1$
$SS = 114$

Sample 2
$n = 15$
$M = 28.5$
$SS = 130$

Sample 3
$n = 15$
$M = 20.8$
$SS = 101$

children. In the context of analysis of variance, an independent variable or a quasi-independent variable is called a *factor*. Thus, Figure 13.1 could represent a study in which temperature is the factor being evaluated or it could represent a study in which age is the factor being examined.

DEFINITION

In analysis of variance, the variable (independent or quasi-independent) that designates the groups being compared is called a **factor.**

In addition, the individual groups or treatment conditions that are used to make up a factor are called the *levels* of the factor. For example, a study that examined performance under three different temperature conditions would have three levels of temperature.

DEFINITION

The individual conditions or values that make up a factor are called the **levels** of the factor.

Like the *t* tests presented in Chapters 10 and 11, ANOVA can be used with either an independent-measures or a repeated-measures design. Recall that an independent-measures design means that there is a separate sample for each of the treatments (or populations) being compared. In a repeated-measures design, on the other hand, the same sample is tested in all of the different treatment conditions. In addition, ANOVA can be used to evaluate the results from a research study that involves more than one factor. For example, a researcher may want to compare two different therapy techniques, examining their immediate effectiveness as well as the persistence of their effectiveness over time. In this situation, the research study could involve two different groups of participants, one for each therapy, and measure each group at several different points in time. The structure of this design is shown in Figure 13.2. Notice that the study uses two factors, one independent-measures factor and one repeated-measures factor:

1. Therapy technique: A separate group is used for each technique (independent measures).

2. Time: Each group is tested at three different times (repeated measures).

FIGURE 13.2

A research design with two factors. The research study uses two factors: One factor uses two levels of therapy technique (I versus II), and the second factor uses three levels of time (before, after, and 6 months after). Also notice that the therapy factor uses two separate groups (independent measures) and the time factor uses the same group for all three levels (repeated measures).

		TIME		
		Before Therapy	After Therapy	6 Months After Therapy
THERAPY TECHNIQUE	Therapy I (Group 1)	Scores for group 1 measured before Therapy I	Scores for group 1 measured after Therapy I	Scores for group 1 measured 6 months after Therapy I
	Therapy II (Group 2)	Scores for group 2 measured before Therapy II	Scores for group 2 measured after Therapy II	Scores for group 2 measured 6 months after Therapy II

The ability to combine different factors and to mix different designs within one study provides researchers with the flexibility to develop studies that address scientific questions that could not be answered by a single design using a single factor.

Although analysis of variance can be used in a wide variety of research situations, this chapter introduces analysis of variance in its simplest form. Specifically, we consider only *single-factor* designs. That is, we examine studies that have only one independent variable (or only one quasi-independent variable). Second, we consider only *independent-measures* designs; that is, studies that use a separate sample for each treatment condition. The basic logic and procedures that are presented in this chapter will form the foundation for more complex applications of ANOVA. For example, in Chapter 14 we extend the analysis to single-factor, repeated-measures designs and two-factor designs. But for now, in this chapter, we will limit our discussion of ANOVA to *single-factor, independent-measures* research studies.

STATISTICAL HYPOTHESES FOR ANOVA

The following example will be used to introduce the statistical hypotheses for ANOVA. Suppose that a psychologist examined learning performance under three temperature conditions: 50°, 70°, and 90°. Three groups of participants are selected, one group for each treatment condition. The purpose of the study is to determine whether room temperature affects learning performance. In statistical terms, we want to decide between two hypotheses: the null hypothesis (H_0), which says that temperature has no effect, and the alternative hypothesis (H_1), which states that temperature does affect learning. In symbols, the null hypothesis states

$$H_0: \quad \mu_1 = \mu_2 = \mu_3$$

In words, the null hypothesis states that temperature has no effect on performance. That is, the population means for the three temperature conditions are all the same. In general, H_0 states that there is no treatment effect. Once again, notice that the hypotheses are always stated in terms of population parameters, even though we use sample data to test them.

For the alternative hypothesis, we may state that

$$H_1: \quad \text{At least one population mean is different from another.}$$

In general, H_1 states that the treatment conditions are not all the same; that is, there is a real treatment effect.

Notice that we have not given any specific alternative hypothesis. This is because many different alternatives are possible, and it would be tedious to list them all. One alternative, for example, would be that the first two populations are identical, but that the third is different. Another alternative states that the last two means are the same, but that the first is different. Other alternatives might be

$$H_1: \quad \mu_1 \neq \mu_2 \neq \mu_3 \qquad \text{(All three means are different.)}$$

$$H_1: \quad \mu_1 = \mu_3, \text{ but } \mu_2 \text{ is different}$$

We should point out that a researcher typically entertains only one (or at most a few) of these alternative hypotheses. Usually a theory or the outcomes of previous studies will dictate a specific prediction concerning the treatment effect. For the sake of simplicity, we will state a general alternative hypothesis rather than try to list all possible specific alternatives.

THE TEST STATISTIC FOR ANOVA

The test statistic for ANOVA is very similar to the t statistics used in earlier chapters. For the t statistic, we first computed the standard error which measures the standard distance that is reasonable to expect between two sample means if there is no treatment effect (that is, if H_0 is true). Then we computed the t statistic with the following structure

$$t = \frac{\text{obtained difference between two sample means}}{\text{standard error (the difference expected with no treatment effect)}}$$

For analysis of variance, the test statistic is called an F-ratio and has the following structure:

$$F = \frac{\text{variance (differences) between sample means}}{\text{variance (differences) expected with no treatment effect}}$$

Note that the F-ratio is based on *variance* instead of sample mean *difference*. The reason for this change is that ANOVA is used when there are more than two sample means and it is impossible to compute a sample mean difference. For example, if there are only two samples and they have means of $M = 20$ and $M = 30$, then there is a 10-point difference between the means. Suppose, however, that we add a third sample with a mean of $M = 35$. Now how much difference is there between the sample means? It should be clear that the concept of *a mean difference* becomes difficult to define and impossible to calculate when there are more than two means. The solution to this problem is to use variance to define and measure the size of the differences among the sample means. Consider the following two sets of sample means:

Set 1	Set 2
$M_1 = 20$	$M_1 = 28$
$M_2 = 30$	$M_2 = 30$
$M_3 = 35$	$M_3 = 31$

If you compute the variance for the three numbers in each set, then the variance you obtain for set 1 is $s^2 = 58.33$ and the variance for set 2 is $s^2 = 2.33$. Notice that the two variances provide an accurate representation of the size of the differences. In set 1 there are relatively large differences between sample means and the variance is relatively large. In set 2 the mean differences are small and the variance is small. Thus, the variance in the numerator of the F-ratio provides a single number that describes how big the differences are among all of the sample means.

In much the same way, the variance in the denominator of the F-ratio and the standard error in the denominator of the t statistic both measure the differences that would be expected just by chance or sampling error. Remember that two samples are not expected to be identical even if there is no treatment effect whatsoever. In the independent-measures t statistic we computed an estimated standard error to measure how much difference is reasonable to expect between two sample means. In analysis of variance, we will compute a variance to measure how big the mean differences should be if there is no treatment effect.

Finally, you should realize that the t statistic and the F-ratio provide the same basic information. In each case, the numerator of the ratio measures the actual difference obtained from the sample data, and the denominator measures the difference that would be expected if there were no treatment effect. With either the F-ratio or the t statistic, a large value provides evidence that the sample mean difference is more than would be expected by chance alone (Box 13.1).

BOX
13.1

TYPE I ERRORS AND MULTIPLE-HYPOTHESIS TESTS

If we already have *t* tests for comparing mean differences, you might wonder why analysis of variance is necessary. Why create a whole new hypothesis-testing procedure that simply duplicates what the *t* tests can already do? The answer to this question is based in a concern about Type I errors.

Remember that each time you do a hypothesis test, you select an alpha level that determines the risk of a Type I error. With $\alpha = .05$, for example, there is a 5%, or a 1-in-20, risk of a Type I error. Thus, for every hypothesis test you do, there is a risk of a Type I error. The more tests you do, the more risk there is of a Type I error. For this reason, researchers often make a distinction between the *testwise* alpha level and the *experimentwise* alpha level. The testwise alpha level is simply the alpha level you select for each individual hypothesis test. The experimentwise alpha level is the total probability of a Type I error accumulated from all of the separate tests in the experiment. As the number of sepa-

rate tests increases, so does the experimentwise alpha level.

For an experiment involving three treatments, you would need three separate *t* tests to compare all of the mean differences:

Test 1 compares treatment I versus treatment II.

Test 2 compares treatment I versus treatment III.

Test 3 compares treatment II versus treatment III.

The three separate tests accumulate to produce a relatively large experimentwise alpha level. The advantage of analysis of variance is that it performs all three comparisons simultaneously in the same hypothesis test. Thus, no matter how many different means are being compared, ANOVA uses one test with one alpha level to evaluate the mean differences and thereby avoids the problem of an inflated experimentwise alpha level.

13.2 THE LOGIC OF ANALYSIS OF VARIANCE

The formulas and calculations required in ANOVA are somewhat complicated, but the logic that underlies the whole procedure is fairly straightforward. Therefore, this section gives a general picture of analysis of variance before we start looking at the details. We will introduce the logic of ANOVA with the help of the hypothetical data in Table 13.1. These data represent the results of an independent-measures experiment comparing learning performance under three temperature conditions.

One obvious characteristic of the data in Table 13.1 is that the scores are not all the same. In everyday language, the scores are different; in statistical terms, the scores are

TABLE 13.1

Hypothetical data from an experiment examining learning performance under three temperature conditions.*

Treatment 1 50° (Sample 1)	Treatment 2 70° (Sample 2)	Treatment 3 90° (Sample 3)
0	4	1
1	3	2
3	6	2
1	3	0
0	4	0
$M = 1$	$M = 4$	$M = 1$

*Note that there are three separate samples, with $n = 5$ in each sample. The dependent variable is the number of problems solved correctly.

variable. Our goal is to measure the amount of variability (the size of the differences) and to explain where it comes from.

The first step is to determine the total variability for the entire set of data. To compute the total variability, we will combine all the scores from all the separate samples to obtain one general measure of variability for the complete experiment. Once we have measured the total variability, we can begin to break it apart into separate components. The word *analysis* means dividing into smaller parts. Because we are going to analyze variability, the process is called *analysis of variance*. This analysis process divides the total variability into two basic components.

1. Between-Treatments Variance. Looking at the data in Table 13.1, we clearly see that much of the variability in the scores is due to general differences between treatment conditions. For example, the scores in the 70° condition tend to be much higher ($M = 4$) than the scores in the 50° condition ($M = 1$). We will calculate the variance between treatments to provide a measure of the overall differences between treatment conditions. Notice that the variance between treatments is really measuring the differences between sample means.

2. Within-Treatment Variance. In addition to the general differences between treatment conditions, there is variability within each sample. Looking again at Table 13.1, we see that the scores in the 70° condition are not all the same; they are variable. The within-treatments variance will provide a measure of the variability inside each treatment condition.

Analyzing the total variability into these two components is the heart of analysis of variance. We will now examine each of the components in more detail.

BETWEEN-TREATMENTS VARIANCE

Remember that calculating variance is simply a method for measuring how big the differences are for a set of numbers. When you see the term *variance,* you can automatically translate it into the term *differences*. Thus, the *between-treatments variance* simply measures how much difference exists between the treatment conditions.

In addition to measuring the differences between treatments, the overall goal of ANOVA is to evaluate the differences between treatments. Specifically, the purpose for the analysis is to distinguish between two alternative explanations:

1. The differences between treatments are simply due to chance. That is, the differences are not caused by any treatment effect but are simply the naturally occurring differences that exist between one sample and another.

2. The differences between treatments are significantly greater than can be explained by chance alone; that is, the differences have been caused by the *treatment effects.*

Thus, there are always two possible explanations for the difference (or variance) that exists between treatments:

1. Treatment Effect. The differences are *caused by the treatments*. For the data in Table 13.1, the people in sample 1 were placed in a 50° room and the people in sample 2 were placed in a 70° room. It is possible that the difference between the scores for the two samples was caused by the different temperatures.

2. Chance. The differences are *simply due to chance*. If there is no treatment effect at all, you would still expect some differences between samples. The samples consist of different individuals with different scores, and it should not be surprising that differences exist between samples just by chance. In general, "chance differences" can be defined as unplanned and unpredictable differences that are not caused or explained by any systematic factors. Researchers commonly identify two primary sources for chance differences.

a. *Individual differences:* Because each treatment condition has a different sample of participants, you would expect the individuals in one treatment to have different scores than the individuals in another treatment. Although it is reasonable to expect different samples to produce different scores, it is impossible to predict exactly what the differences will be.

b. *Experimental error:* Whenever you make a measurement, there is potential for some degree of error. Even if you measure the same individual under the same conditions, it is possible that you will obtain two different measurements. Because these differences are unexplained and unpredictable, they are considered to be chance occurrences.

Thus, when we compute the between-treatments variance, we are measuring differences that could be caused by a treatment effect or could simply be due to chance. To demonstrate that there really is a treatment effect, we must establish that the differences between treatments are bigger than would be expected by chance alone. To accomplish this goal, we will determine how big the differences are when there is no treatment effect involved; that is, we will measure how much difference (or variance) occurs by chance alone. To measure chance differences, we compute the variance within treatments.

WITHIN-TREATMENTS VARIANCE

Inside each treatment condition, we have a set of individuals who all receive exactly the same treatment; that is, the researcher does not do anything that would cause these individuals to have different scores. In Table 13.1, for example, the data show that five individuals were tested in a 70° room (treatment 2). Although these five individuals were all treated exactly the same, their scores are different. Why are the scores different? The answer is that the differences within a treatment are simply due to chance.

Thus, the *within-treatments variance* provides a measure of how much difference is reasonable to expect just by chance. In particular, the within-treatments variance measures how big the differences are when there is no treatment effect; that is, how big the differences are when H_0 is true.

Figure 13.3 shows the overall analysis of variance and identifies the sources of variability that are measured by each of the two basic components.

FIGURE 13.3

The independent-measures analysis of variance partitions, or analyzes, the total variability into two components: variance between treatments and variance within treatments.

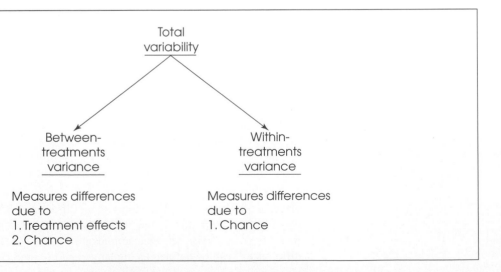

THE *F*-RATIO: THE TEST STATISTIC FOR ANOVA

Once we have analyzed the total variability into two basic components (between treatments and within treatments), we simply compare them. The comparison is made by computing a statistic called an *F-ratio*. For the independent-measures ANOVA, the *F*-ratio has the following structure:

$$F = \frac{\text{variance between treatments}}{\text{variance within treatments}} = \frac{\text{differences including any treatment effects}}{\text{differences with no treatment effects}} \quad (13.1)$$

When we express each component of variability in terms of its sources (see Figure 13.3), the structure of the *F*-ratio is

$$F = \frac{\text{treatment effect} + \text{differences due to chance}}{\text{differences due to chance}} \quad (13.2)$$

The value obtained for the *F*-ratio will help determine whether any treatment effects exist. Consider the following two possibilities:

1. When the treatment has no effect, then the differences between treatments (numerator) are entirely due to chance. In this case, the numerator and the denominator of the *F*-ratio are both measuring chance differences and should be roughly the same size. With the numerator and denominator roughly equal, the *F*-ratio should have a value around 1.00. In terms of the formula, when the treatment effect is zero, we obtain

$$F = \frac{0 + \text{differences due to chance}}{\text{differences due to chance}}$$

Thus, an *F*-ratio near 1.00 indicates that the differences between treatments (numerator) are about the same as the differences that are expected by chance (the denominator). With an *F*-ratio near 1.00, we will conclude that there is no evidence to suggest that the treatment has any effect.

2. When the treatment does have an effect, causing differences between samples, then the between-treatment differences (numerator) should be larger than those due to chance (denominator). In this case, the numerator of the *F*-ratio should be noticeably larger than the denominator, and we should obtain an *F*-ratio noticeably larger than 1.00. Thus, a large *F*-ratio indicates that the differences between treatments are greater than expected by chance; that is, the treatment does have a significant effect.

In more general terms, the denominator of the *F*-ratio measures only uncontrolled and unexplained (often called *unsystematic*) variability. For this reason, the denominator of the *F*-ratio is called the *error term*. The numerator of the *F*-ratio always includes the same unsystematic variability as in the error term, but it also includes any systematic differences caused by the treatment effect. The goal of ANOVA is to find out whether a treatment effect exists.

DEFINITION

For ANOVA, the denominator of the *F*-ratio is called the **error term**. The error term provides a measure of the variance due to chance. When the treatment effect is zero (H_0 is true), the error term measures the same sources of variance as the numerator of the *F*-ratio, so the value of the *F*-ratio is expected to be nearly equal to 1.00.

LEARNING CHECK

1. ANOVA is a statistical procedure that compares two or more treatment conditions for differences in variance. (True or false?)

2. In ANOVA, what value is expected, on the average, for the F-ratio when the null hypothesis is true?

3. What happens to the value of the F-ratio if differences between treatments are increased? What happens to the F-ratio if variability inside the treatments is increased?

4. In ANOVA, the total variability is partitioned into two parts. What are these two variability components called, and how are they used in the F-ratio?

ANSWERS

1. False. Although ANOVA uses variance in the computations, the purpose of the test is to evaluate differences in *means* between treatments.

2. When H_0 is true, the expected value for the F-ratio is 1.00 because the top and bottom of the ratio are both measuring the same variance.

3. As differences between treatments increase, the F-ratio will increase. As variability within treatments increases, the F-ratio will decrease.

4. The two components are between-treatments variability and within-treatments variability. Between-treatments variance is the numerator of the F-ratio, and within-treatments variance is the denominator.

13.3 ANOVA NOTATION AND FORMULAS

Because ANOVA most often is used to examine data from more than two treatment conditions (and more than two samples), we need a notational system to help keep track of all the individual scores and totals. To help introduce this notational system, we use the hypothetical data from Table 13.1 again. The data are reproduced in Table 13.2 along with some of the notation and statistics that will be described.

1. The letter k is used to identify the number of treatment conditions—that is, the number of levels of the factor. For an independent-measures study, k also specifies the number of separate samples. For the data in Table 13.2, there are three treatments, so $k = 3$.

TABLE 13.2

Hypothetical data from an experiment examining learning performance under three temperature conditions.*

Temperature Conditions			
1 50°	2 70°	3 90°	
0	4	1	$\Sigma X^2 = 106$
1	3	2	$G = 30$
3	6	2	$N = 15$
1	3	0	$k = 3$
0	4	0	
$T_1 = 5$	$T_2 = 20$	$T_3 = 5$	
$SS_1 = 6$	$SS_2 = 6$	$SS_3 = 4$	
$n_1 = 5$	$n_2 = 5$	$n_3 = 5$	
$M_1 = 1$	$M_2 = 4$	$M_3 = 1$	

*Summary values and notation for an analysis of variance are also presented.

2. The number of scores in each treatment is identified by a lowercase letter n. For the example in Table 13.2, $n = 5$ for all the treatments. If the samples are of different sizes, you can identify a specific sample by using a subscript. For example, n_2 is the number of scores in treatment 2.

3. The total number of scores in the entire study is specified by a capital letter N. When all the samples are the same size (n is constant), $N = kn$. For the data in Table 13.2, there are $n = 5$ scores in each of the $k = 3$ treatments, so we have a total of $N = 3(5) = 15$ scores in the entire study.

4. The sum of the scores (ΣX) for each treatment condition is identified by the capital letter T (for treatment total). The total for a specific treatment can be identified by adding a numerical subscript to the T. For example, the total for the second treatment in Table 13.2 is $T_2 = 20$.

5. The sum of all the scores in the research study (the grand total) is identified by G. You can compute G by adding up all N scores or by adding up the treatment totals: $G = \Sigma T$.

6. Although there is no new notation involved, we also have computed SS and M for each sample, and we have calculated ΣX^2 for the entire set of $N = 15$ scores in the study. These values are given in Table 13.2 and will be important in the formulas and calculations for ANOVA.

Because ANOVA formulas require ΣX for each treatment and ΣX for the entire set of scores, we have introduced new notation (T and G) to help identify which ΣX is being used. Remember: T stands for *treatment total*, and G stands for *grand total*.

Finally, we should note that there is no universally accepted notation for analysis of variance. Although we are using Gs and Ts, for example, you may find that other sources use other symbols.

ANOVA FORMULAS   Because analysis of variance requires extensive calculations and many formulas, one common problem for students is simply keeping track of the different formulas and numbers. Therefore, we will examine the general structure of the procedure and look at the organization of the calculations before we introduce the individual formulas.

1. The final calculation for ANOVA is the F-ratio, which is composed of two variances:

$$F = \frac{\text{variance between treatments}}{\text{variance within treatments}}$$

2. Recall that variance for sample data has been defined as

$$\text{sample variance} = s^2 = \frac{SS}{df}$$

Therefore, we will need to compute an SS and a df for the variance between treatments (numerator of F), and we will need another SS and df for the variance within treatments (denominator of F). To obtain these SS and df values, we must go through two separate analyses: First, compute SS for the total study, and analyze it into two components (between and within). Then compute df for the total study, and analyze it into two components (between and within).

Thus, the entire process of analysis of variance will require nine calculations: three values for SS, three values for df, two variances (between and within), and a final F-ratio. However, these nine calculations are all logically related and are all directed toward finding the final F-ratio. Figure 13.4 shows the logical structure of ANOVA calculations.

FIGURE 13.4

The structure and sequence of calculations for the analysis of variance.

The final goal for the analysis of variance is an *F*-ratio	$F = \dfrac{\text{Variance between treatments}}{\text{Variance within treatments}}$	
Each variance in the *F*-ratio is computed as *SS/df*	$\begin{array}{l}\text{Variance}\\\text{between}\\\text{treatments}\end{array} = \dfrac{SS\,\text{between}}{df\,\text{between}}$	$\begin{array}{l}\text{Variance}\\\text{within}\\\text{treatments}\end{array} = \dfrac{SS\,\text{within}}{df\,\text{within}}$
To obtain each of the *SS* and *df* values, the total variability is analyzed into the two components	*SS* total ⟋ ⟍ *SS* between *SS* within	*df* total ⟋ ⟍ *df* between *df* within

ANALYSIS OF SUM OF SQUARES (*SS*)

The ANOVA requires that we first compute a total sum of squares and then partition this value into two components: between treatments and within treatments. This analysis is outlined in Figure 13.5. We will examine each of the three components separately.

1. Total Sum of Squares, SS_{total}. As the name implies, SS_{total} is the sum of squares for the entire set of *N* scores. We calculate this value by using the computational formula for *SS*:

$$SS = \Sigma X^2 - \frac{(\Sigma X)^2}{N}$$

To make this formula consistent with the ANOVA notation, we substitute the letter *G* in place of ΣX and obtain

$$SS_{\text{total}} = \Sigma X^2 - \frac{G^2}{N} \tag{13.3}$$

FIGURE 13.5

Partitioning the sum of squares (*SS*) for the independent-measures analysis of variance.

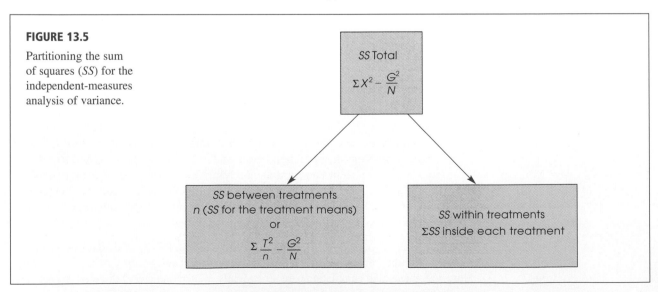

SS Total

$\Sigma X^2 - \dfrac{G^2}{N}$

SS between treatments
n (*SS* for the treatment means)
or
$\Sigma \dfrac{T^2}{n} - \dfrac{G^2}{N}$

SS within treatments
ΣSS inside each treatment

Applying this formula to the set of data in Table 13.2, we obtain

$$SS_{\text{total}} = 106 - \frac{30^2}{15}$$

$$= 106 - 60$$

$$= 46$$

2. Within-Treatments Sum of Squares, $SS_{\text{within treatments}}$. Now we are looking at the variability inside each of the treatment conditions. We already have computed the SS within each of the three treatment conditions (Table 13.2): $SS_1 = 6$, $SS_2 = 6$, and $SS_3 = 4$. To find the overall within-treatment sum of squares, we simply add these values together:

$$SS_{\text{within treatments}} = \Sigma SS_{\text{inside each treatment}} \tag{13.4}$$

For the data in Table 13.2, this formula gives

$$SS_{\text{within treatments}} = 6 + 6 + 4$$

$$= 16$$

3. Between-Treatments Sum of Squares, $SS_{\text{between treatments}}$. Before we introduce any equations for $SS_{\text{between treatments}}$, consider what we have found so far. The total variability for the data in Table 13.2 is $SS_{\text{total}} = 46$. We intend to partition this total into two parts (see Figure 13.5). One part, $SS_{\text{within treatments}}$, has been found to be equal to 16. This means that $SS_{\text{between treatments}}$ must be equal to 30 in order for the two parts (16 and 30) to add up to the total (46). Thus, the value for $SS_{\text{between treatments}}$ can be found simply by subtraction:

To simplify the notation we will use the subscripts *between* and *within* in place of *between treatments* and *within treatments*.

$$SS_{\text{between}} = SS_{\text{total}} - SS_{\text{within}} \tag{13.5}$$

However, it is also possible to compute SS_{between} directly, then check your calculations by ensuring that the two components, between and within, add up to the total. Therefore, we present two different formulas for calculating SS_{between}.

Recall that the variability between treatments is measuring the differences between treatment means. Conceptually, the most direct way of measuring the amount of variability among the treatment means is to compute the sum of squares for the set of sample means. Specifically,

Caution: Equation 13.6 can be used only when all treatments have the same number of scores.

$$SS_{\text{between}} = n(SS_{\text{means}}) \tag{13.6}$$

For the data in Table 13.2, the sample means are 1, 4, and 1, and $n = 5$. The calculation of SS_{means} is shown as follows:

Mean (X)	X^2
1	1
4	16
1	1
6	18

$$SS = \Sigma X^2 - \frac{(\Sigma X)^2}{n}$$

$$= 18 - \frac{(6)^2}{3}$$

$$= 18 - 12 = 6$$

Thus, the sum of squares for the three treatment means in Table 13.2 is $SS_{\text{means}} = 6$, and each treatment contains $n = 5$ scores. Therefore,

$$SS_{\text{between}} = n(SS_{\text{means}}) = 5(6) = 30$$

The intent of Equation 13.6 is to emphasize that SS_{between} measures the mean differences. In this case, we are measuring the differences among three treatment means. However, Equation 13.6 can only be used when all of the samples are exactly the same size (equal ns), and the equation can be very awkward, especially when the treatment means are not whole numbers. Therefore, we also present a computational formula for SS_{between} that uses the treatment totals (T) instead of the treatment means.

$$SS_{\text{between}} = \Sigma \frac{T^2}{n} - \frac{G^2}{N} \tag{13.7}$$

In the formula, each treatment total (T) is squared and then divided by the number of scores in the treatment. These values are added to produce the first term in the formula. Next, the grand total (G) is squared and divided by the total number of scores in the entire study to produce the second term in the formula. Finally, the second term is subtracted from the first. The formula is demonstrated using the data from Table 13.2 as follows:

$$
\begin{aligned}
SS_{\text{between}} &= \frac{5^2}{5} + \frac{20^2}{5} + \frac{5^2}{5} - \frac{30^2}{15} \\
&= 5 + 80 + 5 - 60 \\
&= 90 - 60 \\
&= 30
\end{aligned}
$$

Note that all three techniques produce the same result, $SS_{\text{between}} = 30$. Also note that the two components, between and within, add up to the total. For the data in Table 13.2,

$$SS_{\text{total}} = SS_{\text{within}} + SS_{\text{between}}$$
$$46 = 16 + 30$$

THE ANALYSIS OF DEGREES OF FREEDOM (*df*)

The analysis of degrees of freedom (*df*) follows the same pattern as the analysis of *SS*. First, we will find *df* for the total set of *N* scores, and then we will partition this value into two components: degrees of freedom between treatments and degrees of freedom within treatments. In computing degrees of freedom, there are two important considerations to keep in mind:

1. Each *df* value is associated with a specific *SS* value.

2. Normally, the value of *df* is obtained by counting the number of items that were used to calculate *SS* and then subtracting 1. For example, if you compute *SS* for a set of *n* scores, then $df = n - 1$.

With this in mind, we will examine the degrees of freedom for each part of the analysis.

1. Total Degrees of Freedom, df_{total}. To find the *df* associated with SS_{total}, you must first recall that this *SS* value measures variability for the entire set of *N* scores. Therefore, the *df* value is

$$df_{\text{total}} = N - 1 \tag{13.8}$$

For the data in Table 13.2, the total number of scores is $N = 15$, so the total degrees of freedom are

$$df_{\text{total}} = 15 - 1$$
$$= 14$$

2. Within-Treatments Degrees of Freedom, df_{within}. To find the df associated with SS_{within}, we must look at how this SS value is computed. Remember, we first find SS inside of each of the treatments and then add these values together. Each of the treatment SS values measures variability for the n scores in the treatment, so each SS will have $df = n - 1$. When all these individual treatment values are added together, we obtain

$$df_{\text{within}} = \Sigma(n - 1) = \Sigma df_{\text{in each treatment}} \qquad (13.9)$$

For the experiment we have been considering, each treatment has $n = 5$ scores. This means there are $n - 1 = 4$ degrees of freedom inside each treatment. Because there are three different treatment conditions, this gives a total of 12 for the within-treatments degrees of freedom. Notice that this formula for df simply adds up the number of scores in each treatment (the n values) and subtracts 1 for each treatment. If these two stages are done separately, you obtain

$$df_{\text{within}} = N - k \qquad (13.10)$$

(Adding up all the n values gives N. If you subtract 1 for each treatment, then altogether you have subtracted k because there are k treatments.) For the data in Table 13.2, $N = 15$ and $k = 3$, so

$$df_{\text{within}} = 15 - 3$$
$$= 12$$

3. Between-Treatments Degrees of Freedom, df_{between}. The df associated with SS_{between} can be found by considering the SS formula. This SS formula measures the variability for the set of treatment means or treatment totals. To find df_{between}, simply count the number of means or T values and subtract 1. Because the number of treatments is specified by the letter k, the formula for df is

$$df_{\text{between}} = k - 1 \qquad (13.11)$$

For the data in Table 13.2, there are three different treatment conditions (three T values), so the between-treatments degrees of freedom are computed as follows:

$$df_{\text{between}} = 3 - 1$$
$$= 2$$

Notice that the two parts we obtained from this analysis of degrees of freedom add up to equal the total degrees of freedom:

$$df_{\text{total}} = df_{\text{within}} + df_{\text{between}}$$
$$14 = 12 + 2$$

The complete analysis of degrees of freedom is shown in Figure 13.6.

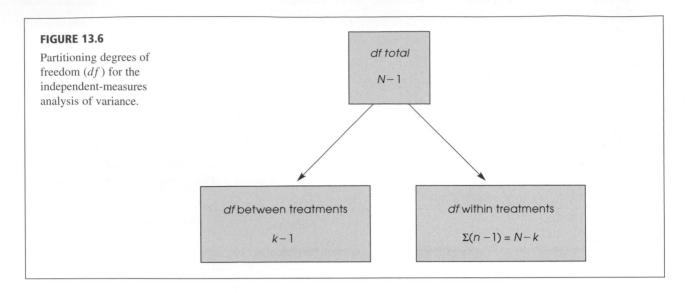

FIGURE 13.6

Partitioning degrees of freedom (df) for the independent-measures analysis of variance.

As you are computing the SS and df values for analysis of variance, keep in mind that the labels that are used for each value can help you to understand the formulas. Specifically,

1. The term **total** refers to the entire set of scores. We compute SS for the whole set of N scores, and the df value is simply $N - 1$.

2. The term **within treatments** refers to differences that exist inside the individual treatment conditions. Thus, we compute SS and df inside each of the separate treatments.

3. The term **between treatments** refers to differences from one treatment to another. With three treatments, for example, we are comparing three different means (or totals) and have $df = 3 - 1 = 2$.

CALCULATION OF VARIANCES (MS) AND THE F-RATIO

The next step in the analysis of variance procedure is to compute the two variances (between and within) that are used to calculate the F-ratio (see Figure 13.4).

In ANOVA, it is customary to use the term *mean square,* or simply *MS,* in place of the term *variance.* Recall (from Chapter 4) that variance is defined as the mean of the squared deviations. In the same way that we use SS to stand for the sum of the squared deviations, we now will use MS to stand for the mean of the squared deviations. For the final F-ratio we will need an MS (variance) between treatments for the numerator and an MS (variance) within treatments for the denominator. In each case

$$MS \text{ (variance)} = s^2 = \frac{SS}{df} \tag{13.12}$$

For the data we have been considering,

$$MS_{\text{between}} = s^2_{\text{between}} = \frac{SS_{\text{between}}}{df_{\text{between}}} = \frac{30}{2} = 15$$

and

$$MS_{\text{within}} = s^2_{\text{within}} = \frac{SS_{\text{within}}}{df_{\text{within}}} = \frac{16}{12} = 1.33$$

We now have a measure of the variance (or differences) between the treatments and a measure of the variance within the treatments. The F-ratio simply compares these two variances:

$$F = \frac{MS_{\text{between}}}{MS_{\text{within}}} \tag{13.13}$$

For the experiment we have been examining, the data give an F-ratio of

$$F = \frac{15}{1.33} = 11.28$$

It is useful to organize the results of the analysis in one table called an *ANOVA summary table*. The table shows the source of variability (between treatments, within treatments, and total variability), *SS, df, MS,* and *F*. For the previous computations, the ANOVA summary table is constructed as follows:

Source	SS	df	MS	
Between treatments	30	2	15	$F = 11.28$
Within treatments	16	12	1.33	
Total	46	14		

Although these tables are no longer used in published reports, they are a common part of computer printouts, and they do provide a concise method for presenting the results of an analysis. (Note that you can conveniently check your work: Adding the first two entries in the *SS* column (30 + 16) yields the total *SS*. The same applies to the *df* column.) When using analysis of variance, you might start with a blank ANOVA summary table and then fill in the values as they are calculated. With this method, you will be less likely to "get lost" in the analysis, wondering what to do next.

For this example, the obtained value of $F = 11.28$ indicates that the numerator of the F-ratio is substantially bigger than the denominator. If you recall the conceptual structure of the F-ratio as presented in Equations 13.1 and 13.2, the F value we obtained indicates that the differences between treatments are more than 11 times bigger than what would be expected if there is no treatment effect. Stated in terms of the experimental variables, it appears that temperature does have an effect on learning performance. However, to properly evaluate the F-ratio, we must examine the F distribution.

LEARNING CHECK

1. Calculate SS_{total}, SS_{between}, and SS_{within} for the following set of data:

Treatment 1	Treatment 2	Treatment 3	
$n = 10$	$n = 10$	$n = 10$	$N = 30$
$T = 10$	$T = 20$	$T = 30$	$G = 60$
$SS = 27$	$SS = 16$	$SS = 23$	$\Sigma X^2 = 206$

2. A researcher uses an ANOVA to compare three treatment conditions with a sample of $n = 8$ in each treatment. For this analysis, find df_{total}, df_{between}, and df_{within}.

3. A researcher reports an F-ratio with $df_{between} = 2$ and $df_{within} = 30$ for an independent-measures analysis of variance. How many treatment conditions were compared in the experiment? How many subjects participated in the experiment?

4. A researcher conducts an experiment comparing four treatment conditions with a separate sample of $n = 6$ in each treatment. An analysis of variance is used to evaluate the data, and the results of the ANOVA are presented in the following table. Complete all missing values in the table. *Hint:* Begin with the values in the df column.

Source	SS	df	MS	
Between treatments	__	__	__	$F =$ ____
Within treatments	__	__	2	
Total	58	__		

ANSWERS   1. $SS_{total} = 86$; $SS_{between} = 20$; $SS_{within} = 66$

2. $df_{total} = 23$; $df_{between} = 2$; $df_{within} = 21$

3. There were 3 treatment conditions ($df_{between} = k - 1 = 2$). A total of $N = 33$ individuals participated ($df_{within} = 30 = N - k$).

Source	SS	df	MS	
Between treatments	18	3	6	$F = 3.00$
Within treatments	40	20	2	
Total	58	23		

13.4   THE DISTRIBUTION OF *F*-RATIOS

In analysis of variance, the F-ratio is constructed so that the numerator and denominator of the ratio are measuring exactly the same variance when the null hypothesis is true (see Equation 13.2). In this situation, we expect the value of F to be around 1.00. The problem now is to define precisely what we mean by "around 1.00." What values are considered to be close to 1.00, and what values are far away? To answer this question, we need to look at all the possible F values—that is, the *distribution of F-ratios*.

Before we examine this distribution in detail, you should note two obvious characteristics:

1. Because F-ratios are computed from two variances (the numerator and denominator of the ratio), F values always will be positive numbers. Remember that variance is always positive.

2. When H_0 is true, the numerator and denominator of the F-ratio are measuring the same variance. In this case, the two sample variances should be about the same size, so the ratio should be near 1. In other words, the distribution of F-ratios should pile up around 1.00.

With these two factors in mind, we can sketch the distribution of F-ratios. The distribution is cut off at zero (all positive values), piles up around 1.00, and then tapers off to the right (Figure 13.7). The exact shape of the F distribution depends on the degrees

FIGURE 13.7

The distribution of *F*-ratios with $df = 2, 12$. Of all the values in the distribution, only 5% are larger than $F = 3.88$, and only 1% are larger than $F = 6.93$.

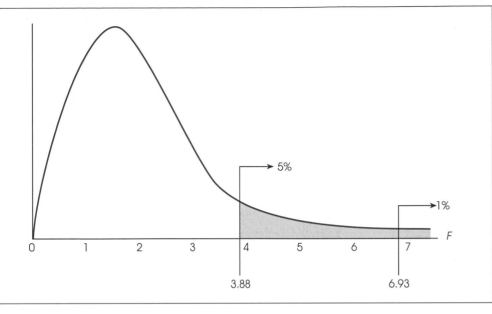

of freedom for the two variances in the *F*-ratio. You should recall that the precision of a sample variance depends on the number of scores or the degrees of freedom. In general, the variance for a large sample (large *df*) provides a more accurate estimate of the population variance. Because the precision of the *MS* values depends on *df,* the shape of the *F* distribution also will depend on the *df* values for the numerator and denominator of the *F*-ratio. With very large *df* values, nearly all the *F*-ratios will be clustered very near to 1.00. With the smaller *df* values, the *F* distribution is more spread out.

THE *F* DISTRIBUTION TABLE

For analysis of variance, we expect *F* near 1.00 if H_0 is true, and we expect a large value for *F* if H_0 is not true. In the *F* distribution, we need to separate those values that are reasonably near 1.00 from the values that are significantly greater than 1.00. These critical values are presented in an *F* distribution table in Appendix B, page 533. A portion of the *F* distribution table is shown in Table 13.3. To use the table, you must know the *df* values for the *F*-ratio (numerator and denominator), and you must know the alpha level for the hypothesis test. It is customary for an *F* table to have the *df* values for the numerator of the *F*-ratio printed across the top of the table. The *df* values for the denominator of *F* are printed in a column on the left-hand side. For the temperature experiment we have been considering, the numerator of the *F*-ratio (between treatments) has $df = 2$, and the denominator of the *F*-ratio (within treatments) has $df = 12$. This *F*-ratio is said to have "degrees of freedom equal to 2 and 12." The degrees of freedom would be written as $df = 2$, 12. To use the table, you would first find $df = 2$ across the top of the table and $df = 12$ in the first column. When you line up these two values, they point to a pair of numbers in the middle of the table. These numbers give the critical cutoffs for $\alpha = .05$ and $\alpha = .01$. With $df = 2, 12$, for example, the numbers in the table are 3.88 and 6.93. These values indicate that the most unlikely 5% of the distribution ($\alpha = .05$) begins at a value of 3.88. The most extreme 1% of the distribution begins at a value of 6.93 (see Figure 13.7).

In the temperature experiment, we obtained an *F*-ratio of 11.28. According to the critical cutoffs in Figure 13.7, this value is extremely unlikely (it is in the most extreme 1%). Therefore, we would reject H_0 with α set at either .05 or .01 and conclude that temperature does have a significant effect on learning performance.

TABLE 13.3

A portion of the F distribution table. Entries in roman type are critical values for the .05 level of significance, and bold type values are for the .01 level of significance. The critical values for $df = 2, 12$ have been highlighted (see text).

Degrees of Freedom: Denominator	Degrees of Freedom: Numerator					
	1	2	3	4	5	6
10	4.96	4.10	3.71	3.48	3.33	3.22
	10.04	**7.56**	**6.55**	**5.99**	**5.64**	**5.39**
11	4.84	3.98	3.59	3.36	3.20	3.09
	9.65	**7.20**	**6.22**	**5.67**	**5.32**	**5.07**
12	4.75	3.88	3.49	3.26	3.11	3.00
	9.33	**6.93**	**5.95**	**5.41**	**5.06**	**4.82**
13	4.67	3.80	3.41	3.18	3.02	2.92
	9.07	**6.70**	**5.74**	**5.20**	**4.86**	**4.62**
14	4.60	3.74	3.34	3.11	2.96	2.85
	8.86	**6.51**	**5.56**	**5.03**	**4.69**	**4.46**

LEARNING CHECK

1. A researcher obtains $F = 4.18$ with $df = 2, 15$. Is this value sufficient to reject H_0 with $\alpha = .05$? Is it big enough to reject H_0 if $\alpha = .01$?

2. With $\alpha = .05$, what value forms the boundary for the critical region in the distribution of F-ratios with $df = 2, 24$?

ANSWERS

1. For $\alpha = .05$, the critical value is 3.68 and you should reject H_0. For $\alpha = .01$, the critical value is 6.36 and you should fail to reject H_0.

2. The critical value is 3.40.

13.5 EXAMPLES OF HYPOTHESIS TESTING AND EFFECT SIZE WITH ANOVA

Although we have now seen all the individual components of ANOVA, the following example demonstrates the complete ANOVA process using the standard four-step procedure for hypothesis testing.

EXAMPLE 13.1

The data depicted in Table 13.4 were obtained from an independent-measures experiment designed to measure the effectiveness of three pain relievers (A, B, and C). A fourth group that received a placebo (sugar pill) also was tested.

TABLE 13.4

The effect of drug treatment on the amount of time (in seconds) a stimulus is endured.

Placebo	Drug A	Drug B	Drug C	
3	4	6	7	$N = 20$
0	3	3	6	$G = 60$
2	1	4	5	$\Sigma X^2 = 262$
0	1	3	4	
0	1	4	3	
$T = 5$	$T = 10$	$T = 20$	$T = 25$	
$SS = 8$	$SS = 8$	$SS = 6$	$SS = 10$	

The purpose of the analysis is to determine whether these sample data provide evidence of any significant differences among the four drugs. The dependent variable is the amount of time (in seconds) that subjects can withstand a painfully hot stimulus.

Before we begin the hypothesis test, note that we have already computed several summary statistics for the data in Table 13.4. Specifically, the treatment totals (T) and SS values are shown for each sample, and the grand total (G) as well as N and ΣX^2 are shown for the entire set of data. Having these summary values will simplify the computations in the hypothesis test, and we suggest that you always compute these summary statistics before you begin an analysis of variance.

STEP 1 The first step is to state the hypotheses and select an alpha level:

$$H_0: \quad \mu_1 = \mu_2 = \mu_3 = \mu_4 \quad \text{(There is no treatment effect.)}$$

$$H_1: \quad \text{At least one of the treatment means is different.}$$

We will use $\alpha = .05$.

STEP 2 To locate the critical region for the F-ratio, we first must determine degrees of freedom for MS_{between} and MS_{within} (the numerator and denominator of F). For these data, the total degrees of freedom are

Often it is easier to postpone finding the critical region until after step 3, where you compute the df values as part of the calculations for the F-ratio.

$$df_{\text{total}} = N - 1$$
$$= 20 - 1$$
$$= 19$$

Analyzing this total into two components, we obtain

$$df_{\text{between}} = k - 1$$
$$= 4 - 1$$
$$= 3$$

$$df_{\text{within}} = \Sigma df_{\text{inside each treatment}} = 4 + 4 + 4 + 4 = 16$$

The F-ratio for these data have $df = 3, 16$. The distribution of all the possible F-ratios with $df = 3, 16$ is presented in Figure 13.8. Note that F-ratios larger than 3.24 are extremely rare ($p < .05$) if H is true and, therefore, will form the critical region for the test.

FIGURE 13.8

The distribution of F-ratios with $df = 3, 16$. The critical value for $\alpha = .05$ is $F = 3.24$.

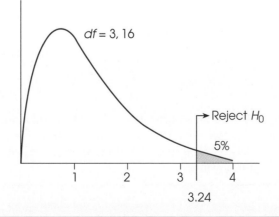

STEP 3   To compute the F-ratio for these data, you must go through the series of calculations outlined in Figure 13.4. The calculations can be summarized as follows:

    a. Analyze the SS to obtain $SS_{between}$ and SS_{within}.

    b. Use the SS values and the df values (from step 2) to calculate the two variances, $MS_{between}$ and MS_{within}.

    c. Finally, use the two MS values (variances) to compute the F-ratio.

Analysis of SS. First, we will compute the total SS and then the two components, as indicated in Figure 13.5.

SS_{total} is simply the SS for the total set of $N = 20$ scores.

$$SS_{total} = \Sigma X^2 - \frac{G^2}{N}$$
$$= 262 - \frac{60^2}{20}$$
$$= 262 - 180$$
$$= 82$$

SS_{within} combines the SS values from inside each of the treatment conditions.

$$SS_{within} = \Sigma SS_{inside\ each\ treatment} = 8 + 8 + 6 + 10 = 32$$

$SS_{between}$ measures the differences between the four treatment means (or treatment totals).

$$SS_{between} = \Sigma \frac{T^2}{n} - \frac{G^2}{N}$$
$$= \frac{5^2}{5} + \frac{10^2}{5} + \frac{20^2}{5} + \frac{25^2}{5} - \frac{60^2}{20}$$
$$= 5 + 20 + 80 + 125 - 180$$
$$= 50$$

Calculation of mean squares. Now we must compute the variance or MS for each of the two components:

The df values ($df_{between} = 3$ and $df_{within} = 16$) were computed in step 2 when we located the critical region.

$$MS_{between} = \frac{SS_{between}}{df_{between}} = \frac{50}{3} = 16.67$$

$$MS_{within} = \frac{SS_{within}}{df_{within}} = \frac{32}{16} = 2.00$$

Calculation of F. We compute the F-ratio:

$$F = \frac{MS_{between}}{MS_{within}} = \frac{16.67}{2.00} = 8.33$$

STEP 4   Finally, we make the statistical decision. The F value we obtained, $F = 8.33$, is in the critical region (see Figure 13.8). It is very unlikely ($p < .05$) that we will obtain a value this large if H_0 is true. Therefore, we reject H_0 and conclude that there is a significant treatment effect.

Example 13.1 demonstrated the complete, step-by-step application of the ANOVA procedure. There are two additional points that can be made using this example.

First, you should look carefully at the statistical decision. We have rejected H_0 and concluded that not all the treatments are the same. But we have not determined which ones are different. Is drug A different from the placebo? Is drug A different from drug B? Unfortunately, these questions remain unanswered. We do know that at least one difference exists (we rejected H_0), but additional analysis is necessary to find out exactly where this difference is. We address this problem in Section 13.6.

Second, as noted earlier, all of the components of the analysis (the *SS, df, MS,* and *F*) can be presented together in one summary table. The summary table for the analysis in Example 13.1 is as follows:

Source	SS	df	MS	
Between treatments	50	3	16.67	$F = 8.33$
Within treatments	32	16	2.00	
Total	82	19		

Although these tables are very useful for organizing the components of an analysis of variance, they are not commonly used in published reports. The current method for reporting the results from an ANOVA is presented on page 358.

MEASURING EFFECT SIZE FOR ANALYSIS OF VARIANCE

As we noted previously, a *significant* mean difference simply indicates that the difference observed in the sample data is very unlikely to have occurred just by chance. Thus, the term significant does not necessarily mean *large,* it simply means larger than expected by chance. To provide an indication of how large the effect actually is, it is recommended that researchers report a measure of effect size in addition to the measure of significance.

For analysis of variance, the simplest and most direct way to measure effect size is to compute r^2, the percentage of variance accounted for. In simpler terms, r^2 measures how much of the differences between scores is accounted for by the differences between treatments. For analysis of variance, the calculation and the concept of r^2 is extremely straightforward.

SS_{between} measures the variability accounted for by the treatment differences, and SS_{total} measures the total variability. Therefore,

$$r^2 = \frac{SS_{\text{between}}}{SS_{\text{total}}} \tag{13.14}$$

For the data from Example 13.1, we obtain

$$r^2 = \frac{50}{82} = 0.61 \quad (\text{or } 61\%)$$

In published reports of research results, the percentage of variance accounted for by the treatment effect is usually called η^2 (the Greek letter eta squared) instead of using r^2. Thus, for the study in Example 13.1, $\eta^2 = 0.61$.

IN THE LITERATURE:
REPORTING THE RESULTS OF ANALYSIS OF VARIANCE

The APA format for reporting the results of ANOVA begins with a presentation of the treatment means and standard deviations in the narrative of the article, a table or a graph. These descriptive statistics are not needed in the calculations of the actual analysis of variance, but you can easily determine them from n, T, and SS values for each treatment. Next, report the results of the ANOVA. For the study described in Example 13.1, the report might state the following:

The means and standard deviations are presented in Table 1. The analysis of variance revealed a significant difference, $F(3, 16) = 8.33$, $p < .05$, $\eta^2 = 0.61$.

TABLE 1

Amount of time (seconds) the stimulus was endured

	Placebo	Drug A	Drug B	Drug C
M	1.00	2.00	4.00	5.00
SD	1.41	1.41	1.22	1.58

Note how the F-ratio is reported. In this example, degrees of freedom for between and within treatments are $df = 3, 16$, respectively. These values are placed in parentheses immediately following the symbol F. Next, the calculated value for F is reported, followed by the probability of committing a Type I error and the measure of effect size.

When an analysis of variance is done using a computer program, the F-ratio is usually accompanied by an exact value for p. The data from Example 13.1 were analyzed using the SPSS program (see Resources at the end of this chapter) and the computer output included a significance level of $p = .001$. Using the exact p value from the computer output, the research report would conclude, "The analysis of variance revealed a significant difference, $F(3, 16) = 8.33$, $p = .001$, $\eta^2 = 0.61$." ❏

A CONCEPTUAL VIEW OF ANOVA

Because analysis of variance requires relatively complex calculations, students encountering this statistical technique for the first time often tend to be overwhelmed by the formulas and arithmetic and lose sight of the general purpose for the analysis. The following two examples are intended to minimize the role of the formulas and shift attention back to the conceptual goal of the ANOVA process.

EXAMPLE 13.2

The following data represent the outcome of an experiment using two separate samples to evaluate the mean difference between two treatment conditions. Take a minute to look at the data and, without doing any calculations, try to predict the outcome of an ANOVA for these values. Specifically, predict what values should be obtained for

$SS_{between}$, $MS_{between}$, and the F-ratio. If you do not "see" the answer after 20 or 30 seconds, try reading the hints that follow the data.

Treatment I	Treatment II	
4	2	$N = 8$
0	1	$G = 16$
1	0	$\Sigma X^2 = 56$
3	5	
$T = 8$	$T = 8$	
$SS = 10$	$SS = 14$	

If you are having trouble predicting the outcome of the ANOVA, read the following hints, and then go back and look at the data.

Hint 1: Remember: $SS_{between}$ and $MS_{between}$ provide a measure of how much difference there is *between* treatment conditions.

Hint 2: Find the mean or total (T) for each treatment, and determine how much difference there is between the two treatments.

You should realize by now that the data have been constructed so that there is zero difference between treatments. The two sample means (and totals) are identical, so $SS_{between} = 0$, $MS_{between} = 0$, and the F-ratio is zero.

Conceptually, the numerator of the F-ratio always measures how much difference exists between treatments. In Example 13.2, we constructed an extreme set of scores with zero difference. However, you should be able to look at any set of data and quickly compare the means (or totals) to determine whether there are big differences between treatments or small differences between treatments.

Being able to estimate the magnitude of between-treatment differences is a good first step in understanding ANOVA and should help you to predict the outcome of an analysis of variance. However, the *between-treatment* differences are only one part of the analysis. You must also understand the *within-treatment* differences that form the denominator of the F-ratio. The following example is intended to demonstrate the concepts underlying SS_{within} and MS_{within}. In addition, the example should give you a better understanding of how the between-treatment differences and the within-treatment differences act together within the ANOVA.

EXAMPLE 13.3   The purpose of this example is to present a visual image for the concepts of between-treatments variability and within-treatments variability. In this example, we compare two hypothetical outcomes for the same experiment. In each case, the experiment uses two separate samples to evaluate the mean difference between two treatments. The following data represent the two outcomes, which we call experiment A and experiment B.

The data from experiment A are displayed in a frequency distribution graph in Figure 13.9(a). Notice that there is a 4-point difference between the treatment means ($M_1 = 8$ and $M_2 = 12$). This is the *between-treatments* difference that contributes to the numerator of the F-ratio. Also notice that the scores in each treatment are clustered close around the mean, indicating that the variance inside each treatment is

FIGURE 13.9

A visual representation of the between-treatments variability and the within-treatments variability that form the numerator and denominator, respectively, of the F-ratio. In (a), the difference between treatments is relatively large and easy to see. In (b), the same 4-point difference between treatments is relatively small and is overwhelmed by the within-treatments variability.

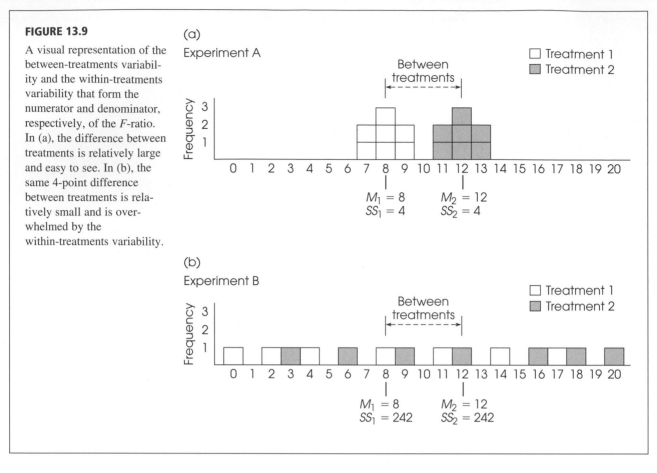

relatively small. This is the *within-treatments* variance that contributes to the denominator of the F-ratio. Finally, you should realize that it is easy to see the mean difference between the two samples. The fact that there is a clear mean difference between the two treatments is confirmed by computing the F-ratio for experiment A.

$$F = \frac{\text{between-treatments difference}}{\text{within-treatments differences}} = \frac{MS_{\text{between}}}{MS_{\text{within}}} = \frac{56}{0.667} = 83.96$$

An F-ratio of $F = 83.96$ is sufficient to reject the null hypothesis with $\alpha = .05$, so we conclude that there is a significant difference between the two treatments.

Now consider the data from experiment B which are shown in Figure 13.9(b) and present a very different picture. This experiment has the same 4-point difference between treatment means that we found in experiment A ($M_1 = 8$ and $M_2 = 12$). However, for these data the scores in each treatment are scattered across the entire scale, indicating relatively large variance inside each treatment. Notice that the large variance within treatments makes it almost impossible to see the mean difference between treatments. The F-ratio for these data confirms that there is no clear mean difference between treatments.

$$F = \frac{\text{between-treatments difference}}{\text{within-treatments differences}} = \frac{MS_{\text{between}}}{MS_{\text{within}}} = \frac{56}{40.33} = 1.39$$

For experiment B, the F-ratio is not large enough to reject the null hypothesis, so we conclude that there is no significant difference between the two treatments. Once again, the statistical conclusion is consistent with the appearance of the data in Figure 13.9(b).

As a final point, note that the denominator of the F-ratio, MS_{within}, is a measure of the variability (or variance) within each of the separate samples. As we have noted in previous chapters, high variability makes it difficult to see any patterns in the data. In Figure 13.9(a), the 4-point mean difference between treatments is easy to see because the sample variability is small. In Figure 13.9(b), the 4-point difference gets lost because the sample variability is large.

Although Examples 13.2 and 13.3 present somewhat simplified demonstrations with exaggerated data, the general point of the examples is to help you *see* what happens when you perform an analysis of variance. Specifically:

1. The numerator of the F-ratio ($MS_{between}$) simply measures how much difference exists between the treatment means. The bigger the mean differences, the bigger is the F-ratio.

2. The denominator of the F-ratio (MS_{within}) measures the variance of the scores inside each treatment; that is, the variance for each of the separate samples. As seen in Example 13.3, large sample variances can make it difficult to see a mean difference. In general, the larger the sample variances, the smaller is the F-ratio.

AN EXAMPLE WITH UNEQUAL SAMPLE SIZES

In the previous examples, all the samples were exactly the same size (equal ns). However, the formulas for ANOVA can be used when the sample size varies within an experiment. With unequal sample sizes, you must take care to be sure that each value of n is matched with the proper T value in the equations. You also should note that the general ANOVA procedure is most accurate when used to examine experimental data with equal sample sizes. Therefore, researchers generally try to plan experiments with equal ns. However, there are circumstances in which it is impossible or impractical to have an equal number of subjects in every treatment condition. In these situations, ANOVA still provides a valid test, especially when the samples are relatively large and when the discrepancy between sample sizes is not extreme.

The following example demonstrates an ANOVA with samples of different sizes.

EXAMPLE 13.4

A psychologist conducts a research study to compare learning performance for three species of monkeys. The animals are tested individually on a delayed-response task. A raisin is hidden in one of three containers while the animal watches from its cage window. A shade is then pulled over the window for 1 minute to block the view. After this delay period, the monkey is allowed to respond by tipping over one container. If its response is correct, the monkey is rewarded with the raisin. The number of trials it takes before the animal makes five consecutive correct responses is recorded. The researcher used all of the available animals from each species, which resulted in unequal sample sizes (n). The data are summarized in Table 13.5.

STEP 1

State the hypotheses, and select the alpha level.

H_0: $\mu_1 = \mu_2 = \mu_3$

H_1: At least one population is different.

$\alpha = .05$

TABLE 13.5

The performance of different species of monkeys on a delayed-response task.

Vervet	Rhesus	Baboon	
$n = 4$	$n = 10$	$n = 6$	$N = 20$
$M = 9$	$M = 14$	$M = 4$	$G = 200$
$T = 36$	$T = 140$	$T = 24$	$\Sigma X^2 = 3400$
$SS = 200$	$SS = 500$	$SS = 320$	

STEP 2 Locate the critical region. To find the critical region, we first must determine the df values for the F-ratio:

$$df_{total} = N - 1 = 20 - 1 = 19$$

$$df_{between} = k - 1 = 3 - 1 = 2$$

$$df_{within} = N - k = 20 - 3 = 17$$

The F-ratio for these data will have $df = 2, 17$. With $\alpha = .05$, the critical value for the F-ratio is 3.59.

STEP 3 Compute the F-ratio. First, compute the three SS values. As usual, SS_{total} is the SS for the total set of $N = 20$ scores, and SS_{within} combines the SS values from inside each of the treatment conditions.

$$SS_{total} = \Sigma X^2 - \frac{G^2}{N} \qquad SS_{within} = \Sigma SS_{inside\ each\ treatment}$$

$$= 3400 - \frac{200^2}{20} \qquad\qquad = 200 + 500 + 320$$

$$= 3400 - 2000 \qquad\qquad\quad = 1020$$

$$= 1400$$

$SS_{between}$ can be found by subtraction.

$$SS_{between} = SS_{total} - SS_{within}$$

$$= 1400 - 1020$$

$$= 380$$

Or, $SS_{between}$ can be calculated using the computational formula (Equation 13.7). If you use the computational formula, be careful to match each treatment total with the appropriate sample size.

Finally, compute the MS values and the F-ratio:

$$MS_{between} = \frac{SS}{df} = \frac{380}{2} = 190$$

$$MS_{within} = \frac{SS}{df} = \frac{1020}{17} = 60$$

$$F = \frac{MS_{between}}{MS_{within}} = \frac{190}{60} = 3.17$$

STEP 4   Make a decision. Because the obtained F-ratio is not in the critical region, we fail to reject H_0 and conclude that these data do not provide evidence of significant differences among the three populations of monkeys in terms of average learning performance.

**ASSUMPTIONS FOR THE
INDEPENDENT-MEASURES
ANOVA**

The independent-measures ANOVA requires the same three assumptions that were necessary for the independent-measures t hypothesis test:

1. The observations within each sample must be independent (see page 210).
2. The populations from which the samples are selected must be normal.
3. The populations from which the samples are selected must have equal variances (homogeneity of variance).

Ordinarily, researchers are not overly concerned with the assumption of normality, especially when large samples are used, unless there are strong reasons to suspect the assumption has not been satisfied. The assumption of homogeneity of variance is an important one. If a researcher suspects it has been violated, it can be tested by Hartley's F-max test for homogeneity of variance (Chapter 10, page 276).

LEARNING CHECK

1. A researcher used analysis of variance and computed $F = 4.25$ for the following data.

	Treatments	
I	II	III
$n = 10$	$n = 10$	$n = 10$
$M = 20$	$M = 28$	$M = 35$
$SS = 1005$	$SS = 1391$	$SS = 1180$

a. If the mean for treatment III were changed to $M = 25$, what would happen to the size of the F-ratio (increase or decrease)? Explain your answer.

b. If the SS for treatment I were changed to $SS = 1400$, what would happen to the size of the F-ratio (increase or decrease)? Explain your answer.

2. A research study comparing three treatment conditions produces $T = 20$ with $n = 4$ for the first treatment, $T = 10$ with $n = 5$ for the second treatment, and $T = 30$ with $n = 6$ for the third treatment. Calculate $SS_{between}$ for these data.

ANSWERS

1. a. If the mean for treatment III were changed to $M = 25$, it would reduce the size of the mean differences (the three means would be closer together). This would reduce the size of $MS_{between}$ and would reduce the size of the F-ratio.

   b. If the SS in treatment I were increased to $SS = 1400$, it would increase the size of the variability within treatments. This would increase MS_{within} and would reduce the size of the F-ratio.

2. With $G = 60$ and $N = 15$, $SS_{between} = 30$.

13.6 POST HOC TESTS

As noted earlier, the primary advantage of ANOVA (compared to t tests) is it allows researchers to test for significant mean differences when there are *more than two* treatment conditions. Analysis of variance accomplishes this feat by comparing all the individual mean differences simultaneously within a single test. Unfortunately, the process of combining several mean differences into a single test statistic creates some difficulty when it is time to interpret the outcome of the test. Specifically, when you obtain a significant F-ratio (reject H_0), it simply indicates that somewhere among the entire set of mean differences there is at least one that is greater than would be expected by chance. In other words, the overall F-ratio only tells you that a significant difference exists; it does not tell exactly which means are significantly different and which are not.

Consider, for example, a research study that uses three samples to compare three treatment conditions. Suppose that the three sample means are $M_1 = 3$, $M_2 = 5$, and $M_3 = 10$. In this hypothetical study there are three mean differences:

1. There is a 2-point difference between M_1 and M_2.
2. There is a 5-point difference between M_2 and M_3.
3. There is a 7-point difference between M_1 and M_3.

If an analysis of variance were used to evaluate these data, a significant F-ratio would indicate that at least one of the sample mean differences is too large to be reasonably explained just by chance and therefore indicates a significant difference between treatments. In this example, the 7-point difference is the biggest of the three and, therefore, it must indicate a significant difference between the first treatment and the third treatment ($\mu_1 \neq \mu_3$). But what about the 5-point difference? Is it also large enough to be significant? And what about the 2-point difference between M_1 and M_2? Is it also significant? The purpose of *post hoc tests* is to answer these questions.

DEFINITION

> **Post hoc tests** (or **posttests**) are additional hypothesis tests that are done after an analysis of variance to determine exactly which mean differences are significant and which are not.

As the name implies, post hoc tests are done after an analysis of variance. More specifically, these tests are done after ANOVA when

1. You reject H_0 and
2. There are three or more treatments ($k \geq 3$).

Rejecting H_0 indicates that at least one difference exists among the treatments. With $k = 3$ or more, the problem is to find where the differences are. Note that when you have two treatments, rejecting H_0 indicates that the two means are not equal ($\mu_1 \neq \mu_2$). In this case there is no question about *which* means are different, and there is no need to do posttests.

POSTTESTS AND TYPE I ERRORS

In general, a post hoc test enables you to go back through the data and compare the individual treatments two at a time. In statistical terms, this is called making *pairwise comparisons*. For example, with $k = 3$, we would compare μ_1 versus μ_2, then μ_2 versus μ_3, and then μ_1 versus μ_3. In each case, we are looking for a significant mean difference. The process of conducting pairwise comparisons involves performing a series of separate hypothesis tests, and each of these tests includes the risk of a Type I error.

As you do more and more separate tests, the risk of a Type I error accumulates and is called the *experimentwise alpha level* (see Box 13.1).

DEFINITION

The **experimentwise alpha level** is the overall probability of a Type I error that accumulates over a series of separate hypothesis tests. Typically, the experimentwise alpha level is substantially greater than the value of alpha used for any one of the individual tests.

We have seen, for example, that a research study with three treatment conditions produces three separate mean differences, each of which could be evaluated using a post hoc test. If each test uses $\alpha = .05$, then there is a 5% risk of a Type I error for the first posttest, another 5% risk for the second test, and one more 5% risk for the third test. Although the probability of error is not simply the sum across the three tests, it should be clear that increasing the number of separate tests will definitely increase the total, experimentwise probability of a Type I error.

Whenever you are conducting posttests, you must be concerned about the experimentwise alpha level. Statisticians have worked with this problem and have developed several methods for trying to control Type I errors in the context of post hoc tests. We will consider two alternatives.

TUKEY'S HONESTLY SIGNIFICANT DIFFERENCE (HSD) TEST

The first post hoc test we consider is *Tukey's HSD test*. We selected Tukey's HSD test because it is a commonly used test in psychological research. Tukey's test allows you to compute a single value that determines the minimum difference between treatment means that is necessary for significance. This value, called the *honestly significant difference,* or HSD, is then used to compare any two treatment conditions. If the mean difference exceeds Tukey's HSD, you conclude that there is a significant difference between the treatments. Otherwise, you cannot conclude that the treatments are significantly different. The formula for Tukey's HSD is

$$HSD = q \sqrt{\frac{MS_{\text{within}}}{n}} \tag{13.15}$$

The q value used in Tukey's HSD test is called a Studentized range statistic.

where the value of q is found in Table B.5 (Appendix B, page 536), MS_{within} is the within-treatments variance from the ANOVA, and n is the number of scores in each treatment. Tukey's test requires that the sample size, n, be the same for all treatments. To locate the appropriate value of q, you must know the number of treatments in the overall experiment (k) and the degrees of freedom for MS_{within} (the error term in the F-ratio) and select an alpha level (generally the same α used for the ANOVA).

EXAMPLE 13.5

To demonstrate the procedure for conducting post hoc tests with Tukey's HSD, we use the hypothetical data shown in Table 13.6. The data represent the results of a

TABLE 13.6

Hypothetical results from a research study comparing three treatment conditions. Summary statistics are presented for each treatment along with the outcome from the analysis of variance.

Treatment A	Treatment B	Treatment C
$n = 9$	$n = 9$	$n = 9$
$T = 27$	$T = 49$	$T = 63$
$M = 3.00$	$M = 5.44$	$M = 7.00$

Source	SS	df	MS
Between	73.19	2	36.60
Within	96.00	24	4.00
Total	169.19	26	
Overall $F(2, 24) = 9.15$			

study comparing scores in three different treatment conditions. Note that the table displays summary statistics for each sample and the results from the overall ANOVA. With $\alpha = .05$ and $k = 3$ treatments, the value of q for the test is $q = 3.53$ (check the table). Therefore, Tukey's HSD is

$$HSD = q\sqrt{\frac{MS_{within}}{n}} = 3.53\sqrt{\frac{4.00}{9}} = 2.36$$

Thus, the mean difference between any two samples must be at least 2.36 to be significant. Using this value, we can make the following conclusions:

1. Treatment A is significantly different from treatment B ($M_A - M_B = 2.44$).
2. Treatment A is also significantly different from treatment C ($M_A - M_C = 4.00$).
3. Treatment B is not significantly different from treatment C ($M_B - M_C = 1.56$).

THE SCHEFFÉ TEST   Because it uses an extremely cautious method for reducing the risk of a Type I error, the *Scheffé test* has the distinction of being one of the safest of all possible post hoc tests (smallest risk of a Type I error). The Scheffé test uses an *F*-ratio to evaluate the significance of the difference between any two treatment conditions. The numerator of the *F*-ratio is an *MS* between treatments that is calculated using *only the two treatments you want to compare*. The denominator is the same *MS* within treatments that was used for the overall ANOVA. The "safety factor" for the Scheffé test comes from the following two considerations:

1. Although you are comparing only two treatments, the Scheffé test uses the value of k from the original experiment to compute *df* between treatments. Thus, *df* for the numerator of the *F*-ratio is $k - 1$.

2. The critical value for the Scheffé *F*-ratio is the same as was used to evaluate the *F*-ratio from the overall ANOVA. Thus, Scheffé requires that every posttest satisfy the same criterion that was used for the complete analysis of variance. The following example uses the data from Table 13.6 to demonstrate the Scheffé posttest procedure.

EXAMPLE 13.6   Remember that the Scheffé procedure requires a separate $SS_{between}$, $MS_{between}$, and *F*-ratio for each comparison being made. Although Scheffé computes $SS_{between}$ using the regular computational formula (Equation 13.7), you must remember that all the numbers in the formula are entirely determined by the two treatment conditions being compared. To demonstrate the Scheffé test, we will use the data in Table 13.6. We begin by comparing treatment A (with $T = 27$ and $n = 9$) and treatment B (with $T = 49$ and $n = 9$). The first step is to compute $SS_{between}$ for these two groups. In the formula for *SS*, notice that the grand total for the two groups is $G = 27 + 49 = 76$, and the total number of scores for the two groups is $N = 9 + 9 = 18$.

$$SS_{between} = \Sigma\frac{T^2}{n} - \frac{G^2}{N}$$

$$= \frac{27^2}{9} + \frac{49^2}{9} - \frac{76^2}{18}$$

$$= 81 + 266.78 - 320.89$$

$$= 26.89$$

Although we are comparing only two groups, these two were selected from a study consisting of $k = 3$ samples. The Scheffé test uses the overall study to determine the degrees of freedom between treatments. Therefore, $df_{between} = 3 - 1 = 2$, and the MS between treatments is

$$MS_{between} = \frac{SS_{between}}{df_{between}} = \frac{26.89}{2} = 13.45$$

Finally, the Scheffé procedure uses the error term from the overall ANOVA to compute the F-ratio. In this case, $MS_{within} = 4.00$ with $df_{within} = 24$. Thus, the Scheffé test produces an F-ratio of

$$F_{A \text{ verus } B} = \frac{MS_{between}}{MS_{within}} = \frac{13.45}{4.00} = 3.36$$

With $df = 2, 24$ and $\alpha = .05$, the critical value for F is 3.40 (see Table B.4). Therefore, our obtained F-ratio is not in the critical region, and we must conclude that these data show no significant difference between treatment A and treatment B.

The second comparison involves treatment B ($T = 49$) versus treatment C ($T = 63$). This time the data produce $SS_{between} = 10.89$, $MS_{between} = 5.45$, and $F(2, 24) = 1.36$ (check the calculations for yourself). Once again the critical value for F is 3.40, so we must conclude that the data show no significant difference between treatment B and treatment C.

The final comparison is treatment A ($T = 27$) versus treatment C ($T = 63$). This time the data produce $SS_{between} = 72$, $MS_{between} = 36$, and $F(2, 24) = 9.00$ (check the calculations for yourself). Once again the critical value for F is 3.40, and this time we conclude that the data show a significant difference.

Thus, the Scheffé posttest indicates that the only significant difference is between treatment A and treatment C.

There are two interesting points to be made from the posttest outcomes presented in the preceding two examples. First, the Scheffé test was introduced as being one of the safest of the posttest techniques because it provides the greatest protection from Type I errors. To provide this protection, the Scheffé test simply requires a larger sample mean difference before you may conclude that the difference is significant. In Example 13.5 we found that the difference between treatment A and treatment B was large enough to be significant according to Tukey's test, but this same difference failed to reach significance according to Scheffé (Example 13.6). The discrepancy between the results is an example of Scheffé's extra demands: The Scheffé test simply requires more evidence and, therefore, its use is less likely to lead to a Type I error.

The second point concerns the pattern of results from the three Scheffé tests in Example 13.6. You may have noticed that the posttests produce what are apparently contradictory results. Specifically, the tests show no significant difference between A and B and they show no significant difference between B and C. This combination of outcomes might lead you to suspect that there is no significant difference between A and C. However, the test did show a significant difference. The answer to this apparent contradiction lies in the criterion of statistical significance. The differences between A and B and between B and C are too small to satisfy the criterion of significance. However, when these differences are combined, the total difference between A and C is large enough to meet the criterion for significance.

LEARNING CHECK

1. With $k = 2$ treatments, are post hoc tests necessary when the null hypothesis is rejected? Explain why or why not.

2. An analysis of variance comparing three treatments produces an overall F-ratio with $df = 2, 27$. If the Scheffé test was used to compare two of the three treatments, then the Scheffé F-ratio would also have $df = 2, 27$. (True or false?)

3. Using the data and the results from Example 13.1,

   a. Use Tukey's HSD test to determine whether there is a significant mean difference between drug B and the placebo. Use $\alpha = .05$.

   b. Use the Scheffé test to determine whether there is a significant mean difference between drug B and the placebo. Use $\alpha = .05$.

ANSWERS

1. No. Post hoc tests are used to determine which treatments are different. With only two treatment conditions, there is no uncertainty as to which two treatments are different.

2. True.

3. a. For this test, $q = 4.05$ and HSD $= 2.55$. There is a 3-point mean difference between drug B and the placebo, which is large enough to be significant.

   b. The Scheffé $F = 3.75$, which is greater than the critical value of 3.24. Conclude that the mean difference between drug B and the placebo is significant.

SUMMARY

1. Analysis of variance (ANOVA) is a statistical technique that is used to test for mean differences among two or more treatment conditions. The null hypothesis for this test states that in the general population there are no mean differences among the treatments. The alternative states that at least one mean is different from another.

2. The test statistic for analysis of variance is a ratio of two variances called an F-ratio. The variances in the F-ratio are called mean squares, or MS values. Each MS is computed by

$$MS = \frac{SS}{df}$$

3. For the independent-measures analysis of variance, the F-ratio is

$$F = \frac{MS_{between}}{MS_{within}}$$

The $MS_{between}$ measures differences between the treatments by computing the variability of the treatment means or totals. These differences are assumed to be produced by
   a. Treatment effects (if they exist)
   b. Differences due to chance

The MS_{within} measures variability inside each of the treatment conditions. Because individuals inside a treatment condition are all treated exactly the same, any differences within treatments cannot be caused by treatment effects. Thus, the within-treatments MS is produced only by differences due to chance. With these factors in mind, the F-ratio has the following structure:

$$F = \frac{\text{treatment effect} + \text{differences due to chance}}{\text{differences due to chance}}$$

When there is no treatment effect (H_0 is true), the numerator and the denominator of the F-ratio are measuring the same variance, and the obtained ratio should be near 1.00. If there is a significant treatment effect, the numerator of the ratio should be larger than the denominator, and the obtained F value should be much greater than 1.00.

4. The formulas for computing each SS, df, and MS value are presented in Figure 13.10, which also shows the general structure for the analysis of variance.

5. The F-ratio has two values for degrees of freedom, one associated with the MS in the numerator and one associated with the MS in the denominator. These df values are used to find the critical value for the F-ratio in the F distribution table.

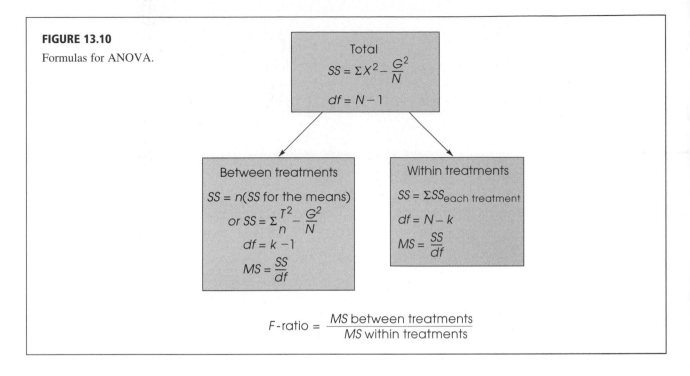

FIGURE 13.10

Formulas for ANOVA.

$$F\text{-ratio} = \frac{MS \text{ between treatments}}{MS \text{ within treatments}}$$

6. Effect size for the independent-measures ANOVA is measured by computing eta squared, the percentage of variance accounted for by the treatment effect.

$$\eta^2 = \frac{SS_{\text{between}}}{SS_{\text{between}} + SS_{\text{within}}}$$

$$= \frac{SS_{\text{between}}}{SS_{\text{total}}}$$

7. When the decision from an analysis of variance is to reject the null hypothesis and when the experiment contained more than two treatment conditions, it is necessary to continue the analysis with a post hoc test, such as Tukey's HSD test or the Scheffé test. The purpose of these tests is to determine exactly which treatments are significantly different and which are not.

KEY TERMS

analysis of variance (ANOVA)	between-treatments variance	error term	post hoc tests
	treatment effect	mean square (MS)	pairwise comparisons
factor	individual differences	ANOVA summary table	experimentwise alpha level
levels	experimental error	distribution of F-ratios	Tukey's HSD test
F-ratio	within-treatments variance	eta squared (η^2)	Scheffé test

RESOURCES

There are a tutorial quiz and other learning exercises for Chapter 13 at the Wadsworth website, www.thomsonedu.com/psychology/gravetter. The site also provides access to a workshop entitled *One-Way ANOVA* that reviews the material presented in this chapter. See page 27 for more information about accessing items on the website.

If you are using WebTutor along with this book, there is a WebTutor section correspon-ding to this chapter. The WebTutor contains a brief summary of Chapter 13, hints for learning the concepts and the formulas for analysis of variance, cautions about common errors, and sample exam items including solutions.

SPSS

General instructions for using SPSS are presented in Appendix D. Following are detailed instructions for using SPSS to perform **The Single-Factor, Independent-Measures Analysis of Variance (ANOVA)** presented in this chapter.

Data Entry

1. The scores are entered in a *stacked format* in the data editor, which means that all the scores from all of the different treatments are entered in a single column (VAR00001). Enter the scores for treatment #2 directly beneath the scores from treatment #1 with no gaps or extra spaces. Continue in the same column with the scores from treatment #3, and so on.
2. In the second column (VAR00002), enter a number to identify the treatment condi-tion for each score. For example, enter a 1 beside each score from the first treat-ment, enter a 2 beside each score from the second treatment, and so on.

Data Analysis

1. Click **Analyze** on the tool bar, select **Compare Means,** and click on **One-Way ANOVA.**
2. Highlight the column label for the set of scores (VAR0001) in the left box and click the arrow to move it into the **Dependent List** box.
3. Highlight the label for the column containing the treatment numbers (VAR0002) in the left box and click the arrow to move it into the **Factor** box.
4. If you want descriptive statistics for each treatment, click on the **Options** box, select **Descriptives,** and click **Continue.**
5. Click **OK.**

SPSS Output

If you selected the Descriptives Option, SPSS will produce a table showing descriptive statistics for each of the samples. This table includes the number of scores, the mean, the standard deviation, and the standard error for the mean for each of the individual samples as well as the same statistics for the entire group of participants. This table also includes a 95% confidence interval for each mean. The second part of the output presents a summary table showing the results from the analysis of variance including all three SS and df val-ues, the two MS values (variances), the F-ratio, and the level of significance (the p value or alpha level for the test).

FOCUS ON PROBLEM SOLVING

---

1. It can be helpful to compute all three SS values separately, then check to verify that the two components (between and within) add up to the total. However, you can greatly simply the calculations if you simply find SS_{total} and SS_{within}, then obtain $SS_{between}$ by subtraction.

2. Remember that an *F*-ratio has two separate values for *df:* a value for the numerator and one for the denominator. Properly reported, the $df_{between}$ value is stated first. You will need both *df* values when consulting the *F* distribution table for the critical *F* value. You should recognize immediately that an error has been made if you see an *F*-ratio reported with a single value for *df*.

3. When you encounter an *F*-ratio and its *df* values reported in the literature, you should be able to reconstruct much of the original experiment. For example, if you see "$F(2, 36) = 4.80$," you should realize that the experiment compared $k = 3$ treatment groups (because $df_{between} = k - 1 = 2$), with a total of $N = 39$ subjects participating in the experiment (because $df_{within} = N - k = 36$).

DEMONSTRATION 13.1

ANALYSIS OF VARIANCE

A human factors psychologist studied three computer keyboard designs. Three samples of individuals were given material to type on a particular keyboard, and the number of errors committed by each participant was recorded. The data are as follows:

Keyboard A	Keyboard B	Keyboard C	
0	6	6	$N = 15$
4	8	5	$G = 60$
0	5	9	$\Sigma X^2 = 356$
1	4	4	
0	2	6	
$T = 5$	$T = 25$	$T = 30$	
$SS = 12$	$SS = 20$	$SS = 14$	

Are these data sufficient to conclude that there are significant differences in typing performance among the three keyboard designs?

STEP 1   State the hypotheses, and specify the alpha level.

The null hypothesis states that there is no difference among the keyboards in terms of number of errors committed. In symbols, we would state

$$H_0: \quad \mu_1 = \mu_2 = \mu_3 \quad \text{(Type of keyboard used has no effect.)}$$

As noted previously in this chapter, there are a number of possible statements for the alternative hypothesis. Here we state the general alternative hypothesis:

$$H_1: \quad \text{At least one of the treatment means is different.}$$

We will set alpha at $\alpha = .05$.

STEP 2   Locate the critical region.

To locate the critical region, we must obtain the values for $df_{between}$ and df_{within}.

$$df_{between} = k - 1 = 3 - 1 = 2$$

$$df_{within} = N - k = 15 - 3 = 12$$

The *F*-ratio for this problem will have $df = 2, 12$. Consult the *F*-distribution table for $df = 2$ in the numerator and $df = 12$ in the denominator. The critical *F* value for $\alpha = .05$ is $F = 3.88$. The obtained *F*-ratio must exceed this value to reject H_0.

STEP 3   Perform the analysis.

The analysis involves the following steps:

1. Perform the analysis of SS.

2. Perform the analysis of df.

3. Calculate mean squares.

4. Calculate the F-ratio.

Perform the analysis of SS. We will compute SS_{total} followed by its two components.

$$SS_{total} = \Sigma X^2 - \frac{G^2}{N} = 356 - \frac{60^2}{15} = 356 - \frac{3600}{15}$$

$$= 356 - 240 = 116$$

$$SS_{within} = \Sigma SS_{inside\ each\ treatment}$$

$$= 12 + 20 + 14$$

$$= 46$$

$$SS_{between} = \Sigma \frac{T^2}{n} - \frac{G^2}{N}$$

$$= \frac{5^2}{5} + \frac{25^2}{5} + \frac{30^2}{5} - \frac{60^2}{15}$$

$$= \frac{25}{5} + \frac{625}{5} + \frac{900}{5} - \frac{3600}{15}$$

$$= 5 + 125 + 180 - 240$$

$$= 70$$

Analyze degrees of freedom. We will compute df_{total}. Its components, $df_{between}$ and df_{within}, were previously calculated (step 2).

$$df_{total} = N - 1 = 15 - 1 = 14$$

$$df_{between} = 2$$

$$df_{within} = 12$$

Calculate the MS values. The values for $MS_{between}$ and MS_{within} are determined.

$$MS_{between} = \frac{SS_{between}}{df_{between}} = \frac{70}{2} = 35$$

$$MS_{within} = \frac{SS_{within}}{df_{within}} = \frac{46}{12} = 3.83$$

Compute the F-ratio. Finally, we can compute F.

$$F = \frac{MS_{between}}{MS_{within}} = \frac{35}{3.83} = 9.14$$

STEP 4   Make a decision about H_0, and state a conclusion.

The obtained F of 9.14 exceeds the critical value of 3.88. Therefore, we can reject the null hypothesis. The type of keyboard used has a significant effect on the number of errors committed, $F(2, 12) = 9.14$, $p < .05$. The following table summarizes the results of the analysis:

Source	SS	df	MS	
Between treatments	70	2	35	$F = 9.14$
Within treatmens	46	12	3.83	
Total	116	14		

DEMONSTRATION 13.2

COMPUTING EFFECT SIZE FOR ANALYSIS OF VARIANCE

We will compute eta squared (η^2), the percentage of variance explained, for the data that were analyzed in Demonstration 13.1. The data produced a between-treatments SS of 70 and a total SS of 116. Thus,

$$\eta^2 = \frac{SS_{between}}{SS_{total}} = \frac{70}{116} = 0.60 \quad (\text{or } 60\%)$$

PROBLEMS

1. Several factors influence the size of the F-ratio. For each of the following, indicate whether it would influence the numerator or the denominator of the F-ratio, and indicate whether the size of the F-ratio would increase or decrease.
  a. Increase the differences between the sample means.
  b. Increase the size of the sample variances.

2. Explain why you should use ANOVA instead of several t tests to evaluate mean differences when an experiment consists of three or more treatment conditions.

3. Explain why the expected value for an F-ratio is equal to 1.00 when there is no treatment effect.

4. Describe the similarities between an F-ratio and a t statistic.

5. Posttests are done after an analysis of variance.
  a. What is the purpose for posttests?
  b. Explain why you would not do posttests if the analysis is comparing only two treatments.
  c. Explain why you would not do posttests if the decision from the ANOVA was to fail to reject the null hypothesis.

6. The following data are constructed so that all three treatments have exactly the same mean, $M = 4$.
  a. Before you begin any calculations, predict what value should be obtained for $SS_{between}$. (*Hint:* How big are the differences between treatments?)
  b. Calculate SS_{total} and SS_{within}. You should find that all of the variability in the data is within-treatments variability ($SS_{total} = SS_{within}$).
  c. Complete the analysis of variance with $\alpha = .05$ to determine whether there are any significant differences among the three treatments. (Does your answer agree with your prediction in part a?)

Treatment			
I	II	III	
0	2	3	$N = 12$
6	6	2	$G = 48$
4	4	5	$\Sigma X^2 = 234$
6	4	6	
$M = 4$	$M = 4$	$M = 4$	
$SS = 24$	$SS = 8$	$SS = 10$	

7. The following data are from an experiment comparing three treatment conditions with a separate sample of $n = 4$ in each treatment.
   a. Use an ANOVA with $\alpha = .05$ to determine whether there are any significant differences among the three treatments.
   b. Compute η^2 for these data.

Treatment			
I	II	III	
2	3	7	$N = 12$
6	7	5	$G = 60$
2	6	4	$\Sigma X^2 = 344$
6	4	8	
$M = 4$	$M = 5$	$M = 6$	
$SS = 16$	$SS = 10$	$SS = 10$	

8. In the preceding problem, the three sample means are close together and there are no significant mean differences. To construct the following data, we started with the scores in Problem 7, then increased the size of the mean differences. Specifically, we lowered the smallest mean by subtracting 2 points from each score in treatment I, and we increased the largest mean by adding 2 points to each score in treatment III. As a result, the three sample means are now much more spread out.
   a. Use an ANOVA with $\alpha = .05$ to determine whether there are any significant differences among the three treatments. Compare the outcome with the results in Problem 7.
   b. Compute η^2 for these data. Compare the outcome with the result from Problem 7.

Treatment			
I	II	III	
0	3	9	$N = 12$
4	7	7	$G = 60$
0	6	6	$\Sigma X^2 = 408$
4	4	10	
$M = 2$	$M = 5$	$M = 8$	
$SS = 16$	$SS = 10$	$SS = 10$	

9. The following data represent the results from an independent-measures experiment comparing three treatment conditions. Use an analysis of variance with $\alpha = .05$ to determine whether these data are sufficient to conclude that there are significant differences between the treatments.

Treatment			
I	II	III	
0	2	5	$N = 15$
0	4	6	
2	0	4	$G = 45$
1	1	7	
2	3	8	$\Sigma X^2 = 229$
$M = 1$	$M = 2$	$M = 6$	
$SS = 4$	$SS = 10$	$SS = 10$	

10. In the previous problem the treatments were significantly different primarily because the mean for sample III is noticeably different from the other two samples ($M_1 = 1$, $M_2 = 2$, and $M_3 = 6$). For the following data we have taken the scores from Problem 9 and reduced the differences between treatments by moving sample III closer to the other two samples. Specifically, we have subtracted 3 points from each score in the third sample to produce sample means of $M_1 = 1$, $M_2 = 2$, and $M_3 = 3$.
   a. Before you begin any calculations, predict how the changes in the data should influence the outcome of the analysis. That is, how will the F-ratio for these data compare with the F-ratio from Problem 9?
   b. Use an analysis of variance with $\alpha = .05$ to determine whether there are any significant differences among the three treatments. (Does your answer agree with your prediction in part a?)

Treatment			
I	II	III	
0	2	2	$N = 15$
0	4	3	
2	0	1	$G = 30$
1	1	4	
2	3	5	$\Sigma X^2 = 94$
$M = 1$	$M = 2$	$M = 3$	
$SS = 4$	$SS = 10$	$SS = 10$	

11. The following data were obtained in a study using three separate samples to compare three different treatments.
   a. Use an analysis of variance with $\alpha = .05$ to determine whether there are any significant differences among the treatments.
   b. Compute the value for η^2 for these data.

Treatment			
I	II	III	
4	3	8	$N = 12$
3	1	4	$G = 48$
5	3	6	$\Sigma X^2 = 238$
4	1	6	
$M = 4$	$M = 2$	$M = 6$	
$SS = 2$	$SS = 4$	$SS = 8$	

Low Moderate	High Moderate	Moderately Severe	Severe	
0	1	4	5	$N = 16$
2	3	6	6	$G = 48$
2	2	2	6	$\Sigma X^2 = 204$
0	2	4	3	
$M = 1$	$M = 2$	$M = 4$	$M = 5$	
$SS = 4$	$SS = 2$	$SS = 8$	$SS = 6$	

12. The data from Problem 11 show significant differences between treatments. To construct the following data, we started with the numbers in Problem 11 but we increased the variance within each sample. Specifically, we kept the same means as in Problem 11, but we spread out the scores inside each of the treatments.

    a. Before you begin any calculations, predict how the changes in the data should influence the outcome of the analysis. That is, how will the F-ratio for these data compare with the F-ratio from Problem 11?

    b. Use an analysis of variance with $\alpha = .05$ to determine whether there are any significant differences among the three treatments. (Does your answer agree with your prediction in part a?)

Treatment			
I	II	III	
4	4	9	$N = 12$
2	0	3	$G = 48$
6	3	6	$\Sigma X^2 = 260$
4	1	6	
$M = 4$	$M = 2$	$M = 6$	
$SS = 8$	$SS = 10$	$SS = 18$	

13. Recent research indicates that the effectiveness of antidepressant medication is directly related to the severity of the depression (Khan, Brodhead, Kolts, & Brown, 2005). Based on pre-treatment depression scores, patients were divided into four groups based on their level of depression. After receiving the antidepressant medication, depression scores were measured again and the amount of improvement was recorded for each patient. The following data are similar to the results of the study.

    a. Do the data indicate significant differences among the four levels of severity? Test with $\alpha = .05$.

    b. Compute η^2, the percentage of variance explained by the group differences.

14. A research study comparing three treatment conditions produced means of $M_1 = 2$, $M_2 = 4$, and $M_3 = 6$.

    a. Compute the variance for the set of three means. (Treat the means as a sample of $n = 3$ values and compute the sample variance.)

    b. Now we will change the third mean from $M_3 = 6$ to $M_3 = 15$. Notice that we have substantially increased the differences among the three means. Compute the variance for the new set of $n = 3$ means. You should find that the variance is much larger than the value obtained in part a. Note: The variance provides a measure of the size of the mean differences.

15. The following data are constructed so that there is no variability inside any of the treatment conditions.

    a. Before you begin any calculations, predict what value should be obtained for SS_{within}. (*Hint:* How big are the differences within treatments?)

    b. Calculate SS_{total} and $SS_{between}$. You should find that all of the variability in the data is between-treatments variability ($SS_{total} = SS_{between}$).

Treatment			
I	II	III	
1	2	3	$N = 15$
1	2	3	
1	2	3	$G = 30$
1	2	3	
1	2	3	$\Sigma X^2 = 70$
$M = 1$	$M = 2$	$M = 3$	
$SS = 0$	$SS = 0$	$SS = 0$	

16. The results from an independent-measures research study indicate that there are significant differences between treatments, $F(3, 36) = 3.28$, $p < .05$.

    a. How many treatment conditions were compared in the study?

    b. How many individuals participated in the entire study?

17. A researcher reports an F-ratio with $df = 2, 24$ for an independent-measures research study.
   a. How many treatment conditions were compared in the study?
   b. How many subjects participated in the entire study?

18. A psychologist would like to examine how the rate of presentation affects people's ability to memorize a list of words. A list of 20 words is prepared. For one group of participants the list is presented at the rate of one word every $\frac{1}{2}$ second. The next group gets one word every second. The third group has one word every 2 seconds, and the fourth group has one word every 3 seconds. After the list is presented, the psychologist asks each person to recall the entire list. The dependent variable is the number of errors in recall. The data from this experiment are as follows:

$\frac{1}{2}$ Second	1 Second	2 Seconds	3 Seconds	
4	0	3	0	
6	2	1	2	$G = 32$
2	2	2	1	$\Sigma X^2 = 104$
4	0	2	1	
$M = 4$	$M = 1$	$M = 2$	$M = 1$	
$SS = 8$	$SS = 4$	$SS = 2$	$SS = 2$	

   a. Can the psychologist conclude that the rate of presentation has a significant effect on memory? Test at the .05 level.
   b. Use the Tukey HSD test to determine which rates of presentation are statistically different and which are not.

19. First-born children tend to develop language skills faster than their younger siblings. One possible explanation for this phenomenon is that first-borns have undivided attention from their parents. If this explanation is correct, then it is also reasonable that twins should show slower language development than single children and that triplets should be even slower. Davis (1937) found exactly this result. The following hypothetical data demonstrate the relationship. The dependent variable is a measure of language skill at age 3 for each child. Do the data indicate any significant differences? Test with $\alpha = .05$.

Single Child	Twin	Triplet
8	4	4
7	6	4
10	7	7
6	4	2
9	9	3

20. There is some evidence that high school students justify cheating in class on the basis of poor teacher skills or low levels of teacher caring (Murdock, Miller, and Kohlhardt, 2004). Students appear to rationalize their illicit behavior based on perceptions of how their teachers view cheating. Poor teachers are thought not to know or care whether students cheat, so cheating in their classes is okay. Good teachers, on the other hand, do care and are alert to cheating, so students tend not to cheat in their classes. Following are hypothetical data similar to the actual research results. The scores represent judgments of the acceptability of cheating for the students in each sample. Use an ANOVA with $\alpha = .05$ to determine whether there are significant differences in student judgments depending on how they see their teachers.

Poor Teacher	Average Teacher	Good Teacher	
$n = 6$	$n = 8$	$n = 10$	$N = 24$
$M = 6$	$M = 2$	$M = 2$	$G = 72$
$SS = 30$	$SS = 33$	$SS = 42$	$\Sigma X^2 = 393$

21. The following data represent three separate samples used to evaluate the differences between three treatment conditions. Use an analysis of variance with $\alpha = .05$ to determine whether there are any significant differences among the three conditions.

Treatment			
I	II	III	
3	4	7	$N = 12$
4	2	2	$G = 36$
0	0	3	$\Sigma X^2 = 150$
3			
3			
5			
$n = 6$	$n = 3$	$n = 3$	
$T = 18$	$T = 6$	$T = 12$	
$SS = 14$	$SS = 8$	$SS = 14$	

22. The following summary table presents the results from an ANOVA comparing three treatment conditions with $n = 8$ participants in each treatment. Complete all missing values. (*Hint:* Start with the df column.)

Source	SS	df	MS	
Between treatments	____	____	20	$F = $ ____
Within treatments	____	____	____	
Total	124	____		

23. A pharmaceutical company has developed a drug that is expected to reduce hunger. To test the drug, three samples of rats are selected with $n = 15$ in each sample. The first sample receives the drug every day. The second sample is given the drug once a week, and the third sample receives no drug at all. The dependent variable is the amount of food eaten by each rat over a 1-month period. These data are analyzed by an analysis of variance, and the results are reported in the following summary table. Fill in all missing values in the table. (*Hint:* Start with the *df* column.)

Source	SS	df	MS	
Between treatments	____	____	20	$F = 4.00$
Within treatments	____	____	____	
Total	____	____		

24. A common science-fair project involves testing the effects of music on the growth of plants. For one of these projects, a sample of 40 newly sprouted bean plants is obtained. These plants are randomly assigned to four treatments, with $n = 10$ in each group. The four conditions are rock, heavy metal, country, and classical music. The dependent variable is the height of each plant after 2 weeks. The data from this experiment were examined using an ANOVA, and the results are summarized in the following table. Fill in all missing values.

Source	SS	df	MS	
Between treatments	72	____	____	$F = $ ____
Within treatments	____	____	3	
Total	____	____		

25. One possible explanation for why some birds migrate and others maintain year round residency in a single location is intelligence. Specifically, birds with small brains, relative to their body size, are simply not smart enough to find food during the winter and must migrate to warmer climates where food is easily available (Sol, Lefebvre, & Rodriguez-Teijeiro, 2005). Birds with bigger brains, on the other hand, are more creative and can find food even when the weather turns harsh. Following are hypothetical data similar to the actual research results. The numbers represent relative brain size for the individual birds in each sample.

Non-Migrating	Short-Distance Migrants	Long-Distance Migrants	
8	5	2	$N = 15$
11	7	4	$G = 150$
17	16	2	$\Sigma X^2 = 2110$
23	6	14	
16	16	3	
$M = 15$	$M = 10$	$M = 5$	
$SS = 134$	$SS = 122$	$SS = 104$	

a. Use an analysis of variance with $\alpha = .05$ to determine whether there are any significant differences among the three groups of birds.
b. Compute η^2, the percentage of variance explained by the differences between groups, for these data.

CHAPTER

14

Repeated-Measures and Two-Factor Analysis of Variance

Tools You Will Need

The following items are considered essential background material for this chapter. If you doubt your knowledge of any of these items, you should review the appropriate chapter or section before proceeding.

- Independent-measures analysis of variance (Chapter 13)

- Repeated-measures designs (Chapter 11)
  - Individual differences

14.1   OVERVIEW

In the preceding chapter we introduced analysis of variance (ANOVA) as a hypothesis-testing procedure for evaluating mean differences. The specific advantage of ANOVA, especially in contrast to *t* tests, is that ANOVA can be used to evaluate the significance of mean differences in situations where there are more than two sample means being compared. However, the presentation of analysis of variance in Chapter 13 was limited to one specific type of research design. In particular, we discussed ANOVA only in relation to single-factor, independent-measures research designs. Recall that *single factor* indicates that the research study involves only one independent variable (or only one quasi-independent variable), and the term *independent-measures* indicates that the study uses a separate sample for each of the different treatment conditions being compared. In fact, ANOVA is an extremely flexible technique, with applications far beyond this single research design. In this chapter, we will begin to explore some more sophisticated research situations in which ANOVA is used. Specifically, we will introduce the following ANOVA topics:

An independent variable is the manipulated variable in an experiment. A quasi-independent variable is not manipulated but defines the groups of scores in a nonexperimental design.

1. **Repeated-Measures ANOVA** It is possible to compare several different treatment conditions using a repeated-measures research design where the same group of individuals participates in every treatment. We will demonstrate how the analysis of variance procedure can be adapted to test for mean differences from a repeated-measures study.

2. **Two-Factor ANOVA** Often, research questions are concerned with how behavior is influenced by several different variables acting simultaneously. For example, a doctor may want to examine how measurements of cholesterol respond to different levels of diet and medication. In this situation, two variables are manipulated (diet and medication) while a third variable is observed. In statistical terminology, the research study has two independent variables or two factors. In the final section of this chapter, we will show how the general ANOVA procedure from Chapter 13 can be used to test for mean differences in a two-factor research study.

14.2   REPEATED-MEASURES ANALYSIS OF VARIANCE (ANOVA)

Chapter 13 introduced the general logic underlying ANOVA and presented the equations used for analyzing data from a single-factor, independent-measures research study. As we noted, the defining characteristic of an independent-measures research design is that the study uses a separate sample for each of the different treatment conditions. One concern with an independent-measures design is that the participants in one treatment condition may have characteristics that are noticeably different from participants in another condition. For example, the individuals in treatment 1 may be smarter than the individuals in treatment 2. In this case, it is impossible to explain any differences that are found between the two treatments. For example: (1) It could be that treatment 1 causes people to have higher scores, or (2) It could be that smarter people have higher scores. To avoid this problem, researchers often chose to use a *repeated-measures design.* You should recall (Chapter 11), that a repeated-measures design uses the same group of participants in all of the treatment conditions. In a repeated-measures study, it is impossible for one group to be different from another because exactly the same group is used in every treatment condition.

In this section we will extend the analysis of variance procedure to single-factor, repeated-measures designs. The analysis is used to evaluate mean differences in two general research situations:

1. The research study is comparing two or more treatment conditions, with the same group of individuals tested in all of the conditions.

2. The research study simply observes the same group of individuals at two or more different times.

Examples of these two research situations are presented in Table 14.1. Table 14.1(a) shows data from a study in which the researcher changes the type of distraction to create three treatment conditions. One group of participants is then tested in all three conditions. In this study, the factor being examined is the type of distraction.

Table 14.1(b) shows a study in which a researcher observes depression scores for the same group of individuals at three different times. In this study, the time-of-measurement is the factor being examined. Another common example of this type of design is found in developmental psychology when the participants' age is the factor being studied. For example, a researcher could study the development of vocabulary skill by measuring vocabulary for a sample of 3-year-old children, then measuring the same children again at ages 4 and 5.

TABLE 14.1

Two sets of data representing typical examples of single-factor, repeated-measures research designs.

(a) Data from an experimental study evaluating the effects of different types of distraction on the performance of a visual detection task.

Participant	Visual detection scores		
	No distraction	Visual distraction	Auditory distraction
A	47	22	41
B	57	31	52
C	38	18	40
D	45	32	43

(b) Data from a nonexperimental design evaluating the effectiveness of a clinical therapy for treating depression.

Participant	Depression scores		
	Before therapy	After therapy	6-month follow up
A	71	53	55
B	62	45	44
C	82	56	61
D	77	50	46
E	81	54	55

HYPOTHESES FOR THE REPEATED-MEASURES ANOVA

The hypotheses for the repeated-measures ANOVA are exactly the same as those for the independent-measures ANOVA presented in Chapter 13. Specifically, the null hypothesis states that for the general population there are no mean differences among the treatment conditions being compared. In symbols,

$$H_0: \quad \mu_1 = \mu_2 = \mu_3 = \cdots$$

According to the null hypothesis, on average, all of the treatments have exactly the same effect. As a consequence of H_0, any differences that may exist among the sample means are not caused by the treatments but rather are simply due to sampling error or chance.

The alternative hypothesis states that there are mean differences among the treatment conditions. Rather than specifying exactly which treatments are different, we will use a generic version of H_1, which simply states that differences exist:

$$H_1: \quad \text{At least one treatment mean } (\mu) \text{ is different from another.}$$

Note that the alternative says that, on average, the treatments do have different effects. Thus, the treatment conditions are responsible for causing mean differences among the samples. As always, the goal of the analysis of variance is to use the sample data to determine which of the two hypotheses is more likely to be correct.

THE _F_-RATIO FOR THE REPEATED-MEASURES ANOVA

The test statistic for the repeated-measures analysis of variance has the same structure that was used for the independent-measures ANOVA in Chapter 13. In each case, the F-ratio compares the actual mean differences between treatments with the amount of difference that would be expected if there is no treatment effect. As always, the F-ratio uses variance to measure the size of the differences. Thus, the F-ratio for the repeated-measures ANOVA has the general structure

$$F = \frac{\text{variance (differences) between treatments}}{\text{variance (differences) expected if there is no treatment effect}}$$

A large value for the F-ratio indicates that the differences between treatments are greater than would be expected by chance or error alone. If the F-ratio is larger than the critical value in the F distribution table, we can conclude that the differences between treatments are _significant_.

Although the structure of the F-ratio is the same for independent-measures and repeated-measures designs, there is a fundamental difference between the two designs that produces a corresponding difference in the two F-ratios. Specifically, one of the characteristics of a repeated-measures design is that it eliminates or removes the variance caused by individual differences. This point was first made when we introduced the repeated-measures design in Chapter 11 (pages 300–301), but we will repeat it briefly now.

First, recall that the term _individual differences_ refers to characteristics such as age, personality, and gender that vary from one person to another and may influence the measurements that you obtain for each person. For example, one person may be smarter or older or taller than another. As we noted earlier, however, in a repeated-measures design every treatment contains exactly the same group of individuals. Thus, it is impossible for individual differences to influence the variance or differences between treatments. In terms of the F-ratio for a repeated-measures analysis, the numerator (between treatments) does not contain any individual differences.

A repeated-measures design also allows you to remove individual differences from the variance in the denominator of the F-ratio. Because the same individuals are measured in every treatment condition, it is possible to measure the size of the individual differences. In Table 14.1(a), for example, participant A has scores that average 10 points lower than participant B. Because there is a consistent difference between participants across all the treatment conditions, we can be reasonably confident that the 10-point difference is not simply chance or random error, but rather is a systematic and predictable measure of the individual differences between these two people. Thus, in a repeated-measures research study, individual differences are not random and unpredictable, but instead they can be measured and separated from other sources of error.

Because individual differences can be eliminated or removed from a repeated-measures study, the structure of the final F-ratio can be modified as follows:

$$F = \frac{\text{variance/differences between treatments (without individual differences)}}{\text{variance/differences expected by chance (with individual differences removed)}}$$

The process of removing individual differences is an important part of the procedure for a repeated-measures analysis of variance.

THE LOGIC OF THE REPEATED-MEASURES ANOVA

The general purpose of a repeated-measures analysis of variance is to determine whether the differences that are found between treatment conditions are significantly greater than would be expected by chance alone. In the numerator of the F-ratio, the between-treatments variance measures the size of the actual mean differences between the treatment conditions in a research study. The variance in the denominator of the F-ratio is intended to measure how much difference is reasonable to expect without any treatment effect. In this section we will examine the elements that make up each of these two variances.

Variance between treatments: The numerator of the F-ratio   Logically, any differences that are found between treatment conditions can be explained by only two factors:

1. Treatment Effect. It is possible that the different treatment conditions really do have different effects and, therefore, cause the individuals' scores in one condition to be higher (or lower) than in another. Remember that the purpose for the research study is to determine whether a treatment effect exists.

2. Error or Chance. Even if there is no treatment effect, it is still possible for the scores in one treatment condition to be different from the scores in another. For example, suppose that I measure your IQ score on a Monday morning. A week later I come back and measure your IQ again under exactly the same conditions. Will you get exactly the same IQ score both times? In fact, minor differences between the two measurement situations will probably cause you to end up with two different scores. For example, for one of the IQ tests you might be more tired, or hungry, or worried, or distracted than you were on the other test. These differences can cause your scores to vary. The same thing can happen in a repeated-measures research study. The same individuals are being measured two different times and, even though there may be no difference between the two treatment conditions, you can still end up with different scores. Because these differences are unsystematic and unpredictable, they are classified as chance or experimental error.

Thus, it is possible that any differences (or variance) found between treatments could be caused by treatment effects, and it is possible that the differences could be due to random error. On the other hand, it is *impossible* for the differences between treatments to be caused by individual differences. Because the same individuals are used in every treatment, individual differences are *automatically eliminated* from the variance between treatments in the numerator of the F-ratio.

Variance due to chance/error: The denominator of the F-ratio   The denominator of the F-ratio is intended to measure the magnitude of the differences (or variance) that would be expected by chance alone. For a repeated-measures analysis of variance, this means that we must measure the variance due to random sources of error without including any individual differences or any systematic treatment effects. For a repeated-measures ANOVA, the denominator for the F-ratio is obtained in a two-step process.

1. First we measure the variance within treatments, exactly as we did in Chapter 13. Because the participants within each treatment are treated exactly the same, this variance does not contain any treatment effects. However, the variance within treatments does include individual differences as well as other sources of experimental error.

2. We measure and subtract out the individual differences.

The result is a measure of variance that does not include any treatment effects or any individual differences. In particular, we are measuring how much variance exists by chance alone. This is exactly what we want for the denominator of the repeated-measures F-ratio.

In summary, the F-ratio for a repeated-measures ANOVA has the same basic structure as the F-ratio for independent measures (Chapter 13) except that it includes no variability due to individual differences. The individual differences are automatically eliminated from the variance between treatments (numerator) because the repeated-measures design uses the same individuals in all treatments. In the denominator, the individual differences are subtracted out during the analysis. As a result, the repeated-measures F-ratio has the following structure:

$$F = \frac{\text{variance between treatments}}{\text{variance due to chance/error}}$$

$$= \frac{\text{treatment effect} + \text{chance/error (excluding individual diff's.)}}{\text{chance/error (excluding individual diff's.)}} \tag{14.1}$$

When there is no treatment effect, the F-ratio is balanced because the numerator and denominator are both measuring exactly the same variance. In this case, the F-ratio should have a value near 1.00. When research results produce an F-ratio near 1.00, we conclude that there is no evidence of a treatment effect and we fail to reject the null hypothesis. On the other hand, when a treatment effect does exist, it will contribute only to the numerator and should produce a large value for the F-ratio. Thus, a large value for F indicates that there is a real treatment effect and therefore we should reject the null hypothesis.

LEARNING CHECK

1. What sources contribute to between-treatments variability for the repeated-measures design?

2. What sources of variability contribute to within-treatments variability?

3. **a.** Describe the structure of the F-ratio for a repeated-measures ANOVA.

   b. Compare it to the F-ratio structure for the independent-measures ANOVA (Chapter 13). How do they differ?

ANSWERS

1. Treatment effect, error/chance

2. Individual differences, error/chance

3. **a.** $F = \dfrac{\text{treatment effect } + \text{ error/chance}}{\text{error/chance}}$

   b. For the independent-measures ANOVA, individual differences contribute variability to both the numerator and the denominator of the F-ratio.

THE STRUCTURE OF THE REPEATED-MEASURES ANOVA

The overall structure of the repeated-measures analysis of variance is shown in Figure 14.1. Note that the ANOVA can be viewed as a two-stage process. In the first stage, the total variability is partitioned into two components: variance between treatments and variance within treatments. This stage is identical to the analysis that we conducted for an independent-measures design in Chapter 13.

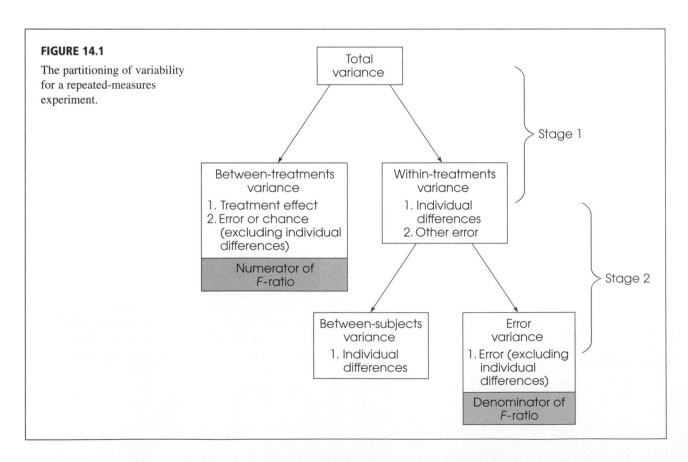

FIGURE 14.1

The partitioning of variability for a repeated-measures experiment.

The second stage of the analysis is intended to remove the individual differences from the denominator of the F-ratio. In the second stage, we begin with the variance within treatments and then measure and subtract out the individual differences. The remaining variance, often called the *residual variance* or *error variance,* provides a measure of how much variance is reasonable to expect after the treatment effects and individual differences have been removed. The second stage of the analysis is what differentiates the repeated-measures ANOVA from the independent-measures ANOVA.

DEFINITION

In a repeated-measures analysis of variance, the denominator of the F-ratio is called the **residual variance** or the **error variance** and measures how much variance is to be expected after the treatment effects and individual differences have been removed.

NOTATION AND FORMULAS FOR THE REPEATED-MEASURES ANOVA

We will use the data in Table 14.2 to introduce the notation for the repeated-measures ANOVA. The data represent the results of a study comparing three brands of pain reliever as well as a fourth condition in which the participants receive a placebo (sugar pill). Note that the same group of $n = 5$ individuals is tested in all four conditions.

You should recognize that most of the notation in Table 14.2 is identical to the notation used in an independent-measures analysis (Chapter 13). For example, there are $n = 5$ participants who are tested in $k = 4$ treatment conditions, producing a total of $N = 20$ scores that sum to a grand total of $G = 60$.

The repeated-measures ANOVA introduces only one new notational symbol. The letter P is used to represent the total of all the scores for each individual in the study. You can think of the P values as "Person totals" or "Participant totals." In Table 14.2, for example, participant A had scores of 3, 4, 6, and 7 for a total of $P = 20$. The P values will be used to define and measure the magnitude of the individual differences in the second stage of the analysis.

EXAMPLE 14.1

We will use the data in Table 14.2 to demonstrate the repeated-measures analysis of variance. Again, the goal of the test is to determine whether there are any significant differences among the four drugs being compared. Specifically, are any of the sample mean differences greater than would be expected without any treatment effect?

TABLE 14.2

The effect of drug treatment on the amount of time (in seconds) a stimulus is endured. *Note:* For comparison, the numerical scores are identical to those used in Example 13.1 on page 354.

Person	Placebo	Drug A	Drug B	Drug C	Person totals	
A	3	4	6	7	$P = 20$	$n = 5$
B	0	3	3	6	$P = 12$	$k = 4$
C	2	1	4	5	$P = 12$	$N = 20$
D	0	1	3	4	$P = 8$	$G = 60$
E	0	1	4	3	$P = 8$	$\Sigma X^2 = 262$
	$T = 5$	$T = 10$	$T = 20$	$T = 25$		
	$SS = 8$	$SS = 8$	$SS = 6$	$SS = 10$		

STAGE 1 OF THE REPEATED-MEASURES ANALYSIS

The first stage of the repeated-measures analysis is identical to the independent-measures ANOVA presented in Chapter 13. Specifically, the SS and df for the total set of scores are analyzed into within-treatments and between-treatments components.

To help demonstrate the similarity between the independent-measures ANOVA and the repeated-measures ANOVA, the numerical values in Table 14.2 are identical to the values used in Example 13.1 (page 354). As a result, the computations for the first stage of the repeated-measures analysis are identical to those in Example 13.1. Rather than repeating the same arithmetic, the results of the first stage of the repeated-measures analysis can be summarized as follows:

Total:

For more details on the formulas and calculations see Example 13.1, pages 354–356.

$$SS_{\text{total}} = \Sigma X^2 - \frac{G^2}{N} = 262 - \frac{(60)^2}{20} = 262 - 180 = 82$$

$$df_{\text{total}} = N - 1 = 19$$

Within treatments:

$$SS_{\text{within treatments}} = \Sigma SS_{\text{inside each treatment}} = 8 + 8 + 6 + 10 = 32$$

$$df_{\text{within treatments}} = \Sigma df_{\text{inside each treatment}} = 4 + 4 + 4 + 4 = 16$$

Between treatments:

$$SS_{\text{between treatments}} = \Sigma \frac{T^2}{n} - \frac{G^2}{N} = \frac{5^2}{5} + \frac{10^2}{5} + \frac{20^2}{5} + \frac{25^2}{5} - \frac{60^2}{20} = 50$$

$$df_{\text{between treatments}} = k - 1 = 3$$

This completes the first stage of the repeated-measures analysis. Note that the two components, between and within, add up to the total for the SS values and for the df values. Also note that the between-treatments SS and df values provide a measure of the mean differences between treatments and will be used to compute the variance in the numerator of the final F-ratio.

STAGE 2 OF THE REPEATED-MEASURES ANALYSIS

The second stage of the analysis involves removing the individual differences from the denominator of the F-ratio. Because the same individuals are used in every treatment, it is possible to measure the size of the individual differences. For the data in Table 14.2, for example, person A tends to have the highest scores and participants D and E tend to have the lowest scores. These individual differences are reflected in the P values, or person totals in the right-hand column. We will use these P values to calculate an SS between subjects in much the same way that we used the treatment totals, the T values, to compute the SS between treatments. Specifically, the formula for SS between subjects is

$$SS_{\text{between subjects}} = \Sigma \frac{P^2}{k} - \frac{G^2}{N} \qquad (14.2)$$

Notice that the formula for the between-subjects SS has exactly the same structure as the formula for the between-treatments SS. In this case we use the person totals (P values) instead of the treatment totals (T values). Each P value is squared and divided by the number of scores that were added to obtain the total. In this case, each person has k scores, one for each treatment. Box 14.1 presents another

> ### BOX 14.1 $SS_{between\ subjects}$ AND $SS_{between\ treatments}$

The data for a repeated-measures study are normally presented in a matrix, with the treatment conditions determining the columns and the participants defining the rows. The data in Table 14.2 demonstrate this normal presentation. The calculation of $SS_{between\ treatments}$ provides a measure of the differences between treatment conditions—that is, a measure of the mean differences between the *columns* in the data matrix. For the data in Table 14.2, the column totals are 5, 10, 20, and 25. These values are variable, and $SS_{between\ treatments}$ measures the amount of variability.

The following table reproduces the data from Table 14.2, but now we have turned the data matrix on its side so that the people define the columns and the treatment conditions define the rows.

In this new format, the differences between the columns represent the between-subjects variability. The

column totals are now P values (instead of T values) and the number of scores in each column is now identified by k (instead of n). With these changes in notation, the formula for $SS_{between\ subjects}$ has exactly the same structure as the formula for $SS_{between\ treatments}$. If you examine the two equations (13.7 and 14.2), the similarity should be clear.

			Person			
	A	B	C	D	E	
Placebo	3	0	2	0	0	$T = 5$
Drug A	4	3	1	1	1	$T = 10$
Drug B	6	3	4	3	4	$T = 20$
Drug C	7	6	5	4	3	$T = 25$

$$P = 20 \quad P = 12 \quad P = 12 \quad P = 8 \quad P = 8$$

demonstration of the similarity of the formulas for SS between subjects and SS between treatments. For the data in Table 14.2,

$$SS_{between\ subjects} = \frac{20^2}{4} + \frac{12^2}{4} + \frac{12^2}{4} + \frac{8^2}{4} + \frac{8^2}{4} - \frac{60^2}{20}$$

$$= 100 + 36 + 36 + 16 + 16 - 180$$

$$= 24$$

The value of $SS_{between\ subjects}$ provides a measure of the size of the individual differences—that is, the differences between subjects. In the second stage of the analysis we simply subtract out the individual differences to obtain the measure of error that will form the denominator of the F-ratio. Thus, the final step in the analysis of SS is

$$SS_{error} = SS_{within\ treatments} - SS_{between\ subjects} \tag{14.3}$$

For the data in Table 14.2,

$$SS_{error} = 32 - 24 = 8$$

The analysis of degrees of freedom follows exactly the same pattern that was used to analyze SS. Remember that we are using the P values to measure the magnitude of the individual differences. The number of P values corresponds to the number of subjects, n, so the corresponding df is

$$df_{between\ subjects} = n - 1 \tag{14.4}$$

For the data in Table 14.2, there are $n = 5$ subjects and

$$df_{between\ subjects} = 5 - 1 = 4$$

Next, we subtract the individual differences from the within-subjects component to obtain a measure of error. In terms of degrees of freedom,

$$df_{\text{error}} = df_{\text{within treatments}} - df_{\text{between subjects}} \tag{14.5}$$

For the data in Table 14.2,

$$df_{\text{error}} = 16 - 4 = 12$$

Remember: The purpose for the second stage of the analysis is to measure the individual differences and then remove the individual differences from the denominator of the F-ratio. This goal is accomplished by computing SS and df between subjects (the individual differences) and then subtracting these values from the within-treatments values. The result is a measure of variability due to error with the individual differences removed. This error variance (SS and df) will be used in the denominator of the F-ratio.

CALCULATION OF THE VARIANCES (*MS* VALUES) AND THE *F*-RATIO

The final calculation in the analysis is the F-ratio, which is a ratio of two variances. Each variance is called a mean square or MS, and is obtained by dividing the appropriate SS by its corresponding df value. The MS in the numerator of the F-ratio measures the size of the differences between treatments and is calculated as

$$MS_{\text{between treatments}} = \frac{SS_{\text{between treatments}}}{df_{\text{between treatments}}} \tag{14.6}$$

For the data in Table 14.2,

$$MS_{\text{between treatments}} = \frac{50}{3} = 16.67$$

The denominator of the F-ratio measures how much difference is reasonable to expect just by chance, after the individual differences have been removed. This is the error variance or the residual obtained in stage 2 of the analysis.

$$MS_{\text{error}} = \frac{SS_{\text{error}}}{df_{\text{error}}} \tag{14.7}$$

For the data in Table 14.2,

$$MS_{\text{error}} = \frac{8}{12} = 0.67$$

Finally, the F-ratio is computed as

$$F = \frac{MS_{\text{between treatments}}}{MS_{\text{error}}} \tag{14.8}$$

For the data in Table 14.2,

$$F = \frac{16.67}{0.67} = 24.88$$

Once again, notice that the repeated-measures ANOVA uses MS_{error} in the denominator of the F-ratio. This MS value is obtained in the second stage of the analysis, after the individual differences have been removed. As a result, individual differences are completely eliminated from the repeated-measures F-ratio, so that the general structure is

$$F = \frac{\text{treatment effect} + \text{chance/error (without individual differences)}}{\text{chance/error (without individual differences)}}$$

For the data we have been examining, the F-ratio is $F = 24.88$, indicating that the differences between treatments (numerator) are almost 25 times bigger than you would expect without any treatment effect (denominator). A ratio this large would seem to provide clear evidence that there is a real treatment effect. To verify this conclusion you must consult the F distribution table to determine the appropriate critical value for the test. The degrees of freedom for the F-ratio are determined by the two variances that form the numerator and the denominator. For a repeated-measures ANOVA, the df values for the F-ratio are reported as

$$df = df_{\text{between treatments}}, df_{\text{error}}$$

For the example we are considering, the F-ratio has $df = 3, 12$ ("degrees of freedom equal two and twelve"). Using the F distribution table (page 533) with $\alpha = .05$, the critical value is $F = 3.49$, and with $\alpha = .01$ the critical value is $F = 5.95$. Our obtained F-ratio, $F = 24.88$, is well beyond either of the critical values, so we can conclude that the differences between treatments are *significantly* greater than expected by chance using either $\alpha = .05$ or $\alpha = .01$.

The summary table for the repeated-measures ANOVA from Example 14.1 is presented in Table 14.3. Although these tables are no longer commonly used in research reports, they provide a concise format for displaying all of the elements of the analysis.

MEASURING EFFECT SIZE FOR THE REPEATED-MEASURES ANOVA

The most common method for measuring effect size with analysis of variance is to compute the percentage of variance that is explained by the treatment differences. The percentage of explained variance is usually identified by r^2, but in the context of analysis of variance it is commonly identified as η^2 (eta squared). In Chapter 13, for the independent-measures design, we computed η^2 as

$$\eta^2 = \frac{SS_{\text{between treatments}}}{SS_{\text{between treatments}} + SS_{\text{within treatments}}} = \frac{SS_{\text{between treatments}}}{SS_{\text{total}}}$$

The intent is to measure how much of the total variability is explained by the differences between treatments. With a repeated-measures design however, there is another component that can explain some of the variability in the data. Specifically, part of the variability is caused by differences between individuals. In Table 14.2, for example, person A consistently scored higher than person B. This consistent difference explains some of the variability in the data. When computing the size of the treatment effect, it is customary to remove any variability that can be explained by other factors, and then

TABLE 14.3

A summary table for the repeated-measures ANOVA for the data from Example 14.1.

Source	SS	df	MS	F
Between treatments	50	3	16.67	$F(3,12) = 24.88$
Within treatments	32	16		
Between subjects	24	4		
Error	8	12	0.67	
Total	82	19		

compute the percentage of the remaining variability that can be explained by the treatment effects. Thus, for a repeated-measures ANOVA, the variability from the individual differences is removed before computing η^2. As a result, η^2 is computed as

$$\eta^2 = \frac{SS_{\text{between treatments}}}{SS_{\text{total}} - SS_{\text{between subjects}}} \qquad (14.9)$$

Because Equation 14.9 computes a percentage that is not based on the total variability of the scores (one part, $SS_{\text{between subjects}}$, is removed), the result is often called a *partial eta squared*.

The general goal of Equation 14.9 is to calculate a percentage of the variability that has not already been explained by other factors. Thus, the denominator of Equation 14.9 is limited to variability from the treatment differences and variability that is exclusively due to chance or error. With this in mind, an equivalent version of the η^2 formula is

$$\eta^2 = \frac{SS_{\text{between treatments}}}{SS_{\text{between treatments}} + SS_{\text{error}}} \qquad (14.10)$$

In this new version of the eta-squared formula, the denominator consists of the variability that is explained by the treatment differences plus the other *unexplained* variability. Using either formula, the data from Example 14.1 produce

$$\eta^2 = \frac{50}{58} = 0.862 \quad (\text{or } 86.2\%)$$

This result means that 86.2% of the variability in the data (except for the individual differences) is accounted for by the differences between treatments.

IN THE LITERATURE
REPORTING THE RESULTS OF A REPEATED-MEASURES ANOVA

As described in Chapter 13 (page 358), the format for reporting ANOVA results in journal articles consists of

1. A summary of descriptive statistics (at least treatment means and standard deviations, and tables or graphs as needed)

2. A concise statement of the outcome of the analysis of variance

For the study in Example 14.1, the report could state:

> The means and standard deviations for the four drug conditions are shown in Table 1. A repeated-measures analysis of variance indicated significant differences in pain tolerance among the four drugs, $F(3, 12) = 24.88$, $p < .01$, $\eta^2 = 0.862$.

TABLE 1

Amount of pain tolerated

	Placebo	Drug A	Drug B	Drug C
M	1.00	2.00	4.00	5.00
SD	1.41	1.41	1.22	1.58

When an analysis of variance is done on a computer, the output usually includes an exact level of significance or p value along with the F-ratio. In this case, the exact p value should be reported instead of using the $p < \alpha$ convention. For the data in Example 14.1, the exact probability value was so small that the computer rounded the p value to .000. However, the exact level of significance is really not zero, so the research report should state $p < .001$.   ❏

POST HOC TESTS WITH REPEATED MEASURES

Recall that ANOVA provides an overall test of significance for the treatment. When the null hypothesis is rejected, it indicates only that there is a difference between at least two of the treatment means. If $k = 2$, it is obvious where the difference lies in the experiment. However, when k is greater than 2, the situation becomes more complex. To determine exactly where significant differences exist, the researcher must follow the ANOVA with post hoc tests. In Chapter 13, we used Tukey's HSD and the Scheffé test to make these multiple comparisons among treatment means. These two procedures attempt to control the overall alpha level by making adjustments for the number of potential comparisons.

For a repeated-measures ANOVA, Tukey's HSD and the Scheffé test can be used in the exact same manner as was done for the independent-measures ANOVA, *provided* that you substitute MS_{error} in place of MS_{within} in the formulas and use df_{error} in place of df_{within} when locating the critical value in a statistical table. It should be noted that statisticians are not in complete agreement about the appropriate error term in post hoc tests for repeated-measures designs (for a discussion, see Keppel, 1973, or Keppel & Zedeck, 1989).

LEARNING CHECK

1. How is SS_{error} calculated for the repeated-measures ANOVA?

2. What two df components are associated with the repeated-measures F-ratio? How are they computed?

3. For the following set of data, compute all of the SS components for a repeated-measures ANOVA:

		Treatment			
Subject	1	2	3	4	
A	2	2	2	2	$G = 32$
B	4	0	0	4	$\Sigma X^2 = 96$
C	2	0	2	0	
D	4	2	2	4	

4. Which two MS components are used to form the F-ratio of the repeated-measures ANOVA? How are they computed?

ANSWERS

1. $SS_{error} = SS_{within\ treatments} - SS_{between\ subjects}$

2. Between-treatments df and error df; $df_{between\ treatments} = k - 1$; $df_{error} = (N - k) - (n - 1)$

3. $SS_{total} = 32$, $SS_{between\ treatments} = 10$, $SS_{within\ treatments} = 22$, $SS_{between\ subjects} = 8$, $SS_{error} = 14$

4. Between-treatments *MS* and error *MS*;

$$MS_{\text{between treatments}} = \frac{SS_{\text{between treatments}}}{df_{\text{between treatments}}}$$

$$MS_{\text{error}} = \frac{SS_{\text{error}}}{df_{\text{error}}}$$

14.3 TWO-FACTOR ANALYSIS OF VARIANCE (INDEPENDENT MEASURES)

In most research situations, the goal is to examine the relationship between two variables. Typically, the research study will attempt to isolate the two variables in order to eliminate or reduce the influence of any outside variables that may distort the relationship being studied. A typical experiment, for example, will focus on one independent variable (which is expected to influence behavior) and one dependent variable (which is a measure of the behavior). In real life, however, variables rarely exist in isolation. That is, behavior usually is influenced by a variety of different variables acting and interacting simultaneously. To examine these more complex, real-life situations, researchers often design research studies that include more than one independent variable. Thus, researchers will systematically change two (or more) variables and then observe how the changes influence another (dependent) variable.

In the preceding chapter, we examined analysis of variance for *single-factor* research designs—that is, designs that included only one independent variable or only one quasi-independent variable. When a research study involves more than one factor, it is called a *factorial design*. In this chapter, we consider the simplest version of a factorial design. Specifically, we will examine analysis of variance as it applies to research studies with exactly two factors. In addition, we will limit our discussion to studies that use a separate sample for each treatment condition—that is, independent-measures designs. Finally, we only will consider research designs for which the sample size (*n*) is the same for all treatment conditions. In the terminology of ANOVA, this chapter will examine *two-factor, independent-measures, equal n designs*. The following example demonstrates the general structure of this kind of research study.

EXAMPLE 14.2   Most of us find it difficult to think clearly or to work efficiently on hot summer days. If you listen to people discussing this problem, you will occasionally hear comments like "It's not the heat; it's the humidity." To evaluate this claim scientifically, you would need to design a study in which both heat and humidity are manipulated within the same experiment and then observe behavior under a variety of different heat and humidity combinations. Table 14.4 shows the structure of a hypothetical study intended to examine the heat-versus-humidity question. Note that the study involves two independent variables: The temperature (heat) is varied from 70° to 80° to 90°, and the humidity is varied from low to high. The two independent variables are used to create a *matrix* with the different values of temperature defining the columns and the different levels of humidity defining the rows. The resulting two-by-three matrix shows six different combinations of the variables, producing six treatment conditions. Thus, the research study would require six separate samples, one for each of the *cells* or boxes in the matrix. The dependent variable for our study

TABLE 14.4

The structure of a two-factor experiment presented as a matrix. The factors are humidity and temperature. There are two levels for the humidity factor (low and high), and there are three levels for the temperature factor (70°, 80°, and 90°).

		Factor B: temperature		
		70° room	80° room	90° room
Factor A: humidity	Low humidity	Scores for $n = 15$ subjects tested in a 70° room with low humidity	Scores for $n = 15$ subjects tested in an 80° room with low humidity	Scores for $n = 15$ subjects tested in a 90° room with low humidity
	High humidity	Scores for $n = 15$ subjects tested in a 70° room with high humidity	Scores for $n = 15$ subjects tested in an 80° room with high humidity	Scores for $n = 15$ subjects tested in a 90° room with high humidity

would be a measure of thinking/working proficiency (such as performance on a problem-solving task) for people observed in each of the six conditions.

A two-factor research study, such as the heat-and-humidity example in Table 14.4, allows us to evaluate a variety of mean differences. For example, this study would allow us to examine

1. What happens to the mean level of performance as the temperature is changed from 70° to 80° to 90°?
2. What happens to the mean level of performance as the humidity is changed from low to high?
3. How do specific combinations of temperature and humidity affect performance? (For example, increasing humidity may have no effect on performance when the temperature is low but could be very disruptive when the temperature is high.)

Thus, the two-factor analysis of variance allows us to examine three types of mean differences within one analysis. In particular, we will conduct three separate hypotheses tests for the same data, with a separate F-ratio for each test. The three F-ratios will all have the same basic structure:

$$F = \frac{\text{variance (differences) between treatments}}{\text{variance (differences) expected if there is no treatment effect}} \qquad (14.11)$$

In each case, the numerator of the F-ratio measures the actual mean differences in the data, and the denominator measures the differences that would be expected if there was no treatment effect. As always in ANOVA, a large value for the F-ratio indicates that the sample mean differences are greater than would be expected by chance alone, and therefore provide evidence of a treatment effect. To determine whether the obtained F-ratios are *significant,* we will need to compare each F-ratio with the critical values found in the F-distribution table in Appendix B.

MAIN EFFECTS AND INTERACTIONS

As noted in the previous section, a two-factor ANOVA actually involves three distinct hypothesis tests. In this section, we examine these three tests in more detail.

Traditionally, the two independent variables in a two-factor experiment are identified as factor A and factor B. For the experiment presented in Table 14.4, humidity would be factor A, and temperature would be factor B. The goal of the experiment is to evaluate the mean differences that may be produced by either of these factors independently or by the two factors acting together.

MAIN EFFECTS

One purpose of the experiment is to determine whether differences in humidity (factor A) result in differences in performance. To answer this question, we will compare the mean score for all participants tested with low humidity versus the mean score for those tested with high humidity. Note that this process evaluates the mean difference between the top row and the bottom row in Table 14.4.

To make this process more concrete, we have presented a set of hypothetical data in Table 14.5. The table shows the mean score for each of the treatment conditions (cells) as well as the overall mean for each column (each temperature) and the overall mean for each row (humidity level). These data indicate that participants in the low-humidity condition (the top row) obtained an average score of $M = 80$. This overall mean was obtained by computing the average of the three means in the top row. In contrast, high humidity resulted in a mean score of $M = 70$ (the overall mean for the bottom row). The difference between these means constitutes what is called the *main effect* for humidity, or the *main effect for factor A*.

Similarly, the main effect for factor B (temperature) is defined by the mean differences among columns of the matrix. For the data in Table 14.5, the two groups of participants tested with a temperature of 70° obtained an overall mean score of $M = 80$. Participants tested with the temperature at 80° averaged $M = 75$, and those tested at 90° achieved an overall mean score of $M = 70$. The differences among these means constitute the *main effect* for temperature, or the *main effect for factor B*.

DEFINITION

The mean differences among the levels of one factor are referred to as the **main effect** of that factor. When the design of the research study is represented as a matrix with one factor determining the rows and the second factor determining the columns, then the mean differences among the rows describe the main effect of one factor, and the mean differences among the columns describe the main effect for the second factor.

The mean differences between columns or rows simply *describe* the main effects for a two-factor study. As we have observed in earlier chapters, the existence of sample mean differences does not necessarily imply that the differences are *statistically significant*. In general, two samples are not expected to have exactly the same means. There will always be small differences from one sample to another, and you should not automatically assume that these differences are an indication of a systematic treatment effect. In the case of a two-factor study, any main effects that are observed in the data

TABLE 14.5

Hypothetical data from an experiment examining two different levels of humidity (factor A) and three different levels of temperature (factor B).

	70°	80°	90°	
Low humidity	$M = 85$	$M = 80$	$M = 75$	$M = 80$
High humidity	$M = 75$	$M = 70$	$M = 65$	$M = 70$
	$M = 80$	$M = 75$	$M = 70$	

must be evaluated with a hypothesis test to determine whether they are statistically significant effects. Unless the hypothesis test demonstrates that the main effects are significant, you must conclude that the observed mean differences are simply the result of sampling error.

The evaluation of main effects will make up two of the three hypothesis tests contained in a two-factor ANOVA. We will state hypotheses concerning the main effect of factor A and the main effect of factor B and then calculate two separate F-ratios to evaluate the hypotheses.

For the example we are considering, factor A involves the comparison of two different levels of humidity. The null hypothesis would state that there is no difference between the two levels; that is, humidity has no effect on performance. In symbols,

$$H_0: \quad \mu_{A_1} = \mu_{A_2}$$

The alternative hypothesis is that the two different levels of humidity do produce different scores:

$$H_1: \quad \mu_{A_1} \neq \mu_{A_2}$$

To evaluate these hypotheses, we will compute an F-ratio that compares the actual mean differences between the two humidity levels versus the amount of difference that would be expected by chance or sampling error.

$$F = \frac{\text{variance (differences) between the means for factor } A}{\text{variance (differences) expected by chance/error}}$$

$$F = \frac{\text{variance (differences) between row means}}{\text{variance (differences) expected by chance/error}}$$

Similarly, factor B involves the comparison of the three different temperature conditions. The null hypothesis states that overall there are no differences in mean performance among the three temperatures. In symbols,

$$H_0: \quad \mu_{B_1} = \mu_{B_2} = \mu_{B_3}$$

As always, the alternative hypothesis states that there are differences:

$$H_1: \quad \text{At least one mean is different from another.}$$

Again, the F-ratio will compare the obtained mean differences among the three temperature conditions versus the amount of difference that would be expected by chance.

$$F = \frac{\text{variance (differences) between the means for factor } B}{\text{variance (differences) expected by chance/error}}$$

$$F = \frac{\text{variance (differences) between column means}}{\text{variance (differences) expected by chance/error}}$$

INTERACTIONS   In addition to evaluating the main effect of each factor individually, the two-factor ANOVA allows you to evaluate other mean differences that may result from unique combinations of the two factors. For example, specific combinations of heat and humidity may have effects that are different from the overall effects of heat or humidity acting alone. Any "extra" mean differences that are not explained by the main effects are called an *interaction between factors*. The real advantage of combining two factors within the same study is the ability to examine the unique effects caused by an interaction.

DEFINITION

An **interaction between two factors** occurs whenever the mean differences between individual treatment conditions, or cells, are different from what would be predicted from the overall main effects of the factors.

To make the concept of an interaction more concrete, we will reexamine the data shown in Table 14.5. For these data, there is no interaction; that is, there are no extra mean differences that are not explained by the main effects. For example, within each temperature condition (each column of the matrix) the participants scored 10 points higher in the low-humidity condition than in the high-humidity condition. This 10-point mean difference is exactly what is predicted by the overall main effect for humidity.

Now consider the data shown in Table 14.6. These new data show exactly the same main effects that existed in Table 14.5 (the column means and the row means have not been changed). But now there is an interaction between the two factors. For example, when the temperature is 90° (third column), there is a 20-point difference between the low-humidity and high-humidity conditions. This 20-point difference cannot be explained by the 10-point main effect for humidity. Also, when the temperature is 70° (first column), the data show no difference between the two humidity conditions. Again, this zero difference is not what would be expected based on the 10-point main effect for humidity. Mean differences that are not explained by the main effects are an indication of an interaction between the two factors.

To evaluate the interaction, the two-factor ANOVA first identifies the extra mean differences that are not explained by the main effects. The extra mean differences are then evaluated by an F-ratio with the following structure:

$$F = \frac{\text{variance (mean differences) not explained by main effects}}{\text{variance (differences) expected by chance/error}}$$

The null hypothesis for this F-ratio simply states that there is no interaction:

H_0: There is no interaction between factors A and B. All mean differences between treatment conditions are explained by the main effects of the two factors.

TABLE 14.6

Hypothetical data from an experiment examining two different levels of humidity (factor A) and three different temperature conditions (factor B). (The data show the same main effects as the data in Table 14.5, but the individual treatment means have been modified to produce an interaction.)

	70°	80°	90°	
Low humidity	$M = 80$	$M = 80$	$M = 80$	$M = 80$
High humidity	$M = 80$	$M = 70$	$M = 60$	$M = 70$
	$M = 80$	$M = 75$	$M = 70$	

The alternative hypothesis is that there is an interaction between the two factors:

H_1: There is an interaction between factors. The mean differences between treatment conditions are not what would be predicted from the overall main effects of the two factors.

MORE ABOUT INTERACTIONS

In the previous section, we introduced the concept of an interaction as the unique effect produced by two factors working together. This section will present two alternative definitions of an interaction. These alternatives are intended to help you understand the concept of an interaction and to help you identify an interaction when you encounter one in a set of data. The new definitions are equivalent to the original and simply present slightly different perspectives on the same concept.

The first new perspective on the concept of an interaction focuses on the notion of independence for the two factors. More specifically, if the two factors are independent, so that one factor does not influence the effect of the other, then there will be no interaction. On the other hand, when the two factors are not independent, so that the effect of one factor *depends on* the other, then there is an interaction. The notion of dependence between factors is consistent with our earlier discussion of interactions. If one factor influences the effect of the other, then unique combinations of the factors will produce unique effects.

D E F I N I T I O N

When the effect of one factor depends on the different levels of a second factor, then there is an **interaction between the factors**.

This definition of an interaction should be familiar in the context of a "drug interaction." Your doctor and pharmacist are always concerned that the effect of one medication may be altered or distorted if a second medication is being taken at the same time. Thus, the effect of one drug (factor 1) depends on a second drug (factor 2), and you have an interaction between the two drugs.

Returning to the data in Table 14.5 (with no interaction), notice that the size of the humidity effect (top row versus bottom row) *does not depend on* the temperature. For these data, the change in humidity shows the same 10-point effect for all three levels of temperature. Thus, the humidity effect does not depend on temperature, and there is no interaction. Now consider the data in Table 14.6. This time, the effect of changing humidity *depends on* the temperature, and there is an interaction. At 70°, for example, there is no difference between the high and low humidity conditions. However, there is a 10-point difference between high and low humidity when the temperature is 80°, and there is a 20-point effect at 90°. Thus, the effect of humidity depends on the temperature, which means that there is an interaction between the two factors.

The second alternative definition of an interaction refers to a graph showing the means from a two-factor study. In this case, the concept of an interaction can be defined in terms of the pattern displayed in the graph. Figure 14.2 shows the two sets of data we have been considering. The original data from Table 14.5, where there is no interaction, are presented in Figure 14.2(a). To construct this figure, we selected one of the factors to be displayed on the horizontal axis; in this case, it is the different levels of temperature. The dependent variable, mean level of performance, is shown on the vertical axis. Note that the figure actually contains two separate graphs: The top line shows the relationship between temperature and mean performance when the humidity is low,

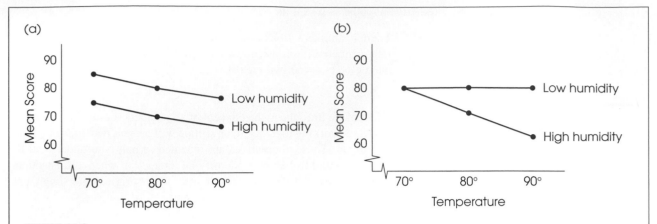

FIGURE 14.2

(a) Graph showing the data from Table 14.5, where there is no interaction. (b) Graph showing the data from Table 14.6, where there is an interaction.

and the bottom line shows the relationship when the humidity is high. In general, the picture in the graph matches the structure of the data matrix; the columns of the matrix appear as values along the *X*-axis, and the rows of the matrix appear as separate lines in the graph.

For this particular set of data, Figure 14.2(a), note that the two lines are parallel; that is, the distance between lines is constant. In this case, the distance between lines reflects the 10-point difference in mean performance between high and low humidity, and this 10-point difference is the same for all three temperature conditions.

Now look at a graph that is obtained when there is an interaction in the data. Figure 14.2(b) shows the data from Table 14.6. This time, note that the lines in the graph are not parallel. The distance between the lines changes as you scan from left to right. For these data, the distance between the lines corresponds to the humidity effect—that is, the mean difference in performance for low humidity versus high humidity. The fact that this difference depends on temperature indicates an interaction between factors.

D E F I N I T I O N	When the results of a two-factor study are presented in a graph, the existence of nonparallel lines (lines that cross or converge) indicates an **interaction between the two factors**.

The *A* × *B* interaction typically is called "*A* by *B*" interaction. If there is an interaction of temperature and humidity, it may be called the "temperature by humidity" interaction.

For many students, the concept of an interaction is easiest to understand using the perspective of interdependency; that is, an interaction exists when the effects of one variable *depend* on another factor. However, the easiest way to identify an interaction within a set of data is to draw a graph showing the treatment means. The presence of nonparallel lines is an easy way to spot an interaction.

LEARNING CHECK

1. Each of the following matrices represents a possible outcome of a two-factor experiment. For each experiment:

   a. Describe the main effect for factor *A*.

   b. Describe the main effect for factor *B*.

c. Does there appear to be an interaction between the two factors?

Experiment I

	B_1	B_2
A_1	$M = 10$	$M = 20$
A_2	$M = 30$	$M = 40$

Experiment II

	B_1	B_2
A_1	$M = 10$	$M = 30$
A_2	$M = 20$	$M = 20$

2. In a graph showing the means from a two-factor experiment, parallel lines indicate that there is no interaction. (True or false?)

3. A two-factor ANOVA consists of three hypothesis tests. What are they?

4. It is impossible to have an interaction unless you also have main effects for at least one of the two factors. (True or false?)

ANSWERS **1.** For Experiment I:

    a. There is a main effect for factor A; the scores in A_2 average 20 points higher than in A_1.

    b. There is a main effect for factor B; the scores in B_2 average 10 points higher than in B_1.

    c. There is no interaction; there is a constant 20-point difference between A_1 and A_2 that does not depend on the levels of factor B.

For Experiment II:

    a. There is no main effect for factor A; the scores in A_1 and in A_2 both average 20.

    b. There is a main effect for factor B; on average, the scores in B_2 are 10 points higher than in B_1.

    c. There is an interaction. The difference between A_1 and A_2 depends on the level of factor B. (There is a $+10$ difference in B_1 and a -10 difference in B_2.)

2. True

3. The two-factor ANOVA evaluates the main effect for factor A, the main effect for factor B, and the interaction between the two factors.

4. False. The existence of main effects and interactions is completely independent.

STRUCTURE OF THE TWO-FACTOR ANALYSIS

The general structure of the two-factor ANOVA is shown in Figure 14.3. Note that the overall analysis is divided into two stages. In the first stage, the total variability is separated into two components: between-treatments variability and within-treatments variability. This first stage is identical to the single-factor analysis of variance introduced in Chapter 13 with each cell in the two-factor matrix viewed as a separate treatment condition. The within-treatments variability that is obtained in stage 1 of the analysis will be used as the denominator for all three F-ratios. As we noted in Chapter 13, within each treatment, all of the participants are treated exactly the same. Thus, any differences that exist within the treatments cannot be caused by treatment effects. As a result, the within-treatments variability provides a measure of the differences that are due exclusively to chance or error, without any treatment effects (see Equation 14.11).

The between-treatments variability obtained in stage 1 of the analysis combines all the mean differences produced by factor A, factor B, and the interaction. The purpose

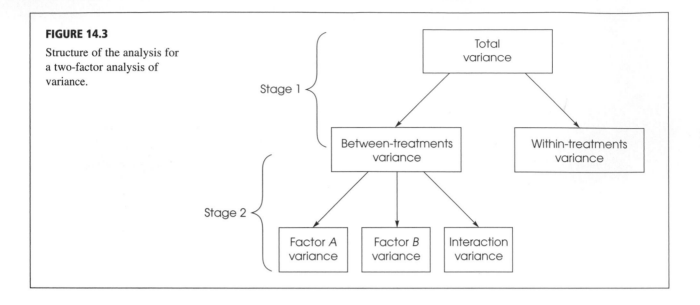

FIGURE 14.3

Structure of the analysis for a two-factor analysis of variance.

of the second stage is to partition the differences into three separate components: differences attributed to factor *A*, differences attributed to factor *B*, and any remaining mean differences that define the interaction. These three components form the numerators for the three *F*-ratios in the analysis.

The goal of this analysis is to compute the variance values needed for the three *F*-ratios. We will need three between-treatments variances (one for factor *A*, one for factor *B*, and one for the interaction), and we will need a within-treatments variance. Each of these variances (or mean squares) will be determined by a sum of squares value (*SS*) and a degrees of freedom value (*df*):

Remember that in ANOVA a variance is called a mean square, or *MS*.

$$\text{mean square} = MS = \frac{SS}{df}$$

NOTATION AND FORMULAS FOR THE TWO-FACTOR ANOVA

E X A M P L E   1 4 . 3   The hypothetical data shown in Table 14.7 will be used to demonstrate the two-factor ANOVA. The data are representative of many studies examining the relationship between arousal and performance. The general result of these studies is that increasing the level of arousal (or motivation) tends to improve the level of performance. For very difficult tasks, however, increasing arousal beyond a certain point tends to lower the level of performance. (This relationship is generally known as the Yerkes–Dodson law.) The data are displayed in a matrix with the two levels of task difficulty (factor *A*) making up the rows and the three levels of arousal (factor *B*) making up the columns. For the easy task, note that performance scores increase consistently as arousal increases. For the difficult task, on the other hand, performance peaks at a medium level of arousal and drops when arousal is increased to a high level. Note that the data matrix has a total of six *cells* or treatment conditions with a separate sample of $n = 5$ subjects in each condition. Most of the notation should be familiar from the single-factor ANOVA presented in Chapter 13. Specifically, the treatment totals are identi-

TABLE 14.7

Hypothetical data for a two-factor research study comparing two levels of task difficulty (easy and hard) and three levels of arousal (low, medium, and high). The study involves a total of six different treatment conditions with $n = 5$ subjects in each condition.

		Factor B: Arousal level				
		Low	Medium	High		
		3	2	9		
		1	5	9		
	Easy	1	9	13	$T_{ROW1} = 90$	
		6	7	6		
		4	7	8		
		$T = 15$	$T = 30$	$T = 45$		$N = 30$
		$SS = 18$	$SS = 28$	$SS = 26$		$G = 120$
Factor A:						$\Sigma X^2 = 840$
Task difficulty		0	3	0		
		2	8	0		
	Difficult	0	3	0	$T_{ROW2} = 30$	
		0	3	5		
		3	3	0		
		$T = 5$	$T = 20$	$T = 5$		
		$SS = 8$	$SS = 20$	$SS = 20$		

$$T_{COL1} = 20 \quad T_{COL2} = 50 \quad T_{COL3} = 50$$

fied by T values, the total number of scores in the entire study is $N = 30$, and the grand total (sum) of all 30 scores is $G = 120$. In addition to these familiar values, we have included the totals for each row and for each column in the matrix. The goal of the ANOVA is to determine whether the mean differences observed in the data are significantly greater than would be expected if there are no treatment effects.

STAGE 1 OF THE TWO-FACTOR ANALYSIS

The first stage of the two-factor analysis separates the total variability into two components: between-treatments and within-treatments. The formulas for this stage are identical to the formulas used in the single-factor ANOVA in Chapter 13 with the provision that each cell in the two-factor matrix is treated as a separate treatment condition. The formulas and the calculations for the data in Table 14.7 are as follows:

Total variability

$$SS_{total} = \Sigma X^2 - \frac{G^2}{N}$$

For these data,

$$SS_{total} = 840 - \frac{120^2}{30}$$

$$= 840 - 480$$

$$= 360$$

This SS value measures the variability for all $N = 30$ scores and has degrees of freedom given by

$$df_{total} = N - 1$$

For the data in Table 14.7, $df_{total} = 29$.

Between-treatments variability   Remember that each treatment condition corresponds to a cell in the matrix. With this in mind, the between-treatments SS is computed as

$$SS_{\text{between treatments}} = \Sigma \frac{T^2}{n} - \frac{G^2}{N}$$

For the data in Table 14.7, there are six treatments (six T values), and the between-treatments SS is

$$SS_{\text{between treatments}} = \frac{15^2}{5} + \frac{30^2}{5} + \frac{45^2}{5} + \frac{5^2}{5} + \frac{20^2}{5} + \frac{5^2}{5} - \frac{120^2}{30}$$

$$= 45 + 180 + 405 + 5 + 80 + 5 - 480$$

$$= 240$$

The between-treatments df value is determined by the number of treatments (or the number of T values) minus one. For a two-factor study, the number of treatments is equal to the number of cells in the matrix. Thus,

$$df_{\text{between treatments}} = \text{number of cells} - 1$$

For these data, $df_{\text{between treatments}} = 5$.

Within-treatments variability   To compute the variance within treatments, we first compute SS and $df = n - 1$ for each of the individual treatment conditions. Then the within-treatments SS is defined as

$$SS_{\text{within treatments}} = \Sigma SS_{\text{each treatment}}$$

And the within-treatments df is defined as

$$df_{\text{within treatments}} = \Sigma df_{\text{each treatment}}$$

For the data in Table 14.7,

$$SS_{\text{within treatments}} = 18 + 28 + 26 + 8 + 20 + 20$$

$$= 120$$

$$df_{\text{within treatments}} = 4 + 4 + 4 + 4 + 4 + 4$$

$$= 24$$

This completes the first stage of the analysis. Note that the two components add to equal the total for both SS values and df values.

$$SS_{\text{between treatments}} + SS_{\text{within treatments}} = SS_{\text{total}}$$

$$240 + 120 = 360$$

$$df_{\text{between treatments}} + df_{\text{within treatments}} = df_{\text{total}}$$

$$5 + 24 = 29$$

STAGE 2 OF THE TWO-FACTOR ANALYSIS

The second stage of the analysis will determine the numerators for the three F-ratios. Specifically, this stage will determine the between-treatments variance for factor A, factor B, and the interaction.

1. Factor A. The main effect for factor A evaluates the mean differences between the levels of factor A. For this example, factor A defines the rows of the matrix, so we are evaluating the mean differences between rows. To compute the SS for factor A, we will calculate a between-treatments SS using the row totals exactly the same as we computed $SS_{\text{between treatments}}$ using the treatment totals (T values) earlier. For factor A, the row totals are 90 and 30, and each total was obtained by adding up 15 scores. Therefore,

$$SS_{\text{factor } A} = \Sigma \frac{T^2_{\text{ROW}}}{n_{\text{ROW}}} - \frac{G^2}{N} \tag{14.12}$$

For our data,

$$SS_{\text{factor } A} = \frac{90^2}{15} + \frac{30^2}{15} - \frac{120^2}{30}$$

$$= 540 + 60 - 480$$

$$= 120$$

Factor A involves two treatments (or two rows), easy and difficult, so the df value is

$$df_{\text{factor } A} = \text{number of rows} - 1 \tag{14.13}$$

$$= 2 - 1$$

$$= 1$$

2. Factor B. SS and df for factor B are computed using the column totals.

$$SS_{\text{factor } B} = \Sigma \frac{T^2_{\text{COL}}}{n_{\text{COL}}} - \frac{G^2}{N} \tag{14.14}$$

For our data, the column totals are 20, 50, and 50, and each total was obtained by summing 10 scores. Thus,

$$SS_{\text{factor } B} = \frac{20^2}{10} + \frac{50^2}{10} + \frac{50^2}{10} - \frac{120^2}{30}$$

$$= 40 + 250 + 250 - 480$$

$$= 60$$

$$df_{\text{factor } B} = \text{number of columns} - 1 \tag{14.15}$$

$$= 3 - 1$$

$$= 2$$

3. The $A \times B$ Interaction. The $A \times B$ interaction is defined as the "extra" mean differences not accounted for by the main effects of the two factors. We will use this definition to find the SS and df values for the interaction by simple subtraction. Specifically, the between-treatments variability is partitioned into three parts: the A effect, the B effect, and the interaction (see Figure 14.3). We have already computed the SS and df values for A and B, so we can find the interaction values by subtracting to find out how much is left. Thus,

$$SS_{A \times B} = SS_{\text{between treatments}} - SS_{\text{factor } A} - SS_{\text{factor } B} \tag{14.16}$$

For our hypothetical data,

$$SS_{A \times B} = 240 - 120 - 60$$

$$= 60$$

Similarly,

$$df_{A \times B} = df_{\text{between treatments}} - df_{\text{factor } A} - df_{\text{factor } B} \tag{14.17}$$
$$= 5 - 1 - 2$$
$$= 2$$

MEAN SQUARES AND
F-RATIOS FOR THE
TWO-FACTOR ANALYSIS

The two-factor ANOVA consists of three separate hypothesis tests with three separate F-ratios. The denominator for each F-ratio is intended to measure the variance (differences) that would be expected just by chance. As we saw in Chapter 13, the within-treatments variance forms the denominator for an independent-measures design. Remember that inside each treatment all the individuals are treated exactly the same, which means any differences that occur are simply due to chance (see Chapter 13, page 342). The within-treatments variance is called a *mean square*, or *MS*, and is computed as follows:

$$MS_{\text{within treatments}} = \frac{SS_{\text{within treatments}}}{df_{\text{within treatments}}}$$

For the data in Table 14.7,

$$MS_{\text{within treatments}} = \frac{120}{24} = 5.00$$

This value will form the denominator for all three F-ratios.

The numerators of the three F-ratios all measured variance or differences between treatments: differences between levels of factor A, or differences between levels of factor B, or extra differences that are attributed to the $A \times B$ interaction. These three variances are computed as follows:

$$MS_A = \frac{SS_A}{df_A} \qquad MS_B = \frac{SS_B}{df_B} \qquad MS_{A \times B} = \frac{SS_{A \times B}}{df_{A \times B}}$$

For the data in Table 14.7, the three MS values are

$$MS_A = \frac{SS_A}{df_A} = \frac{120}{1} = 120 \qquad MS_B = \frac{SS_B}{df_B} = \frac{60}{2} = 30$$

$$MS_{A \times B} = \frac{SS_{A \times B}}{df_{A \times B}} = \frac{60}{2} = 30$$

Finally, the three F-ratios are

$$F_A = \frac{MS_A}{MS_{\text{within treatments}}} = \frac{120}{5} = 24.00$$

$$F_B = \frac{MS_B}{MS_{\text{within treatments}}} = \frac{30}{5} = 6.00$$

$$F_{A \times B} = \frac{MS_{A \times B}}{MS_{\text{within treatments}}} = \frac{30}{5} = 6.00$$

To determine the significance of each F-ratio, we must consult the F distribution table using the df values for each of the individual F-ratios. For this example, the F-ratio for factor A has $df = 1$ for the numerator and $df = 24$ for the denominator.

Checking the table with $df = 1, 24$, we find a critical value of 4.26 for $\alpha = .05$ and a critical value of 7.82 for $\alpha = .01$. Our obtained F-ratio, $F = 24.00$ exceeds both of these values, so we conclude that there is a significant difference between the levels of factor A. That is, performance on the easy task (top row) is significantly different from performance on the difficult task (bottom row).

Similarly, the F-ratio for factor B has $df = 2, 24$. The critical values obtained from the table are 3.40 for $\alpha = .05$ and 5.61 for $\alpha = .01$. Again, our obtained F-ratio, $F = 6.00$, exceeds both values, so we can conclude that there are significant differences among the levels of factor B. For this study, the three levels of arousal result in significantly different levels of performance.

Finally, the F-ratio for the $A \times B$ interaction has $df = 2, 24$ (the same as factor B). With critical values of 3.40 for $\alpha = .05$ and 5.61 for $\alpha = .01$, our obtained F-ratio of $F = 6.00$ is sufficient to conclude that there is a significant interaction between task difficulty and level of arousal.

Table 14.8 is a summary table for the complete two-factor analysis of variance from Example 14.3. Although these tables are no longer commonly used in research reports, they provide a concise format for displaying all of the elements of the analysis.

INTERPRETATION OF RESULTS FROM A TWO-FACTOR ANOVA

Because the two-factor analysis of variance involves three separate tests, you must consider the overall pattern of results rather than focusing on the individual main effects or the interaction. In particular, whenever there is a significant interaction, you should be cautious about accepting the main effects at face value (whether they are significant or not). Remember, an interaction means that the effect of one factor *depends on* the levels of the second factor. Because the effect changes from one level to the next, there is no consistent "main effect."

Figure 14.4 shows the sample means obtained from the task difficulty and arousal study. Recall that the analysis showed that both main effects and the interaction were significant. The main effect for factor A (task difficulty) can be seen by the fact that the scores on the easy task are generally higher than scores on the difficult task.

On the other hand, the main effect for factor B (arousal) is not that easy to see. Although there is a tendency for scores to increase as the level of arousal increases, this is not a completely consistent trend. In fact, the scores on the difficult task show a sharp *decrease* when arousal is increased from moderate to high. This is an example of the complications that can occur when you have a significant interaction. Remember that an interaction means that a factor does not have a uniformly consistent effect. Instead, the effect of one factor *depends on* the other factor. For the data in Figure 14.4, the ef-

TABLE 14.8

A summary table for the repeated-measures ANOVA for the data from Example 14.3.

Source	SS	df	MS	F
Between treatments	240	5		
Factor A (difficulty)	120	1	120.0	$F(1, 24) = 24.00$
Factor B (arousal)	60	2	30.0	$F(2, 24) = 6.00$
$A \times B$ interaction	60	2	30.0	$F(2, 24) = 6.00$
Within treatments	120	24	5.0	
Total	360	29		

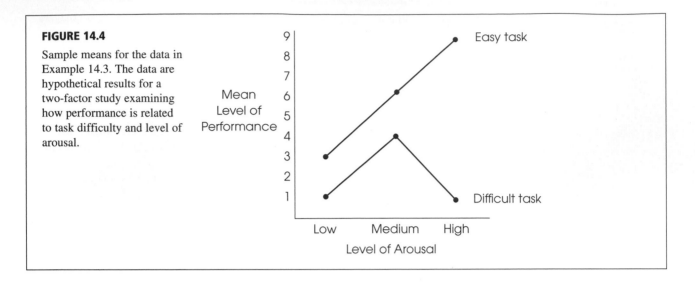

FIGURE 14.4

Sample means for the data in Example 14.3. The data are hypothetical results for a two-factor study examining how performance is related to task difficulty and level of arousal.

fect of increasing arousal depends on the task difficulty. For the easy task, increasing arousal produces increased performance. For the difficult task, however, increasing arousal beyond a moderate level produces decreased performance. This interdependence between factors is the source of the significant interaction.

MEASURING EFFECT SIZE FOR THE TWO-FACTOR ANOVA

The general technique for measuring effect size with an analysis of variance is to compute a value for η^2, the percentage of variance that is explained by the treatment effects. For a two-factor ANOVA, we compute three separate values for eta squared: one measuring how much of the variance is explained by the main effect for factor A, one for factor B, and a third for the interaction. As we did with the repeated-measures ANOVA (page 389) we remove any variability that can be explained by other sources before we calculate the percentage for each of the three specific effects. Thus, for example, before we compute the η^2 for factor A, we remove the variability that is explained by factor B and the variability explained by the interaction. The resulting equation is,

$$\text{for factor } A, \ \eta^2 = \frac{SS_A}{SS_{\text{total}} - SS_B - SS_{A \times B}} \tag{14.18}$$

Note that the denominator of Equation 14.18 consists of the variability that is explained by factor A and the other *unexplained* variability. Thus, an equivalent version of the equation is,

$$\text{for factor } A, \ \eta^2 = \frac{SS_A}{SS_A + SS_{\text{within treatments}}} \tag{14.19}$$

Similarly, the η^2 formulas for factor B and for the interaction are as follows:

$$\text{for factor } B, \ \eta^2 = \frac{SS_B}{SS_{\text{total}} - SS_A - SS_{A \times B}} = \frac{SS_B}{SS_B + SS_{\text{within treatments}}} \tag{14.20}$$

$$\text{for } A \times B, \ \eta^2 = \frac{SS_{A \times B}}{SS_{\text{total}} - SS_A - SS_B} = \frac{SS_{A \times B}}{SS_{A \times B} + SS_{\text{within treatments}}} \tag{14.21}$$

Because each of the η^2 equations computes a percentage that is not based on the total variability of the scores, the results are often called *partial* eta squares. For the data in Example 15.2, the equations produce the following values:

$$\eta^2 \text{ for factor } A \text{ (difficulty)} = \frac{120}{360 - 60 - 60} = \frac{120}{240} = 0.50 \quad \text{(or 50\%)}$$

$$\eta^2 \text{ for factor } B \text{ (arousal)} = \frac{60}{360 - 120 - 60} = \frac{60}{180} = 0.33 \quad \text{(or 33\%)}$$

$$\eta^2 \text{ for the interaction} = \frac{60}{360 - 120 - 60} = \frac{60}{180} = 0.33 \quad \text{(or 33\%)}$$

IN THE LITERATURE
REPORTING THE RESULTS OF A TWO-FACTOR ANOVA

The APA format for reporting the results of a two-factor analysis of variance follows the same basic guidelines as the single-factor report. First, the means and standard deviations are reported. Because a two-factor design typically involves several treatment conditions, these descriptive statistics usually are presented in a table or a graph. Next, the results of all three hypothesis tests (*F*-ratios) are reported. For the research study in Example 14.3, the report would have the following form:

The means and standard deviations for all treatment conditions are shown in Table 1. The two-factor analysis of variance showed a significant main effect for task difficulty, $F(1, 24) = 24.00$, $p < .01$, $\eta^2 = 0.50$; a significant main effect for level of arousal, $F(2, 24) = 6.00$, $p < .01$, $\eta^2 = 0.33$; and a significant interaction between difficulty and arousal, $F(2, 24) = 6.00$, $p < .01$, $\eta^2 = 0.33$.

TABLE 1

Mean performance score for each treatment condition

		Level of Arousal		
		Low	Medium	High
Difficulty	Easy	$M = 3.0$ $SD = 2.12$	$M = 6.00$ $SD = 2.65$	$M = 9.00$ $SD = 2.55$
	Hard	$M = 1.00$ $SD = 1.41$	$M = 4.00$ $SD = 2.24$	$M = 1.00$ $SD = 2.24$

ASSUMPTIONS FOR THE TWO-FACTOR ANOVA

The validity of the analysis of variance presented in this chapter depends on the same three assumptions we have encountered with other hypothesis tests for independent-measures designs (the *t* test in Chapter 10 and the single-factor ANOVA in Chapter 13):

1. The observations within each sample must be independent (see page 210).

2. The populations from which the samples are selected must be normal.

3. The populations from which the samples are selected must have equal variances (homogeneity of variance).

As before, the assumption of normality generally is not a cause for concern, especially when the sample size is relatively large. The homogeneity of variance assumption is more important, and if it appears that your data fail to satisfy this requirement, you should conduct a test for homogeneity before you attempt the ANOVA. Hartley's F-max test (see page 276) allows you to use the sample variances from your data to determine whether there is evidence for any differences among the population variances.

1. The following data summarize the results from a two-factor independent-measures experiment:

Factor B

		B_1	B_2	B_3
	A_1	$n = 10$ $T = 0$ $SS = 30$	$n = 10$ $T = 10$ $SS = 40$	$n = 10$ $T = 20$ $SS = 50$
Factor A	A_2	$n = 10$ $T = 40$ $SS = 60$	$n = 10$ $T = 30$ $SS = 50$	$n = 10$ $T = 20$ $SS = 40$

a. Calculate the total for each level of factor A (the row totals), and compute SS for factor A.

b. Calculate the total for each level of factor B (the column totals), and compute SS for factor B. (*Note:* You should find that the totals for B are all the same, so there is no variability for this factor.)

c. For the data, $SS_{\text{between treatments}}$ is equal to 100. Given this information, what is the SS for the interaction?

d. Calculate the within-treatments SS, df, and MS for the data. (*Note:* $MS_{\text{within treatments}}$ is the denominator for each of the three F-ratios.)

ANSWERS 1. a. The totals for factor A are 30 and 90, and each total is obtained by summing 30 scores. $SS_A = 60$.

b. All three totals for factor B are equal to 40. Because they are all the same, there is no variability, and $SS_B = 0$.

c. The interaction is determined by differences that remain after the main effects have been accounted for. For the data,

$$SS_{A \times B} = SS_{\text{between treatments}} - SS_A - SS_B$$

$$= 100 - 60 - 0$$

$$= 40$$

d. $SS_{\text{within treatments}} = \Sigma SS_{\text{each cell}} = 30 + 40 + 50 + 60 + 50 + 40$

$$= 270$$

$df_{\text{within treatments}} = \Sigma df_{\text{each cell}} = 9 + 9 + 9 + 9 + 9 + 9$

$$= 54$$

$$MS_{\text{within treatments}} = \frac{SS_{\text{within treatments}}}{df_{\text{within treatments}}} = \frac{270}{54} = 5.00$$

SUMMARY

1. The repeated-measures ANOVA is used to evaluate the mean differences obtained in a research study comparing two or more treatment conditions using the same sample of individuals in each condition. The test statistic is an F-ratio, where the numerator measures the variance (differences) between treatments and the denominator measures the variance (differences) expected by chance or error (without any treatment effects or individual differences).

$$F = \frac{MS_{\text{between treatments}}}{MS_{\text{error}}}$$

2. The first stage of the repeated-measures ANOVA is identical to the independent-measures analysis and separates the total variability into two components: between-treatments and within-treatments. Because a repeated-measures design uses the same subjects in every treatment condition, the differences between treatments cannot be caused by individual differences. Thus, individual differences are automatically eliminated from the between-treatments variance in the numerator of the F-ratio.

3. In the second stage of the repeated-measures analysis, individual differences are computed and removed from the denominator of the F-ratio. To remove the individual differences, you first compute the variability between subjects (SS and df) and then subtract these values from the corresponding within-treatments values. The residual provides a measure of error excluding individual differences, which is the appropriate denominator for the repeated-measures F-ratio.

4. A research study with two independent variables is called a two-factor design. Such a design can be diagramed as a matrix with the levels of one factor defining the rows and the levels of the other factor defining the columns. Each cell in the matrix corresponds to a specific combination of the two factors.

5. Traditionally, the two factors are identified as factor A and factor B. The purpose of the analysis of variance is to determine whether there are any significant mean differences among the treatment conditions or cells in the experimental matrix. These treatment effects are classified as follows:
   a. The A-effect: Overall mean differences among the levels of factor A.
   b. The B-effect: Overall mean differences among the levels of factor B.
   c. The $A \times B$ interaction: Extra mean differences that are not accounted for by the main effects.

6. The two-factor analysis of variance produces three F-ratios: one for factor A, one for factor B, and one for the $A \times B$ interaction. Each F-ratio has the same basic structure:

$$F = \frac{MS_{\text{treatment effect}}(\text{either } A \text{ or } B \text{ or } A \times B)}{MS_{\text{within}}}$$

KEY TERMS

individual differences	error variability	matrix	main effect
between-subjects variability	two-factor design	cells	interaction

RESOURCES

There are a tutorial quiz and other learning exercises for Chapter 14 at the Wadsworth website, www.thomsonedu.com/psychology/gravetter. The site also provides access to two workshops titled *Two Way ANOVA* and *Factorial ANOVA* that both review the two-factor analysis presented in this chapter. See page 27 for more information about accessing the website.

WebTUTOR

For those using WebTutor along with this book, there is a WebTutor section corresponding to this chapter. The WebTutor contains a brief summary of Chapter 14, hints for learning the concepts and formulas for the repeated-measures and the two-factor ANOVA, cautions about common errors, and sample exam items including solutions.

General instructions for using SPSS are presented in Appendix D. Following are detailed instructions for using SPSS to perform the **Single-Factor, Repeated-Measures Analysis of Variance (ANOVA)** presented in this chapter.

Data Entry

1. Enter the scores for each treatment condition in a separate column, with the scores for each individual in the same row. All the scores for the first treatment go in the VAR00001 column, the second treatment scores in the VAR00002 column, and so on.

Data Analysis

1. Click **Analyze** on the tool bar, select **General Linear Model,** and click on **Repeated-Measures.**
2. SPSS will present a box titled **Repeated-Measures Define Factors.** Within the box, the Within-Subjects Factor Name should already contain **Factor 1.** If not, type in Factor 1.
3. Enter the **Number of levels** (number of different treatment conditions) in the next box.
4. Click on **Add.**
5. Click **Define.**
6. One by one, move the column labels for your treatment conditions into the **Within Subjects Variables** box. (Highlight the column label on the left and click the arrow to move it into the box.)
7. If you want descriptive statistics for each treatment, click on the **Options** box, select **Descriptives,** and click **Continue.**
8. Click **OK.**

SPSS Output

If you selected the Descriptives Option, SPSS will produce a table showing the mean and standard deviation for each treatment condition. The rest of the SPSS output is relatively complex and includes a lot of statistical information that goes well beyond the scope of this book. Therefore, direct your attention to the table titled **Test of Within-Subjects Effects.** The top line of the **Factor**1 box (sphericity assumed) shows the between-treatments sum of squares, degrees of freedom, and mean square that form the numerator of the F-ratio. The same line reports the value of the F-ratio and the level of significance (the p value or alpha level). Similarly, the top line of the Error(**Factor**1) box shows the sum of squares, the degrees of freedom, and the mean square for the error term (the denominator of the F-ratio).

Following are detailed instructions for using SPSS to perform **the Two-Factor, Independent-Measures Analysis of Variance (ANOVA)** presented in this chapter.

Data Entry

1. The scores are entered into the SPSS data editor in a *stacked format,* which means that all the scores from all the different treatment conditions are entered in a single column (VAR00001).
2. In a second column (VAR00002) enter a code number to identify the level of factor A for each score. If factor A defines the rows of the data matrix, enter a 1 beside each score from the first row, enter a 2 beside each score from the second row, and so on.

3. In a third column (VAR00003) enter a code number to identify the level of factor B for each score. If factor B defines the columns of the data matrix, enter a 1 beside each score from the first column, enter a 2 beside each score from the second column, and so on.

Thus, each row of the SPSS data editor will have one score and two code numbers, with the score in the first column, the code for factor A in the second column, and the code for factor B in the third column.

Data Analysis

1. Click **Analyze** on the tool bar, select **General Linear Model,** and click on **Univariant.**
2. Highlight the column label for the set of scores (VAR0001) in the left box and click the arrow to move it into the **Dependent Variable** box.
3. One by one, highlight the column labels for the two factor codes and click the arrow to move them into the **Fixed Factors** box.
4. If you want descriptive statistics for each treatment, click on the **Options** box, select **Descriptives,** and click **Continue.**
5. Click **OK.**

SPSS Output

If you selected the Descriptives Options, SPSS will produce a table showing the means and standard deviations for each treatment condition (each cell) as well as the mean and standard deviation for each level of both factors. The results of the ANOVA are shown in the table labeled **Tests of Between-Subjects Effects.** The top row (*Corrected Model*) presents the between-treatments *SS* and *df* values. The second row (*Intercept*) is not relevant for our purposes. The next three rows present the two main effects and the interaction (the *SS, df,* and *MS* values, as well as the *F*-ratio and the level of significance), with each factor identified by its column number from the SPSS data editor. The next row (*Error*) describes the error term (denominator of the *F*-ratio), and the final row (*Corrected Total*) describes the total variability for the entire set of scores. (Ignore the row labeled *Total.*)

FOCUS ON PROBLEM SOLVING

1. Before you begin a repeated-measures ANOVA, complete all the preliminary calculations needed for the ANOVA formulas. This requires that you find the total for each treatment (*T*s), the total for each person (*P*s), the grand total (*G*), the *SS* for each treatment condition, and ΣX^2 for the entire set of *N* scores. As a partial check on these calculations, be sure that the *T* values add up to *G* and that the *P* values have a sum of *G*.

2. To help remember the structure of repeated-measures ANOVA, keep in mind that a repeated-measures experiment eliminates the contribution of individual differences. There are no individual differences contributing to the numerator of the *F*-ratio ($MS_{\text{between treatments}}$) because the same individuals are used for all treatments. Therefore, you must also eliminate individual differences in the denominator. This is accomplished by partitioning within-treatments variability into two components: between-subjects variability and error variability. It is the *MS* value for error variability that is used in the denominator of the *F*-ratio.

3. Before you begin a two-factor ANOVA, take time to organize and summarize the data. It is best if you summarize the data in a matrix with rows corresponding to the levels of one factor and columns corresponding to the levels of the other factor. In each cell of the matrix, show the number of scores (n), the total and mean for the cell, and the SS within the cell. Also compute the row totals and column totals that will be needed to calculate main effects.

4. For a two-factor ANOVA, there are three separate F-ratios. These three F-ratios use the same error term in the denominator (MS_{within}). On the other hand, these F-ratios will have different numerators and may have different df values associated with each of these numerators. Therefore, you must be careful when you look up the critical F values in the table. The two factors and the interaction may have different critical F values.

DEMONSTRATION 14.1

REPEATED-MEASURES ANOVA

The following data were obtained from a research study examining the effect of sleep deprivation on motor skills performance. A sample of five participants was tested on a motor-skills task after 24 hours of sleep deprivation, tested again after 36 hours, and tested once more after 48 hours. The dependent variable is the number of errors made on the motor-skills task. Do these data indicate that the number of hours of sleep deprivation has a significant effect on motor skills performance?

Participant	24 Hours	36 Hours	48 Hours	P totals	
A	0	0	6	6	$N = 15$
B	1	3	5	9	$G = 45$
C	0	1	5	6	$\Sigma X^2 = 245$
D	4	5	9	18	
E	0	1	5	6	
	$T = 5$	$T = 10$	$T = 30$		
	$SS = 12$	$SS = 16$	$SS = 12$		

STEP 1 State the hypotheses, and specify alpha.
The null hypothesis states that for the general population there are no differences among the three deprivation conditions. Any differences that exist among the samples are simply due to chance or error. In symbols,

$$H_0 = \mu_1 = \mu_2 = \mu_3$$

The alternative hypothesis states that there are differences among the conditions.

$$H_1: \quad \text{At least one of the treatment means is different.}$$

We will use $\alpha = .05$.

STEP 2 The repeated-measures analysis.
Rather than compute the df values and look for a critical value for F at this time, we will proceed directly to the ANOVA.

STAGE 1 The first stage of the analysis is identical to the independent-measures ANOVA presented in Chapter 13.

$$SS_{total} = \Sigma X^2 - \frac{G^2}{N}$$

$$= 245 - \frac{45^2}{15} = 110$$

$$SS_{within} = \Sigma SS_{inside\ each\ treatment} = 12 + 16 + 12 = 40$$

$$SS_{between} = \Sigma \frac{T^2}{n} - \frac{G^2}{N}$$

$$= \frac{5^2}{5} + \frac{10^2}{5} + \frac{30^2}{5} - \frac{45^2}{15}$$

$$= 70$$

and the corresponding degrees of freedom are

$$df_{total} = N - 1 = 14$$

$$df_{within} = \Sigma df = 4 + 4 + 4 = 12$$

$$df_{between} = k - 1 = 2$$

STAGE 2 The second stage of the repeated-measures analysis measures and removes the individual differences from the denominator of the F-ratio.

$$SS_{between\ subjects} = \Sigma \frac{P^2}{k} - \frac{G^2}{N}$$

$$= \frac{6^2}{3} + \frac{9^2}{3} + \frac{6^2}{3} + \frac{18^2}{3} + \frac{6^2}{3} - \frac{45^2}{15}$$

$$= 36$$

$$SS_{error} = SS_{within} - SS_{between\ subjects}$$

$$= 40 - 36$$

$$= 4$$

and the corresponding df values are

$$df_{between\ subjects} = n - 1 = 4$$

$$df_{error} = df_{within} - df_{between\ subjects}$$

$$= 12 - 4$$

$$= 8$$

The mean square values that will form the F-ratio are as follows:

$$MS_{between} = \frac{SS_{between}}{df_{between}} = \frac{70}{2} = 35$$

$$MS_{error} = \frac{SS_{error}}{df_{error}} = \frac{4}{8} = 0.50$$

Finally, the *F*-ratio is

$$F = \frac{MS_{\text{between}}}{MS_{\text{error}}} = \frac{35}{0.50} = 70.00$$

STEP 3   Make a decision and state a conclusion.
With $df = 2, 8$ and $\alpha = .05$, the critical value is $F = 4.46$. Our obtained *F*-ratio ($F = 70.00$) is well into the critical region, so our decision is to reject the null hypothesis and conclude that there are significant differences among the three levels of sleep deprivation.

DEMONSTRATION 14.2

TWO-FACTOR ANOVA

The following data are representative of the results obtained in a research study examining the relationship between eating behavior and body weight (Schachter, 1968). The two factors in this study were:

1. The participant's weight (normal or obese)

2. The participant's state of hunger (full stomach or empty stomach)

All participants were led to believe that they were taking part in a taste test for several types of crackers, and they were allowed to eat as many crackers as they wanted. The dependent variable was the number of crackers eaten by each participant. There were two specific predictions for this study. First, it was predicted that normal participants' eating behavior would be determined by their state of hunger. That is, people with empty stomachs would eat more and people with full stomachs would eat less. Second, it was predicted that eating behavior for obese participants would not be related to their state of hunger. Specifically, it was predicted that obese participants would eat the same amount whether their stomachs were full or empty. Note that the researchers are predicting an interaction: The effect of hunger will be different for the normal participants and the obese participants. The data are as follows:

		Factor *B*: Hunger			
		Empty stomach	Full stomach		
Factor *A*: Weight	Normal	$n = 20$ $M = 22$ $T = 440$ $SS = 1540$	$n = 20$ $M = 15$ $T = 300$ $SS = 1270$	$T_{\text{normal}} = 740$	$G = 1440$ $N = 80$ $\Sigma X^2 = 31{,}836$
	Obese	$n = 20$ $M = 17$ $T = 340$ $SS = 1320$	$n = 20$ $M = 18$ $T = 360$ $SS = 1266$	$T_{\text{obese}} = 700$	
		$T_{\text{empty}} = 780$	$T_{\text{full}} = 660$		

STEP 1   State the hypotheses, and select alpha.
For a two-factor study, there are three separate hypotheses, the two main effects and the interaction.

For factor A, the null hypothesis states that there is no difference in the amount eaten for normal participants versus obese participants. In symbols,

$$H_0: \quad \mu_{normal} = \mu_{obese}$$

For factor B, the null hypothesis states that there is no difference in the amount eaten for full-stomach versus empty-stomach conditions. In symbols,

$$H_0: \quad \mu_{full} = \mu_{empty}$$

For the $A \times B$ interaction, the null hypothesis can be stated two different ways. First, the difference in eating between the full-stomach and empty-stomach conditions will be the same for normal and obese participants. Second, the difference in eating between the normal and obese participants will be the same for the full-stomach and empty-stomach conditions. In more general terms,

H_0:   The effect of factor A does not depend on the levels of factor B (and B does not depend on A).

We will use $\alpha = .05$ for all tests.

STEP 2   The two-factor analysis.

Rather than compute the *df* values and look up critical values for *F* at this time, we will proceed directly to the ANOVA.

STAGE 1   The first stage of the analysis is identical to the independent-measures ANOVA presented in Chapter 13, where each cell in the data matrix is considered a separate treatment condition.

$$SS_{total} = \Sigma X^2 - \frac{G^2}{N}$$

$$= 31,836 - \frac{1440^2}{80} = 5916$$

$$SS_{within\ treatments} = \Sigma SS_{inside\ each\ treatment} = 1540 + 1270 + 1320 + 1266 = 5396$$

$$SS_{between\ treatments} = \Sigma \frac{T^2}{n} - \frac{G^2}{N}$$

$$= \frac{440^2}{20} + \frac{300^2}{20} + \frac{340^2}{20} + \frac{360^2}{20} - \frac{1440^2}{80}$$

$$= 520$$

The corresponding degrees of freedom are

$$df_{total} = N - 1 = 79$$

$$df_{within\ treatments} = \Sigma df = 19 + 19 + 19 + 19 = 76$$

$$df_{between\ treatments} = \text{number of treatments} - 1 = 3$$

STAGE 2   The second stage of the analysis partitions the between-treatments variability into three components: the main effect for factor A, the main effect for factor B, and the $A \times B$ interaction.

For factor A (normal/obese),

$$SS_A = \Sigma \frac{T^2_{\text{ROWS}}}{n_{\text{ROWS}}} - \frac{G^2}{N}$$

$$= \frac{740^2}{40} + \frac{700^2}{40} - \frac{1440^2}{80}$$

$$= 20$$

For factor B (full/empty),

$$SS_B = \Sigma \frac{T^2_{\text{COLS}}}{n_{\text{COLS}}} - \frac{G^2}{N}$$

$$= \frac{780^2}{40} + \frac{660^2}{40} - \frac{1440^2}{80}$$

$$= 180$$

For the $A \times B$ interaction,

$$SS_{A \times B} = SS_{\text{between treatments}} - SS_A - SS_B$$

$$= 520 - 20 - 180$$

$$= 320$$

The corresponding degrees of freedom are

$$df_A = \text{number of rows} - 1 = 1$$

$$df_B = \text{number of columns} - 1 = 1$$

$$df_{A \times B} = df_{\text{between treatments}} - df_A - df_B$$

$$= 3 - 1 - 1$$

$$= 1$$

The MS values needed for the F-ratios are

$$MS_A = \frac{SS_A}{df_A} = \frac{20}{1} = 20$$

$$MS_B = \frac{SS_B}{df_B} = \frac{180}{1} = 180$$

$$MS_{A \times B} = \frac{SS_{A \times B}}{df_{A \times B}} = \frac{320}{1} = 320$$

$$MS_{\text{within treatments}} = \frac{SS_{\text{within treatments}}}{df_{\text{within treatments}}} = \frac{5396}{76} = 71$$

Finally, the F-ratios are

$$F_A = \frac{MS_A}{MS_{\text{within treatments}}} = \frac{20}{71} = 0.28$$

$$F_B = \frac{MS_B}{MS_{\text{within treatments}}} = \frac{180}{71} = 2.54$$

$$F_{A \times B} = \frac{MS_{A \times B}}{MS_{\text{within treatments}}} = \frac{320}{71} = 4.51$$

STEP 3 Make a decision and state a conclusion.

All three F-ratios have $df = 1, 76$. With $\alpha = .05$, the critical F value is 3.98 for all three tests.

For these data, factor A (weight) has no significant effect; $F(1, 76) = 0.28$. Statistically, there is no difference in the number of crackers eaten by normal versus obese participants.

Similarly, factor B (fullness) has no significant effect; $F(1, 76) = 2.54$. Statistically, the number of crackers eaten by full participants is no different from the number eaten by hungry participants. (*Note:* This conclusion concerns the combined group of normal and obese participants. The interaction concerns these two groups separately.)

These data produce a significant interaction; $F(1, 76) = 4.51, p < .05$. This means that the effect of fullness does depend on weight. A closer look at the original data shows that the degree of fullness did affect the normal participants, but it had no effect on the obese participants.

PROBLEMS

1. A researcher conducts an experiment comparing three treatment conditions. The data consist of $n = 20$ scores for each treatment condition.
   a. If the researcher used an independent-measures design, then how many individuals were needed for the study and what are the df values for the F-ratio?
   b. If the researcher used a repeated-measures design, then how many individuals were needed for the study and what are the df values for the F-ratio?

2. The repeated-measures analysis of variance can be viewed as a two-stage process. What is the purpose for the second stage?

3. How does the denominator of the F-ratio (the error term) differ for a repeated-measures analysis of variance compared to an independent-measures ANOVA?

4. A researcher reports an F-ratio with $df = 1, 10$ for a repeated-measures ANOVA.
   a. How many treatment conditions were compared in the study?
   b. How many individuals participated in the study?

5. A researcher reports an F-ratio with $df = 2, 12$ for a repeated-measures ANOVA.
   a. How many treatment conditions were compared in the study?
   b. How many individuals participated in the study?

6. A researcher conducts a repeated-measures experiment using a sample of $n = 12$ subjects to evaluate the differences among three treatment conditions. If the results are examined with an ANOVA, what are the df values for the F-ratio?

7. An analysis of variance was used to evaluate the mean differences from a repeated-measures research study. The results were reported as $F(3, 24) = 6.40$.
   a. How many treatment conditions were compared in the study?
   b. How many individuals participated in the study?

8. The following data were obtained from a repeated-measures study comparing three treatment conditions.

Subject	Treatment I	Treatment II	Treatment III	P	
A	6	8	10	24	$G = 48$
B	5	5	5	15	$\Sigma X^2 = 294$
C	1	2	3	6	
D	0	1	2	3	
	$T = 12$	$T = 16$	$T = 20$		
	$SS = 26$	$SS = 30$	$SS = 38$		

Use a repeated-measures analysis of variance with $\alpha = .05$ to determine whether these data are sufficient to demonstrate significant differences between the treatments.

9. In Problem 8 the data show large and consistent differences between subjects. For example, subject A has the largest score in every treatment and subject D always has the smallest score. In the second stage of the ANOVA, the large individual differences get subtracted out of the denominator of the F-ratio, which results in a larger value for F.

The following data were created by using the same numbers that appeared in Problem 8. However, we eliminated the consistent individual differences by scrambling the scores within each treatment.

Subject	Treatment I	II	III	P	
A	6	2	3	11	$G = 48$
B	5	1	5	11	$\Sigma X^2 = 294$
C	0	5	10	15	
D	1	8	2	11	
	$T = 12$	$T = 16$	$T = 20$		
	$SS = 26$	$SS = 30$	$SS = 38$		

a. Use a repeated-measures analysis of variance with $\alpha = .05$ to determine whether these data are sufficient to demonstrate significant differences between the treatments.
b. Explain how the results of this analysis compare with the results from Problem 8.

10. The following summary table presents the results from an ANOVA from a repeated-measures study comparing three treatments with a sample of $n = 8$ participants. Fill in all missing values in the table.

Source	SS	df	MS	
Between treatments	____	____	15	$F = $ ____
Within treatments	70	____		
Between subjects	42	____		
Error	____	____	____	
Total	____	____		

11. The following data are from an experiment comparing three different treatment conditions:

A	B	C	
0	1	2	$N = 15$
2	5	5	$\Sigma X^2 = 354$
1	2	6	
5	4	9	
2	8	8	
$T = 10$	$T = 20$	$T = 30$	
$SS = 14$	$SS = 30$	$SS = 30$	

a. If the experiment uses an *independent-measures design,* can the researcher conclude that the treatments are significantly different? Test at the .05 level of significance.

b. If the experiment is done with a *repeated-measures design,* should the researcher conclude that the treatments are significantly different? Set alpha at .05 again.
c. Explain why the results are different in the analyses of parts a and b.

12. In a study examining cardiovascular responses to embarrassment, Harris (2001) asked participants to sing the Star Spangled Banner in front of a video camera while she recorded their heart rate and blood pressure. The data indicate that heart rate increases quickly during the first minute of an embarrassing episode, then drops quickly during the second minute. Blood pressure, on the other hand, increases steadily for a full 2 minutes before gradually returning to normal. Following are heart rate data similar to the research results. Do the data show significant changes in heart rate over time? Use a repeated-measures ANOVA with $\alpha = .05$.

Person	Baseline	1 Minute	2 Minutes	P	
A	74	88	75	237	$N = 12$
B	76	90	77	243	$G = 960$
C	78	89	76	243	$\Sigma X^2 = 77,208$
D	76	85	76	237	
	$M = 76$	$M = 88$	$M = 76$		
	$SS = 8$	$SS = 14$	$SS = 2$		

13. Loss of hearing can be a significant problem for older adults. Although hearing aids can correct the physical problem, people who have lived with hearing impairment often develop poor communication strategies and social skills. To address this problem, a home education program has been developed to help people who are receiving hearing aids for the first time. The program emphasizes communication skills. To evaluate the program, overall quality of life and satisfaction were measured before treatment, again at the end of the training program, and once more at a 6-month follow-up (Kramer, Allessie, Dondorp, Zekveld, & Kapteyn, 2005). Data similar to the results obtained in the study are shown below. Do the data indicate a significant improvement in quality of life following the training program? Test at the .05 level of significance.

Person	Before	After	6-Months	
A	3	7	8	$N = 12$
B	0	5	7	$G = 60$
C	4	9	5	$\Sigma X^2 = 384$
D	1	7	4	

Quality-of-Life Scores

$T = 8$ $T = 28$ $T = 24$
$SS = 10$ $SS = 8$ $SS = 10$

14. A behavior analyst would like to evaluate the effectiveness of a new technique for controlling classroom outbursts of unruly children. For a sample of $n = 4$ children, the number of outbursts is recorded 1 day before treatment, and again 1 week, 1 month, and 6 months after treatment. Use a repeated-measures ANOVA with $\alpha = .05$ to determine whether there are significant changes in behavior over time. The data are as follows:

Child	Before	1-Week	1-Month	6-Months	P Totals	
A	8	2	1	1	12	$N = 16$
B	4	1	1	0	6	$G = 44$
C	6	2	0	2	10	$\Sigma X^2 = 222$
D	8	3	4	1	16	

$T = 26$ $T = 8$ $T = 6$ $T = 4$
$SS = 11$ $SS = 2$ $SS = 9$ $SS = 2$

15. A teacher used an ANOVA to evaluate the effectiveness of a reading skills course. A standardized reading comprehension test was given to a sample of $n = 12$ students before the course started and again at the end of the course. The following summary table presents a portion of the results from the ANOVA. Fill in the missing values in the table. (*Hint:* Start with the *df* values.)

Source	SS	df	MS	
Between treatments	___	___	24	$F = $ ___
Within treatments	___	___		
Between subjects	60	___		
Error	___	___	___	
Total	128	___		

16. Explain the advantage of using a two-factor design instead of using two single-factor designs (one for each of the two factors).

17. For the data in the following matrix:

	No Treatment	Treatment	
Male	10	20	Overall $M = 15$
Female	14	16	Overall $M = 15$
	Overall $M = 12$	Overall $M = 18$	

a. What numbers are compared to evaluate the main effect for the treatment?
b. What numbers are compared to evaluate the main effect for gender?

18. Define each of the following terms:
a. Factor
b. Level
c. Two-factor study

19. The structure of a two-factor study can be presented as a matrix, with one factor determining the rows and the second factor determining the columns. With this structure in mind, identify the three separate hypothesis tests that make up a two-factor ANOVA, and explain the purpose of each test.

20. The results of a two-factor experiment are examined using an ANOVA, and the researcher reports an *F*-ratio for factor A with $df = 1, 54$ and an *F*-ratio for factor B with $df = 2, 108$. Explain why this report cannot be correct.

21. A psychologist conducts a two-factor study comparing the effectiveness of two different therapy techniques (factor A) for treating mild and severe phobias (factor B). The dependent variable is a measure of fear for each participant. If the study uses $n = 10$ participants in each of the four conditions, then identify the *df* values for each of the three *F*-ratios.
a. What are the *df* values for the *F*-ratio for factor A?
b. What are the *df* values for the *F*-ratio for factor B?
c. What are the *df* values for the *F*-ratio for the A × B interaction?

22. The following matrix presents the results of a two-factor experiment with two levels of factor A, two levels of factor B, and $n = 10$ subjects in each treatment condition. Each value in the matrix is the mean score for the subjects in that treatment condition. Notice that one of the mean values is missing.

	Factor B B₁	B₂
A₁	10	50
A₂	40	

Factor A

a. What value should be assigned to the missing mean so that the resulting data would show no main effect for factor A?

b. What value should be assigned to the missing mean so that the data would show no interaction?

23. For the data in the following graph:

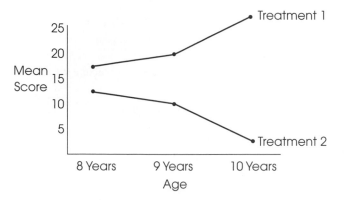

a. Is there a main effect for the treatment factor?

b. Is there a main effect for the age factor?

c. Is there an interaction between age and treatment?

24. Shrauger (1972) conducted an experiment that examined the effect of an audience on the performance of two different personality types. Hypothetical data from this experiment are as follows. The dependent variable is the number of errors made by each participant.

Self-Esteem		Alone	With Audience
High		3	9
		6	4
		2	5
		2	8
		4	4
		7	6
Low		7	10
		7	14
		2	11
		6	15
		8	11
		6	11

Use an ANOVA with $\alpha = .05$ to evaluate these data. Describe the effect of the audience and the effect of personality on performance.

25. The following data are from a two-factor, independent-measures experiment.

		Factor B	
		B_1	B_2
Factor A	A_1	7	1
		12	0
		10	4
		9	3
		12	2
	A_2	1	8
		4	11
		2	11
		3	9
		5	16

a. For these data, compute the cell means and place them in an $A \times B$ matrix.

b. Looking at the cell means, row means, and column means, describe whether there might be an interaction, a main effect for factor A, and a main effect for factor B.

c. Perform a two-factor analysis of variance with $\alpha = .01$.

d. Describe the results of the analysis.

26. A researcher conducted a two-factor research study using two levels of factor A and four levels of factor B with a separate sample of $n = 6$ subjects in each of the eight treatment conditions (cells). The following table summarizes the results of the analysis, but it is not complete. Fill in the missing values. (*Hint:* Start with the df values.)

Source	SS	df	MS	
Between Treatments	620	___		
Factor A	___	___	___	F = ___
Factor B	___	___	100	F = ___
A × B Interaction	120	___	___	F = ___
Within Treatments	___	___	___	
Total	780	___		

27. A researcher conducted a two-factor research study using two levels of factor A and three levels of factor B with a separate sample of $n = 10$ subjects in each of the six treatment conditions (cells). The following table summarizes the results of the analysis, but it is not complete. Fill in the missing values. (*Hint:* Start with the df values.)

Source	SS	df	MS	
Between Treatments	180	___		
Factor A	___	___	20	$F =$ ___
Factor B	___	___	___	$F =$ ___
A × B Interaction	100	___	___	$F =$ ___
Within Treatments	___	___	5	
Total	___	___		

28. A recent study of driving behavior suggests that self-reported measures of high driving skills and low ratings of safety skills create a dangerous combination (Šumer, Özkan, & Lajunen, 2006). Note: Those who rate themselves as highly skilled drivers are probably overly confident. Drivers were classified as high or low in self-rated skill based on responses to a driver-skill inventory, then classified as high or low in safety skill based on responses to a driver-aggression scale. An overall measure of driving risk was obtained by combining several variables such as number of accidents, tickets, tendency to speed, and tendency to pass other cars. The following data represent results similar to those obtained in the study. Use a two-factor analysis of variance with $\alpha = .05$ to evaluate the results.

		Driving Skill		
		Low	High	
Driving Safety	Low	$n = 8$ $M = 5$ $T = 40$ $SS = 52$	$n = 8$ $M = 8.5$ $T = 68$ $SS = 71$	$N = 32$ $G = 160$ $\Sigma X^2 = 1151$
	High	$n = 8$ $M = 3$ $T = 24$ $SS = 34$	$n = 8$ $M = 3.5$ $T = 28$ $SS = 46$	

29. The following data show the results of a two-factor experiment with $n = 10$ in each treatment condition (cell):

		Factor B	
		B_1	B_2
Factor A	A_1	$M = 4$ $SS = 40$	$M = 2$ $SS = 50$
	A_2	$M = 3$ $SS = 50$	$M = 1$ $SS = 40$

$$\Sigma X^2 = 480$$

a. Sketch a graph showing the results of this experiment.

b. Look at your graph: does there appear to be an A × B interaction? Does factor A appear to have any effect? Does factor B appear to have any effect?

c. Evaluate these data using an ANOVA with $\alpha = .05$.

CHAPTER

15

Correlation and Regression

Tools You Will Need

The following items are considered essential background material for this chapter. If you doubt your knowledge of any of these items, you should review the appropriate chapter or section before proceeding.

- Sum of squares (SS) (Chapter 4)
  - Computational formula
  - Definitional formula
- *z*-scores (Chapter 5)
- Hypothesis testing (Chapter 8)

15.1 INTRODUCTION

Correlation is a statistical technique that is used to measure and describe a relationship between two variables. Usually the two variables are simply observed as they exist naturally in the environment—there is no attempt to control or manipulate the variables. For example, a researcher interested in the relationship between sugar consumption and activity level could measure (and record) the types of food eaten by a group of preschool children and then observe their activity levels on the playground. Notice that the researcher is not trying to manipulate the children's diet or activity level, but is simply observing what occurs naturally. Also note that a correlation requires two scores for each individual (one score from each of the two variables). These scores normally are identified as X and Y. The pairs of scores can be listed in a table, or they can be presented in a graph called a scatter plot (Figure 15.1). In the scatter plot, the values for the X variable are listed on the horizontal axis and the Y values are listed on the vertical axis. Each individual is then identified by a single point on the graph so that the coordinates of the point (the X and Y values) match the individual's X score and Y score. The value of the scatter plot is that it allows you to see any patterns or trends that exist in the data (see Figure 15.1).

THE CHARACTERISTICS OF A RELATIONSHIP

A correlation is a numerical value that describes and measures three characteristics of the relationship between X and Y. These three characteristics are as follows:

1. The Direction of the Relationship. The sign of the correlation, positive or negative, describes the direction of the relationship.

DEFINITIONS

In a **positive correlation,** the two variables tend to change in the same direction: As the value of the X variable increases from one individual to another, the Y variable also tends to increase; when the X variable decreases, the Y variable also decreases.

In a **negative correlation,** the two variables tend to go in opposite directions. As the X variable increases, the Y variable decreases. That is, it is an inverse relationship.

The following examples illustrate positive and negative relationships.

FIGURE 15.1

The same set of $n = 6$ pairs of scores (X and Y values) is shown in a table and in a scatter plot. Note that the scatter plot allows you to see the relationship between X and Y.

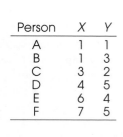

Person	X	Y
A	1	1
B	1	3
C	3	2
D	4	5
E	6	4
F	7	5

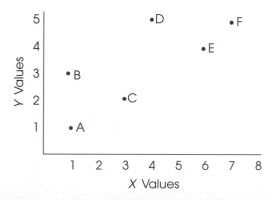

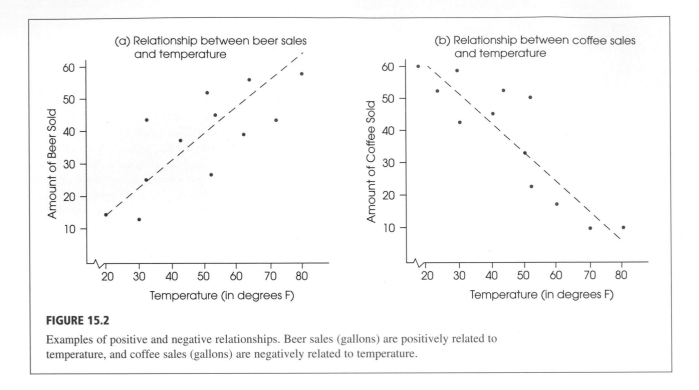

FIGURE 15.2

Examples of positive and negative relationships. Beer sales (gallons) are positively related to temperature, and coffee sales (gallons) are negatively related to temperature.

EXAMPLE 15.1 Suppose you run the drink concession at the football stadium. After several seasons, you begin to notice a relationship between the temperature at game time and the beverages you sell. Specifically, you have noted that when the temperature is low, you sell relatively little beer. However, as the temperature goes up, beer sales also go up (Figure 15.2). This is an example of a positive correlation. You also have noted a relationship between temperature and coffee sales: On cold days you sell a lot of coffee, but coffee sales go down as the temperature goes up. This is an example of a negative relationship.

2. The Form of the Relationship. In the preceding coffee and beer examples, the relationships tend to have a linear form; that is, the points in the scatter plot tend to cluster around a straight line. We have drawn a line through the middle of the data points in each figure to help show the relationship. The most common use of correlation is to measure straight-line relationships. However, other forms of relationships do exist and there are special correlations used to measure them. (We will examine alternatives in Section 15.5.)

3. The Strength or Consistency of the Relationship. Finally, the correlation measures the consistency of the relationship. For a linear relationship, for example, the data points could fit perfectly on a straight line. Every time X increases by one point, the value of Y also changes by a consistent and predictable amount. Figure 15.3(a) shows an example of a perfect linear relationship. However, relationships are usually not perfect. Although there may be a tendency for the value of Y to increase whenever X increases, the amount that Y changes is not always the same, and occasionally, Y decreases when X increases. In this situation, the data points will not fall perfectly on a straight line. The consistency of the relationship is measured by the numerical value

FIGURE 15.3

Examples of different values for linear correlations: (a) a perfect negative correlation, −1.00; (b) no linear trend, 0.00; (c) a strong positive relationship, approximately +0.90; (d) a relatively weak negative correlation, approximately −0.40.

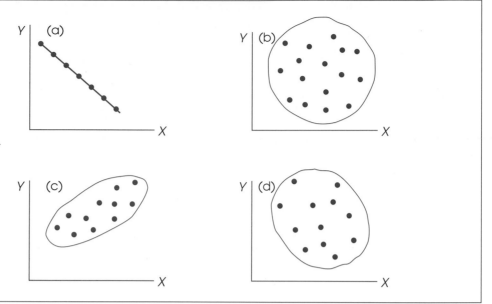

of the correlation. A perfect correlation always is identified by a correlation of 1.00 and indicates a perfectly consistent relationship. For a correlation of 1.00 (or −1.00), each change in X is accompanied by a perfectly predictable change in Y. At the other extreme, a correlation of 0 indicates no consistency at all. For a correlation of 0, the data points are scattered randomly with no clear trend [see Figure 15.3(b)]. Intermediate values between 0 and 1 indicate the degree of consistency.

Examples of different values for linear correlations are shown in Figure 15.3. In each example we have sketched a line around the data points. This line, called an *envelope* because it encloses the data, often helps you to see the overall trend in the data. As a rule of thumb, when the envelope is shaped roughly like a football, the correlation is around 0.7. Envelopes that are fatter than a football indicate correlations closer to 0, and narrower shapes indicate correlations closer to 1.00.

LEARNING CHECK

1. For each of the following, indicate whether you would expect a positive or a negative correlation.
   a. Height and weight for a group of adults
   b. Sugar consumption and activity level for a group of children
   c. Daily high temperature and daily energy consumption for 30 days in the summer
   d. Daily high temperature and daily energy consumption for 30 days in the winter

2. The data points would be clustered more closely around a straight line for a correlation of −0.80 than for a correlation of +.05. (True or false?)

3. If the data points are tightly clustered around a line that slopes down from left to right, then a good estimate of the correlation would be +.90. (True or false?)

4. A correlation can never be greater than +1.00. (True or false?)

ANSWERS
1. **a.** Positive: Taller people tend to weigh more.

   b. Positive: Activity tends to increase as sugar consumption increases.

   c. Positive: Higher temperature tends to increase the use of air conditioning.

   d. Negative: Higher temperature tends to decrease the need for heating.

2. True. The numerical value indicates the strength of the relationship. The sign only indicates direction.

3. False. The sign of the correlation would be negative.

4. True.

15.2 THE PEARSON CORRELATION

By far the most common correlation is the Pearson correlation (or the Pearson product–moment correlation) which measures the degree of straight-line relationship.

DEFINITION

The **Pearson correlation** measures the degree and the direction of the linear relationship between two variables.

The Pearson correlation is identified by the letter r. Conceptually, this correlation is computed by

$$r = \frac{\text{degree to which } X \text{ and } Y \text{ vary together}}{\text{degree to which } X \text{ and } Y \text{ vary separately}}$$

$$= \frac{\text{covariability of } X \text{ and } Y}{\text{variability of } X \text{ and } Y \text{ separately}}$$

When there is a perfect linear relationship, every change in the X variable is accompanied by a corresponding change in the Y variable. In Figure 15.3(a), for example, every time the value of X increases, there is a perfectly predictable decrease in the value of Y. The result is a perfect linear relationship, with X and Y always varying together. In this case, the covariability (X and Y together) is identical to the variability of X and Y separately, and the formula produces a correlation with a magnitude of 1.00 or -1.00. At the other extreme, when there is no linear relationship, a change in the X variable does not correspond to any predictable change in the Y variable. In this case, there is no covariability, and the resulting correlation is zero.

THE SUM OF PRODUCTS OF DEVIATIONS

To calculate the Pearson correlation, it is necessary to introduce one new concept: the *sum of products* of deviations, or *SP*. This new value is similar to *SS* (the sum of squared deviations) which is used to measure variability for a single variable. Now, we will use *SP* to measure the amount of covariability between two variables. The value for *SP* can be calculated with either a definitional formula or a computational formula.

The *definitional formula* for the sum of products is

$$SP = \Sigma(X - M_X)(Y - M_Y) \tag{15.1}$$

where M_X is the mean for the X scores and M_Y is the mean for the Ys.

| BOX 15.1 | COMPARING THE *SP* AND *SS* FORMULAS |

It will help you to learn the formulas for *SP* if you note the similarity between the two *SP* formulas and the corresponding formulas for *SS* that were presented in Chapter 4. The definitional formula for *SS* is

$$SS = \Sigma(X - M)^2$$

In this formula, you must square each deviation, which is equivalent to multiplying it by itself. With this in mind, the formula can be rewritten as

$$SS = \Sigma(X - M)(X - M)$$

The similarity between the *SS* formula and the *SP* formula should be obvious—the *SS* formula uses squares and the *SP* formula uses products. This same relation-ship exists for the computational formulas. For *SS*, the computational formula is

$$SS = \Sigma X^2 - \frac{(\Sigma X)^2}{n}$$

As before, each squared value can be rewritten so that the formula becomes

$$SS = \Sigma XX - \frac{\Sigma X \Sigma X}{n}$$

Again, note the similarity in structure between the *SS* formula and the *SP* formula. If you remember that *SS* uses squares and *SP* uses products, the two new formu-las for the sum of products should be easy to learn.

The definitional formula instructs you to perform the following sequence of operations:

1. Find the *X* deviation and the *Y* deviation for each individual.

2. Find the product of the deviations for each individual.

3. Sum the products.

Notice that this process "defines" the value being calculated: the sum of the products of the deviations.

The *computational formula* for the sum of products of deviations is

Caution: The *n* in this formula refers to the number of pairs of scores.

$$SP = \Sigma XY - \frac{\Sigma X \Sigma Y}{n} \tag{15.2}$$

Because the computational formula uses the original scores (*X* and *Y* values), it usually results in easier calculations than those required with the definitional formula. However, both formulas will always produce the same value for *SP*.

You may have noted that the formulas for *SP* are similar to the formulas you have learned for *SS* (sum of squares). The relationship between the two sets of formulas is described in Box 15.1. The following example demonstrates the calculation of *SP* with both formulas.

EXAMPLE 15.2   The same set of $n = 4$ pairs of scores will be used to calculate *SP*, first using the definitional formula and then using the computational formula.

For the definitional formula, you need deviation scores for each of the *X* values and each of the *Y* values. Note that the mean for the *X*s is $M_X = 3$ and the mean for the *Y*s is $M_Y = 5$. The deviations and the products of deviations are shown in the following table:

Caution: The signs (+ and −) are critical in determining the sum of products, *SP*.

Scores		Deviations		Products
X	Y	$X - M_X$	$Y - M_Y$	$(X - M_X)(Y - M_Y)$
1	3	−2	−2	+4
2	6	−1	+1	−1
4	4	+1	−1	−1
5	7	+2	+2	+4
				+6 = SP

For these scores, the sum of the products of the deviations is $SP = +6$.

For the computational formula, you need the *X* value, the *Y* value, and the *XY* product for each individual. Then you find the sum of the *X*s, the sum of the *Y*s, and the sum of the *XY* products. These values are as follows:

X	Y	XY	
1	3	3	
2	6	12	
4	4	16	
5	7	35	
12	20	66	Totals

Substituting the sums in the formula gives

$$SP = \Sigma XY - \frac{\Sigma X \Sigma Y}{n}$$

$$= 66 - \frac{12(20)}{4}$$

$$= 66 - 60$$

$$= 6$$

Both formulas produce the same result, $SP = 6$.

CALCULATION OF THE PEARSON CORRELATION

As noted earlier, the Pearson correlation consists of a ratio comparing the covariability of *X* and *Y* (the numerator) with the variability of *X* and *Y* separately (the denominator). In the formula for the Pearson *r*, we will use *SP* to measure the covariability of *X* and *Y*. The variability of *X* and *Y* will be measured by computing *SS* for the *X* scores and *SS* for the *Y* scores separately. With these definitions, the formula for the Pearson correlation becomes

Note that you *multiply SS* for *X* by *SS* for *Y* in the denominator of the Pearson formula.

$$r = \frac{SP}{\sqrt{SS_X SS_Y}} \tag{15.3}$$

The following example demonstrates the use of this formula with a simple set of scores.

EXAMPLE 15.3

X	Y
0	2
10	6
4	2
8	4
8	6

The Pearson correlation is computed for the set of $n = 5$ pairs of scores shown in the margin.

Before starting any calculations, it is useful to put the data in a scatter plot and make a preliminary estimate of the correlation. These data have been graphed in Figure 15.4. Looking at the scatter plot, it appears that there is a very good (but not perfect) positive correlation. You should expect an approximate value of $r = +.8$ or $+.9$. To find the Pearson correlation, we will need *SP, SS* for *X*, and *SS* for *Y*. The following table presents the calculations for each of these values using the definitional formulas. (Note that the mean for the *X* values is $M_X = 6$ and the mean for the *Y* scores is $M_Y = 4$.)

Scores		Deviations		Squared Deviations		Products
X	Y	$X - M_X$	$Y - M_Y$	$(X - M_X)^2$	$(Y - M_Y)^2$	$(X - M_X)(Y - M_Y)$
0	2	−6	−2	36	4	+12
10	6	+4	+2	16	4	+8
4	2	−2	−2	4	4	+4
8	4	+2	0	4	0	0
8	6	+2	+2	4	4	+4
				$SS_X = 64$	$SS_Y = 16$	$SP = +28$

Using these values, the Pearson correlation is

$$r = \frac{SP}{\sqrt{(SS_X)(SS_Y)}} = \frac{28}{\sqrt{(64)(16)}} = \frac{28}{32} = +0.875$$

Note that the value we obtained for the correlation is perfectly consistent with the pattern shown in Figure 15.4. First, the positive value of the correlation indicates that the points are clustered around a line that slopes up to the right. Second, the high value for the correlation (near 1.00) indicates that the points are very tightly clustered close to the line. Thus, the value of the correlation describes the relationship that exists in the data.

FIGURE 15.4

Scatterplot of the data from Example 15.3.

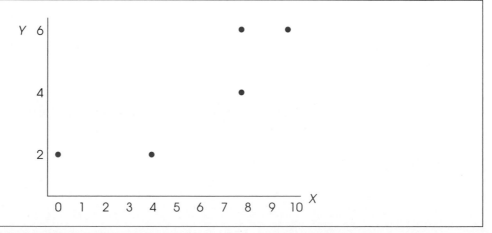

**THE PEARSON
CORRELATION AND
z-SCORES**

The Pearson correlation measures the relationship between an individual's location in the X distribution and his or her location in the Y distribution. For example, a positive correlation means that individuals who score high on X also tend to score high on Y. Similarly, a negative correlation indicates that individuals with high X scores tend to have low Y scores.

Recall from Chapter 5 that z-scores provide a precise way to identify the location of an individual score within a distribution. Because the Pearson correlation measures the relationship between locations and because z-scores are used to specify locations, the formula for the Pearson correlation can be expressed entirely in terms of z-scores:

$$r = \frac{\Sigma z_X z_Y}{n} \tag{15.4}$$

In this formula, z_X identifies each individual's z-score position within the X distribution, and z_Y identifies his or her position within the Y distribution. The product of the z-scores (like the product of the deviation scores) determines the strength and direction of the correlation.

Because z-scores are considered to be the best way to describe a location within a distribution, Formula 15.4 often is considered to be the best way to define the Pearson correlation. However, this formula requires a lot of tedious calculations (changing each score to a z-score), so it rarely is used to calculate a correlation.

Note: Computing a correlation with z-scores (Equation 15.4) requires that you use the population standard deviation to obtain the z-scores for both X and Y. If you compute the z-scores with the sample standard deviation (using $df = n - 1$), then the correct equation is

$$r = \frac{\Sigma z_X z_Y}{(n - 1)}$$

LEARNING CHECK

1. Describe what is measured by a Pearson correlation.

2. Can *SP* ever have a value less than zero?

3. Calculate the sum of products of deviations (*SP*) for the following set of scores. Use the definitional formula and then the computational formula. Verify that you get the same answer with both formulas.

X	Y
1	0
3	1
7	6
5	2
4	1

Remember: It is useful to sketch a scatterplot and make an estimate of the correlation before you begin calculations.

4. Compute the Pearson correlation for the following data:

X	Y
2	9
1	10
3	6
0	8
4	2

ANSWERS   1. The Pearson correlation measures the degree and direction of the linear relationship between two variables.

2. Yes. *SP* can be positive, negative, or zero depending on the relationship between *X* and *Y*.

3. $SP = 19$

4. $r = -\dfrac{16}{20} = -0.80$

15.3 USING AND INTERPRETING THE PEARSON CORRELATION

WHERE AND WHY CORRELATIONS ARE USED

Although correlations have a number of different applications, a few specific examples are presented next to give an indication of the value of this statistical measure.

1. Prediction. If two variables are known to be related in some systematic way, it is possible to use one of the variables to make accurate predictions about the other. For example, when you applied for admission to college, you were required to submit a great deal of personal information, including your scores on the Scholastic Achievement Test (SAT). College officials want this information so they can predict your chances of success in college. It has been demonstrated over several years that SAT scores and college grade point averages are correlated. Students who do well on the SAT tend to do well in college; students who have difficulty with the SAT tend to have difficulty in college. Based on this relationship, college admissions officers can make a prediction about the potential success of each applicant. You should note that this prediction is not perfectly accurate. Not everyone who does poorly on the SAT will have trouble in college. Thus, you also submit letters of recommendation, high school grades, and other information with your application.

2. Validity. Suppose a psychologist develops a new test for measuring intelligence. How could you show that this test truly measures what it claims; that is, how could you demonstrate the validity of the test? One common technique for demonstrating validity is to use a correlation. If the test actually measures intelligence, then the scores on the test should be related to other measures of intelligence—for example, standardized IQ tests, performance on learning tasks, problem-solving ability, and so on. The psychologist could measure the correlation between the new test and each of these other measures of intelligence to demonstrate that the new test is valid.

3. Reliability. In addition to evaluating the validity of a measurement procedure, correlations are used to determine reliability. A measurement procedure is considered reliable to the extent that it produces stable, consistent measurements. That is, a reliable measurement procedure will produce the same (or nearly the same) scores when the same individuals are measured under the same conditions. For example, if your IQ were measured as 113 last week, you would expect to obtain nearly the same score if your IQ were measured again this week. One way to evaluate reliability is to use correlations to determine the relationship between two sets of measurements. When reliability is high, the correlation between two measurements should be strong and positive. Further discussion of the concept of reliability is presented in Box 15.2.

BOX 15.2

RELIABILITY AND ERROR IN MEASUREMENT

The idea of reliability of measurement is tied directly to the notion that each individual measurement includes an element of error. Expressed as an equation,

measured score = true score + error

For example, if I try to measure your intelligence with an IQ test, the score that I get is determined partially by your actual level of intelligence (your true score) but it also is influenced by a variety of other factors such as your current mood, your level of fatigue, your general health, and so on. These other factors are lumped together as *error,* and are typically a part of any measurement.

It is generally assumed that the error component changes randomly from one measurement to the next and this causes your score to change. For example, your IQ score is likely to be higher when you are well rested and feeling good compared to a measurement that is taken when you are tired and depressed. Although your actual intelligence hasn't changed, the error component causes your score to change from one measurement to another.

As long as the error component is relatively small, then your scores will be relatively consistent from one measurement to the next, and the measurements are said to be reliable. If you are feeling especially happy and well rested, it may affect your IQ score by a few points, but it is not going to boost your IQ from 110 to 170.

On the other hand, if the error component is relatively large, then you will find huge differences from one measurement to the next and the measurements are not reliable. Suppose, for example, that I am trying to measure the strength of your leg by determining how far you can kick a football. Your first kick goes off the side of your foot then hits the ground at a bad angle and bounces backwards. The next time you hit the ball squarely and get a good roll. In this situation, it is likely that I will find enormous differences between measurements; one kick can easily be two or three times longer than another. When measurements are unreliable you cannot trust any single measurement to provide an accurate indication of the individual's true score.

Correlations can be used to help researchers measure and describe reliability. By taking two measurements for each individual, it is possible to compute the correlation between the first score and the second score. A strong, positive correlation indicates a good level of reliability: people who scored high on the first measurement also scored high on the second. A weak correlation indicates that there is not a consistent relationship between the first score and the second score; that is, a weak correlation indicates poor reliability.

---

4. **Theory Verification.** Many psychological theories make specific predictions about the relationship between two variables. For example, a theory may predict a relationship between brain size and learning ability; a developmental theory may predict a relationship between the parents' IQs and the child's IQ; a social psychologist may have a theory predicting a relationship between personality type and behavior in a social situation. In each case, the prediction of the theory could be tested by determining the correlation between the two variables.

INTERPRETING CORRELATIONS

When you encounter correlations, there are four additional considerations that you should bear in mind:

1. Correlation simply describes a relationship between two variables. It does not explain why the two variables are related. Specifically, a correlation should not and cannot be interpreted as proof of a cause-and-effect relationship between the two variables.

2. The value of a correlation can be affected greatly by the range of scores represented in the data.

3. One or two extreme data points, often called *outliers,* can have a dramatic effect on the value of a correlation.

4. When judging how "good" a relationship is, it is tempting to focus on the numerical value of the correlation. For example, a correlation of $+.5$ is halfway between 0 and 1.00 and therefore appears to represent a moderate degree of relationship. However, a correlation should not be interpreted as a proportion. Although a correlation of 1.00 does mean that there is a 100% perfectly predictable relationship between X and Y, a correlation of .5 does not mean that you can make predictions with 50% accuracy. To describe how accurately one variable predicts the other, you must square the correlation. Thus, a correlation of $r = .5$ provides only $r^2 = .5^2 = 0.25$, or 25% accuracy.

We will now discuss each of these four points in detail.

CORRELATION AND CAUSATION

One of the most common errors in interpreting correlations is to assume that a correlation necessarily implies a cause-and-effect relationship between the two variables. We constantly are bombarded with reports of relationships: Cigarette smoking is related to heart disease; alcohol consumption is related to birth defects; carrot consumption is related to good eyesight. Do these relationships mean that cigarettes cause heart disease or carrots cause good eyesight? The answer is *no*. Although there may be a causal relationship, the simple existence of a correlation does not prove it. This point should become clear in the following hypothetical example.

EXAMPLE 15.4

Suppose we select a variety of different cities and towns throughout the United States and measure the number of churches (X variable) and the number of serious crimes (Y variable) for each. A scatter plot showing hypothetical data for this study is presented in Figure 15.5. Notice that this scatter plot shows a strong, positive correlation between churches and crime. You also should note that these are realistic data. It is reasonable that the small towns would have less crime and fewer churches and that

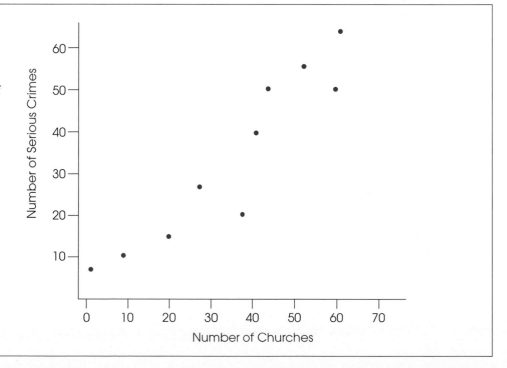

FIGURE 15.5

Hypothetical data showing the logical relationship between the number of churches and the number of serious crimes for a sample of U.S. cities.

the large cities would have large values for both variables. Does this relationship mean that churches cause crime? Does it mean that crime causes churches? It should be clear that both answers are no. Although a strong correlation exists between churches and crime, the real cause of the relationship is the size of the population.

CORRELATION AND RESTRICTED RANGE

Whenever a correlation is computed from scores that do not represent the full range of possible values, you should be cautious in interpreting the correlation. Suppose, for example, you are interested in the relationship between IQ and creativity. If you select a sample of your fellow college students, your data probably will represent only a limited range of IQ scores (most likely from 110 to 130). The correlation within this restricted range could be completely different from the correlation that would be obtained from a full range of IQ scores. For example, Figure 15.6 shows a strong positive relationship between X and Y when the entire range of scores is considered. However, this relationship is obscured when the data are limited to a restricted range.

To be safe, you should not generalize any correlation beyond the range of data represented in the sample. For a correlation to provide an accurate description for the general population, there should be a wide range of X and Y values in the data.

OUTLIERS

An outlier is an individual with X and/or Y values that are substantially different (larger or smaller) from the values obtained for the other individuals in the data set. The data point of a single outlier can have a dramatic influence on the value obtained for the correlation. This effect is illustrated in Figure 15.7. Figure 15.7(a) shows a set of $n = 5$ data points where the correlation between the X and Y variables is nearly zero (actually $r = -0.08$). In Figure 15.7(b), one extreme data point (14, 12) has been added to the original data set. When this outlier is included in the analysis, a strong, positive correlation emerges (now $r = +0.85$). Note that the single outlier drastically alters the value for the correlation and thereby can affect one's interpretation of the relationship between variables X and Y. Without the outlier, one would conclude there is no relationship between the two variables. With the extreme data point, $r = +0.85$ implies that as X increases, Y will increase—and do so consistently. The problem of outliers is a good reason why you should always look at a scatter plot, instead of simply basing your interpretation on the numerical value of the correlation. If you only "go by the numbers," you might overlook the fact that one extreme data point inflated the size of the correlation.

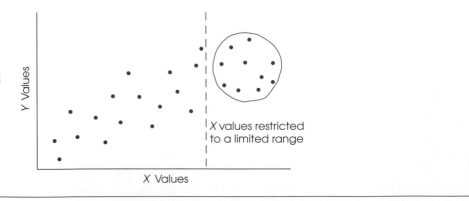

FIGURE 15.6

In this example, the full range of X and Y values shows a strong, positive correlation, but the restricted range of scores produces a correlation near zero.

Y Values

X values restricted to a limited range

X Values

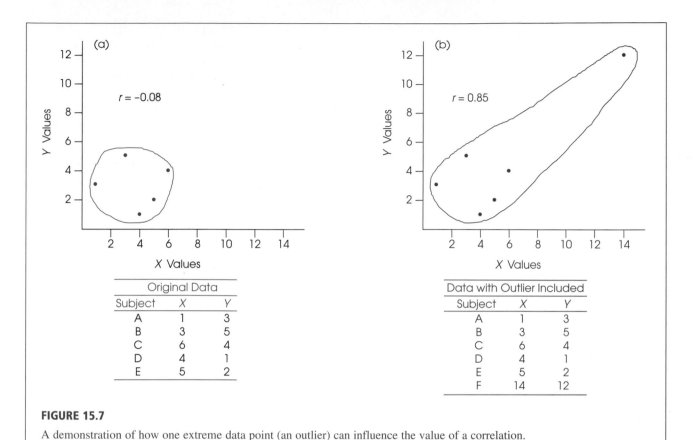

FIGURE 15.7

A demonstration of how one extreme data point (an outlier) can influence the value of a correlation.

CORRELATION AND THE STRENGTH OF THE RELATIONSHIP

A correlation measures the degree of relationship between two variables on a scale from 0 to 1.00. Although this number provides a measure of the degree of relationship, many researchers prefer to square the correlation and use the resulting value to measure the strength of the relationship.

One of the common uses of correlation is for prediction. If two variables are correlated, you can use the value of one variable to predict the other. For example, college admissions officers do not guess which applicants are likely to do well; they use other variables (SAT scores, high school grades, etc.) to predict which students are most likely to be successful. These predictions are based on correlations. By using correlations, the admissions officers expect to make more accurate predictions than would be obtained by guessing. In general, the squared correlation (r^2) measures the gain in accuracy that is obtained from using the correlation for prediction rather than guessing.

DEFINITION

The value r^2 is called the **coefficient of determination** because it measures the proportion of variability in one variable that can be determined from the relationship with the other variable. A correlation of $r = .80$ (or $-.80$), for example, means that $r^2 = 0.64$ (or 64%) of the variability in the Y scores can be predicted from the relationship with X.

In earlier chapters (see pages 245, 269, and 295) we introduced r^2 as a method for measuring effect size for research studies where mean differences were used to compare treatments. Specifically, we measured how much of the variance in the scores was accounted for by the differences between treatments. In experimental terminology, r^2 measures how much of the variance in the dependent variable is accounted for by the independent variable. Now we are doing the same thing, except that there is no independent or dependent variable. Instead, we simply have two variables, X and Y, and we use r^2 to measure how much of the variance in one variable can be determined from its relationship with the other variable. The following example demonstrates this concept.

EXAMPLE 15.5   Figure 15.8 shows three sets of data representing different degrees of linear relationship. The first set of data [Figure 15.8(a)] shows the relationship between IQ and shoe size. In this case, the correlation is $r = 0$ (and $r^2 = 0$), and you have no ability to predict a person's IQ based on his or her shoe size. Knowing a person's shoe size provides no information (0%) about the person's IQ. In this case, shoe size provides no information (0%) to help explain why different people have different IQs.

Now consider the data in Figure 15.8(b). These data show a moderate, positive correlation, $r = +0.60$, between IQ scores and college grade point averages (GPA). Students with high IQs tend to have higher grades than students with low IQs. From this relationship, it is possible to predict a student's GPA based on his or her IQ. However, you should realize that the prediction is not perfect. Although students with high IQs *tend* to have high GPAs, this is not always true. Thus, knowing a student's IQ provides some information about the student's grades, or knowing a student's grades provides some information about the student's IQ. In this case, IQ scores help explain the fact that different students have different grade point averages. Specifically, you can say that *part* of the differences in GPA are accounted for by IQ. With a correlation of $r = +0.60$, we obtain $r^2 = 0.36$, which means that 36% of the variance in GPA can be explained by IQ.

Finally, consider the data in Figure 15.8(c). This time we show a perfect linear relationship ($r = +1.00$) between monthly salary and yearly salary for a group of college employees. With $r = 1.00$ and $r^2 = 1.00$, there is 100% predictability. If you

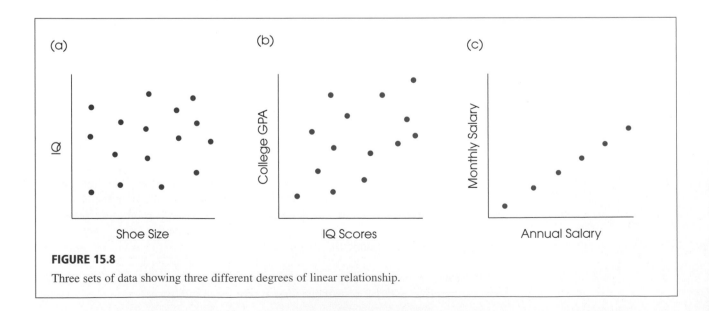

FIGURE 15.8
Three sets of data showing three different degrees of linear relationship.

know a person's monthly salary, you can predict perfectly the person's annual salary. If two people have different annual salaries, the difference can be completely explained (100%) by the difference in their monthly salaries.

15.4   HYPOTHESIS TESTS WITH THE PEARSON CORRELATION

The Pearson correlation is generally computed for sample data. As with most sample statistics, however, a sample correlation is often used to answer questions about the corresponding population correlation. For example, a psychologist would like to know whether there is a relationship between IQ and creativity. This is a general question concerning a population. To answer the question, a sample would be selected, and the sample data would be used to compute the correlation value. You should recognize this process as an example of inferential statistics: using samples to draw inferences about populations. In the past, we have been concerned primarily with using sample means as the basis for answering questions about population means. In this section, we examine the procedures for using a sample correlation as the basis for testing hypotheses about the corresponding population correlation.

THE HYPOTHESES   The basic question for this hypothesis test is whether a correlation exists in the population. The null hypothesis is "No, there is no correlation in the population" or "The population correlation is zero." The alternative hypothesis is "Yes, there is a real, nonzero correlation in the population." Because the population correlation is traditionally represented by ρ (the Greek letter rho), these hypotheses would be stated in symbols as

H_0: $\rho = 0$ (There is no population correlation.)

H_1: $\rho \neq 0$ (There is a real correlation.)

When there is a specific prediction about the direction of the correlation, it is possible to do a directional, or one-tailed test. For example, if a researcher is predicting a positive relationship, the hypotheses would be

H_0: $\rho \leq 0$ (The population correlation is not positive.)

H_1: $\rho > 0$ (The population correlation is positive.)

The correlation from the sample data will be used to evaluate the hypotheses. For the regular, nondirectional test, a sample correlation near zero provides support for H_0 and a sample value far from zero tends to refute H_0. For a directional test, a positive value for the sample correlation would tend to refute a null hypothesis stating that the population correlation is not positive.

DEGREES OF FREEDOM FOR THE CORRELATION TEST   The hypothesis test for the Pearson correlation has degrees of freedom defined by $df = n - 2$. An intuitive explanation for this value is that a sample with only $n = 2$ data points has no degrees of freedom. Specifically, if there are only two points, they will fit perfectly on a straight line, and the sample will produce a perfect correlation of $r = +1.00$ or $r = -1.00$. Because the first two points always produce a perfect correlation, the sample correlation is free to vary only when the data set contains more than two points. Thus, $df = n - 2$.

THE HYPOTHESIS TEST

The table lists critical values in terms of degrees of freedom: $df = n - 2$. Remember to subtract 2 when using this table.

Although it is possible to conduct the hypothesis test by computing either a t statistic or an F-ratio, the computations have been completed and are summarized in Table B.6 in Appendix B. The table is based on the concept that a sample is expected to be representative of the population from which it was obtained. In particular, a sample correlation should be similar to the population correlation. If the population correlation is zero, as specified in the null hypothesis, then the sample correlation should be near to zero. Thus, a sample correlation that is close to zero provides support for H_0 and a sample correlation that is far from zero contradicts the null hypothesis. Table B6 identifies exactly which sample correlations are likely to be obtained from a population with $\rho = 0$ and which values are very unlikely. To use the table, you need to know the sample size (n) and the alpha level. With a sample size of $n = 20$ and an alpha level of .05, for example, you locate $df = n - 2 = 18$ in the left-hand column and the value .05 for either one tail or two tails across the top of the table. For $df = 18$ and $\alpha = .05$ for a two-tailed test, the table shows a value of 0.444. Thus, if the null hypothesis is true and there is no correlation in the population, then the sample correlation should be near to zero. According to the table, the sample correlation should have a value between +0.444 and −0.444. If H_0 is true, it is very unlikely ($\alpha = .05$) to obtain a sample correlation outside this range. Therefore, a sample correlation beyond ±0.444 will lead to rejecting the null hypothesis. The following examples demonstrate the use of the table.

EXAMPLE 15.6

A researcher is using a regular, two-tailed test with $\alpha = .05$ to determine whether or not a nonzero correlation exists in the population. A sample of $n = 30$ individuals is obtained. With $\alpha = .05$ and $n = 30$, the table lists a value of 0.361. Thus, the sample correlation (independent of sign) must have a value greater than or equal to 0.361 to reject H_0 and conclude that there is a significant correlation in the population. Any sample correlation between 0.361 and −0.361 is considered within the realm of sampling error and therefore not significant.

EXAMPLE 15.7

This time the researcher is using a directional, one-tailed test to determine whether or not there is a positive correlation in the population.

H_0: $\rho \leq 0$ (There is not a positive correlation.)

H_1: $\rho > 0$ (There is a positive correlation.)

With $\alpha = .05$ and a sample of $n = 30$, the table lists a value of 0.306 for a one-tailed test. Thus, the researcher must obtain a sample correlation that is positive (as predicted) and has a value greater than or equal to 0.306 to reject H_0 and conclude that there is a significant positive correlation in the population.

IN THE LITERATURE
REPORTING CORRELATIONS

When correlations are computed, the results are reported using APA format. The statement should include the sample size, the calculated value for the correlation, whether or not it is a statistically significant relationship, the probability level, and the type of test used (one- or two-tailed). For example, a correlation might be reported as follows:

A correlation for the data revealed that amount of education and annual income were significantly related, $r = +.65$, $n = 30$, $p < .01$, two tails.

Sometimes a study might look at several variables, and correlations between all possible variable pairings are computed. Suppose, for example, that a study measured people's annual income, amount of education, age, and intelligence. With four variables, there are six possible pairings leading to six different correlations. The results from multiple correlations are most easily reported in a table called a *correlation matrix*, using footnotes to indicate which correlations are significant. For example, the report might state:

The analysis examined the relationships among income, amount of education, age, and intelligence for $n = 30$ participants. The correlations between pairs of variables are reported in Table 1. Significant correlations are noted in the table.

TABLE 1

Correlation matrix for income, amount of education, age, and intelligence

	Education	Age	IQ
Income	+.65*	+.41**	+.27
Education		+.11	+.38**
Age			−.02

$n = 30$
*$p < .01$, two tails
**$p < .05$, two tails

❏

1. A researcher obtains a correlation of $r = -.41$ for a sample of $n = 25$ individuals. Does this sample provide sufficient evidence to conclude that there is a significant, nonzero correlation in the population? Assume a nondirectional test with $\alpha = .05$.

2. For a sample of $n = 20$, how large a correlation is needed to conclude at the .05 level that there is a nonzero correlation in the population? Assume a nondirectional test.

3. As sample size gets smaller, what happens to the magnitude of the correlation necessary for significance? Explain why this occurs.

ANSWERS

1. Yes. For $n = 25$, the critical value is $r = .396$. The sample value is in the critical region.

2. For $n = 20$, the critical value is $r = .444$.

3. As the sample size gets smaller, the magnitude of the correlation needed for significance gets larger. With a small sample, it is easy to get a relatively large correlation just by chance. Therefore, a small sample requires a very large correlation before you can be confident there is a real (nonzero) relationship in the population.

15.5 ALTERNATIVES TO THE PEARSON CORRELATION

The Pearson correlation measures the degree of linear relationship between two variables when the data (X and Y values) consist of numerical scores from an interval or ratio scale of measurement. However, other correlations have been developed for nonlinear relationships and for other types of data. In this section we will examine three additional correlations: the Spearman correlation, the point-biserial correlation, and the phi-coefficient. As you will see, all three can be viewed as special applications of the Pearson correlation.

THE SPEARMAN CORRELATION

When the Pearson correlation formula is used with data from an ordinal scale (ranks), the result is called the Spearman correlation. The Spearman correlation is used in two situations.

First, the Spearman correlation is used to measure the relationship between X and Y when both variables are measured on an ordinal scale. Recall from Chapter 1 that an ordinal scale typically involves ranking individuals rather than obtaining numerical scores. Rank-order data are fairly common because they are often easier to obtain than interval or ratio scale data. For example, a teacher may feel confident about rank-ordering students' leadership abilities but would find it difficult to measure leadership on some other scale.

In addition to measuring relationships for ordinal data, the Spearman correlation can be used as a valuable alternative to the Pearson correlation, even when the original raw scores are on an interval or a ratio scale. As we have noted, the Pearson correlation measures the degree of *linear relationship* between two variables—that is, how well the data points fit on a straight line. However, a researcher often expects the data to show a consistently one-directional relationship but not necessarily a linear relationship. For example, Figure 15.9 shows the typical relationship between practice and performance. For nearly any skill, increasing amounts of practice tend to be associated with improvements in performance (the more you practice, the better you get). However, it is not a straight-line relationship. When you are first learning a new skill, practice produces large improvements in performance. After you have been performing a skill for several years, however, additional practice produces only minor changes in perfor-

FIGURE 15.9

Hypothetical data showing the relationship between practice and performance. Although this relationship is not linear, there is a consistent positive relationship. An increase in performance tends to accompany an increase in practice.

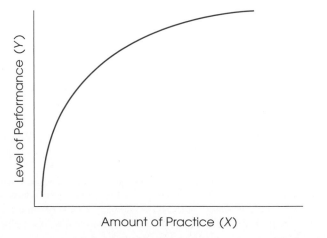

mance. Although there is a consistent relationship between the amount of practice and the quality of performance, it clearly is not linear. If the Pearson correlation were computed for these data it would not produce a correlation of 1.00 because the data do not fit perfectly on a straight line. In a situation like this, the Spearman correlation can be used to measure the consistency of the relationship, independent of its form.

The reason that the Spearman correlation measures consistency, rather than form, comes from a simple observation: When two variables are consistently related, their ranks will be linearly related. For example, a perfectly consistent positive relationship means that every time the X variable increases, the Y variable also increases. Thus, the smallest value of X is paired with the smallest value of Y, the second-smallest value of X is paired with the second smallest value of Y, and so on. Every time the rank for X goes up by 1 point, the rank for Y also goes up by 1 point. As a result, the ranks fit perfectly on a straight line. This phenomenon is demonstrated in the following example.

EXAMPLE 15.8 Table 15.1 presents X and Y scores for a sample of $n = 4$ people. Note that the data show a perfectly consistent relationship. Each increase in X is accompanied by an increase in Y. However the relationship is not linear, as can be seen in the graph of the data in Figure 15.10(a).

TABLE 15.1

Scores and ranks for Example 15.8.

Person	X	Y	X-Rank	Y-Rank
A	2	2	1	1
B	3	8	2	2
C	4	9	3	3
D	10	10	4	4

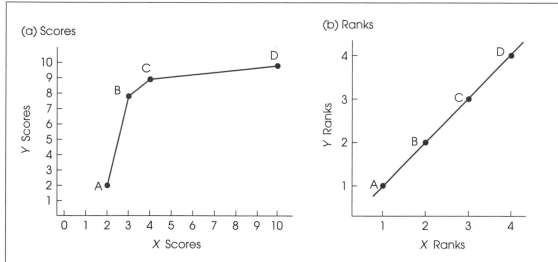

FIGURE 15.10

Scatter plots showing (a) the scores and (b) the ranks for the data in Example 15.8. Notice that there is a consistent, positive relationship between the X and Y scores, although it is not a linear relationship. Also notice that the scatter plot of the ranks shows a perfect linear relationship.

Next, we convert the scores to ranks. The lowest X is assigned a rank of 1, the next lowest a rank of 2, and so on. The ranking procedure is then repeated with the Y scores. The ranks are listed in Table 15.1 and shown in Figure 15.10(b). Note that the perfect consistency for the scores produces a perfect linear relationship for the ranks.

The preceding example demonstrated that a consistent relationship among scores produces a linear relationship when the scores are converted to ranks. Thus, if you want to measure the consistency of a relationship for a set of scores, you can simply convert the scores to ranks and then use the Pearson correlation formula to measure the linear relationship for the ranked data. The degree of linear relationship for the ranks provides a measure of the degree of consistency for the original scores.

To summarize, the Spearman correlation measures the relationship between two variables when both are measured on ordinal scales (ranks). There are two general situations in which the Spearman correlation is used:

1. Spearman is used when the original data are ordinal; that is, when the X and Y values are ranks. In this case, you simply apply the Pearson correlation formula to the set of ranks.

2. Spearman is used when a researcher wants to measure the consistency of a relationship between X and Y, independent of the specific form of the relationship. In this case, the original scores are first converted to ranks; then the Pearson correlation formula is used with the ranks. Because the Pearson formula measures the degree to which the ranks fit on a straight line, it also measures the degree of consistency in the relationship for the original scores. Incidentally, when there is a consistently one-directional relationship between two variables, the relationship is said to be *monotonic*. Thus, the Spearman correlation can be used to measure the degree of monotonic relationship between two variables.

The word *monotonic* describes a sequence that is consistently increasing (or decreasing). Like the word *monotonous*, it means constant and unchanging.

In either case, the Spearman correlation is identified by the symbol r_S to differentiate it from the Pearson correlation. The complete process of computing the Spearman correlation, including ranking scores, is demonstrated in Example 15.9.

EXAMPLE 15.9   The following data show a nearly perfect monotonic relationship between X and Y. When X increases, Y tends to decrease, and there is only one reversal in this general trend. To compute the Spearman correlation, we first rank the X and Y values, and we then compute the Pearson correlation for the ranks.

We have listed the X values in order so that the trend is easier to recognize.

Original Data		Ranks		
X	Y	X	Y	XY
3	12	1	5	5
4	10	2	3	6
8	11	3	4	12
10	9	4	2	8
13	3	5	1	5
				$36 = \Sigma XY$

To compute the correlation, we will need SS for X, SS for Y, and SP. Remember that all these values are computed with the ranks, not the original scores.

The X ranks are simply the integers 1, 2, 3, 4, and 5. These values have $\Sigma X = 15$ and $\Sigma X^2 = 55$. The SS for the X ranks is

$$SS_X = \Sigma X^2 - \frac{(\Sigma X)^2}{n} = 55 - \frac{(15)^2}{5} = 10$$

Note that the ranks for Y are identical to the ranks for X; that is, they are the integers 1, 2, 3, 4, and 5. Therefore, the SS for Y will be identical to the SS for X:

$$SS_Y = 10$$

To compute the SP value, we need ΣX, ΣY, and ΣXY for the ranks. The XY values are listed in the table with the ranks, and we already have found that both the Xs and the Ys have a sum of 15. Using these values, we obtain

$$SP = \Sigma XY - \frac{(\Sigma X)(\Sigma Y)}{n} = 36 - \frac{(15)(15)}{5} = -9$$

The final Spearman correlation is

$$r_S = \frac{SP}{\sqrt{(SS_X)(SS_Y)}}$$

$$= \frac{-9}{\sqrt{10(10)}}$$

$$= -0.9$$

The Spearman correlation indicates that the data show a strong (nearly perfect) negative trend.

RANKING TIED SCORES   When you are converting scores into ranks for the Spearman correlation, you may encounter two (or more) identical scores. Whenever two scores have exactly the same value, their ranks should also be the same. This is accomplished by the following procedure:

1. List the scores in order from smallest to largest. Include tied values in the list.
2. Assign a rank (first, second, etc.) to each position in the ordered list.
3. When two (or more) scores are tied, compute the mean of their ranked positions, and assign this mean value as the final rank for each score.

The process of finding ranks for tied scores is demonstrated here. These scores have been listed in order from smallest to largest.

Scores	Rank Position	Final Rank	
3	1	1.5	Mean of 1 and 2
3	2	1.5	
5	3	3	
6	4	5	
6	5	5	Mean of 4, 5, and 6
6	6	5	
12	7	7	

Note that this example has seven scores and uses all seven ranks. For $X = 12$, the largest score, the appropriate rank is 7. It cannot be given a rank of 6 because that rank has been used for the tied scores.

SPECIAL FORMULA FOR THE SPEARMAN CORRELATION

After the original X values and Y values have been ranked, the calculations necessary for SS and SP can be greatly simplified. First, you should note that the X ranks and the Y ranks are really just a set of integers: $1, 2, 3, 4, \ldots, n$. To compute the mean for these integers, you can locate the midpoint of the series by $M = (n + 1)/2$. Similarly, the SS for this series of integers can be computed by

$$SS = \frac{n(n^2 - 1)}{12} \qquad \text{(Try it out.)}$$

Also, because the X ranks and the Y ranks are the same values, the SS for X will be identical to the SS for Y.

Because calculations with ranks can be simplified and because the Spearman correlation uses ranked data, these simplifications can be incorporated into the final calculations for the Spearman correlation. Instead of using the Pearson formula after ranking the data, you can put the ranks directly into a simplified formula:

Caution: In this formula, you compute the value of the fraction and then subtract from 1. The 1 is not part of the fraction.

$$r_S = 1 - \frac{6\Sigma D^2}{n(n^2 - 1)} \tag{15.5}$$

where D is the difference between the X rank and the Y rank for each individual. This special formula will produce the same result that would be obtained from the Pearson formula. However, note that this special formula can be used only after the scores have been converted to ranks and only when there are no ties among the ranks. If there are relatively few tied ranks, the formula still may be used, but it loses accuracy as the number of ties increases. The application of this formula is demonstrated in the following example.

EXAMPLE 15.10

To demonstrate the special formula for the Spearman correlation, we will use the same data that were presented in Example 15.9. The ranks for these data are shown again here:

Ranks		Difference	
X	Y	D	D^2
1	5	4	16
2	3	1	1
3	4	1	1
4	2	−2	4
5	1	−4	16
			$38 = \Sigma D^2$

Using the special formula for the Spearman correlation, we obtain

$$r_S = 1 - \frac{6\Sigma D^2}{n(n^2 - 1)}$$

$$= 1 - \frac{6(38)}{5(25 - 1)}$$

$$= 1 - \frac{228}{120}$$

$$= 1 - 1.90$$

$$= -0.90$$

This is exactly the same answer that we obtained in Example 15.9, using the Pearson formula on the ranks.

---

1. Describe what is measured by a Spearman correlation, and explain how this correlation is different from the Pearson correlation.

2. Identify the two procedures that can be used to compute the Spearman correlation.

3. Compute the Spearman correlation for the following set of scores:

X	Y
2	7
12	38
9	6
10	19

ANSWERS

1. The Spearman correlation measures the consistency of the direction of the relationship between two variables. The Spearman correlation does not depend on the form of the relationship, whereas the Pearson correlation measures how well the data fit a linear form.

2. After the X and Y values have been ranked, you can compute the Spearman correlation by using either the special formula or the Pearson formula.

3. $r_S = 0.80$

THE POINT-BISERIAL CORRELATION AND MEASURING EFFECT SIZE WITH r^2

In Chapters 9, 10, and 11 we introduced r^2 as a measure of effect size that often accompanies a hypothesis test using the t statistic. The r^2 used to measure effect size and the r used to measure a correlation are directly related, and we now have an opportunity to demonstrate the relationship. Specifically, we compare the independent-measures t test (Chapter 10) and a special version of the Pearson correlation known as the *point-biserial correlation.*

The point-biserial correlation is used to measure the relationship between two variables in situations where one variable consists of regular, numerical scores, but the second variable has only two values. A variable with only two values is called a *dichotomous variable*. Some examples of dichotomous variables are

1. Male versus female

2. College graduate versus not a college graduate

3. First-born child versus later-born child

4. Success versus failure on a particular task

5. Over 30 years old versus under 30 years old

It is customary to use the numerical values 0 and 1, but any two different numbers would work equally well and would not affect the value of the correlation.

To compute the point-biserial correlation, the dichotomous variable is first converted to numerical values by assigning a value of zero (0) to one category and a value of one (1) to the other category. Then the regular Pearson correlation formula is used with the converted data.

To demonstrate the point-biserial correlation and its association with the r^2 measure of effect size, we will use the data from Example 10.1 (page 266). The original example evaluated the effect of mental imagery on memory performance by comparing memory scores for two groups of participants; one group was instructed to use images and the other was not. The data from the independent-measures study are presented on the left side of Table 15.2. Notice that the data consist of two separate samples, and the independent-measures t was used to determine whether there was a significant mean difference between the two treatment conditions.

On the right-hand side of Table 15.2 we have reorganized the data into a form that is suitable for a point-biserial correlation. Specifically, we have used the original memory score as the X value for each individual, and we have created a new variable, Y, to represent the treatment condition for each individual. In this case, we have used $Y = 1$ for participants in the imagery condition and $Y = 0$ for participants in the no-imagery condition.

When the data in Table 15.2 were originally presented in Chapter 10, we conducted an independent-measures t hypothesis test and obtained $t = 4.00$ with $df = 18$. We measured the size of the treatment effect by calculating r^2, the percentage of variance accounted for, and obtained $r^2 = 0.47$.

TABLE 15.2

The same data are organized in two different formats. On the left-hand side, the data appear as two separate samples (Group 1 and Group 2), appropriate for an independent-measures t hypothesis test. On the right-hand side, the same data are shown as a single sample, with two scores for each individual: the original memory score (X) and a dichotomous score (Y) that designates the treatment condition (images or no-images) in which the participant is located. The data on the right are appropriate for a point-biserial correlation.

Data for the independent-measures t. The data consist of two separate samples with $n = 10$ scores in each sample.			
Data (Number of Words Recalled)			
Group 1 (Images)		Group 2 (No Images)	
19	32	23	12
20	30	22	16
24	27	15	19
30	22	16	14
31	25	18	25
$n = 10$		$n = 10$	
$M = 26$		$M = 18$	
$SS = 200$		$SS = 160$	

Data for the point-biserial correlation. The data consist of two scores (X and Y) for each of the 20 participants.		
Participant	Memory Score	Treatment Condition
A	19	1
B	20	1
C	24	1
D	30	1
E	31	1
F	32	1
G	30	1
H	27	1
I	22	1
J	25	1
K	23	0
L	22	0
M	15	0
N	16	0
O	18	0
P	12	0
Q	16	0
R	19	0
S	14	0
T	25	0

Calculating the point-biserial correlation for these data also produces a value for r. Specifically, the X scores produce $SS = 680$; the Y values produce $SS = 5.00$, and the sum of the products of the X and Y deviations produces $SP = 40$. The point-biserial correlation is

$$r = \frac{SP}{\sqrt{(SS_X)(SS_Y)}} = \frac{40}{\sqrt{(680)(5)}} = \frac{40}{58.31} = 0.686$$

Notice that squaring the value of the point-biserial correlation produces $r^2 = (0.686)^2 = 0.47$, which is exactly the value of r^2 we obtained measuring effect size.

In some respects, the point-biserial correlation and the independent-measures hypothesis test are evaluating the same thing. Specifically, both are examining the relationship between mental imagery and memory scores.

1. The correlation is measuring the *strength* of the relationship between the two variables. A large correlation (near 1.00 or −1.00) would indicate that there is a consistent, predictable relationship between memory performance and mental imagery. In particular, the value of r^2 measures how much of the variance in the memory scores can be predicted by knowing whether the participants used imagery.

2. The t test evaluates the *significance* of the relationship. The hypothesis test determines whether the mean difference in memory scores between the imagery group and the no-imagery group is greater than can be reasonably explained by chance alone.

As we noted in Chapter 10 (pages 268–269), the outcome of the hypothesis test and the value of r^2 are often reported together. The t value measures statistical significance and r^2 measures the effect size. Also, as we noted in Chapter 10, the values for t and r are directly related. In fact, either one can be calculated from the other by the equations

$$r^2 = \frac{t^2}{t^2 + df} \qquad \text{and} \qquad t^2 = \frac{r^2}{(1 - r^2)/df}$$

where df is the degrees of freedom for the t statistic.

However, you should note that r^2 is determined entirely by the size of the correlation, whereas t is influenced by the size of the correlation and the size of the sample. For example, a correlation of $r = 0.30$ produces $r^2 = 0.09$ (9%) no matter how large the sample may be. On the other hand, a point-biserial correlation of $r = 0.30$ for a total sample of 10 people ($n = 5$ in each group) produces a nonsignificant value of $t = 0.791$. If the sample is increased to 50 people ($n = 25$ in each group), the same correlation produces a significant t value of $t = 4.75$. Although t and r are related, they are measuring different things.

THE PHI-COEFFICIENT When both variables (X and Y) measured for each individual are dichotomous, the correlation between the two variables is called the *phi-coefficient*. To compute phi (ϕ), you follow a two-step procedure:

1. Convert each of the dichotomous variables to numerical values by assigning a 0 to one category and a 1 to the other category for each of the variables.

2. Use the regular Pearson formula with the converted scores.

This process is demonstrated in the following example.

EXAMPLE 15.11   A researcher is interested in examining the relationship between birth-order position and personality. A random sample of $n = 8$ individuals is obtained, and each individual is classified in terms of birth-order position as first-born or only child versus later-born. Then each individual's personality is classified as either introvert or extrovert.

The original measurements are then converted to numerical values by the following assignments:

Birth Order	Personality
1st or only child $= 0$	Introvert $= 0$
Later-born child $= 1$	Extrovert $= 1$

The original data and the converted scores are as follows:

Original Data		Converted Scores	
Birth Order X	Personality Y	Birth Order X	Personality Y
1st	Introvert	0	0
3rd	Extrovert	1	1
Only	Extrovert	0	1
2nd	Extrovert	1	1
4th	Extrovert	1	1
2nd	Introvert	1	0
Only	Introvert	0	0
3rd	Extrovert	1	1

The Pearson correlation formula would then be used with the converted data to compute the phi-coefficient.

Because the assignment of numerical values is arbitrary (either category could be designated 0 or 1), the sign of the resulting correlation is meaningless. As with most correlations, the *strength* of the relationship is best described by the value of r^2, the coefficient of determination, which measures how much of the variability in one variable is predicted or determined by the association with the second variable.

We also should note that although the phi-coefficient can be used to assess the relationship between two dichotomous variables, the more common statistical procedure is a chi-square statistic, which is examined in Chapter 16.

LEARNING CHECK

1. Define a *dichotomous* variable.

2. The following data represent job-related stress scores for a sample of $n = 8$ individuals. These people also are classified by salary level.

   a. Convert the data into a form suitable for the point-biserial correlation.

   b. Compute the point-biserial correlation for these data.

Salary More than $40,000	Salary Less than $40,000
8	4
6	2
5	1
3	3

ANSWERS   1. A dichotomous variable has only two possible values.

2. a. Salary level is a dichotomous variable and can be coded as $Y = 1$ for individuals with salary more than \$40,000 and $Y = 0$ for salary less than \$40,000. The stress scores produce $SS_X = 36$, the salary codes produce $SS_Y = 2$, and $SP = 6$.   b. The point-biserial correlation is 0.71.

15.6 INTRODUCTION TO LINEAR EQUATIONS AND REGRESSION

Earlier in this chapter, we introduced the Pearson correlation as a technique for describing and measuring the linear relationship between two variables. Figure 15.11 presents hypothetical data showing the relationship between SAT scores and college grade point average (GPA). Note that the figure shows a good, but not perfect, positive relationship. Also note that we have drawn a line through the middle of the data points. This line serves several purposes:

1. The line makes the relationship between SAT and GPA easier to see.

2. The line identifies the center, or *central tendency,* of the relationship, just as the mean describes central tendency for a set of scores. Thus, the line provides a simplified description of the relationship. For example, if the data points were removed, the straight line would still give a general picture of the relationship between SAT and GPA.

3. Finally, the line can be used for prediction. The line establishes a precise, one-to-one relationship between each X value (SAT score) and a corresponding Y value (GPA). For example, an SAT score of 620 corresponds to a GPA of 3.25 (see Figure 15.11). Thus, the college admissions officers could use the straight-line relationship to predict that a student entering college with an SAT score of 620 should achieve a college GPA of approximately 3.25.

Our goal in this section is to develop a procedure that identifies and defines the straight line that provides the best fit for any specific set of data. This straight line does

FIGURE 15.11

Hypothetical data showing the relationship between SAT scores and GPA with a regression line drawn through the data points. The regression line defines a precise, one-to-one relationship between each X value (SAT score) and its corresponding Y value (GPA).

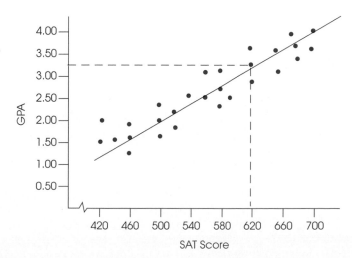

not have to be drawn on a graph; it can be presented in a simple equation. Thus, our goal is to find the equation for the line that best describes the relationship for a set of X and Y data.

LINEAR EQUATIONS

In general, a *linear relationship* between variables X and Y can be expressed by the equation $Y = bX + a$, where b and a are fixed constants.

For example, a local tennis club charges a fee of $5 per hour plus an annual membership fee of $25. With this information, the total cost of playing tennis can be computed using a *linear equation* that describes the relationship between the total cost (Y) and the number of hours (X).

$$Y = 5X + 25$$

Note that a positive slope means that Y increases when X increases, and a negative slope indicates that Y decreases when X increases.

In the general linear equation, the value of b is called the *slope*. The slope determines how much the Y variable will change when X is increased by one point. For the tennis club example, the slope is $b = \$5$ and indicates that your total cost will increase by $5 for each hour you play. The value of a in the general equation is called the Y-intercept because it determines the value of Y when $X = 0$. (On a graph, the a value identifies the point where the line intercepts the Y-axis.) For the tennis club example, $a = \$25$; there is a $25 charge even if you never play tennis.

Figure 15.12 shows the general relationship between cost and number of hours for the tennis club example. Notice that the relationship results in a straight line. To obtain this graph, we picked any two values of X and then used the equation to compute the corresponding values for Y. For example, when $X = 10$, the equation produces $Y = 75$. When $X = 30$, the equation produces $Y = 175$.

When drawing a graph of a linear equation, it is wise to compute and plot at least three points to be certain you have not made a mistake.

Next, these two points are plotted on the graph: one point at $X = 10$ and $Y = 75$, the other point at $X = 30$ and $Y = 175$. Because two points completely determine a straight line, we simply drew the line so that it passed through these two points.

FIGURE 15.12

Relationship between total cost and number of hours playing tennis. The tennis club charges a $25 membership fee plus $5 per hour. The relationship is described by a linear equation:

total cost = $5 (number of hours) + $25
$$Y = bX + a$$

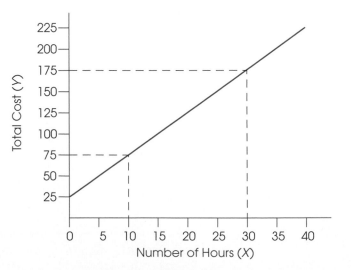

LEARNING CHECK

1. Identify the slope and Y-intercept for the following linear equation:

   $$Y = -3X + 7$$

2. Use the linear equation $Y = 2X - 7$ to determine the value of Y for each of the following values of X: 1, 3, 5, 10.

3. If the slope constant (b) in a linear equation is positive, then a graph of the equation will be a line tilted from lower left to upper right. (True or false?)

ANSWERS

1. Slope $= -3$ and Y-intercept $= +7$.

2.

X	Y
1	-5
3	-1
5	3
10	13

3. True. A positive slope indicates that Y increases (goes up in the graph) when X increases (goes to the right in the graph).

REGRESSION

Because a straight line can be extremely useful for describing a relationship between two variables, a statistical technique has been developed that provides a standardized method for determining the best-fitting straight line for any set of data. The statistical procedure is regression, and the resulting straight line is called the regression line.

DEFINITION

The statistical technique for finding the best-fitting straight line for a set of data is called **regression**, and the resulting straight line is called the **regression line**.

The goal for regression is to find the best-fitting straight line for a set of data. To accomplish this goal, however, it is first necessary to define precisely what is meant by "best fit." For any particular set of data, it is possible to draw lots of different straight lines that all appear to pass through the center of the data points. Each of these lines can be defined by a linear equation of the form

$$Y = bX + a$$

where b and a are constants that determine the slope and Y-intercept of the line, respectively. Each individual line has its own unique values for b and a. The problem is to find the specific line that provides the best fit to the actual data points.

THE LEAST-SQUARES SOLUTION

To determine how well a line fits the data points, the first step is to define mathematically the distance between the line and each data point. For every X value in the data, the linear equation will determine a Y value on the line. This value is the predicted Y and is called $\hat{Y}$ ("Y hat"). The distance between this predicted value and the actual Y value in the data is determined by

$$\text{distance} = Y - \hat{Y}$$

Note that we simply are measuring the vertical distance between the actual data point (Y) and the predicted point on the line. This distance measures the error between the line and the actual data (see Figure 15.13).

Because some of these distances will be positive and some will be negative, the next step is to square each distance to obtain a uniformly positive measure of error. Finally, to determine the total error between the line and the data, we sum the squared errors for all of the data points. The result is a measure of overall squared error between the line and the data:

$$\text{total squared error} = \Sigma(Y - \hat{Y})^2$$

Now we can define the *best-fitting* line as the one that has the smallest total squared error. For obvious reasons, the resulting line is commonly called the *least-squared-error* solution. In symbols, we are looking for a linear equation of the form

$$\hat{Y} = bX + a$$

For each value of X in the data, this equation will determine the point on the line ($\hat{Y}$) *that gives the best prediction of Y*. The problem is to find the specific values for a and b that will make this the best-fitting line.

The calculations that are needed to find this equation require calculus and some sophisticated algebra, so we will not present the details of the solution. The results, however, are relatively straightforward, and the solutions for b and a are as follows:

$$b = \frac{SP}{SS_X} \tag{15.6}$$

where SP is the sum of products and SS_X is the sum of squares for the X scores.

A commonly used alternative formula for the slope is based on the standard deviations for X and Y. The alternative formula is

$$b = r\frac{s_Y}{s_X} \tag{15.7}$$

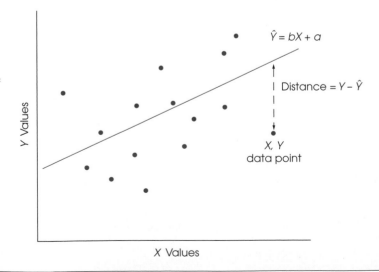

FIGURE 15.13

The distance between the actual data point (Y) and the predicted point on the line ($\hat{Y}$) is defined as $Y - \hat{Y}$. The goal of regression is to find the equation for the line that minimizes these distances.

$\hat{Y} = bX + a$

Distance $= Y - \hat{Y}$

X, Y data point

Y Values

X Values

where s_Y is the standard deviation for the Y scores and s_X is the standard deviation for the X scores. The value of the constant a in the equation is determined by

$$a = M_Y - bM_X \qquad (15.8)$$

Note that these formulas determine the linear equation that provides the best prediction of Y values. This equation is called the *regression equation for* Y.

DEFINITION

The **regression equation for Y** is the linear equation

$$\hat{Y} = bX + a \qquad (15.9)$$

where the constant b is determined by Equation 15.6 or 15.7, and the constant a is determined by Equation 15.8. This equation results in the least squared error between the data points and the line.

Note that the values of SS and SP are needed in the formulas for b and a, just as they are needed to compute the Pearson correlation. Now we present an example demonstrating the calculation and use of this best-fitting line.

EXAMPLE 15.12   The following table shows X and Y scores for a sample of $n = 5$ individuals. These data will be used to demonstrate the procedure for determining the linear regression equation for predicting Y values.

X	Y	$X - M_X$	$Y - M_Y$	$(X - M_X)(Y - M_Y)$	$(X - M_X)^2$
7	11	2	5	10	4
4	3	−1	−3	3	1
6	5	1	−1	−1	1
3	4	−2	−2	4	4
5	7	0	1	0	0
				$16 = SP$	$10 = SS_X$

For these data, $\Sigma X = 25$, so $M_X = 5$. Also, $\Sigma Y = 30$, so $M_Y = 6$. These means have been used to compute the deviation scores for each X and Y value. The final two columns show the products of the deviation scores and the squared deviations for X. Based on these values,

$$SP = \Sigma(X - M_X)(Y - M_Y) = 16$$
$$SS_X = \Sigma(X - M_X)^2 = 10$$

Our goal is to find the values for b and a in the linear equation so that we obtain the best-fitting straight line for the data.

By using Equations 15.7 and 15.8, the solutions for b and a are

$$b = \frac{SP}{SS_X} = \frac{16}{10} = 1.6$$

$$a = M_Y - bM_X$$
$$= 6 - 1.6(5)$$
$$= 6 - 8$$
$$= -2$$

The resulting regression equation is

$$\hat{Y} = 1.6X - 2$$

The original data and the regression line are shown in Figure 15.14.

As we noted at the beginning of this section, one common use of regression equations is for prediction. For any given value of X, we can use the equation to compute a predicted value for Y. For the equation from Example 15.12, an individual with an X score of $X = 5$ would be predicted to have a Y score of

$$\hat{Y} = 1.6X - 2$$
$$= 1.6(5) - 2$$
$$= 8 - 2$$
$$= 6$$

Although regression equations can be used for prediction, a few cautions should be considered whenever you are interpreting the predicted values:

1. The predicted value is not perfect (unless $r = +1.00$ or -1.00). If you examine Figure 15.14, it should be clear that the data points do not fit perfectly on the line. In general, there will be some error between the predicted Y values (on the line) and the actual data. Although the amount of error will vary from point to point, on average the errors will be directly related to the magnitude of the correlation. With a correlation near 1.00 (or -1.00), the data points will generally be clustered close to the line and the error will be small. As the correlation gets nearer to zero, the points will move away from the line and the magnitude of the error will increase.

2. The regression equation should not be used to make predictions for X values that fall outside the range of values covered by the original data. For Example 15.12, the X values ranged from $X = 3$ to $X = 7$, and the regression equation

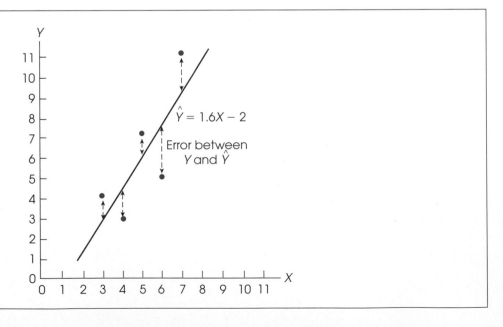

FIGURE 15.14

The scatter plot for the data in Example 15.12 is shown with the best-fitting straight line. The predicted Y values ($\hat{Y}$) are on the regression line. Unless the correlation is perfect ($+1.00$ or -1.00), there will be some error between the actual Y values and the predicted Y values. The larger the correlation is, the smaller the error will be.

was calculated as the best-fitting line within this range. Because you have no information about the X-Y relationship outside this range, the equation should not be used to predict Y for any X value lower than 3 or greater than 7.

STANDARDIZED FORM OF THE REGRESSION EQUATION

So far we have presented the regression equation in terms of the original values, or raw scores, for X and Y. Occasionally, however, researchers standardize the scores by transforming the X and Y values into z-scores before finding the regression equation. The resulting equation is often called the standardized form of the regression equation and is greatly simplified compared to the raw-score version. The simplification comes from the fact that z-scores have standardized characteristics. Specifically, the mean for a set of z-scores is always zero and the standard deviation is always 1. As a result, the standardized form of the regression equation becomes

$$\hat{z}_Y = (\text{beta})z_X \tag{15.10}$$

First notice that we are now using the z-score for each X value to predict the z-score for the corresponding Y value. Also, note that the slope constant that was identified as b in the raw-score formula is now identified as beta. Because both sets of z-scores have a mean of zero, the constant a disappears from the regression equation. Finally, when one variable, X, is being used to predict a second variable, Y, the value of beta is equal to the Pearson correlation for X and Y. Thus, the standardized form of the regression equation can also be written as

$$\hat{z}_Y = rz_X \tag{15.11}$$

Because the process of transforming all of the original scores into z-scores can be tedious, researchers usually compute the raw-score version of the regression equation (Equation 15.9) instead of the standardized form. However, most computer programs report the value of beta as part of the output from linear regression, and you should understand what this value represents.

LEARNING CHECK

1. Sketch a scatter plot for the following data—that is, a graph showing the X, Y data points:

X	Y
1	4
3	9
5	8

   a. Find the regression equation for predicting Y from X. Draw this line on your graph. Does it look like the best-fitting line?
   b. Use the regression equation to find the predicted Y value corresponding to each X in the data.

ANSWERS

1. **a.** $SS_X = 8$, $SP = 8$, $b = 1$, $a = 4$. The equation is

$$\hat{Y} = X + 4$$

   b. The predicted Y values are 5, 7, and 9.

15.7 TESTING THE SIGNIFICANCE OF THE REGRESSION EQUATION: ANALYSIS OF REGRESSION

As we noted earlier in this chapter, a sample correlation is expected to be representative of its population correlation. For example, if the population correlation is zero, the sample correlation is expected to be near zero. Note that we do not expect the sample correlation to be exactly equal to zero. This is the general concept of *sampling error* that was introduced in Chapter 1 (page 6). The principle of sampling error is that there will typically be some discrepancy or error between the value obtained for a sample statistic and the corresponding population parameter. Thus, when there is no relationship whatsoever in the population ($\rho = 0$), you are still likely to obtain a nonzero value for the sample correlation. In this situation, however, the sample correlation is meaningless and a hypothesis test will usually demonstrate that the correlation is not significant.

Whenever you obtain a nonzero value for a sample correlation, you will also obtain real, numerical values for the regression equation. However, if there is no real relationship in the population, both the sample correlation and the regression equation are meaningless—they are simply the result of sampling error and should not be viewed as an indication of any relationship between X and Y. In the same way that we tested the significance of a Pearson correlation, we can test the significance of the regression equation. In fact, when a single variable X is being used to predict a single variable Y, the two tests are equivalent. In each case, the purpose for the test is to determine whether the sample correlation represents a real relationship or is simply the result of sampling error. For both tests, the null hypothesis states that there is no relationship between the two variables in the population. A more specific null hypothesis for testing the significance of a regression equation is that the equation does not account for a significant proportion of the variance in the Y scores. An alternative version of H_0 states that the values of b or beta that are computed for the regression equation do not represent any real relationship between X and Y, but rather are simply the result of chance or sampling error. In other words, the true population value of b, or beta, is zero.

ANALYSIS OF REGRESSION

The process of testing the significance of a regression equation is called analysis of regression and is very similar to the analysis of variance (ANOVA) presented in Chapter 13. As with ANOVA, the regression analysis uses an F-ratio to determine whether the amount of variance accounted for by the regression equation is significantly greater than would be expected by chance alone. The F-ratio is a ratio of two variances, or mean square (MS) values, and each variance is obtained by dividing an SS value by its corresponding degrees of freedom. To obtain the SS and df values needed for the F-ratio, we analyze the variability for the Y scores into two components:

1. The variability in the Y scores that is predicted or accounted for by the relationship with X.

2. The variability in the Y scores that is not predicted.

Earlier we defined the squared correlation, r^2, as the coefficient of determination because it measures the proportion of variability in one variable that can be determined by the relationship with the other variable. We can now use this value to determine the variability in the Y scores that is predicted by the relationship with X. This value is known as $SS_{\text{regression}}$.

$$\text{Predicted variability} = SS_{\text{regression}} = r^2 SS_Y \qquad (15.12)$$

Because r^2 measures the portion of the variability in the Y scores that is predicted by the regression equation, the remaining, unpredicted proportion is determined by $(1 - r^2)$. Thus,

$$\text{Unpredicted variability} = SS_{\text{residual}} = (1 - r^2)SS_Y \qquad (15.13)$$

These two SS values have degrees of freedom determined by

$$df_{\text{regression}} = 1 \qquad (15.14)$$

$$df_{\text{residual}} = n - 2 \qquad (15.15)$$

Note that the $n - 2$ value is the same as the degrees of freedom used to test the significance of the Pearson correlation. Once again, an intuitive explanation for this value is that a sample correlation is not free to vary until the data set contains more than two points. With only two data points, the values will fit perfectly on a straight line and the correlation will always be 1.00 or -1.00.

The complete analysis of SS and df is shown in Figure 15.15. Note that the two components, regression and residual, will always add up to the total for both SS and df.

Separating the variability in the Y score into two components provides the SS and df values needed to compute the variances (MS values) for the F-ratio. The two MS values are defined as

$$MS_{\text{regressiion}} = \frac{SS_{\text{regression}}}{df_{\text{regression}}} \qquad \text{and} \qquad MS_{\text{residuals}} = \frac{SS_{\text{residuals}}}{df_{\text{residuals}}}$$

Finally, the F-ratio is

$$F = \frac{MS_{\text{regression}}}{MS_{\text{residuals}}} \qquad \text{with } df = 1, n - 2 \qquad (15.16)$$

The following example demonstrates the complete analysis of regression.

FIGURE 15.15

The partitioning of SS and df for analysis of regression. The variability in the original Y scores (both SS_Y and df_Y) is partitioned into two components: (1) the variability that is explained by the regression equation, and (2) the residual variability.

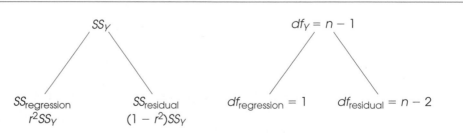

EXAMPLE 15.13   The following table shows the same data that were used in Example 15.12 along with the deviations for both X and Y, the squared deviations, and the products of the deviations.

X	Y	$X - M_X$	$Y - M_Y$	$(X - M_X)^2$	$(Y - M_Y)^2$	$(X - M_X)(Y - M_Y)$
7	11	2	5	4	25	10
4	3	-1	-3	1	9	3
6	5	1	-1	1	1	-1
3	4	-2	-2	4	4	4
5	7	0	1	0	1	0
				$SS_X = 10$	$SS_Y = 40$	$SP = 16$

For these data, the Pearson correlation is

$$r = \frac{SP}{\sqrt{SS_X SS_Y}} = \frac{16}{\sqrt{10(40)}} = \frac{16}{20} = 0.80$$

With $SS_Y = 40$ and a correlation of 0.80, the *predicted variability* from the regression equation is

$$SS_{\text{regression}} = r^2 SS_Y = (0.8^2)(40) = 0.64(40) = 25.60$$

Similarly, the *unpredicted variability* is

$$SS_{\text{residual}} = (1 - r^2)SS_Y = (1 - 0.8^2)(40) = 0.36(40) = 14.40$$

The corresponding *df* values are

$$df_{\text{regression}} = 1 \quad \text{and} \quad df_{\text{residual}} = n - 2 = 3$$

Using these values, we obtain

$$MS_{\text{regression}} = \frac{SS_{\text{regression}}}{df_{\text{regression}}} = \frac{25.60}{1} = 25.60$$

$$MS_{\text{residual}} = \frac{SS_{\text{residual}}}{df_{\text{residual}}} = \frac{14.40}{3} = 4.80$$

Finally, the *F*-ratio for evaluating the significance of the regression equation is:

$$F = \frac{MS_{\text{regression}}}{MS_{\text{residual}}} = \frac{25.60}{4.80} = 5.33$$

With $df = 1, 3$ and $\alpha = .05$, the critical value is 10.13, so we fail to reject the null hypothesis and conclude that the regression equation does not account for a significant portion of the variance for the Y scores. Note that this conclusion is perfectly consistent with the corresponding test for the significance of the Pearson correlation. For these data, the Pearson correlation is $r = 0.80$ with $n = 5$. Checking Table B6 in Appendix B, you can verify that the correlation is also not significant. Thus, the data we have been evaluating do not provide sufficient evidence to conclude that there is a significant relationship between X and Y either in terms of a significant correlation or in terms of a significant regression equation. The complete analysis of regression is summarized in Table 15.3, which is a common format for computer printouts of regression analysis.

TABLE 15.3

A summary table showing the results from an analysis of regression.

Source	SS	df	MS	F
Regression	25.60	1	25.60	5.33
Residual	14.40	3	4.80	
Total	40.00	4		

LEARNING CHECK

1. A set of $n = 12$ pairs of scores produces a Pearson correlation of $r = 0.40$ with $SS_Y = 120$. Find $SS_{regression}$ and $SS_{residual}$ and compute the F-ratio to evaluate the significance of the regression equation for predicting Y.

ANSWER

1. $SS_{regression} = 19.2$ with $df = 1$. $SS_{residual} = 100.8$ with $df = 10$. $F = 1.90$. With $df = 1, 10$ the F-ratio is not significant.

$SS_{residual}$ AND THE STANDARD ERROR OF ESTIMATE

Conceptually, a regression equation produces a predicted Y score for each person. However, the prediction usually is not perfect, so the regression equation also fails to predict part of each person's Y score. These two parts, the predicted and the unpredicted portions of each Y score, produce the values for $SS_{regression}$ and $SS_{residual}$. With this in mind, the residual or unpredicted portion of each score can be determined by the difference between that actual Y value and the predicted Y value ($\hat{Y}$) from the regression equation. For each individual,

$$\text{residual} = (Y - \hat{Y})$$

Thus, an alternative procedure for computing the sum of the squared residuals ($SS_{residual}$) is simply to square each residual and then add the squared values.

$$SS_{residual} = \Sigma(Y - \hat{Y})^2 \qquad (15.17)$$

The following example demonstrates this new formula for SS using the data from Example 15.12 (in which we found the regression equation) and Example 15.13 (the analysis of regression).

EXAMPLE 15.14

Table 15.4 shows the same set of scores that were used in the two previous examples. In Example 15.12 we found the regression equation for these data, $\hat{Y} = 1.6X - 2$, and in Example 15.13 we computed $SS_{residual} = 14.40$. In the table, we also show the predicted Y values from the regression equation, the residual ($Y - \hat{Y}$) for each individual, and the squared residuals. Note that the squared residuals add up to $SS_{residual} = 14.40$ which is exactly the value we obtained in the analyis of regression using Equation 15.13.

TABLE 15.4

Data		Predicted Y Values $\hat{Y} = 1.6X - 2$	Residual $Y - \hat{Y}$	Squared Residual $(Y - \hat{Y})^2$
X	Y			
7	11	9.2	1.8	3.24
4	3	4.4	−1.4	1.96
6	5	7.6	−2.6	6.76
3	4	2.8	1.2	1.44
5	7	6.0	1.0	1.00

$$14.40 = SS_{\text{residual}}$$

THE STANDARD ERROR OF ESTIMATE

A regression equation, by itself, allows you to make predictions, but it does not provide any information about the accuracy of the predictions. Specifically, it does not tell you how much error exists between the predicted Y values on the regression line and the actual Y values in the data. To measure the precision of the prediction, it is customary to compute a standard error of estimate.

DEFINITION

The **standard error of estimate** is a measure of the standard distance between a regression line and the actual data points.

Conceptually, the standard error of estimate is very much like a standard deviation. Both provide a measure of standard distance. You will also see that the calculation of the standard error of estimate is very similar to the calculation of standard deviation.

To compute the standard error of estimate, we begin with SS_{residual}. As demonstrated in Example 15.14, this SS measures the sum of the squared distances between the regression line and the actual Y values. Next, we divide SS by its df to obtain a measure of variance. As usual, variance provides a measure of the average squared distance.

$$\text{Variance} = MS_{\text{residuals}} = \frac{SS_{\text{residuals}}}{df_{\text{residuals}}} = \frac{\Sigma(Y - \hat{Y})^2}{n - 2} \quad \text{or} \quad \frac{(1 - r^2)SS_Y}{n - 2}$$

Finally, we take the square root of the variance to obtain the measure of standard distance that we want:

$$\text{Standard error of estimate} = \sqrt{\frac{SS_{\text{residuals}}}{n - 2}} = \sqrt{MS_{\text{residuals}}} \tag{15.18}$$

As noted earlier, the standard error of estimate provides a measure of the standard distance between the predicted Y values on the regression line and the actual Y values in the data and, therefore, provide a measure of the accuracy of prediction. In general, a strong correlation between X and Y (near 1.00 or −1.00) means that the data points will be close to the regression line and the standard error of estimate will be small. A small correlation, near 0, means that the points are not near the line and the standard error of estimate will be large.

SUMMARY

1. A correlation measures the relationship between two variables, X and Y. The relationship is described by three characteristics:
   a. *Direction.* A relationship can be either positive or negative. A positive relationship means that X and Y vary in the same direction. A negative relationship means that X and Y vary in opposite directions. The sign of the correlation ($+$ or $-$) specifies the direction.
   b. *Form.* The most common form for a relationship is a straight line. However, special correlations exist for measuring other forms. The form is specified by the type of correlation used. For example, the Pearson correlation measures linear form.
   c. *Strength or consistency.* The numerical value of the correlation measures the strength or consistency of the relationship. A correlation of 1.00 indicates a perfectly consistent relationship and 0.00 indicates no relationship at all. For the Pearson correlation, $r = 1.00$ (or -1.00) means that the data points fit perfectly on a straight line.

2. The most commonly used correlation is the Pearson correlation, which measures the degree of linear relationship. The Pearson correlation is identified by the letter r and is computed by

$$r = \frac{SP}{\sqrt{SS_X SS_Y}}$$

In this formula, SP is the sum of products of deviations and can be calculated with either a definitional formula or a computational formula:

definitional formula: $SP = \Sigma(X - M_X)(Y - M_Y)$

computational formula: $SP = \Sigma XY - \dfrac{\Sigma X \Sigma Y}{n}$

3. A correlation between two variables should not be interpreted as implying a causal relationship. Simply because X and Y are related does not mean that X causes Y or that Y causes X.

4. To evaluate the strength of a relationship, you square the value of the correlation. The resulting value, r^2, is called the *coefficient of determination* because it measures the portion of the variability in one variable that can be predicted using the relationship with the second variable.

5. The Spearman correlation (r_S) measures the consistency of direction in the relationship between X and Y—that is, the degree to which the relationship is one-

directional, or monotonic. The Spearman correlation is computed by a two-stage process:
   a. Rank the X scores and the Y scores separately.
   b. Compute the Pearson correlation using the ranks.

6. The point-biserial correlation is used to measure the strength of the relationship when one of the two variables is dichotomous. The dichotomous variable is coded using values of 0 and 1, and the regular Pearson formula is applied. Squaring the point-biserial correlation produces the same r^2 value that is obtained to measure effect size for the independent-measures t test. When both variables, X and Y, are dichotomous, the phi-coefficient can be used to measure the strength of the relationship. Both variables are coded 0 and 1, and the Pearson formula is used to compute the correlation.

7. When there is a general linear relationship between two variables, X and Y, it is possible to construct a linear equation that allows you to predict the Y value corresponding to any known value of X:

$$\text{predicted } Y \text{ value} = \hat{Y} = bX + a$$

The technique for determining this equation is called regression. By using a *least-squares* method to minimize the error between the predicted Y values and the actual Y values, the best-fitting line is achieved when the linear equation has

$$b = \frac{SP}{SS_X} \quad \text{and} \quad a = M_Y - bM_X$$

8. The linear equation generated by regression (called the regression equation) can be used to compute a predicted Y value for any value of X. However, the prediction is not perfect, so for each Y value, there is a predicted portion and an unpredicted, or residual, portion. Overall, the predicted portion of the Y score variability is measured by r^2, and the residual portion is measured by $1 - r^2$.

$$\text{Predicted variability} = SS_{\text{regression}} = r^2 SS_Y$$

$$\text{Unpredicted variability} = SS_{\text{residual}} = (1 - r^2) SS_Y$$

9. The residual variability can be used to compute the standard error of estimate, which provides a measure of the standard distance (or error) between the predicted Y values on the line and the actual data points. The standard error of estimate is computed by

$$\text{standard error of estimate} = \sqrt{\frac{SS_{\text{residual}}}{n - 2}}$$

$$= \sqrt{MS_{\text{residual}}}$$

10. It is also possible to compute an F-ratio to evaluate the significance of the regression equation. The process is called analysis of regression and determines whether the equation predicts a significant portion of the variance for the Y scores. First a variance, or MS, value is computed for the predicted variability and the residual variability,

$$MS_{\text{regression}} = \frac{SS_{\text{regression}}}{df_{\text{regression}}} \qquad MS_{\text{residual}} = \frac{SS_{\text{residual}}}{df_{\text{residual}}}$$

where $df_{\text{regression}} = 1$ and $df_{\text{residual}} = n - 2$. Next, an F-ratio is computed to evaluate the significance of the regression equation.

$$F = \frac{MS_{\text{regression}}}{MS_{\text{residual}}} \qquad \text{with } df = 1, n - 2$$

KEY TERMS

correlation	restricted range	linear equation	regression
positive correlation	coefficient of determination	slope	regression line
negative correlation	Spearman correlation	Y-intercept	predicted variability ($SS_{\text{regression}}$)
perfect correlation	point-biserial correlation	least-squares solution	unpredicted variability (SS_{residual})
Pearson correlation	phi-coefficient	regression equation for Y	standard error of estimate
sum of products (SP)	linear relationship		

RESOURCES

There are a tutorial quiz and other learning exercises for Chapter 15 at the Wadsworth website, www.thomsonedu.com/psychology/gravetter. The site also provides access to two workshops entitled *Correlation* and *Bivariate Scatter Plots* that includes information on regression. See page 27 for more information about accessing items on the website.

WebTUTOR

For those using WebTutor along with this book, there is a WebTutor section corresponding to this chapter. The WebTutor contains a brief summary of Chapter 15, hints for learning the concepts and the formulas for correlation and regression, cautions about common errors, and sample exam items including solutions.

SPSS

General instructions for using SPSS are presented in Appendix D. Following are detailed instructions for using SPSS to perform **The Pearson, Spearman, and the point-biserial correlations.** Note: We will focus on the Pearson correlation and then describe how slight modifications to this procedure can be made to compute the Spearman and point-biserial correlations. Separate instructions for the **phi-coefficient** are presented at the end of this section.

Data Entry

1. The data are entered into two columns in the data editor, one for the X values (VAR00001) and one for the Y values (VAR00002), with the two scores for each individual in the same row.

Data Analysis

1. Click **Analyze** on the tool bar, select **Correlate,** and click on **Bivariate.**
2. One by one, move the labels for the two data columns into the **Variables** box. (Hightlight each label and click the arrow to move it into the box.)
3. The **Pearson** box should be checked but, at this point, you can switch to the Spearman correlation by clicking the appropriate box.
4. Click **OK.**

SPSS Output

The program will produce a correlation matrix showing all the possible correlations, including the correlation of X with X and the correlation of Y with Y (both are perfect correlations). You want the correlation of X and $Y,$ which is contained in the upper right corner (or the lower left). The output includes the significance level (p value or alpha level) for the correlation.

To compute the **Spearman** correlation, enter either the X and Y ranks or the X and Y scores into the first two columns. Then follow the same Data Analysis instructions that were presented for the Pearson correlation. At step 3 in the instructions, click on the **Spearman** box before the final OK. (*Note:* If you enter X and Y scores into the data editor, SPSS will convert the scores to ranks before computing the Spearman correlation.)

To compute the **point-biserial** correlation, enter the scores (X values) in the first column and enter the numerical values (usually 0 and 1) for the dichotomous variable in the second column. Then, follow the same Data Analysis instructions that were presented for the Pearson correlation.

The **phi-coefficient** can also be computed by entering the complete string of 0s and 1s into two columns of the SPSS data editor, then following the same Data Analysis instructions that were presented for the Pearson correlation. However, this can be tedious, especially with a large set of scores. The following is an alternative procedure for computing the phi-coefficient with large data sets.

Data Entry

1. Enter the values, 0, 0, 1, 1 (in order) into the first column of the SPSS data editor.
2. Enter the values 0, 1, 0, 1 (in order) into the second column.
3. Count the number of individuals in the sample who are classified with $X = 0$ and $Y = 0$. Enter this frequency in the top box in the third column of the data editor. Then, count how many have $X = 0$ and $Y = 1$ and enter the frequency in the second box of the third column. Continue with the number who have $X = 1$ and $Y = 0$, and finally the number who have $X = 1$ and $Y = 1$. You should end up with 4 values in column three.
4. Click **Data** on the Tool Bar at the top of the SPSS Data Editor page and select **Weight Cases** at the bottom of the list.
5. Click the **weight cases by** circle, then highlight the label for the column containing your frequencies (VAR00003) on the left and move it into the **Frequency Variable** box by clicking on the arrow.
6. Click **OK.**
7. Click **Analyze** on the tool bar, select **Correlate,** and click on **Bivariate.**

8. One by one move the labels for the two data columns containing the 0s and 1s (probably VAR00001 and VAR00002) into the **Variables** box. (Highlight each label and click the arrow to move it into the box.)

9. Verify that the **Pearson** box is checked.

10. Click **OK.**

SPSS Output

The program will produce the same correlation matrix that was described for the Pearson correlation. Again, you want the correlation between X and Y which is in the upper right corner (or lower left). Remember, with the phi-coefficient, the sign of the correlation is meaningless.

Following are detailed instructions for using SPSS to perform **The Linear Regression** presented in this chapter.

Data Entry

1. Enter the X values in one column and the Y values in a second column of the SPSS data editor.

Data Analysis

1. Click **Analyze** on the tool bar, select **Regression,** and click on **Linear.**

2. In the left-hand box, hightlight the column label for the Y values, then click the arrow to move the column label into the **Dependent Variable** box.

3. Highlight the column label for the X values and click the arrow to move it into the **Independent Variable(s)** box.

4. Click **OK.**

SPSS Output

The first table in the output simply identifies the predictor variables that were entered into the regression equation (the X values). The second table (Model Summary) presents the values for R, R^2, and the standard error of estimate. (Note: R is simply the Pearson correlation between X and Y.) The third table (ANOVA) presents the analysis of regression evaluating the significance of the regression equation, including the F-ratio and the level of significance (the p value or alpha level for the test). The final table summarizes the unstandardized and the standardized coefficients for the regression equation. The table shows the values for the constant (a) and the coefficient (b). The standardized coefficient is the beta value. Again, beta is simply the Pearson correlation between X and Y. Finally, the table uses a t statistic to evaluate the significance of the predictor variable. This is identical to the significance of the regression equation and you should find that t is equal to the square root of the F-ratio from the analysis of regression.

FOCUS ON PROBLEM SOLVING

1. A correlation always has a value from $+1.00$ to -1.00. If you obtain a correlation outside this range, then you have made a computational error.

2. When interpreting a correlation, do not confuse the sign ($+$ or $-$) with its numerical value. The sign and the numerical value must be considered separately. Remember that the sign indicates the direction of the relationship between X and Y. On the other hand, the numerical value reflects the strength of the relationship or how well the points approximate a linear (straight-line) relationship. Therefore, a correlation of -0.90 is as strong as a correlation of $+0.90$. The signs tell us that the first correlation is an inverse relationship.

3. Before you begin to calculate a correlation, sketch a scatterplot of the data and make an estimate of the correlation. (Is it positive or negative? Is it near 1 or near 0?) After computing the correlation, compare your final answer with your original estimate.

4. The definitional formula for the sum of products (SP) should be used only when you have a small set (n) of scores and the means for X and Y are both whole numbers. Otherwise, the computational formula will produce quicker, easier, and more accurate results.

5. For computing a correlation, n is the number of individuals (and therefore the number of *pairs* of X and Y values).

6. Rather than memorizing the formula for the Y-intercept in the regression equation, simply remember that the graphed line of the regression equation always goes through the point M_X, M_Y. Therefore, if you plug the mean value for X (M_X) into the regression equation, the result equals the mean value for Y (M_Y).

$$M_Y = bM_X + a$$

If you solve this equation for a, you get the formula for the Y-intercept.

$$a = M_Y - bM_X$$

7. You can calculate $SS_{residual}$ directly by finding the residual (the difference between the actual Y and the predicted Y for each individual), squaring the residuals, and adding the squared values. However, it usually is much easier to compute r^2 (or R^2) and then find $SS_{residual} = (1 - r^2)SS_Y$.

8. The F-ratio for analysis of regression is usually calculated using the actual $SS_{regression}$ and $SS_{residual}$. However, you can simply use r^2 in place of $SS_{regression}$ and you can use $1 - r^2$ in place of $SS_{residual}$. *Note:* You must still use the correct df value for the numerator and the denominator.

DEMONSTRATION 15.1

CORRELATION AND REGRESSION

For the following data, calculate the Pearson correlation and find the regression equation:

Person	X	Y
A	0	4
B	2	1
C	8	10
D	6	9
E	4	6

$M_X = 4$ with $SS_X = 40$
$M_Y = 6$ with $SS_Y = 54$
$SP = 40$

STEP 1 Sketch a scatter plot.

We have constructed a scatter plot for the data (Figure 15.16) and placed an envelope around the data points to make a preliminary estimate of the correlation. Note that the envelope is narrow and elongated. This indicates that the correlation is large—perhaps 0.80 to 0.90. Also, the correlation is positive because increases in X are generally accompanied by increases in Y.

We can sketch a straight line through the middle of the envelope and data points. Now we can roughly approximate the slope and Y-intercept of the best-fit line. This is only an educated guess, but it will tell us what values are reasonable when we actually compute the regression line. The line has a positive slope (as X increases, Y increases), and it intersects the Y-axis in the vicinity of $+2$.

STEP 2 Compute the Pearson correlation.

For these data, the Pearson correlation is

$$r = \frac{SP}{\sqrt{SS_X SS_Y}} = \frac{40}{\sqrt{40(54)}} = \frac{40}{\sqrt{2160}} = \frac{40}{46.48}$$

$$= 0.861$$

In step 1, our preliminary estimate for the correlation was between $+0.80$ and $+0.90$. The calculated correlation is consistent with this estimate.

STEP 3 *Compute the values for the regression equation.* The general form of the regression equation is

$$\hat{Y} = bX + a \qquad \text{where } b = \frac{SP}{SS_X} \qquad \text{and} \quad a = M_Y - bM_X$$

For these data, $b = \dfrac{40}{40} = 1.00$ and $a = 6 - 1(4) = +2.00$

Thus, the regression equation is $\hat{Y} = (1)X + 2.00$ or simply, $\hat{Y} = X + 2$

FIGURE 15.16

The scatter plot for the data of Demonstration 15.1. An envelope is drawn around the points to estimate the magnitude of the correlation. A line is drawn through the middle of the envelope to roughly estimate the Y-intercept for the regression equation.

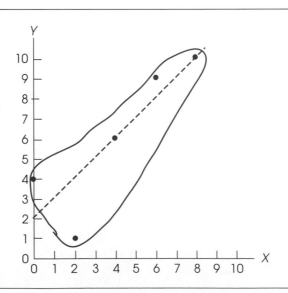

STEP 4 *Evaluate the significance of the regression equation.* The null hypothesis states that the regression equation does not predict a significant portion of the variance for the Y scores. To conduct the test, the total variability for the Y scores, $SS_Y = 54$, is partitioned into the portion predicted by the regression equation and the residual portion.

$$SS_{\text{regression}} = r^2(SS_Y) = 0.741(54) = 40.01 \qquad \text{with } df = 1$$

$$SS_{\text{residual}} = (1 - r^2)(SS_Y) = 0.259(54) = 13.99 \qquad \text{with } df = n - 2 = 3$$

The two MS values (variances) for the F-ratio are

$$MS_{\text{regression}} = \frac{SS_{\text{regression}}}{df} = \frac{40.01}{1} = 40.01$$

$$MS_{\text{residual}} = \frac{SS_{\text{residual}}}{df} = \frac{13.99}{3} = 4.66$$

And the F-ratio is

$$F = \frac{MS_{\text{regression}}}{MS_{\text{residual}}} = \frac{40.01}{4.66} = 8.59$$

With $df = 1, 3$ and $\alpha = .05$, the critical value for the F-ratio is 10.13. Therefore, we fail to reject the null hypothesis and conclude that the regression equation does not predict a significant portion of the variance for the Y scores.

PROBLEMS

1. What information is provided by the sign ($+$ or $-$) of the Pearson correlation?

2. For the following set of data,

X	Y
1	0
2	2
4	6
5	8
3	4

   a. Sketch a graph showing the location of the five X, Y points.
   b. Just looking at your graph, estimate the value of the Pearson correlation.
   c. Compute the Pearson correlation for this data set.

3. The value of the Pearson correlation (including the sign) should give you enough information to visualize or to sketch a scatter plot that accurately represents the appearance of the X and Y scores.
   a. Sketch a scatter plot representing a set of X and Y scores with $r = +0.70$.
   b. Sketch a scatter plot representing a set of X and Y scores with $r = -0.90$.

4. What information is provided by the numerical value of the Pearson correlation?

5. For each of the following sets of scores, calculate SP using the definitional formula and then using the computational formula:

Set 1		Set 2	
X	Y	X	Y
1	0	1	4
3	1	1	4
4	5	3	0
6	3	4	2
6	6	6	0

6. For each of the following, determine whether the sample provides enough evidence to conclude that there is a significant, nonzero correlation in the population. In each case, use a two-tailed test with $\alpha = .05$.
   a. A sample of $n = 18$ with $r = -0.50$.
   b. A sample of $n = 15$ with $r = -0.50$.
   c. A sample of $n = 30$ with $r = 0.375$
   d. A sample of $n = 25$ with $r = 0.375$

7. Assuming a two-tailed test with $\alpha = .05$, how large a correlation is needed to be statistically significant for each of the following samples?
   a. A sample of $n = 15$ individuals
   b. A sample of $n = 30$ individuals
   c. A sample of $n = 92$ individuals

8. It is well known that similarity in attitudes, beliefs, and interests plays an important role in interpersonal attraction (see Byrne, 1971, for example). Thus, correlations for attitudes between married couples should be strong. Suppose a researcher developed a questionnaire that measures how liberal or conservative one's attitudes are. Low scores indicate that the person has liberal attitudes, whereas high scores indicate conservatism. The following hypothetical data are scores for married couples.

Couple	Wife	Husband
A	11	14
B	6	7
C	16	15
D	4	7
E	1	3
F	10	9
G	5	9
H	3	8

Compute the Pearson correlation for these data, and determine whether there is a significant correlation between attitudes for husbands and wives. Set alpha at .05, two tails.

9. Correlation studies are often used to help determine whether certain characteristics are controlled more by genetic influences or by environmental influences. These studies often examine adopted children and compare their behaviors with the behaviors of their birth parents and their adoptive parents. One study examined how much time individuals spend watching TV (Plomin, Corley, DeFries, & Fulker, 1990). The following data are similar to the results obtained in the study.

Amount of Time Spent Watching TV		
Adopted Children	Birth Parents	Adoptive Parents
2	0	1
3	3	4
6	4	2
1	1	0
3	1	0
0	2	3
5	3	2
2	1	3
5	3	3

a. Compute the correlation between the children and their birth parents.
b. Compute the correlation between the children and their adoptive parents.

c. Based on the two correlations, does TV watching appear to be inherited from the birth parents or is it learned from the adoptive parents?

10. In the following data, there are three scores (X, Y, and Z) for each of the $n = 5$ individuals:

X	Y	Z
3	5	5
4	3	2
2	4	6
1	1	3
0	2	4

a. Sketch a graph showing the relationship between X and Y. Compute the Pearson correlation between X and Y.
b. Sketch a graph showing the relationship between Y and Z. Compute the Pearson correlation between Y and Z.
c. Given the results of parts a and b, what would you predict for the correlation between X and Z?
d. Sketch a graph showing the relationship between X and Z. Compute the Pearson correlation for these data.
e. What general conclusion can you make concerning relationships among correlations? If X is related to Y and Y is related to Z, does this necessarily mean that X is related to Z?

11. A common concern for students (and teachers) is the assignment of grades for essays or term papers. Because there are no absolute right or wrong answers, these grades must be based on a judgment of quality. To demonstrate that these judgments actually are reliable, an English instructor asked a colleague to rank-order a set of term papers. The ranks and the instructor's grades for these papers are as follows:

Rank	Grade
1	A
2	B
3	A
4	B
5	B
6	C
7	D
8	C
9	C
10	D
11	E

a. Calculate the Spearman correlation for these data. *(Note:* You must convert the letter grades to ranks.)

b. Based on this correlation, does it appear that there is reasonable agreement between these two instructors in their judgment of the papers?

12. Convert the following scores to ranks and compute the Spearman correlation.

X	Y
7	19
2	4
11	34
15	28
32	104

13. What is the major distinction between the Pearson and Spearman correlations?

14. A researcher would like to evaluate the relationship between a person's age and his or her preference between two leading brands of cola. In a sample of 12 people, the researcher found that 5 out of 8 people 30 years or older preferred brand A and only 1 out of 4 people younger than 30 years old preferred brand A.

a. Convert the data to a form suitable for computing the phi-coefficient. (Code the two age categories as 0 and 1 for the X variable, and code the preferred brand of soft drink as 0 and 1 for the Y variable.)

b. Compute the phi-coefficient for the data.

15. A researcher is comparing two sets of instructions for assembling a bicycle. Of the 10 people using the first set of instructions, only 2 were able to assemble the bike completely in 30 minutes. Of the 10 people using the second set of instructions, 7 completed assembly in 30 minutes. Convert the data into a form suitable for the phi-coefficient and compute the phi-correlation for these data.

16. To test the effectiveness of a new studying strategy, a psychologist randomly divides a sample of 8 students into two groups, with $n = 4$ in each group. The students in one group receive training in the new studying strategy. Then all students are given 30 minutes to study a chapter from a history textbook before they take a quiz on the chapter. The quiz scores for the two groups are as follows:

Training	No Training
9	4
7	7
6	3
10	6

a. Convert these data into a form suitable for the point-biserial correlation. (Use $X = 1$ for training, $X = 0$ for no training, and the quiz score for Y.)

b. Calculate the point-biserial correlation for these data.

17. Problem 14 in Chapter 10 described a study by Rozin, Bauer, and Catanese (2003) comparing attitudes toward eating for male and female college students. The results showed that females are much more concerned about weight gain and other negative aspects of eating than are men. The following data represent the results from one measure of concern about weight gain.

Males	Females
22	54
44	57
39	32
27	53
35	49
19	41
	35
	36
	48

Convert the data into a form suitable for the point-biserial correlation and compute the correlation.

18. A set of scores produces a regression equation of $\hat{Y} = 7X - 2$. Use the equation to find the predicted value of Y for each of the following X scores: 0, 2, 5, 8, 10.

19. For the following set of data, find the linear regression equation for predicting Y from X.

X	Y
3	0
8	10
7	8
5	3
7	7
6	8

20. Sketch a graph showing the line for the equation $Y = 2X - 3$. On the same graph, show the line for $Y = -2X + 8$.

21. A set of $n = 10$ pairs of scores, X and Y values, produces $SS_X = 16$, $SS_Y = 25$, and $SP = 6$. If the mean for the X scores is $M_X = 8$ and the mean for the Y scores is $M_Y = 10$,
   a. Calculate the Pearson correlation for the scores.
   b. Find the regression equation for predicting Y values from the X scores.

22. A professor obtains SAT scores and freshman grade point averages (GPAs) for a group of $n = 15$ college students. The SAT scores have a mean of $M = 580$ with $SS = 22{,}400$, and the GPAs have a mean of 3.10 with $SS = 1.26$, and $SP = 84$.
   a. Find the regression equation for predicting GPA from SAT scores.
   b. What percentage of the variance in GPAs is accounted for by the regression equation? (Compute the correlation, r, then find r^2.)
   c. Does the regression equation account for a significant portion of the variance in GPA? Use $\alpha = .05$ to evaluate the F-ratio.

23. Problem 8 examined the relationship between political attitudes for husbands and wives for a sample of $n = 8$ married couples. The wives had a mean score of $M = 7$ with $SS = 172$, the husbands had a mean score of $M = 9$ with $SS = 106$, and $SP = 122$.
   a. Find the regression equation for predicting a husband's political attitude from his wife's score. (Identify the wives' scores as X values and the husbands' scores as Y values.)
   b. What percentage of the variance in the husbands' scores is accounted for by the regression equation? (Compute the correlation, r, then find r^2.)
   c. Does the regression equation account for a significant portion of the variance in the husbands' scores? Use $\alpha = .05$ to evaluate the F-ratio.

24. For the following data:
   a. Find the regression equation for predicting Y from X.
   b. Use the regression equation to find a predicted Y for each X.
   c. Find the difference between the actual Y value and the predicted Y value for each individual, square the differences, and add the squared values to obtain $SS_{residual}$.
   d. Calculate the Pearson correlation for these data. Use r^2 and SS_Y to compute $SS_{residual}$ with Equation 15.13. You should obtain the same value as in part c.

X	Y
7	16
5	2
6	1
3	2
4	9

25. A researcher finds a correlation of $r = 0.40$ between IQ and creativity scores for a sample of $n = 20$ college students. Using these data, the researcher computes the regression equation for predicting creativity from IQ.
   a. What percentage of the variance in creativity scores is predicted from IQ, and what percentage is not predicted?
   b. If $SS_Y = 10$, does the regression equation predict a significant proportion of the variance in creativity?
   c. If $SS_Y = 100$, does the regression equation predict a significant proportion of the variance in creativity?

   Note: Comparing your answers for part b and part c, you should find that the value of SS_Y has no influence on the F-ratio for analysis of variance. In fact, SS_Y appears in both the numerator and the denominator of the F-ratio and simply cancels out.

26. a. One set of 12 pairs of scores, X and Y values, produces a correlation of $r = 0.90$. If $SS_Y = 200$, find the standard error of estimate for the regression line.
   b. A second set of 12 pairs of X and Y values produces of correlation of $r = 0.60$. If $SS_Y = 200$, find the standard error of estimate for the regression line.

27. A set of $n = 6$ paris of X and Y values has a Pearson correlation of $r = +0.60$ and $SS_Y = 100$. If you are using these data as the basis for a regression equation,
   a. On average, how much error would you expect if the regression equation were used to predict the Y score for a specific individual? That is, find the standard error of estimate.
   b. How much error would you expect if the sample size were $n = 102$ instead of $n = 6$?

28. A researcher who is evaluating the significance of a regression equation with one predictor variable obtains an F-ratio with $df = 1, 18$. How many pairs of scores, X and Y values, are in the data?

C H A P T E R

16

The Chi-Square Statistic: Tests for Goodness of Fit and Independence

Tools You Will Need

The following items are considered essential background material for this chapter. If you doubt your knowledge of any of these items, you should review the appropriate chapter or section before proceeding.

- Proportions (math review, Appendix A)

- Frequency distributions (Chapter 2)

16.1   PARAMETRIC AND NONPARAMETRIC STATISTICAL TESTS

All the statistical tests we have examined thus far are designed to test hypotheses about specific population parameters. For example, we used t tests to assess hypotheses about μ and later about $\mu_1 - \mu_2$. In addition, these tests typically make assumptions about other population parameters. Recall that, for analysis of variance, the population distributions are assumed to be normal and homogeneity of variance is required. Because these tests all concern parameters and require assumptions about parameters, they are called *parametric tests*.

Another general characteristic of parametric tests is that they require a numerical score for each individual in the sample. The scores then are added, squared, averaged, and otherwise manipulated using basic arithmetic. In terms of measurement scales, parametric tests require data from an interval or a ratio scale (see Chapter 1).

Often, researchers are confronted with experimental situations that do not conform to the requirements of parametric tests. In these situations, it may not be appropriate to use a parametric test. Remember that when the assumptions of a test are violated, the test may lead to an erroneous interpretation of the data. Fortunately, there are several hypothesis-testing techniques that provide alternatives to parametric tests. These alternatives are called *nonparametric tests*.

In this chapter, we will introduce two commonly used examples of nonparametric tests. Both tests are based on a statistic known as chi-square and both tests use sample data to evaluate hypotheses about the proportions or relationships that exist within populations. Note that the two chi-square tests, like most nonparametric tests, do not state hypotheses in terms of a specific parameter and that they make few (if any) assumptions about the population distribution. For the latter reason, nonparametric tests sometimes are called *distribution-free tests*.

One of the most obvious differences between parametric and nonparametric tests is the type of data they use. All of the parametric tests that we have examined so far require numerical scores. For nonparametric tests, on the other hand, the participants are usually just classified into categories such as Democrat and Republican, or High, Medium, and Low IQ. Note that these classifications involve measurement on nominal or ordinal scales, and they do not produce numerical values that can be used to calculate means and variances. Instead, the data for many nonparametric tests are simply frequencies—for example, the number of Democrats and the number of Republicans in a sample of $n = 100$ registered voters.

Occasionally, you have a choice between using a parametric and a nonparametric test. Changing to a nonparametric test usually involves transforming the data from numerical scores to nonnumerical categories. For example, you could start with numerical scores measuring self-esteem and create three categories consisting of high, medium, and low self-esteem. In most situations, the parametric test is preferred because it is more likely to detect a real difference or a real relationship. However, there are situations for which transforming scores into categories might be a better choice.

1. Ocassionally, it is simpler to obtain category measurements. For example it is easier to classify students as high, medium, or low in leadership ability than to obtain a numerical score measuring each student's ability.

2. The original scores may violate some of the basic assumptions that underlie certain statistical procedures. For example, the t tests and analysis of variance assume that the data come from normal distributions. Also, the independent-measures tests assume that the different populations all have the same variance

(the homogeneity-of-variance assumption). If a researcher suspects that the data do not satisfy these assumptions, it may be safer to transform the scores into categories and use a nonparametric test to evaluate the data.

3. The original scores may have unusually high variance. Variance is a major component of the standard error in the denominator of t statistics and the error term in the denominator of F-ratios. Thus, large variance can greatly reduce the likelihood that these parametric tests will find significant differences. Converting the scores to categories essentially eliminates the variance. For example, all individuals fit into three categories (high, medium, and low) no matter how variable the original scores are.

4. Occasionally, an experiment produces an undetermined, or infinite, score. For example, a rat may show no sign of solving a particular maze after hundreds of trials. This animal has an infinite, or undetermined, score. Although there is no absolute score that can be assigned, you can say that this rat is in the highest category, and then classify the other scores according to their numerical values.

16.2   THE CHI-SQUARE TEST FOR GOODNESS OF FIT

Parameters such as the mean and the standard deviation are the most common way to describe a population, but there are situations in which a researcher has questions about the proportions or relative frequencies for a distribution. For example,

How does the number of women lawyers compare with the number of men in the profession?

Of the two leading brands of cola, which is preferred by most Americans?

In the past 10 years, has there been a significant change in the proportion of college students who declare a business major?

The name of the test comes from the Greek letter χ (chi, pronounced "kye"), which is used to identify the test statistic.

Note that each of the preceding examples asks a question about proportions in the population. In particular, we are not measuring a numerical score for each individual. Instead, the individuals are simply classified into categories and we want to know what proportion of the population is in each category. The *chi-square test for goodness of fit* is specifically designed to answer this type of question. In general terms, this chi-square test uses the proportions obtained for sample data to test hypotheses about the corresponding proportions in the population.

DEFINITION

The **chi-square test for goodness of fit** uses sample data to test hypotheses about the shape or proportions of a population distribution. The test determines how well the obtained sample proportions fit the population proportions specified by the null hypothesis.

Recall from Chapter 2 that a frequency distribution is defined as a tabulation of the number of individuals located in each category of the scale of measurement. In a frequency distribution graph, the categories that make up the scale of measurement are listed on the X-axis. In a frequency distribution table, the categories are listed in the first column. With chi-square tests, however, it is customary to present the scale of measurement as a series of boxes, with each box corresponding to a separate category on the scale. The frequency corresponding to each category is simply presented as a num-

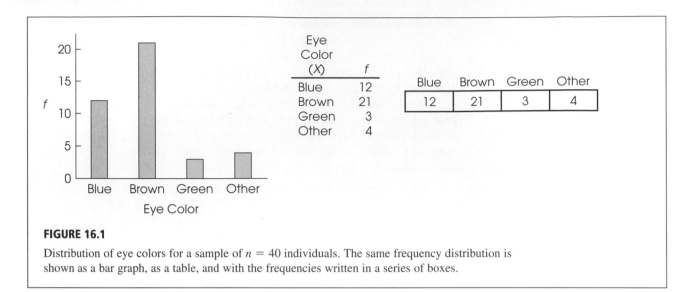

FIGURE 16.1

Distribution of eye colors for a sample of $n = 40$ individuals. The same frequency distribution is shown as a bar graph, as a table, and with the frequencies written in a series of boxes.

ber written inside the box. Figure 16.1 shows how a distribution of eye colors for a set of $n = 40$ students can be presented as a graph, a table, or a series of boxes. The scale of measurement for this example consists of four categories of eye color (blue, brown, green, other).

THE NULL HYPOTHESIS FOR THE GOODNESS-OF-FIT TEST

For the chi-square test of goodness of fit, the null hypothesis specifies the proportion (or percentage) of the population in each category. For example, a hypothesis might state that 90% of all lawyers are men and only 10% are women. The simplest way of presenting this hypothesis is to put the hypothesized proportions in the series of boxes representing the scale of measurement:

	Men	Women
H_0:	90%	10%

Although it is conceivable that a researcher could choose any proportions for the null hypothesis, there usually is some well-defined rationale for stating a null hypothesis. Generally H_0 will fall into one of the following categories:

1. No Preference. The null hypothesis often states that there is no preference among the different categories. In this case, H_0 states that the population is divided equally among the categories. For example, a hypothesis stating that there is no preference among the three leading brands of soft drinks would specify a population distribution as follows:

	Brand X	Brand Y	Brand Z
H_0:	$\frac{1}{3}$	$\frac{1}{3}$	$\frac{1}{3}$

(Preferences in the population are equally divided among the three soft drinks.)

The no-preference hypothesis is used in situations in which a researcher wants to determine whether there are any preferences among the categories, or whether the proportions differ from one category to another.

2. No Difference from a Known Population. The null hypothesis can state that the proportions for one population are not different from the proportions that are known to exist for another population. For example, suppose it is known that 60% of Americans favor the president's foreign policy and 40% are in opposition. A researcher might wonder whether this same pattern of attitudes exists among Europeans. The null hypothesis would state that there is no difference between the two populations and would specify that the Europeans are distributed as follows:

	Favor	Oppose	
H_0:	60%	40%	(Proportions for the European population are not different from the American proportions.)

The no-difference hypothesis is used when a specific population distribution is already known. For example, you may have a known distribution from an earlier time, and the question is whether there has been any change in the proportions. Or you may have a known distribution for one population (Americans) and the question is whether a second population (Europeans) has the same proportions.

Because the null hypothesis for the goodness-of-fit test specifies an exact distribution for the population, the alternative hypothesis (H_1) simply states that the population distribution has a different shape from that specified in H_0. If the null hypothesis states that the population is equally divided among three categories, the alternative hypothesis will say that the population is not divided equally.

THE DATA FOR THE GOODNESS-OF-FIT TEST

The data for a chi-square test are remarkably simple. There is no need to calculate a sample mean or *SS;* you just select a sample of n individuals and count how many are in each category. The resulting values are called *observed frequencies*. The symbol for observed frequency is f_o. For example, the following data represent observed frequencies for a sample of $n = 40$ participants. Each person was given a personality questionnaire and classified into one of three personality categories: A, B, or C.

Category A	Category B	Category C	
15	19	6	$n = 40$

Notice that each individual in the sample is classified into one and only one of the categories. Thus, the frequencies in this example represent three completely separate groups of individuals: 15 who were classified as category A, 19 classified as B, and 6 classified as C. Also note that the observed frequencies add up to the total sample size: $\Sigma f_o = n$. Finally, you should realize that we are not assigning individuals to categories. Instead, we are simply measuring individuals to determine the category in which they belong.

DEFINITION

The **observed frequency** is the number of individuals from the sample who are classified in a particular category. Each individual is counted in one and only one category.

EXPECTED FREQUENCIES

The general goal of the chi-square test for goodness of fit is to compare the data (the observed frequencies) with the null hypothesis. The problem is to determine how well the data fit the distribution specified in H_0—hence the name *goodness of fit.*

The first step in the chi-square test is to construct a hypothetical sample that represents how the sample distribution would look if it was in perfect agreement with the proportions stated in the null hypothesis. Suppose, for example, the null hypothesis states that the population is distributed in three categories with the following proportions:

Category A	Category B	Category C
25%	50%	25%

If this hypothesis is correct, how would you expect a random sample of $n = 40$ individuals to be distributed among the three categories? It should be clear that your best strategy is to predict that 25% of the sample would be in category A, 50% would be in category B, and 25% would be in category C. To find the exact frequency expected for each category, multiply the sample size (n) by the proportion (or percentage) from the null hypothesis. For this example, you would expect

25% of 40 = 0.25(40) = 10 individuals in category A

50% of 40 = 0.50(40) = 20 individuals in category B

25% of 40 = 0.25(40) = 10 individuals in category C

The frequency values predicted from the null hypothesis are called *expected frequencies*. The symbol for expected frequency is f_e, and the expected frequency for each category is computed by

$$\text{expected frequency} = f_e = pn \qquad (16.1)$$

where p is the proportion stated in the null hypothesis and n is the sample size.

DEFINITION

The **expected frequency** for each category is the frequency value that is predicted from the null hypothesis and the sample size (n). The expected frequencies define an ideal, *hypothetical* sample distribution that would be obtained if the sample proportions were in perfect agreement with the proportions specified in the null hypothesis.

Note that the no-preference null hypothesis will always produce equal f_e values for all categories because the proportions (p) are the same for all categories. On the other hand, the no-difference null hypothesis typically will not produce equal values for the expected frequencies because the hypothesized proportions typically vary from one category to another. You also should note that the expected frequencies are calculated, hypothetical values and the numbers that you obtain may be decimals or fractions. The observed frequencies, on the other hand, always represent real individuals and always will be whole numbers.

THE CHI-SQUARE STATISTIC

The general purpose of any hypothesis test is to determine whether the sample data support or refute a hypothesis about the population. In the chi-square test for goodness of fit, the data provide a set of observed frequencies (f_o values), and the null hypothesis is used to generate a set of expected frequencies (f_e values). The *chi-square statis-*

tic simply measures how well the data (f_o) fit the hypothesis (f_e). The symbol for the chi-square statistic is χ^2. The formula for the chi-square statistic is

$$\text{chi-square} = \chi^2 = \Sigma \frac{(f_o - f_e)^2}{f_e} \qquad (16.2)$$

As the formula indicates, the value of chi-square is computed by the following steps:

1. Find the difference between f_o (the data) and f_e (the hypothesis) for each category.
2. Square the difference. This ensures that all values are positive.
3. Next, divide the squared difference by f_e. A justification for this step is given in Box 16.1.
4. Finally, sum the values from all the categories.

THE CHI-SQUARE DISTRIBUTION AND DEGREES OF FREEDOM

It should be clear from the chi-square formula that the numerical value of chi-square is a measure of the discrepancy between the observed frequencies (data) and the expected frequencies (H_0). As usual, the sample data are not expected to provide a perfectly accurate representation of the population. In this case, the proportions or observed frequencies in the sample are not expected to be exactly equal to the proportions in the population. Thus, if there are small discrepancies between the f_o and f_e values, we will obtain a small value for chi-square and we will conclude that there is a good fit between the data and the hypothesis (fail to reject H_0). However, when there are large discrepancies between f_o and f_e, we will obtain a large value for chi-square and conclude that the data do not fit the hypothesis (reject H_0). To decide whether a particular chi-square value is "large" or "small," we must refer to a *chi-square distribution*. This distribution is the set of chi-square values for all the possible random samples when H_0 is true. Much like other distributions we have examined (*t* distribution, *F* distribution), the chi-

---

BOX 16.1   THE CHI-SQUARE FORMULA

The numerator of the chi-square formula is fairly easy to understand. Specifically, the numerator simply measures how much difference there is between the data (the f_o values) and the hypothesis (represented by the f_e values). A large value indicates that the data do not fit the hypothesis, and will lead us to reject the hypothesis.

The denominator of the formula, on the other hand, is not as easy to understand. Why must we divide by f_e before we sum the category values? The answer to this question is that the obtained discrepancy between f_o and f_e is viewed as *relatively* large or *relatively* small depending on the size of the expected frequency. This point is demonstrated in the following analogy.

Suppose you were going to throw a party and you *expected* 1000 people to show up. However, at the party you counted the number of guests and *observed* that 1040 actually showed up. Forty more guests than expected are no major problem when all along you were planning for 1000. There will still probably be enough beer and potato chips for everyone. On the other hand, suppose you had a party and you expected 10 people to attend but instead 50 actually showed up. Forty more guests in this case spell big trouble. How "significant" the discrepancy is depends in part on what you were originally expecting. With very large expected frequencies, allowances are made for more error between f_o and f_e. This is accomplished in the chi-square formula by dividing the squared discrepancy for each category, $(f_o - f_e)^2$, by its expected frequency.

square distribution is a theoretical distribution with well-defined characteristics. Some of these characteristics are easy to infer from the chi-square formula.

1. The formula for chi-square involves adding squared values, so you can never obtain a negative value. Thus, all chi-square values are zero or larger.

2. When H_0 is true, you expect the data (f_o values) to be close to the hypothesis (f_e values). Thus, we expect chi-square values to be small when H_0 is true.

These two factors suggest that the typical chi-square distribution will be positively skewed (Figure 16.2). Note that small values, near zero, are expected when H_0 is true and large values (in the right-hand tail) are very unlikely. Thus, unusually large values of chi-square will form the critical region for the hypothesis test.

Although the typical chi-square distribution is positively skewed, there is one other factor that plays a role in the exact shape of the chi-square distribution—the number of categories. Recall that the chi-square formula requires that you sum values from every category. The more categories you have, the more likely it is that you will obtain a large sum for the chi-square value. On average, chi-square will be larger when you are summing over 10 categories than when you are summing over only 3 categories. As a result, there is a whole family of chi-square distributions, with the exact shape of each distribution determined by the number of categories used in the study. Technically, each specific chi-square distribution is identified by degrees of freedom (df) rather than the number of categories. For the goodness-of-fit test, the degrees of freedom are determined by

$$df = C - 1 \tag{16.3}$$

Caution: The df for a chi-square test is *not* related to sample size (n), as it is in most other tests.

where C is the number of categories. A brief discussion of this df formula is presented in Box 16.2. Figure 16.3 shows the general relationship between df and the shape of the chi-square distribution. Note that the chi-square values tend to get larger (shift to the right) as the number of categories and the degrees of freedom increase.

LOCATING THE CRITICAL REGION FOR A CHI-SQUARE TEST

Recall that a large value for the chi-square statistic indicates a big discrepancy between the data and the hypothesis, and suggests that we reject H_0. To determine whether a particular chi-square value is significantly large, you must consult the table entitled The Chi-Square Distribution (Appendix B). A portion of the chi-square table is shown in Table 16.1. The first column lists df values for the chi-square test, and the top row of

FIGURE 16.2

Chi-square distributions are positively skewed. The critical region is placed in the extreme tail, which reflects large chi-square values.

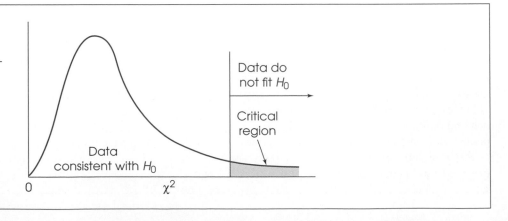

BOX 16.2	**A CLOSER LOOK AT DEGREES OF FREEDOM**

Degrees of freedom for the chi-square test literally measure the number of free choices that exist when you are determining the null hypothesis or the expected frequencies. For example, when you are classifying individuals into three categories, you have exactly two free choices in stating the null hypothesis. You may select any two proportions for the first two categories, but then the third proportion is determined. If you hypothesize 25% in the first category and 50% in the second category, then the third category must be 25% to account for 100% of the population.

Category A	Category B	Category C
25%	50%	?

In general, you are free to select proportions for all but one of the categories, but then the final proportion is determined by the fact that the entire set must total 100%. Thus, you have $C - 1$ free choices, where C is the number of categories: Degrees of freedom, df, equal $C - 1$.

FIGURE 16.3

The shape of the chi-square distribution for different values of df. As the number of categories increases, the peak (mode) of the distribution has a larger chi-square value.

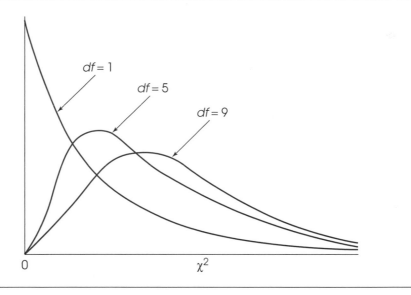

TABLE 16.1

A portion of the table of critical values for the chi-square distribution.

	Proportion in critical region				
df	0.10	0.05	0.025	0.01	0.005
1	2.71	3.84	5.02	6.63	7.88
2	4.61	5.99	7.38	9.21	10.60
3	6.25	7.81	9.35	11.34	12.84
4	7.78	9.49	11.14	13.28	14.86
5	9.24	11.07	12.83	15.09	16.75
6	10.64	12.59	14.45	16.81	18.55
7	12.02	14.07	16.01	18.48	20.28
8	13.36	15.51	17.53	20.09	21.96
9	14.68	16.92	19.02	21.67	23.59

the table lists proportions (alpha levels) in the extreme right-hand tail of the distribution. The numbers in the body of the table are the critical values of chi-square. The table shows, for example, that when the null hypothesis is true and $df = 3$, only 5% (.05) of the chi-square values are greater than 7.81, and only 1% (.01) are greater than 11.34.

EXAMPLE OF THE CHI-SQUARE TEST FOR GOODNESS OF FIT

We will use the same step-by-step process for testing hypotheses with chi-square as we used for other hypothesis tests. In general, the steps consist of stating the hypotheses, locating the critical region, computing the test statistic, and making a decision about H_0. The following example demonstrates the complete process of hypothesis testing with the goodness-of-fit test.

EXAMPLE 16.1

A psychologist examining art appreciation selected an abstract painting that had no obvious top or bottom. Hangers were placed on the painting so that it could be hung with any one of the four sides at the top. The painting was shown to a sample of $n = 50$ participants, and each was asked to hang the painting in the orientation that looked correct. The following data indicate how many people chose each of the four sides to be placed at the top:

Top up (correct)	Bottom up	Left side up	Right side up
18	17	7	8

The question for the hypothesis test is whether there are any preferences among the four possible orientations. Are any of the orientations selected more (or less) often than would be expected simply by chance?

STEP 1   State the hypotheses and select an alpha level. The hypotheses can be stated as follows:

H_0:   In the general population, there is no preference for any specific orientation. Thus, the four possible orientations are selected equally often, and the population distribution has the following proportions:

Top up (correct)	Bottom up	Left side up	Right side up
25%	25%	25%	25%

H_1:   In the general population, one or more of the orientations is preferred over the others.

We will use $\alpha = .05$.

STEP 2   Locate the critical region. For this example, the value for degrees of freedom is

$$df = C - 1 = 4 - 1 = 3$$

For $df = 3$ and $\alpha = .05$, the table of critical values for chi-square indicates that the critical χ^2 has a value of 7.81. The critical region is sketched in Figure 16.4.

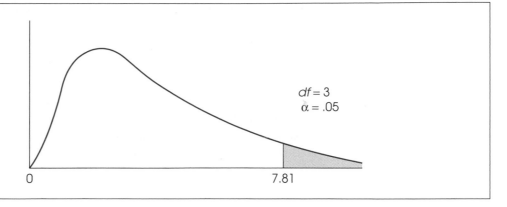

FIGURE 16.4

For Example 16.1, the critical region begins at a chi-square value of 7.81.

$df = 3$
$\alpha = .05$

0   7.81

STEP 3   Calculate the chi-square statistic. The calculation of chi-square is actually a two-stage process. First, you must compute the expected frequencies from H_0 and then calculate the value of the chi-square statistic. For this example, the null hypothesis specifies that one-quarter of the population ($p = 25\%$) will be in each of the four categories. According to this hypothesis, we should expect one-quarter of the sample to be in each category. With a sample of $n = 50$ individuals, the expected frequency for each category is

Expected frequencies are computed and may be decimal values. Observed frequencies are always whole numbers.

$$f_e = pn = \tfrac{1}{4}(50) = 12.5$$

The observed frequencies and the expected frequencies are presented in Table 16.2. Using these values, the chi-square statistic may now be calculated.

$$\chi^2 = \Sigma \frac{(f_o - f_e)^2}{f_e}$$

$$= \frac{(18 - 12.5)^2}{12.5} + \frac{(17 - 12.5)^2}{12.5} + \frac{(7 - 12.5)^2}{12.5} + \frac{(8 - 12.5)^2}{12.5}$$

$$= \frac{30.25}{12.5} + \frac{20.25}{12.5} + \frac{30.25}{12.5} + \frac{20.25}{12.5}$$

$$= 2.42 + 1.62 + 2.42 + 1.62$$

$$= 8.08$$

STEP 4   State a decision and a conclusion. The obtained chi-square value is in the critical region. Therefore, H_0 is rejected, and the researcher may conclude that the four orien-

TABLE 16.2

The observed frequencies and the expected frequencies for the chi-square test in Example 16.1.

		Top up (correct)	Bottom up	Left side up	Right side up
Observed frequencies		18	17	7	8
		Top up (correct)	Bottom up	Left side up	Right side up
Expected frequencies		12.5	12.5	12.5	12.5

tations are not equally likely to be preferred. Instead, there are significant differences among the four orientations, with some selected more often and others less often than would be expected by chance.

IN THE LITERATURE
REPORTING THE RESULTS FOR CHI-SQUARE

APA style specifies the format for reporting the chi-square statistic in scientific journals. For the results of Example 16.1, the report might state:

> The participants showed significant preferences among the four orientations for hanging the painting, $\chi^2(3, n = 50) = 8.08, p < .05$.

Note that the form of the report is similar to that of other statistical tests we have examined. Degrees of freedom are indicated in parentheses following the chi-square symbol. Also contained in the parentheses is the sample size (n). This additional information is important because the degrees of freedom value is based on the number of categories (C), not sample size. Next, the calculated value of chi-square is presented, followed by the probability that a Type I error has been committed. Because the null hypothesis was rejected, the probability is *less than* the alpha level.

Additionally, the report should provide the observed frequencies (f_o) for each category. This information may be presented in a simple sentence or in a table.   ❑

GOODNESS OF FIT AND THE SINGLE-SAMPLE *t* TEST

We begin this chapter with a general discussion of the difference between parametric tests and nonparametric tests. In this context, the chi-square test for goodness of fit is an example of a nonparametric test; that is, it makes no assumptions about the parameters of the population distribution, and it does not require data from an interval or ratio scale. In contrast, the single-sample *t* test introduced in Chapter 9 is an example of a parametric test: It assumes a normal population, it tests hypotheses about the population mean (a parameter), and it requires numerical scores that can be summed, squared, divided, and so on.

Although the chi-square test and the single-sample *t* are clearly distinct, they are also very similar. In particular, both tests are intended to use the data from a single sample to test hypotheses about a single population.

The primary factor that determines whether you should use the chi-square test or the *t* test is the type of measurement that is obtained for each participant. If the sample data consist of numerical scores (from an interval or ratio scale), it is appropriate to compute a sample mean and use a *t* test to evaluate a hypothesis about the population mean. For example, a researcher could measure the IQ for each individual in a sample of registered voters. A *t* test could then be used to evaluate a hypothesis about the mean IQ for the entire population of registered voters. On the other hand, if the individuals in the sample are classified into nonnumerical categories (on a nominal or ordinal scale), you would use a chi-square test to evaluate a hypothesis about the population proportions. For example, a researcher could classify people according to gender by simply counting the number of males and females in a sample of registered voters. A chi-square test would then be appropriate to evaluate a hypothesis about the population proportions.

LEARNING CHECK

1. A researcher uses a chi-square test for goodness of fit with a sample of $n = 120$ people to determine whether there are any preferences among four different brands of chocolate-chip cookies. What is the df value for the chi-square statistic?

2. Is it possible for expected frequencies to be fractions or decimal values?

3. A researcher has developed three different designs for a computer keyboard. A sample of $n = 60$ participants is obtained, and each individual tests all three keyboards and identifies his or her favorite. The frequency distribution of preferences is as follows:

Design A	Design B	Design C	
23	12	25	$n = 60$

Use a chi-square test for goodness of fit with $\alpha = .05$ to determine whether there are any significant preferences among the three designs.

ANSWERS

1. With four categories, $df = 3$.

2. Yes. Expected frequencies are computed and may be fractions or decimal values.

3. The null hypothesis states that there are no preferences; one-third of the population would prefer each design. With $df = 2$, the critical value is 5.99. The expected frequencies are all 20, and the chi-square statistic is 4.90. Fail to reject the null hypothesis. There are no significant preferences.

16.3 THE CHI-SQUARE TEST FOR INDEPENDENCE

The chi-square statistic may also be used to test whether there is a relationship between two variables. In this situation, each individual in the sample is measured or classified on two separate variables. For example, a group of students could be classified in terms of personality (introvert, extrovert) and in terms of color preference (red, yellow, green, or blue). Usually, the data from this classification are presented in the form of a matrix, where the rows correspond to the categories of one variable and the columns correspond to the categories of the second variable. Table 16.3 presents some hypothetical data for a sample of $n = 200$ students who have been classified by personality and color preference. The number in each box, or cell, of the matrix depicts the frequency of that particular group. In Table 16.3, for example, there are 10 students who were classified as introverted and who selected red as their preferred color. To obtain these data, the researcher first selects a random sample of $n = 200$ students. Each student is then given a personality test and is asked to select a preferred color from among the four choices. Note that the classification is based on the measurements for each student; the researcher does not assign students to categories. Also, note that the data consist of fre-

TABLE 16.3

Color preferences according to personality types.

	Red	Yellow	Green	Blue	
Introvert	10	3	15	22	50
Extrovert	90	17	25	18	150
	100	20	40	40	$n = 200$

quencies, not scores, from a sample. These sample data will be used to test a hypothesis about the corresponding population frequency distribution. Once again, we will be using the chi-square statistic for the test, but in this case, the test is called the chi-square *test for independence*.

THE NULL HYPOTHESIS FOR THE TEST FOR INDEPENDENCE

The null hypothesis for the chi-square test for independence states that the two variables being measured are independent; that is, for each individual, the value obtained for one variable is not related to (or influenced by) the value for the second variable. This general hypothesis can be expressed in two different conceptual forms, each viewing the data and the test from slightly different perspectives. The data in Table 16.3 describing color preference and personality will be used to present both versions of the null hypothesis.

H_0 **version 1**   For this version of H_0, the data are viewed as a single sample with each individual measured on two variables. The goal of the chi-square test is to evaluate the relationship between the two variables. For the example we are considering, the goal is to determine whether there is a consistent, predictable relationship between personality and color preference. That is, if I know your personality, will it help me to predict your color preference? The null hypothesis states that there is no relationship. The alternative hypothesis, H_1, states that there is a relationship between the two variables.

> H_0:   For the general population of students, there is no relationship between color preference and personality.

This version of H_0 demonstrates the similarity between the chi-square test for independence and a correlation. In each case, the data consist of two measurements (X and Y) for each individual, and the goal is to evaluate the relationship between the two variables. The correlation, however, requires numerical scores for X and Y. The chi-square test, on the other hand, simply uses frequencies for individuals classified into categories.

H_0 **version 2**   For this version of H_0, the data are viewed as two (or more) separate samples representing two (or more) separate populations. The goal of the chi-square test is to determine whether there are significant differences between the populations. For the example we are considering, the data in Table 16.3 would be viewed as a sample of $n = 50$ introverts (top row) and a separate sample of $n = 150$ extroverts (bottom row). The chi-square test will determine whether the distribution of color preferences for introverts is significantly different from the distribution of color preferences for extroverts. From this perspective, the null hypothesis is stated as follows:

> H_0:   In the population of students, there is no difference between the distribution of color preferences for introverts and the distribution of color preferences for extroverts. The two distributions have the same shape (same proportions).

This version of H_0 demonstrates the similarity between the chi-square test and an independent-measures t test (or ANOVA). In each case, the data consist of two (or more) separate samples that are being used to test for differences between two (or more) populations. The t test (or ANOVA) requires numerical scores to compute means and mean differences. However, the chi-square test simply uses frequencies for individuals classified into categories. The null hypothesis for the chi-square test states that the populations have the same proportions (same shape). The alternative hypothesis, H_1, simply states that the populations have different proportions. For the example we are considering, H_1 states that the distribution of color preferences for introverts is different from the distribution of color preferences for extroverts.

Equivalence of H_0 version 1 and H_0 version 2   Although we have presented two different statements of the null hypothesis, these two versions are equivalent. The first version of H_0 states that color preference is not related to personality. If this hypothesis is correct, then the distribution of color preferences should not depend on personality. In other words, the distribution of color preferences should be the same for introverts and extroverts, which is the second version of H_0.

For example, if we found that 60% of the introverts preferred red, then H_0 would predict that we also should find that 60% of the extroverts prefer red. In this case, knowing that an individual prefers red does not help you predict his/her personality. Note that finding the *same proportions* indicates *no relationship*.

On the other hand, if the proportions were different, it would suggest that there is a relationship. For example, if red is preferred by 60% of the extroverts but only 10% of the introverts, then there is a clear, predictable relationship between personality and color preference. (If I know your personality, I can predict your color preference.) Thus, finding *different proportions* means that there is *a relationship* between the two variables.

D E F I N I T I O N

Two variables are **independent** when there is no consistent, predictable relationship between them. In this case, the frequency distribution for one variable is not related to (or dependent on) the categories of the second variable. As a result, when two variables are independent, the frequency distribution for one variable will have the same shape (same proportions) for all categories of the second variable.

Thus, stating that there is no relationship between two variables (version 1 of H_0) is equivalent to stating that the distributions have equal proportions (version 2 of H_0).

OBSERVED AND EXPECTED FREQUENCIES

The chi-square test for independence uses the same basic logic that was used for the goodness-of-fit test. First, a sample is selected, and each individual is classified or categorized. Because the test for independence considers two variables, every individual is classified on both variables, and the resulting frequency distribution is presented as a two-dimensional matrix (see Table 16.3). As before, the frequencies in the sample distribution are called *observed frequencies* and are identified by the symbol f_o.

The next step is to find the expected frequencies, or f_e values, for this chi-square test. As before, the *expected frequencies* define an ideal hypothetical distribution that is in perfect agreement with the null hypothesis. Once the expected frequencies are obtained, we will compute a chi-square statistic to determine how well the data (observed frequencies) fit the null hypothesis (expected frequencies).

Although you can use either version of the null hypothesis to find the expected frequencies, the logic of the process is much easier when you use H_0 stated in terms of equal proportions. For the example we are considering, the null hypothesis states

H_0:   The frequency distribution of color preference has the same shape (same proportions) for both categories of personality.

To find the expected frequencies, we first determine the overall distribution of color preferences and then apply this distribution to both categories of personality. Table 16.4

TABLE 16.4

An empty frequency distribution matrix showing only the row totals and column totals. (These numbers describe the basic characteristics of the sample from Table 16.3.)

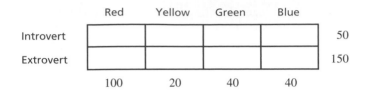

shows an empty matrix corresponding to the data from Table 16.3. Notice that the empty matrix includes all of the row totals and column totals from the original sample data.

The row totals and column totals are essential for computing the expected frequencies.

The column totals for the matrix describe the overall distribution of color preferences. For these data, 100 people selected red as their preferred color. Because the total sample consists of 200 people, it is easy to determine that the proportion selecting red is 100 out of 200 or 50%. The complete set of color preference proportions is as follows:

$$100 \text{ out of } 200 = 50\% \text{ prefer red}$$

$$20 \text{ out of } 200 = 10\% \text{ prefer yellow}$$

$$40 \text{ out of } 200 = 20\% \text{ prefer green}$$

$$40 \text{ out of } 200 = 20\% \text{ prefer blue}$$

The row totals in the matrix define the two samples of personality types. For example, the matrix in Table 16.4 shows a total of 50 introverts (the top row) and a sample of 150 extroverts (the bottom row). According to the null hypothesis, both personality groups should have the same proportions for color preferences. To find the expected frequencies, we simply apply the overall distribution of color preferences to each sample. Beginning with the sample of 50 introverts in the top row, we obtain expected frequencies of

$$50\% = 0.50 \text{ choose red:} \qquad f_e = 0.50(50) = 25$$

$$10\% = 0.10 \text{ choose yellow:} \quad f_e = 0.10(50) = 5$$

$$20\% = 0.20 \text{ choose green:} \qquad f_e = 0.20(50) = 10$$

$$20\% = 0.20 \text{ choose blue:} \qquad f_e = 0.20(50) = 10$$

Using exactly the same proportions for the sample of 150 extroverts in the bottom row, we obtain expected frequencies of

$$50\% = 0.50 \text{ choose red:} \qquad f_e = 0.50(150) = 75$$

$$10\% = 0.10 \text{ choose yellow:} \quad f_e = 0.10(150) = 15$$

$$20\% = 0.20 \text{ choose green:} \qquad f_e = 0.20(150) = 30$$

$$20\% = 0.20 \text{ choose blue:} \qquad f_e = 0.20(150) = 30$$

The complete set of expected frequencies is shown in Table 16.5. Notice that the row totals and the column totals for the expected frequencies are the same as those for the original data (the observed frequencies) in Table 16.3.

TABLE 16.5

Expected frequencies corresponding to the data in Table 16.3. (This is the distribution predicted by the null hypothesis.)

	Red	Yellow	Green	Blue	
Introvert	25	5	10	10	50
Extrovert	75	15	30	30	150
	100	20	40	40	

A SIMPLE FORMULA FOR DETERMINING EXPECTED FREQUENCIES

Although expected frequencies are derived directly from the null hypothesis and the sample characteristics, it is not necessary to go through extensive calculations in order to find f_e values. In fact, there is a simple formula that determines f_e for any cell in the frequency distribution table:

$$f_e = \frac{f_c f_r}{n} \tag{16.4}$$

where f_c is the frequency total for the column (column total), f_r is the frequency total for the row (row total), and n is the number of individuals in the entire sample. To demonstrate this formula, we will compute the expected frequency for introverts selecting yellow in Table 16.5. First, note that this cell is located in the top row and second column in the table. The column total is $f_c = 20$, the row total is $f_r = 50$, and the sample size is $n = 200$. Using these values in formula 16.4, we obtain

$$f_e = \frac{f_c f_r}{n} = \frac{20(50)}{200} = 5$$

This is identical to the expected frequency we obtained using percentages from the overall distribution.

THE CHI-SQUARE STATISTIC AND DEGREES OF FREEDOM

The chi-square test of independence uses exactly the same chi-square formula as the test for goodness of fit:

$$\chi^2 = \Sigma \frac{(f_o - f_e)^2}{f_e}$$

As before, the formula measures the discrepancy between the data (f_o values) and the hypothesis (f_e values). A large discrepancy will produce a large value for chi-square and will indicate that H_0 should be rejected. To determine whether a particular chi-square statistic is significantly large, you must first determine degrees of freedom (df) for the statistic and then consult the chi-square distribution in the appendix. For the chi-square test of independence, degrees of freedom are based on the number of cells for which you can freely choose expected frequencies. Recall that the f_e values are partially determined by the sample size (n) and by the row totals and column totals from the original data. These various totals restrict your freedom in selecting expected frequencies. This point is illustrated in Table 16.6. Once three of the f_e values have been selected, all the other f_e values in the table are also determined. In general, the row totals and the column totals restrict the final choices in each row and column. Thus, we may freely choose all but one f_e in each row and all but one f_e in each column. The total number of f_e values that you can freely choose is $(R - 1)(C - 1)$, where R is the number of rows and C is the number of columns. The degrees of freedom for the chi-square test of independence are given by the formula

$$df = (R - 1)(C - 1) \tag{16.5}$$

TABLE 16.6

Degrees of freedom and expected frequencies. (Once three values have been selected, all the remaining expected frequencies are determined by the row totals and the column totals. This example has only three free choices, so $df = 3$.)

Red	Yellow	Green	Blue	
25	5	10	?	50
?	?	?	?	150
100	20	40	40	

AN EXAMPLE OF THE CHI-SQUARE TEST FOR INDEPENDENCE

The steps for the chi-square test of independence should be familiar by now. First, the hypotheses are stated, and an alpha level is selected. Second, the value for degrees of freedom is computed, and the critical region is located. Third, expected frequencies are determined, and the chi-square statistic is computed. Finally, a decision is made regarding the null hypothesis. The following example demonstrates the complete hypothesis-testing procedure.

EXAMPLE 16.2

Research has demonstrated strong gender differences in teenagers' approaches to dealing with mental health issues (Chandra & Minkovitz, 2006). In a typical study, eighth-grade students are asked to report their willingness to use mental health services in the event they were experiencing emotional or other mental health problems. Typical data for a sample of $n = 150$ students are shown in Table 16.7. Do the data show a significant relationship between gender and willingness to seek mental health assistance?

STEP 1

State the hypotheses, and select a level of significance. According to the null hypothesis, the two variables are independent. This general hypothesis can be stated in two different ways:

Version 1

H_0: In the general population, there is no relationship between gender and willingness to use mental health services.

This version of H_0 emphasizes the similarity between the chi-square test and a correlation. The corresponding alternative hypothesis would state:

H_1: In the general population, there is a consistent, predictable relationship between gender and willingness to use mental health services.

TABLE 16.7

A frequency distribution showing willingness to use mental health services according to gender for a sample of $n = 150$ students.

	Willingness to Use Mental Health Services			
	Probably No	Maybe	Probably Yes	
Males	17	32	11	60
Females	13	43	34	90
	30	75	45	$n = 150$

Version 2

H_0:   In the general population, the distribution of reported willingness to use mental health services is the same for males and females.

The corresponding alternative hypothesis would state:

H_1:   In the general population, the distribution of reported willingness to use mental health services for males is different from the distribution for females.

The second version of H_0 emphasizes the similarity between the chi-square test and the independent-measures *t* test.

Remember that the two versions for the hypotheses are equivalent. The choice between them is largely determined by how the researcher wants to describe the outcome. For example, a researcher may want to emphasize the *relationship* between variables or may want to emphasis the *difference* between groups.

For this test, we will use $\alpha = .05$.

STEP 2   Determine the degrees of freedom, and locate the critical region. For the chi-square test for independence,

$$df = (R - 1)(C - 1)$$

Therefore, for this study,

$$df = (2 - 1)(3 - 1) = 2$$

With $df = 2$ and $\alpha = .05$, the critical value for chi-square is 5.99 (see Table B.7, p. 538).

STEP 3   Determine the expected frequencies, and compute the chi-square statistic. The following table shows an empty matrix with the same row totals and column totals as the original data. The calculation of expected frequencies requires that this table be filled in so the resulting values provide an ideal frequency distribution that perfectly represents the null hypothesis.

Willingness to Use Mental Health Services

	Probably No	Maybe	Probably Yes	
Males				60
Females				90
	30	75	45	$n = 150$

The column totals indicate that 30 out of the 150 students reported that they would probably not use mental health services. This proportion corresponds to 30/150 or 20% of the total sample. Similarly, 75/150 = 50% reported that they may use mental health services, and 45/150 = 30% reported that they probably would use the services. The null hypothesis (version 2) states that this distribution is the same for males and females. Therefore, we simply apply the proportions to each group to obtain the expected frequencies. For the group of 60 males, we obtain

20% of 60 = 12 males who would probably not seek services

50% of 60 = 30 males who may seek services

30% of 60 = 18 males who probably would seek services

TABLE 16.8

The expected frequencies (f_e values) that would be expected if willingness to use mental services were completely independent of gender.

	Willingness to Use Mental Health Services			
	Probably No	Maybe	Probably Yes	
Males	12	30	18	60
Females	18	45	27	90
	30	75	45	

For the group of 90 females, we would expect

20% of 90 = 18 females who would probably not seek services

50% of 90 = 45 females who may seek services

30% of 90 = 27 females who probably would seek services

These expected frequencies are summarized in Table 16.8.

The chi-square statistic is now used to measure the discrepancy between the data (the observed frequencies in Table 16.7) and the null hypothesis that was used to generate the expected frequencies in Table 16.8.

$$\chi^2 = \frac{(17 - 12)^2}{12} + \frac{(32 - 30)^2}{30} + \frac{(11 - 18)^2}{18}$$
$$+ \frac{(13 - 18)^2}{18} + \frac{(43 - 45)^2}{45} + \frac{(34 - 27)^2}{27}$$
$$= 2.08 + 0.13 + 2.72 + 1.39 + 0.09 + 1.82$$
$$= 8.23$$

STEP 4   Make a decision regarding the null hypothesis and the outcome of the study. The obtained chi-square value exceeds the critical value (5.99). Therefore, the decision is to reject the null hypothesis. In the literature, this would be reported as a significant result with $\chi^2(2, n = 150) = 8.23$, $p < .05$. According to version 1 of H_0, this means that we have decided there is a significant relationship between gender and willingness to use mental health services. Expressed in terms of version 2 of H_0, the data show a significant difference between males' and females' attitudes toward using mental health services. To describe the details of the significant result, you must compare the original data (Table 16.7) with the expected frequencies in Table 16.8. Looking at the two tables, it should be clear that males were less willing to use mental health services and females were more willing than would be expected if the two variables were independent.

LEARNING CHECK

1. A researcher suspects that color blindness is inherited by a sex-linked gene. This possibility is examined by looking for a relationship between gender and color vision. The researcher tests a sample of 1000 people for color blindness, and then classifies them according to their sex and color vision status (normal, red-green

blind, other color blindness). Is color blindness related to gender? The data are as follows:

Observed Frequencies of Color
Vision Status According to Gender

	Normal color vision	Red-green color blindness	Other color blindness	Totals
Male	320	70	10	400
Female	580	10	10	600
Totals	900	80	20	

a. State the hypotheses.

b. Determine the value for df, and locate the critical region.

c. Compute the f_e values and then chi-square.

d. Make a decision regarding H_0.

ANSWERS **1. a.** H_0: In the population, there is no relationship between gender and color vision.

H_1: In the population, gender and color vision are related.

b. $df = 2$; critical $\chi^2 = 5.99$ for $\alpha = .05$.

c. f_e values are as follows:

Expected frequencies

	Normal	Red-Green	Other
Male	360	32	8
Female	540	48	12

Obtained $\chi^2 = 83.44$

d. Reject H_0.

16.4 MEASURING EFFECT SIZE FOR THE CHI-SQUARE TEST FOR INDEPENDENCE

A hypothesis test, like the chi-square test for independence, evaluates the statistical significance of the results from a research study. Specifically, the intent of the test is to determine whether the patterns or relationships observed in the sample data are likely to have occurred simply by chance; that is, without any corresponding patterns or relationships in the population. Tests of significance are influenced not only by the size or strength of the treatment effects but also by the size of the samples. As a result, even a small effect can be statistically significant if it is observed in a very large sample. Because a significant effect does not necessarily mean a large effect, it is generally recommended that the outcome of a hypothesis test be accompanied by a measure of the effect size. This general recommendation also applies to the chi-square test for independence.

**THE PHI-COEFFICIENT
AND CRAMÉR'S V**

In Chapter 15 (page 447), we introduced the *phi-coefficient* as a measure of correlation for data consisting of two dichotomous variables (both variables have exactly two values). This same situation exists when the data for a chi-square test for independence form a 2×2 matrix (again, each variable has exactly two values). In this case, it is possible to compute the correlation phi (ϕ) in addition to the chi-square hypothesis test for the same set of data. Because phi (ϕ) is a correlation, it measures the strength of the relationship, rather than the significance, and thus provides a measure of effect size. The value for the phi-coefficient can be computed directly from chi-square by the following formula:

Caution: The value of χ^2 is already a squared value. Do not square it again.

$$\phi = \sqrt{\frac{\chi^2}{n}}$$

(16.6)

The value of the phi-coefficient is determined entirely by the *proportions* in the 2×2 data matrix and is completely independent of the absolute size of the frequencies. The chi-square value, however, is influenced by the proportions and by the size of the frequencies. This distinction is demonstrated in the following example.

E X A M P L E   1 6 . 3

The following data show a frequency distribution evaluating the relationship between gender and preference between two candidates for student president.

	Candidate	
	A	B
Male	5	10
Female	10	5

Note that the data show that males prefer candidate B by a 2-to-1 margin and females prefer candidate A by 2 to 1. Also note that the sample includes a total of 15 males and 15 females. We will not perform all the arithmetic here, but these data produce chi-square equal to 3.33 (which is not significant) and a phi-coefficient of 0.3332.

Next we will keep exactly the same proportions in the data, but double all of the frequencies. The resulting data are as follows:

	Candidate	
	A	B
Male	10	20
Female	20	10

Once again, males prefer candidate B by 2 to 1 and females prefer candidate A by 2 to 1. However, the sample now contains 30 males and 30 females. For these new data, the value of chi-square is 6.66, twice as big as it was before (and now significant with $\alpha = .05$), but the value of the phi-coefficient is still 0.3332.

Because the proportions are the same for the two samples, the value of the phi-coefficient is unchanged. However, the larger sample provides more convincing evidence than the smaller sample, so the larger sample is more likely to produce a significant result.

The interpretation of ϕ follows the same standards used to evaluate a correlation (Table 9.3, page 245 shows the standards for squared correlations): 0.10 is a small effect, 0.30 is a medium effect, and 0.50 is a large effect. Occasionally, the value of ϕ is squared (ϕ^2) and is reported as a percentage of variance accounted for, exactly the same as r^2.

When the chi-square test involves a matrix larger than 2×2, a modification of the phi-coefficient, known as Cramér's V, can be used to measure effect size.

$$V = \sqrt{\frac{\chi^2}{n(df^*)}} \qquad (16.7)$$

Note that the formula for Cramér's V (16.7) is identical to the formula for the phi-coefficient (16.6) except for the addition of df^* in the denominator. The df^* value is *not* the same as the degrees of freedom for the chi-square test, but it is related. Recall that the chi-square test for independence has $df = (R - 1)(C - 1)$, where R is the number of rows in the table and C is the number of columns. For Cramér's V, the value of df^* is the smaller of either $(R - 1)$ or $(C - 1)$.

Cohen (1988) has also suggested standards for interpreting Cramér's V that are shown in Table 16.9. Note that when $df^* = 1$, as in a 2×2 matrix, the criteria for interpreting V are exactly the same as the criteria for interpreting a regular correlation or a phi-coefficient.

We will use the results from Example 16.2 (page 448) to demonstrate the calculation of Cramér's V. The example evaluated the relationship between gender and willingness to use mental health services. There were two levels of gender and three levels of willingness producing a 2×3 table with a total of $n = 150$ participants. The data produced $\chi^2 = 8.23$. Using these values we obtain

$$V = \sqrt{\frac{\chi^2}{n(df^*)}} = \sqrt{\frac{8.23}{150(1)}} = \sqrt{0.055} = 0.23$$

According to Cohen's guidelines (see Table 16.9), this value indicates a small relationship.

TABLE 16.9

Standards for interpreting Cramér's V as proposed by Cohen (1988).

For $df^* = 1$	$V = 0.10$	Small effect
	$V = 0.30$	Medium effect
	$V = 0.50$	Large effect
For $df^* = 2$	$V = 0.07$	Small effect
	$V = 0.21$	Medium effect
	$V = 0.35$	Large effect
For $df^* = 3$	$V = 0.06$	Small effect
	$V = 0.17$	Medium effect
	$V = 0.29$	Large effect

16.5 ASSUMPTIONS AND RESTRICTIONS FOR CHI-SQUARE TESTS

To use a chi-square test for goodness of fit or a test of independence, several conditions must be satisfied. For any statistical test, violation of assumptions and restrictions will cast doubt on the results. For example, the probability of committing a Type I error may be distorted when assumptions of statistical tests are not satisfied. Some important assumptions and restrictions for using chi-square tests are the following:

1. Independence of Observations. This is *not* to be confused with the concept of independence between *variables*, as seen in the test for independence (Section 16.3). One consequence of independent observations is that each observed frequency is generated by a different individual. A chi-square test would be inappropriate if a person could produce responses that can be classified in more than one category or contribute more than one frequency count to a single category. (See page 210 for more information on independence.)

2. Size of Expected Frequencies. A chi-square test should not be performed when the expected frequency of any cell is less than 5. The chi-square statistic can be distorted when f_e is very small. Consider the chi-square computations for a single cell. Suppose that the cell has values of $f_e = 1$ and $f_o = 5$. The contribution of this cell to the total chi-square value is

$$\text{cell} = \frac{(f_o - f_e)^2}{f_e} = \frac{(5 - 1)^2}{1} = \frac{4^2}{1} = 16$$

Now consider another instance, where $f_e = 10$ and $f_o = 14$. The difference between the observed and the expected frequencies is still 4, but the contribution of this cell to the total chi-square value differs from that of the first case:

$$\text{cell} = \frac{(f_o - f_e)^2}{f_e} = \frac{(14 - 10)^2}{10} = \frac{4^2}{10} = 1.6$$

It should be clear that a small f_e value can have a great influence on the chi-square value. This problem becomes serious when f_e values are less than 5. When f_e is very small, what would otherwise be a minor discrepancy between f_o and f_e will now result in large chi-square values. The test is too sensitive when f_e values are extremely small. One way to avoid small expected frequencies is to use large samples.

SUMMARY

1. Chi-square tests are a type of nonparametric technique that tests hypotheses about the form of the entire frequency distribution. Two types of chi-square tests are the test for goodness of fit and the test for independence. The data for these tests consist of the frequency or number of individuals who are located in each category.

2. The test for goodness of fit compares the frequency distribution for a sample to the population distribution that is predicted by H_0. The test determines how well the observed frequencies (sample data) fit the expected frequencies (data predicted by H_0).

3. The expected frequencies for the goodness-of-fit test are determined by

$$\text{expected frequency} = f_e = pn$$

where p is the hypothesized proportion (according to H_0) of observations falling into a category and n is the size of the sample.

4. The chi-square statistic is computed by

$$\text{chi-square} = \chi^2 = \Sigma \frac{(f_o - f_e)^2}{f_e}$$

where f_o is the observed frequency for a particular category and f_e is the expected frequency for that category. Large values for χ^2 indicate that there is a large discrepancy between the observed (f_o) and the expected (f_e) frequencies and may warrant rejection of the null hypothesis.

5. Degrees of freedom for the test for goodness of fit are

$$df = C - 1$$

where C is the number of categories in the variable. Degrees of freedom measure the number of categories for which f_e values can be freely chosen. As can be seen from the formula, all but the last f_e value to be determined are free to vary.

6. The chi-square distribution is positively skewed and begins at the value of zero. Its exact shape is determined by degrees of freedom.

7. The test for independence is used to assess the relationship between two variables. The null hypothesis states that the two variables in question are independent of each other. That is, the frequency distribution for one variable does not depend on the categories of the second variable. On the other hand, if a relationship does exist, then the form of the distribution for one variable will depend on the categories of the other variable.

8. For the test for independence, the expected frequencies for H_0 can be directly calculated from the marginal frequency totals,

$$f_e = \frac{f_c f_r}{n}$$

where f_c is the total column frequency and f_r is the total row frequency for the cell in question.

9. Degrees of freedom for the test for independence are computed by

$$df = (R - 1)(C - 1)$$

where R is the number of row categories and C is the number of column categories.

10. For the test of independence, a large chi-square value means there is a large discrepancy between the f_o and f_e values. Rejecting H_0 in this test provides support for a relationship between the two variables.

11. Both chi-square tests (for goodness of fit and independence) are based on the assumption that each observation is independent of the others. That is, each observed frequency reflects a different individual, and no individual can produce a response that would be classified in more than one category or more than one frequency in a single category.

12. The chi-square statistic is distorted when f_e values are small. Chi-square tests, therefore, are restricted to situations in which f_e values are 5 or greater. The test should not be performed when the expected frequency of any cell is less than 5.

13. The effect size for a chi-square test for independence can be measured computing a phi-coefficient for data that form a 2 × 2 matrix or computing Cramér's V for a matrix that is larger than 2 × 2.

$$\text{phi} = \sqrt{\frac{\chi^2}{n}} \qquad \text{Cramér's } V = \sqrt{\frac{\chi^2}{n(df^*)}}$$

where df^* is the smaller of $(R - 1)$ and $(C - 1)$. Both phi and Cramér's V are evaluated using the criteria in Table 16.9.

KEY TERMS

parametric test	observed frequencies	distribution of chi-square	phi-coefficient
nonparametric test	expected frequencies	test for independence	Cramér's V
goodness-of-fit test	chi-square statistic		

RESOURCES

There are a tutorial quiz and other learning exercises for Chapter 16 at the Wadsworth website, www.thomsonedu.com/psychology/gravetter. The site also provides access to a workshop entitled *Chi-Square* that reviews the chi-square tests presented in this chapter. See page 27 for more information about accessing items on the website.

WebTUTOR

For those using WebTutor along with this book, there is a WebTutor section corresponding to this chapter. The WebTutor contains a brief summary of Chapter 16, hints for learning the concepts and the formulas for the chi-square tests, cautions about common errors, and sample exam items including solutions.

General instructions for using SPSS are presented in Appendix D. Following are detailed instructions for using SPSS to perform **The Chi-Square Tests for Goodness of Fit and for Independence** that are presented in this chapter.

The Chi-Square Test for Goodness of Fit

Data Entry

1. Enter the set of observed frequencies in the first column of the SPSS data editor. If there are four categories, for example, enter the four observed frequencies.
2. In the second column, enter the numbers 1, 2, 3, and so on so there is a number beside each of the observed frequencies in the first column.

Data Analysis

1. Click **Data** on the tool bar at the top of the page and select **weight cases** at the bottom of the list.
2. Click the **weight cases by** circle, then highlight the label for the column containing the observed frequencies (VAR0000) on the left and move it into the **Frequency Variable** box by clicking on the arrow.
3. Click **OK.**
4. Click **Analyze** on the tool bar, select **Nonparametric Tests,** and click on **Chi-Square.**
5. Highlight the label for the column containing the digits 1, 2, 3, and move it into the Test Variables box by clicking on the arrow.
6. To specify the expected frequencies, you can either use the **all categories equal** option which will automatically compute expected frequencies, or you can enter your own values. To enter your own expected frequencies, click on the **values** option, and one by one enter the expected frequencies into the small box and click **Add** to add each new value to the bottom of the list.
7. Click **OK.**

SPSS Output

The program will produce a table showing the complete set of observed and expected frequencies. A second table provides the value for the chi-square statistic, the degrees of freedom, and the level of significance (the *p* value or alpha level for the test).

The Chi-Square Test for Independence

Data Entry

1. Enter the complete set of observed frequencies in one column of the SPSS data editor (VAR00001).

2. In a second column, enter a number (1, 2, 3, etc.) that identifies the row corresponding to each observed frequency. For example, enter a 1 beside each observed frequency that came from the first row.

3. In a third column, enter a number (1, 2, 3, etc.) that identifies the column corresponding to each observed frequency. Each value from the first column gets a 1, and so on.

Data Analysis

1. Click **Data** on the tool bar at the top of the page and select **weight cases** at the bottom of the list.

2. Click the **weight cases by** circle, then highlight the label for the column containing the observed frequencies (VAR00001) on the left and move it into the **Frequency Variable** box by clicking on the arrow.

3. Click **OK.**

4. Click **Analyze** on the tool bar at the top of the page, select **Descriptive Statistics,** and click on **Crosstabs.**

5. Highlight the label for the column containing the rows (VAR00002) and move it into the **Rows** box by clicking on the arrow.

6. Highlight the label for the column containing the columns (VAR00003) and move it into the **Columns** box by clicking on the arrow.

7. Click on **Statistics,** select **Chi-Square,** and click **Continue.**

8. Click **OK.**

SPSS Output

The program will produce a table presenting valid and missing cases. You should have no missing cases. A second table presents a summary of the observed frequencies. The final table, labeled **Chi-Square Tests,** reports the results. Focus on the top row, the **Pearson Chi-Square,** which reports the calculated chi-square value, the degrees of freedom, and the level of significance (the *p* value or the alpha level for the test).

FOCUS ON PROBLEM SOLVING

1. The expected frequencies that you calculate must satisfy the constraints of the sample. For the goodness-of-fit test, $\Sigma f_e = \Sigma f_o = n$. For the test of independence, the row totals and column totals for the expected frequencies should be identical to the corresponding totals for the observed frequencies.

2. It is entirely possible to have fractional (decimal) values for expected frequencies. Observed frequencies, however, are always whole numbers.

3. Whenever $df = 1$, the difference between observed and expected frequencies $(f_o - f_e)$ will be identical (the same value) for all cells. This makes the calculation of chi-square easier.

4. Although you are advised to compute expected frequencies for all categories (or cells), you should realize that it is not essential to calculate all f_e values separately. Remember that df for chi-square identifies the number of f_e values that are free to vary. Once you have calculated that number of f_e values, the remaining f_e values are determined. You can get these remaining values by subtracting the calculated f_e values from their corresponding row or column totals.

5. Remember that, unlike previous statistical tests, the degrees of freedom (df) for a chi-square test are *not* determined by the sample size (n). Be careful!

DEMONSTRATION 16.1

TEST FOR INDEPENDENCE

A manufacturer of watches would like to examine preferences for digital versus analog watches. A sample of $n = 200$ people is selected, and these individuals are classified by age and preference. The manufacturer would like to know whether there is a relationship between age and watch preference. The observed frequencies (f_o) are as follows:

	Digital	Analog	Undecided	Totals
Under 30	90	40	10	140
30 or over	10	40	10	60
Column totals	100	80	20	$n = 200$

STEP 1 State the hypotheses, and select an alpha level.
> The null hypothesis states that there is no relationship between the two variables.

> H_0: Preference is independent of age. That is, the frequency distribution of preference has the same form for people under 30 as for people 30 or over.

The alternative hypothesis states that there is a relationship between the two variables.

> H_1: Preference is related to age. That is, the type of watch preferred depends on a person's age.

We will set alpha to $\alpha = .05$.

STEP 2 Locate the critical region.
> Degrees of freedom for the chi-square test for independence are determined by

$$df = (C - 1)(R - 1)$$

For these data,

$$df = (3 - 1)(2 - 1) = 2(1) = 2$$

For $df = 2$ with $\alpha = .05$, the critical chi-square value is 5.99. Thus, our obtained chi-square must exceed 5.99 to be in the critical region and to reject H_0.

STEP 3 Compute the test statistic. Computing chi-square requires two calculations: finding the expected frequencies and calculating the chi-square statistic.
> *Expected frequencies, f_e.* For the test for independence, the expected frequencies can be found using the column totals (f_c), the row totals (f_r), and the following formula:

$$f_e = \frac{f_c f_r}{n}$$

For people younger than 30, we obtain the following expected frequencies:

$$f_e = \frac{100(140)}{200} = \frac{14,000}{200} = 70 \text{ for digital}$$

$$f_e = \frac{80(140)}{200} = \frac{11,200}{200} = 56 \text{ for analog}$$

$$f_e = \frac{20(140)}{200} = \frac{2800}{200} = 14 \text{ for undecided}$$

For individuals 30 or older, the expected frequencies are as follows:

$$f_e = \frac{100(60)}{200} = \frac{6000}{200} = 30 \text{ for digital}$$

$$f_e = \frac{80(60)}{200} = \frac{4800}{200} = 24 \text{ for analog}$$

$$f_e = \frac{20(60)}{200} = \frac{1200}{200} = 6 \text{ for undecided}$$

The following table summarizes the expected frequencies:

	Digital	Analog	Undecided
Under 30	70	56	14
30 or over	30	24	6

The chi-square statistic. The chi-square statistic is computed from the formula

$$\chi^2 = \Sigma \frac{(f_o - f_e)^2}{f_e}$$

The following table summarizes the calculations:

Cell	f_o	f_e	$(f_o - f_e)$	$(f_o - f_e)^2$	$(f_o - f_e)^2/f_e$
Under 30—digital	90	70	20	400	5.71
Under 30—analog	40	56	−16	256	4.57
Under 30—undecided	10	14	−4	16	1.14
30 or over—digital	10	30	−20	400	13.33
30 or over—analog	40	24	16	256	10.67
30 or over—undecided	10	6	4	16	2.67

Finally, we can sum the last column to get the chi-square value.

$$\chi^2 = 5.71 + 4.57 + 1.14 + 13.33 + 10.67 + 2.67$$

$$= 38.09$$

STEP 4   Make a decision about H_0, and state the conclusion.

The chi-square value is in the critical region. Therefore, we can reject the null hypothesis. There is a relationship between watch preference and age, $\chi^2(2, n = 200) = 38.09$, $p < .05$.

PROBLEMS

1. The color red is often associated with anger and male dominance. Based on this observation, Hill and Barton (2005) monitored the outcome of four combat sports (boxing, tae kwan do, Greco-Roman wrestling, and freestyle wrestling) during the 2004 Olympic games and found that participants wearing red outfits won significantly more often than those wearing blue.
   a. In 50 wrestling matches involving red versus blue, suppose that the red outfit won 31 times and lost 19 times. Is this result sufficient to conclude that red wins significantly more than would be expected by chance? Test at the .05 level of significance.
   b. In 100 matches, suppose red won 62 times and lost 38. Is this sufficient to conclude that red wins significantly more than would be expected by chance? Again, use $\alpha = .05$.
   c. Note that the winning percentage for red uniforms in part a is identical to the percentage in part b (31 out of 50 is 62%, and 62 out of 100 is also 62%). Although the two samples have an identical winning percentages, one is significant and the other is not. Explain why the two samples lead to different conclusions.

2. A social psychologist suspects that people who serve on juries tend to be much older than citizens in the general population. Jurors are selected from the list of registered voters, so the ages for jurors should have the same distribution as the ages for voters. The psychologist obtains voter registration records and finds that 20% of registered voters are between 18 and 29 years old, 45% are between 30 and 49 years old, and 35% are age 50 or older. The psychologist also monitors jury composition over several weeks and observes the following distribution of ages for actual juries:

   Age Categories for Jurors

18–29	30–49	50 and Over
12	36	32

   Are the data sufficient to conclude that the age distribution for jurors is significantly different from the distribution for the population of registered voters? Test with $\alpha = .05$.

3. Parametric tests (such as *t* or ANOVA) differ from nonparametric tests (such as chi-square) primarily in terms of the assumptions they require and the data they use. Explain these differences.

4. A professor noticed that the representatives on the college student government consist of 31 males and only 9 females. The general college population, on the other hand, consists of 55% females and 45% males. Is the gender distribution for student government representatives significantly different from the distribution for the college population? Test at the .05 level of significance.

5. A researcher is investigating the physical characteristics that influence whether a person's face is judged as beautiful. The researcher selects a photograph of a woman and then creates two modifications of the photo by (1) moving the eyes slightly farther apart and (2) moving the eyes slightly closer together. The original photograph and the two modifications are then shown to a sample of $n = 150$ college students, and each student is asked to select the "most beautiful" of the three faces. The distribution of responses was as follows:

Original Photo	Eyes Moved Apart	Eyes Moved Together
51	72	27

   Do the data indicate any significant preferences among the three versions of the photograph? Test at the .05 level of significance.

6. Data from the Department of Motor Vehicles indicate that 80% of all licensed drivers are older than age 25.
   a. In a sample of $n = 50$ people who recently received speeding tickets, 32 were older than 25 years and the other 18 were age 25 or younger. Is the age distribution for this sample significantly different from the distribution for the population of licensed drivers? Use $\alpha = .05$.
   b. In sample of $n = 50$ people who recently received parking tickets, 38 were older than 25 years and the other 12 were age 25 or younger. Is the age distribution for this sample significantly different from the distribution for the population of licensed drivers? Use $\alpha = .05$.

7. To investigate the phenomenon of "home team advantage," a researcher recorded the outcomes from 64 college football games on one Saturday in October. Of the 64 games, 42 were won by home teams. Does this result provide enough evidence to conclude that home teams win significantly more than would be expected by chance? Assume that winning and losing are equally likely events if there is no home team advantage. Use $\alpha = .05$.

8. A researcher obtained a random sample of $n = 60$ students to determine whether there were any significant preferences among three leading brands of colas. Each student tasted all three brands and then selected

his or her favorite. The resulting frequency distribution is as follows:

Brand A	Brand B	Brand C
28	14	18

Are the data sufficient to indicate any preferences among the three brands? Test with $\alpha = .05$.

9. Suppose the researcher from the previous problem repeated the cola-preference study using twice as many students and obtaining observed frequencies that exactly doubled the original values. The resulting data are as follows:

Brand A	Brand B	Brand C
56	28	36

a. Use a chi-square test to determine whether the data indicate any significant preferences among the three brands.

b. You should find that the conclusion from the hypothesis test is that there are significant preferences (reject H_0). However, in Problem 6 the decision was to fail to reject H_0. How do you explain the difference between the two tests?

10. Langewitz, Izakovic, and Wyler (2005) reported that self-hypnosis can significantly reduce hay fever symptoms. Patients with moderate to severe allergic reactions were trained to focus their minds on specific locations where their allergies do not bother them, such as a beach or a ski resort. In a sample of 64 patients who received this training, suppose that 47 showed reduced allergic reactions and 17 showed an increase in allergic reactions. Are these results sufficient to conclude that the self-hypnosis has a significant effect? Assume that increasing and decreasing allergic reactions are equally likely if the training has no effect. Use $\alpha = .05$.

11. Automobile insurance is much more expensive for teenage drivers than for older drivers. To justify this cost difference, insurance companies claim that the younger drivers are much more likely to be involved in costly accidents. To test this claim, a researcher obtains information about registered drivers from the department of motor vehicles and selects a sample of $n = 300$ accident reports from the police department. The motor vehicle department reports the percentage of registered drivers in each age category as follows: 16% are under age 20; 28% are 20 to 29 years old; and 56% are age 30 or older. The number of accident reports for each age group is as follows:

Under Age 20	Age 20–29	Age 30 or Older
68	92	140

Do the data indicate that the distribution of accidents for the three age groups is significantly different from the distribution of drivers? Test with $\alpha = .05$.

12. A psychology professor is trying to decide which textbook to use for next year's introductory class. To help make the decision, the professor asks the current students to review three texts and identify which one they prefer. The distribution of preferences for the current class is as follows:

Book 1	Book 2	Book 3
52	41	27

Do the data indicate any significant preferences among the three books? Test with $\alpha = .05$.

13. In Problem 12, a professor asked students to rate three textbooks to determine whether there were any preferences among them. Although the data appear to indicate an overall preference for book 1, the professor would like to know whether this opinion is shared by students with different levels of academic ability. To answer this question, the median grade was used to separate the students into two groups: the upper half and the lower half of the class. The distribution of preferences for these two groups is as follows:

	Book 1	Book 2	Book 3	
Upper Half	17	31	12	60
Lower Half	35	10	15	60
	52	41	27	

Do the data indicate that the distribution of preferences for students in the upper half of the class is significantly different from the distribution for students in the lower half? Test at the .05 level of significance.

14. Research has demonstrated that involvement in religious activities seems to benefit health and well-being. For example, Reyes-Ortiz, Ayele, Mulligan, Espino, Berges, and Markides (2006) found that church attendance was significantly related to fear of falling in a sample of Mexican-Americans aged 70 and over. The following frequency distribution represents data similar to the results obtained in the study. Do the data indicate a significant relationship between church attendance and fear of falling? Test at the .05 level of significance.

	Fear of Falling				
	No Fear	Somewhat Afraid	Fairly Afraid	Very Afraid	
Church	51	68	52	29	200
No Church	15	28	29	28	100
					$n = 300$

15. Gender differences in dream content are well documented (see Winget & Kramer, 1979). Suppose a researcher studies aggression content in the dreams of men and women. Each participant reports his or her most recent dream. Then each dream is judged by a panel of experts to have low, medium, or high aggression content. The observed frequencies are shown in the following matrix:

		Aggression Content		
		Low	Medium	High
Gender	Female	18	4	2
	Male	4	17	15

Is there a relationship between gender and the aggression content of dreams? Test with $\alpha = .01$.

16. Friedman and Rosenman (1974) have suggested that personality type is related to heart disease. Specifically, type A people, who are competitive, driven, pressured, and impatient, are more prone to heart disease. On the other hand, type B individuals, who are less competitive and more relaxed, are less likely to have heart disease. Suppose that an investigator would like to examine the relationship between personality type and disease. For a random sample of individuals, personality type is assessed with a standardized test. These individuals are then examined and categorized as to whether they have a heart disorder. The observed frequencies are as follows:

	No Heart Disease	Heart Disease	
Type A	32	18	50
Type B	128	22	150
	160	40	

Is there a relationship between personality and disorder? Test at the .05 level of significance.

17. Research results suggest that IQ scores for boys are more variable than IQ scores for girls (Arden & Plomin, 2006). A typical study looking at 10-year-old children classifies participants by gender and by low, average, or high IQ. Following are hypothetical data representing the research results. Do the data indicate a significant difference between the frequency distributions for males and females? Test at the .05 level of significance and describe the difference.

		IQ		
	Low	Average	High	
Boys	18	42	20	80
Girls	12	54	14	80
				$n = 160$

18. Apparently there is a huge amount of misunderstanding concerning how the process of visual perception works. Specifically, many people believe (incorrectly) that at least part of looking at things involves energy going out of the eyes rather than energy coming into the eyes. This misunderstanding seems to be more common among children than among adults, but a surprisingly large number of college students still do not understand the process of seeing. Winer and Cottrell (1996) asked first-graders and college students to decide what happens when we look at something: does energy go out of our eyes, come into our eyes, or go both directions? The following frequency data are similar to those obtained by Winer and Cottrell. Do the data indicate a significant difference in the distribution of answers for the college students and for the children? Test at the .05 level of significance.

	Direction of Energy Flow			
	Into Our Eyes	Out of Our Eyes	Both Directions	
First-graders	45	40	15	100
College Students	75	20	5	100
	120	60	20	

19. There is some evidence to suggest that left-handed people tend to turn to the left, and right-handed people turn to the right when they need to turn around. A researcher would like to examine this phenomenon by having people stand in the center of a square room with a speaker centered on each wall. The researcher plays a brief sound in one of the speakers and the participant is instructed to turn toward the sound. The key trials involve measuring which direction people turn when responding to a sound from directly behind them. Suppose that the researcher obtained a sample of $n = 150$ people and recorded the handedness and turning preference for each individual. The results

showed that 20 out of 30 left-handed people turned to the left, and 70 out of 120 right handed-people turned to the right.

a. Use the data provided to fill in a 2 × 2 matrix of frequencies with the columns corresponding to left- and right-handed, and the rows corresponding to turning left and turning right.

b. Use a chi-square test with α = .05 to determine whether there is a significant relationship between handedness and turning preference.

20. In a study similar to one conducted by Fallon and Rozin (1985), a psychologist prepared a set of silhouettes showing different female body shapes ranging from somewhat thin to somewhat heavy and asked a group of women to indicate which body figure they thought men would consider the most attractive. Then a group of men were shown the same set of profiles and asked which image they considered most attractive. The following hypothetical data show the number of individuals who selected each of the four body image profiles. Do the data indicate a significant difference between the actual preferences for the men and the preferences predicted by the women? Test at the .05 level of significance.

Body Image Profiles

	Some-what Thin	Slightly Thin	Slightly Heavy	Some-what Heavy	
Women	29	25	18	8	80
Men	11	15	22	12	60
	40	40	40	20	

21. Cialdini, Reno, and Kallgren (1990) examined how people conform to norms concerning littering. The researchers wanted to determine whether a person's tendency to litter depended on the amount of litter already in the area. People were handed a handbill as they entered an amusement park. The entrance area had already been prepared with either no litter, a small amount of litter, or a lot of litter lying on the ground. The people were observed to determine whether they dropped their handbills. The frequency data are as follows:

Amount of Litter

	None	Small Amount	Large Amount
Littering	17	28	49
Not Littering	73	62	41

a. Do the data indicate that people's tendency to litter depends on the amount of litter already on the ground? That is, is there a significant relationship between littering and the amount of existing litter? Test at the .05 level of significance.

b. Compute Cramér's V to measure the size of the treatment effect.

22. Recent reports suggest that children who grow up with pets in the home tend to develop resistence to allergies. To test this phenomenon, a researcher interviews a sample of $n = 120$ college students. Each student is asked about pets during childhood and about his or her current allergies.

Number of Dogs or Cats in Childhood Home

	0	1	2 or More	
No Allergies	22	50	18	90
Allergies	18	10	2	30
	40	60	20	

a. Do the data indicate a significant relationship between having pets and developing resistance to allergies? Test at the .05 level of significance.

b. Compute Cramér's V to measure the effect size.

23. Although the phenomenon is not well understood, it appears that people born during the winter months are slightly more likely to develop schizophrenia than people born at other times (Bradbury & Miller, 1985). The following hypothetical data represent a sample of 50 individuals diagnosed with schizophrenia and a sample of 100 people with no psychotic diagnosis. Each individual is also classified according to season in which he or she was born. Do the data indicate a significant relationship between schizophrenia and the season of birth? Test at the .05 level of significance.

Season of Birth

	Summer	Fall	Winter	Spring	
No Disorder	26	24	22	28	100
Schizophrenia	9	11	18	12	50
	35	35	40	40	

APPENDIX A # Basic Mathematics Review

A.1   Symbols and Notation

A.2   Proportions: Fractions, Decimals, and Percentages

A.3   Negative Numbers

A.4   Basic Algebra: Solving Equations

A.5   Exponents and Square Roots

Preview

This appendix reviews some of the basic math skills that are necessary for the statistical calculations presented in this book. Many students already will know some or all of this material. Others will need to do extensive work and review. To help you assess your own skills, we include a skills assessment exam here. You should allow approximately 30 minutes to complete the test. When you finish, grade your test using the answer key on page 525.

The test is divided into five sections. If you miss more than three questions in any section of the test, you probably need help in that area. Turn to the section of this appendix that corresponds to your problem area. In each section, you will find a general review, examples, and additional practice problems. After reviewing the appropriate section and doing the practice problems, turn to the end of this appendix. You will find another version of the skills assessment exam. If you still miss more than three questions in any section of the exam, continue studying. Get assistance from an instructor or a tutor if necessary. At the end of this appendix is a list of recommended books for individuals who need a more extensive review than can be provided here. We must stress that mastering this material now will make the rest of the course much easier.

SKILLS ASSESSMENT PREVIEW EXAM

SECTION 1

(corresponding to Section A.1 of this appendix)

1. $3 + 2 \times 7 = ?$
2. $(3 + 2) \times 7 = ?$
3. $3 + 2^2 - 1 = ?$
4. $(3 + 2)^2 - 1 = ?$
5. $12/4 + 2 = ?$
6. $12/(4 + 2) = ?$
7. $12/(4 + 2)^2 = ?$
8. $2 \times (8 - 2^2) = ?$
9. $2 \times (8 - 2)^2 = ?$
10. $3 \times 2 + 8 - 1 \times 6 = ?$
11. $3 \times (2 + 8) - 1 \times 6 = ?$
12. $3 \times 2 + (8 - 1) \times 6 = ?$

SECTION 2

(corresponding to Section A.2 of this appendix)

1. The fraction $\frac{3}{4}$ corresponds to a percentage of _____ .
2. Express 30% as a fraction.
3. Convert $\frac{12}{40}$ to a decimal.
4. $\frac{2}{13} + \frac{8}{13} = ?$
5. $1.375 + 0.25 = ?$
6. $\frac{2}{5} \times \frac{1}{4} = ?$
7. $\frac{1}{8} + \frac{2}{3} = ?$
8. $3.5 \times 0.4 = ?$
9. $\frac{1}{5} \div \frac{3}{4} = ?$
10. $3.75/0.5 = ?$
11. In a group of 80 students, 20% are psychology majors. How many psychology majors are in this group?
12. A company reports that two-fifths of its employees are women. If there are 90 employees, how many are women?

SECTION 3

(corresponding to Section A.3 of this appendix)

1. $3 + (-2) + (-1) + 4 = ?$
2. $6 - (-2) = ?$
3. $-2 - (-4) = ?$
4. $6 + (-1) - 3 - (-2) - (-5) = ?$
5. $4 \times (-3) = ?$

6. $-2 \times (-6) = ?$
7. $-3 \times 5 = ?$
8. $-2 \times (-4) \times (-3) = ?$
9. $12 \div (-3) = ?$
10. $-18 \div (-6) = ?$
11. $-16 \div 8 = ?$
12. $-100 \div (-4) = ?$

SECTION 4

(corresponding to Section A.4 of this appendix)
For each equation, find the value of X.

1. $X + 6 = 13$
2. $X - 14 = 15$
3. $5 = X - 4$
4. $3X = 12$
5. $72 = 3X$
6. $X/5 = 3$
7. $10 = X/8$
8. $3X + 5 = -4$
9. $24 = 2X + 2$
10. $(X + 3)/2 = 14$
11. $(X - 5)/3 = 2$
12. $17 = 4X - 11$

SECTION 5

(corresponding to Section A.5 of this appendix)

1. $4^3 = ?$
2. $\sqrt{25 - 9} = ?$
3. If $X = 2$ and $Y = 3$, then $XY^3 = ?$
4. If $X = 2$ and $Y = 3$, then $(X + Y)^2 = ?$
5. If $a = 3$ and $b = 2$, then $a^2 + b^2 = ?$
6. $(-3)^3 = ?$
7. $(-4)^4 = ?$
8. $\sqrt{4} \times 4 = ?$
9. $36/\sqrt{9} = ?$
10. $(9 + 2)^2 = ?$
11. $5^2 + 2^3 = ?$
12. If $a = 3$ and $b = -1$, then $a^2b^3 = ?$

The answers to the skills assessment exam are at the end of Appendix A, on page 525.

A.1   SYMBOLS AND NOTATION

Table A.1 presents the basic mathematical symbols that you should know, and it provides examples of their use. Statistical symbols and notation will be introduced and explained throughout this book as they are needed. Notation for exponents and square roots is covered separately at the end of this appendix.

Parentheses are a useful notation because they specify and control the order of computations. Everything inside the parentheses is calculated first. For example,

$$(5 + 3) \times 2 = 8 \times 2 = 16$$

Changing the placement of the parentheses also changes the order of calculations. For example,

$$5 + (3 \times 2) = 5 + 6 = 11$$

ORDER OF OPERATIONS   Often a formula or a mathematical expression will involve several different arithmetic operations, such as adding, multiplying, squaring, and so on. When you encounter these situations, you must perform the different operations in the correct sequence. Following is a list of mathematical operations, showing the order in which they are to be performed.

1. Any calculation contained within parentheses is done first.
2. Squaring (or raising to other exponents) is done second.
3. Multiplying and/or dividing is done third. A series of multiplication and/or division operations should be done in order from left to right.
4. Adding and/or subtracting is done fourth.

The following examples demonstrate how this sequence of operations is applied in different situations.

To evaluate the expression

$$(3 + 1)^2 - 4 \times 7/2$$

first, perform the calculation within parentheses:

$$(4)^2 - 4 \times 7/2$$

TABLE A.1

Symbol	Meaning	Example
$+$	Addition	$5 + 7 = 12$
$-$	Subtraction	$8 - 3 = 5$
$\times, (\ )$	Multiplication	$3 \times 9 = 27,\ 3(9) = 27$
$\div, /$	Division	$15 \div 3 = 5,\ 15/3 = 5,\ \frac{15}{3} = 5$
$>$	Greater than	$20 > 10$
$<$	Less than	$7 < 11$
$\neq$	Not equal to	$5 \neq 6$

Next, square the value as indicated:

$$16 - 4 \times 7/2$$

Then perform the multiplication and division:

$$16 - 14$$

Finally, do the subtraction:

$$16 - 14 = 2$$

A sequence of operations involving multiplication and division should be performed in order from left to right. For example, to compute $12/2 \times 3$, you divide 12 by 2 and then multiply the result by 3:

$$12/2 \times 3 = 6 \times 3 = 18$$

Notice that violating the left-to-right sequence can change the result. For this example, if you multiply before dividing, you will obtain

$$12/2 \times 3 = 12/6 = 2 \qquad \text{(This is wrong.)}$$

A sequence of operations involving only addition and subtraction can be performed in any order. For example, to compute $3 + 8 - 5$, you can add 3 and 8 and then subtract 5:

$$(3 + 8) - 5 = 11 - 5 = 6$$

Or you can subtract 5 from 8 and then add the result to 3:

$$3 + (8 - 5) = 3 + 3 = 6$$

A mathematical expression or formula is simply a concise way to write a set of instructions. When you evaluate an expression by performing the calculation, simply follow the instructions. For example, assume you are given the instructions that follow:

1. First, add 3 and 8.
2. Next, square the result.
3. Next, multiply the resulting value by 6.
4. Finally, subtract 50 from the value you have obtained.

You can write these instructions as a mathematical expression.

1. The first step involved addition. Because addition is normally done last, use parentheses to give this operation priority in the sequence of calculations:

$$(3 + 8)$$

2. The instruction to square a value is noted by using the exponent 2 beside the value to be squared:

$$(3 + 8)^2$$

3. Because squaring has priority over multiplication, you can simply introduce the multiplication into the expression:

$$6 \times (3 + 8)^2$$

4. Addition and subtraction are done last, so simply write in the requested subtraction:

$$6 \times (3 + 8)^2 - 50$$

To calculate the value of the expression, work through the sequence of operations in the proper order:

$$6 \times (3 + 8)^2 - 50 = 6 \times (11)^2 - 50$$
$$= 6 \times (121) - 50$$
$$= 726 - 50$$
$$= 676$$

As a final note, you should realize that the operation of squaring (or raising to any exponent) applies only to the value that immediately precedes the exponent. For example,

$$2 \times 3^2 = 2 \times 9 = 18 \qquad \text{(Only the 3 is squared.)}$$

If the instructions require multiplying values and then squaring the product, you must use parentheses to give the multiplication priority over squaring. For example, to multiply 2 times 3 and then square the product, write

$$(2 \times 3)^2 = (6)^2 = 36$$

LEARNING CHECK

1. Evaluate each of the following expressions:

a. $4 \times 8/2^2$

b. $4 \times (8/2)^2$

c. $100 - 3 \times 12/(6 - 4)^2$

d. $(4 + 6) \times (3 - 1)^2$

e. $(8 - 2)/(9 - 8)^2$

f. $6 + (4 - 1)^2 - 3 \times 4^2$

g. $4 \times (8 - 3) + 8 - 3$

ANSWERS   **1. a.** 8   **b.** 64   **c.** 91   **d.** 40   **e.** 6   **f.** −33   **g.** 25

A.2   PROPORTIONS: FRACTIONS, DECIMALS, AND PERCENTAGES

A proportion is a part of a whole and can be expressed as a fraction, a decimal, or a percentage. For example, in a class of 40 students, only 3 failed the final exam.

The proportion of the class that failed can be expressed as a fraction

$$\text{fraction} = \frac{3}{40}$$

or as a decimal value

$$\text{decimal} = 0.075$$

or as a percentage

$$\text{percentage} = 7.5\%$$

In a fraction, such as $\frac{3}{4}$, the bottom value (the denominator) indicates the number of equal pieces into which the whole is split. Here the "pie" is split into 4 equal pieces:

If the denominator has a larger value—say, 8—then each piece of the whole pie is smaller:

A larger denominator indicates a smaller fraction of the whole.

The value on top of the fraction (the numerator) indicates how many pieces of the whole are being considered. Thus, the fraction $\frac{3}{4}$ indicates that the whole is split evenly into 4 pieces and that 3 of them are being used:

A fraction is simply a concise way of stating a proportion: "Three out of four" is equivalent to $\frac{3}{4}$. To convert the fraction to a decimal, divide the numerator by the denominator:

$$\frac{3}{4} = 3 \div 4 = 0.75$$

To convert the decimal to a percentage, simply multiply by 100, and place a percent sign (%) after the answer:

$$0.75 \times 100 = 75\%$$

The U.S. money system is a convenient way of illustrating the relationship between fractions and decimals. "One quarter," for example, is one-fourth $\left(\frac{1}{4}\right)$ of a dollar, and its decimal equivalent is 0.25. Other familiar equivalencies are as follows:

	Dime	Quarter	50 cents	75 cents
Fraction	$\frac{1}{10}$	$\frac{1}{4}$	$\frac{1}{2}$	$\frac{3}{4}$
Decimal	0.10	0.25	0.50	0.75
Percentage	10%	25%	50%	75%

FRACTIONS

1. Finding Equivalent Fractions. The same proportional value can be expressed by many equivalent fractions. For example,

$$\frac{1}{2} = \frac{2}{4} = \frac{10}{20} = \frac{50}{100}$$

To create equivalent fractions, you can multiply the numerator and denominator by the same value. As long as both the numerator and the denominator of the fraction are multiplied by the same value, the new fraction will be equivalent to the original. For example,

$$\frac{3}{10} = \frac{9}{30}$$

because both the numerator and the denominator of the original fraction have been multiplied by 3. Dividing the numerator and denominator of a fraction by the same value will also result in an equivalent fraction. By using division, you can reduce a fraction to a simpler form. For example,

$$\frac{40}{100} = \frac{2}{5}$$

because both the numerator and the denominator of the original fraction have been divided by 20.

You can use these rules to find specific equivalent fractions. For example, find the fraction that has a denominator of 100 and is equivalent to $\frac{3}{4}$. That is,

$$\frac{3}{4} = \frac{?}{100}$$

Note that the denominator of the original fraction must be multiplied by 25 to produce the denominator of the desired fraction. For the two fractions to be equal, both the numerator and the denominator must be multiplied by the same number. Therefore, we also multiply the top of the original fraction by 25 and obtain

$$\frac{3 \times 25}{4 \times 25} = \frac{75}{100}$$

2. Multiplying Fractions. To multiply two fractions, you first multiply the numerators and then multiply the denominators. For example,

$$\frac{3}{4} \times \frac{5}{7} = \frac{3 \times 5}{4 \times 7} = \frac{15}{28}$$

3. Dividing Fractions. To divide one fraction by another, invert the second fraction and then multiply. For example,

$$\frac{1}{2} \div \frac{1}{4} = \frac{1}{2} \times \frac{4}{1} = \frac{1 \times 4}{2 \times 1} = \frac{4}{2} = \frac{2}{1} = 2$$

4. Adding and Subtracting Fractions. Fractions must have the same denominator before you can add or subtract them. If the two fractions already have a common denominator, simply add (or subtract as the case may be) *only* the values in the numerators. For example,

$$\frac{2}{5} + \frac{1}{5} = \frac{3}{5}$$

Suppose you divided a pie into five equal pieces (fifths). If you first ate two-fifths of the pie and then another one-fifth, the total amount eaten would be three-fifths of the pie:

If the two fractions do not have the same denominator, you must first find equivalent fractions with a common denominator before you can add or subtract. The product of the two denominators will always work as a common denominator for equivalent fractions (although it may not be the lowest common denominator). For example,

$$\frac{2}{3} + \frac{1}{10} = ?$$

Because these two fractions have different denominators, it is necessary to convert each into an equivalent fraction and find a common denominator. We will use $3 \times 10 = 30$ as the common denominator. Thus, the equivalent fraction of each is

$$\frac{2}{3} = \frac{20}{30} \quad \text{and} \quad \frac{1}{10} = \frac{3}{30}$$

Now the two fractions can be added:

$$\frac{20}{30} + \frac{3}{30} = \frac{23}{30}$$

5. Comparing the Size of Fractions. When comparing the size of two fractions with the same denominator, the larger fraction will have the larger numerator. For example,

$$\frac{5}{8} > \frac{3}{8}$$

The denominators are the same, so the whole is partitioned into pieces of the same size. Five of these pieces are more than three of them:

When two fractions have different denominators, you must first convert them to fractions with a common denominator to determine which is larger. Consider the following fractions:

$$\frac{3}{8} \quad \text{and} \quad \frac{7}{16}$$

If the numerator and denominator of $\frac{3}{8}$ are multiplied by 2, the resulting equivalent fraction will have a denominator of 16:

$$\frac{3}{8} = \frac{3 \times 2}{8 \times 2} = \frac{6}{16}$$

Now a comparison can be made between the two fractions:

$$\frac{6}{16} < \frac{7}{16}$$

Therefore,

$$\frac{3}{8} < \frac{7}{16}$$

DECIMALS

1. Converting Decimals to Fractions. Like a fraction, a decimal represents part of the whole. The first decimal place to the right of the decimal point indicates how many tenths are used. For example,

$$0.1 = \frac{1}{10} \qquad 0.7 = \frac{7}{10}$$

The next decimal place represents $\frac{1}{100}$, the next $\frac{1}{1000}$, the next $\frac{1}{10,000}$, and so on. To change a decimal to a fraction, just use the number without the decimal point for the numerator. Use the denominator that the last (on the right) decimal place represents. For example,

$$0.32 = \frac{32}{100} \qquad 0.5333 = \frac{5333}{10,000} \qquad 0.05 = \frac{5}{100} \qquad 0.001 = \frac{1}{1000}$$

2. Adding and Subtracting Decimals. To add and subtract decimals, the only rule is that you must keep the decimal points in a straight vertical line. For example,

$$
\begin{array}{r}
0.27 \\
+1.326 \\
\hline
1.596
\end{array}
\qquad
\begin{array}{r}
3.595 \\
-0.67 \\
\hline
2.925
\end{array}
$$

3. Multiplying Decimals. To multiply two decimal values, first multiply the two numbers, ignoring the decimal points. Then position the decimal point in the answer so that the number of digits to the right of the decimal point is equal to the total number of decimal places in the two numbers being multiplied. For example,

$$
\begin{array}{r}
1.73 \quad \text{(two decimal places)} \\
\times\, 0.251 \quad \text{(three decimal places)} \\
\hline
173 \\
865 \\
346 \\
\hline
0.43423 \quad \text{(five decimal places)}
\end{array}
\qquad
\begin{array}{r}
0.25 \quad \text{(two decimal places)} \\
\times\, 0.005 \quad \text{(three decimal places)} \\
\hline
125 \\
00 \\
00 \\
\hline
0.00125 \quad \text{(five decimal places)}
\end{array}
$$

4. Dividing Decimals. The simplest procedure for dividing decimals is based on the fact that dividing two numbers is identical to expressing them as a fraction:

$$0.25 \div 1.6 \text{ is identical to } \frac{0.25}{1.6}$$

You now can multiply both the numerator and the denominator of the fraction by 10, 100, 1000, or whatever number is necessary to remove the decimal places. Remember that multiplying both the numerator and the denominator of a fraction by the *same* value will create an equivalent fraction. Therefore,

$$\frac{0.25}{1.6} = \frac{0.25 \times 100}{1.6 \times 100} = \frac{25}{160} = \frac{5}{32}$$

The result is a division problem without any decimal places in the two numbers.

PERCENTAGES

1. Converting a Percentage to a Fraction or a Decimal. To convert a percentage to a fraction, remove the percent sign, place the number in the numerator, and use 100 for the denominator. For example,

$$52\% = \frac{52}{100} \qquad 5\% = \frac{5}{100}$$

To convert a percentage to a decimal, remove the percent sign, and divide by 100, or simply move the decimal point two places to the left. For example,

$$83\% = 83. = 0.83$$

$$14.5\% = 14.5 = 0.145$$

$$5\% = 5. = 0.05$$

2. Performing Arithmetic Operations with Percentages. In certain situations, it is best to express percent values as decimals in order to perform certain arithmetic operations. For example, what is 45% of 60? This question may be stated as

$$45\% \times 60 = ?$$

The 45% should be converted to decimal form to find the solution to this question. Therefore,

$$0.45 \times 60 = 27$$

LEARNING CHECK

1. Convert $\frac{3}{25}$ to a decimal.

2. Convert $\frac{3}{8}$ to a percentage.

3. Next to each set of fractions, write "True" if they are equivalent and "False" if they are not:

   a. $\frac{3}{8} = \frac{9}{24}$ _____

   b. $\frac{7}{9} = \frac{17}{19}$ _____

   c. $\frac{2}{7} = \frac{4}{14} =$ _____

4. Compute the following:

 a. $\frac{1}{6} \times \frac{7}{10}$ **b.** $\frac{7}{8} - \frac{1}{2}$ **c.** $\frac{9}{10} \div \frac{2}{3}$ **d.** $\frac{7}{22} + \frac{2}{3}$

5. Identify the larger fraction of each pair:

 a. $\frac{7}{10}, \frac{21}{100}$ **b.** $\frac{3}{4}, \frac{7}{12}$ **c.** $\frac{22}{3}, \frac{19}{3}$

6. Convert the following decimals into fractions:

 a. 0.012   **b.** 0.77   **c.** 0.005

7. $2.59 \times 0.015 = ?$

8. $1.8 \div 0.02 = ?$

9. What is 28% of 45?

ANSWERS   **1.** 0.12   **2.** 37.5%   **3. a.** True.   **b.** False.   **c.** True.

4. a. $\frac{7}{60}$ **b.** $\frac{3}{8}$ **c.** $\frac{27}{20}$ **d.** $\frac{65}{66}$ **5. a.** $\frac{7}{10}$ **b.** $\frac{3}{4}$ **c.** $\frac{22}{3}$

6. a. $\frac{12}{1000} = \frac{3}{250}$ **b.** $\frac{77}{100}$ **c.** $\frac{5}{1000} = \frac{1}{200}$ **7.** 0.03885   **8.** 90   **9.** 12.6

A.3   NEGATIVE NUMBERS

Negative numbers are used to represent values less than zero. Negative numbers may occur when you are measuring the difference between two scores. For example, a researcher may want to evaluate the effectiveness of a propaganda film by measuring people's attitudes with a test both before and after viewing the film:

	Before	After	Amount of change
Person A	23	27	+4
Person B	18	15	−3
Person C	21	16	−5

Note that the negative sign provides information about the direction of the difference: A plus sign indicates an increase in value, and a minus sign indicates a decrease.

 Because negative numbers are frequently encountered, you should be comfortable working with these values. This section reviews basic arithmetic operations using negative numbers. You should also note that any number without a sign (+ or −) is assumed to be positive.

 1. Adding Negative Numbers. When adding numbers that include negative values, simply interpret the negative sign as subtraction. For example,

$$3 + (-2) + 5 = 3 - 2 + 5 = 6$$

When adding a long string of numbers, it often is easier to add all the positive values to obtain the positive sum and then to add all of the negative values to obtain the negative sum. Finally, you subtract the negative sum from the positive sum. For example,

$$-1 + 3 + (-4) + 3 + (-6) + (-2)$$

positive sum = 6   negative sum = 13

Answer: $6 - 13 = -7$

2. Subtracting Negative Numbers. To subtract a negative number, change it to a positive number, and add. For example,

$$4 - (-3) = 4 + 3 = 7$$

This rule is easier to understand if you think of positive numbers as financial gains and negative numbers as financial losses. In this context, taking away a debt is equivalent to a financial gain. In mathematical terms, taking away a negative number is equivalent to adding a positive number. For example, suppose you are meeting a friend for lunch. You have $7, but you owe your friend $3. Thus, you really have only $4 to spend for lunch. But your friend forgives (takes away) the $3 debt. The result is that you now have $7 to spend. Expressed as an equation,

$$\$4 \text{ minus a } \$3 \text{ debt} = \$7$$

$$4 - (-3) = 4 + 3 = 7$$

3. Multiplying and Dividing Negative Numbers. When the two numbers being multiplied (or divided) have the same sign, the result is a positive number. When the two numbers have different signs, the result is negative. For example,

$$3 \times (-2) = -6$$

$$-4 \times (-2) = +8$$

The first example is easy to explain by thinking of multiplication as repeated addition. In this case,

$$3 \times (-2) = (-2) + (-2) + (-2) = -6$$

You add three negative 2s, which results in a total of negative 6. In the second example, we are multiplying by a negative number. This amounts to repeated subtraction. That is,

$$-4 \times (-2) = -(-2) - (-2) - (-2) - (-2)$$

$$= 2 + 2 + 2 + 2 = 8$$

By using the same rule for both multiplication and division, we ensure that these two operations are compatible. For example,

$$-6 \div 3 = -2$$

which is compatible with

$$3 \times (-2) = -6$$

Also,

$$8 \div (-4) = -2$$

which is compatible with

$$-4 \times (-2) = +8$$

LEARNING CHECK

1. Complete the following calculations:

   a. $3 + (-8) + 5 + 7 + (-1) + (-3)$ **f.** $9 \times (-3)$

   b. $5 - (-9) + 2 - (-3) - (-1)$ **g.** $-7 \times (-4)$

   c. $3 - 7 - (-21) + (-5) - (-9)$ **h.** $-6 \times (-2) \times (-3)$

   d. $4 - (-6) - 3 + 11 - 14$ **i.** $-12 \div (-3)$

   e. $9 + 8 - 2 - 1 - (-6)$ **j.** $18 \div (-6)$

ANSWERS   **1. a.** 3   **b.** 20   **c.** 21   **d.** 4   **e.** 20   **f.** −27   **g.** 28   **h.** −36   **i.** 4   **j.** −3

A.4   BASIC ALGEBRA: SOLVING EQUATIONS

An equation is a mathematical statement that indicates two quantities are identical. For example,

$$12 = 8 + 4$$

Often an equation will contain an unknown (or variable) quantity that is identified with a letter or symbol, rather than a number. For example,

$$12 = 8 + X$$

In this event, your task is to find the value of X that makes the equation "true," or balanced. For this example, an X value of 4 will make a true equation. Finding the value of X is usually called *solving the equation*.

To solve an equation, there are two points to be kept in mind:

1. Your goal is to have the unknown value (X) isolated on one side of the equation. This means that you need to remove all of the other numbers and symbols that appear on the same side of the equation as the X.

2. The equation will remain balanced, provided you treat both sides exactly the same. For example, you could add 10 points to *both* sides, and the solution (the X value) for the equation would be unchanged.

FINDING THE SOLUTION FOR AN EQUATION

We will consider four basic types of equations and the operations needed to solve them.

1. When X Has a Value Added to It.   An example of this type of equation is

$$X + 3 = 7$$

Your goal is to isolate X on one side of the equation. Thus, you must remove the $+3$ on the left-hand side. The solution is obtained by subtracting 3 from *both* sides of the equation:

$$X + 3 - 3 = 7 - 3$$
$$X = 4$$

The solution is $X = 4$. You should always check your solution by returning to the original equation and replacing X with the value you obtained for the solution. For this example,

$$X + 3 = 7$$
$$4 + 3 = 7$$
$$7 = 7$$

2. When X Has a Value Subtracted From It. An example of this type of equation is

$$X - 8 = 12$$

In this example, you must remove the -8 from the left-hand side. Thus, the solution is obtained by adding 8 to *both* sides of the equation:

$$X - 8 + 8 = 12 + 8$$
$$X = 20$$

Check the solution:

$$X - 8 = 12$$
$$20 - 8 = 12$$
$$12 = 12$$

3. When X Is Multiplied by a Value. An example of this type of equation is

$$4X = 24$$

In this instance, it is necessary to remove the 4 that is multiplied by X. This may be accomplished by dividing both sides of the equation by 4:

$$\frac{4X}{4} = \frac{24}{4}$$
$$X = 6$$

Check the solution:

$$4X = 24$$
$$4(6) = 24$$
$$24 = 24$$

4. When X Is Divided by a Value. An example of this type of equation is

$$\frac{X}{3} = 9$$

Now the X is divided by 3, so the solution is obtained by multiplying by 3. Multiplying both sides yields

$$3\left(\frac{X}{3}\right) = 9(3)$$

$$X = 27$$

For the check,

$$\frac{X}{3} = 9$$

$$\frac{27}{3} = 9$$

$$9 = 9$$

SOLUTIONS FOR MORE COMPLEX EQUATIONS

Equations that are more complex can be solved by using a combination of the preceding simple operations. Remember: At each stage you are trying to isolate X on one side of the equation, For example,

$$3X + 7 = 22$$

$$3X + 7 - 7 = 22 - 7 \qquad \text{(Remove} + 7 \text{ by subtracting 7 from both sides.)}$$

$$3X = 15$$

$$\frac{3X}{3} = \frac{15}{3} \qquad \text{(Remove 3 by dividing both sides by 3.)}$$

$$X = 5$$

To check this solution, return to the original equation, and substitute 5 in place of X:

$$3X + 7 = 22$$

$$3(5) + 7 = 22$$

$$15 + 7 = 22$$

$$22 = 22$$

Following is another type of complex equation that is frequently encountered in statistics:

$$\frac{X + 3}{4} = 2$$

First, remove the 4 by multiplying both sides by 4:

$$4\left(\frac{X + 3}{4}\right) = 2(4)$$

$$X + 3 = 8$$

Now remove the $+ 3$ by subtracting 3 from both sides:

$$X + 3 - 3 = 8 - 3$$

$$X = 5$$

To check this solution, return to the original equation, and substitute 5 in place of X:

$$\frac{X + 3}{4} = 2$$

$$\frac{5 + 3}{4} = 2$$

$$\frac{8}{4} = 2$$

$$2 = 2$$

1. Solve for X, and check the solutions:

a. $3X = 18$	**b.** $X + 7 = 9$	**c.** $X - 4 = 18$	**d.** $5X - 8 = 12$
e. $\dfrac{X}{9} = 5$	**f.** $\dfrac{X + 1}{6} = 4$	**g.** $X + 2 = -5$	**h.** $\dfrac{X}{5} = -5$
i. $\dfrac{2X}{3} = 12$	**j.** $\dfrac{X}{3} + 1 = 3$		

ANSWERS   **1. a.** $X = 6$ **b.** $X = 2$ **c.** $X = 22$ **d.** $X = 4$ **e.** $X = 45$
f. $X = 23$ **g.** $X = -7$ **h.** $X = -25$ **i.** $X = 18$ **j.** $X = 6$

A.5   EXPONENTS AND SQUARE ROOTS

EXPONENTIAL NOTATION

A simplified notation is used whenever a number is being multiplied by itself. The notation consists of placing a value, called an *exponent,* on the right-hand side of and raised above another number, called a *base.* For example,

$$7^3 \leftarrow \text{exponent}$$
$$\uparrow$$
$$\text{base}$$

The exponent indicates how many times the base is used as a factor in multiplication. Following are some examples:

$7^3 = 7(7)(7)$ (Read "7 cubed" *or* "7 raised to the third power.")

$5^2 = 5(5)$ (Read "5 squared.")

$2^5 = 2(2)(2)(2)(2)$ (Read "2 raised to the fifth power.")

There are a few basic rules about exponents that you will need to know for this course. They are outlined here.

1. Numbers Raised to One or Zero. Any number raised to the first power equals itself. For example,

$$6^1 = 6$$

Any number (except zero) raised to the zero power equals 1. For example,

$$9^0 = 1$$

2. Exponents for Multiple Terms. The exponent applies only to the base that is just in front of it. For example,

$$XY^2 = XYY$$

$$a^2b^3 = aabbb$$

3. Negative Bases Raised to an Exponent. If a negative number is raised to a power, then the result will be positive for exponents that are even and negative for exponents that are odd. For example,

$$
\begin{aligned}
(-4)^3 &= (-4)(-4)(-4) \\
&= 16(-4) \\
&= -64
\end{aligned}
$$

and

$$
\begin{aligned}
(-3)^4 &= (-3)(-3)(-3)(-3) \\
&= 9(-3)(-3) \\
&= 9(9) \\
&= 81
\end{aligned}
$$

Note: The parentheses are used to ensure that the exponent applies to the entire negative number, including the sign. Without the parentheses there is some ambiguity as to how the exponent should be applied. For example, the expression -3^2 could have two interpretations:

$$-3^2 = (-3)(-3) = 9 \quad \text{or} \quad -3^2 = -(3)(3) = -9$$

4. Exponents and Parentheses. If an exponent is present outside of parentheses, then the computations within the parentheses are done first, and the exponential computation is done last:

$$(3 + 5)^2 = 8^2 = 64$$

Note that the meaning of the expression is changed when each term in the parentheses is raised to the exponent individually:

$$3^2 + 5^2 = 9 + 25 = 34$$

Therefore,

$$X^2 + Y^2 \neq (X + Y)^2$$

5. Fractions Raised to a Power. If the numerator and denominator of a fraction are each raised to the same exponent, then the entire fraction can be raised to that exponent. That is,

$$\frac{a^2}{b^2} = \left(\frac{a}{b}\right)^2$$

For example,

$$\frac{3^2}{4^2} = \left(\frac{3}{4}\right)^2$$

$$\frac{9}{16} = \frac{3}{4}\left(\frac{3}{4}\right)$$

$$\frac{9}{16} = \frac{9}{16}$$

SQUARE ROOTS

The square root of a value equals a number that when multiplied by itself yields the original value. For example, the square root of 16 equals 4 because 4 times 4 equals 16. The symbol for the square root is called a *radical,* $\sqrt{}$. The square root is taken for the number under the radical. For example,

$$\sqrt{16} = 4$$

Finding the square root is the inverse of raising a number to the second power (squaring). Thus,

$$\sqrt{a^2} = a$$

We will typically use positive square roots although you should realize that $\sqrt{9}$ could be either $+3$ or -3.

For example,

$$\sqrt{3^2} = \sqrt{9} = 3$$

Also,

$$(\sqrt{b})^2 = b$$

For example,

$$(\sqrt{64})^2 = 8^2 = 64$$

Computations under the same radical are performed *before* the square root is taken. For example,

$$\sqrt{9 + 16} = \sqrt{25} = 5$$

Note that with addition (or subtraction) separate radicals yield a different result:

$$\sqrt{9} + \sqrt{16} = 3 + 4 = 7$$

Therefore,

$$\sqrt{X} + \sqrt{Y} \neq \sqrt{X + Y}$$
$$\sqrt{X} - \sqrt{Y} \neq \sqrt{X - Y}$$

If the numerator and denominator of a fraction each have a radical, then the entire fraction can be placed under a single radical:

$$\frac{\sqrt{16}}{\sqrt{4}} = \sqrt{\frac{16}{4}}$$

$$\frac{4}{2} = \sqrt{4}$$

$$2 = 2$$

Therefore,

$$\frac{\sqrt{X}}{\sqrt{Y}} = \sqrt{\frac{X}{Y}}$$

Also, if the square root of one number is multiplied by the square root of another number, then the same result would be obtained by taking the square root of the product of both numbers. For example,

$$\sqrt{9} \times \sqrt{16} = \sqrt{9 \times 16}$$

$$3 \times 4 = \sqrt{144}$$

$$12 = 12$$

Therefore,

$$\sqrt{a} \times \sqrt{b} = \sqrt{ab}$$

LEARNING CHECK

1. Perform the following computations:

a. $(-6)^3$

b. $(3 + 7)^2$

c. $a^3 b^2$ when $a = 2$ and $b = -5$

d. $a^4 b^3$ when $a = 2$ and $b = 3$

e. $(XY)^2$ when $X = 3$ and $Y = 5$

f. $X^2 + Y^2$ when $X = 3$ and $Y = 5$

g. $(X + Y)^2$ when $X = 3$ and $Y = 5$

h. $\sqrt{5 + 4}$

i. $(\sqrt{9})^2$

j. $\dfrac{\sqrt{16}}{\sqrt{4}}$

ANSWERS   **1. a.** -216 **b.** 100   **c.** 200   **d.** 432   **e.** 225   **f.** 34   **g.** 64   **h.** 3   **i.** 9   **j.** 2

PROBLEMS FOR APPENDIX A   Basic Mathematics Review

1. $50/(10 - 8) = ?$

2. $(2 + 3)^2 = ?$

3. $20/10 \times 3 = ?$

4. $12 - 4 \times 2 + 6/3 = ?$

5. $24/(12 - 4) + 2 \times (6 + 3) = ?$

6. Convert $\frac{7}{20}$ to a decimal.

7. Express $\frac{9}{25}$ as a percentage.

8. Convert 0.91 to a fraction.

9. Express 0.0031 as a fraction.

10. Next to each set of fractions, write "True" if they are equivalent and "False" if they are not:

a. $\dfrac{4}{1000} = \dfrac{2}{100}$ _____

b. $\dfrac{5}{6} = \dfrac{52}{62}$ _____

c. $\dfrac{1}{8} = \dfrac{7}{56}$ _____

11. Perform the following calculations:

    a. $\dfrac{4}{5} \times \dfrac{2}{3} = ?$ **b.** $\dfrac{7}{9} \div \dfrac{2}{3} = ?$

    c. $\dfrac{3}{8} + \dfrac{1}{5} = ?$ **d.** $\dfrac{5}{18} - \dfrac{1}{6} = ?$

12. $2.51 \times 0.017 = ?$

13. $3.88 \times 0.0002 = ?$

14. $3.17 + 17.0132 = ?$

15. $5.55 + 10.7 + 0.711 + 3.33 + 0.031 = ?$

16. $2.04 \div 0.2 = ?$

17. $0.36 \div 0.4 = ?$

18. $5 + 3 - 6 - 4 + 3 = ?$

19. $9 - (-1) - 17 + 3 - (-4) + 5 = ?$

20. $5 + 3 - (-8) - (-1) + (-3) - 4 + 10 = ?$

21. $8 \times (-3) = ?$

22. $-22 \div (-2) = ?$

23. $-2(-4) \times (-3) = ?$

24. $84 \div (-4) = ?$

Solve the equations in Problems 25–32 for X.

25. $X - 7 = -2$ 26. $9 = X + 3$

27. $\dfrac{X}{4} = 11$ 28. $-3 = \dfrac{X}{3}$

29. $\dfrac{X + 3}{5} = 2$ 30. $\dfrac{X + 1}{3} = -8$

31. $6X - 1 = 11$ 32. $2X + 3 = -11$

33. $(-5)^2 = ?$ 34. $(-5)^3 = ?$

35. If $a = 4$ and $b = 3$, then $a^2 + b^4 = ?$

36. If $a = -1$ and $b = 4$, then $(a + b)^2 = ?$

37. If $a = -1$ and $b = 5$, then $ab^2 = ?$

38. $\dfrac{18}{\sqrt{4}} = ?$ 39. $\sqrt{\dfrac{20}{5}} = ?$

SKILLS ASSESSMENT FINAL EXAM

SECTION 1

1. $4 + 8/4 = ?$ 2. $(4 + 8)/4 = ?$

3. $4 \times 3^2 = ?$ 4. $(4 \times 3)^2 = ?$

5. $10/5 \times 2 = ?$ 6. $10/(5 \times 2) = ?$

7. $40 - 10 \times 4/2 = ?$ 8. $(5 - 1)^2/2 = ?$

9. $3 \times 6 - 3^2 = ?$ 10. $2 \times (6 - 3)^2 = ?$

11. $4 \times 3 - 1 + 8 \times 2 = ?$

12. $4 \times (3 - 1 + 8) \times 2 = ?$

SECTION 2

1. Express $\frac{14}{80}$ as a decimal.

2. Convert $\frac{6}{25}$ to a percentage.

3. Convert 18% to a fraction.

4. $\frac{3}{5} \times \frac{2}{3} = ?$ 5. $\frac{5}{24} + \frac{5}{6} = ?$

6. $\frac{7}{12} \div \frac{5}{6} = ?$ 7. $\frac{5}{9} - \frac{1}{3} = ?$

8. $6.11 \times 0.22 = ?$

9. $0.18 \div 0.9 = ?$

10. $8.742 + 0.76 = ?$

11. In a statistics class of 72 students, three-eighths of the students received a *B* on the first test. How many *B*s were earned?

12. What is 15% of 64?

SECTION 3

1. $3 - 1 - 3 + 5 - 2 + 6 = ?$

2. $-8 - (-6) = ?$

3. $2 - (-7) - 3 + (-11) - 20 = ?$

4. $-8 - 3 - (-1) - 2 - 1 = ?$

5. $8(-2) = ?$ 6. $-7(-7) = ?$

7. $-3(-2)(-5) = ?$ 8. $-3(5)(-3) = ?$

9. $-24 \div (-4) = ?$ 10. $36 \div (-6) = ?$

11. $-56/7 = ?$ 12. $-7/(-1) = ?$

SECTION 4

Solve for X.

1. $X + 5 = 12$ 2. $X - 11 = 3$

3. $10 = X + 4$ 4. $4X = 20$

5. $\dfrac{X}{2} = 15$ 6. $18 = 9X$

7. $\dfrac{X}{5} = 35$ 8. $2X + 8 = 4$

9. $\dfrac{X + 1}{3} = 6$ 10. $4X + 3 = -13$

11. $\dfrac{X + 3}{3} = -7$ 12. $23 = 2X - 5$

SECTION 5

1. $5^3 = ?$ **2.** $(-4)^3 = ?$

3. $(-2)^5 = ?$ **4.** $(-2)^6 = ?$

5. If $a = 4$ and $b = 2$, then $ab^2 = ?$

6. If $a = 4$ and $b = 2$, then $(a + b)^3 = ?$

7. If $a = 4$ and $b = 2$, then $a^2 + b^2 = ?$

8. $(11 + 4)^2 = ?$

9. $\sqrt{7^2} = ?$

10. If $a = 36$ and $b = 64$, then $\sqrt{a + b} = ?$

11. $\dfrac{25}{\sqrt{25}} = ?$

12. If $a = -1$ and $b = 2$, then $a^3b^4 = ?$

ANSWER KEY   Skills Assessment Exams

PREVIEW EXAM

SECTION 1

1. 17	**2.** 35	**3.** 6
4. 24	**5.** 5	**6.** 2
7. $\dfrac{1}{3}$	**8.** 8	**9.** 72
10. 8	**11.** 24	**12.** 48

SECTION 2

1. 75%	**2.** $\dfrac{30}{100}$, or $\dfrac{3}{10}$	**3.** 0.3
4. $\dfrac{10}{13}$	**5.** 1.625	**6.** $\dfrac{2}{20}$, or $\dfrac{1}{10}$
7. $\dfrac{19}{24}$	**8.** 1.4	**9.** $\dfrac{4}{15}$
10. 7.5	**11.** 16	**12.** 36

SECTION 3

1. 4	**2.** 8	**3.** 2
4. 9	**5.** -12	**6.** 12
7. -15	**8.** -24	**9.** -4
10. 3	**11.** -2	**12.** 25

SECTION 4

1. $X = 7$	**2.** $X = 29$	**3.** $X = 9$
4. $X = 4$	**5.** $X = 24$	**6.** $X = 15$
7. $X = 80$	**8.** $X = -3$	**9.** $X = 11$
10. $X = 25$	**11.** $X = 11$	**12.** $X = 7$

SECTION 5

1. 64	**2.** 4	**3.** 54
4. 25	**5.** 13	**6.** -27
7. 256	**8.** 8	**9.** 12
10. 121	**11.** 33	**12.** -9

FINAL EXAM

SECTION 1

1. 6	**2.** 3	**3.** 36
4. 144	**5.** 4	**6.** 1
7. 20	**8.** 8	**9.** 9
10. 18	**11.** 27	**12.** 80

SECTION 2

1. 0.175	**2.** 24%	**3.** $\dfrac{18}{100}$, or $\dfrac{9}{50}$
4. $\dfrac{6}{15}$, or $\dfrac{2}{5}$	**5.** $\dfrac{25}{24}$	**6.** $\dfrac{42}{60}$, or $\dfrac{7}{10}$
7. $\dfrac{2}{9}$	**8** 1.3442	**9.** 0.2
10. 9.502	**11.** 27	**12.** 9.6

SECTION 3

1. 8	**2.** -2	**3.** -25
4. -13	**5.** -16	**6.** 49
7. -30	**8.** 45	**9.** 6
10. -6	**11.** -8	**12.** 7

SECTION 4

1. $X = 7$	**2.** $X = 14$	**3.** $X = 6$
4. $X = 5$	**5.** $X = 30$	**6.** $X = 2$
7. $X = 175$	**8.** $X = -2$	**9.** $X = 17$
10. $X = -4$	**11.** $X = -24$	**12.** $X = 14$

SECTION 5

1. 125	**2.** -64	**3.** -32
4. 64	**5.** 16	**6.** 216
7. 20	**8.** 225	**9.** 7
10. 10	**11.** 5	**12.** -16

SOLUTIONS TO SELECTED PROBLEMS FOR APPENDIX A   Basic Mathematics Review

1. 25

5. 21

7. 36%

10. b. False

11. a. $\frac{8}{15}$ **b.** $\frac{21}{18}$ **c.** $\frac{23}{40}$

12. 0.04267

3. 6

6. 0.35

9. $\frac{31}{10,000}$

14. 20.1832

17. 0.9

21. -24

25. $X = 5$

30. $X = -25$

34. -125

37. -25

19. 5

22. 11

28. $X = -9$

31. $X = 2$

36. 9

39. 2

SUGGESTED REVIEW BOOKS

There are many basic mathematics review books available if you need a more extensive review than this appendix can provide. The following books are but a few of the many that you may find helpful:

Gustafson, R. D., & Frisk, P. D. (2005). *Beginning Algebra* (7th ed.). Belmont, CA: Brooks/Cole.

Lial, M. L., Salzman, S. A., & Hestwood, D. L. (2006) *Basic College Mathematics* (7th ed.). Reading, MA: Addison-Wesley.

McKeague, C. P. (2003). *Basic College Mathematics: A Text/Workbook.* Belmont, CA: Brooks/Cole.

TABLE B.1   THE UNIT NORMAL TABLE*

*Column A lists z-score values. A vertical line drawn through a normal distribution at a z-score location divides the distribution into two sections.
Column B identifies the proportion in the larger section, called the *body*.
Column C identifies the proportion in the smaller section, called the *tail*.
Column D identifies the proportion between the mean and the z-score.
Note: Because the normal distribution is symmetrical, the proportions for negative z-scores are the same as those for positive z-scores.

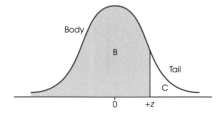 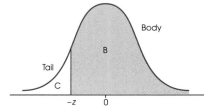 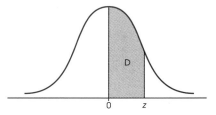

(A) z	(B) Proportion in Body	(C) Proportion in Tail	(D) Proportion Between Mean and z	(A) z	(B) Proportion in Body	(C) Proportion in Tail	(D) Proportion Between Mean and z
0.00	.5000	.5000	.0000	0.25	.5987	.4013	.0987
0.01	.5040	.4960	.0040	0.26	.6026	.3974	.1026
0.02	.5080	.4920	.0080	0.27	.6064	.3936	.1064
0.03	.5120	.4880	.0120	0.28	.6103	.3897	.1103
0.04	.5160	.4840	.0160	0.29	.6141	.3859	.1141
0.05	.5199	.4801	.0199	0.30	.6179	.3821	.1179
0.06	.5239	.4761	.0239	0.31	.6217	.3783	.1217
0.07	.5279	.4721	.0279	0.32	.6255	.3745	.1255
0.08	.5319	.4681	.0319	0.33	.6293	.3707	.1293
0.09	.5359	.4641	.0359	0.34	.6331	.3669	.1331
0.10	.5398	.4602	.0398	0.35	.6368	.3632	.1368
0.11	.5438	.4562	.0438	0.36	.6406	.3594	.1406
0.12	.5478	.4522	.0478	0.37	.6443	.3557	.1443
0.13	.5517	.4483	.0517	0.38	.6480	.3520	.1480
0.14	.5557	.4443	.0557	0.39	.6517	.3483	.1517
0.15	.5596	.4404	.0596	0.40	.6554	.3446	.1554
0.16	.5636	.4364	.0636	0.41	.6591	.3409	.1591
0.17	.5675	.4325	.0675	0.42	.6628	.3372	.1628
0.18	.5714	.4286	.0714	0.43	.6664	.3336	.1664
0.19	.5753	.4247	.0753	0.44	.6700	.3300	.1700
0.20	.5793	.4207	.0793	0.45	.6736	.3264	.1736
0.21	.5832	.4168	.0832	0.46	.6772	.3228	.1772
0.22	.5871	.4129	.0871	0.47	.6808	.3192	.1808
0.23	.5910	.4090	.0910	0.48	.6844	.3156	.1844
0.24	.5948	.4052	.0948	0.49	.6879	.3121	.1879

(A) z	(B) Proportion in Body	(C) Proportion in Tail	(D) Proportion Between Mean and z	(A) z	(B) Proportion in Body	(C) Proportion in Tail	(D) Proportion Between Mean and z
0.50	.6915	.3085	.1915	1.00	.8413	.1587	.3413
0.51	.6950	.3050	.1950	1.01	.8438	.1562	.3438
0.52	.6985	.3015	.1985	1.02	.8461	.1539	.3461
0.53	.7019	.2981	.2019	1.03	.8485	.1515	.3485
0.54	.7054	.2946	.2054	1.04	.8508	.1492	.3508
0.55	.7088	.2912	.2088	1.05	.8531	.1469	.3531
0.56	.7123	.2877	.2123	1.06	.8554	.1446	.3554
0.57	.7157	.2843	.2157	1.07	.8577	.1423	.3577
0.58	.7190	.2810	.2190	1.08	.8599	.1401	.3599
0.59	.7224	.2776	.2224	1.09	.8621	.1379	.3621
0.60	.7257	.2743	.2257	1.10	.8643	.1357	.3643
0.61	.7291	.2709	.2291	1.11	.8665	.1335	.3665
0.62	.7324	.2676	.2324	1.12	.8686	.1314	.3686
0.63	.7357	.2643	.2357	1.13	.8708	.1292	.3708
0.64	.7389	.2611	.2389	1.14	.8729	.1271	.3729
0.65	.7422	.2578	.2422	1.15	.8749	.1251	.3749
0.66	.7454	.2546	.2454	1.16	.8770	.1230	.3770
0.67	.7486	.2514	.2486	1.17	.8790	.1210	.3790
0.68	.7517	.2483	.2517	1.18	.8810	.1190	.3810
0.69	.7549	.2451	.2549	1.19	.8830	.1170	.3830
0.70	.7580	.2420	.2580	1.20	.8849	.1151	.3849
0.71	.7611	.2389	.2611	1.21	.8869	.1131	.3869
0.72	.7642	.2358	.2642	1.22	.8888	.1112	.3888
0.73	.7673	.2327	.2673	1.23	.8907	.1093	.3907
0.74	.7704	.2296	.2704	1.24	.8925	.1075	.3925
0.75	.7734	.2266	.2734	1.25	.8944	.1056	.3944
0.76	.7764	.2236	.2764	1.26	.8962	.1038	.3962
0.77	.7794	.2206	.2794	1.27	.8980	.1020	.3980
0.78	.7823	.2177	.2823	1.28	.8997	.1003	.3997
0.79	.7852	.2148	.2852	1.29	.9015	.0985	.4015
0.80	.7881	.2119	.2881	1.30	.9032	.0968	.4032
0.81	.7910	.2090	.2910	1.31	.9049	.0951	.4049
0.82	.7939	.2061	.2939	1.32	.9066	.0934	.4066
0.83	.7967	.2033	.2967	1.33	.9082	.0918	.4082
0.84	.7995	.2005	.2995	1.34	.9099	.0901	.4099
0.85	.8023	.1977	.3023	1.35	.9115	.0885	.4115
0.86	.8051	.1949	.3051	1.36	.9131	.0869	.4131
0.87	.8078	.1922	.3078	1.37	.9147	.0853	.4147
0.88	.8106	.1894	.3106	1.38	.9162	.0838	.4162
0.89	.8133	.1867	.3133	1.39	.9177	.0823	.4177
0.90	.8159	.1841	.3159	1.40	.9192	.0808	.4192
0.91	.8186	.1814	.3186	1.41	.9207	.0793	.4207
0.92	.8212	.1788	.3212	1.42	.9222	.0778	.4222
0.93	.8238	.1762	.3238	1.43	.9236	.0764	.4236
0.94	.8264	.1736	.3264	1.44	.9251	.0749	.4251
0.95	.8289	.1711	.3289	1.45	.9265	.0735	.4265
0.96	.8315	.1685	.3315	1.46	.9279	.0721	.4279
0.97	.8340	.1660	.3340	1.47	.9292	.0708	.4292
0.98	.8365	.1635	.3365	1.48	.9306	.0694	.4306
0.99	.8389	.1611	.3389	1.49	.9319	.0681	.4319

(A) z	(B) Proportion in Body	(C) Proportion in Tail	(D) Proportion Between Mean and z	(A) z	(B) Proportion in Body	(C) Proportion in Tail	(D) Proportion Between Mean and z
1.50	.9332	.0668	.4332	2.00	.9772	.0228	.4772
1.51	.9345	.0655	.4345	2.01	.9778	.0222	.4778
1.52	.9357	.0643	.4357	2.02	.9783	.0217	.4783
1.53	.9370	.0630	.4370	2.03	.9788	.0212	.4788
1.54	.9382	.0618	.4382	2.04	.9793	.0207	.4793
1.55	.9394	.0606	.4394	2.05	.9798	.0202	.4798
1.56	.9406	.0594	.4406	2.06	.9803	.0197	.4803
1.57	.9418	.0582	.4418	2.07	.9808	.0192	.4808
1.58	.9429	.0571	.4429	2.08	.9812	.0188	.4812
1.59	.9441	.0559	.4441	2.09	.9817	.0183	.4817
1.60	.9452	.0548	.4452	2.10	.9821	.0179	.4821
1.61	.9463	.0537	.4463	2.11	.9826	.0174	.4826
1.62	.9474	.0526	.4474	2.12	.9830	.0170	.4830
1.63	.9484	.0516	.4484	2.13	.9834	.0166	.4834
1.64	.9495	.0505	.4495	2.14	.9838	.0162	.4838
1.65	.9505	.0495	.4505	2.15	.9842	.0158	.4842
1.66	.9515	.0485	.4515	2.16	.9846	.0154	.4846
1.67	.9525	.0475	.4525	2.17	.9850	.0150	.4850
1.68	.9535	.0465	.4535	2.18	.9854	.0146	.4854
1.69	.9545	.0455	.4545	2.19	.9857	.0143	.4857
1.70	.9554	.0446	.4554	2.20	.9861	.0139	.4861
1.71	.9564	.0436	.4564	2.21	.9864	.0136	.4864
1.72	.9573	.0427	.4573	2.22	.9868	.0132	.4868
1.73	.9582	.0418	.4582	2.23	.9871	.0129	.4871
1.74	.9591	.0409	.4591	2.24	.9875	.0125	.4875
1.75	.9599	.0401	.4599	2.25	.9878	.0122	.4878
1.76	.9608	.0392	.4608	2.26	.9881	.0119	.4881
1.77	.9616	.0384	.4616	2.27	.9884	.0116	.4884
1.78	.9625	.0375	.4625	2.28	.9887	.0113	.4887
1.79	.9633	.0367	.4633	2.29	.9890	.0110	.4890
1.80	.9641	.0359	.4641	2.30	.9893	.0107	.4893
1.81	.9649	.0351	.4649	2.31	.9896	.0104	.4896
1.82	.9656	.0344	.4656	2.32	.9898	.0102	.4898
1.83	.9664	.0336	.4664	2.33	.9901	.0099	.4901
1.84	.9671	.0329	.4671	2.34	.9904	.0096	.4904
1.85	.9678	.0322	.4678	2.35	.9906	.0094	.4906
1.86	.9686	.0314	.4686	2.36	.9909	.0091	.4909
1.87	.9693	.0307	.4693	2.37	.9911	.0089	.4911
1.88	.9699	.0301	.4699	2.38	.9913	.0087	.4913
1.89	.9706	.0294	.4706	2.39	.9916	.0084	.4916
1.90	.9713	.0287	.4713	2.40	.9918	.0082	.4918
1.91	.9719	.0281	.4719	2.41	.9920	.0080	.4920
1.92	.9726	.0274	.4726	2.42	.9922	.0078	.4922
1.93	.9732	.0268	.4732	2.43	.9925	.0075	.4925
1.94	.9738	.0262	.4738	2.44	.9927	.0073	.4927
1.95	.9744	.0256	.4744	2.45	.9929	.0071	.4929
1.96	.9750	.0250	.4750	2.46	.9931	.0069	.4931
1.97	.9756	.0244	.4756	2.47	.9932	.0068	.4932
1.98	.9761	.0239	.4761	2.48	.9934	.0066	.4934
1.99	.9767	.0233	.4767	2.49	.9936	.0064	.4936

(A)	(B)	(C)	(D)	(A)	(B)	(C)	(D)
z	Proportion in Body	Proportion in Tail	Proportion Between Mean and z	z	Proportion in Body	Proportion in Tail	Proportion Between Mean and z
2.50	.9938	.0062	.4938	2.95	.9984	.0016	.4984
2.51	.9940	.0060	.4940	2.96	.9985	.0015	.4985
2.52	.9941	.0059	.4941	2.97	.9985	.0015	.4985
2.53	.9943	.0057	.4943	2.98	.9986	.0014	.4986
2.54	.9945	.0055	.4945	2.99	.9986	.0014	.4986
2.55	.9946	.0054	.4946	3.00	.9987	.0013	.4987
2.56	.9948	.0052	.4948	3.01	.9987	.0013	.4987
2.57	.9949	.0051	.4949	3.02	.9987	.0013	.4987
2.58	.9951	.0049	.4951	3.03	.9988	.0012	.4988
2.59	.9952	.0048	.4952	3.04	.9988	.0012	.4988
2.60	.9953	.0047	.4953	3.05	.9989	.0011	.4989
2.61	.9955	.0045	.4955	3.06	.9989	.0011	.4989
2.62	.9956	.0044	.4956	3.07	.9989	.0011	.4989
2.63	.9957	.0043	.4957	3.08	.9990	.0010	.4990
2.64	.9959	.0041	.4959	3.09	.9990	.0010	.4990
2.65	.9960	.0040	.4960	3.10	.9990	.0010	.4990
2.66	.9961	.0039	.4961	3.11	.9991	.0009	.4991
2.67	.9962	.0038	.4962	3.12	.9991	.0009	.4991
2.68	.9963	.0037	.4963	3.13	.9991	.0009	.4991
2.69	.9964	.0036	.4964	3.14	.9992	.0008	.4992
2.70	.9965	.0035	.4965	3.15	.9992	.0008	.4992
2.71	.9966	.0034	.4966	3.16	.9992	.0008	.4992
2.72	.9967	.0033	.4967	3.17	.9992	.0008	.4992
2.73	.9968	.0032	.4968	3.18	.9993	.0007	.4993
2.74	.9969	.0031	.4969	3.19	.9993	.0007	.4993
2.75	.9970	.0030	.4970	3.20	.9993	.0007	.4993
2.76	.9971	.0029	.4971	3.21	.9993	.0007	.4993
2.77	.9972	.0028	.4972	3.22	.9994	.0006	.4994
2.78	.9973	.0027	.4973	3.23	.9994	.0006	.4994
2.79	.9974	.0026	.4974	3.24	.9994	.0006	.4994
2.80	.9974	.0026	.4974	3.30	.9995	.0005	.4995
2.81	.9975	.0025	.4975	3.40	.9997	.0003	.4997
2.82	.9976	.0024	.4976	3.50	.9998	.0002	.4998
2.83	.9977	.0023	.4977	3.60	.9998	.0002	.4998
2.84	.9977	.0023	.4977	3.70	.9999	.0001	.4999
2.85	.9978	.0022	.4978	3.80	.99993	.00007	.49993
2.86	.9979	.0021	.4979	3.90	.99995	.00005	.49995
2.87	.9979	.0021	.4979	4.00	.99997	.00003	.49997
2.88	.9980	.0020	.4980				
2.89	.9981	.0019	.4981				
2.90	.9981	.0019	.4981				
2.91	.9982	.0018	.4982				
2.92	.9982	.0018	.4982				
2.93	.9983	.0017	.4983				
2.94	.9984	.0016	.4984				

TABLE B.2   **THE *t* DISTRIBUTION**

Table entries are values of *t* corresponding to proportions in one tail or in two tails combined.

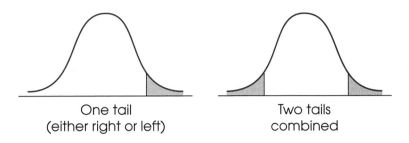

One tail
(either right or left)

Two tails
combined

df	Proportion in One Tail					
	0.25	0.10	0.05	0.025	0.01	0.005
	Proportion in Two Tails Combined					
	0.50	0.20	0.10	0.05	0.02	0.01
1	1.000	3.078	6.314	12.706	31.821	63.657
2	0.816	1.886	2.920	4.303	6.965	9.925
3	0.765	1.638	2.353	3.182	4.541	5.841
4	0.741	1.533	2.132	2.776	3.747	4.604
5	0.727	1.476	2.015	2.571	3.365	4.032
6	0.718	1.440	1.943	2.447	3.143	3.707
7	0.711	1.415	1.895	2.365	2.998	3.499
8	0.706	1.397	1.860	2.306	2.896	3.355
9	0.703	1.383	1.833	2.262	2.821	3.250
10	0.700	1.372	1.812	2.228	2.764	3.169
11	0.697	1.363	1.796	2.201	2.718	3.106
12	0.695	1.356	1.782	2.179	2.681	3.055
13	0.694	1.350	1.771	2.160	2.650	3.012
14	0.692	1.345	1.761	2.145	2.624	2.977
15	0.691	1.341	1.753	2.131	2.602	2.947
16	0.690	1.337	1.746	2.120	2.583	2.921
17	0.689	1.333	1.740	2.110	2.567	2.898
18	0.688	1.330	1.734	2.101	2.552	2.878
19	0.688	1.328	1.729	2.093	2.539	2.861
20	0.687	1.325	1.725	2.086	2.528	2.845
21	0.686	1.323	1.721	2.080	2.518	2.831
22	0.686	1.321	1.717	2.074	2.508	2.819
23	0.685	1.319	1.714	2.069	2.500	2.807
24	0.685	1.318	1.711	2.064	2.492	2.797
25	0.684	1.316	1.708	2.060	2.485	2.787
26	0.684	1.315	1.706	2.056	2.479	2.779
27	0.684	1.314	1.703	2.052	2.473	2.771
28	0.683	1.313	1.701	2.048	2.467	2.763
29	0.683	1.311	1.699	2.045	2.462	2.756
30	0.683	1.310	1.697	2.042	2.457	2.750
40	0.681	1.303	1.684	2.021	2.423	2.704
60	0.679	1.296	1.671	2.000	2.390	2.660
120	0.677	1.289	1.658	1.980	2.358	2.617
∞	0.674	1.282	1.645	1.960	2.326	2.576

Table III of R. A. Fisher and F. Yates, *Statistical Tables for Biological, Agricultural and Medical Research*, 6th ed. London: Longman Group Ltd., 1974 (previously published by Oliver and Boyd Ltd., Edinburgh). Adapted and reprinted with permission of the Addison Wesley Longman Publishing Co.

TABLE B.3 CRITICAL VALUES FOR THE *F*-MAX STATISTIC*

*The critical values for $\alpha = .05$ are in lightface type, and for $\alpha = .01$, they are in boldface type.

n − 1	2	3	4	5	6	*k* = Number of Samples 7	8	9	10	11	12
4	9.60	15.5	20.6	25.2	29.5	33.6	37.5	41.4	44.6	48.0	51.4
	23.2	**37.**	**49.**	**59.**	**69.**	**79.**	**89.**	**97.**	**106.**	**113.**	**120.**
5	7.15	10.8	13.7	16.3	18.7	20.8	22.9	24.7	26.5	28.2	29.9
	14.9	**22.**	**28.**	**33.**	**38.**	**42.**	**46.**	**50.**	**54.**	**57.**	**60.**
6	5.82	8.38	10.4	12.1	13.7	15.0	16.3	17.5	18.6	19.7	20.7
	11.1	**15.5**	**19.1**	**22.**	**25.**	**27.**	**30.**	**32.**	**34.**	**36.**	**37.**
7	4.99	6.94	8.44	9.70	10.8	11.8	12.7	13.5	14.3	15.1	15.8
	8.89	**12.1**	**14.5**	**16.5**	**18.4**	**20.**	**22.**	**23.**	**24.**	**26.**	**27.**
8	4.43	6.00	7.18	8.12	9.03	9.78	10.5	11.1	11.7	12.2	12.7
	7.50	**9.9**	**11.7**	**13.2**	**14.5**	**15.8**	**16.9**	**17.9**	**18.9**	**19.8**	**21.**
9	4.03	5.34	6.31	7.11	7.80	8.41	8.95	9.45	9.91	10.3	10.7
	6.54	**8.5**	**9.9**	**11.1**	**12.1**	**13.1**	**13.9**	**14.7**	**15.3**	**16.0**	**16.6**
10	3.72	4.85	5.67	6.34	6.92	7.42	7.87	8.28	8.66	9.01	9.34
	5.85	**7.4**	**8.6**	**9.6**	**10.4**	**11.1**	**11.8**	**12.4**	**12.9**	**13.4**	**13.9**
12	3.28	4.16	4.79	5.30	5.72	6.09	6.42	6.72	7.00	7.25	7.48
	4.91	**6.1**	**6.9**	**7.6**	**8.2**	**8.7**	**9.1**	**9.5**	**9.9**	**10.2**	**10.6**
15	2.86	3.54	4.01	4.37	4.68	4.95	5.19	5.40	5.59	5.77	5.93
	4.07	**4.9**	**5.5**	**6.0**	**6.4**	**6.7**	**7.1**	**7.3**	**7.5**	**7.8**	**8.0**
20	2.46	2.95	3.29	3.54	3.76	3.94	4.10	4.24	4.37	4.49	4.59
	3.32	**3.8**	**4.3**	**4.6**	**4.9**	**5.1**	**5.3**	**5.5**	**5.6**	**5.8**	**5.9**
30	2.07	2.40	2.61	2.78	2.91	3.02	3.12	3.21	3.29	3.36	3.39
	2.63	**3.0**	**3.3**	**3.5**	**3.6**	**3.7**	**3.8**	**3.9**	**4.0**	**4.1**	**4.2**
60	1.67	1.85	1.96	2.04	2.11	2.17	2.22	2.26	2.30	2.33	2.36
	1.96	**2.2**	**2.3**	**2.4**	**2.4**	**2.5**	**2.5**	**2.6**	**2.6**	**2.7**	**2.7**

TABLE B.4   THE *F* DISTRIBUTION*

*Table entries in lightface type are critical values for the .05 level of significance.
Boldface type values are for the .01 level of significance.

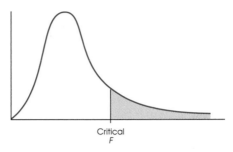

Critical
F

Degrees of Freedom: Denominator	\ Degrees of Freedom: Numerator														
	1	2	3	4	5	6	7	8	9	10	11	12	14	16	20
1	161	200	216	225	230	234	237	239	241	242	243	244	245	246	248
	4052	**4999**	**5403**	**5625**	**5764**	**5859**	**5928**	**5981**	**6022**	**6056**	**6082**	**6106**	**6142**	**6169**	**6208**
2	18.51	19.00	19.16	19.25	19.30	19.33	19.36	19.37	19.38	19.39	19.40	19.41	19.42	19.43	19.44
	98.49	**99.00**	**99.17**	**99.25**	**99.30**	**99.33**	**99.34**	**99.36**	**99.38**	**99.40**	**99.41**	**99.42**	**99.43**	**99.44**	**99.45**
3	10.13	9.55	9.28	9.12	9.01	8.94	8.88	8.84	8.81	8.78	8.76	8.74	8.71	8.69	8.66
	34.12	**30.92**	**29.46**	**28.71**	**28.24**	**27.91**	**27.67**	**27.49**	**27.34**	**27.23**	**27.13**	**27.05**	**26.92**	**26.83**	**26.69**
4	7.71	6.94	6.59	6.39	6.26	6.16	6.09	6.04	6.00	5.96	5.93	5.91	5.87	5.84	5.80
	21.20	**18.00**	**16.69**	**15.98**	**15.52**	**15.21**	**14.98**	**14.80**	**14.66**	**14.54**	**14.45**	**14.37**	**14.24**	**14.15**	**14.02**
5	6.61	5.79	5.41	5.19	5.05	4.95	4.88	4.82	4.78	4.74	4.70	4.68	4.64	4.60	4.56
	16.26	**13.27**	**12.06**	**11.39**	**10.97**	**10.67**	**10.45**	**10.27**	**10.15**	**10.05**	**9.96**	**9.89**	**9.77**	**9.68**	**9.55**
6	5.99	5.14	4.76	4.53	4.39	4.28	4.21	4.15	4.10	4.06	4.03	4.00	3.96	3.92	3.87
	13.74	**10.92**	**9.78**	**9.15**	**8.75**	**8.47**	**8.26**	**8.10**	**7.98**	**7.87**	**7.79**	**7.72**	**7.60**	**7.52**	**7.39**
7	5.59	4.74	4.35	4.12	3.97	3.87	3.79	3.73	3.68	3.63	3.60	3.57	3.52	3.49	3.44
	12.25	**9.55**	**8.45**	**7.85**	**7.46**	**7.19**	**7.00**	**6.84**	**6.71**	**6.62**	**6.54**	**6.47**	**6.35**	**6.27**	**6.15**
8	5.32	4.46	4.07	3.84	3.69	3.58	3.50	3.44	3.39	3.34	3.31	3.28	3.23	3.20	3.15
	11.26	**8.65**	**7.59**	**7.01**	**6.63**	**6.37**	**6.19**	**6.03**	**5.91**	**5.82**	**5.74**	**5.67**	**5.56**	**5.48**	**5.36**
9	5.12	4.26	3.86	3.63	3.48	3.37	3.29	3.23	3.18	3.13	3.10	3.07	3.02	2.98	2.93
	10.56	**8.02**	**6.99**	**6.42**	**6.06**	**5.80**	**5.62**	**5.47**	**5.35**	**5.26**	**5.18**	**5.11**	**5.00**	**4.92**	**4.80**
10	4.96	4.10	3.71	3.48	3.33	3.22	3.14	3.07	3.02	2.97	2.94	2.91	2.86	2.82	2.77
	10.04	**7.56**	**6.55**	**5.99**	**5.64**	**5.39**	**5.21**	**5.06**	**4.95**	**4.85**	**4.78**	**4.71**	**4.60**	**4.52**	**4.41**
11	4.84	3.98	3.59	3.36	3.20	3.09	3.01	2.95	2.90	2.86	2.82	2.79	2.74	2.70	2.65
	9.65	**7.20**	**6.22**	**5.67**	**5.32**	**5.07**	**4.88**	**4.74**	**4.63**	**4.54**	**4.46**	**4.40**	**4.29**	**4.21**	**4.10**
12	4.75	3.88	3.49	3.26	3.11	3.00	2.92	2.85	2.80	2.76	2.72	2.69	2.64	2.60	2.54
	9.33	**6.93**	**5.95**	**5.41**	**5.06**	**4.82**	**4.65**	**4.50**	**4.39**	**4.30**	**4.22**	**4.16**	**4.05**	**3.98**	**3.86**
13	4.67	3.80	3.41	3.18	3.02	2.92	2.84	2.77	2.72	2.67	2.63	2.60	2.55	2.51	2.46
	9.07	**6.70**	**5.74**	**5.20**	**4.86**	**4.62**	**4.44**	**4.30**	**4.19**	**4.10**	**4.02**	**3.96**	**3.85**	**3.78**	**3.67**
14	4.60	3.74	3.34	3.11	2.96	2.85	2.77	2.70	2.65	2.60	2.56	2.53	2.48	2.44	2.39
	8.86	**6.51**	**5.56**	**5.03**	**4.69**	**4.46**	**4.28**	**4.14**	**4.03**	**3.94**	**3.86**	**3.80**	**3.70**	**3.62**	**3.51**
15	4.54	3.68	3.29	3.06	2.90	2.79	2.70	2.64	2.59	2.55	2.51	2.48	2.43	2.39	2.33
	8.68	**6.36**	**5.42**	**4.89**	**4.56**	**4.32**	**4.14**	**4.00**	**3.89**	**3.80**	**3.73**	**3.67**	**3.56**	**3.48**	**3.36**
16	4.49	3.63	3.24	3.01	2.85	2.74	2.66	2.59	2.54	2.49	2.45	2.42	2.37	2.33	2.28
	8.53	**6.23**	**5.29**	**4.77**	**4.44**	**4.20**	**4.03**	**3.89**	**3.78**	**3.69**	**3.61**	**3.55**	**3.45**	**3.37**	**3.25**
17	4.45	3.59	3.20	2.96	2.81	2.70	2.62	2.55	2.50	2.45	2.41	2.38	2.33	2.29	2.23
	8.40	**6.11**	**5.18**	**4.67**	**4.34**	**4.10**	**3.93**	**3.79**	**3.68**	**3.59**	**3.52**	**3.45**	**3.35**	**3.27**	**3.16**
18	4.41	3.55	3.16	2.93	2.77	2.66	2.58	2.51	2.46	2.41	2.37	2.34	2.29	2.25	2.19
	8.28	**6.01**	**5.09**	**4.58**	**4.25**	**4.01**	**3.85**	**3.71**	**3.60**	**3.51**	**3.44**	**3.37**	**3.27**	**3.19**	**3.07**

TABLE B.4   (continued)

Degrees of Freedom: Denominator	Degrees of Freedom: Numerator														
	1	2	3	4	5	6	7	8	9	10	11	12	14	16	20
19	4.38	3.52	3.13	2.90	2.74	2.63	2.55	2.48	2.43	2.38	2.34	2.31	2.26	2.21	2.15
	8.18	**5.93**	**5.01**	**4.50**	**4.17**	**3.94**	**3.77**	**3.63**	**3.52**	**3.43**	**3.36**	**3.30**	**3.19**	**3.12**	**3.00**
20	4.35	3.49	3.10	2.87	2.71	2.60	2.52	2.45	2.40	2.35	2.31	2.28	2.23	2.18	2.12
	8.10	**5.85**	**4.94**	**4.43**	**4.10**	**3.87**	**3.71**	**3.56**	**3.45**	**3.37**	**3.30**	**3.23**	**3.13**	**3.05**	**2.94**
21	4.32	3.47	3.07	2.84	2.68	2.57	2.49	2.42	2.37	2.32	2.28	2.25	2.20	2.15	2.09
	8.02	**5.78**	**4.87**	**4.37**	**4.04**	**3.81**	**3.65**	**3.51**	**3.40**	**3.31**	**3.24**	**3.17**	**3.07**	**2.99**	**2.88**
22	4.30	3.44	3.05	2.82	2.66	2.55	2.47	2.40	2.35	2.30	2.26	2.23	2.18	2.13	2.07
	7.94	**5.72**	**4.82**	**4.31**	**3.99**	**3.76**	**3.59**	**3.45**	**3.35**	**3.26**	**3.18**	**3.12**	**3.02**	**2.94**	**2.83**
23	4.28	3.42	3.03	2.80	2.64	2.53	2.45	2.38	2.32	2.28	2.24	2.20	2.14	2.10	2.04
	7.88	**5.66**	**4.76**	**4.26**	**3.94**	**3.71**	**3.54**	**3.41**	**3.30**	**3.21**	**3.14**	**3.07**	**2.97**	**2.89**	**2.78**
24	4.26	3.40	3.01	2.78	2.62	2.51	2.43	2.36	2.30	2.26	2.22	2.18	2.13	2.09	2.02
	7.82	**5.61**	**4.72**	**4.22**	**3.90**	**3.67**	**3.50**	**3.36**	**3.25**	**3.17**	**3.09**	**3.03**	**2.93**	**2.85**	**2.74**
25	4.24	3.38	2.99	2.76	2.60	2.49	2.41	2.34	2.28	2.24	2.20	2.16	2.11	2.06	2.00
	7.77	**5.57**	**4.68**	**4.18**	**3.86**	**3.63**	**3.46**	**3.32**	**3.21**	**3.13**	**3.05**	**2.99**	**2.89**	**2.81**	**2.70**
26	4.22	3.37	2.98	2.74	2.59	2.47	2.39	2.32	2.27	2.22	2.18	2.15	2.10	2.05	1.99
	7.72	**5.53**	**4.64**	**4.14**	**3.82**	**3.59**	**3.42**	**3.29**	**3.17**	**3.09**	**3.02**	**2.96**	**2.86**	**2.77**	**2.66**
27	4.21	3.35	2.96	2.73	2.57	2.46	2.37	2.30	2.25	2.20	2.16	2.13	2.08	2.03	1.97
	7.68	**5.49**	**4.60**	**4.11**	**3.79**	**3.56**	**3.39**	**3.26**	**3.14**	**3.06**	**2.98**	**2.93**	**2.83**	**2.74**	**2.63**
28	4.20	3.34	2.95	2.71	2.56	2.44	2.36	2.29	2.24	2.19	2.15	2.12	2.06	2.02	1.96
	7.64	**5.45**	**4.57**	**4.07**	**3.76**	**3.53**	**3.36**	**3.23**	**3.11**	**3.03**	**2.95**	**2.90**	**2.80**	**2.71**	**2.60**
29	4.18	3.33	2.93	2.70	2.54	2.43	2.35	2.28	2.22	2.18	2.14	2.10	2.05	2.00	1.94
	7.60	**5.42**	**4.54**	**4.04**	**3.73**	**3.50**	**3.33**	**3.20**	**3.08**	**3.00**	**2.92**	**2.87**	**2.77**	**2.68**	**2.57**
30	4.17	3.32	2.92	2.69	2.53	2.42	2.34	2.27	2.21	2.16	2.12	2.09	2.04	1.99	1.93
	7.56	**5.39**	**4.51**	**4.02**	**3.70**	**3.47**	**3.30**	**3.17**	**3.06**	**2.98**	**2.90**	**2.84**	**2.74**	**2.66**	**2.55**
32	4.15	3.30	2.90	2.67	2.51	2.40	2.32	2.25	2.19	2.14	2.10	2.07	2.02	1.97	1.91
	7.50	**5.34**	**4.46**	**3.97**	**3.66**	**3.42**	**3.25**	**3.12**	**3.01**	**2.94**	**2.86**	**2.80**	**2.70**	**2.62**	**2.51**
34	4.13	3.28	2.88	2.65	2.49	2.38	2.30	2.23	2.17	2.12	2.08	2.05	2.00	1.95	1.89
	7.44	**5.29**	**4.42**	**3.93**	**3.61**	**3.38**	**3.21**	**3.08**	**2.97**	**2.89**	**2.82**	**2.76**	**2.66**	**2.58**	**2.47**
36	4.11	3.26	2.86	2.63	2.48	2.36	2.28	2.21	2.15	2.10	2.06	2.03	1.98	1.93	1.87
	7.39	**5.25**	**4.38**	**3.89**	**3.58**	**3.35**	**3.18**	**3.04**	**2.94**	**2.86**	**2.78**	**2.72**	**2.62**	**2.54**	**2.43**
38	4.10	3.25	2.85	2.62	2.46	2.35	2.26	2.19	2.14	2.09	2.05	2.02	1.96	1.92	1.85
	7.35	**5.21**	**4.34**	**3.86**	**3.54**	**3.32**	**3.15**	**3.02**	**2.91**	**2.82**	**2.75**	**2.69**	**2.59**	**2.51**	**2.40**
40	4.08	3.23	2.84	2.61	2.45	2.34	2.25	2.18	2.12	2.07	2.04	2.00	1.95	1.90	1.84
	7.31	**5.18**	**4.31**	**3.83**	**3.51**	**3.29**	**3.12**	**2.99**	**2.88**	**2.80**	**2.73**	**2.66**	**2.56**	**2.49**	**2.37**
42	4.07	3.22	2.83	2.59	2.44	2.32	2.24	2.17	2.11	2.06	2.02	1.99	1.94	1.89	1.82
	7.27	**5.15**	**4.29**	**3.80**	**3.49**	**3.26**	**3.10**	**2.96**	**2.86**	**2.77**	**2.70**	**2.64**	**2.54**	**2.46**	**2.35**

TABLE B.4   (continued)

Degrees of Freedom: Denominator	Degrees of Freedom: Numerator														
	1	2	3	4	5	6	7	8	9	10	11	12	14	16	20
44	4.06	3.21	2.82	2.58	2.43	2.31	2.23	2.16	2.10	2.05	2.01	1.98	1.92	1.88	1.81
	7.24	**5.12**	**4.26**	**3.78**	**3.46**	**3.24**	**3.07**	**2.94**	**2.84**	**2.75**	**2.68**	**2.62**	**2.52**	**2.44**	**2.32**
46	4.05	3.20	2.81	2.57	2.42	2.30	2.22	2.14	2.09	2.04	2.00	1.97	1.91	1.87	1.80
	7.21	**5.10**	**4.24**	**3.76**	**3.44**	**3.22**	**3.05**	**2.92**	**2.82**	**2.73**	**2.66**	**2.60**	**2.50**	**2.42**	**2.30**
48	4.04	3.19	2.80	2.56	2.41	2.30	2.21	2.14	2.08	2.03	1.99	1.96	1.90	1.86	1.79
	7.19	**5.08**	**4.22**	**3.74**	**3.42**	**3.20**	**3.04**	**2.90**	**2.80**	**2.71**	**2.64**	**2.58**	**2.48**	**2.40**	**2.28**
50	4.03	3.18	2.79	2.56	2.40	2.29	2.20	2.13	2.07	2.02	1.98	1.95	1.90	1.85	1.78
	7.17	**5.06**	**4.20**	**3.72**	**3.41**	**3.18**	**3.02**	**2.88**	**2.78**	**2.70**	**2.62**	**2.56**	**2.46**	**2.39**	**2.26**
55	4.02	3.17	2.78	2.54	2.38	2.27	2.18	2.11	2.05	2.00	1.97	1.93	1.88	1.83	1.76
	7.12	**5.01**	**4.16**	**3.68**	**3.37**	**3.15**	**2.98**	**2.85**	**2.75**	**2.66**	**2.59**	**2.53**	**2.43**	**2.35**	**2.23**
60	4.00	3.15	2.76	2.52	2.37	2.25	2.17	2.10	2.04	1.99	1.95	1.92	1.86	1.81	1.75
	7.08	**4.98**	**4.13**	**3.65**	**3.34**	**3.12**	**2.95**	**2.82**	**2.72**	**2.63**	**2.56**	**2.50**	**2.40**	**2.32**	**2.20**
65	3.99	3.14	2.75	2.51	2.36	2.24	2.15	2.08	2.02	1.98	1.94	1.90	1.85	1.80	1.73
	7.04	**4.95**	**4.10**	**3.62**	**3.31**	**3.09**	**2.93**	**2.79**	**2.70**	**2.61**	**2.54**	**2.47**	**2.37**	**2.30**	**2.18**
70	3.98	3.13	2.74	2.50	2.35	2.23	2.14	2.07	2.01	1.97	1.93	1.89	1.84	1.79	1.72
	7.01	**4.92**	**4.08**	**3.60**	**3.29**	**3.07**	**2.91**	**2.77**	**2.67**	**2.59**	**2.51**	**2.45**	**2.35**	**2.28**	**2.15**
80	3.96	3.11	2.72	2.48	2.33	2.21	2.12	2.05	1.99	1.95	1.91	1.88	1.82	1.77	1.70
	6.96	**4.88**	**4.04**	**3.56**	**3.25**	**3.04**	**2.87**	**2.74**	**2.64**	**2.55**	**2.48**	**2.41**	**2.32**	**2.24**	**2.11**
100	3.94	3.09	2.70	2.46	2.30	2.19	2.10	2.03	1.97	1.92	1.88	1.85	1.79	1.75	1.68
	6.90	**4.82**	**3.98**	**3.51**	**3.20**	**2.99**	**2.82**	**2.69**	**2.59**	**2.51**	**2.43**	**2.36**	**2.26**	**2.19**	**2.06**
125	3.92	3.07	2.68	2.44	2.29	2.17	2.08	2.01	1.95	1.90	1.86	1.83	1.77	1.72	1.65
	6.84	**4.78**	**3.94**	**3.47**	**3.17**	**2.95**	**2.79**	**2.65**	**2.56**	**2.47**	**2.40**	**2.33**	**2.23**	**2.15**	**2.03**
150	3.91	3.06	2.67	2.43	2.27	2.16	2.07	2.00	1.94	1.89	1.85	1.82	1.76	1.71	1.64
	6.81	**4.75**	**3.91**	**3.44**	**3.14**	**2.92**	**2.76**	**2.62**	**2.53**	**2.44**	**2.37**	**2.30**	**2.20**	**2.12**	**2.00**
200	3.89	3.04	2.65	2.41	2.26	2.14	2.05	1.98	1.92	1.87	1.83	1.80	1.74	1.69	1.62
	6.76	**4.71**	**3.88**	**3.41**	**3.11**	**2.90**	**2.73**	**2.60**	**2.50**	**2.41**	**2.34**	**2.28**	**2.17**	**2.09**	**1.97**
400	3.86	3.02	2.62	2.39	2.23	2.12	2.03	1.96	1.90	1.85	1.81	1.78	1.72	1.67	1.60
	6.70	**4.66**	**3.83**	**3.36**	**3.06**	**2.85**	**2.69**	**2.55**	**2.46**	**2.37**	**2.29**	**2.23**	**2.12**	**2.04**	**1.92**
1000	3.85	3.00	2.61	2.38	2.22	2.10	2.02	1.95	1.89	1.84	1.80	1.76	1.70	1.65	1.58
	6.66	**4.62**	**3.80**	**3.34**	**3.04**	**2.82**	**2.66**	**2.53**	**2.43**	**2.34**	**2.26**	**2.20**	**2.09**	**2.01**	**1.89**
∞	3.84	2.99	2.60	2.37	2.21	2.09	2.01	1.94	1.88	1.83	1.79	1.75	1.69	1.64	1.57
	6.64	**4.60**	**3.78**	**3.32**	**3.02**	**2.80**	**2.64**	**2.51**	**2.41**	**2.32**	**2.24**	**2.18**	**2.07**	**1.99**	**1.87**

Table A14 of *Statistical Methods,* 7th ed. by George W. Snedecor and William G. Cochran. Copyright © 1980 by the Iowa State University Press, 2121 South State Avenue, Ames, Iowa 50010. Reprinted with permission of the Iowa State University Press.

TABLE B.5 THE STUDENTIZED RANGE STATISTIC (*q*)*

*The critical values for *q* corresponding to α = .05 (lightface type) and α = .01 (boldface type).

df for Error Term	k = Number of Treatments										
	2	3	4	5	6	7	8	9	10	11	12
5	3.64	4.60	5.22	5.67	6.03	6.33	6.58	6.80	6.99	7.17	7.32
	5.70	**6.98**	**7.80**	**8.42**	**8.91**	**9.32**	**9.67**	**9.97**	**10.24**	**10.48**	**10.70**
6	3.46	4.34	4.90	5.30	5.63	5.90	6.12	6.32	6.49	6.65	6.79
	5.24	**6.33**	**7.03**	**7.56**	**7.97**	**8.32**	**8.61**	**8.87**	**9.10**	**9.30**	**9.48**
7	3.34	4.16	4.68	5.06	5.36	5.61	5.82	6.00	6.16	6.30	6.43
	4.95	**5.92**	**6.54**	**7.01**	**7.37**	**7.68**	**7.94**	**8.17**	**8.37**	**8.55**	**8.71**
8	3.26	4.04	4.53	4.89	5.17	5.40	5.60	5.77	5.92	6.05	6.18
	4.75	**5.64**	**6.20**	**6.62**	**6.96**	**7.24**	**7.47**	**7.68**	**7.86**	**8.03**	**8.18**
9	3.20	3.95	4.41	4.76	5.02	5.24	5.43	5.59	5.74	5.87	5.98
	4.60	**5.43**	**5.96**	**6.35**	**6.66**	**6.91**	**7.13**	**7.33**	**7.49**	**7.65**	**7.78**
10	3.15	3.88	4.33	4.65	4.91	5.12	5.30	5.46	5.60	5.72	5.83
	4.48	**5.27**	**5.77**	**6.14**	**6.43**	**6.67**	**6.87**	**7.05**	**7.21**	**7.36**	**7.49**
11	3.11	3.82	4.26	4.57	4.82	5.03	5.20	5.35	5.49	5.61	5.71
	4.39	**5.15**	**5.62**	**5.97**	**6.25**	**6.48**	**6.67**	**6.84**	**6.99**	**7.13**	**7.25**
12	3.08	3.77	4.20	4.51	4.75	4.95	5.12	5.27	5.39	5.51	5.61
	4.32	**5.05**	**5.50**	**5.84**	**6.10**	**6.32**	**6.51**	**6.67**	**6.81**	**6.94**	**7.06**
13	3.06	3.73	4.15	4.45	4.69	4.88	5.05	5.19	5.32	5.43	5.53
	4.26	**4.96**	**5.40**	**5.73**	**5.98**	**6.19**	**6.37**	**6.53**	**6.67**	**6.79**	**6.90**
14	3.03	3.70	4.11	4.41	4.64	4.83	4.99	5.13	5.25	5.36	5.46
	4.21	**4.89**	**5.32**	**5.63**	**5.88**	**6.08**	**6.26**	**6.41**	**6.54**	**6.66**	**6.77**
15	3.01	3.67	4.08	4.37	4.59	4.78	4.94	5.08	5.20	5.31	5.40
	4.17	**4.84**	**5.25**	**5.56**	**5.80**	**5.99**	**6.16**	**6.31**	**6.44**	**6.55**	**6.66**
16	3.00	3.65	4.05	4.33	4.56	4.74	4.90	5.03	5.15	5.26	5.35
	4.13	**4.79**	**5.19**	**5.49**	**5.72**	**5.92**	**6.08**	**6.22**	**6.35**	**6.46**	**6.56**
17	2.98	3.63	4.02	4.30	4.52	4.70	4.86	4.99	5.11	5.21	5.31
	4.10	**4.74**	**5.14**	**5.43**	**5.66**	**5.85**	**6.01**	**6.15**	**6.27**	**6.38**	**6.48**
18	2.97	3.61	4.00	4.28	4.49	4.67	4.82	4.96	5.07	5.17	5.27
	4.07	**4.70**	**5.09**	**5.38**	**5.60**	**5.79**	**5.94**	**6.08**	**6.20**	**6.31**	**6.41**
19	2.96	3.59	3.98	4.25	4.47	4.65	4.79	4.92	5.04	5.14	5.23
	4.05	**4.67**	**5.05**	**5.33**	**5.55**	**5.73**	**5.89**	**6.02**	**6.14**	**6.25**	**6.34**
20	2.95	3.58	3.96	4.23	4.45	4.62	4.77	4.90	5.01	5.11	5.20
	4.02	**4.64**	**5.02**	**5.29**	**5.51**	**5.69**	**5.84**	**5.97**	**6.09**	**6.19**	**6.28**
24	2.92	3.53	3.90	4.17	4.37	4.54	4.68	4.81	4.92	5.01	5.10
	3.96	**4.55**	**4.91**	**5.17**	**5.37**	**5.54**	**5.69**	**5.81**	**5.92**	**6.02**	**6.11**
30	2.89	3.49	3.85	4.10	4.30	4.46	4.60	4.72	4.82	4.92	5.00
	3.89	**4.45**	**4.80**	**5.05**	**5.24**	**5.40**	**5.54**	**5.65**	**5.76**	**5.85**	**5.93**
40	2.86	3.44	3.79	4.04	4.23	4.39	4.52	4.63	4.73	4.82	4.90
	3.82	**4.37**	**4.70**	**4.93**	**5.11**	**5.26**	**5.39**	**5.50**	**5.60**	**5.69**	**5.76**
60	2.83	3.40	3.74	3.98	4.16	4.31	4.44	4.55	4.65	4.73	4.81
	3.76	**4.28**	**4.59**	**4.82**	**4.99**	**5.13**	**5.25**	**5.36**	**5.45**	**5.53**	**5.60**
120	2.80	3.36	3.68	3.92	4.10	4.24	4.36	4.47	4.56	4.64	4.71
	3.70	**4.20**	**4.50**	**4.71**	**4.87**	**5.01**	**5.12**	**5.21**	**5.30**	**5.37**	**5.44**
∞	2.77	3.31	3.63	3.86	4.03	4.17	4.28	4.39	4.47	4.55	4.62
	3.64	**4.12**	**4.40**	**4.60**	**4.76**	**4.88**	**4.99**	**5.08**	**5.16**	**5.23**	**5.29**

TABLE B.6   CRITICAL VALUES FOR THE PEARSON CORRELATION*

---

*To be significant, the sample correlation, r, must be greater than or equal to the critical value in the table.

	Level of Significance for One-Tailed Test			
	.05	.025	.01	.005
	Level of Significance for Two-Tailed Test			
df = n − 2	.10	.05	.02	.01
1	.988	.997	.9995	.9999
2	.900	.950	.980	.990
3	.805	.878	.934	.959
4	.729	.811	.882	.917
5	.669	.754	.833	.874
6	.622	.707	.789	.834
7	.582	.666	.750	.798
8	.549	.632	.716	.765
9	.521	.602	.685	.735
10	.497	.576	.658	.708
11	.476	.553	.634	.684
12	.458	.532	.612	.661
13	.441	.514	.592	.641
14	.426	.497	.574	.623
15	.412	.482	.558	.606
16	.400	.468	.542	.590
17	.389	.456	.528	.575
18	.378	.444	.516	.561
19	.369	.433	.503	.549
20	.360	.423	.492	.537
21	.352	.413	.482	.526
22	.344	.404	.472	.515
23	.337	.396	.462	.505
24	.330	.388	.453	.496
25	.323	.381	.445	.487
26	.317	.374	.437	.479
27	.311	.367	.430	.471
28	.306	.361	.423	.463
29	.301	.355	.416	.456
30	.296	.349	.409	.449
35	.275	.325	.381	.418
40	.257	.304	.358	.393
45	.243	.288	.338	.372
50	.231	.273	.322	.354
60	.211	.250	.295	.325
70	.195	.232	.274	.302
80	.183	.217	.256	.283
90	.173	.205	.242	.267
100	.164	.195	.230	.254

Table VI of R.A. Fisher and F. Yates, *Statistical Tables for Biological, Agricultural and Medical Research,* 6th ed. London: Longman Group Ltd., 1974 (previously published by Oliver and Boyd Ltd., Edinburgh). Adapted and reprinted with permission of the Addison Wesley Longman Publishing Co.

TABLE B.7   THE CHI-SQUARE DISTRIBUTION*

*The table entries are critical values of χ^2.

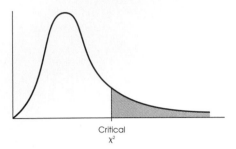

Critical
χ^2

df	Proportion in Critical Region				
	0.10	0.05	0.025	0.01	0.005
1	2.71	3.84	5.02	6.63	7.88
2	4.61	5.99	7.38	9.21	10.60
3	6.25	7.81	9.35	11.34	12.84
4	7.78	9.49	11.14	13.28	14.86
5	9.24	11.07	12.83	15.09	16.75
6	10.64	12.59	14.45	16.81	18.55
7	12.02	14.07	16.01	18.48	20.28
8	13.36	15.51	17.53	20.09	21.96
9	14.68	16.92	19.02	21.67	23.59
10	15.99	18.31	20.48	23.21	25.19
11	17.28	19.68	21.92	24.72	26.76
12	18.55	21.03	23.34	26.22	28.30
13	19.81	22.36	24.74	27.69	29.82
14	21.06	23.68	26.12	29.14	31.32
15	22.31	25.00	27.49	30.58	32.80
16	23.54	26.30	28.85	32.00	34.27
17	24.77	27.59	30.19	33.41	35.72
18	25.99	28.87	31.53	34.81	37.16
19	27.20	30.14	32.85	36.19	38.58
20	28.41	31.41	34.17	37.57	40.00
21	29.62	32.67	35.48	38.93	41.40
22	30.81	33.92	36.78	40.29	42.80
23	32.01	35.17	38.08	41.64	44.18
24	33.20	36.42	39.36	42.98	45.56
25	34.38	37.65	40.65	44.31	46.93
26	35.56	38.89	41.92	45.64	48.29
27	36.74	40.11	43.19	46.96	49.64
28	37.92	41.34	44.46	48.28	50.99
29	39.09	42.56	45.72	49.59	52.34
30	40.26	43.77	46.98	50.89	53.67
40	51.81	55.76	59.34	63.69	66.77
50	63.17	67.50	71.42	76.15	79.49
60	74.40	79.08	83.30	88.38	91.95
70	85.53	90.53	95.02	100.42	104.22
80	96.58	101.88	106.63	112.33	116.32
90	107.56	113.14	118.14	124.12	128.30
100	118.50	124.34	129.56	135.81	140.17

Solutions for
Odd-Numbered Problems
in the Text

Note: Many of the problems in the text require several stages of computation. At each stage there is an opportunity for rounding answers. Depending on the exact sequence of operations used to solve a problem, different individuals will round their answers at different times and in different ways. As a result, you or your students may obtain answers that are slightly different from those presented here. To help minimize this problem, we have tried to include the numerical values obtained at different stages of complex problems rather than presenting a single final answer.

CHAPTER 1: **INTRODUCTION TO STATISTICS**

1. Descriptive statistics are used to simplify and summarize data. Inferential statistics use sample data to make general conclusions about populations.

3. **a.** The population is the entire set of laboratory rats.
   b. The sample is the group of 25 rats that were tested in the study.

5. This is an experimental study. Dr. Jones has created two treatment conditions by manipulating the quality of breakfast and has controlled most other variables by dividing the boys into "equivalent" groups. Dr. Jones will compare the two groups of scores.

7. You cannot automatically conclude that the hormone caused the difference. Even when two samples are selected from the same population, you should not expect the two samples to have exactly the same statistics. The samples consist of different individuals with different scores and the two samples will have different statistics. The naturally occurring differences between a sample and it population, and the differences between two samples, are called *sampling error*.

9. The distinguishing characteristics of the experimental method are *manipulation* and *control*. In the experimental method, the researcher manipulates one variable and observes a second variable. All other variables are controlled to prevent them from affecting the outcome.

11. **a.** The dependent variable is the number of colds each subject has during the winter.
    b. Discrete.
    c. Ratio scale (zero means none).

13. The researcher manipulates the *independent variable* by changing its value to create two (or more) treatment conditions. The *dependent variable* is then measured for a group of individuals to obtain a set of scores within each condition.

15. **a.** The independent variable is whether the rats receive the antioxidant supplements, and the dependent variable is amount of time needed to find the submerged platform.
    b. Time is measured on a ratio scale.

17. A hypothetical construct is an internal attribute or characteristic that cannot be observed directly. Because constructs cannot be directly observed or measured, researchers must find some indirect method for measuring and defining them so that constructs can be examined in research studies. An operational definition provides an indirect method for measuring and defining a construct.

19. **a.** $\Sigma X + 3$
    b. $\Sigma(X - 2)^2$
    c. $\Sigma X^2 - 10$

21. **a.** $\Sigma X = 11$
    b. $\Sigma X^2 = 45$
    c. $\Sigma(X + 1) = 15$
    d. $\Sigma(X + 1)^2 = 71$

23. **a.** $\Sigma X^2 = 84$
    b. $(\Sigma X)^2 = 144$
    c. $\Sigma(X - 3) = 0$
    d. $\Sigma(X - 3)^2 = 48$

25. **a.** $\Sigma X = 22$
    b. $\Sigma Y = 20$
    c. $\Sigma XY = 79$

CHAPTER 2: **FREQUENCY DISTRIBUTIONS**

1. A grouped frequency distribution is used when the original scale of measurement consists of more categories than can be listed simply in a regular table. Around 20 or more categories is generally considered too many for a regular table.

3.

X	f	p	%
9	1	.05	5
8	2	.10	10
7	4	.20	20
6	5	.25	25
5	3	.15	15
4	2	.10	10
3	2	.10	10
2	1	.05	5

5. a.

X	f
55–59	2
50–54	2
45–49	4
40–44	3
35–39	3
30–34	5
25–29	1
20–24	4
15–19	2
10–14	1

b.

X	f
50–59	4
40–49	7
30–39	8
20–29	5
10–19	3

7. a.

X	f
7	2
6	2
5	3
4	7
3	3
2	2
1	1

b.

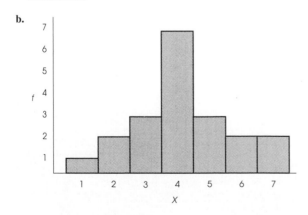

9. a.

X	f
10	1
9	0
8	1
7	3
6	1
5	2
4	5
3	4
2	2
1	1

b.

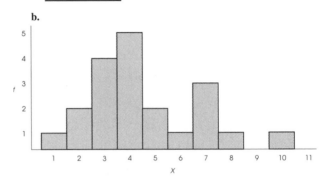

11. A bar graph leaves a space between adjacent bars and is used with data from nominal or ordinal scales. In a histogram, adjacent bars touch at the real limits. Histograms are used to display data from interval or ratio scales.

13.

X	f	p	%
6	2	.08	8%
5	3	.12	12%
4	3	.12	12%
3	4	.16	16%
2	5	.20	20%
1	8	.32	32%

The distribution is positively skewed.

15. a. $n = 10$

b. $\Sigma X = 25$

c. $\Sigma X^2 = 75$

17. a. A bar graph should be used for measurements from an ordinal scale.

b.

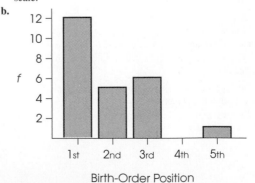

Birth-Order Position

19. a. Section I

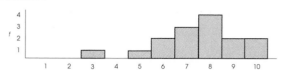

Section II

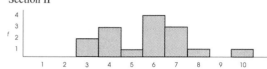

The scores in Section I are centered around $X = 8$ and form a negatively skewed distribution. In Section II, the scores are lower (centered around $X = 6$) and the distribution is more symmetrical with some tendency toward a positively skewed distribution.

21. a.

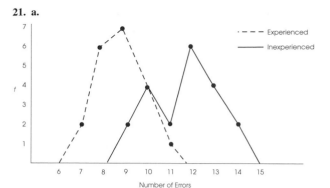

b. Yes, it appears that the inexperienced rats tend to make more errors than the experienced rats do.

CHAPTER 3: **CENTRAL TENDENCY**

1. The purpose of central tendency is to identify a single score that serves as the best representative for an entire distribution, usually a score from the center of the distribution.

3. The mean, median, and mode are identical for a symmetrical distribution with one mode.

5. With a skewed distribution, the extreme scores in the tail can displace the mean. Specifically, the mean is displaced away from the main pile of scores and moved out toward the tail. The result is that the mean is often not a very representative value.

7. $\Sigma X = 48$

9. The mean is $\frac{27}{10} = 2.7$, the median is 2.5, and the mode is 2.

11. The mean is $\frac{40}{12} = 3.33$, the median $= 3.50$, and the mode is 4.

13. The new mean is $\frac{198}{9} = 22$.

15. The new mean is $\frac{176}{8} = 22$. Changing $X = 14$ to $X = 30$ adds 16 points to ΣX.

17. The original set of ten scores has $\Sigma X = 90$. After one is removed, the eight remaining scores have $\Sigma X = 72$. The score that was removed must be $X = 18$.

19. The new mean is $\frac{42}{6} = 7$.

21. a. Median (a few extreme scores would distort the mean).
b. Mode (nominal scale).
c. Mean.

23. a.

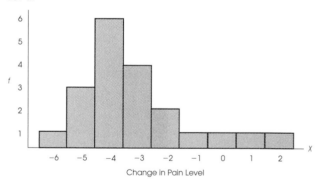

b. The mean difference in pain level is $M = \frac{-59}{20} = -2.95$. On average, pain decreased by 2.95 points.
c. Yes, the pain level appears to have decreased for nearly all participants.

25. The combined mean is $\frac{(56 + 36)}{10} = 9.2$.

CHAPTER 4: **VARIABILITY**

1. SS cannot be less than zero because it is computed by adding squared deviations. Squared deviations are always greater than or equal to zero.

3. A standard deviation of $s = 5$ indicates that the scores are scattered around the mean with the average distance between X and M equal to 5 points. More specifically, around 70% of the scores should be within 5 points of the mean and about 95% of the scores should be within 10 points of the mean.

5. a. *SS* is the sum of squared deviation scores.
  b. Variance is the mean squared deviation.
  c. Standard deviation is the square root of the variance. It provides a measure of the standard distance from the mean.

7. a. Your score is 5 points above the mean. If the standard deviation is 2, then your score is an extremely high value (out in the tail of the distribution). However, if the standard deviation is 10, then your score is only slightly above average. Thus, you would prefer $\sigma = 2$.
  b. If you are located 5 points below the mean then the situation is reversed. A standard deviation of 2 gives you an extremely low score, but with a standard deviation of 10 you are only slightly below average. Here, you would prefer $\sigma = 10$.

9. a. The range is 5 points, the interquartile range is 1 point (from 2.5 to 3.5), and the standard deviation is $\sqrt{1.25} = 1.12$.
  b. After adding two points to every score, the range is still 4, the interquartile range is still 1, and the standard deviation is still 1.12. Adding a constant to every score does not affect variability.

11. a. The mean is $M = 4$ and the standard deviation is $s = \sqrt{9} = 3$.
  b. The new mean is $M = 6$ and the new standard deviation is $\sqrt{49} = 7$.
  c. Changing one score changes both the mean and the standard deviation.

13. a. The definitional formula is easy to use when the mean is a whole number and there are relatively few scores.
  b. The computational formula is preferred when the mean is not a whole number.

15. a. $\Sigma X = 10$ and $\Sigma X^2 = 52$.
  b. $SS = 27$

17. a. With $\sigma = 20$, your sketch should show all four scores located near the center of the distribution (within one standard deviation of the mean).

b. With $\sigma = 2$, only one of the scores ($X = 47$) is located near the center of the distribution. All of the other scores are extreme values.

19. a.

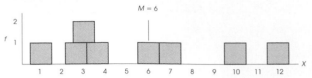

  b. The mean is $\dfrac{42}{7} = 6$ and the standard deviation appears to be about 4 or 5.
  c. $SS = 96$, $s^2 = 16$, $s = 4$

21. $SS = 8$, the sample variance is 1, and the standard deviation is 1.

23. a.

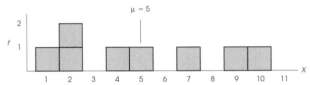

  b. The mean is $\dfrac{40}{8} = 5$ and the standard deviation appears to be about 3 or 4.
  c. $SS = 80$, $\sigma^2 = 10$, $\sigma = 3.16$.

25. $SS = 9$, the sample variance is 3, and the standard deviation is 1.73.

27. a. For the exercise group, $M = 3.125$ with $s = 1.25$. For the no exercise group, $M = 5.25$ with $s = 1.28$.
  b. On average, the exercise group appears to have fewer symptoms of depression.

CHAPTER 5: *z*-SCORES

1. a. Above the mean by 8 points.
  b. Above the mean by 2 points.
  c. Below the mean by 8 points.
  d. Below the mean by 2 points.

3. A *z*-score describes a precise location within a distribution. The sign of the *z*-score tells whether the location is above (+) or below (−) the mean, and the magnitude tells the distance from the mean in terms of the number of standard deviations.

5. a. $X = 49$.
  b. $X = 70$.
  c. $X = 86$.
  d. $X = 92$.

7.

X	z	X	z	X	z
65	0.56	70	1.11	53	−0.78
48	−1.33	75	1.67	58	−0.22

9. a.

X	z	X	z	X	z
43	0.25	49	0.75	52	1.00
34	−0.50	28	−1.00	64	2.00

b.

X	z	X	z	X	z
49	0.75	58	1.50	16	−2.00
37	−0.25	34	−0.50	55	1.25

11.

X	z	X	z	X	z
84	0.80	86	1.20	90	2.00
78	−0.40	77	−0.60	71	−1.80

13. $\sigma = 3$.

15. $\sigma = 8$.

17. $M = 56$.

19. $\mu = 60$ and $\sigma = 4$. The distance between the two scores is 10 points, which is equal to 2.5 standard deviations.

21. $X = 43$ corresponds to $z = 1.50$, and $X = 60$ corresponds to $z = 0.50$. $X = 43$ has a higher position in its distribution and should receive the higher grade.

23. $\sigma = 2$

25. a. $\mu = 4$ and $\sigma = 2$.
   b. & c.

Original X	z-score	Transformed X
6	1.00	60
1	−1.50	35
3	−0.50	45
4	0	50
7	1.50	65
3	−0.50	45

27. a. $X = 80$ ($z = -1.00$).
   b. $X = 40$ ($z = -3.00$).
   c. $X = 140$ ($z = 2.00$).
   d. $X = 110$ ($z = 0.50$).

CHAPTER 6: **PROBABILITY**

1. The two requirements for a random sample are: (1) each individual has an equal chance of being selected, and (2) if more than one individual is selected, the probabilities must stay constant for all selections.

3. a. $p = 30/50 = 0.60$.
   b. $p = 20/50 = 0.40$.
   c. $p = 10/50 = 0.20$.

5. a. $z = 1.28$.
   b. $z = 0.84$.
   c. $z = -0.84$.
   d. $z = -0.52$.

7. a. Tail to the right, $p = 0.0668$.
   b. Tail to the left, $p = 0.0401$.
   c. Tail to the right, $p = 0.4207$.
   d. Tail to the left, $p = 0.3085$.

9. a. $p(z > 1.00) = 0.1587$.
   b. $p(z > 0.80) = 0.2119$.
   c. $p(z < -0.25) = 0.4013$.
   d. $p(z < -1.25) = 0.1056$.

11. You cannot use the unit normal table to find proportions or z-scores because the distribution is not normal.

13. a. $p = 0.3830$.
   b. $p = 0.6826$.
   c. $p = 0.4332$.
   d. $p = 0.5586$.

15. a. $X = 628$.
   b. $X = 552$.
   c. $X = 525$.

17. a. Body to the left, $p = 0.6915$
   b. Body to the left, $p = 0.8849$
   c. Body to the right, $p = 0.5793$
   d. Body to the right, $p = 0.7881$

19. a. $z = 1.00, p = 0.1587$.
   b. $z = 2.00, p = 0.0228$.
   c. $z = 3.00, p = 0.0013$.

21. a. $z = 1.65, X = 124.75$ (IQ of 125 or higher).
   b. $z = 1.28, X = 119.2$ (IQ of 120 or higher).
   c. $z = 0.67, X = 110.05$ (IQ of 111 or higher).

23. a. $z = 1.00, p = 0.1587$.
   b. $z = -0.82, p = 0.2061$.

CHAPTER 7: **PROBABILITY AND SAMPLES**

1. With $n = 36$, the distribution of sample means will be approximately normal even if the population is not. The expected value is $\mu = 80$ and the standard error is $\frac{24}{6} = 4$.

3. a. The distribution of sample means consists of the sample means for all the possible random samples of a specific size (n) from a specific population.
   b. The expected value of M is the mean of the distribution of sample means (μ).
   c. The standard error of M is the standard deviation of the distribution of sample means ($\sigma_M = \frac{\sigma}{\sqrt{n}}$).

5. a. The standard error is 50 points.
   b. The standard error is 20 points.
   c. The standard error is 10 points.

7. a. The standard deviation is $\sigma = 5$.
   b. The standard deviation is $\sigma = 10$.
   c. The standard deviation is $\sigma = 50$.

9. a. $\sigma_M = 4$ and $z = -0.50$.
   b. $\sigma_M = 2$ and $z = -1.00$.
   c. $\sigma_M = 1$ and $z = -2.00$.

11. a. Standard error $= \dfrac{20}{\sqrt{4}} = 10$
   b. Standard error $= \dfrac{20}{\sqrt{16}} = 5$
   c. Standard error $= \dfrac{20}{\sqrt{100}} = 2$

13. a. $z = 0.25$, $p = 0.4013$.
   b. $\sigma_M = 6$, $z = 0.50$, $p = 0.3085$.
   c. $\sigma_M = 2$, $z = 1.50$, $p = 0.0668$.

15. a. $\sigma_M = 2$, $z = -2.00$, $p = 0.9772$.
   b. $\sigma_M = 4$, $z = 0.50$, $p = 0.3085$.
   c. $\sigma_M = 1$, $z = 2.00$, $p = 0.0228$.

17. a. $p = 0.9544$.
   b. $p = 0.5762$.
   c. The middle 95% of all sample means range from 45.1 to 54.9.

19. a. $z = 1.00$. This is a typical sample.
   b. $z = 1.00$. This is a typical sample.
   c. $z = 2.00$. This is an extreme sample.

21. a. With a standard error of 3.1, this sample mean corresponds to a z-score of $z = 2.97$. A z-score this extreme has a probability of only $p = 0.0015$.
   b. It would be almost impossible to obtain a sample mean this large by random sampling.

23. a. The distribution is normal with a mean of 80 and $\sigma_M = 3$.
   b. The middle 95% is bounded by $z = \pm 1.96$.
   c. $z = 9/3 = 3.00$. The sample mean is not in the middle 95%.
   d. $z = 4/3 = 1.33$. The sample mean is in the middle 95%.

25.

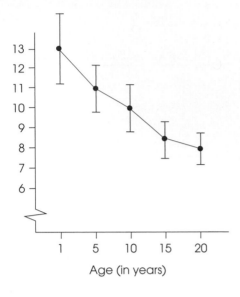

CHAPTER 8:   INTRODUCTION TO HYPOTHESIS TESTING

1. a. A Type I error is rejecting a true H_0. This can occur if you obtain a very unusual sample with scores that are much different from the general population.
   b. A Type II error is failing to reject a false H_0. This can happen when the treatment effect is very small. In this case the treated sample is not noticeably different from the original population.

3. a. $M - \mu$ measures the difference between the sample mean and the hypothesized population mean.
   b. A sample mean is not expected to be identical to the population mean. The standard error measures how much difference, on average, is reasonable to expect between M and μ.

5. Lowering the alpha level causes the boundaries of the critical region to move farther out into the tails of the distribution. Lowering α reduces the probability of a Type I error.

7. a. With a standard error of 2.5, a sample mean of $M = 54$ produces $z = 1.60$. This is not beyond the critical value of 1.96, so we conclude that there is not a significant effect.
   b. With $M = 56$, $z = 2.40$ and we conclude that there is a significant effect.

9. a. H_0 $\mu = 40$. The sample mean $M = 42$ corresponds to $z = 1.00$. This is not sufficient to reject the null hypothesis. You cannot conclude that the program has a significant effect.
   b. H_0 $\mu = 40$. The sample mean $M = 44$ corresponds to $z = 2.00$. This is sufficient to reject the null hypothesis and conclude that the program does have a significant effect.
   c. The 2-point difference between the sample and the hypothesis in part a was not sufficient to reject H_0, however, the 4-point difference in part b is significantly more than chance.

11. a. The null hypothesis states that the herb has no effect on memory scores.
   b. H_0: $\mu = 80$ (even with the herbs, the mean is still 80).
   H_1: $\mu \neq 80$ (the mean has changed)
   c. The critical region consists of z-scores beyond ± 1.96. For these data, the standard error is 3 and $z = \frac{4}{3} = 1.33$. Fail to reject the null hypothesis. The herbal supplements do not have a significant effect on memory scores.

13. a. The null hypothesis states that there is no increase in REM activity, $\mu \leq 110$. The critical region consists of z-scores beyond $z = 2.33$. For these data, the standard error is 12.5 and $z = 33/12.5 = 2.64$. Reject H_0. There is a significant increase in REM activity.
   b. Cohen's $d = 33/50 = 0.66$.

15. a. For the one-tailed test, the critical region consists of z-scores beyond $z = 1.65$. Reject H_0. The standard error is 4 and $z = \frac{7}{4} = 1.75$.
   b. For the two-tailed test, the critical region consists of z-scores beyond $z = \pm 1.96$. Fail to reject H_0.
   c. The one-tailed requires a smaller treatment effect as long as it is in the predicted direction.

17. a. Cohen's $d = \frac{4}{12} = 0.33$.
   b. Cohen's $d = \frac{4}{12} = 0.33$. Sample size has no influence on Cohen's d.
   c. Cohen's $d = \frac{4}{24} = 0.165$. The larger the standard deviation, the smaller the effect size.
   d. Cohen's $d = \frac{8}{12} = 0.67$. The larger the mean difference, the larger the effect size.

19. a. $M = 30$

   b. The histogram shows the scores centered around $M = 30$, with most of the scores within 5 or 6 points in either direction.

   c. The sample appears to be shifted to the right, away from $\mu = 25$.

   d. The null hypothesis says that the treatment has no effect and the population mean is still $\mu = 25$. The standard error is 2 points and $z = \frac{5}{2} = 2.50$. Reject the null hypothesis.

   e. The treatment effect appears to be about 5 points (from $\mu = 25$ to $M = 30$).

   f. Cohen's $d = \frac{5}{6} = 0.83$.

21. a. With $n = 4$, the standard error is 6, and $z = \frac{6}{6} = 1.00$. Fail to reject H_0.

   b. With $n = 36$, the standard error is 2, and $z = \frac{6}{2} = 3.00$. Reject H_0.

   c. Cohen's $d = \frac{6}{12} = 0.50$ for both tests.

   d. A larger sample increases the likelihood of rejecting H_0 but has no influence on Cohen's d.

23. As the size of the treatment effect gets smaller, the treatment distribution moves closer to the null distribution and power decreases. When the difference between the two distributions is extremely small, the size of the critical region (alpha) corresponds almost exactly with the portion of the treatment distribution that is located in the critical region (power). Thus, the smallest possible power is equal to alpha.

CHAPTER 9:   **INTRODUCTION TO THE *t* STATISTIC**

1. a. $s = 8$ and $s_M = 2$.

   b. The sample standard deviation describes the average distance between X and M for the scores in the sample. The standard error describes the average distance between a sample mean, M, and the population mean, μ, for a sample with these characteristics ($n = 16$ and $s = 8$).

3. A z-score is used when the population standard deviation (or variance) is known. The t statistic is used when the population variance or standard deviation is unknown. You use the sample data to estimate the variance and the standard error.

5. The sample variance (s^2) in the t formula is an estimated value and contributes to the variability.

7. a. 6 points

   b. $s_M = 4$

   c. For these data, $t = 1.50$. With $df = 3$ the critical value is $t = \pm 3.182$. Fail to reject H_0 and conclude that there is not a significant effect.

9. a. $M = 5$ and $s = \sqrt{20} = 4.47$

   b. $s_M = 2$.

11. a. With $n = 4$, $s_M = 4$ and $t = \frac{6}{4} = 1.50$. This is not greater than the critical value of 3.182, so there is no significant effect.

   b. With $n = 16$, $s_M = 2$ and $t = \frac{6}{2} = 3.00$. This value is greater than the critical value of 2.131, so we reject the null hypothesis and conclude that there is a significant treatment effect.

13. The sample variance is 27, the estimated standard error is $\sqrt{3} = 1.73$, and $t = \frac{6.3}{1.73} = 3.64$. For a two-tailed test, the critical value is 2.306. Reject the null hypothesis, there is a significant preference for the terry cloth mother.

15. The sample variance is 64, the estimated standard error is 1.60, and $t = \frac{6}{1.60} = 3.75$. For a two-tailed test, the critical value is 2.797. Reject the null hypothesis and conclude that children with a history of day care have significantly different cognitive skills.

17. a. With a variance of 64, the standard deviation is 8 and $d = \frac{2}{8} = 0.25$. The estimated standard error is 2 and

   $t = \frac{2}{2} = 1$. $r^2 = \frac{1}{16} = 0.0625$.

   b. With a variance of 1600, the standard deviation is 40 and $d = \frac{2}{40} = 0.05$. The estimated standard error is 10 and

   $t = \frac{2}{10} = 0.20$. $r^2 = \frac{0.04}{15.04} = 0.0027$.

   c. Measures of effect size tend to decrease as sample variance increases.

19. a. With $df = 15$, the one-tailed critical value is 2.602. For these data, the sample variance is 400, the estimated standard error is 5, and $t = \frac{21}{5} = 4.20$. Reject the null hypothesis and conclude that the sample mean is significantly greater than would be expected from a population with $\mu = 100$.

21. a. $H_0: \mu \geq 15$. The critical region consists of t values less than -1.943. For these data, $M = 11.71$, $s^2 = 12.24$, the standard error is 1.32, and $t(6) = -2.49$. Reject H_0 and conclude right hemisphere brain damage does significantly reduce spatial skills.

23. a. $H_0: \mu = 21$. Because $df = 99$ is not in the table, use $df = 60$ to obtain critical boundaries of ± 2.00. With a standard error of 0.50, $t(99) = -4.60$. Reject H_0 and conclude that humidity has a significant effect on the rats eating behavior.

   b. Cohen's $d = \frac{2.3}{5} = 0.46$ and $r^2 = \frac{21.16}{120.16} = 0.176$.

CHAPTER 10: **THE *t* TEST FOR TWO INDEPENDENT SAMPLES**

1. An independent-measures study requires a separate sample for each of the treatments or populations being compared. An independent-measures t statistic is appropriate when a researcher has two samples and wants to use the sample mean difference to test hypotheses about the population mean difference.

3. a. The first sample has $s^2 = 16$ and the second has $s^2 = 14$. The pooled variance is $\frac{90}{6} = 15$ (halfway between).

   b. The first sample has $s^2 = 16$ and the second has $s^2 = 6$. The pooled variance is $\frac{90}{10} = 9$.

5. The homogeneity of variance assumption specifies that the variances are equal for the two populations from which the samples are obtained. If this assumption is violated, the t statistic can cause misleading conclusions for a hypothesis test.

7. **a.** The pooled variance is 120.
   b. The estimated standard error is 4.00.
   c. A mean difference of 8 would produce $t = \frac{8}{4} = 2$. With $df = 28$, the critical values are ± 2.048. Fail to reject H_0.
   d. A mean difference of 12 would produce $t = \frac{12}{4} = 3$. With $df = 28$, the critical values are ± 2.048. Reject H_0.
   e. With a mean difference of 8 points, $r^2 = 0.125$. With a difference of 12 points, $r^2 = 0.24$.

9. **a.** The pooled variance is 45 and the estimated standard error is 3.
   b. The pooled variance is 154 and the estimated standard error is 6.

11. **a.** The pooled variance is 100.
    b. The standard deviation is 10. One sample is centered at $M = 75$ with the majority of the scores scattered between 65 and 85. The second sample is centered at $M = 87$ with the majority of the scores scattered between 77 and 97. There is some overlap between distributions but the two means are more than one standard deviation apart. They form two distinct distributions.
    c. The estimated standard error for the sample mean difference is $\sqrt{10} = 3.16$, and $t = \frac{-12}{3.16} = -3.80$. With a critical value of 2.042 (using $df = 30$ because 38 is not in the table), we reject the null hypothesis and conclude that there is a significant difference between the two teaching methods.

13. **a.** The pooled variance is 20, the estimated standard error is 2, and $t = \frac{4}{2} = 2.00$. The critical t value is 2.101, so we fail to reject the null hypothesis.
    b. With an 8-point difference, $t = \frac{8}{2} = 4.00$. Reject the null hypothesis and conclude that the medication has a significant effect.

15. The pooled variance is 32, the estimated standard error is 2, and $t = \frac{6}{2} = 3.00$. With $df = 30$ the critical value is 2.042. Reject the null hypothesis. There is a significant difference between the two treatments.

17. The pooled variance is 10, the estimated standard error is 1, and $t = \frac{-2.8}{1} = -2.80$. With $df = 38$ the critical value is 2.042 (using $df = 30$ in the table). Reject the null hypothesis and conclude that there is a significant difference between the two groups.

19. **a.** The pooled variance is 1.2, the estimated standard error is 0.4, and $t = \frac{0.9}{0.4} = 2.25$. With $df = 28$, the critical value is 2.048. Reject the null hypothesis and conclude that there is a significant difference between group performance and individual performance.
    b. The estimated Cohen's $d = \frac{0.9}{\sqrt{1.2}} = 0.822$.

21. **a.** The null hypothesis states that there is no difference between the two sets of instructions, $H_0: \mu_1 - \mu_2 = 0$. With $df = 6$ and $\alpha = .05$, the critical region consists of t values beyond ± 2.447. For the first set, $M = 6$ and $SS = 16$. For the second set, $M = 10$ with $SS = 32$. For these data, the pooled variance is 8, the estimated standard error is 2, and $t(6) = 2.00$. Fail to reject H_0. The data are not sufficient to conclude that there is a significant difference between the two sets of instructions.
    b. For these data, the estimated $d = \frac{4}{\sqrt{8}} = 1.41$ (a very large effect) and $r^2 = \frac{4}{10} = 0.40$ (40%).

23. **a.** The humorous sentences produced a mean of $M = 4.25$ with $SS = 35$, and the nonhumorous sentences had $M = 3.00$ with $SS = 26$. The pooled variance is 2.03, the estimated standard error is 0.504, and $t = 2.48$. With $df = 30$, the critical value is 2.042. Reject the null hypothesis and conclude that there is a significant difference in memory for the two types of sentences.
    b. The estimated $d = \frac{1.25}{1.42} = 0.88$.
    c. $r^2 = \frac{6.15}{36.15} = 0.17$

25. **a.** The null hypothesis states that owning a pet has no effect on health, $H_0: \mu_1 - \mu_2 = 0$. The critical boundaries are $t = \pm 2.228$. For the control group, $M = 11.14$ and $SS = 56.86$. For the dog owners, $M = 6.4$ and $SS = 17.2$. The pooled variance is 7.41 and $t(10) = 2.98$. Reject H_0. The data show a significant difference between the dog owners and the control group.
    b. For these data, $r^2 = 0.47$ (47%).

CHAPTER 11: **THE t TEST FOR TWO RELATED SAMPLES**

1. For a repeated-measures design the same subjects are used in both treatment conditions. In a matched-subjects design, two different sets of subjects are used. However, in a matched-subjects design, each subject in one condition is matched with respect to a specific variable with a subject in the second condition so that the two separate samples are equivalent with respect to the matching variable.

3. **a.** This is an independent-measures experiment with two separate samples.
   b. This is repeated measures. The same individuals are measured twice.
   c. This is repeated measures. The same individuals are measured twice.

5. **a.** The estimated standard error is 2 and the critical value for $df = 14$ is 2.145. With $M_D = 3$, you obtain $t = \frac{3}{2} = 1.50$. Fail to reject the null hypothesis.
   b. With $M_D = 6$, $t = \frac{6}{2} = 3.00$ and you would reject the null hypothesis.

7. **a.** For the first sample, the scores pile up around $M_D = 4$ and the majority of the scores are spread over a range from -6 to 14. A value of zero is located slightly to the left of the center of the distribution. For the second sample, the scores pile up around $M_D = 4$ but now the majority of the scores are contained between 2 and 6. A value of zero is an extreme value, clearly outside the center of the distribution.

b. Because a sample is usually representative of its population, the first sample is more likely to have come from a population with $\mu_D = 0$.

9. The null hypothesis states that there is no difference in the perceived intelligence between attractive and unattractive photos. For these data, the estimated standard error is 0.4 and $t = \dfrac{2.7}{0.4} = 6.75$. With $df = 24$, the critical value is 2.064. Reject the null hypothesis.

11. The null hypothesis says that the magnetic therapy has no effect, $H_0: \mu_D = 0$. With $df = 8$ and $\alpha = .01$, the critical values are $t = \pm 3.355$. For these data, the standard error is 4, and $t(8) = 3.13$. Fail to reject H_0 and conclude that the magnetic therapy has no significant effect on chronic pain.

13. a. The null hypothesis says that there is no difference in judgments for smiling versus frowning. For these data, the sample variance is 64, the estimated standard error is 2, and $t = \dfrac{3.6}{2} = 1.80$. For a one-tailed test with $df = 15$, the critical value is 1.753. Reject the null hypothesis.

   b. $r^2 = \dfrac{3.24}{18.24} = 0.178$ (17.8%)

15. The null hypothesis says that pets do not have an effect on mood, $H_0: \mu_D = 0$. With $df = 5$ and $\alpha = .05$, the critical values are $t = \pm 2.571$. For these data, $M_D = 5$, $SS = 120$, the estimated standard error is 2.00, and $t(5) = 2.50$. Fail to reject H_0 and conclude that pet do not have a significant effect on mood.

17. a. The difference scores are 3, 7, 3, and 3. $M_D = 4$.

   b. $SS = 12$, sample variance is 4, and the estimated standard error is 1.

c. With $df = 3$ and $\alpha = .05$, the critical values are $t = \pm 3.182$. For these data, $t = 4.00$. Reject H_0. There is a significant treatment effect.

19. a. For problem 17, Cohen's d is 2.00 and for problem 18, $d = \dfrac{4}{\sqrt{40}} = 0.63$. The percentage of variance accounted for is $r^2 = .842$ for problem 17 and $r^2 = .349$ for problem 18.

   b. In general, the larger sample variance (problem 18) produces a smaller effect size.

21. The null hypothesis says that stress has no effect on lymphocyte count, $H_0: \mu_D = 0$. With $\alpha = .05$ the critical region consists of t values beyond ± 2.093. For these data, the standard error is 0.018, and $t(19) = 5.00$. Reject H_0 and conclude that the data show a significant change in lymphocyte count.

23. The null hypothesis says that deprivation has no effect on hearing threshold, $H_0: \mu_D = 0$. With $\alpha = .05$, the critical region consists of t values beyond ± 2.447. For these data, $M_D = -2.29$, $SS = 51.43$, $s^2 = 8.57$, the standard error is 1.11, and $t(6) = -2.06$. Fail to reject H_0 and conclude that the data show no significant change in hearing threshold.

25. The null hypothesis says that forming images has no effect on visual perception, $H_0: \mu_D = 0$. With $df = 5$ and $\alpha = .05$, the critical values are $t = \pm 2.571$. For these data, $M_D = -4$, $SS = 78$, the estimated standard error is 1.61, and $t(5) = -2.48$. Fail to reject H_0 and conclude that the mental images do not have a significant effect on visual perception.

CHAPTER 12: **ESTIMATION**

1. a. The larger the sample, the narrower the interval.

   b. The larger the sample standard deviation (s), the wider the interval.

   c. The higher the percentage of confidence, the wider the interval.

3. The general purpose of a hypothesis test is to determine whether a treatment effect exists. A hypothesis test always addresses a "yes/no" question. The purpose of estimation is to determine the size of the effect. Estimation addresses a "how much" question.

5. a. If the sample size is increased, the width of the interval will decrease.

   b. If the level of confidence is increased, the width of the interval will also increase.

7. a. Use the sample mean, $M = 3.1$ hours for the point estimate.

   b. Using a single-sample t statistic with $df = 24$, the standard error is 0.60, the t score boundaries for 90% confidence are ± 1.711, and the interval extends from 2.073 to 4.127.

9. For the point estimate, use $M = 15.3$ hours. For the interval estimate, the standard error is 1.732 and with $df = 8$, the t score boundaries for 80% confidence are ± 1.397. The interval extends from 12.88 hours to 17.72 hours.

11. a. Use the sample mean difference, 5.2, for the point estimate.

   b. Using an independent-measures t statistic with $df = 28$, the pooled variance is 30, the estimated standard error is 2.00, the

t score boundaries for 95% confidence are ± 2.048, and the interval extends from 1.104 to 9.296.

   c. The t score boundaries for 99% confidence are ± 2.763, and the interval extends from -0.326 to 10.726.

   d. The change is significant for $\alpha = .05$ because a mean difference of zero is outside the interval and therefore rejected with 95% confidence. However, a mean difference of zero is within the 99% interval and therefore is an acceptable value (fail to reject) with 99% confidence.

13. a. $M = 7.00$ and $s^2 = 9$

   b. Use $M = 7.00$ as the point estimate for μ.

   c. With $df = 8$ and an estimated standard error of 1.00, the t score boundaries for 80% confidence are $t = \pm 1.397$, and the interval extends from 5.603 and 8.397.

15. a. Use the sample mean difference, $M_1 - M_2 = 14$ points for the point estimate.

   b. For the interval estimate, the pooled variance is 90 and the standard error is 5. With $df = 13$, the t score boundaries for 90% confidence are ± 1.771. The interval extends from 5.145 to 22.855.

17. Use the sample mean difference, 11.2 points, as the point estimate of the population mean difference. With $df = 18$, the t values for the 90% interval are ± 1.734. With a standard error of 5 points, the interval extends from 2.53 to 19.87 points.

19. a. Use the sample mean difference, $M = \frac{13}{8} = 1.625$, as the point estimate of the population mean difference.

   b. The sample of difference scores has $SS = 59.88$, a variance of 8.55, and an estimated standard error of 1.03. With $df = 7$, the t score boundaries for 95% confidence are ± 2.365 and the interval extends from -0.811 to 4.061.

21. a. For the men, the estimated standard error is 1.30. With $df = 9$, the t score boundaries for 95% confidence are ± 2.262. The interval extends from -0.0406 to 5.8406.

   b. A population mean difference of zero is included in the 95% confidence interval and therefore is an acceptable value. A hypothesis test would fail to reject the null hypothesis.

   c. For the women, the estimated standard error is 1.64. With $df = 9$, the t score boundaries for 95% confidence are ± 2.262. The interval extends from 2.6903 to 10.1097.

   d. A population mean difference of zero is not included in the 95% confidence interval and therefore is not an acceptable value. A hypothesis test would reject the null hypothesis.

23. a. Use the sample mean difference, 24, for the point estimate.

   b. Using a repeated-measures t statistic with $df = 35$, the estimated standard error is 1.33, the t score boundaries for 95% confidence are ± 2.042 (using $df = 30$ because 35 is not listed), and the interval extends from 21.284 to 26.716.

CHAPTER 13: INTRODUCTION TO ANALYSIS OF VARIANCE

1. a. As the differences between sample means increase, $MS_{between}$ also increases, and the F-ratio increases.

   b. Increases in sample variability cause MS_{within} to increase and, thereby, decrease the F-ratio.

3. When there is no treatment effect, the numerator and the denominator of the F-ratio are both measuring the same sources of variability (individual differences and experimental error). In this case, the F-ratio is balanced and should have a value near 1.00.

5. a. Posttests are used to determine exactly which treatment conditions are significantly different.

   b. If there are only two treatments, then there is no questions as to which two treatments are different.

   c. If the decision is to fail to reject H_0, then there are no significant differences.

7. a.

Source	SS	df	MS	
Between treatments	8	2	4	$F(2, 9) = 1.00$
Within treatments	36	9	4	
Total	44	11		

With $\alpha = .05$, the critical value is $F = 4.26$. Fail to reject the null hypothesis and conclude that there are no significant differences among the three treatments.

   b. For these data, eta squared is $\frac{8}{44} = 0.18$ or 18%.

9.

Source	SS	df	MS	
Between treatments	70	2	35	$F(2, 12) = 17.50$
Within treatments	24	12	2	
Total	94	14		

With $\alpha = .05$, the critical value is $F = 3.88$. Reject the null hypothesis and conclude that there are no significant differences among the three treatments.

11. a.

Source	SS	df	MS	
Between treatments	32	2	16	$F(2, 9) = 10.26$
Within treatments	14	9	1.56	
Total	46	11		

With $\alpha = .05$, the critical value is $F = 4.26$. Reject the null hypothesis and conclude that there are significant differences among the three treatments.

   b. For these data, eta squared is $\frac{32}{46} = 0.70$.

13. a.

Source	SS	df	MS	
Between treatments	40	3	13.33	$F(3, 12) = 7.98$
Within treatments	20	12	1.67	
Total	60	15		

With $\alpha = .05$, the critical value is $F = 3.49$. Reject the null hypothesis and conclude that there are significant differences among the four levels.

   b. For these data, eta squared is $\frac{40}{60} = 0.67$.

15. a. If there are no differences within the treatments, then SS_{within} should be zero.

   b. $SS_{total} = MS_{between} = 10$.

17. a. With $df_{between} = 2$, there must be 3 treatment conditions.

   b. Adding the two df values (2 and 24) gives $df_{total} = 26$. Therefore, the total number of subjects must be $N = 27$.

19. The means and SS values are:

	Single	Twin	Triplet
	$M = 8$	$M = 6$	$M = 4$
	$SS = 10$	$SS = 18$	$SS = 14$

The null hypothesis states that there are no differences in language development among the three groups, $H_0: \mu_1 = \mu_2 = \mu_3$. The critical value for $\alpha = .05$ is 3.88. The analysis of variance produces,

Source	SS	df	MS	
Between treatments	40	2	20	$F(2, 12) = 5.71$
Within treatments	42	12	3.5	
Total	82	14		

Reject H_0 and conclude that there are significant differences in language development among the three groups.

21.

Source	SS	df	MS	
Between treatments	6	2	3	$F(2, 9) = 0.75$
Within treatments	36	9	4	
Total	42	11		

With $\alpha = .05$, the critical value is $F = 4.26$. Fail to reject the null hypothesis and conclude that there are no significant differences among the three treatments.

23.

Source	SS	df	MS	
Between treatments	40	2	20	$F(2, 42) = 4.00$
Within treatments	210	42	5	
Total	250	44		

With $\alpha = .05$, the critical value is $F = 3.88$. Reject the null hypothesis and conclude that there are significant differences among the three types of birds.

b. For these data, eta squared is $\frac{250}{610} = 0.410$ or 41.0%.

25. a.

Source	SS	df	MS	
Between treatments	250	2	125	$F(2, 12) = 4.17$
Within treatments	360	12	30	
Total	610	14		

CHAPTER 14: **REPEATED-MEASURES AND TWO-FACTOR ANALYSIS OF VARIANCE**

1. a. A total of 60 participants is needed; three separate samples, each with $n = 20$. The F-ratio has $df = 2, 57$.

b. One sample of $n = 20$ is needed. The F-ratio has $df = 2, 38$.

3. For an independent measures design, the variability within treatments is the appropriate error term. For repeated measures, however, you must subtract variability due to individual differences from the variability within treatments to obtain a measure of error.

5. a. 3 treatments.
b. 7 participants.

7. a. 4 treatments.
b. 9 participants.

9. a. The null hypothesis states that there are no differences among the three treatments, $H_0: \mu_1 = \mu_2 = \mu_3$. With $df = 2, 6$, the critical value is 5.14.

Source	SS	df	MS	
Between treatments	8	2	4	$F(2, 6) = 0.27$
Within treatments	94	9		
Between subjects	4	3		
Error	90	6	15	
Total	102	11		

Fail to reject H_0. There are no significant differences among the three treatments.

b. In Problem 8 the individual differences were relatively large and consistent. When the individual differences were subtracted out, the error was greatly reduced.

11. a. The null hypothesis states that there are no differences between treatments, $H_0: \mu_1 = \mu_2 = \mu_3$. For an independent-measures design, the critical value is 3.88.

Source	SS	df	MS	
Between treatments	40	2	20.00	$F(2, 12) = 3.24$
Within treatments	74	12	6.17	
Total	114	14		

b. The null hypothesis states that there are no differences between treatments, $H_0: \mu_1 = \mu_2 = \mu_3$. For a repeated-measures design, the critical value is 4.46.

Source	SS	df	MS	
Between treatments	40	2	20.0	$F(2, 8) = 8.00$
Within treatments	74	12		
Between subjects	54	4		
Error	20	8	2.5	
Total	114	14		

c. The independent measures design includes all the individual differences in the error term (MS_{within}). As a result the F-ratio, $F(2, 12) = 3.24$ is not significant. With a repeated-measures design, the individual differences are removed and the result is a significant F-ratio, $F(2, 8) = 8.00, p < .05$.

13.

Source	SS	df	MS	
Between treatments	56	2	28	$F(2, 6) = 10.49$
Within treatments	28	9		
Between subjects	12	3		
Error	16	6	2.67	
Total	84	11		

Reject H_0 and conclude that quality of life changes significantly over the three measurements.

15.

Source	SS	df	MS	
Between treatments	24	1	24	$F(1, 11) = 6.00$
Within treatments	104	22		
Between subjects	60	11		
Error	44	11	4	
Total	128	23		

17. a. The main effect for treatment is evaluated by comparing the two overall column means, $M = 12$ and $M = 18$.

b. The main effect for gender is evaluated by comparing the two overall row means, $M = 15$ and $M = 15$. (There is no main effect for gender.)

19. One hypothesis test evaluates mean differences among the rows and a second test evaluates mean differences among the columns. The test for an interaction evaluates the significance of any mean differences that are not explained by row and/or column differences.

21. a. $df = 1, 36$.
b. $df = 1, 36$.
c. $df = 1, 36$.

23. a. The scores in treatment 1 are consistently higher than the scores in treatment 2. There is a main effect for treatment.

b. The overall mean is around $M = 15$ for all three age groups. There is no main effect for age.

c. The two lines are not parallel. Instead, the difference between the treatments increases as the participants get older. Yes, there is an interaction.

25. a. The cell means are as follows:

	B_1	B_2
A_1	10	2
A_2	3	11

b. There appears to be no main effect for factor A (the means are nearly equal) and no effect for factor B (the means are equal). There does appear to be an interaction because the means decrease across levels of B for A_1 but the means increase across B for A_2.

c. The null hypotheses state that factor A has no effect (H_0: $\mu_{A1} = \mu_{A2}$), factor B has no effect (H_0: $\mu_{B1} = \mu_{B2}$), and that there is no interaction. For $df = 1,16$ and $\alpha = .01$, the critical value is $F = 8.53$.

Source	SS	df	MS	
Between treatments	325	3		
Factor A	5	1	5	$F(1,16) = 1.05$
Factor B	0	1	0	$F(1,16) = 0$
$A \times B$ Interaction	320	1	320	$F(1,16) = 67.36$
Within Treatments	76	16	4.75	
Total	401	19		

d. The A and B main effects are not significant, but there is a significant interaction.

27.

Source	SS	df	MS	
Between treatments	180	5		
Factor A	20	1	20	$F(1,40) = 4.00$
Factor B	60	2	30	$F(2,40) = 6.00$
$A \times B$ Interaction	100	2	50	$F(2,40) = 10.00$
Within Treatments	270	54	5	
Total	450	59		

29. a.

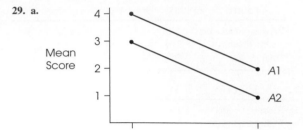

b. The lines are parallel, so there does not appear to be any interaction. There is a small difference between the lines for A_1 and A_2, so there may be a small main effect for factor A. The difference between B_1 and B_2 is larger, so there probably is a main effect for factor B.

c. The null hypotheses state that there is no difference between levels of factor A (H_0: $\mu_{A1} = \mu_{A2}$), no difference between levels of factor B (H_0: $\mu_{B1} = \mu_{B2}$), and no interaction. All F-ratios have $df = 1,36$ and the critical value is $F = 4.11$.

Source	SS	df	MS	
Between treatments	50	3		
Factor A	10	1	10	$F(1,36) = 2.00$
Factor B	40	1	40	$F(1,36) = 8.00$
$A \times B$ Interaction	0	1	0	$F(1,36) = 0$
Within Treatments	180	36	5	
Total	230	39		

The main effect for Factor B is significant, but the A effect and the interaction are not.

CHAPTER 15:   **CORRELATION AND REGRESSION**

1. A positive correlation indicates that X and Y change in the same direction: As X increases, Y also increases. A negative correlation indicates that X and Y tend to change in opposite directions: As X increases, Y decreases.

3. a. The scatter plot should show data points clustered around a line sloping up to the right. The pattern formed by the points should be roughly the shape of a football.

b. The scatter plot should show data points clustered very close to a line sloping down to the right.

5. For set 1, $SP = 17$. For set 2, $SP = -14$.

7. a. With $n = 15$, the correlation must be equal to or greater than 0.514.

b. With $n = 30$, the correlation must be equal to or greater than 0.361.

c. With $n = 92$, the correlation must be equal to or greater than 0.205.

9. a. For the children, $SS = 32$, and for the birth parents, $SS = 14$. $SP = 15$. The correlation is $r = 0.709$.

b. For the children, $SS = 32$, and for the adoptive parents, $SS = 16$. $SP = 3$. The correlation is $r = 0.133$.

c. The children's behavior is strongly related to their birth parents and only weakly related to their adoptive parents. The data suggest that the behavior is inherited rather than learned.

11. a. $r_S = +0.907$.

  b. Yes, there is a strong positive relationship between the grades assigned by the two instructors.

13. The Pearson correlation measures the degree of linear relationship. The Spearman correlation measures the degree to which the relationship is monotonic, or one directional, independent of form.

15. Using the X value to designate the instructions, 1 and 2, and using the Y value to indicate failure (0) or success (1), the converted data show 8 people with scores of 1, 0; 2 people with scores of 1, 1; 3 people with scores of 2, 0; and 7 people with scores of 2, 1. (Note: Any two different numbers can be used for the X and Y values.) The correlation is 0.503.

17. Using the eating concern scores as the X variable and coding males as 1 and females as 0 for the Y variable produces $SS_X = 1875.6$, $SS_Y = 3.6$, and $SP = -50.4$. The point-biserial correlation is $r = -0.613$. (Reversing the codes for males and females will change the sign of the correlation.)

19. $SS_X = 16$ $SP = 32$ $\hat{Y} = 2X - 6$.

21. a. $r = 0.30$.

  b. $\hat{Y} = 0.375X + 7$.

23. a. $b = 122/172 = 0.709$ and $a = 9 - 0.709(7) = 4.037$.

  b. $r = 0.904$ and $r^2 = 0.817$ or 81.7%.

  c. $SS_{regression} = 86.602$ with $df = 1$, and $SS_{residual} = 19.398$ with $df = 6$. $F = 86.602/3.233 = 26.79$. With $df = 1, 6$ the F-ratio is significant with $\alpha = .05$ or with $\alpha = .01$.

25. a. The predicted portion is determined by $r^2 = 0.16$ or 16%. The unpredicted (residual) portion is determined by $(1 - r^2) = 0.84$ or 84%.

  b. $SS_{regression} = 1.6$ with $df = 1$, and $SS_{residual} = 8.4$ with $df = 18$. $F = 1.6/0.467 = 3.43$. With $df = 1, 18$ the F-ratio is not significant.

  c. $SS_{regression} = 16$ with $df = 1$, and $SS_{residual} = 84$ with $df = 18$. $F = 16/4.67 = 3.43$. With $df = 1, 18$ the F-ratio is not significant.

  Note: The F-ratios are exactly the same. SS_Y has no effect on the significance of the regression equation.

27. a. The standard error of estimate is 4.00.

  b. The standard error of estimate is 0.80.

CHAPTER 16: THE CHI-SQUARE STATISTIC: TESTS FOR GOODNESS OF FIT AND INDEPENDENCE

1. a. The null hypothesis states that there is no advantage (no preference) for red or blue. With $df = 1$, the critical value is 3.84. The expected frequency is 25 wins for each color, and chi-square = 2.88. Fail to reject H_0 and conclude that there is no significant advantage for one color over the other.

  b. The null hypothesis states that there is no advantage (no preference) for red or blue. With $df = 1$, the critical value is 3.84. The expected frequency is 50 wins for each color, and chi-square = 5.76. Reject H_0 and conclude that there is a significant advantage for the color red.

  c. Although the proportions are identical for the two samples, the sample in part b is twice as big as the sample in part a. The larger sample provides more convincing evidence of an advantage for red than does the smaller sample.

3. Nonparametric tests make few if any assumptions about the populations from which the data are obtained. For example, the populations do not need to form normal distributions, nor is it required that different populations in the same study have equal variances (homogeneity of variance assumption). Parametric tests require data measured on an interval or ratio scale. For nonparametric tests, any scale of measurement is acceptable.

5. The null hypothesis states that there is no preference among the three photographs; $p = \dfrac{1}{3}$ for all categories. The expected frequencies are $f_e = 50$ for all categories, and chi-square = 20.28. With $df = 2$, the critical value is 5.99. Reject H_0 and conclude that there are significant preferences

7. The null hypothesis states that wins and loses are equally likely. With 64 games, the expected frequencies are 32 wins and 32 losses. With $df = 1$ the critical value is 3.84, and the data produce a chi-square of 6.25. Reject the null hypothesis and conclude that home team wins are significantly more common that would be expected by chance.

9. a. The null hypothesis states that there is no preference among the three colas; one third of the population prefers each of the three colas. For a sample of $n = 120$, the expected frequency is 40 for each cola. For $df = 2$ and $\alpha = .05$, the critical value for chi-square is 5.99. For these data, the chi-square statistic is 10.40. Reject H_0 and conclude that there are significant preferences among the colas.

  b. A larger sample should be more representative of the population. If the sample continues to be different from the hypothesis as the sample size increases, eventually the difference will be significant.

11. H_0 states that the distribution of automobile accidents is the same as the distribution of registered drivers: 16% under age 20, 28% age 20 to 29, and 56% age 30 or older. With $df = 2$, the critical value is 5.99. The expected frequencies for these three categories are 48, 84, and 168. Chi-square = 13.76. Reject H_0 and conclude that the distribution of automobile accidents is significantly different from the distribution of registered drivers.

13. The null hypothesis states that the distribution of preferences is the same for both groups of students (the two variables are independent). With $df = 2$, the critical value is 5.99. The expected frequencies are:

	Book 1	Book 2	Book 3
Upper half	26.0	20.5	13.5
Lower half	26.0	20.5	13.5

Chi-square = 17.32. Reject H_0.

15. The null hypothesis states that there is no relationship between dream content and gender; the distribution of aggression content should be the same for males and females. The critical value is 9.21. The expected frequencies are:

	Low	Medium	High
Female	8.8	8.4	6.8
Male	13.2	12.6	10.2

The chi-square statistic is 25.52. Reject H_0 with $\alpha = .01$ and $df = 2$.

17. The null hypothesis states that IQ and gender are independent. The distribution of IQ scores for boys should be the same as the distribution for girls. With $df = 2$ and and $\alpha = .05$, the critical value is 5.99. The expected frequencies are 15 low IQ, 48 medium, and 17 high for both boys and girls. For these data, chi-square is 3.76. Fail to reject the null hypothesis. These data do not provide evidence for a significant relationship between IQ and gender.

19. a.

	Handedness	
	Left	Right
Turn left	20	50
Turn right	10	70

b. The null hypothesis states that there is no relationship between handedness and turning preference. With $df = 1$ and $\alpha = .05$ the critical value is 3.84. The expected frequencies for left handed participants are 14 turning left and 16 turning right. For right handed participants the expected frequencies are 56 turning left and 64 turning right. Chi-square = 6.03. These data indicate a significant relationship between handedness and turning preference.

21. a. The null hypothesis states that littering is independent of the amount of litter already on the ground. With $df = 2$, the critical value is 5.99. The expected frequencies are:

	Amount of Litter		
	None	Small	Large
Litter	31.33	31.33	31.33
Not litter	58.67	58.67	58.67

Chi-square = 25.88. Reject H_0.

b. $V = 0.310$ (a medium effect).

23. The null hypothesis states that there is no relationship between the season of birth and schizophrenia. With $df = 3$ and $\alpha = .05$, the critical value is 7.81. The expected frequencies are:

	Summer	Fall	Winter	Spring
No disorder	23.33	23.33	26.67	26.67
Schizophrenia	11.67	11.67	13.33	13.33

Chi-square = 3.62. Fail to reject H_0 and conclude that these data do not provide enough evidence to conclude that there is a significant relationship between the season of birth and schizophrenia.

General Instructions for Using SPSS

The Statistical Package for the Social Sciences, commonly known as SPSS, is a computer program that performs statistical calculations, and is widely available on college campuses. Detailed instructions for using SPSS for specific statistical calculations (such as computing sample variance or performing an independent-measures t test) are presented at the end of the appropriate chapter in the text. Look for the SPSS logo in the Resources section at the end of each chapter. In this appendix, we provide a general overview of the SPSS program.

SPSS consists of two basic components: A data editor and a set of statistical commands. The **data editor** is a huge matrix of numbered rows and columns. To begin any analysis, you must type your data into the data editor. Typically, the scores are entered into columns of the editor. Before scores are entered, each of the columns is labeled "VAR." After scores are entered, the first column becomes VAR00001, the second column becomes VAR00002, and so on. In order to enter data into the editor, the **Data View** tab must be set at the bottom left of the screen. If you want to name a column (instead of using VAR00001), click on the **Variable View** tab at the bottom of the data editor. You will get a description of each variable in the editor, including a box for the name. You may type in a new name using up to 8 lowercase characters (no spaces, no hyphens). Click the **Data View** tab to go back to the data editor.

The **statistical commands** are listed in menus that are made available by clicking on **Analyze** in the tool bar at the top of the screen. When you select a statistical command, SPSS typically asks you to identify exactly where the scores are located and exactly what other options you want to use. This is accomplished by identifying the column(s) in the data editor that contain the needed information. Typically, you are presented with a display similar to the following figure. On the left is a box that lists all of the columns in the data editor that contain information. In this example, we have typed values into columns 1, 2, 3, and 4. On the right is an empty box that is waiting for you to identify the correct column. For example, suppose that you wanted to do a statistical calculation using the scores in column 3. You should highlight VAR00003 by clicking on it in the left-hand box, then click the arrow to move the column label into the right hand box. (If you make a mistake, you can highlight the variable in the right-hand box and the arrow reverses so that you can move the variable back to the left-hand box.)

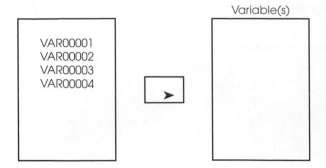

SPSS DATA FORMATS The SPSS program uses two basic formats for entering scores into the data matrix. Each is described and demonstrated as follows:

1. The first format is used when the data consist of several scores (more than one) for each individual. This includes data from a repeated-measures study, in which each person is measured in all of the different treatment conditions, and data from a correlational study where there are two scores, *X* and *Y,* for each individual. Table D1 illustrates this kind of data and shows how the scores would appear in the SPSS data matrix. Note that the scores in the data matrix have exactly the same structure as the scores in the original data. Specifically, each row of the data matrix contains the scores for an individual participant, and each column contains the scores for one treatment condition.

TABLE D1

Data for a repeated-measures or correlational study with several scores for each individual. The left half of the table (a) shows the original data, with three scores for each person; and the right half (b) shows the scores as they would be entered into the SPSS data matrix. Note: SPSS automatically adds the two decimal points for each score. For example, you type in 10 and it appears as 10.00 in the matrix.

(a) Original data

Person	I	II	III
A	10	14	19
B	9	11	15
C	12	15	22
D	7	10	18
E	13	18	20

(Treatments)

(b) Data as entered into the SPSS data matrix

	VAR0001	VAR0002	VAR0003	var
1	10.00	14.00	19.00	
2	9.00	11.00	15.00	
3	12.00	15.00	22.00	
4	7.00	10.00	18.00	
5	13.00	18.00	20.00	

2. The second format is used for data from an independent-measures study using a separate group of participants for each treatment condition. This kind of data is entered into the data matrix in a *stacked* format. Instead of having the scores from different treatments in different columns, all of the scores from all of the treatment conditions are entered into a single column so that the scores from one treatment condition are literally stacked on top of the scores from another treatment condition. A code number is then entered into a second column beside each score to tell the computer which treatment condition corresponds to each score. For example, you could enter a value of 1 beside each score from treatment #1, enter a 2 beside each score from treatment #2, and so on. Table D2 illustrates this kind of data and shows how the scores would be entered into the SPSS data matrix.

TABLE D2

Data for an independent-measures study with a different group of participants in each treatment condition. The left half of the table shows the original data, with three separate groups, each with five participants, and the right half shows the scores as they would be entered into the SPSS data matrix. Note that the data matrix lists all 15 scores in the same column, then uses code numbers in a second column to indicate the treatment condition corresponding to each score.

(a) Original data

Treatments		
I	II	III
10	14	19
9	11	15
12	15	22
7	10	18
13	18	20

(b) Data as entered into the SPSS data matrix

	VAR0001	VAR0002	var
1	10.00	1.00	
2	9.00	1.00	
3	12.00	1.00	
4	7.00	1.00	
5	13.00	1.00	
6	14.00	2.00	
7	11.00	2.00	
8	15.00	2.00	
9	10.00	2.00	
10	18.00	2.00	
11	19.00	3.00	
12	15.00	3.00	
13	22.00	3.00	
14	18.00	3.00	
15	20.00	3.00	

Statistics Organizer

The following pages present an organized summary of the statistical procedures covered in this book. This organizer is divided into four sections, each of which groups together statistical techniques that serve a common purpose. The four groups are

   I. Descriptive Statistics
   II. Parametric Tests: Inferences about Population Means and Mean Differences
   III. Evaluating Relationships Between Variables
   IV. Nonparametric Chi-Square Tests: Inferences about Population Proportions

Each of the four sections begins with a general overview that discusses the purpose for the statistical techniques that follow and points out some common characteristics of the different techniques. Next, there is a decision map that leads you, step by step, through the task of deciding which statistical technique is appropriate for the data you wish to analyze. Finally, there is a brief description of each technique and a reference to a complete example in the text.

I   DESCRIPTIVE STATISTICS

The purpose of descriptive statistics is to simplify and organize a set of scores. Scores may be organized in a table or graph, or they may be summarized by computing one or two values that describe the entire set. The most commonly used descriptive techniques are as follows:

A. Frequency Distribution Tables and Graphs

A frequency distribution is an organized tabulation of the number of individuals in each category on the scale of measurement. A frequency distribution can be presented as either a table or a graph. The advantage of a frequency distribution is that it presents the entire set of scores rather than condensing the scores into a single descriptive value. The disadvantage of a frequency distribution is that it can be somewhat complex, especially with large sets of data.

B. Measures of Central Tendency

The purpose of measuring central tendency is to identify a single score that represents an entire data set. The goal is to obtain a single value that is the best example of the average, or most typical, score from the entire set. Measures of central tendency are used to describe a single data set, and they are the most commonly used measures for comparing two (or more) different sets of data.

CHOOSING DESCRIPTIVE STATISTICS: A DECISION MAP

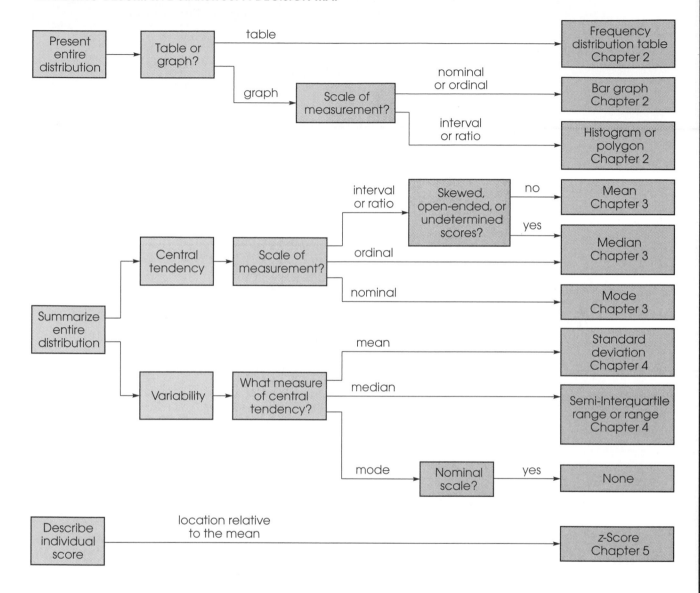

C. Measures of Variability

Variability is used to provide a description of how spread out the scores are in a distribution. It also provides a measure of how accurately a single score selected from a distribution represents the entire set.

D. *z*-Scores

Most descriptive statistics are intended to provide a description of an entire set of scores. However, *z*-scores are used to describe individual scores within a distribution. The purpose of a *z*-score is to identify the precise location of an individual within a distribution by using a single number.

1. The Mean (Chapter 3)

The mean is the most commonly used measure of central tendency. It is computed by finding the total (ΣX) for the set of scores and then dividing the total by the number of individuals. Conceptually, the mean is the amount each individual will receive if the total is divided equally. See Demonstration 3.1 on page 81.

2. **The Median** (Chapter 3)

Exactly 50% of the scores in a data set have values less than or equal to the median. The median is the 50th percentile. The median usually is computed for data sets when the mean cannot be found (undetermined scores, open-ended distribution) or when the mean does not provide a good, representative value (ordinal scale, skewed distribution). See Demonstration 3.1 on page 81.

3. **The Mode** (Chapter 3)

The mode is the score with the greatest frequency. The mode is used when the scores consist of measurements on a nominal scale. See Demonstration 3.1 on page 81.

4. **The Range** (Chapter 4)

The range is the distance from the lowest to the highest score in a data set. The range is considered to be a relatively crude measure of variability. See the example on page 86.

5. **The Semi-Interquartile Range** (Chapter 4)

The semi-interquartile range is half of the range covered by the middle 50% of the distribution. The semi-interquartile range is often used to measure variability in situations where the median is used to report central tendency. See the example on page 88.

6. **Standard Deviation** (Chapter 4)

The standard deviation is a measure of the standard distance from the mean. Standard deviation is obtained by first computing *SS* (the sum of squared deviations) and variance (the mean squared deviation). Standard deviation is the square root of variance. See Demonstration 4.1 on page 110.

7. ***z*-Scores** (Chapter 5)

The sign of a *z*-score indicates whether an individual is above ($+$) or below ($-$) the mean. The numerical value of the *z*-score indicates how many standard deviations there are between the score and the mean. See Demonstration 5.1 on page 130.

II PARAMETRIC TESTS: INFERENCES ABOUT MEANS AND MEAN DIFFERENCES

All of the hypothesis tests covered in this section use the means obtained from sample data as the basis for testing hypotheses about population means. Although there are a variety of tests used in a variety of research situations, all use the same basic logic, and all of the test statistics have the same basic structure. In each case, the test statistic (*z, t,* or *F*) involves computing a ratio with the following structure:

$$\text{test statistic} = \frac{\text{obtained mean difference}}{\text{mean difference expected with no treatment effect}}$$

The goal of each test is to determine whether the obtained sample mean differences are larger than would be expected if there were no systematic mean differences in the population. In general terms, a *significant* result indicates that the mean differences found in the sample data are very unlikely to have occurred if there are not corresponding mean differences in the population.

You should be aware that all parametric tests place stringent restrictions on the sample data and the population distributions being considered. First, these tests all require measurements on an interval or a ratio scale (numerical values that allow you to compute means and differences). Second, each test makes assumptions about population distributions and sampling techniques. Consult the appropriate section of this book to verify that the specific assumptions are satisfied before proceeding with any parametric test.

1. The *z*-Score Test (Chapter 8)

The *z*-score test is used to evaluate the significance of a treatment effect in situations in which the population standard deviation (σ) is known. A sample is selected from a population, and the treatment is administered to the individuals in the sample. The test evaluates the difference between the sample mean and a hypothesized population mean. The null hypothesis provides a specific value for the unknown population mean by stating that the population mean has not been changed by the treatment. See Demonstration 8.1 on page 227.

CHOOSING A PARAMETRIC TEST TO EVALUATE MEAN DIFFERENCES BETWEEN TREATMENT CONDITIONS OR BETWEEN POPULATIONS: A DECISION MAP

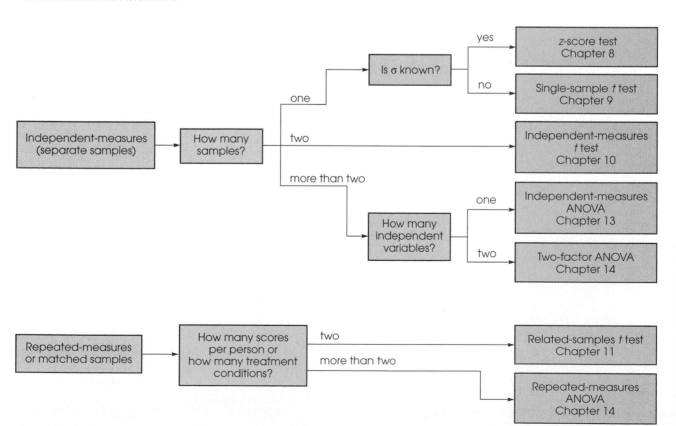

Effect Size for the z-Score Test

In addition to the hypothesis test, a measure of effect size is recommended to determine the actual magnitude of the effect. Cohen's d provides a measure of the mean difference measured in standard deviation units. See Demonstration 8.2 on page 228.

2. The Single-Sample t Test (Chapter 9)

The single sample t test is used to evaluate the significance of a treatment effect in situations in which the population standard deviation (σ) is not known. A sample is selected from a population, and the treatment is administered to the individuals in the sample. The test evaluates the difference between the sample mean and a hypothesized population mean. The null hypothesis provides a specific value for the unknown population mean by stating that the population mean has not been changed by the treatment. The t test uses the sample variance to estimate the unknown population variance. See Demonstration 9.1 on page 252.

Effect Size for the Single-Sample t

The effect size for the single-sample t test can be described by either estimating Cohen's d or by computing r^2, which measures the percentage of variability that is accounted for by the treatment effect. See Demonstration 9.2 on page 253.

3. The Independent-Measures t Test (Chapter 10)

The independent-measures t test uses data from two separate samples to test a hypothesis about the difference between two population means. The variability within the two samples is combined to obtain a single (pooled) estimate of population variance. The null hypothesis states that there is no difference between the two population means. See Demonstration 10.1 on page 280.

Effect Size for the Independent-Measures t

The effect size for the independent-measures t test can be described by either estimating Cohen's d or by computing r^2, which measures the percentage of variability that is accounted for by the treatment effect. See Demonstraton 10.2 on page 282.

4. The Related-Samples t Test (Chapter 11)

This test evaluates the mean difference between two treatment conditions using the data from a repeated-measures or a matched-subjects experiment. A difference score (D) is obtained for each subject (or each matched pair) by subtracting the score in treatment 1 from the score in treatment 2. The variability of the sample difference scores is used to estimate the population variability. The null hypothesis states that the population mean difference (μ_D) is zero. See Demonstration 11.1 on page 304.

Effect Size for the Related-Samples t

The effect size for the repeated-measures (related samples) t test can be described by either estimating Cohen's d or by computing r^2, which measures the percentage of variability that is accounted for by the treatment effect. See Demonstration 11.2 on page 306.

5. **Single-Factor, Independent-Measures Analysis of Variance** (Chapter 13)

This test uses data from two or more separate samples to test for mean differences among two or more populations. The null hypothesis states that there are no differences among the population means. The test statistic is an F-ratio that uses the variability between treatment conditions (sample mean differences) in the numerator and the variability within treatment conditions (error variability) as the denominator. With only two samples, this test is equivalent to the independent-measures t test. See Demonstration 13.1 on page 371.

Effect Size for Analysis of Variance

The effect size for an analysis of variance is described by a measure of the percentage of variability that is accounted for by the treatment effect. In the context of ANOVA, the percentage is called η^2 (eta squared) instead of r^2. See Demonstration 13.2 on page 373.

6. **Single-Factor, Repeated-Measures Analysis of Variance** (Chapter 14)

This test is used to evaluate mean differences among two or more treatment conditions using sample data from a repeated-measures (or matched-subjects) experiment. The null hypothesis states that there are no differences among the population means. The test statistic is an F-ratio using variability between treatment conditions (mean differences) in the numerator exactly like the independent-measures ANOVA. The denominator of the F-ratio (error term) is obtained by measuring variability within treatments and then subtracting out the variability between subjects. The research design and the test statistic remove variability due to individual differences and thereby provide a more sensitive test for treatment differences than is possible with an independent-measures design. See Demonstration 14.1 on page 412.

Effect Size for Repeated-Measures Analysis of Variance

The effect size for the repeated-measures ANOVA is described by η^2 (eta squared), which measures the percentage of variability that is accounted for by the treatment effect. The percentage is computed after other explained sources of variability have been removed. See the example on page 389.

7. **Two-Factor, Independent-Measures Analysis of Variance** (Chapter 14)

This test is used to evaluate mean differences among populations or treatment conditions using sample data from research designs with two independent variables (factors). The two-factor ANOVA tests three separate hypotheses: mean differences among the levels of factor A (main effect for factor A), mean differences among the levels of factor B (main effect for factor B), and mean differences resulting from specific combinations of the two factors (interaction). Each of the three separate null hypotheses states that there are no population mean differences. Each of the three tests uses an F-ratio as the test statistic, with the variability between samples (sample mean differences) in the numerator and the variability within samples (error variability) in the denominator. See Demonstration 14.2 on page 414.

Effect Size for the Two-Factor Analysis of Variance

The effect size for each main effect (A and B) and for the interaction are described by η^2 (eta squared), which measures the percentage of variability that is accounted for by the specific treatment effect. The percentage is computed after other explained sources of variability have been removed. See the example on page 406.

III   EVALUATING RELATIONSHIPS BETWEEN VARIABLES

As we noted in Chapter 1, a major purpose for scientific research is to investigate and establish orderly relationships between variables. The statistical techniques covered in this section all serve the purpose of measuring and describing relationships. The data for these statistics involve two observations for each individual—one observation for each of the two variables being examined. The goal is to determine whether a consistent, predictable relationship exists and to describe the nature of the relationship.

Each of the different statistical methods described in this section is intended to be used with a specific type of data. To determine which method is appropriate, you must first examine your data and identify what type of variable is involved and what scale of measurement was used for recording the observations.

1. **The Pearson Correlation** (Chapter 15)

   The Pearson correlation measures the degree of linear relationship between two variables. The sign ($+$ or $-$) of the correlation indicates the direction of the relationship. The magnitude of the correlation (from 0 to 1) indicates the degree to which the data points fit on a straight line. See Demonstration 15.1 on page 465.

2. **The Spearman Correlation** (Chapter 15)

   The Spearman correlation measures the degree to which the relationship between two variables is one-directional or monotonic. The Spearman correlation is used when both variables, X and Y, are measured on an ordinal scale or after the two variables have been transformed to ranks. See Example 15.9 on page 442.

3. **The Point-Biserial Correlation** (Chapter 15)

   The point-biserial correlation is a special application of the Pearson correlation that is used when one variable is dichotomous (only two values) and the second variable is measured on an interval or ratio scale. The value of the correlation measures the strength of the relationship between the two variables. The point-biserial correlation often is used as an alternative or a supplement to the independent-measures t hypothesis test. See the example on pages 446–447.

4. **The Phi-Coefficient** (Chapter 15)

   The phi-coefficient is a special application of the Pearson correlation that is used when both variables, X and Y, are dichotomous (only two values). The value of the correlation measures the strength of the relationship between the two variables. The phi-coefficient is often used as an alternative or a supplement to the chi-square test for independence. See Example 15.11 on page 448.

5. **The Chi-Square Test for Independence** (Chapter 16)

   This test uses frequency data to determine whether there is a significant relationship between two variables. The null hypothesis states that the two variables are independent. The chi-square test for independence is used when the scale of measurement consists of relatively few categories for both variables and can be used with nominal, ordinal, interval, or ratio scales. See Demonstration 16.1 on page 498.

6. **Linear Regression** (Chapter 15)

   The purpose of linear regression is to find the equation for the best-fitting straight line for predicting Y scores from X scores. The regression process determines the linear equation with the least-squared error between the actual

CHOOSING A METHOD FOR EVALUATING RELATIONSHIPS BETWEEN VARIABLES: A DECISION MAP

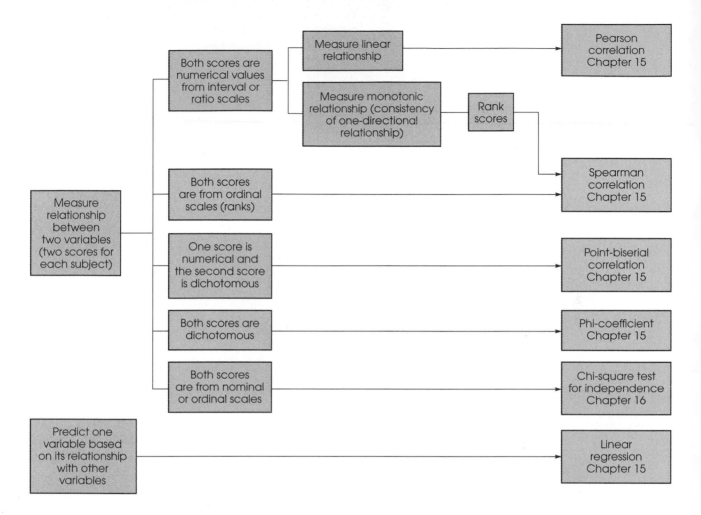

Y values and the predicted Y values on the line. The standard error of estimate provides a measure of the standard distance (or error) between the actual Y values and the predicted Y values. Analysis of regression determines whether the regression equation predicts a significant proportion of the variance for the Y scores by comparing the predicted portion (r^2) with the residual portion, $(1 - r^2)$. See Demonstration 15.1 on page 465.

IV NONPARAMETRIC CHI-SQUARE TESTS: INFERENCES ABOUT POPULATION PROPORTIONS

Chi-square tests are used to evaluate hypotheses about the relative frequencies (proportions) that exist in the population. The sample data consist of observed frequencies that simply identify the number of individuals found in each category. The hypotheses specify the expected proportions for the categories in the population. The chi-square test for goodness of fit uses the frequencies found in one sample to test a null hypothesis that specifies the corresponding proportions in the population. The chi-square test for independence can be viewed in two different ways:

1. The test uses two or more different samples representing different treatments or different populations to determine whether there are systematic differences between the treatments or populations. The null hypothesis states that the treatments (or populations) all have frequency distributions with the same proportions (same shape).

2. The test uses one sample measuring two variables for each individual to determine whether there is a consistent, systematic relationship between the two variables. The null hypothesis states that the two variables are independent in the population.

A DECISION MAP FOR CHI-SQUARE TESTS

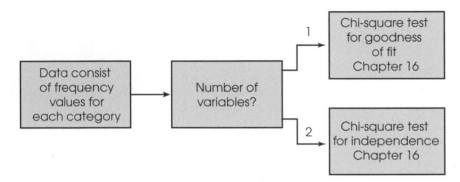

1. **The Chi-Square Test for Goodness of Fit** (Chapter 16)

   This chi-square test is used in situations where the measurement procedure results in classifying individuals into distinct categories. The test uses frequency data from a single sample to test a hypothesis about the population distribution. The null hypothesis specifies the proportion or percentage of the population for each category on the scale of measurement. See Example 16.1 on page 480.

2. **The Chi-Square Test for Independence** (Chapter 16)

   This test serves as an alternative to the independent-measures t test (or ANOVA) in situations in which the dependent variable involves classifying individuals into distinct categories. The sample data consist of frequency distributions (proportions across categories) for two or more separate samples. The null hypothesis states that the separate populations all have the same proportions (same shape). That is, the proportions across categories are independent of the different populations. See Demonstration 16.1 on page 498.

   Effect Size for the Chi-Square Test for Independence

   Effect size for the chi-square test for independence is measured by the phi-coefficient for data from a 2×2 matrix or Cramér's V for data from a larger matrix. Both values are interpreted as correlations. See the examples on pages 491–493.

References

American Psychological Association (APA). (2001). *Publication manual of the American Psychological Association* (5th ed.) Washington, DC: Author.

Arden, R. & Plomin, R. (2006). Sex differences in variance of intelligence across childhood. *Personality and Individual Differences, 41,* 39–48.

Bahrick, H. P., & Hall, L. K. (1991). Lifetime maintenance of high school mathematics content. *Journal of Experimental Psychology: General, 120,* 20–33.

Belsky, J., Weinraub, M., Owen, M., & Kelly, J. (2001). Quality of child care and problem behavior. In J. Belsky (Chair), *Early childcare and children's development prior to school entry.* Symposium conducted at the 2001 Biennial Meetings of the Society for Research in Child Development, Minneapolis, MN.

Bradbury, T. N., & Miller, G. A. (1985). Season of birth in schizophrenia: A review of evidence, methodology, and etiology. *Psychological Bulletin, 98,* 569–594.

Broberg, A. G., Wessels, H., Lamb, M. E., & Hwang, C. P. (1997). Effects of day care on the development of cognitive abilities in 8-year-olds: A longitudinal study. *Development Psychology, 33,* 62–69.

Byrne, D. (1971). *The attraction paradigm.* New York: Academic Press.

Cerveny, R. S., & Balling, Jr., R. C. (1998). Weekly cycles of air pollutants, precipitation and tropical cyclones in the coastal NW Atlantic region. *Nature, 394,* 561–563.

Chandra, A., & Minkovitz, C. S. (2006). Stigma starts early: Gender differences in teen willingness to use mental health services. *Journal of Adolescent Health, 38,* 754.e1–754.e8.

Chaplin, W. F., Phillips, J. B., Brown, J. D., Clanton, N. R., & Stein, J. L. (2000). Handshaking, gender, personality, and first impressions. *Journal of Personality and Social Psychology, 79,* 110–117.

Cialdini, R. B., Reno, R. R., & Kallgren, C. A. (1990). A focus theory of normative conduct: Recycling the concept of norms to reduce littering in public places. *Journal of Personality and Social Psychology, 58,* 1015–1026.

Cohen, J. (1988). *Statistical power analysis for the behavioral sciences.* Hillsdale, NJ: Lawrence Erlbaum Associates.

Cowles, M., & Davis, C. (1982). On the origins of the .05 level of statistical significance. *American Psychologist, 37,* 553–558.

Davis, E. A. (1937). *The development of linguistic skills in twins, single twins with siblings, and only children from age 5 to 10 years.* Institute of Child Welfare Series, No. 14. Minneapolis: University of Minnesota Press.

Duncker, K. (1945). On problem-solving. *Psychological Monographs, 58* (No. 270).

Eagly, A. H., Ashmore, R. D., Makhijani, M. G., & Longo, L. C. (1991). What is beautiful is good but . . . : A meta-analytic review of research on the physical attractiveness stereotype. *Psychological Bulletin, 110,* 109–128.

Evans, S. W., Pelham, W. E., Smith, B. H., Bukstein, O., Gnagy, E. M., Greiner, A. R., Atenderfer, L. B., & Baron-Myak, C. (2001). Dose-response effects of methylphenidate on ecologically valid measures of academic performance and classroom behavior in adolescents with ADHD. *Experimental and Clinical Psychopharmacology, 9,* 163–175.

Fallon, A. E., & Rozin, P. (1985). Sex differences in perceptions of desirable body shape. *Journal of Abnormal Psychology, 94,* 102–105.

Flynn, J. R. (1984). The mean IQ of Americans: Massive gains 1932 to 1978. *Psychological Bulletin, 95,* 29–51.

Flynn, J. R. (1999). Searching for justice: The discovery of IQ gains over time. *American Psychologist, 54,* 5–20.

Friedman, M., & Rosenman, R. H. (1974). *Type A behavior and your heart.* New York: Knopf.

Frieswijk, N., Buunk, B. P., Steverink, N., & Slaets, J. P. J. (2004). The effect of social comparison information on the life satisfaction of frail older persons. *Psychology and Aging, 19,* 183–190.

Fukukawa, Y., Nakashina, C., Tsubio, S., Kozakai, R., Doyo, W., Naoakira, N., Ando, F., & Shimokata, H. (2004). Age differences in the effect of physical activity on depressive symptoms. *Psychology and Aging, 19,* 346–351.

Harlow, H. F. (1959). Love in infant monkeys. *Scientific American, 200,* 68–86.

Harris, C. R. (2001). Cardiovascular responses of embarrassment and effects of emotional suppression in a social setting. *Journal of Personality and Social Psychology, 81,* 886–897.

Harris, R. J., Schoen, L. M., & Hensley, D. L. (1992). A cross-cultural study of story memory. *Journal of Cross-Cultural Psychology, 23,* 133–147.

Heaton, R. K., Chelune, G. J., Talley, J. L., Kay, G. G., & Curtiss, G. (1993). *Wisconsin Card Sorting Test (WCST) manual: Revised and expanded.* Odessa, FL: Psychological Assessment Resources.

Heaton, R. K., Gladsjo, J. A., Palmer, B. W., Kuck, J., Marcotte, T. D., & Jeste, D. V. (2002). Stability and course of neuropsychological deficits in schizophrenia. *Archives of General Psychiatry, 58,* 24–32.

Hill, R. A., & Barton, R. A. (2005). Red enhances human performance in contests. *Nature, 435,* 293.

Hunter, J. E. (1997). Needed: A ban on the significance test. *Psychological Science, 8,* 3–7.

Johnston, J. J. (1975). Sticking with first responses on multiple-choice exams: for better or worse? *Teaching of Psychology, 2,* 178–179.

Joseph, J. A., Shukitt-Hale, B., Denisova, N. A., Bielinnski, D., Martin, A., McEwen, J. J., & Bickford, P. C. (1999). Reversals of age-related declines in neuronal signal transduction, cognitive, and motor behavioral deficits with blueberry, spinach, or strawberry dietary supplementation. *Journal of Neuroscience, 19,* 8114–8121.

Keppel, G. (1973). *Design and analysis: A researcher's handbook.* Englewood Cliffs, NJ: Prentice-Hall.

Keppel, G., & Zedeck, S. (1989). *Data analysis for research designs.* New York: Freeman.

Kerr, D. P., Walsh, D. M., & Baxter, D. (2003). Acupuncture in the management of chronic low back pain: A blinded randomized controlled trial. *Clinical Journal of Pain, 19,* 364–370.

Khan, A., Brodhead, A. E., Kolts, R. L., & Brown, W. A. (2005). Severity of depressive symptoms and response to antidepressants and placebo in antidepressant trials. *Journal of Psychiatric Research, 39,* 145–150.

Killeen, P. R. (2005). An alternative to null-hypothesis significance tests. *Psychological Science, 16,* 345–353.

Kosfeld, M., Heinrichs, M., Zak, P. J., Fischbacher, U., & Fehr, R. (2005). Oxytocin increases trust in humans. *Nature, 435,* 673–676.

Kramer, S. E., Allessie, G. H. M., Dondorp, A. W., Zekveld, A. A., & Kapteyn, T. S. (2005). A home education program for older adults with hearing impairment and their significant others: A randomized evaluating short- and long-term effects. *International Journal of Audiology, 44,* 255–264.

Kuo, M., Adlaf, E. M., Lee, H., Gliksman, L., Demers, A., & Wechsler, H. (2002). More Canadian students drink but American students drink more: Comparing college alcohol use in two countries. *Addiction, 97,* 1583–1592.

Langewitz, W., Izakovic, J., & Wyler, J. (2005). Effect of self-hypnosis on hay fever symptoms—a randomized controlled intervention. *Psychotherapy and Psychosomatics, 74,* 165–172.

Laughlin, P. R., Zander, M. L., Knievel, E. M., & Tan, T. K. (2003). Groups perform better than the best individuals on letters-to-numbers problems: Informative equations and effective strategies. *Journal of Personality and Social Psychology, 85,* 684–694.

Lieber, C. S. (1990). Cited in Barroom biology: How alcohol goes to a woman's head (January 14). *The New York Times,* p E24.

Linde, L., & Bergstroem, M. (1992). The effect of one night without sleep on problem-solving and immediate recall. *Psychological Research, 54,* 127–136.

Loftus, G. R. (1996). Psychology will be a much better science when we change the way we analyze data. *Current Directions in Psychological Science, 5,* 161–171.

McGee, R., Williams, S., Howden-Chapman, P., Martin, J., & Kawachi, I. (2006). Participation in clubs and groups from childhood to adolescence and its effects on attachment and self-esteem. *Journal of Adolescence, 29,* 1–17.

Murdock, T. B., Miller, M., & Kohlhardt, J. (2004). Effects of classroom context variables on high school students' judgments of the acceptability and likelihood of cheating. *Journal of Educational Psychology, 96,* 765–777.

Pelton, T. (1983). The shootists. *Science83, 4*(4), 84–86.

Persson, J., Bringlov, E., Nilsson, L., & Nyberg, L. (2004). The memory-enhancing effects of Ginseng and Ginkgo biloba in health volunteers. *Psychopharmacology, 172,* 430–434.

Plomin, R., Corley, R., DeFries, J. C., & Fulker, D. W. (1990). Individual differences in television viewing in early childhood: Nature as well as nurture. *Psychological Science, 1,* 371–377.

Raine, A., Reynolds, C., Verables, P. H., & Mednick, S. A. (2002). Stimulation seeking and intelligence: A prospective longitudinal study. *Journal of Personality and Social Psychology, 82,* 663–674.

Reifman, A. S., Larrick, R. P., & Fein, S. (1991). Temper and temperature on the diamond: The heat–aggression relationship in major league baseball. *Personality and Social Psychology Bulletin, 17,* 580–585.

Reyes-Ortiz, C. A., Ayele, H., Mulligan, T., Espino, D. V., Berges, I. M., & Markides, K. S. (2006). Higher church attendance predicts lower fear of falling in older Mexican-Americans. *Aging and Mental Health, 10,* 13–18.

Rozin, P. Bauer, R., & Cantanese, D. (2003). Food and life, pleasure and worry, among American college students: Gender differences and regional similarities. *Journal of Personality and Social Psychology, 85,* 132–141.

Scaife, M. (1976). The response to eye-like shapes by birds. I. The effect of context: A predator and a strange bird. *Animal Behaviour, 24,* 195–199.

Schachter, S. (1968). Obesity and eating. *Science, 161,* 751–756.

Schleifer, S. J., Keller, S. E., Camerino, M., Thorton, J. C., & Stein, M. (1983). Suppression of lymphocyte stimulation following bereavement. *Journal of the American Medical Association, 250,* 374–377.

Schmidt, S. R. (1994). Effects of humor on sentence memory. *Journal of Experimental Psychology: Learning, Memory, & Cognition, 20,* 953–967.

Segal, S. J., & Fusella, V. (1970). Influence of imaged pictures and sounds on detection of visual and auditory signals. *Journal of Experimental Psychology, 83,* 458–464.

Shrauger, J. S. (1972). Self-esteem and reactions to being observed by others. *Journal of Personality and Social Psychology, 23,* 192–200.

Siegel, J. M. (1990). Stress life events and use of physician services among the elderly: The moderating role of pet ownership. *Journal of Personality and Social Psychology, 58,* 1081–1086.

Smith, C., & Lapp, L. (1991). Increases in number of REMs and REM density in humans following an intensive learning period. *Sleep: Journal of Sleep Research & Sleep Medicine, 14,* 325–330.

Sol, D., Lefebvre, L., & Rodriguez-Teijeiro, J. D. (2005). Brain size, innovative propensity and migratory behavior in temperate Palaearctic birds. *Proceedings [Proc Biol Sci], 272,* 1433–1441.

Stickgold, R., Whidbee, D., Schirmer B., Patel, V., & Hobson, J. A. (2000). Visual discrimination task improvement: A multi-step process occurring during sleep. *Journal of Cognitive Neuroscience, 12,* 246–254.

Strack, F., Martin, L. L., & Stepper, S. (1998). Inhibiting and facilitating conditions of the human smile: A nonobtrusive test of the facial feedback hypothesis. *Journal of Personality & Social Psychology, 54,* 768–777.

Sümer, N., Özkan, T., & Lajunen, T. (2006). Asymetric relationship between driving and safety skills. *Accident Analysis and Prevention, 38,* 703–711.

Twenge, J. M. (2000). The age of anxiety? Birth cohort change in anxiety and neuroticism, 1952–1993. *Journal of Personality and Social Psychology, 79,* 1007–1021.

von Hippel, P. T. (2005). Mean, median, and skew: Correcting a textbook rule. *Journal of Statistics Education, 13*(2). Retrieved from www.amstat.org/publications/jse/vl3n2/vonhippel.html.

Welsh, R. S., Davis, M. J., Burke, J. R., & Williams, H. G. (2002). Carbohydrates and physical/mental performance during intermittent exercise to fatigue. *Medicine & Science in Sports & Exercise, 34,* 723–731.

Wilkinson, L., and the Task Force on Statistical Inference. (1999). Statistical methods in psychology journals. *American Psychologist, 54,* 594–604.

Winer, G. A., & Cottrell, J. E. (1996). Does anything leave the eye when we see? Extramission beliefs of children and adults. *Current Directions in Psychological Science, 5,* 137–142.

Winget, C., & Kramer, M. (1979). *Dimensions of dreams.* Gainesville: University Press of Florida.

Index

CHOOSING DESCRIPTIVE STATISTICS: A DECISION MAP

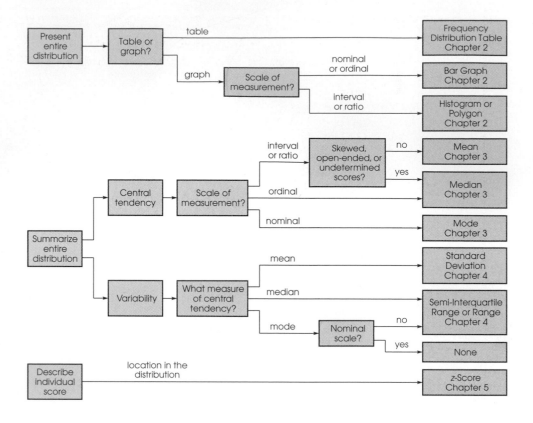

CHOOSING A PARAMETRIC TEST TO EVALUATE MEAN DIFFERENCES BETWEEN TREATMENT CONDITIONS OR BETWEEN POPULATIONS: A DECISION MAP

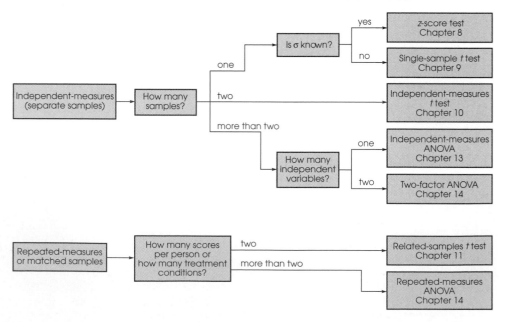